CW01496071

The Palgrave Handbook of Criminal and Terrorism Financing Law

Colin King • Clive Walker • Jimmy Gurulé
Editors

The Palgrave Handbook of Criminal and Terrorism Financing Law

Volume 1

palgrave
macmillan

Editors
Colin King
University of Sussex
Falmer, UK

Clive Walker
University of Leeds
Leeds, UK

Jimmy Gurulé
Notre Dame Law School
Notre Dame, IN, USA

ISBN 978-3-319-64497-4   ISBN 978-3-319-64498-1   (eBook)
https://doi.org/10.1007/978-3-319-64498-1

Library of Congress Control Number: 2017958007

Cover illustration: RubberBall / Alamy Stock Photo

Printed on acid-free paper

This Palgrave Macmillan imprint is published by the registered company Springer International Publishing AG part of Springer Nature.
The registered company address is: Gewerbestrasse 11, 6330 Cham, Switzerland

Contents

List of Figures

List of Tables

Part I

Introductory Section

1

Criminal and Terrorism Financing Law: An Introduction

Clive Walker, Colin King, and Jimmy Gurulé

Background

Popular depictions abound of criminal financing through racketeering and organised crime, as have been delivered by Hollywood productions such as *The Godfather*, *The Sopranos*, and *The Wire*. Counter-terrorism financing (CTF) is a somewhat less glamorised aspect of the genre, as represented by the likes of *24* and *Homeland*. Nevertheless, much public interest was aroused by the real deal, such as the *Osama bin Laden Document Release* by the US Director of National Intelligence and based on materials seized in the Abbottabad raid of 2011, which revealed some fascinating insights into the business of terrorism.[1]

The generation of public attention through not only popular culture but also governmental promotion might be viewed by some commentators as whipping up a climate of undue fear for ulterior political motives.[2] However, governments seem to have been vehement about their own rhetoric. For instance, the UK government in its policy statement, *National Security Strategy and Strategic Defence and Security Review 2015: A Secure and Prosperous United Kingdom*,[3] depicts terrorism as a Tier 1 national security threat, while serious

C. Walker
University of Leeds, Leeds, UK

C. King
University of Sussex, Brighton, UK

J. Gurulé
Notre Dame Law School, Notre Dame, IN, USA

© The Author(s) 2018
C. King et al. (eds.), *The Palgrave Handbook of Criminal and Terrorism Financing Law*,
https://doi.org/10.1007/978-3-319-64498-1_1

and organised crime is within Tier 2. These ratings entail real consequences in terms of political priorities, the allocation of resources, and the endless generation of legislation.

Consequently, organised crime and transnational terrorism are perceived as posing significant and unrelenting threats to the integrity, security, and stability of contemporary societies. In response, conventional policing responses have struggled to make a sufficient impact, as demonstrated by the churn of organisational and operational models. As a result, there arise the predominantly criminal threats from drug trafficking, fraud, human trafficking, identity theft, intellectual property crime, and counterfeiting, which have been tackled by successive policing and executive agencies which implement specialist legislation. The current approach is to adopt anti-money laundering measures to prevent 'dirty money' from infiltrating the legitimate economy, and asset recovery powers to target the accumulated financial assets of those engaged in criminal activity.

Following the financial trails of terrorists has been less prominent as a driver of change, at least until 9/11, since the sums involved are much lower. There is some melding with criminal activities, especially in the case of hierarchical and geographically focused terrorism such as in Northern Ireland and the Basque region of Spain.[4] However, following 9/11, the international community has now in an increasingly shrill voice demanded action by way of CTF. The demand was first signalled by the UN Convention on the Suppression of Terrorist Finance 1999[5] and by UN Security Council Resolution 1267 of 15 October 1999, followed up by a stream of further resolutions, notably, 1333 of 19 December 2000 (dealing with Al-Qa'ida) and 1373 of 28 September 2001 (against terrorism in all guises) through to numbers 2178 and 2253 in 2014 and 2015 (dealing with 'foreign terrorist fighters and Islamic State). This range of international edicts must be reflected and applied by national legislation. There remain distinctions between criminal money laundering and counter-terrorism financing, such as an emphasis on intelligence gathering as much as the negation of the value of criminal enterprise. At the same time, there are also parallels and cross-fertilisation of 'lessons learnt', highlighted by the frequent application of criminal proceeds of crime laws in the UK to terrorism assets[6] and by the decision in 2013 of the UK government to apply formal counter-terrorism strategy to tackling serious and organised crime.[7] Those aspects of terrorism which relate to financing may operate as just a subsidiary aspect of the full risk picture, but it is one which has become of enduring interest. Thus, one angle of the investigation into the London Bridge attacks in June 2017 immediately became the use of a credit card to hire a heavy lorry (which was declined and resulted in the hiring of a light van).[8] This may seem like a minor detail in the circumstances of such an outrage, but one can predict that such data will not only figure in subsequent investigations but also will translate eventually into extra regulatory checks, just as bomb ingredients based on fertiliser or bleach products have resulted in the imposition of extra restrictions over time.[9]

In the US context, the expressed resolve to deal with these threats of criminal and terrorism financing is arguably even more trenchant. 'Crime incorporated'[10] is a long-standing prime mission of the Federal Bureau of Investigation (FBI), at least when not preoccupied with race and Reds.[11] That agenda is outstripped now by counter-terrorism, which mobilises not only the FBI but also the whole nation under the joint resolution of the House of Representatives and the Senate, the Authorization for the Use of Military Force (AUMF). This instrument affords the President broad powers as Commander in Chief to '… use all necessary and appropriate force against those nations, organizations, or persons he determines planned, authorized, committed, or aided the terrorist attacks that occurred on September 11, 2001, or harboured such organizations or persons'.[12] The ensuing 'war on terror'[13] has persisted without end for more than a decade, despite doubts during the era of President Obama that the AUMF was not tenable in the future and that a major tactic, detention of suspects at Guantánamo, must be ended.[14] Yet, the AUMF outlived the Obama administration, and the emergence of drones during his tenure has affected far more terrorist suspects than were ever held at Guantánamo.[15]

Based on the foregoing survey, the importance of the agendas of anti-money laundering (AML), asset recovery (AR), and counter-terrorism financing (CTF) cannot be doubted. But there is room for doubt about many aspects of these agendas. Our scepticism may be driven by the inadequate collection or release of official data and by an absence of comprehensive evidence-led independent research. The gaps are especially apparent in 'follow the money' approaches to tackling financial-based crime. 'Following the money' represents an alternative approach to conventional policing stratagems to tackling organised crime and/ or terrorism and are blithely presumed: to operate as a deterrent, to disrupt criminal networks/markets, to improve detection rates, and to result in increased intelligence flows to policing agencies. Yet, criminological research to date suggests that these outcomes do not necessarily follow. So, despite extensive lawmaking in this field (such as, in the UK, the Proceeds of Crime Act 2002, the Terrorism Act 2000, the Anti-Terrorism, Crime and Security Act 2001, and the Terrorist Asset-Freezing etc. Act 2010, and in the USA, the pervasive Racketeer Influenced and Corrupt Organizations Act 1970),[16] organised crime and terrorism activities are, as already indicated, depicted as rising threats despite every effort of the 'follow the money' approaches.

Agendas

It follows that there is an evident need for deeper analysis of the relevant 'follow the money' policies, legislation, and institutions. There is a need to evaluate their impacts and to identify future directions in policy, practice, and research. Key issues for discussion include the following themes.

In terms of the substantive agenda, the broad policy of 'follow the money' requires reflection upon different aspects of its approaches, namely, AML, AR (which can include post-conviction confiscation of assets, civil recovery absent criminal conviction, and taxation of illegally acquired assets), and the CTF equivalents.

There must also be an effort to assess not just designs but also actual impacts. This goal reflects the fact that while there has been much academic discussion on the meaning of 'legal provisions', rather less is known about the impact of follow-the-money approaches to disrupting organised crime groups, deterring future criminal activity, reducing harm to society, and garnering intelligence for police or security agencies. Measuring the success of the responsive regimes will therefore be a key discussion point. This aspect might include a cost-benefit analysis (assuming that all costs and benefits can be identified and weighted)[17] and also whether it is possible to quantify the impact of disrupting organised criminal activity through financial approaches, as compared to more conventional criminal investigation and prosecution.

These first two themes give rise to a third. A prime goal behind our project is to seek to understand legal structures and measures in the context of practice. Through putting the 'law in practice', we seek practical insight into how the law operates in reality. Consequently, our project has at every stage included practitioners as well as academics. Their valuable insights are reflected in our book. Some were even persuaded (and allowed) to contribute their own chapters to our book.

Moving on to institutional aspects of our inquiry, we shall seek to assess the appropriate design of relevant institutions. For instance, in the United Kingdom, the Assets Recovery Agency was initially tasked as the specialist body with targeting illicit assets, but this remit was subsequently taken over by the Serious Organised Crime Agency (SOCA).[18] In 2013, SOCA was replaced by the National Crime Agency (NCA).[19] Institutional designs are clearly difficult to get right since they involve complex choices about the need for specialism and independence, the role of multi- and inter-agency cooperation and the deployment of special and sensitive powers and techniques.

Another important aspect of institutional design is accountability. Set against a high level of institutional fluidity (at least in the UK example), we must examine the degree of accountability of specialist agencies. Their limited transparency and accountability may affect both public confidence and corporate trust which may provoke counter-productive consequences such as the failure to provide information.

More broadly, issues of legitimacy must be tackled. While policy discourse emphasises the positive rationales underpinning the 'follow the money' activities, which may be justified by broad claims to public security and protection, there are inevitable detriments to those affected by the broad powers invoked in enforcement action. Individual rights can be severely compromised. Furthermore, because of the concerted links between public and private stakeholders, the latter may be free to impose detriments on individuals without constraint by the doctrines of individual rights and accountability.

Next, the implications arising from the crossing of borders must be considered when dealing with transnational crime and transnational terrorism.[20] Thus, some comparative work is required so that lessons can be learnt while transcending a variety of jurisdictions. Our multi-national focus is therefore noteworthy. Much of the current research on AML, AR, and CTF tends to be focused on individual jurisdictions (typically the USA or UK). Our project deliberately adopts much needed international and comparative perspectives, drawing upon experiences of not just the UK and USA but also European countries such as Italy, the wider common law world such as Australia and Canada, and international organisations including the EU and UN. There is now an unprecedented international regulatory focus on 'dirty assets' by way of the EU Money Laundering Directives, UN Conventions, and Financial Action Task Force guides. This book will benefit from its comparative approach.

Finally, changing environments demand novel research and practical and legal adaptability by agencies, lawyers and researchers. Novel techniques may include barely encountered modes of asset exchange such as *hawala*. Equally, electronic or virtual currencies (such as Bitcoin), which operate in barely regulated environments, challenge conventional approaches to asset recovery techniques.

Our Research Inquiries

To answer the foregoing agendas, our research fieldwork involved the organisation and delivery of four symposia. These events were funded by an AHRC grant (made to King and Walker),[21] under the title, 'Dirty Assets: Experiences, reflections, and lessons learnt from a decade of legislation on criminal money laundering and terrorism financing.' This project built on an earlier exploratory symposium held in 2011, when Colin King and Clive Walker organised an event, 'The Confiscation of Assets: Policy, Practice and Research', to bring together policymakers, practitioners, and academics to discuss follow-the-money approaches to combating organised crime and terrorism. This event was funded by the publishers of the *Modern Law Review*. The objectives behind this event were twofold: to raise awareness of expertise concerning the four different limbs of follow-the-money approaches and to open discussions about the need for independent research to feed back into policy and practice. Our initial foray was marked by an edited collection, *Dirty Assets: Emerging Issues in the Regulation of Criminal and Terrorist Assets*.[22]

Based on the earlier experience, and reflecting similar objectives, we held four further events which were designed, once again, to bring policymakers, practitioners, and researchers together to explore current, and future, directions in policy, law, and practice. The workshops were held in Manchester (October 2014), London (May 2015), Tilburg, Netherlands (October 2015), and Notre Dame, USA (April 2016).[23]

Book Plan

Based on the insights and discussions at these key events, as well as selected invitees who could provide the authority and depth demanded by our project, the *Handbook of Criminal and Terrorism Financing Law* provides innovative commentary in that it examines in a comprehensive way all aspects of tainted ('dirty') assets. The chapters together explore three distinct, but interlocking, aspects, namely, anti-money laundering, asset recovery, and counter terrorism financing. In this way, comparisons can be drawn from one aspect to the next. Second, the book is also comprehensive in terms of disciplines. The main theme is legal, but the contributors also reflect other disciplines—politics, criminology, business, and economics. In addition, there is practitioner input as well as legal input. Third, the jurisdictional coverage is suitably broad. The main focus is the UK and USA, but we have been determined to include European and Asian contributions as well as experts on international systems. Fourth, the chapters reflect new or substantially updated materials and not simply reprints of previous publications. This feature has been assured through the process of our symposia. As a result, the book will deliver original, theoretically informed, and well-referenced analysis, which we intend to be accessible to both practitioners and scholars alike in multiple jurisdictions.

This Handbook focuses on three distinct, but related, aspects of 'following the money' of organised crime and terrorist related activities: anti-money laundering, asset recovery, and counter-terrorism financing measures. Within each aspect, it examines the policy, institutional, and legal responses, set within policy and practice contexts, and with a view to critique on grounds such as effective delivery and compliance with legality and individual rights. These three broad themes are reflected in the structure of the book. Part II (Chaps. 2 through to 15) covers 'anti-money laundering measures'. Part III (Chaps. 16 through to 29) deals with 'asset recovery'. Part IV (Chaps. 30 through to 47) is devoted to 'counter-terrorism financing'. An overview of the purpose and chapter contents for each part is given in introductory chapters at the start of each part—Chaps. 2, 16, and 30.

Finally, though our project has been some years in the making, every chapter has been updated, most to 31 March 2017. This deadline, plus the fact that the fourth event was in 2016, has allowed us to encompass contemporary and emergent controversies, including the responses to Islamic State funding. Even so, the churn of events means that sustained digestion of the very latest news, whether the UK Criminal Finances Act 2017 or the terrorism financing sanctions levelled against Qatar,[24] must await our next book.

Notes

1. Office of the Director of National Intelligence, 'Bin Laden's Bookshelf' <www.dni.gov/index.php/features/bin-laden-s-bookshelf> accessed 12 June 2017.
2. See especially Frank Furedi, *Invitation to Terror* (Continuum 2007).
3. HM Government, *National Security Strategy and Strategic Defence and Security Review 2015: A Secure and Prosperous United Kingdom* (Cm 9161, 2015) Annex A, 87.
4. See Thomas Baumert and Mikel Buesa, 'Dismantling Terrorist Economics: The Spanish Experience' in Colin King and Clive Walker (eds), *Dirty Assets: Emerging Issues in the Regulation of Criminal and Terrorist Assets* (Ashgate Publishing 2014).
5. UNGA International Convention for the Suppression of the Financing of Terrorism (adopted 9 December 1999, opened for signature 10 January 2000) (2000) 39 ILM 270.
6. Colin King and Clive Walker, 'Counter Terrorism Financing: A Redundant Fragmentation?' (2015) 6(3) New Journal of European Criminal Law 372. See further Tamara Makarenko, 'The Crime-Terror Continuum: Tracing the Interplay between Transnational Organised Crime and Terrorism' (2004) 6(1) Global Crime 129.

7. See Home Office, *Serious and Organised Crime Strategy* (Cm 8715, 2013) para 1.5. The strategy derives from Home Office, *Countering International Terrorism: The United Kingdom's Strategy* (Cm 6888, 2006).

8. See Nicola Hurley, 'First Pictures of Fake Suicide Belts Worn by London Bridge Attackers' *Daily Telegraph* (London, 10 June 2017) <www.telegraph.co.uk/news/2017/06/10/first-pictures-fake-suicide-belts-worn-london-bridge-attackers/> accessed 13 June 2017.

9. Regulation (EC) No 1907/2006 of the European Parliament and of the Council of 18 December 2006 concerning the Registration, Evaluation, Authorisation and Restriction of Chemicals (REACH), establishing a European Chemicals Agency, amending Directive 1999/45/EC and repealing Council Regulation (EEC) No 793/93 and Commission Regulation (EC) No 1488/94 as well as Council Directive 76/769/EEC and Commission Directives 91/155/EEC, 93/67/EEC, 93/105/EC and 2000/21/EC (Text with EEA relevance) [2006] OJ L396/1; Regulation (EU) No 98/2013 of the European Parliament and of the Council of 15 January 2013 on the marketing and use of explosives precursors Text with EEA relevance [2013] OJ L39/1.

10. William Balsamo and George Carpozi Jr., *Crime Incorporated or Under the Clock: The Inside Story of the Mafia's First Hundred Years* (New Horizons Press 1999).

11. Ronald Kessler, *The Bureau: The Secret History of the FBI* (St Martin's Press 2003); *Rhodri Jeffreys-Jones, The FBI: A History* (Yale University Press 2008); Tim Weiner, *Enemies: A History of the FBI* (Penguin 2013).

12. Authorization for the Use of Military Force of 18 September 2001 (Public Law 107–40 [SJ RES 23]), s 2a.

13. See Johan Steyn, 'Guantanamo Bay: The Legal Black Hole' (2004) 53(1) International and Comparative Legal Quarterly 1; Helen Duffy, *The 'War on Terror' and the Framework of International Law* (CUP 2005); Benjamin Wittes (ed), *Legislating the War on Terror: An Agenda for Reform* (Brookings Institution Press 2009); Geoffrey S Corn, *The War on Terror and the Laws of War: A Military Perspective* (2nd edn, OUP 2015).

14. President Barack Obama, 'The Future of Our Fight Against Terrorism' (National Defense University 2013) <https://obamawhitehouse.archives.gov/the-press-office/2013/05/23/remarks-president-barack-obama> accessed 12 June 2017.

15. See Bureau of Investigative Journalism, 'Drone Wars: The Full Data' <www.thebureauinvestigates.com/stories/2017-01-01/drone-wars-the-full-data> accessed 12 June 2017.

16. 18 USC, ss 1961–1968. See Dylan Bensinger and others, 'Racketeer Influenced and Corrupt Organizations' [2016] American Criminal Law Review 1673.

17. An interesting official assessment along those lines is the Department of Business, Energy and Industrial Strategy paper, *Cutting Red Tape: Review of the UK's Anti-Money Laundering and Counter Financing of Terrorism Regime* (2017).
18. See Proceeds of Crime Act 2002, Pt I; Serious Crime Act 2007, s 74.
19. See Crime and Courts Act 2013, Pt I. The Economic Crime Command leads the NCA's activities. In addition, the Joint Money Laundering Intelligence Taskforce (JMLIT) was established in 2015 in partnership with the banking financial sector to tackle high-end money laundering.
20. See Katja F. Aas, *Globalisation and Crime* (Sage 2007); Angela Veng Mei Leong, *The Disruption of International Organised Crime: An Analysis of Legal and Non-Legal Strategies* (Ashgate Publishing 2007); Peter Andreas and Ethan Nadelmann, *Policing the Globe: Criminalization and Crime Control in International Relations* (OUP 2008); Neil Boister, *An Introduction to Transnational Criminal Law* (OUP 2012); Ben Bowling and James Sheptycki, *Global Policing* (Sage 2012); Saskia Hufnagel, *Policing Cooperation Across Borders* (Ashgate Publishing 2013).
21. Grant Ref AH/L014920/1.
22. Colin King and Clive Walker (eds), *Dirty Assets: Emerging Issues in the Regulation of Criminal and Terrorist Assets* (Ashgate Publishing 2014).
23. For details of these events, see 'Dirty Assets: Experiences, Reflections, and Lessons Learnt from a Decade of Legislation on Criminal Money Laundering and Terrorism Financing' <www.law.leeds.ac.uk/research/projects/dirty-assets> accessed 2 June 2017. The events in London and Notre Dame were generously hosted by Professor Jimmy Gurulé and Notre Dame Law School.
24. See Staff writer, 'Arab Countries Release List of Terrorist Financiers Supported by Qatar' *Al Arabiya* (Dubai, 9 June 2017) <http://english.alarabiya.net/en/News/gulf/2017/06/09/Arab-countries-release-list-of-terrorist-financiers-supported-by-Qatar.html> accessed 13 June 2017.

Clive Walker (LL.B., Ph.D., LL.D., Solicitor, QC (Hon)) is Professor Emeritus of Criminal Justice Studies at the University of Leeds. He has published extensively on terrorism issues. In 2003, he was a special adviser to the UK Parliamentary select committee which scrutinised what became the Civil Contingencies Act 2004: see *The Civil Contingencies Act 2004: Risk, Resilience and the Law in the United Kingdom* (Oxford University Press, 2006). His books on terrorism laws are leading authorities: *Terrorism and the Law* (Oxford University Press, 2011), *The Anti-Terrorism Legislation* (3rd ed., Oxford University Press, 2014), and the *Routledge Handbook of Law and Terrorism* (Routledge, 2015). The Home Office appointed him in 2010 as Senior Adviser to the Independent Reviewer of Terrorism Legislation, and he has also worked with other governmental bodies and many parliamentary committees.

Colin King is Reader in Law at the University of Sussex and co-Founder of the Crime Research Centre. He was an Academic Fellow at the Honourable Society of the Inner Temple from 2014–2017. In March 2016 Colin gave oral evidence at the Home Affairs Select Committee Inquiry into the Proceeds of Crime Act. Colin is co-editor of Dirty Assets: Emerging Issues in the Regulation of Criminal and Terrorist Assets (King and Walker, Ashgate, 2014). Also with Clive Walker, Colin led an AHRC-funded research network (2014–2016) entitled 'Dirty Assets: Experiences, reflections, and lessons learnt from a decade of legislation on criminal money laundering and terrorism financing'. In 2017 he was awarded a prestigious AHRC Leadership Fellowship to conduct empirical research on proceeds of crime legislation.

Jimmy Gurulé is an expert in the field of international criminal law, specifically, terrorism, terrorist financing, and anti-money laundering. He has worked in a variety of high-profile public law enforcement positions including as Under Secretary for Enforcement, U.S. Department of the Treasury (2001–2003), where he had oversight responsibilities for the U.S. Secret Service, U.S. Customs Service, Bureau of Alcohol, Tobacco, and Firearms (BATF), Financial Crimes Enforcement Network (FinCEN), Office of Foreign Assets Control (OFAC), and the Federal Law Enforcement Training Center (FLETC); Assistant Attorney General, Office of Justice Programs, U.S. Department of Justice (1990–1992); and Assistant U.S. Attorney, where he served as Deputy Chief of the Major Narcotics Section of the Los Angeles U.S. Attorney's Office (1985–1989). Among his many successes in law enforcement, he was instrumental in developing and implementing the U.S. Treasury Department's global strategy to combat terrorist financing. He has published extensively in these fields, and he is the author or co-author of the following: *National Security Law, Principles and Policy*; *Principles of Counter-Terrorism Law*; *Unfunding Terror: The Legal Response to the Financing of Global Terrorism*; *International Criminal Law, Cases and Materials* (4th ed.); *Complex Criminal Litigation: Prosecuting Drug Enterprises and Organized Crime* (3rd ed.); and *The Law of Asset Forfeiture* (2nd ed.).

Part II

Anti-Money Laundering

2

Anti-Money Laundering: An Overview

Colin King

Over the past three decades or so, there have been extensive developments in the area of anti-money laundering (AML) laws and policies. At the international level, the Financial Action Task Force (FATF) is now regarded as the global standard setter through its Recommendations,[1] the European Union (EU) has issued four money laundering directives (1991, 2001, 2005, and 2015), the United Nations has sponsored Conventions (Vienna Convention; Palermo Convention) as has the Council of Europe (Strasbourg Convention; Warsaw Convention). Other international agencies also play an important role in AML, including the International Monetary Fund,[2] the World Bank,[3] MONEYVAL,[4] and the Egmont Group.[5]

In reflection of the fact that AML law and policy is truly a global issue, in Chap. 3 Bergstrom explores the global development of AML, considering laws, policies, and actors. She notes how the global AML regime 'is constantly being updated and expanded not only geographically, but most importantly both in width and depth'. While the initial focus was on drugs, and the proceeds of drug trafficking, the global AML regime of today has significantly expanded. Another important aspect of AML developments is the expanding involvement of private actors.[6] In the words of Bergstrom, 'one of the most striking features of the EU AML framework is the intensified multilevel cooperation of public and private actors'. She goes on to note how private actors not only work in AML, but also how they play an important role in formulating

C. King
University of Sussex, Brighton, UK

© The Author(s) 2018
C. King et al. (eds.), *The Palgrave Handbook of Criminal and Terrorism Financing Law*,
https://doi.org/10.1007/978-3-319-64498-1_2

rules and procedures. In that way, 'traditional public tasks are shared by public and private actors'. The role of private actors took on even more prominence after the adoption of the risk-based approach in AML.

Bergstrom not only traces the development of global AML laws, but she also considers how AML is prominent in policy documents such as in the EU Justice and Home Affairs programme and the European Agenda on Security 2015–2020. Key issues here include, *inter alia*, enhancing cooperation between financial intelligence authorities, strengthening the powers of financial intelligence units (FIUs), tackling new opportunities for/threats of ML (such as virtual currency platforms, pre-paid cards), ensuring safeguards for financial flows from high-risk jurisdictions, enhancing transparency in relation to beneficial ownership, and ensuring a more targeted and focused risk-based approach. Bergstrom notes how global (and particularly EU) AML developments can be viewed in terms of both prevention and control. But she notes that proposals to expand the EU regulatory framework represent a shift in focus more towards control of money laundering (ML) and terrorist financing (TF) rather than prevention. This shift is not without difficulties, not least for processing of personal data.

Globalisation, and the global nature of AML, is explored further in Chap. 4, where Talani considers how 'global cities' can be involved—wittingly or unwittingly—in money laundering. She notes how globalisation has enabled money, legal and illicit, to move easily across the world. Of course, it is almost impossible to measure the extent to which global cities are involved in, or affected by, money laundering. But, she argues, where a money laundering operation has been successful, in many cases global cities are the final destinations for clean(ed) money. She goes on to claim that 'the City of London and the British financial sector are among the winners (and there are, unfortunately, many losers!) of the process by which money obtained through drug trafficking, sex exploitation, arms dealing, smuggling of migrants and similar practices is given a new, cleaner face'. Talani goes on to suggest that the suspicious activity reports (SARs) regime has not operated effectively to combat such laundering and even that there is more general 'hostility of the City of London towards AMLR'. Drawing upon research by Yeandle et al.,[7] Talani notes how the costs of AML are regarded as too high, that the UK approach is not directed in the most effective way, and that the AML regime does not represent good value for money. Given the sheer array of legislation and statutory instruments pertaining to AML there may be some justification for complaint about delivery.[8] The UK government is currently consulting on transposing the EU Fourth Money Laundering Directive as well as on the draft Money Laundering Regulations 2017.[9] Further, a new 'watchdog'—the Office for Professional Body Anti-Money Laundering Supervision (OPBAS)—is due to be launched in 2018.[10] According to HM Treasury,

The creation of OPBAS will ensure consistent high standards across the regime, whilst imposing the minimum possible burden on legitimate business.[11]

Based on Talani's review of AML and its reception, we can expect further complaint from the City of London.

The next two chapters build upon this discussion by examining the operation of AML requirements in two different sectors, namely banks (Chap. 5 Iafolla) and the legal profession (Chap. 6 Benson). Policymakers and law enforcement agencies have emphasised that financial institutions are vulnerable to ML. For example, in December 2014 the UK National Crime Agency (NCA) published a report on 'high end money laundering', which it defined as: 'the laundering of funds, wittingly or unwittingly, through the UK financial sector and related professional services'.[12] The NCA continued on to say, 'Although there are many ways to launder money, it is often the professional enabler who holds the key to the kind of complex processes that can provide the necessary anonymity for the criminal'.[13]

In Chap. 5, Iafolla considers how banks have risen to the challenge of implementing AML requirements. Her research specifically focuses on the first point of contact between the bank (through cashiers) and customers. While there has been extensive literature on reporting suspicious transactions, much less researched is how front-line staff interpret their AML obligations. Where an employee suspects that a transaction is suspicious, they will file what is known as an Unusual Transaction Report (UTR), which is the focus of Iafolla's research. In her study, Iafolla draws upon the sociology of risk and the sociology of money in an effort to better understand how bank employees can be influenced by, for example, their own personal attitudes, and how they understand and manage ML risks.

One aspect of AML regimes is their emphasis on know your customer (KYC). KYC can play an important function in different ways, including enabling the bank to have a deep understanding of a customer's history, and habits. As Iafolla notes,

> This kind of access to information leads to a different kind of intimate knowledge of the client by the bank teller, particularly in the context of assessing risk, and an understanding of clean or dirty money is imperative for understanding how employees come to view what kinds of transactions are unusual, and thus worth reporting.

Her study thus focuses on how cashiers, and their supervisors, make decisions about AML, drawing upon her empirical research in a Canadian bank. Her focus on the 'coalface' of AML—specifically decisions whether to file an UTR or not—offers new insights into AML in practice. Her analysis demonstrates how the decision to take action can be triggered by the (personal and subjective) experiences, or even prejudices, of the bank cashier. Not only might bank employees be swayed by their perceptions of the customer (including age, appearance, social standing, and lifestyle), but they can also be influenced by the type of instrument involved (cash versus cheque), the sums of money involved, the denominations of cash, or the regularity of transactions. Thus, 'moral judgements' on the part of employees can, and do, play a significant role in AML in practice; as Iafolla states 'This intersection of risk, money, and morality is largely fuelled by discretion'.

Other important actors in the financial sector impacted by AML requirements are considered by the next chapter, in which Benson (Chap. 6) assesses how private, non-state actors have been conscripted into the AML regime, with specific focus on the legal profession.[14] The legal profession has been identified as vulnerable to ML,[15] with the profession now subject to AML requirements in many jurisdictions as a result. The extension of AML requirements to the legal profession has not been without criticism, however, not least given the potential impact upon the solicitor/client relationship. Notwithstanding the official discourse, as Benson points out, 'there remains little understanding of the empirical scale and nature of professional facilitation of money laundering'. Albeit with some exceptions,[16] she notes how 'The nature of professionals' involvement in money laundering has received limited academic attention, and there has been little empirical research in the area'. Her research on ML/AML in the legal profession draws upon empirical research on 20 cases of solicitors convicted of money laundering, alongside interviews with practitioners and professional/regulatory bodies. After outlining the UK legal obligations, she considers the different actions and behaviours of solicitors convicted of ML, the financial benefit obtained, the degree of intent (and indeed the extent of knowledge), and the consequences of conviction. What becomes clear is that facilitation of ML by legal professionals is 'not a homogenous phenomenon'. Ultimately, she concludes that 'It is clear … that there is a need for further research into the involvement of professionals in the facilitation of money laundering, and greater consideration of the obligations of professionals in the prevention of money laundering and the legislative framework which underpins these obligations'.

The next chapter (Chap. 7) by Riccardi and Levi considers this issue of 'facilitating' money laundering from a different perspective—through the means of cash. In 2015 Europol published an aptly titled report, 'Why is cash still king?',[17] where it was noted:

The relationship between physical cash and money laundering, as well as that of the criminal to cash, is complex: cash in itself is not a method of laundering the proceeds of crime, nor is it an illegal commodity; rather it is an entirely legal facilitator which enables criminals to inject illegal proceeds into the legal economy with far fewer risks of detection than other systems.[18]

Accordingly, Riccardi and Levi consider how cash is spread in the legitimate economy, as well as those criminal activities that tend to generate illicit cash proceeds. Of course, cash can, and does, play an important role in criminal activities. For example, the US National Money Laundering Risk Assessment 2015 stated: 'Drug proceeds start and often remain as cash, while proceeds from fraud rarely start out as cash but may end up as cash after laundering, or during the layering stage in an effort to break the audit trail'.[19] Riccardi and Levi thus explore how cash is used as a means of laundering, with specific focus on cash smuggling and cash-intensive businesses/assets. Often, the authors suggest, such laundering is 'a response to increased AML controls on the financial sector and on money service businesses'.

One suggestion that is often put forward to minimise the risk of ML/TF is to minimise the use of cash in the legitimate economy through, for example, controls on purchases, on cross-border-transfers, or on banknote denominations. Alternatively, the government could simply withdraw certain denominations from circulation—as the Indian government did in late 2016 in an effort to combat corruption and illegal cash holdings.[20] These approaches do have obvious appeal; yet, as the authors point out,

> … data shows that cash is successful also in the legal economy. Despite the increasing use of alternative payment methods, such as credit cards, mobile payments or virtual currencies, banknotes still represent the preferred means of payment both in Europe and abroad.

It is important then to consider how—if at all—restrictions on cash use might impact upon money laundering and on crime more generally and outweigh any side effects. The authors suggest that the impact would be heavier on petty money laundering schemes and traditional criminal organisations, but that there would be much less impact upon higher-level ML schemes. So too is it important to consider displacement effects, potential changes to the criminal market and partnerships, and new opportunities for criminal activities. Alongside these, policymakers must consider how cash restrictions might impact upon consumers' behaviour, though it is difficult to assess the extent of this impact. This issue is a recurring one throughout the chapter—a lack of data: 'despite being one of the oldest means of payment, cash is still the one we least know about—both in relation to the legal and the illegal economy'. The authors adopt a pragmatic approach, calling for such issues to receive greater consideration, starting with a presumption 'that there would have to be some very good reasons to believe that these cash controls would have a greater impact than others, whose effectiveness in crime reduction have been heavily critiqued'.

The three previous chapters focus on what might be described as 'traditional' financial sectors (banks and lawyers) and the main form of transfer (cash) in ML schemes. The next two chapters, however, draw attention to emerging areas that provide significant potential for ML. One such obvious site of development is in relation to online fora where the AML legal framework is still unclear. Thus, there is a need to consider how the AML framework applies in virtual worlds (Chap. 8) and in relation to Bitcoin (Chap. 9), areas that have been identified as incurring significant risks and vulnerabilities.[21]

Chambers-Jones (Chap. 8) outlines how virtual worlds can be 'a safe haven for criminal activity', including money laundering. She argues that policy discourse has primarily focused on virtual currencies, with little attention on, or understanding of, virtual worlds. Indeed, she emphasises that there is 'a lack of detailed knowledge of virtual worlds and also digital currencies'. She makes the case that virtual ML can easily satisfy the traditional stages of laundering (placement, layering, and integration). She explores the attractions to money launderers of the virtual platforms, including the ease of international payments and anonymity. Chambers-Jones is critical of the lack of a joined-up multi-national response, which makes it easier for virtual ML. She draws upon examples to demonstrate that virtual ML is 'real' enough in terms of its real-life impact and that the current regulatory framework is inadequate.

Staying within information and communications technologies, in Chap. 9, Egan considers virtual currencies, with particular focus on bitcoins. She too notes the lack of clarity in this area. She considers policy discourse where virtual currencies are often presented as either positive or negative, and she assesses whether there is a need for greater regulation. She notes that perceived threats posed by virtual currencies, such as anonymity which can hamper customer identification and due diligence, have gained momentum. So, discussion now is more on what form regulation should take, rather than whether there should be regulation. Of course, as is well known from AML requirements in other sectors,[22] this will have implications in terms of 'private policing' and AML. Acknowledging the current ambiguity, Egan argues that regulating bitcoin does have potential to prevent the device from being exploited for criminal purposes, so there is a need for coherent and harmonised conceptual understanding and then regulation of virtual currencies. She echoes the argument that regulation must transcend jurisdictional boundaries and be embedded in appropriate legal frameworks. Even if the EU AML framework is expanded to regulate bitcoins, as Egan points out, 'this does not solve the problem of policing bitcoins'. As a result, this area of AML looks set to remain problematic not only in terms of regulation but also in terms of law enforcement challenges, such as technological advancements, the expertise needed, and the significant resources required to effectively police bitcoin activities.

As made clear in the previous two chapters, the opportunities (or threats, depending on your perspective) for online laundering are now very much under consideration at policy and practical levels. The next chapter, however, explores a topic that is not receiving the same level of attention, even though it would appear to be a much larger threat—trade-based money laundering (TBML). According to the 2015 US National Money Laundering Risk Assessment, 'TBML is one of the more complex methods of money laundering to investigate'.[23] Murray (Chap. 10) sets out how TBML is straightforward to describe, but difficult to tackle. Unlike other examples of ML, TBML is concerned with transferring value rather than money which makes it difficult to detect. Murray argues that TBML is 'a problem that is too big an issue for law enforcement and regulatory authorities to ignore'. Yet, AML efforts to date have primarily focused on the financial sector (considered in Chaps. 5 and 6), and TBML has not received the same level of attention. Murray suggests that current AML approaches may be inadequate to effectively deal with TBML, but the risk cannot simply be side-lined, especially as TBML is being used to circumvent more traditional laundering avenues that are more open to detection. Indeed, Murray suggests that if nothing is done to tackle TBML, it might undermine 'the reputation and credibility of the entire AML endeavour'. Moreover, the financial sector might well question why they are putting so much time and resources into AML compliance when international trade is an even bigger medium for ML. However, solutions are not straightforward. The difficulties inherent in AML frameworks would equally apply if TBML were brought within its remit. Indeed, he argues: 'If this problem was to be considered anew with a clean sheet of paper, it would likely be that we would consider different approaches to solving it'.

Earlier chapters in this collection focus on AML regulation in diverse areas. The next two chapters, by Ramachandran *et al.* (Chap. 11) and Levi (Chap. 12) provide a different perspective—exploring 'unintended consequences' of AML laws and policies. Ramachandran *et al.* set out many examples of how

AML regulation negatively impacts upon money transfer businesses and upon correspondent banking sectors. They suggest that de-banking of money transfer businesses and the severing of correspondent banking relationships are significant problems, particularly for developing countries. The reasons for the stance taken by banks can be briefly summed up as being affected by: regulatory risk, reputational risk, and risk of ML/TF abuse. Against a backdrop of drives to reduce compliance costs, the perception that money transfer businesses and correspondent banking relationships are 'high risk' influences banks in decisions whether or not to de-bank or to sever relationships.[24] Crucially though, Ramachandran *et al.* note that 'Risk perceptions by rich world regulators appear to reflect a bias against cross-border transactions (since they imply additional challenges in tracing), even though there is no particular evidence that cross-border transactions are more likely to involve criminal behaviour'. Almost inevitably, then, banks consider money transfer businesses to be 'particularly risky', so it is unsurprising that such businesses face de-banking in the current climate of ever more regulatory pressure. The knock-on effect is that as banks de-bank, money transfer businesses must adopt other arrangements. First, they may turn to other, less mainstream banks which then bear the burden of AML/CTF compliance. The replacement bank might resort to 'nested' relationships which are less transparent, and costs might increase as banks are forced to pay a higher premium for correspondent banking. Second, they may become incorporated into broader financial organisations which are less suited to the customers of the money transfer business. Third, they may go out of business entirely. In this way, regulatory requirements could potentially have an important impact on competition and available customer services in the banking sector. While there have been some efforts to encourage banks to manage, rather than eliminate, risk,[25] the authors contend that a lot more work needs to be done in this area[26] because 'they fall well short of a systematic attempt to understand and mitigate the unintended consequences of AML/CFT'. Given the importance of remittances to alleviating poverty in developing countries and also promoting financial development,[27] there is a need for greater data 'in order to allow researchers and policy makers to work together to reform the AML/CFT system to be as effective and efficient as possible. This should be seen as both a security and a sustainable development priority'.

De-risking is considered further in the next chapter, where Levi (Chap. 12) outlines how financial institutions, particularly banks, came to be a 'line of defence' in reporting suspected activities to financial intelligence units, and how their role has subsequently expanded. However, an important obstacle in this role is that financial institutions themselves are unclear what they ought to be looking for: 'it is seldom clear what banks should be looking out for and the temptation is to look for "out of context" behaviour, or behaviour that is not readily explicable'. And as banks have been sanctioned for engaging in 'risky' behaviour, and as compliance costs have increased, a not unexpected development was that the 'risk appetite' of banks changed. That is the context behind de-risking by many banks.[28] Levi acknowledges that AML/CTF policies may 'have unintentional and costly consequences for people in poor countries, not just offenders but also especially the families of migrant workers, small businesses that need to access working capital or trade finance, and aid recipients'. Further, there are risks that financial flows will become less transparent and that there will be greater hostility towards the West—what the author describes as counter-productive regulation. He emphasises the crime-control approach of the AML/CTF 'community', which has taken 'little account—except when forced to—either of due process/human rights considerations or of the unintended costs of policies and practices to which the controls give rise'. There are many examples of how banks have engaged in de-risking, where banks have acted 'to rid themselves of business that might expose them to sanctions'. These decisions are, Levi notes, made behind closed doors. While there have been calls for banks to look beyond their profit motive,[29] the obvious retort from banks is that such criticism does not take account of the potential sanctions faced by banks, especially from US regulators. This criticism of the risk-based approach is picked up again in later chapters in this Handbook (such as by van Duyne *et al.* in Chapter 15).

Levi argues that the practice of what is to be regarded as 'risky' business 'expose[s] the intellectual and institutional fault-lines' of the policy and practice of the international community's approach to dirty behaviour and assets. He notes how banks speak the language of risk, but feel pressurised to practise zero tolerance. The reality is that, as banks engage in a risk-based approach, it is inevitable that de-risking and de-banking will occur. And banks will often be influenced by the actions of regulators, and expectations about future regulatory actions. Significantly, though, 'there is, as yet, no generally agreed quantitative assessment methodology for assessing financial crime risk'. Even if banks are consistent in their interpretation of 'risk' that too can result in de-risking. Therefore, discussion of de-risking needs to go beyond risk; it is also important to take account of 'harm', the impact of 'credible deterrence', and decision-making by regulators and prosecutors. While authorities have issued guidance about de-risking and de-banking,[30] the impact of such guidance remains unclear in practice. More influential to banking practice is the threat of criminal prosecution, regulatory penalties, and civil actions: 'In the absence of clear and consistent policies in all of these spheres, risk aversion is understandable' and 'there is no point in blaming banks for making defensive decisions to get rid of existing clients or not to take on others if the probability is above zero of suffering serious consequences for making a false negative judgment about the riskiness of a client (including a correspondent bank)'.

The next three chapters engage with specific aspects of the AML regime, taking account of the FATF Recommendations.[31] First, Chaikin (Chap. 13) considers the question of 'effectiveness' of AML measures. Then Ferwerda (Chap. 14) considers the costs and benefits of AML policies. Finally, van Duyne *et al.* (Chap. 15) critique the risk-based approach to AML compliance.

In Chap. 13 Chaikin notes how effectiveness cannot be considered without first looking at the objectives and development of AML at the international level, and how such objectives have been implemented at a national level. Initially, when the focus of the international community was on ML related to drugs (particularly in the 1980s), it was easier to examine the effectiveness of AML measures. Even then, however, as Chaikin notes, it was difficult to assess whether the AML regime was effective in meeting that goal. Today—where the focus is not solely on drugs but also encompasses other serious crimes, Chaikin points out that 'the expansion of the goals of the AML system has meant that the problem of assessment of the effectiveness of the system is yet more difficult'. A key issue here is the difficulty in identifying the goals of the AML regime, not made any easier by the fact that the objectives of the FATF have themselves evolved. The expansion of the global AML regime tends to be linked with three developments: the inclusion of counter terrorist financing measures within the remit of the FATF post 9/11, the inclusion of financing of proliferation of weapons of mass destruction also within the FATF remit, and the Global Financial Crisis resulting in international bodies such as the IMF adopting a policy stance that links issues of financial stability to international financial crime.

In this chapter, Chaikin focuses on the Australian experience of complying with international AML measures, the primary legislation being the Anti-Money Laundering and Counter-Terrorism Financing Act 2006 (Cth) (the 'AML/CTF Act'). The reason for this focus is that Australia is one of the first countries to be assessed under the new FATF criterion of 'effectiveness'. Previously peer review assessments carried out by the FATF focused on technical compliance, where the focus was often on whether a country had enacted legislation that complies with the FATF Recommendations. While this might appear relatively straightforward, such compliance tended to be low, both in developed and developing countries.[32] Since 2013 a new methodology for peer review assessment has been adopted, with the focus not only on technical compliance but also on 'effectiveness'.[33] The underpinning rationales here are to improve the FATF's focus on outcomes, to identify the extent to which national

AML/CTF systems are achieving the objectives of the FATF standards, to identify any systematic weaknesses, and to enable countries to prioritise measures to improve their system.[34] Effectiveness is defined as 'The extent to which the defined outcomes are achieved'.[35] More specifically, in the AML/CTF context, it is 'the extent to which financial systems and economies mitigate the risks and threats of money laundering, and financing of terrorism and proliferation'.[36] This new methodology represents a significant departure from the focus solely on technical compliance; as the FATF states:

> It does not involve checking whether specific requirements are met, or that all elements of a given Recommendation are in place. Instead, it requires a judgement as to whether, or to what extent defined outcomes are being achieved, *i.e.* whether the key objectives of an AML/CFT system, in line with the FATF Standards, are being effectively met in practice.[37]

There is, however, an important link between the two: the 'level of technical compliance contributes to the assessment of effectiveness. ... It is unlikely that a country that is assessed to have a low level of compliance with the technical aspects of the FATF Recommendations will have an effective AML/CFT system'.[38]

Chaikin considers the Mutual Evaluation Report of Australia[39] under the new FATF methodology. It attains a rating of compliant or largely compliant in relation to 24 of the Recommendations but is non-compliant or partially compliant in relation to 16. Overall, it is 'a surprisingly modest result'. Chaikin argues that this assessment shows how the FATF Recommendations 'are difficult to implement for legal, political or other reasons'. As for the process of evaluation, his assessment is that:

> The new methodology represents an ambitious attempt by the FATF to ensure that implementation of the FATF Recommendations is assessed not merely by assessing technical compliance but also enforcement outcomes. It is likely that the new methodology will increase the complexity in AML performance measurement and make the task of peer reviewers more time consuming and difficult. Whether the new methodology will result in countries changing their AML enforcement behaviour is an open question.

In the next chapter, Ferwerda (Chap. 14) adopts an economics approach to assessing AML policies. He too considers the criterion of 'effectiveness' and reinforces the view that the goals of AML policies are not clear. Drawing upon empirical research across the EU, he discovered many different views as to that goal, including: fighting/reducing money laundering; reducing/fighting crime;

confiscating criminal assets; fighting drugs crimes; fighting tax evasion; and complying with international obligations. He notes how the goal of AML policy 'is not sufficiently clear for accurate measurement of effectiveness'. This conclusion, combined with the lack of any (reliable) consensus as to the extent of money laundering, leads Ferwerda to focus on the efficiency of AML policies. He explores both the costs and benefits of AML policies, to enable a fuller understanding of whether such policies are worth the cost. The costs of AML policies are broken down as follows: ongoing policy making, sanction costs (repressive), FIUs, supervision, law enforcement and judiciary, duties of the private sector, reduction in privacy, and efficiency costs for society and the financial system. Benefits are broken down into: fines (preventive and repressive); confiscated proceeds; reduction in the amount of ML; less predicate crimes; the reduced damage effect on the real economy; and less risk for the financial sector. Given the lack of detailed, and sufficient, statistics to undertake a comprehensive cost/benefit analysis, Ferwerda's approach is to undertake such an analysis for a hypothetical country combining information gathered for 27 EU Members States. He finds that it is possible to estimate the costs of AML policies but much more difficult to estimate the benefits. For a hypothetical country with a population of 10 million people and a price level equal to the United States, annual AML costs would be in excess of €44 million.[40] Given the difficulties in measuring benefits, Ferwerda suggests that the cost/benefit analysis boils down to a simple question: are we willing to spend such an amount, along with reductions in privacy and efficiency costs, for unknown benefits? His answer is that only a brave person would suggest that that is too high a price to pay for countering serious crime.

The final chapter in the AML section of this Handbook, by van Duyne *et al.* (Chap. 15), builds upon the previous two chapters by focusing on the risk-based approach and the concept of proportionality. The risk-based approach is now entrenched in FATF parlance.[41] According to its 2007 Guidance,

> By adopting a risk-based approach, competent authorities and financial institutions are able to ensure that measures to prevent or mitigate money laundering and terrorist financing are commensurate to the risks identified. This will allow resources to be allocated in the most efficient ways. The principle is that resources should be directed in accordance with priorities so that the greatest risks receive the highest attention.[42]

This approach, so the Guidance suggests, avoids a simple 'tick-box' approach with a focus on regulatory requirements.[43] A risk-based approach requires: a determination of where ML and TF risks are greatest; identification by countries of the main vulnerabilities and then efforts to address them; and identification by institutions of higher risk customers, products and services. Furthermore, 'These are not static assessments. They will change over time, depending on how circumstances develop, and how threats evolve'.[44] While the FATF does emphasise potential benefits (including better management of risks and cost-benefits, financial institutions focus on real and identified threats, and flexibility to adapt to risks that change over time), it also recognises potential challenges (such as identifying appropriate information to conduct a sound risk analysis, addressing short-term transitional costs, a greater need for more expert staff capable of exercising sound judgement, and regulatory responses to potential diversity of practices).[45]

Van Duyne *et al.* are sceptical of this FATF risk-based approach. They note how global AML policies are now more targeted as a result of the risk-based approach, yet they question whether that approach is proportionate. They suggest that the FATF's use of a 'risk-based approach' differs from how the term 'risk' is used in banking; indeed, they go so far as to say that 'despite a common vocabulary, the interpretation of "risk" within AML is fundamentally different'. It is axiomatic that a proportionate risk-based approach would result in a high-risk threat requiring greater resources, while lesser resources would be devoted to a lower risk. There is a significant practical difficulty here, however, because, as the authors highlight, what is to be regarded as high and low risk is not clear. So, 'Without proper yardsticks, institutions must attempt to second guess whether their perception of risk will match that of the regulator'. Further, the authors are critical of how ambiguity in the FATF guidance, perhaps inevitably, undermines proportionality. Moreover, when considering proportionality, it is necessary to consider the extent of the threat of criminal money. Here the authors are particularly critical of AML policy development, noting how such policies are driven by 'faith rather than fact', and how policy discourse is full of 'earthquake warnings' that lack empirical support. The authors are particularly critical of various efforts to measure the amount of money that is laundered: 'The available meagre evidence is insufficient as a basis for finding a proportional risk-based counter strategy: proportional to what?' The authors go on to critique the fourth round of evaluations carried out by FATF assessors. Drawing again upon the concept of proportionality, they question whether the FATF evaluations are themselves conducted in a proportionate manner. For example, even where countries are regarded as financially isolated by the FATF (such as Armenia or Ethiopia), they can still be subjected to detailed evaluation 'by a platoon of seven to eight experts for about two weeks, producing reports of 105 to 182 pages'. Would it not be better, the authors suggest, to allocate resources to these evaluation reports based on the level of risk? Yet, 'it is difficult to identify any consideration of resource allocation, let alone a proportionality of applied resources set off against risk'. Ultimately, the authors come to a rather sombre conclusion in relation to the relationship between 'risk' and 'proportionality'. While the risk-based approach might look relatively straightforward (at least in FATF publications), the reality is very different and much more complex. They conclude: 'The FATF has failed to unravel this complexity, saddling the global AML community with a defectively elaborated and immature approach'.

In conclusion, there are too many variable sectors and practices and too little sound data to reach resounding or secure conclusions about AML policy and its application. The best that can be claimed here is that the research presented in Part II elucidates the complexities of analysis and evaluation. One can say with more certainty that the debates will continue, not only because of new developments such as virtual currencies but also because of serious costs and strains, not only because of the risks in financial sectors but also amongst customers who suffer the pains of de-risking.

Notes

1. FATF, *International Standards on Combatting Money Laundering and the Financing of Terrorism and Proliferation* (FATF/OECD 2012, updated in June 2017).
2. IMF, 'The IMF and the Fight Against Money Laundering and the Financing of Terrorism: Factsheet' (updated October 2016) <www.imf.org/About/Factsheets/Sheets/2016/08/01/16/31/Fight-Against-Money-Laundering-the-Financing-of-Terrorism?pdf=1> accessed 19 April 2017.
3. World Bank, *Combatting Money Laundering and the Financing of Terrorism— A Comprehensive Training Guide* (World Bank 2009).
4. See, for example, Committee of Experts on the Evaluation of Anti-Money Laundering Measures and the Financing of Terrorism (MONEYVAL), 'Compliance Enhancing Procedures' <www.coe.int/t/dghl/monitoring/moneyval/Evaluations/Compliance_en.asp> accessed 19 April 2017.
5. The Egmont Group, 'Strategic Plan 2014—2017' (2015) <https://egmontgroup.org/en/document-library/8> accessed 19 April 2017.
6. See, for example, Karin Svedberg Helgesson and Ulrika Mörth, 'Involuntary Public Policy-making by For-Profit Professionals: European Lawyers on Anti-Money Laundering and Terrorism Financing' (2016) 54(5) Journal of Common Market Studies 1216; Gilles Favarel-Garrigues, Thierry Godefroy, and Pierre Lascoumes, 'Sentinels in the Banking Industry: Private Actors and the Fight against Money Laundering in France' (2008) 48(1) British Journal of Criminology 1.

7. Mark Yeandle and others, *Anti-Money Laundering Requirements: Costs, Benefits and Perceptions* (Research Series Number Six, Corporation of London 2005).

8. For wider discussion, see Peter Alldridge, *What Went Wrong with Money Laundering Law?* (Palgrave Macmillan 2016).

9. HM Treasury, 'Open Consultation: Money Laundering Regulations 2017' <www.gov.uk/government/consultations/money-laundering-regulations-2017> accessed 30 March 2017.

10. Caroline Binham, 'UK Steps Up Anti-Money Laundering Crackdown with New Watchdog' *Financial Times* (London, 15 March 2017).

11. HM Treasury, 'UK Tightens Defence Against Money Laundering' <www.gov.uk/government/news/uk-tightens-defences-against-money-laundering> accessed 30 March 2017.

12. National Crime Agency, *High End Money Laundering: Strategy and Action Plan* (2014) para 3 <http://nationalcrimeagency.gov.uk/publications/625-high-end-money-laundering-strategy/file> accessed 1 February 2017.

13. Ibid. para 5.

14. Other sectors that have to comply with AML requirements include estate agents, art dealers, accountants, and more. For further discussion see, for example, Martin Gill and Geoff Taylor, 'Preventing Money Laundering or Obstructing Business? Financial Companies' Perspectives on "Know Your Customer" Procedures' (2004) 44(4) British Journal of Criminology 582; Janet Ulph, 'The Impact of the Criminal Law and Money Laundering Measures Upon the Illicit Trade in Art and Antiquities' (2011) XVI(1) Art, Antiquity and the Law 39; Maria Bergstrom and others, 'A New Role for For-Profit Actors? The Case of Anti-Money Laundering and Risk Management' (2011) 49(5) Journal of Common Market Studies 1043. Compare Anja P Jakobi, 'Non-State Actors and Global Crime Governance: Explaining the Variance of Public-Private Interaction' (2016) 18(1) British Journal of Politics and International Relations 72.

15. For example, FATF, *Money Laundering and Terrorist Financing: Vulnerabilities of Legal Professionals* (FATF/OECD 2013); Solicitors Regulation Authority, *Cleaning Up: Law Firms and the Risk of Money Laundering* (2014); HM Treasury and Home Office, *UK National Risk Assessment of Money Laundering and Terrorist Financing* (2015); NCA, *National Strategic Assessment of Serious and Organised Crime 2016* (National Crime Agency 2016).

16. For example, Melvin Soudijn, 'Removing Excuses in Money Laundering' (2012) 15(2) Trends in Organized Crime 146; David Middleton and Michael Levi, 'Let Sleeping Lawyers Lie: Organized Crime, Lawyers and the Regulation of Legal Services' (2015) 55(4) British Journal of Criminology 647.

17. Europol, *Why is Cash Still King? A Strategic Report on the Use of Cash by Criminal Groups as a Facilitator for Money Laundering* (European Police Office 2015).

18. Ibid. 9.

19. US Department of the Treasury, *National Money Laundering Risk Assessment 2015* (2015) 23.
20. BBC News, 'India Scraps 500 and 1000 Rupee Bank Notes Overnight' (London, 9 November 2016) <www.bbc.co.uk/news/business-37906742> accessed 13 June 2017.
21. See FATF, *Virtual Currencies: Key Definitions and Potential AML/CFT Risks* (FATF/OECD 2014); HM Treasury and Home Office (n 15).
22. Favarel-Garrigues, Godefroy, and Lascoumes (n 6); Karin Svedberg Helgesson, 'Banks and the Governance of Crime' in Anja P Jakobi and Klaus Dieter Wolf (eds), *The Transnational Governance of Violence and Crime: Non-State Actors in Security* (Palgrave Macmillan 2013) 214.
23. US Department of the Treasury (n 19) 29.
24. See FATF, *FATF Guidance: Correspondent Banking Services* (FATF/OECD 2016); HM Treasury and Home Office (n 15); Joint Money Laundering Steering Group, *Guidance in Respect of Money Service Businesses* (2014).
25. See FATF, 'FATF Clarifies Risk-Based Approach: Case by Case, not Wholesale De-Risking' (28 October 2014) <www.fatf-gafi.org/publications/fatfgeneral/documents/rba-and-de-risking.html> accessed 13 June 2017; FCA, 'Derisking: Banks' Management of Money Laundering Risk—FCA Expectations' <www.fca.org.uk/firms/money-laundering/derisking-managing-risk, 2015> accessed 11 June 2017.
26. Michaela Erbenová and others, *The Withdrawal of Correspondent Banking Relationships: A Case for Policy Action* IMF Staff Discussion Note (IMF 2016).
27. See Reena Aggarwal, Asli Demirguc-Kunt, and Maria Soledad Martínez Pería, *Do Workers' Remittances Promote Financial Development?* (World Bank 2006); Mohapatra Sanket and Ratha Dilip (eds), *Remittance Markets in Africa* (World Bank 2011).
28. David Artingstall and others, *Drivers and Impacts of De-Risking: A Study of Representative Views and Data in the UK* (John Howell and Co Ltd 2016).
29. See, for example, Tom Keatinge, *Uncharitable Behavior: Counter-Terrorist Regulation Restricts Charity Banking Worldwide* (DEMOS 2014).
30. For example, Office of the Comptroller of the Currency, 'Risk Management Guidance on Periodic Risk Re-evaluation of Foreign Correspondent Banking' (US Department of the Treasury 2016) <http://.gov/news-issuances/bulletins/2016/bulletin-2016-32.html> accessed 20 April 2017.
31. FATF (n 1).
32. For consideration of the FATF Recommendations in developing countries, see, for example, Hennie Bester and others, *Implementing FATF Standards in Developing Countries and Financial Inclusion: Findings and Guidelines* (Genesis Analytics (Pty) Ltd 2008) <www.cenfri.org/documents/AML/AML_CFT%20and%20Financial%20Inclusion.pdf> accessed 16 April 2017; Abdullahi Y. Shehu, 'Promoting Financial Inclusion for Effective Anti-Money Laundering and Counter Financing of Terrorism (AML/CFT)' (2012) 57(3) Crime, Law and Social Change 305.

33. FATF, *Methodology for Assessing Technical Compliance with the FATF Recommendations and the Effectiveness of AML/CFT Systems* (FATF/OECD 2013, updated February 2017).

34. Ibid. para 38.

35. Ibid.

36. Ibid.

37. Ibid. para 40.

38. Ibid. 45. The reverse might not hold true—technical compliance does not necessarily guarantee effectiveness.

39. FATF and APG, *Anti-Money Laundering and Counter-Terrorist Financing Measures, Australia, Mutual Evaluation Report* (FATF and APG 2016).

40. Based on this estimate, estimates are also provided for EU Member States, ranging from Cyprus (€1.47m) to Germany (€378.17m), and the EU as a whole (€2,157,059,590).

41. See, for example, FATF, *Risk-Based Approach Guidance in Relation to Money or Value Transfer Services* (2016); FATF, *Guidance for a Risk-Based Approach to Virtual Currencies* (FATF/OECD 2015); FATF, *Guidance for a Risk-Based Approach to the Banking Sector* (FATF/OECD 2014); FATF, *Guidance for a Risk-Based Approach to Pre-Paid Cards, Mobile Payments and Internet Based Payments Services* (FATF/OECD 2013); FATF, *Guidance for a Risk-Based Approach to the Life Insurance Sector* (FATF/OECD 2009); FATF, *Guidance for a Risk-Based Approach to Legal Professionals* (FATF/OECD 2008); FATF, *Guidance for a Risk-Based Approach to Casinos* (FATF/OECD 2008); FATF, *Guidance for a Risk-Based Approach to Accountants* (FATF/OECD 2008); FATF, *Guidance on the Risk-Based Approach for Real Estate Agents* (FATF/OECD 2008).

42. FATF, *Guidance on the Risk-Based Approach to Combating Money Laundering and Terrorist Financing: High Level Principles and Procedures* (FATF/OECD 2007) para 1.7.

43. Ibid.

44. Ibid. para 1.9.

45. Ibid. para 1.22.

Colin King is Reader in Law at the University of Sussex and co-Founder of the Crime Research Centre. He was an Academic Fellow at the Honourable Society of the Inner Temple from 2014–2017. In March 2016 Colin gave oral evidence at the Home Affairs Select Committee Inquiry into the Proceeds of Crime Act. Colin is co-editor of *Dirty Assets: Emerging Issues in the Regulation of Criminal and Terrorist Assets* (King and Walker, Ashgate, 2014). Also with Clive Walker, Colin led an AHRC-funded research network (2014–2016) entitled 'Dirty Assets: Experiences, reflections, and lessons learnt from a decade of legislation on criminal money laundering and terrorism financing'. In 2017 he was awarded a prestigious AHRC Leadership Fellowship to conduct empirical research on proceeds of crime legislation.

3

The Global AML Regime and the EU AML Directives: Prevention and Control

Maria Bergström

Introduction

In just over 30 years, a global Anti-Money Laundering (AML) Regime has developed that is constantly being updated and expanded not only geographically but most importantly both in width and depth. Today, it affects a large part of modern society including both private and public actors and is key in a steadily growing number of interconnected areas. Initially associated with the fight against drug trafficking and the threat to banking and other financial institutions by drug Money Laundering (ML), and later expanded to the global war on terror, its latest advances form part of the EU Security Agenda, including a wider EU effort to improve tax transparency and the combat of tax abuse.

Constantly finding new roles and purposes, the global AML Regime has become well-known far beyond its influence upon public and private actors in financial markets, and it affects individuals as well as regional and global actors and markets. With its variety of soft and hard law, embracing logics of 'naming and shaming' as well as hard enforcement mechanisms within both administrative and criminal law, its impact upon society and individuals is certainly far reaching.

In December 2016, 25 years after the first EU AML Directive (1MLD) was adopted with reference to the internal market legal basis, the European Commission put forward a proposal for a criminal law AML Directive.[1] This

M. Bergström
Uppsala University, Uppsala, Sweden

© The Author(s) 2018
C. King et al. (eds.), *The Palgrave Handbook of Criminal and Terrorism Financing Law*,
https://doi.org/10.1007/978-3-319-64498-1_3

proposal and the fourth internal market AML Directive form an important part of the wider European Agenda on Security for 2015–2020. These are also key instruments in the 2016 EU Action Plan to further step up the fight against the financing of terrorism.[2] In addition, there are recent measures regarding information accompanying transfers of funds, payment services in the internal market and access to AML information by tax authorities.

Against this backdrop, this chapter aims to illustrate the complex nature of the current AML Regime. Involving international, EU and national actors and laws, embracing public, private and penal rules, self-regulation, administrative and criminal law enforcement mechanisms, this complex regulatory field is now meant not only to prevent but also to control ML and terrorism financing.

The Emergence and Development of the Global and Regional EU AML Regime

Although ML is an international phenomenon and constitutes a major problem around the world, the phenomenon and the term has only come to prominence in the last 30 years. Although in use earlier, the term 'money laundering' seems to have been introduced in legislation in 1986 in the US Money Laundering Control Act of 1986.[3] In the early days, ML was recognised mainly as a domestic problem. However, the dirty money that was laundered often came, and still comes today, from the trade in drugs, human trafficking and other transnational criminal activities.[4]

At the same time, ML is a crime that hinders the proper workings of financial systems.[5] As pointed out by the International Monetary Fund, possible consequences of ML (and the financing of terrorism) include 'risks to the soundness and stability of financial institutions and financial systems, increased volatility of international capital flows, and a dampening effect on foreign direct investment'.[6] In this respect, ML is particularly threatening since a sound financial infrastructure is one of the fundamental features of a stable society. With increased economic globalisation, national borders became less relevant also for financial transactions.[7] Taken together, the threats of ML and the emerging AML regulation have gradually become transnational and even global, strongly affecting also the regional and national levels.[8]

Regulations and Regulators

International Rules and European Regulations

Attention to ML as a global problem began in 1988 with the prohibition of the laundering of drug proceeds in the United Nations Convention against Illicit Traffic in Narcotic Drugs and Psychotropic Substances (the Vienna Convention).[9] The Vienna Convention was, however, limited to drugs and did not specifically refer to the term 'money laundering'. That same year, principles dealing with ML were also adopted by the Basel Committee on Banking Supervision (BCBS).[10] This body consists of banking supervisory authorities in a number of states and aims to produce common standards of supervision of banking and financial institutions. The Council of Europe Convention on Laundering, Search, Seizure and Confiscation of the Proceeds from Crime (the Strasbourg Convention)[11] from 1990 is the first multilateral treaty which deals generally with 'laundering offences'.[12] The Strasbourg Convention also widened the so-called predicate offences beyond drug trafficking.[13] In 1998, another regional actor intervened when the OECD presented a series of recommendations on harmful tax practices.[14] In 1999 the UN International Convention for the Suppression of the Financing of Terrorism was adopted,[15] and in 2000, the UN General Assembly adopted the United Nations Convention against Transnational Organized Crime.

Building upon and updating the Strasbourg Convention, the Council of Europe Convention on Laundering, Search, Seizure and Confiscation of the Proceeds from Crime and on the Financing of Terrorism of 2005 (the Warsaw Convention)[16] constitutes the most comprehensive international convention on ML. It aims to facilitate international cooperation and mutual assistance in investigating crime. The Convention not only includes provisions related to the criminalisation of ML but also provisions on asset freezing and confiscation. The Warsaw Convention is the first international treaty covering both the prevention and the control of ML and terrorism financing. The adoption of the Warsaw Convention reflects the importance of quick access to financial information or information on assets held by criminal organisations.

The Financial Action Task Force (FATF)

Today the FATF is the most important international standard setter for AML and Combatting Terrorism Financing (CTF). The FATF is not created by treaty; instead it was established in July 1989 as a result of an American initiative by decision of the Paris summit of the G-7. The establishment of the FATF was a response to the G-7's recognition of the threat of drug ML to banking and other financial institutions.[17] The FATF is thus a part, albeit autonomous, of the Organisation of Economic Cooperation and Development (OECD).[18] The FATF currently comprises 35 member jurisdictions and 2 regional organisations, thus representing most major financial centres in all parts of the world.[19] Its membership includes the European Commission and 15 Members States (MSs). The remaining 13 MSs are members of 'MONEYVAL', which is an FATF-style regional body that conducts self and mutual assessment exercises of the measures in place in Council of Europe Member States.

The FATF sets standards or model rules and then tests Member States against these. It works by peer review: panels composed of national experts in law and banking are established which periodically evaluate states' laws and practices.[20] The FATF can apply, and has applied, sanctions in the form of warning states which are considered to be failing to comply with the 'non-binding' FATF standards. This results in significantly higher transaction costs for financial institutions in the blacklisted state, as financial institutions in other FATF states demand greater security when dealing with them. This type of 'blacklisting' partially explains relatively high degree of compliance with the FATF standards. As far as EU states are concerned, the standards are, in fact, binding, as they have been incorporated into EU legislation.[21]

The European Union

The EU AML Directive from 1991 (1MLD) was the first stage in combating ML at the European level.[22] Strongly influenced by the international level, the 1MLD was based on the 40 original FATF recommendations and influenced by UN Conventions and the recommendations and principles adopted by the Council of Europe and the banking organisation BCBS. This included taking the definition of ML from the Vienna Convention.

In the European context, a historical and a contextual analysis reveal that the emergence of the European single market required European rules on financial transactions.[23] The elimination of national borders demanded compensatory measures to delimit financial cross-border crimes. Preventive measures to ensure that an open and liberal financial market was not abused by criminal elements were adopted. The preamble of the 1MLD stated that ML must be combated mainly by penal means and within the framework of international cooperation among judicial and law enforcement authorities.

Nevertheless, clearly lacking criminal law competence at the time,[24] the EU adopted the Directive employing the legal bases on the right of establishment and the establishment and functioning of the internal market.[25]

The preamble stated that ML has an evident influence on the rise of organised crime in general and drug trafficking in particular. It continued on to say that there is more and more awareness that combating ML is one of the most effective means of opposing this form of criminal activity, which constitutes a particular threat to Member States' societies. Yet, the Directive recognised that a penal approach should not be the only way to combat ML 'since the financial system can play a highly effective role'.[26] On 1 January 1993, additional rules such as rules on free movement of capital and the liberalisation of the banking, insurance and investment services were adopted.[27]

In 2001, the second AML Directive (2MLD) was adopted, amending the 1MLD.[28] The 2MLD specifically referred to the widened definition of ML, beyond that of drugs offences, as reflected in the 1996 revisions of the 40 FATF recommendations, which were widened in scope to reflect evolving money laundering typologies.[29] The Directive further stated that the suppression of organised crime was particularly closely linked to AML measures.[30] It would be another ten years before the next money laundering directive was passed—more on which below.

Private Actors

Besides the public initiatives by the foregoing international and regional regulators, banking organisations have also been involved in regulatory activities. The current Basel III is a comprehensive set of reform measures, developed by the BCBS, to strengthen the regulation, supervision and risk management of the banking sector.[31]

As a result, one of the most striking features of the EU AML framework is the intensified multilevel cooperation of public and private actors. Not only are private parties expected to work against anti-money launderers and to report suspicious transactions under threats of administrative and criminal sanctions, they also take an active part in formulating the underlying rules and procedures on different levels. In short, traditional public tasks are shared by public and private actors.[32]

In the early days of AML regulation, the private actors were only loosely part of the public sector in preventing crimes on ML. However, the shift towards the risk-based approach (discussed below) entailed several major consequences regarding the relationship between private and public actors.

Inherent in this change is that the 'policing' tasks of private actors, which have always played an important role in crime prevention, are expanding.[33] As a result, this regulatory field is extremely complex, involving international, EU and national actors and laws, embracing public, private and penal rules as well as enforcement mechanisms.[34]

Major Changes After 2000

The shift towards the risk-based approach and the extension to include the financing of terrorism as ML predicate offence were both introduced with the third AML Directive (3MLD) at the European level. Even today these remain two of the major changes within this regulatory field. This shift brought the regional EU rules into line with the global, revised and expanded, FATF recommendations.

Financing of Terrorism

The 2MLD was soon to be replaced when, post 9/11, the FATF explicitly extended its recommendations to include the financing of terrorism, adopting eight special recommendations for that purpose.[35] According to these, each country should take immediate steps to ratify and implement the 1999 UN International Convention for the Suppression of the Financing of Terrorism[36] and to implement the UN Resolutions on the Prevention and Suppression of the Financing of Terrorist Acts.[37] Each country should criminalise the financing of terrorism, terrorist acts and terrorist organisations, and ensure that such offences are designated as ML predicate offences.[38] FATF also agreed upon rules about freezing and confiscating terrorist assets,[39] rules about reporting suspicious transactions related to terrorism[40] and rules concerning international cooperation, alternative remittance, wire transfers and non-profit organisations.[41] On 22 October 2004, a ninth special recommendation on cash couriers was developed with the objective of ensuring that terrorists and other criminals cannot finance their activities or launder the proceeds of their crimes through the physical cross-border transportation of currency and bearer negotiable instruments.[42]

The 3MLD[43] brought the regional EU rules into line with the global, revised and expanded, FATF recommendations.[44] As a result, the preventive measures of the Directive now cover not only the manipulation of money derived from crime but also the collection of money or property for terrorist purposes.[45]

The Risk-Based Approach

Besides extending its provisions to any financial transaction which might be linked to terrorist activities, the biggest change in the 3MLD and the solution to the problem of ML was to establish a standard for risk analysis. This 'risk-based approach'[46] has a prominent position in the 3MLD, as well as in the amended FATF recommendations that it builds upon.[47]

The starting point is that risks differ between countries, customers and business areas over time. The operators themselves are the best analysts of where the risk areas are, or might arise, as they best know their business and their customers.[48] The idea is that resources should be used where needs arise and the framework is supposed to be more flexible and adjustable to risk. Within a risk-based approach, businesses are expected to make risk assessments of their customers and divide them into low and high risk. In order to enable operators to assess whether a situation involves a risk of ML and terrorism financing and to then act accordingly, the Directive introduced more detailed provisions. For this purpose, the directive specified a number of customer due diligence (CDD) measures that are more extensive and far-reaching for situations of higher risk, such as appropriate procedures to determine whether a person is a politically exposed person (PEP). The risk-based approach further emphasises that the evaluation of who is high or low risk is to be a continuous process. As a result, the concept of 'know your customer', as used in the financial sector, in practice became applicable to all covered by the directive. Yet, as mentioned above, AML measures were in place in Europe two decades before the 9/11 attacks, where the rationale for their introduction had nothing to do with terrorist financing.

Despite the internal market legal basis, the wider regulatory framework can therefore be said to have changed from a predominantly single market context via criminal law concerns to the fight against organised crime, terrorism financing and an internal security context based on the risk-based approach. The main focus of the global and regional EU measures based on the risk-based approach is however still set on preventive measures, whereas AML control is still a matter for national jurisdictions and the developing framework of international cooperation among judicial and law enforcement authorities. It remains to be seen if the proposal for a criminal law AML Directive will be adopted that would expand the current EU focus from prevention to control of ML and terrorist financing. Meanwhile, Member States are obliged to implement the fourth AML Directive (4MLD), to which changes have already been proposed.

Recent Developments at the EU Level

The Broader Regulatory Framework

In the multi-year EU Justice and Home Affairs programme adopted in June 2014,[49] the European Council defined the strategic guidelines for legislative and operational planning for the coming years within the Area of Freedom, Security and Justice (AFSJ). These strategic guidelines set out some general principles and a few concrete objectives replacing the more detailed Stockholm programme that was adopted in 2009.[50] Although not specifically mentioned, AML measures and procedures are highly relevant.

In April 2015, the European Commission presented the European Agenda on Security for the period 2015–2020.[51] Highlighting that the primary goal of organised crime is profit and that international criminal networks use legal business structures to conceal the source of their profits, the European Agenda on Security called for a strengthening of the capacity of law enforcement to tackle the finance of organised crime. Besides the fight against organised crime and cybercrime, preventing terrorism and countering radicalisation are identified as the most pressing challenges.

The European Agenda on Security will support Member States' cooperation in tackling these security threats. Key actions include effective measures to 'follow the money' and cutting the financing of criminals, where cooperation between competent authorities, in particular national Financial Intelligence Units (FIUs), which will be connected to Europol, will be strengthened. In addition, Eurojust could offer more expertise and assistance to national authorities when conducting financial investigations.

The idea is that cross-border cooperation between national FIUs and national Asset Recovery Offices (AROs) will help to combat ML and to access the illicit proceeds of crime.[52] The powers of FIUs will thereby be reinforced to better track the financial dealings of organised crime networks and enhance the powers of competent national authorities to freeze and confiscate illicit assets. The European Agenda on Security thus aims at 'tackling the nexus between terrorism and organised crime, highlighting that organised crime feeds terrorism through channels like the supply of weapons, financing through drug smuggling, and the infiltration of financial markets'.[53]

The European Agenda on Security for 2015–2020 specifically called for additional measures in the area of terrorist financing and ML. Indeed the rules against ML and terrorism financing adopted in May 2015, including the 4MLD,[54] and the criminal law AML Directive proposed in December 2016,[55] are key actions.[56] Besides legislation against ML, the EU further contributes to preventing the financing of terrorism through the network of EU FIUs and the EU-US Terrorist Finance Tracking Programme.[57]

In February 2016, the Commission presented an Action Plan to further step up the fight against the financing of terrorism.[58] In brief, the plan has two main objectives. First, it aims to prevent the movement of funds and identify terrorist funding. In this respect, key actions include ensuring virtual currency exchange platforms are covered by the AML Directive, tackling terrorist financing through anonymous pre-paid instruments such as pre-paid cards, improving access to information and cooperation between EU FIUs, ensuring a high level of safeguards for financial flows from high-risk third countries and giving EU FIUs access to centralised bank and payment account registers and central data retrieval systems. Secondly, it aims to disrupt sources of revenue for terrorist organisations. Here key actions include tackling terrorist financing sources such as the illicit trade in goods, cultural goods and wildlife and working with third countries to ensure a global response to tackling terrorist financing sources.[59] Accordingly, the EU AML Regime is central also for the Action Plan for Strengthening the Fight against Terrorist Financing.

The Current EU AML Framework

The current AML framework consists of two legal instruments both based on Article 114 TFEU on the internal market: the 4MLD[60] and the Transfer of Funds Regulation.[61] Both instruments update existing EU legal instruments on ML and the financing of terrorism and aim to implement and extend the newest recommendations issued in February 2012 by the FATF.[62]

In short, the main goal of the 4MLD is to prevent the EU financial system from being used for ML and terrorist financing purposes. Generally, the Directive's scope is extended by reducing the cash payment threshold from EUR 15,000 to EUR 10,000 and including providers of gambling services. In addition, tax crimes are now included as a new predicate offence.[63] Like the previous Directives, the preamble to the 4MLD, scheduled to be in force as from 26 June 2017, emphasises the international character of ML, terrorism financing and AML measures:

> Money laundering and terrorist financing are frequently carried out in an international context. Measures adopted solely at national or even at Union level, without taking into account international coordination and cooperation, would have very limited effect. The measures adopted by the Union in that field should

therefore be compatible with, and at least as stringent as, other actions undertaken in international fora. Union action should continue to take particular account of the FATF Recommendations and instruments of other international bodies active in the fight against money laundering and terrorist financing.[64]

A few important changes introduced with the 4MLD need to be mentioned.

More Cooperation Between National Authorities

There will be more cooperation between the different national FIUs. Their role is to receive, analyse the exchange and disseminate reports raising suspicions of ML or terrorist financing to competent authorities in order to facilitate their cooperation. In this respect, the FIUs have been given strengthened powers to identify and follow suspicious transfers of money and facilitate exchange of information.[65] According to recital 58, Member States should in particular ensure that their FIUs exchange information freely, spontaneously or upon request, with third-country FIUs, having regard to Union law and to the principles relating to information exchange developed by the Egmont Group of Financial Intelligence Units.[66]

Enhancing transparency, specific provisions on the beneficial ownership of companies have been introduced, and information about beneficial ownership will be stored in a central register accessible to competent authorities, FIUs, entities required to take customer due diligence (CDD) measures and other persons with a legitimate interest. According to recital 14, the need for accurate and up-to-date information on the beneficial owner is a key factor in tracing criminals who might otherwise hide their identity behind a corporate structure. In addition, new rules on traceability of fund transfers have been introduced.

A More Targeted and Focused Risk-Based Approach

The new provisions provide for a more targeted and focused risk-based approach using evidence-based decision-making to better target risks, as well as guidance by European supervisory authorities,[67] and reinforce the sanctioning powers of the competent authorities.[68] In this respect, the new framework clarifies how AML supervisory powers apply in cross-border situations.

An additional feature is tougher rules on customer due diligence (CDD) which require that banks and other relevant entities have in place adequate controls and procedures so that they know the customers with whom they are dealing and understand the nature of their business. In particular, these rules have been clarified, and relevant entities are required to take enhanced measures where the risks are greater,[69] and can take simplified measures where risks are demonstrated to be lower.[70] Simplified procedures should thereby not be wrongly perceived as exemptions from CDD.

According to the Council, the strengthened rules 'reflect the need for the EU to adapt its legislation to take account of the development of technology and other means at the disposal of criminals'.[71] In comparison with the 3MLD, scheduled to be in force until 25 June 2017, the risk-based approach has therefore been further developed in the 4MLD. These changes have the aim of updating the EU rules to implement the newest FATF recommendations, with their increased focus on the effectiveness of regimes to counter ML and terrorism financing, as well as addressing the shortcomings connected with the 3MLD identified by the European Commission.[72]

More specifically, and in line with the international standards and the report on the application of the 3MLD,[73] the new framework incorporates more risk-based elements which should allow for a more targeted and focused approach to assessing risks and applying resources where they are most needed. Additional provisions on politically exposed persons (PEPs) at a domestic level and those working for international organisations are adopted.[74] As regards sanctions, the Directive stipulates a maximum administrative pecuniary sanction of up to twice the amount of the benefit derived from the breach where such benefit can be determined, or up to EUR 1 million.[75] In addition, the 4MLD incorporates new provisions on data protection.

According to articles 66 and 67 of the 4MLD, the current Directives will be repealed with effect from 26 June 2017,[76] by which date the 4MLD would need to be implemented by the Member States. By this date, the new Regulation would also come into force.

The Proposed Amendments

On 5 July 2016, the European Commission adopted a proposal amending the 4MLD and Directive 2009/101 in order to reinforce the preventive framework against ML, in particular by addressing emerging risks and increasing the capacity of competent authorities to access and exchange information.[77] This was a coordinated action with the G20 and the OECD, aiming at tackling tax evasion by both legal and natural persons directly and incisively in order to establish a fairer and more effective tax system.

This initiative is the first action to enforce the Action Plan for strengthening the fight against terrorism financing adopted by the Commission on 2 February 2016. It also forms part of a wider EU effort to improve tax transparency and tackle tax abuse. The proposal takes a stricter approach to the problem of effectively countering ML and terrorism financing and focuses on new channels and modalities to transfer illegal funds to the legal economy, such as virtual currencies and money exchange platforms.

The proposed amendments have been criticised by the Data Protection Agency for introducing other policy purposes than countering ML and terrorism financing that do not seem clearly identified:

> Processing personal data collected for one purpose for another, completely unrelated purpose infringes the data protection principle of purpose limitation and threatens the implementation of the principle of proportionality. The amendments, in particular, raise questions as to why certain forms of invasive personal data processing, acceptable in relation to anti-money laundering and fight against terrorism, are necessary out of those contexts and on whether they are proportionate.[78]

Hence, the Data Protection Agency also criticises the proposed amendments due to lack of proportionality in particular concerning the broadened access to beneficial ownership information by both competent authorities and the public as a policy tool to facilitate and optimise enforcement of tax obligations. The Data Protection Agency in this respect sees, 'in the way such solution is implemented, a lack of proportionality, with significant and unnecessary risks for the individual rights to privacy and data protection'.[79]

On 19 December 2016, the Council adopted a compromise text on the proposal aiming at amending only the AML Directive focusing mainly on AML and terrorism financing. Although the purpose of fighting tax evasion is no longer explicitly mentioned, tools that were designed to achieve that purpose remain although somewhat modified.[80] According to the proposal, Member States shall bring into force the laws, regulations and administrative provisions necessary to comply with this Directive by 1 January 2017 at the latest. At the time of writing (8 April 2017), it remains to be seen if the compromise text will be adopted.

The Criminal Law Proposal

The European Agenda on Security[81] called for additional measures in the area of terrorist financing and ML. In its communication on an 'Action Plan to strengthen the fight against terrorist financing',[82] the Commission highlighted the need to counter ML by means of criminal law and the need to ensure that criminals who fund terrorism are deprived of their assets. As stated in the Explanatory Memorandum of the criminal law proposal, the rationale set out was that terrorists often resort to criminal proceeds to fund their activities and use ML schemes in that process. Thus, the underlying idea is that criminalisation of ML would contribute to tackling terrorist financing.[83] Hence, one of the key measures was to consider a possible proposal for a minimum Directive on the definition of the criminal offence of ML,[84] applying it to terrorist offences and other serious criminal offences, and to approximate sanctions.

On 21 December 2016,[85] the Commission proposed an AML criminal law Directive based on Article 83(1) TFEU,[86] which identifies ML as one of the so-called Euro-crimes with particular cross-border dimension. It aims to counter ML by means of criminal law and enables the European Parliament and the Council to establish the necessary minimum rules on the definition of ML by means of directives adopted in accordance with the ordinary legislative procedure. Under the present situation, the Member States should ensure that administrative sanctions and measures in accordance with the 4MLD and criminal sanctions in accordance with national law are in place. If adopted, the AML criminal law Directive will change this situation. The line between administrative and criminal law and sanctions in the AML Regime is however not clear cut.

The Fourth AML Directive and Criminal Law

Article 1(3) of the 4MLD provides for an EU-wide definition of ML.[87] It might therefore be argued that the current AML framework does establish harmonised rules when it comes to the definition of ML, via rules setting out which behaviour is considered to constitute a criminal act, although not stating what type and level of sanctions are applicable for such acts. Under Section 4 on Sanctions, article 58(1) of the 4MLD emphasises that sanctions or measures for breaches of national provisions transposing the Directive must be effective, proportionate and dissuasive. According to the second paragraph of article 58(2), Member States may decide not to lay down rules for administrative sanctions or measures for breaches which are subject to criminal sanctions in their national law. In that case, Member States must communicate to the Commission the relevant criminal law provisions. Despite all assumptions and suggestions that the current EU AML framework is mainly administrative in character, there is a floating and not clear line between administrative and criminal law and sanctions, not least since national laws and EU law are intertwined and interrelated. Still, the 4MLD, although harmonising national criminal law on AML measures, does not require the Member States to have certain criminal law provisions in place with certain specific minimum and maximum sanctions for breaches.[88]

Although the Directive may not establish minimum rules concerning the definition of criminal offences and sanctions in the meaning of Article 83(1) TFEU, article 1(2) of the 4MLD clearly states that Member States shall ensure that ML and terrorist financing are prohibited. According to recital 59, Member States should ensure that the imposition of administrative sanctions and measures in accordance with this Directive, and of criminal sanctions in accordance with national law, does not breach the principle of *ne bis in idem*. In other words, it is the responsibility of the Member States to ensure that parallel systems of administrative and criminal law sanctions do not breach the principle of *ne bis in idem*.

As pointed out by Koen Lenaerts and José Gutiérrez-Fons,[89] the CJEU in *Åkerberg Fransson* recalled that, when EU legislation does not specifically provide any penalty for an infringement of EU law or refers for that purpose to national laws, regulations and administrative provisions, the Member States have the freedom to choose the applicable penalties, that is, administrative, criminal or a combination of the two.[90] Yet, the resulting penalties must comply with the Charter of Fundamental Rights and be effective, proportionate and dissuasive.[91] Any measure based on Article 83(1) TFEU, however, will leave no such freedom to the Member States.

The Proposed EU AML Criminal Law Directive

The proposed EU AML Criminal Law Directive is embedded in the global fight against ML and terrorism financing. It implements international obligations in this area including the Warsaw Convention and Recommendation 3 of the FATF. FATF Recommendation 3 in turn calls on countries to criminalise ML on the basis of the Vienna Convention of 1988 and Palermo Convention of 2000.[92]

As regards the relationship with the 4MLD and the Transfer of Funds Regulation,[93] the Commission emphasises that these legal instruments help prevent ML and facilitate investigations into ML cases, but that they do not address the absence of a uniform definition of the crime of ML and the differences in the type and level of sanctions for this crime throughout the Union.

The current proposal would complement different pieces of EU legislation that require Member States to criminalise some forms of ML. It will partially replace Council Framework Decision 2001/500/JHA as regards the

Member States bound by this proposal.[94] This Framework Decision aims at approximating national rules on confiscation and on certain forms of ML which Member States were required to adopt in accordance with the 1990 Council of Europe Convention on Laundering, Search, Seizure and Confiscation of the Proceeds from Crime. According to the Commission's proposal, the existing instruments at EU level, and in particular the above-mentioned Framework Decision, are limited in scope and do not ensure a comprehensive criminalisation of ML offences.[95]

The Commission claims that 'All Member States criminalise money laundering but there are significant differences in the respective definitions of what constitutes money laundering, on which are the predicate offences—i.e. the underlying criminal activity which generated the property laundered—as well as the level of sanctions'.[96] The Commission further argues that the current legislative framework is neither comprehensive nor sufficiently coherent to be fully effective and that 'The differences in legal frameworks can be exploited by criminals and terrorists, who can choose to carry out their financial transactions where they perceive anti-money laundering measures to be weakest'.[97]

According to the Commission proposal, the definitions, scope and sanctions of ML offences affect cross-border police and judicial cooperation between national authorities and the exchange of information. As an example, it is stated that differences in the scope of predicate offences make it difficult for FIUs and law enforcement authorities in one Member State to coordinate with other EU jurisdictions to tackle cross-border ML.[98] In this respect, the Commission points out that practitioners taking part in the preparatory phase reported that differences in criminalising pose obstacles to effective police cooperation and cross-border investigation.[99]

The proposal further complements Directive 2014/42/EU that aims at creating a common set of minimum rules for the detection, tracing and confiscation of proceeds of crime across the EU and the Council Framework Decision 2008/841/JHA which criminalises the participation in an organised criminal group and racketeering.[100] In addition, it reinforces and complements the criminal law framework with regard to offences relating to terrorist groups, in particular the proposal for a Directive on combating terrorism,[101] which sets a 'comprehensive definition of the crime of terrorist financing, covering not only terrorist offences, but also terrorist-related offences such as recruitment, training and propaganda'.[102]

According to the Progress Report from the Presidency to the Council, work on the proposal is progressing very well in the Working Party on Substantive Criminal Law (DROIPEN):

Three meetings of the group were held since January 2017. A full examination of the Commission's proposal was carried out during the first meeting. In addition, two complete rounds of discussion on the basis of a revised Presidency text were concluded, including compromise proposals on the definition of criminal activity, self-laundering and penalties. Work at expert level will continue with a view to submitting a compromise text to the Council for obtaining a general approach in June 2017.[103]

Conclusions: Preventing and Controlling ML and Terrorism Financing?

If the latest proposal for a proper criminal law AML Directive is adopted, it would expand the current EU focus from prevention to control of ML and terrorist financing. On the other hand, as suggested by the Commission, the proposal, if adopted, will also reinforce the measures in place aimed at detecting, disrupting and preventing the abuse of the financial system for ML and terrorist financing purposes, notably the 4MLD. This Directive, along with the Transfer of Funds Regulation,[104] sets out rules which are designed to prevent the abuse of the financial system for ML and terrorist financing purposes.

The purpose of these legal instruments is to prevent ML and facilitate investigations into ML cases. Accordingly, the focus of the 4MLD is set mainly on enhancing cooperation between national authorities and the development of a more targeted and focused risk-based approach. In this respect, focus is clearly set on prevention and detection and the latest proposal for a criminal AML Directive is in this respect ancillary addressing the absence of a uniform definition of the crime of ML and the differences in the type and level of sanctions for this crime throughout the Union.

As pointed out by the Data Protection Agency regarding the proposal to amend the 4MLD,[105] there are limits, however, concerning the processing of personal data collected for one purpose for another. In this respect, it is reasonable to raise questions as to why certain forms of invasive personal data processing, hitherto acceptable in relation to AML and the fight against terrorism,[106] are necessary out of those contexts and whether they are proportionate.

Notes

1. Commission, 'Proposal for a Directive of the European Parliament and of the Council on countering money laundering by criminal law' COM (2016) 826 final.
2. Commission, 'Communication from the Commission to the European Parliament and the Council on an Action Plan for Strengthening the Fight against Terrorist Financing' COM (2016) 50/2.
3. Armand Kersten, 'Financing of Terrorism—A Predicate Offence to Money Laundering?' in Mark Pieth (ed), *Financing Terrorism* (Kluwer Academic Publishers 2002) 50.
4. John Braithwaite and Peter Drahos, *Global Business Regulation* (CUP 2000) 105.
5. Anon, 'Combating Financial Crime and Money Laundering: Overview' (1997) 2(3) Trends in Organized Crime 5.
6. International Monetary Fund, 'Anti-Money Laundering/Combating the Financing of Terrorism—Topics' <www.imf.org/external/np/leg/amlcft/eng/aml1.htm> accessed 8 April 2017.
7. In this collection, see Chap. 4 (Talani). See also Peter Alldridge, 'Money Laundering and Globalization' (2008) 35(4) Journal of Law and Society 437.
8. This chapter builds upon previous publications: Maria Bergström, 'EU Anti-Money Laundering Regulation: Multilevel Cooperation of Public and Private Actors' in Christina Eckes and Theodore Konstadinides (eds), *Crime Within the Area of Freedom, Security and Justice: A European Public Order* (CUP 2011); Maria Bergström, 'The Place of Sanctions in the EU System for Combating the Financing of Terrorism' in Iain Cameron (ed), *EU Sanctions: Law and Policy Issues Concerning Restrictive Measures* (Intersentia 2013); and Maria Bergström, 'Money Laundering' in Valsamis Mitsilegas, Maria Bergström, and Theodore Konstadinides (eds), *Research Handbook on EU Criminal Law* (Edward Elgar Publishing 2016).
9. UN Convention against Illicit Traffic in Narcotic Drugs and Psychotropic Substances (adopted 20 December 1988, entered into force 11 November 1990) 1582 UNTS 95.
10. Basel Committee on Banking Supervision, 'Prevention of Criminal Use of the Banking System for the Purpose of Money-Laundering' (1988) <www.bis.org/publ/bcbsc137.htm> accessed 8 April 2017. The BCBS is a standard-setting body on banking supervision consisting of senior representatives of bank supervisory authorities and central banks. It was created by the central bank governors of the Group of Ten nations in 1974.
11. Council of Europe, Convention on Laundering, Search, Seizure and Confiscation of the Proceeds from Crime (1990) CETS No 141 (Strasbourg Convention).
12. This section is based on Kersten (n 3) 50.

13. The term 'proceeds' in the Strasbourg definition covers 'any economic advantage from criminal offences', whereas the term 'predicate offence' covers 'any criminal offence as a result of which proceeds were generated that may become the subject of an offence as defined in the 'laundering article': Strasbourg Convention (n 11) art 1.

14. OECD, 'OECD Report on Harmful Tax Competition: An Emerging Global Issue' (1998) <www.oecd.org/tax/transparency/44430243.pdf> accessed 8 April 2017.

15. UNGA International Convention for the Suppression of the Financing of Terrorism (adopted 9 December 1999, opened for signature 10 January 2000) (2000) 39 ILM 270.

16. Council of Europe, Convention on Laundering, Search, Seizure and Confiscation of the Proceeds from Crime and on the Financing of Terrorism (2005) CETS No 198.

17. Jonathan M Winer, 'Globalization, Terrorist Finance, and Global Conflict—Time for a White List?' in Mark Pieth (ed), *Financing Terrorism* (Kluwer Academic Publishers 2002). See also Maria O'Neill, *The Evolving EU Counter-Terrorism Legal Framework* (Routledge 2012).

18. Bergström, 'The Place of Sanctions' (n 8).

19. FATF, 'FATF Members and Observers' <www.fatf-gafi.org/about/membersandobservers/> accessed 8 April 2017.

20. See Chap. 15 (van Duyne, Harvey, and Gelemerova) in this collection.

21. Bergström, 'The Place of Sanctions' (n 8).

22. Council Directive 91/308/EEC of 10 June 1991 on prevention of the use of the financial system for the purpose of money laundering [1991] OJ L166/77.

23. See further Bergström, 'Money Laundering' (n 8).

24. See, however, the limited third pillar measure, Council Framework Decision 2001/500/JHA of 26 June 2001 on money laundering, the identification, tracing, freezing, seizing and confiscation of instrumentalities and the proceeds of crime [2001] OJ L182/1.

25. After the Lisbon Treaty, these articles have been amended and renumbered to arts 53 and 114 TFEU.

26. Directive 91/308/EEC (n 22).

27. Mohamed Sideek, 'Legal Instruments to Combat Money Laundering in the EU Financial Market' (2002) 6(1) Journal of Money Laundering Control 66; Mohamed Sideek, *European Community Law on the Free Movement* of Capital and the EMU' (Brill 1999).

28. Directive 2001/97/EC of the European Parliament and of the Council of 4 December 2001 amending Council Directive 91/308/EEC on prevention of the use of the financial system for the purpose of money laundering [2001] OJ L344/76.

29. Ibid. Recital 7.

30. Ibid. Recital 10.

31. See further, BCBS, 'International Regulatory Framework for Banks (Basel III)' <www.bis.org/bcbs/basel3.htm?m=3%7C14%7C572> accessed 8 April 2017; Bergström, 'EU Anti Money Laundering' (n 8).

32. For the purposes of this section, private actors are simply defined as for-profit actors, whereas public actors are governments, agencies and international organisations.

33. Gilles Favarel-Garrigues, Thierry Godefroy and Pierre Lascoumes, 'Sentinels in the Banking Industry: Private Actors and the Fight against Money Laundering in France' (2008) 48(1) British Journal of Criminology 1.

34. See further Bergström, 'EU Anti Money Laundering' (n 8).

35. Agreed upon at a special meeting after the 11 September attacks.

36. Convention for the Suppression of the Financing of Terrorism (n 15).

37. FATF, *IX Special Recommendations* (FATF/OECD 2001), Recommendation I.

38. Ibid. Recommendation II.

39. Ibid. Recommendation III.

40. Ibid. Recommendation IV.

41. Ibid. Recommendations V to VIII. Recommendation VI has been covered by Directive 2007/64/EC of the European Parliament and of the Council of 13 November 2007 on Payment Services (PSD) in the internal market [2007] OJ L319/1; Recommendation VII was addressed by Regulation (EC) 1781/2006 of the European Parliament and of the Council of 15 November 2006 on information on the payer accompanying transfers of funds [2006] OJ L345/1.

42. FATF Special Recommendation IX is covered by Regulation (EC) 1889/2005 of the European Parliament and of the Council of 26 October 2005 on controls of cash entering or leaving the Community [2005] OJ L309/9.

43. Directive 2005/60/EC of the European Parliament and of the Council of 26 October 2005 on the prevention of the use of the financial system for the purpose of money laundering and terrorist financing [2005] OJ L309/15.

44. FATF, *40 Recommendations* (FATF/OECD 2003), incorporating the amendments of 22 October 2004.

45. Directive 2005/60/EC (n 43) Recital 8.

46. Risk management is expanding in both range and scope across organisations in the public and the private sectors and has become something of a contemporary standard for dealing with uncertainty in an organised manner. See Michael Power, *The Risk Management of Everything* (Demos 2004); Michael Power, *Organized Uncertainty: Designing a World of Risk Management* (OUP 2007). For an integrated analysis of the concepts of risk and securitisation, see Maria Bergström, Ulrika Mörth and Karin Svedberg Helgesson, 'A New Role for For-Profit Actors? The Case of Anti-Money Laundering and Risk Management' (2011) 49(5) Journal of Common Market Studies 1043. In this article a linkage is shown between the concepts of risk and securitisation, both emphasising the structural threats and uncertainties in the case of

AML. See also Valsamis Mitsilegas, *Money Laundering Counter-Measures in the European Union: A New Paradigm of Security Governance versus Fundamental Legal Principles* (Kluwer Law International 2003) 3, on 'reconceptualising security in the risk society'.

47. For a critical analysis of the risk-based approach, see Ester Herlin-Karnell, 'The EU's Anti Money Laundering Agenda: Built on Risks?' in Christina Eckes and Theodore Konstadinides (eds), *Crime within the Area of Freedom, Security and Justice: A European Public Order* (CUP 2011). In this collection, see Chap. 15 (van Duyne, Harvey and Gelemerova).
48. For discussion in the context of banks, see Chap. 5 (Iafolla) in this collection.
49. Included as Chap. 1, European Council, '26/27 June 2014 Conclusions' EUCO 79/14.
50. The Stockholm Programme: An Open and Secure Europe Serving and Protecting Citizens [2010] OJ C115/1.
51. Commission, 'Communication from the Commission to the European Parliament, the Council, the European Economic and Social Committee and the Committee of the Regions (The European Agenda on Security)' COM (2015) 185 final.
52. Ibid.
53. COM (2016) 826 final (n 1) Explanatory memorandum.
54. Directive 2015/849/EU of the European Parliament and of the Council of 20 May 2015 on the prevention of the use of the financial system for the purposes of money laundering or terrorist financing, amending Regulation (EU) 648/2012 of the European Parliament and of the Council and repealing Directive 2005/60/EC of the European Parliament and of the Council and Commission Directive 2006/70/EC (4MLD) [2015] OJ L141/73; Regulation (EU) 2015/847 of the European Parliament and of the Council of 20 May 2015 on information accompanying transfers of funds and repealing Regulation (EC) 1781/2006 [2015] OJ L141/1.
55. COM (2016) 826 final (n 1).
56. COM (2015) 185 final (n 51). Commission, Press Release 'Commission Takes Steps to Strengthen EU Cooperation in the Fight against Terrorism, Organised Crime and Cybercrime' IP/15/4865 (28 April 2015). Suggested also by the European Parliament, Resolution of 17 December 2014 on renewing the EU Internal Security Strategy 2014/2918 (RSP) in which it calls for the new Internal Security Strategy to be forward-looking and strategic, and easily adaptable to evolving situations, by focusing not only on existing security threats but also on emerging ones and taking an integrated, comprehensive and holistic approach to priority areas such as cyber security, trafficking in human beings and counter-terrorism, and to interlinked issues such as organised crime, money laundering and corruption.

57. Commission, 'Fact Sheet: European Agenda on Security: Questions and Answers' MEMO/15/4867 (2015).
58. COM (2016) 50/2 (n 2).
59. Commission, 'Fact Sheet: Action Plan to Strengthen the Fight Against Terrorist Financing. European Agenda on Security' <://ec.europa.eu/justice/criminal/files/aml-factsheet_en.pdf> accessed 8 April 2017.
60. Directive 2015/849/EU (n 54).
61. Regulation (EU) 2015/847 (n 54).
62. FAFT, 'International Standards on Combating Money Laundering and the Financing of Terrorism and Proliferation: the FATF Recommendations' (2012) updated in February 2013, October 2015, June 2016 and October 2016 <www.fatf-gafi.org/media/fatf/documents/recommendations/pdfs/FATF_Recommendations.pdf> accessed 8 April 2017.
63. This section builds on Bergström, 'Money Laundering' (n 8).
64. Directive 2015/849/EU (n 54) Recital 4.
65. See also Council, Decision 2000/642/JHA of 17 October 2000 concerning arrangements for cooperation between FIUs of the Member States in respect of exchanging information [2000] OJ L271/4, which the Commission also plans to update; Commission, 'Report on the Application of the Third Anti-Money Laundering Directive: Frequently Asked Questions' MEMO/12/246 (2012).
66. Egmont Group of Financial Intelligence Units Charter, Approved by the Egmont Group Heads of Financial Intelligence Units (2013) <https://egmontgroup.org/en/document-library/8> accessed 8 April 2017.
67. Directive 2015/849/EU (n 54) Recital 23, for example, states that underpinning the risk-based approach is the need for Member States and the Union to identify, understand and mitigate the risks of money laundering and terrorist financing that they face. The importance of a supranational approach to risk identification has been recognised at international level, and the European Supervisory Authority (European Banking Authority) (EBA), established by Regulation (EU) 1093/2010 of the European Parliament and of the Council; the European Supervisory Authority (European Insurance and Occupational Pensions Authority) (EIOPA), established by Regulation (EU) 1094/2010 of the European Parliament and of the Council; and the European Supervisory Authority (European Securities and Markets Authority) (ESMA), established by Regulation (EU) 1095/2010 of the European Parliament and of the Council, should be tasked with issuing an opinion, through their Joint Committee, on the risks affecting the Union financial sector. Recital 24 of the fourth AML Directive then states that national and Union data protection supervisory authorities should be involved only if the assessment of the risk of money laundering and terrorist financing has an impact on the privacy and data protection of individuals.

68. Els De Busser and Cornelia Riehle, 'Money Laundering: Fourth Anti Money Laundering Directive Released' (2013) 1 Eucrim 6.

69. Directive 2015/849/EU (n 54) section 3.

70. Ibid. section 2 and Annex II.

71. Council, Press Release 'Money Laundering: Council Approves Strengthened Rules' (20 April 2015) <www.consilium.europa.eu/en/press/press-releases/2015/04/20-money-laundering-strengthened-rules> accessed 8 April 2017.

72. See in particular the review of the 3MLD undertaken by the Commission, with a view to addressing any identified shortcomings: MEMO/12/246 (2012) (n 65).

73. See Commission, Press Release 'Anti-Money Laundering: Creating a Modern EU Framework Capable of Responding to New Threats IP/12/357' (11 April 2012) <http://europa.eu/rapid/press-release_IP-12-357_en.htm?locale=en> accessed 8 April 2017.

74. Directive 2015/849/EU (n 54) arts 20–23.

75. Ibid. art 59(2)(e).

76. The Commission, 'Proposal for a Directive of the European Parliament and of the Council amending Directive (EU) 2015/849 on the prevention of the use of the financial system for the purposes of money laundering or terrorist financing and amending Directive 2009/101/EC' COM (2016) 450 final, that proposes to bring forward the date of transposition of the 4MLD to 1 January 2017 has so far not been adopted (8 April 2017).

77. Ibid.

78. European Data Protection Supervisor, Summary of the Opinion of the European Data Protection Supervisor on a Commission Proposal amending Directive (EU) 2015/849 and Directive 2009/101/EC Access to beneficial ownership information and data protection implications [2017] OJ C85/3.

79. Ibid.

80. Council, 'Proposal for a Directive of the European Parliament and of the Council amending Directive (EU) 2015/849 on the prevention of the use of the financial system for the purposes of money laundering or terrorist financing and amending Directive 2009/101/EC—Presidency Compromise text' 2016/0208 (COD). For the procedure, see <http://eur-lex.europa.eu/legal-content/EN/HIS/?uri=CELEX:52016PC0450&qid=1491076566465> accessed 8 April 2017.

81. COM (2015) 185 final (n 51).

82. Commission, 'Communication from the Commission to the European Parliament and the Council on an Action Plan for strengthening the fight against terrorist financing' COM (2016) 50 final.

83. COM (2016) 826 final (n 1) Explanatory memorandum.

84. Announced in COM (2016) 50 final (n 82).

85. On 21 December 2016, the Commission submitted two legislative proposals: the COM (2016) 826 final (n 1) and a 'Proposal for a Regulation on the mutual recognition of freezing and confiscation orders' COM (2016) 819 final.
86. COM (2016) 826 final (n 1).
87. For the purposes of this Directive, the following conduct, when committed intentionally, shall be regarded as money laundering: (a) the conversion or transfer of property, knowing that such property is derived from criminal activity or from an act of participation in such activity, for the purpose of concealing or disguising the illicit origin of the property or of assisting any person who is involved in the commission of such an activity to evade the legal consequences of that person's action; (b) the concealment or disguise of the true nature, source, location, disposition, movement, rights with respect to, or ownership of, property, knowing that such property is derived from criminal activity or from an act of participation in such an activity; (c) the acquisition, possession or use of property, knowing, at the time of receipt, that such property was derived from criminal activity or from an act of participation in such an activity; (d) participation in, association to commit, attempts to commit and aiding, abetting, facilitating and counselling the commission of any of the actions referred to in points (a), (b) and (c).
88. See Ester Herlin-Karnell, 'Is Administrative Law Still Relevant? How the Battle of Sanctions has Shaped EU Criminal Law' in Valsamis Mitsilegas, Maria Bergström, and Theodore Konstadinides (eds), *Research Handbook on EU Criminal Law* (Edward Elgar Publishing 2016).
89. Koen Lenaerts and José Gutiérrez-Fons, 'The European Court of Justice and Fundamental Rights in the Field of Criminal Law' in Valsamis Mitsilegas, Maria Bergström and Theodore Konstadinides (eds), *Research Handbook on EU Criminal Law* (Edward Elgar Publishing 2016).
90. Case C-617/10 *Åkerberg Fransson* (GC, 26 February 2013), para 34.
91. Ibid. para 36.
92. UN Convention Against Transnational Organized Crime (adopted 15 November 2000, entered into force 29 September 2003) 2225 UNTS 209.
93. Regulation (EU) 2015/847 (n 54).
94. Council Framework Decision 2001/500/JHA (n 24).
95. COM (2016) 826 final (n 1) Explanatory memorandum.
96. Ibid. 1.
97. Ibid.
98. Ibid.
99. Ibid. 2.
100. Ibid. 5.
101. Commission, 'Proposal for a Directive of the European Parliament and of the Council on combating terrorism and replacing Council Framework Decision 2002/475/JHA on combating terrorism' COM (2015) 625 final.

102. COM (2016) 826 final (n 1) Explanatory memorandum, 5.
103. Council, 'Combatting financial crime and terrorist financing (a) Proposal for a Directive of the European Parliament and of the Council on countering money laundering by criminal law (First reading); and (b) Proposal for a Regulation of the European Parliament and of the Council on mutual recognition of freezing and confiscation orders (First reading)—Progress report' 2016/0414 (COD) 2016/0412 (COD) (2017).
104. Regulation (EU) 2015/847 (n 54).
105. [2017] OJ C85/3 (n 78).
106. The level of acceptability has seemingly diminished after Case C-362/14 *Schrems v Data Protection Commissioner* (GC, 6 October 2015) and Joined Cases C-203/15 and C-698/15 *Tele2 Sverige AB v Post-och telestyrelsen and Secretary of State for the Home Department v Tom Watson* (GC, 21 December 2016).

Maria Bergström   is Associate Professor of European Law and Senior Lecturer in EU Law at Uppsala University. She holds a Doctor of Laws from the European University Institute. Her recent publications include 'Money Laundering', in Mitsilegas, V, Bergström, M and Konstadinides, T (eds) *Research Handbook on EU Criminal Law*, Edward Elgar Publishing 2016; 'The Relevance of the Criminal Justice Experience—Mutual Recognition in Criminal and Civil Justice', in Hess, B, Bergström, M and Storskrubb, E (eds) *EU Civil Justice—Current Issues and Future Outlook*, Hart Publishing 2016; and 'Judicial Protection for Private Parties in European Commission Rulemaking', in Bergström, CF and Ritleng, D (eds), *Rulemaking by the European Commission—The New System for Delegation of Powers*, Oxford University Press, 2016.

4

Globalization, Money Laundering and the City of London

Leila Simona Talani

Introduction

This chapter will analyse the extent to which the City of London can be considered the 'laundry of choice' for many criminals. Moreover, it addresses the reaction of the City of London, and of the United Kingdom more generally, to the introduction of Anti-Money Laundering Requirements (AMLR). Finally, it considers the motivations behind the City's attitude vis-à-vis both money laundering and anti-money laundering legislation.

In theoretical terms, this contribution adds to widespread literature underlying how globalization has produced a clustering of financial activities in global cities.[1] Globalization is also at the roots of the increased capacity of criminal proceeds to successfully enter the legal economy. The definition of globalization adopted in this chapter is the traditional, qualitative one, recognizing the phenomenon of globalization as producing a number of transformations in both the realm of manufacturing production and in the financial markets.[2] Technological transformation is at the root of the exceptional developments of financial markets in producing what is normally defined as financial globalization, in other words, the existence of around-the-clock access to financial transactions all over the world.[3] This phenomenon, however, does not mean that the physical location of financial markets loses significance. Some scholars argue that financial globalization has 'made geography more,

L. S. Talani
King's College London, London, UK

© The Author(s) 2018
C. King et al. (eds.), *The Palgrave Handbook of Criminal and Terrorism Financing Law*,
https://doi.org/10.1007/978-3-319-64498-1_4

not less, important'.[4] The location of global financial power has remained surprisingly unchanged and concentrated in a handful of urban centres, namely New York, London and, to a more limited extent, Tokyo. This concentration is unparalleled in any other kind of industry, and it is also extremely stable.[5] This resonates with Sassen's assessment of the role of global cities as financial centres.[6]

Moreover, financial globalization, as defined in this chapter, does not imply that financial elites, such as the City of London, become disentangled from national boundaries. On the contrary, their role and bargaining power inside the national polity increase as their economic position improves, leading to a shift in the power relations between the different socio-economic groups whose relevance can hardly be overestimated. This statement is true both for developed countries and for underdeveloped countries, where the establishment of off-shore markets produces incredible transformations in the local economy and social structure.[7] However, 'off-shore' refers not only to the geographical location of economic activities but also to their juridical status. In reality, off-shore financial transactions also take place in the great financial centres of London, New York and Tokyo.[8] Finally, unlimited 24-hour access to financial markets leads to a great sensitivity of capital to interest rates, which, in the long run, reduces the scope for the adoption of differentiated national monetary and macroeconomic policies.[9]

This definition of financial globalization implies that not only legal, but also illicit, money now can move across the world, around the clock with the click of a mouse, rendering it almost impossible to follow among myriad jurisdictions. It is true that states and international organizations have tried, and have adopted, some rules to limit the capacity of dirty money. However, as rightly pointed out in the relevant literature,[10] the reality is that as of yet, no 'global' jurisdiction exists for money, meaning that with respect to global money laundering, there are no globally enforceable rules. Many states adopt practices in contrast with the prescriptions of money laundering prevention.[11] Even when states stick to internationally agreed protocols,[12] loopholes in legislation and gaps in its implementation are so wide that money laundering continues unhindered.[13]

Moreover, as financial businesses are almost by definition 'transnational', legitimate business and banking institutions often have no idea of which money laundering legislation to implement. There is no international enforcement agency tracking international financial criminals and money launderers, and national regulators find it difficult to tackle cross-border transactions effectively.[14] Finally, even if everything was done by the banking system or business organization in question to prevent money laundering, globalization, especially through the Internet, has made it possible to easily circumvent regulation.

According to some scholars, the origins of the term 'money laundering' can be traced back to the United States in the 1920s, when criminals used the laundering business to recycle the proceeds of their activities into the legal economy.[15] But things have changed substantially since money laundering began; there are now a multiplicity of actors and even more techniques available to successful money launderers.

The IMF defines money laundering as '…a process by which the illicit source of assets obtained or generated by criminal activity is concealed to obscure the link between the funds and the original criminal activity'.[16] In reality, laundering illicit money is not always a linear process bringing the proceeds of an illegal transaction directly to the legitimate business and banking system. The process can be extremely complicated and involve a number of actors and techniques that are almost impossible to trace by authorities.[17] Ultimately, however, if the money laundering is successful, the end destination of all illicitly gained money is always a legitimate financial institution. A classic example of a money laundering scheme is the following:

> From May 1994, two people used an accounting firm to launder the proceeds of sales of amphetamines. They regularly handed over to their accountant, brown-paper envelopes or shoeboxes containing US$ 38,000 to US$ 63,000 in cash, without any receipt being delivered. The accountant had set up a company and opened trust accounts for his clients, as well as personal bank accounts in the name of their parents. Some of the funds were used to buy lorry parts abroad, which were then resold in the country of origin, some were used to buy real estate. According to the investigation, the accountant and three of his colleagues had laundered about US$ 633,900 in return for a 10% commission.[18]

Globalization gave new opportunities to money launderers. It is almost a truism to say that globalization (or better, the technological developments associated with it) simplified things substantially to the extent that some authors provocatively provide 'beginners' guides to money laundering on the Internet.[19] How does this happen?

Money laundering is conventionally divided into three stages: (1) the placement of funds derived from the crime; (2) the layering of those funds in order to disguise their origins; and (3) the integration of the funds into the mainstream economy. Many forms of illegal activity are cash intensive, although virtual money can now be a common proceed of an illicit activity.[20] The first aim of the money launderer is to remove the cash from where it was acquired and put it where it will not be detected. The next stage is to disguise the source of funds by creating complex layers of financial transactions. The final stage of money laundering is to integrate funds into the normal economy so that these funds appear to be legitimate.[21]

Placement is usually the riskiest stage when laundering money, as there is an immediate connection between the profits and the crime. Bearing in mind that a successful money launderer first needs to conceal his/her identity, the Internet has made that task extremely easy. One can open an anonymous credit card account online, often for life, which can then be financed with illicit money. Similarly, Internet facilities allow for the opening of bank accounts in the name of corporations based in off-shore centres. Many websites offer false identities selling fake passports (even diplomatic ones) and there is even the possibility of buying legitimate passports from various countries, which in some cases actually confer special diplomatic privileges. Other websites offer anonymous securities trading accounts or allow the establishment of shell business entities off-shore.[22] Another common way to gain access to the banking system is the use of correspondent banking,[23] which has been greatly facilitated by modern technology. Correspondent banking often opens the door of the international bank's global network to customers that the bank cannot directly monitor or police and that can transfer funds at the click of a mouse.[24] Globalization has also made the second stage of money laundering much safer. Normally called 'layering' (or agitation or commingling),[25] this process consists of moving money around by dispersing the bulk of criminal proceeds into different accounts, countries or investments. The classic method of layering money is through a front company. No longer a 'launderette' as in the 1920s, there are now plenty of opportunities for establishing 'brass plate businesses' which are incorporated in a specific jurisdiction but have no tangible physical presence. Some countries even allow corporate trusts that conceal the owner's identity.[26] However, some of these companies are perfectly functioning, and some jurisdictions, like the United Kingdom, are softer than others with regard to the establishment of similar enterprises.[27] Moreover, modern technology makes it possible to invest in Internet pornography or online casinos and sports gambling, where the level of regulation is low and the possibility of remaining anonymous very high.[28] Ultimately, money is integrated into the legal economy through a legitimate transaction of any kind (such as a payment for professional services; a legitimate purchase, especially commodities and precious metals).[29]

Overall, manipulating money has become much easier through globalization, and some of these activities are not even strictly illegal in many contexts. Buying from your own bank, transferring money in different countries through it, making a loan to yourself or to finance one of your businesses, multiplying the number of businesses you are involved in, and even changing the sets of ownership names, moving profits internationally as inter-business finance so as not to pay taxes on them and finally employing a horde of lawyers, accountants, financiers and managers to take care of all the activities and thus legitimize profits—none of this is illegal per se, but allows for any kind of illicitly obtained money to come out whiter than white.[30] In the next section, we consider the extent to which the City of London is involved in similar practices.

Money Laundering in the City of London

It is very difficult to establish through published evidence the extent to which the City of London is involved in, or affected by, the phenomenon of money laundering. As Lilley states, 'by its very nature, the whole point of a successful laundering operation is to convert dirty funds in one part of the world into clean money in a respected and respectable financial center'.[31] The City of London is certainly one of the most respectable and, above all, respected financial services centres in the world, and yet it is also one of the main final 'depots' of washed money. In a way, the City of London (or any other established financial centre such as New York or Tokyo) is by definition the final stop of illicit money if the money laundering process is successful.[32]

One could say that the City's personnel or institutions cannot be held accountable for this, and of course it is very difficult to prove the contrary (although not impossible). This does not, however, eliminate the fact that the City of London and the British financial sector are among the winners (and there are, unfortunately, many losers!) of the process by which money obtained through drug trafficking, sex exploitation, arms dealing, smuggling of migrants and similar practices is given a new, cleaner face.[33]

There is also another way by which the City of London contributes to successful money laundering. Its bankers, lawyers, accountants, company formation agents, tax advisers, fiduciaries and other groups of professionals lend their services, both knowingly and unwittingly, to criminals for substantial commissions.[34] According to a Latin saying '*Pecunia non olet*'—money does not stink—or, at least, not after being laundered.[35] Moreover, many city markets are used as vehicles for money laundering. The gold market is indeed extremely important for money laundering. Gold is both a commodity and, to a lesser extent, a means of exchange for covering transactions involving criminal proceeds between Latin America, the United States and Europe.[36] And the global centre for gold exchange is the London Bullion market.

Finally, we should not forget that the 'off-shore' economy, which contributes to successful money laundering activity,[37] is very often an on-shore activity, concentrated in the most important global financial centres, namely New York, Tokyo and, obviously, the City of London. Off-shore may be defined as 'juridical spaces characterized by a relative lack of regulation and taxation'[38]; and, therefore, off-shore can be a market or a set of transactions which take place in a major financial centre.[39] As an example, it is worth noting that the foreign exchange market, with a daily turnover of $2 trillion, is almost entirely off-shore.[40] Thus, off-shore does not refer to the geographical location of financial activities but to its juridical status. For many of its activities, the City of London enjoys a clear 'off-shore' juridical status: 'there is nothing the City of London would like more than getting rid of its messy hinterland, Great Britain'.[41]

The 'messy hinterland', however, also provides for other locations, apart from the City of London itself, to conduct off-shore financial activities within its territory. The Bailiwick of Guernsey (including the islands of Guernsey, Alderney and Sark), the Isle of Man and Jersey are all dependencies of the British Crown and are all well-known off-shore centres. The UK government provides political stability for all of them as it is responsible for their international relations and defence, but they are all autonomous with regard to taxation and other domestic issues.[42] Moreover, they are part of the European Union customs territory, but they are not subject to other EU rules. A similar status is enjoyed by Gibraltar, which is formally a UK overseas territory.[43]

Here we provide some anecdotal evidence[44] of the involvement of City financial institutions and personnel in the activities connected to money laundering. In 2006, there were widespread allegations that the deposed Prime Minister of Thailand, Thaksin Shinawatra, had acquired his London assets through tax evasion on a $1.9 billon share deal.[45] Another example concerns Diepreye Alamieyeseigha, a Nigerian state governor who bought four properties in London for a total of just under £5 million; at least another £2.7 million passed through a bank account in the name of a company that he controlled. When the police raided one of his properties, a two-storey penthouse valued at £1.75 million, they found also more than 1 million pounds in cash in his safe. Mr. Alamieyeseigha was arrested and charged with money laundering, but he jumped bail and went back to Nigeria.[46] He had opened accounts with no fewer than five major London banks. Under Britain's Money Laundering Regulations of the time, those banks were supposed to file 'suspicious activity reports' (SARs) with the financial intelligence unit if they had any concerns. So too were solicitors obliged to be alert to money laundering. But only one suspicious activity report was lodged by those banks.[47] One would expect banks to verify similar transactions, particularly when it was known that the person behind the companies entering into these transactions was a governor of the state of Nigeria, and thus a Politically Exposed Person (PEP). Next, Stephen Baker, a Jersey-based barrister who specializes in corruption cases, reported that by 2006, when the anti-money laundering legislation had been in place in the United Kingdom for 10 years, not a single banker had been prosecuted in the United Kingdom for not reporting money laundering.[48] He also explicitly stated, 'The complaint that one hears is that the most serious financial crime is not properly investigated or prosecuted in the United Kingdom'.[49] Richard Dowden, director of the Royal African Society, believes Britain may still be viewed as a safe haven by some corrupt foreign politicians seeking to enjoy the proceeds of their crimes. In his words:

> I think until recently Britain has been seen as quite a soft touch. In fact the expression the City of London being the laundry of choice I've heard a couple of times. There's a lot of property being bought, nice houses or land. The way it comes in is to go into offshore trusts and companies where they don't need to name the beneficiaries. That money then flows into the City of London from apparently legal companies in offshore territories and overseas territories, and I think that's the sort of soft underbelly here and that's the one they've got to tighten up on...I think the other one is that the regulatory system has been, not that it's been weak but it hasn't been implemented. And so I think the feeling is yeah, if you're rich and you have a shady past, London is a very good place to come and put your money.[50]

There is also the problem of the ease with which it is possible to establish a UK company via the Internet, even concealing ownership by having another company act as a nominee shareholder.[51] The following are some examples of the consequences of such a practice.

London is a major trading centre for oil from West Africa. In 2005, a High Court judgement revealed that the Congolese government had been able to hide its corruption and dirty dealings by channelling them through a series of companies, one of which was registered in the United Kingdom. In this specific case, the national oil company in Congo, which normally sells oil on behalf of the government directly to oil traders, sold the oil at very low prices to a series of shell companies; Sphynx Bermuda was the main company, but there was also a company registered in the United Kingdom called Sphynx UK. These companies then sold the oil at a profit to oil traders. Around $470 million worth of oil was being sold in this way. The related profits should have gone to the Congolese people, but instead were siphoned to corrupt Congolese politicians through an off-shore UK shell company. Obviously, it was impossible to uncover who was behind the UK company, which was still in existence in 2006 while its Bermuda sister company had been swiftly dismantled by the local government.

Another scandal involving UK shell companies concerned corrupt Kenyan officials who had signed and made payments on an entire series of faked contracts with overseas companies, including several with UK addresses. The scandal was known as Anglo Leasing after one of the companies so involved.[52] 'Anglo Leasing' was, of course, a collective term given to a nexus of scandals that involved dodgy procurement procedures. The total value was astounding: it was about the value of Kenya's total foreign aid in a year, one billion dollars. There was an entire network of companies in Britain and elsewhere—some not even officially registered, and others apparently not able to fulfil the contracts they had signed. A number of UK citizens were named in an official Kenyan government report as signatories to the contracts. Among the key players was Kenyan businessman, Deepak Kamani, whose sister owned a hotel in Liverpool.[53]

Moreover, during the 1990s, 23 London-based banks laundered more than $1.3 billion stolen by former Nigerian dictator General Sani Abacha. Barclays alone was reported to have handled more than $170 million of funds suspected of being looted from the Nigerian treasury by General Abacha's military regime. Not a single institution or individual was named, let alone prosecuted, by British authorities. Only in 2005 did UK institutions start returning some of the £1.3 billion looted by the Nigerian general.[54]

Finally, it is extremely unlikely that the incredible amount of money, around $15 billion (£9.6 billion) that HSBC allegedly accepted in bulk cash transactions, from countries at very high risk of money laundering (such as Mexico and Russia) without any proper checks, did not end up in a way or another in the City of London.[55]

Given the inherent secretive nature of money laundering activities, there is no certainty about the breadth of money laundering globally or in the United Kingdom. In 1996, an IMF study suggested that money laundering was equal to 2–5% of the global GDP which then totalled between US$ 590 billion and US$ 1.5 trillion.[56] This range is often used to estimate the size of the money laundering problem in the United Kingdom. Applying the IMF methodology, HM Customs and Excise estimated that money laundering in the United Kingdom was in the range of £19–£48 billion in 1999. Currently, the scale of money laundering in the United Kingdom is estimated to be between £23 and £57 billion.[57]

The United Kingdom plays a leading role in European and world finance and remains attractive to money launderers because of the size, sophistication and reputation of its financial markets. Although drugs are still the major source of illegal proceeds for money laundering, the proceeds of other offences—such as financial fraud and the smuggling of people and goods—have become increasingly important. The trend over the past few years has witnessed a move away from High Street banks and mainstream financial institutions for the placement of cash. In laundering funds, criminals continue to use a variety of methods, including bureaux de change (small, tourist-type currency exchanges), smuggling cash in and out of the United Kingdom, professional money launderers (including solicitors and accountants) and the purchase of high-value assets or commodities such as gold, as disguises for illegally obtained money.[58] Even the CIA Factbook's Illicit Drugs section refers to the United Kingdom as a 'money laundering centre'.[59]

The overall threat to the United Kingdom from serious organized crime and related money laundering is high. UK law enforcement agencies estimate the economic and social costs of serious organized crime, including the costs of combating it, at upwards of £20 billion a year. It is estimated that the total quantified organized crime market in the United Kingdom is worth approximately £15 billion per year: drugs (50%), excise fraud (25%), fraud (12%), counterfeiting (7%) and organized immigration crime (6%).[60]

Estimated recoverable criminal assets per annum total £4.75 billion, of which an estimated £2.75 billion is sent overseas. Cash remains the main proceeds of most serious organized criminal activities in the United Kingdom. The following typologies are of most concern to UK law enforcement agencies: cash/value couriering, abuse of 'gatekeepers', abuse of money transmission agents (including *hawala* and other alternative remittance systems), cash-rich businesses and front companies, high-value assets and property and abuse of bank accounts and other over-the-counter financial sector products.[61] All this happened despite attempts at policing money laundering, including the Financial Action Task Force (FATF) Recommendations and various EU Money Laundering Directives.[62]

The UK and Anti-Money Laundering Legislation

The United Kingdom implemented the provisions of the EU's Anti-Money Laundering Directives, and the FATF 40 Recommendations, though drug-related money laundering has been a criminal offence in the United Kingdom since 1986.[63] Subsequent legislation criminalized the laundering of proceeds from all other crimes. The United Kingdom also has a requirement for the reporting of suspicious transactions that applies to banks and non-bank financial institutions, and secondary regulations that require systems be in place to prevent and detect money laundering.[64]

In addition, the United Kingdom's banking sector provides accounts to both residents and non-residents, who can open them through various intermediaries that often advertise on the Internet and also offer various off-shore services, or as a part of private banking activities. Private banking[65] constitutes a significant portion of the British banking industry. Both resident and non-resident accounts are subject to the same reporting and record-keeping requirements. Non-resident accounts are typically opened by individuals for taxation or investment purposes.

The United Kingdom is a party to the 1988 UN Drug Convention and a member of the FATF; it also signed the United Nations Convention against Transnational Organized Crime in December 2000, and the Mutual Legal Assistance Treaty (MLAT) between the United Kingdom and the United States has been in force since 1996.[66]

In addition, the financial services industry in the United Kingdom has been subject to Anti-Money Laundering Requirements (AMLR) since the introduction of the First Money Laundering Directive in 1991 (transposed into UK law through the Criminal Justice Act 1993 and the Money Laundering Regulations 1993), designed to give legal force to the FATF 40 Recommendations in the EU. The key features of the First Directive were that: member states must ensure that money laundering is prohibited; financial institutions must require identification of their customers by means of supporting evidence when entering into business relations; financial institutions must maintain adequate records of transactions and identification for at least five years; financial institutions must cooperate with national law enforcement authorities and must inform them of any fact which might be an indication of money laundering; financial institutions must carry out adequate staff training to ensure that their staff are aware of the law and are trained to spot potentially suspicious transactions; and member states must extend the provisions of the directive to any businesses which engage in activities which are particularly likely to be used for money laundering purposes.

In 1997, guidance notes on best practices were issued by the Joint Money Laundering Steering Group (JMLSG) of professional and trade bodies. The Bank of England Act 1998 transferred responsibility for UK bank supervision from the Bank of England to the newly established Financial Services Authority (FSA). The FSA's primary responsibilities were in areas relating to the safety and soundness of the institutions in its jurisdiction. From the full implementation of the Financial Services and Markets Act (in 2001), the FSA administered a new civil-fines regime and had new prosecution powers. The FSA had the power to make regulatory rules in relation to money laundering and enforced those rules with a range of disciplinary measures (including fines).[67]

Anti-Money Laundering Requirements were increased by the passage of the Proceeds of Crime Act (PoCA) in 2002 which extended the definition of money laundering. The PoCA combined and simplified the Criminal Justice Act of 1996 and the Drug Trafficking Act of 1994. Additionally, the guidance notes issued by the Joint Money Laundering Steering Group are used as a practical guide for implementing ML regulations. At that time, suspicious transaction reports were to be filed with the Economic Crime Unit of the National Criminal Intelligence Service (NCIS), which served as the United Kingdom's financial intelligence unit.[68] The role of the NCIS was to analyse reports, develop intelligence and pass information to police forces and HM Customs for investigation.

In 2003, regulations were introduced in the United Kingdom in response to the EU's Second Money Laundering Directive (2MLD) (2001) which was approved to update the First Directive in the light of experiences and global trends in money laundering. In particular, the 2MLD addressed those activities and professions shown to be vulnerable to money laundering. Prior to the Money Laundering Regulations 2003, AMLR applied only to banks and financial services institutions. The 2003 Regulations extended AMLR to a number of other sectors, most notably accounting and legal services.[69]

On 15 December 2007, new Money Laundering Regulations took effect which implemented the requirements of the EU's Third Money Laundering Directive (3MLD) in the United Kingdom. The ML regulations imposed requirements on various types of businesses. Until its dismantlement in 2012/2013, the FSA supervised the money laundering controls in authorized firms (which the FSA already regulated under the Financial Services and Markets Act) as well as certain other types of businesses, such as safety deposit box providers, leasing companies, share registrars and commercial lenders, which were registered with the FSA for the first time. Since 2013, this role has been taken over by the new Financial Conduct Authority (FCA).

The Counter-Terrorism Act 2008 came into effect on 27 November 2008. Schedule 7 set out new powers for the Treasury in directing financial and credit institutions in the application of a range of financial restrictions with respect to business with persons from non-EEA (European Economic Area) countries of money laundering, terrorist financing or proliferation concern. Various monitoring and enforcement provisions are included as well.[70]

Despite the fact that the City considers the aforementioned legislation burdensome, and a potentially deadly competitive threat for its business, when FATF issued the first mutual evaluation of the implementation of Anti-Money Laundering Requirements in the United Kingdom in 2007, a number of gaps were found.[71] For example, with respect to identification, FATF reported that the United Kingdom only partially fulfilled the requirements of the FATF Anti-Money Laundering Recommendations. JMLSG guidance only partly dealt with identification, primarily where there were doubts regarding previously obtained customer identification data. Regarding this, there was no legal requirement on the books; entities were not specifically required to verify that any person purporting to act on behalf of the customer was so authorized. Similarly, there was no legal requirement to identify beneficial owners and no explicit obligation to obtain information regarding the purpose and nature of the business relationship in the United Kingdom.[72]

As outlined above, correspondent banking and shell banks are often used by money launderers to enter the banking system. In the United Kingdom in 2007, there were no enforceable obligations pertaining to correspondent banking. Moreover, there was no enforceable obligation for financial institutions not to enter into, or continue, correspondent banking relationships with shell banks and no obligation to require financial institutions to ensure that correspondent financial institutions in foreign countries do not permit their accounts to be used by shell banks. Further, there were no requirements relating to foreign branches and subsidiaries; and there was no requirement for financial institutions to give special attention to business with countries which did not sufficiently apply FATF Recommendations.[73]

Generally speaking, there was no specific obligation to pay special attention to any complex, unusually large transactions, or unusual patterns of transactions that had no apparent or visible economic or lawful purpose. For casinos, customer identification was not required above the 3000 euro threshold, and it was not clear that casinos had to adequately link the incoming customers to individual transactions. Even more lax, estate agents were not required to certify the identity of buyers.[74]

Overall, the number of FSA disciplinary sanctions seemed fairly low: only 14 enforcement actions had been enacted between 2001 and 2007, including warnings and licence cancellations; administrative sanctions of Her Majesty's Revenue & Customs did not extend to directors and senior managers. Additionally, UK authorities did not have the power to detain cash or bearer negotiable instruments purely on the basis of a false disclosure.[75]

Some of these shortcomings were addressed following the implementation of the 3MLD (adopted in June 2007). In October 2009, FATF recognized that the United Kingdom had made significant progress in addressing deficiencies identified in their Mutual Evaluation Report and thereby removed the country from the regular follow-up process, agreeing that it should now report on a biennial basis.[76] There were, however, still some areas of concern. For example, there was still no direct obligation to verify that any person purporting to act on behalf of the customer was so authorized, and full exemptions to Customer Due Diligence (CDD) still exist for certain customers that go beyond the FATF standards.[77] Further, while the new regulations impose requirements for correspondent banking relationships outside the EEA, there are no similar requirements for correspondent relationships in other EEA countries. In addition, while there is a requirement to assess the respondent's anti-money laundering terrorist financing controls, there is no requirement to subsequently ascertain that those controls are adequate and effective before proceeding with the correspondent relationship.[78]

In determining where third parties who meet the required conditions can be based, competent authorities only partially take into account available information on whether those countries adequately apply FATF Recommendations. Indeed, there is still no specific requirement for financial institutions to give special attention to business with countries which do not sufficiently apply FATF Recommendations.[79] There is no specific requirement to extensively examine the background and purpose of all complex, unusually large transactions, or unusual patterns of transactions that have no apparent or visible economic or lawful purpose and to set forth those findings in writing.[80] There are no new obligations pertaining to branches and subsidiaries of UK financial institutions located in other EEA countries. Nor is there a requirement that financial institutions ensure that their foreign branches and subsidiaries in other EEA countries observe anti-money laundering (AML) and counter financial terrorism (CFT) measures consistent with the home country requirements and, therefore, with FATF Recommendations. Similarly, where AML/CFT requirements of the home and host countries differ, there is no requirement that branches and subsidiaries in the host country apply the higher standard.[81]

Despite these shortcomings in the application of the AMLR by the United Kingdom, and the widespread feeling reported above that not enough is being done to restrain criminal proceedings from ending their laundering journeys somewhere in the City of London, the perception of the City itself is that regulation is too high, and it actively lobbies for looser regulation, as detailed below.

AMLR and the City of London

There is no mistaking the hostility of the City of London towards AMLR. As the officer of a UK-based law firm put it, AMLR is a 'Sledgehammer to crack a nut'.[82] Similarly, a London-based accountant stated, 'The current requirements are a completely disproportionate response to money laundering—there are far too many reports, far too much wasted time and far too much bureaucracy—and you can quote me on that!'[83] The City of London's official position towards AMLR is that the United Kingdom should continue strong enforcement of its comprehensive anti-money laundering programme and its active participation in international organizations that combat domestic and global threats of money laundering. However, in a report published by the City of London in 2005, Michael Snyder, then chairman of the Policy and Resources Committee of the City of London, explicitly noticed that:

> London's reputation must be maintained without undermining its competitive position. The UK is engaged in an on-going competition with other jurisdictions to uphold its status and attract more international business. One important and highly visible measure of the balance between reputation and competitiveness is the effectiveness and cost of Anti-Money Laundering Requirements (AMLR) that countries employ to support their financial systems.[84]

In general, the perception of those actively involved in business in the City of London is that the costs of the AML regime in the United Kingdom are too high. This was true even before the implementation of the 3MLD and the enactment of the anti-money laundering regulations in December 2007.

Neither the financial services sector nor the professions believe there is a need for such a costly effort nor that this effort is directed in the most effective way and represents good value for money.[85] Michael Snyder stated, in 2006,[86] that the implementation of AML regulations was very challenging and difficult for the City of London, as it required a fine balance to ensure effective measures that do not place a disproportionate onus on the industry that must implement them. The 2MLD had proven just how difficult this process can be. In Snyder's opinion, a combination of imprecise terminology in the directive itself and differences in existing national legal and regulatory systems produced a wide range of different implementation results that placed onerous competitive burdens on financial and other City institutions and services.[87] Particular problems were identified with respect to the definition of 'serious crimes' covered by Anti-Money Laundering Requirements, professional privilege exemptions, the verification of identity in non-face-to-face transactions and clashes between the 2MLD prohibition on 'tipping off' and the EU's own Data Protection Directive.[88]

It was also problematic to implement the procedures for defining and reporting suspicious transactions, with some member states imposing the obligation of reporting all transactions above a certain level regardless of suspicions of money laundering.[89] In Snyder's opinion, for an effective AML regime to work, it was essential not to impose unrealistic burdens on honest businesses and their advisers, as this would help to maintain the integrity and effectiveness of the financial system.[90] Within the EU single market, it was also vital that this regime was enacted in all member states in a uniform manner. From Snyder's point of view, the implementation of the 2MLD did not achieve this result, and he hoped this could happen with the implementation of the 3MLD in 2007.[91]

In 2004, the City of London Corporation commissioned a study on the perceptions about AMLR among its practitioners. When this research was planned, the Money Laundering Regulations of 2007 had not yet come into force. Therefore, there was still little experience with the more burdensome provisions of the new legislation or with the effects of including in the new 'regulated sector' other professionals, such as lawyers advising on commercial transactions, accountants or tax advisers. In spite of this, the perceptions of those within the regulated sector were that the costs of the anti-money laundering regime in the United Kingdom were high. This produced substantial lobbying activity by the City's institutions on government, law enforcement authorities and the writers of guidance, to try and steer the regime towards the City's needs.[92]

The study assessed the perceived costs and benefits of UK Anti-Money Laundering Requirements and what impact the UK AMLR has had on the competitive standing of the UK financial services industry. Research was carried out between September 2004 and April 2005 and involved 34 personal interviews and an online survey which elicited 386 responses.[93] The research highlighted the following results: first, almost two-thirds of UK respondents said that AMLR were too severe in proportion to the risks of money laundering. Perceptions of current costs, past cost increases and future cost increases were higher from UK respondents than from international respondents. Second, further intervention in anti-money laundering should focus on improving the perceived effectiveness of current requirements, rather than increasing the level of regulation. Third, the effectiveness of AMLR could be significantly enhanced by closing regulatory gaps.

It is important to underline that British financial services found costs related to the introduction of identity checks to be burdensome, a practice that is hardly considered a cost in other jurisdictions (or in general for that matter).[94] Also, many of the professional services companies contacted said that their highest costs were 'lost-opportunity costs' of fee earners attending AML training in order to comply with AMLR.[95] Overall, the message was clear: 77% of UK-based accountants and 84% of UK-based lawyers felt AMLR was too severe for the risks involved in their sectors.[96]

With respect to compliance, UK banks were generally not worried about sanctions from the authorities and were increasingly taking a 'risk-based' approach, meeting the bare minimum AMLR requirements and only in the riskiest activities from a money laundering perspective. As we saw above, this approach is recommended in the JMLSG proposals and is supported by FSA.

Regarding effectiveness, the survey results indicated that the percentage of international respondents who believed that AMLR in their country was effective in deterring and detecting money laundering was far higher than the percentage of UK respondents who believed the same. However, many UK financial services professionals believed that AMLR is potentially effective but the way in which the regulations are implemented by the City makes them ineffective. The key area of customer identification (Know Your Customer or KYC) provides a good example of this. As one Money Laundering Reporting Officer (MLRO) stated, 'The idea of customer identification is clearly sensible but the actual customer identification process that most banks employ is simply not effective—it is a box ticking exercise'.[97]

Overall, the number of respondents who perceived positive effects from AMLR was extremely low. For example, out of a total of 87 quotes on AMLR-related costs, there was only 1 positive quote. Out of 39 quotes on AMLR-related benefits, there were only 7 positive quotes. As for AMLR effectiveness, there were only 2 positive quotes out of a total of 129 quotes. And, finally, there were only 3 positive quotes out of 36 as regards the effects on competitiveness.[98]

One of the explanations for the City of London's negative attitude towards AMLR is clear from the research itself: increased regulation, especially with regard to money laundering, decreased the attractiveness of the City's services and institutions. This was the opinion held by more than one-third (36%) of the respondents.[99] Compared to those surveyed in Germany, three times as many people in the United Kingdom felt that with the implementation of AMLR the attractiveness had decreased (36% versus 12%).[100] The survey results and all of the evidence from professionals within the industry seemed to agree that UK financial services industry was 'on the edge' of losing competitiveness because of the level of AMLR. Many interviewees perceived that the United Kingdom was approaching a level of regulation which would adversely affect competitiveness.[101]

If this was the response to the 2MLD, then the implementation of the 3MLD and the new Money Laundering Regulations of 2007 produced an array of outright protests in the City of London. This was especially the case among the regulated professions, as they are the ones mostly affected by the new regulations. Lawyers have since been fighting a battle to convince FATF that the same anti-money laundering rules designed for the financial sector should not be applied to them.[102] Their resolve was such that eventually lawyers succeeded in making their case and, after much lobbying, in October 2008 FATF published its Risk-Based Approach Guidance for Legal Professionals (the same day the gambling industry got its own version). The guidance sets out a risk-based approach to assessing the likelihood of money laundering taking place in any case or with any client. Geography, the nature of the client and its business, and the nature of the service requested represented the primary markers for the application of AMLR. The guidance also sets forth recommended approaches to the implementation of effective monitoring processes and training programmes in law firms. However, lawyers were not yet satisfied. According to Stephen Revell, Chair of the International Bar Association Anti-Money Laundering Legislation Implementation Group (IBA-AMLLIG), the reality is that 'in many countries, the rules that lawyers are being asked to adhere to are disproportionate and inconsistent with their duties'.[103] Revell, a partner at leading London law firm Freshfields Bruckhaus Deringer, has supported the AMLLIG's lobbying activity in this area in recent years because of his concerns that he was increasingly 'seeing new laws coming through which were onerous for lawyers and damaging to clients without sufficient thought or consultation with lawyers'.[104] In general, the IBA-AMLLIG questions whether lawyers should be the target of AMLR at all. Revell says the group began its work with two fundamental concerns, neither of which was close to being resolved.[105]

First, lawyers in the City deny that they are unwittingly facilitating money laundering. Revell raises the question of whether all the work and expenditure to put lawyers at the forefront of the fight against AML is a proportionate response to the actual risk. This point assumes greater weight given that the guidance revolves around a risk-based approach. Peter McNamee, senior legal adviser at the CCBE, stresses that 'it is a question we raise at every opportunity. Based on the evidence we have, there are very few lawyers unwittingly involved in money laundering. The FATF guidance, like the EU directives, is a very disproportionate response to the problem'.[106] The second concern is whether lawyers should be obliged to blow the whistle on clients they suspect may be involved in money laundering. Though there is some protection for lawyers, limiting it to certain types of work, for example, reporting has provoked some very strong principled opposition from lawyers who believe that the lawyer–client relationship should be sacrosanct.

The lawyers' community would require reasonable grounds for a suspicion to be reported.[107] Revell believes that 'this may take a long time, but it's a worthwhile goal to say we need to revisit with the FATF the whole suspicious transaction reporting regime they've established'.[108] McNamee comes to the same conclusion. He argues that it was important to hold an absolute line against any reporting, stressing that 'once you've eroded the principle, you chip away at it with other legislation'.[109] There are signs that FATF may follow the lawyers' advice on this issue. The Council of Bars and Law Societies of Europe (CCBE) is expected to broach the subject at a European level with the European Commission.

In the meantime, English firms with a significant international presence continue to point to how unnecessarily expensive and awkward anti-money laundering laws can be when applied to lawyers too zealously. As Revell puts it, 'There is some momentum beginning to build to re-examine the fundamental rule on whistle blowing'.[110] He believes there is room to make it less mandatory and restrict it to serious matters, if not to dispose of it completely. In his opinion, the AML regulation as applied to lawyers is 'broken so we should work on fixing it—but I wouldn't like to predict what the fix is and when it will come'.[111]

Is it the legislation which is costly, ineffective and 'broken', or is it simply that the City does not want to have it and even less to apply it? Indeed, the City of London's incredible capacity to adapt to the changing 'situation' (the Gramscian 'situazione') requires the British financial sector and services to keep the level of regulation to a minimum. It should not therefore take anyone by surprise that AMLR are viewed at least with suspicion, if not with straightforward uneasiness, within the 'square mile'. Not to mention the fact that some in the City might find it more rewarding to turn a blind eye to the sources of the money they are dealing with.

Conclusion

In conclusion, can the City of London be defined a 'Launderer of last resort'? Anecdotal evidence points to the existence of a widespread perception of London as the final stage of the money laundering process. Also the conclusions of the FATF with respect to the implementation of AMLR by the United Kingdom are not reassuring in terms of the extent to which the British financial sector is involved in curtailing the phenomenon. Finally, the high level of opposition that exists in the City of London with respect to AMLR certainly gives hints to the extent to which the City perceives it more as a burden than as a necessity.[112] *Pecunia non olet*. 'POSTSCRIPT: After writing this chapter, the 2017 AML Regs were brought into force on 26 June 2017.'

Notes

1. Saskia Sassen, *The Global City: New York, London, Tokyo* (Princeton University Press 1991); Peter Dicken, *Global Shift: Mapping the Changing Contours of the World Economy* (6th edn, Guildford 2011); Ronen Palan, *The Offshore World: Sovereign Markets, Virtual Places, and Nomad Millionaires* (Cornell University Press 2006); Ronen Palan, Richard Murphy and Christian Chavagneux, *Tax Havens: How Globalization Really Works* (Cornell University Press 2010).

2. James Mittelman, *The Globalization Syndrome: Transformation and Resistance* (Princeton University Press 2000); Henk Overbeek, 'Globalization and the Restructuring of the European Labor Markets: The Role of Migration' in Mihaly Simal, Valentine Moghadam and Arvo Kuddo (eds), *Global Employment. An International Investigation into the Future of Work* (vol 1, United Nations University Press 1995).

3. Benjamin Cohen, 'Phoenix Risen: The Resurrection of Global Finance' (1996) 48(2) World Politics 268, 269; Benjamin Cohen, 'Electronic Money: New Day or False Dawn?' (2001) 8(2) Review of International Political Economy 197; Susan Strange, *Casino Capitalism* (Manchester University Press 1986); Susan Strange, *Mad Money* (Manchester University Press 1998).

4. Peter Dicken, *Global Shift: Reshaping the Global Economic Map in the 21st Century* (Sage 2003) 59; William Coleman, *Financial Services, Globalization and Domestic Policy Change* (Palgrave Macmillan 1996) 7.

5. Dicken (n 4) 462.

6. Sassen (n 1); Saskia Sassen, *Cities in a World Economy* (Pine Forge Press 2000).

7. Peter Lilley, *Dirty Dealing: The Untold Truth about Global Money Laundering* (Kogan Page 2000). See further the evidence of the 'Panama Papers' <https://panamapapers.icij.org/> accessed 28 January 2017.

8. Palan (n 1) 2; Palan, Murphy, and Chavagneux (n 1).

9. Tommaso Padoa-Schioppa, *The Road to Monetary Union in Europe: The Emperor, the Kings and the Genies* (Clarendon Press 1994); Cohen (n 3); Maurice Obstfeld and Alan Taylor, *Global Capital Markets. Integration, Crisis and Growth* (Cambridge University Press 2004).

10. Lilley (n 7) 3.

11. Moises Naim, *Illicit: How Smugglers, Traffickers and Copycats are Hijacking the Global Economy* (William Heinemann 2005).

12. International AML agreements are discussed in other chapters in this collection.

13. Mark Yeandle and others, *Anti-Money Laundering Requirements: Costs, Benefits and Perceptions* (Corporation of London Research Series Number Six, 2005).

14. Ibid. 48.
15. Lilley (n 7) 5.
16. IMF, 'The IMF and the Fight Against Money Laundering and the Financing of Terrorism' *IMF* (6 October 2016) <www.imf.org/external/np/exr/facts/aml.htm> accessed 12 October 2016.
17. Carolyn Nordstrom, *Global Outlaws, Crime, Money and Power in the Contemporary World* (University of California Press 2007) 97.
18. OECD, 'Ten Years of Combatting Money Laundering' (1999) 217–218 OECD Observer <http://oecdobserver.org/news/archivestory.php/aid/63/Ten_years_of_combating_money_laundering.html> accessed 28 January 2017. For a discussion of the role of gatekeepers, or professional enablers, see Chap. 6 (Benson) in this collection.
19. Lilley (n 7); Nordstrom (n 17) 167. For the legal dimension, see also Peter Alldridge, 'Money Laundering and Globalization' (2008) 35(4) Journal of Law and Society 437.
20. For discussion of Bitcoin and the AML framework, see Chap. 9 (Egan) in this collection, and for discussion of how virtual currency can be used in laundering, see Chap. 8 (Chambers-Jones).
21. Yeandle and others (n 13) 36.
22. Lilley (n 7); Nordstrom (n 17) 167–79.
23. Correspondent banking is defined as the provision of banking-related services by one bank (Correspondent) to an overseas bank (Respondent) to enable the Respondent to provide its own customers with cross-border products and services that it cannot provide them with itself, typically due to a lack of an international network.
24. Naim (n 11) 145.
25. Lilley (n 7) 49.
26. Naim (n 11) 147.
27. Ibid. 148.
28. Ibid.
29. Lilley (n 7) 49; Nordstrom (n 17).
30. Nordstrom (n 17) 179.
31. Lilley (n 7) 17.
32. See, for example, the money laundering publications on the Transparency International UK website <http://www.transparency.org.uk/corruption/resources/money-laundering/> accessed 12 December 2016.
33. Ibid.
34. The role of professional enablers is emphasized in National Crime Agency, *High End Money Laundering: Strategy and Action Plan* (December 2014) <http://nationalcrimeagency.gov.uk/publications/625-high-end-money-laundering-strategy/file> accessed 1 February 2017; National Crime Agency, *National Strategic Assessment of Serious and Organised Crime 2016* (September 2016) <http://www.nationalcrimeagency.gov.uk/ publications/731-national-

strategic-assessment-of-serious-and-organised-crime-2016/file> accessed 1 February 2017. See Chap. 6 (Benson) in this collection.

35. See Michael Levi, 'Pecunia Non Olet? The Control of Money Laundering Revisited' in Frank Bovenkerk and Michael Levi (eds), *The Organized Crime Community: Essays in Honour of Alan Block* (Springer 2007).
36. Nordstrom (n 17); OECD (n 18).
37. OECD (n 18).
38. Palan (n 1) 9.
39. Palan (n 1); Palan, Murphy, and Chavagneux (n 1).
40. Palan (n 1) 7.
41. Ibid. 175.
42. Chizu Nakajima, 'Politics: Offshore Centers, Transparency and Integrity: The Case of the UK Territories' in Donato Masciandaro (ed), *Global Financial Crime: Terrorism, Money Laundering and Offshore Centers* (Ashgate Publishing 2004).
43. Ibid.
44. See also Transparency International UK <http://www.transparency.org.uk/> accessed 22 January 2017; NCA, 'Money Laundering' <http://www.national crimeagency.gov.uk/crime-threats/money-laundering> accessed 22 January 2017.
45. BBC Radio 4, 'File on Four: UK "haven" for Money Laundering' *BBC* (31 October 2006) <http://news.bbc.co.uk/2/shared/bsp/hi/pdfs/31_10_06_fo4_money.pdf> accessed 12 October 2016.
46. Ibid. 5.
47. Ibid.
48. Ibid.
49. Ibid. 6.
50. Ibid. 7.
51. Ibid. 8.
52. Ibid. 16.
53. Ibid.
54. See the relevant case law, *Compagnie Noga D'Importation Et D'Exportation SA and another v Australia and New Zealand Banking Group Ltd and others (No 5)* [2005] EWHC 225 (Comm); *Blue Holding (1) Pte Ltd and another v United States of America* [2014] EWCA Civ 1291; *Blue Holdings (1) Pte Ltd and another v National Crime Agency* [2016] EWCA Civ 760; Naim (n 11) 147.
55. See also Chap. 12 (Levi) in this collection.
56. Michel Camdessus, 'ML—The Importance of International Countermeasures' *IMF* (10 February 1998) <www.imf.org/external/np/speeches/1998/021098.htm> accessed 11 August 2016. For a discussion of the 'threat of crime-money' and its extent, see Chap. 15 (van Duyne and others) in this collection.

57. See <http://www.fsa.gov.uk/pages/About/What/financial_crime/money_laundering/faqs/index.shtml> accessed 21 December 2016.

58. UNODCCP, *Report on Money Laundering in the UK* (UNODCCP 2001) (unpublished).

59. See CIA <https://www.cia.gov/library/publications/the-world-factbook/geos/uk.html> accessed 21 December 2016.

60. See HM Treasury and Home Office, *UK National Risk Assessment of Money Laundering and Terrorist Financing* (October 2015) <https://www.gov.uk/government/uploads/system/uploads/attachment_data/file/4682 10/UK_NRA_October_2015_final_web.pdf> accessed 1 February 2017; Financial Services Authority, *The FSA's New Role Under the Money Laundering Regulations 2007: Our Approach* (September 2007) 2 <http://www.betterregulation.com/external/approach.pdf> accessed 1 February 2017.

61. FSA (n 60) 2.

62. For consideration of such developments, see other chapters in this collection.

63. Drug Trafficking Offences Act 1986.

64. UNODCCP (n 58).

65. Private banking is personalized financial and banking services that are traditionally offered to a bank's wealthy high net worth individual (HNWI) clients.

66. UNODCCP (n 58).

67. Yeandle and others (n 13) 12–14.

68. For a detailed breakdown of the current SARs regime in practice, see National Crime Agency, *Suspicious Activity Reports (SARs) Annual Report 2015* <http://www.nationalcrimeagency.gov.uk/publications/677-sars-annual-report-2015/file> accessed 28 January 2017.

69. Yeandle and others (n 13) 12–14.

70. FSA (n 60) 5.

71. Ibid. Appendix.

72. Ibid.

73. FATF, *Annual Report 2009–2010* (FATF/OECD 2010) Appendix.

74. Ibid.

75. Ibid.

76. Ibid.

77. Ibid. 10–11.

78. Ibid. 12.

79. Ibid. 17.

80. Ibid. 14.

81. Ibid. 18.

82. Yeandle and others (n 13) 30.

83. Ibid. 31.

84. Michael Snyder, 'Foreword' in Yeandle and others (n 13) 4.

85. Yeandle and others (n 13) 5.

86. Snyder (n 84).

87. Ibid.

88. Ibid.

89. Ibid.

90. Ibid.

91. Ibid.

92. Yeandle and others (n 13) 6.

93. Ibid.

94. Ibid. 20.

95. Ibid. 27.

96. Ibid. 30.

97. Ibid. 42.

98. Ibid. 22.

99. Ibid. 34.

100. Ibid. 35.

101. Ibid. 36.

102. For consideration of lawyers and AML, see Chap. 6 (Benson) in this collection; Neil Rose, 'Making the Case For Appropriate Anti-Money Laundering Rules for Lawyers' (2009) International Bar News 37, 38.

103. Rose (n 102) 38.

104. Ibid.

105. Ibid.

106. Ibid.

107. The problem in this sector is the underreporting of SARs.

108. Rose (n 102) 39.

109. Ibid.

110. Ibid.

111. Ibid.

112. For the future, maybe Brexit will make things worse if becoming a tax haven and increasing the position of the City as an off-shore market might be the only way to keep the competitiveness of the British financial sector.

Leila Simona Talani is a full Professor of International Political Economy at King's College London. She was appointed as Jean Monnet Chair of European Political Economy in the Department of European and International Studies in 2012. Leila Simona Talani got her PhD with distinction at the European University Institute of Florence in 1998. Her research interests currently focus on the global political economy and migration and on the consequences of the global financial crisis on the capitalist structures of European countries, especially Italy and the United Kingdom.

5

The Production of Suspicion in Retail Banking: An Examination of Unusual Transaction Reporting

Vanessa Iafolla

Introduction

Anti-money laundering (AML) and counter-terrorism financing (CTF) activities have of late gained prominence in Canadian politics and policy. Throughout the 1990s, financial activities related to money laundering and, since 9/11, to the financing of terror have become increasingly regulated. The financial services sector has been identified as susceptible to abuse by money launderers and financiers of terrorism.[1] The enactment of the Proceeds of Crime (Money Laundering) and Terrorism Financing Act (PCMLTFA) in 2000 created a legal requirement for financial institutions to report suspicious financial transactions to the Financial Transactions and Reports Analysis Centre of Canada (FINTRAC), Canada's AML/counter-terrorist financing (AML/CTF) reporting entity. While there are guidelines provided to reporting entities that present specific indicators of suspicion,[2] there is a mandate from both FINTRAC[3] and within the broader banking culture that industry norms are instructive and can strongly indicate when a client's requested transaction is not only atypical but suspicious.

Canadian financial institutions are dominated by a small group of major players—'the Big Five'—though a series of smaller financial institutions (many of which operate in various partnerships with larger banks to provide some services) and credit unions provide regional and national service. The market dominance

V. Iafolla
Department of Sociology and Legal Studies, University of Waterloo, Waterloo, ON, Canada

© The Author(s) 2018
C. King et al. (eds.), *The Palgrave Handbook of Criminal and Terrorism Financing Law*, https://doi.org/10.1007/978-3-319-64498-1_5

of these large financial institutions[4] has meant that these institutions conduct the bulk of financial transactions. The sheer volume of these transactions has necessitated the development of an internal reporting structure to manage the task of suspicious transaction reporting. Canada's largest financial institutions have therefore developed internal systems and structures for reporting these transactions, and the reporting process begins at the point of contact with clients, when employees are asked to examine each transaction and use their discretion to determine whether the transaction merits further scrutiny and report.

This chapter examines the process of generating data for the production of Suspicious Transaction Reports (STRs). In compliance with regulatory requirements,[5] large Canadian financial institutions provide training for their employees with respect to the reporting of suspicious financial transactions, entailing training on patterns of suspicious financial behaviour, risk indicators, and reporting practices. The standard for reporting is *reasonable suspicion*, a relatively low legal threshold that is based on the individual perspective of the employee conducting the transaction. The initial report filed by employees—in this chapter, by retail branch tellers—is known as an Unusual Transaction Report (UTR), and very little is known about how these initial reports of suspicion are generated or used within financial institutions. Thus, this chapter explores, through discourse analysis and interviews with bank employees, how such UTRs are generated.

In keeping with the work of the Financial Action Task Force (FATF), Canada first enacted AML legislation in 1991; since then, the Canadian AML/CTF complex has expanded to require the reporting of suspicious financial transactions related to instances of money laundering and terrorist financing, including mandatory reporting for all cash transactions at or over $10,000.00,[6] and all suspicious financial transactions of any amount.[7] The PCMLTFA, derived from the FATF 40 Recommendations, requires employees working in specific cash-intensive industries[8] to report suspicious financial transactions.[9] While there is some guidance provided, largely the mandate is that identified financial entities must report 'every financial transaction that occurs or that is attempted in the course of their activities and in respect of which there are reasonable grounds to suspect attempted or actual money laundering or terrorist financing'.[10] The 'reasonable grounds' upon which an individual should submit a report of suspicion vary widely by industry. While the PCMLTFA does identify particular transactions that must be reported, such as cash deposit transactions at or above $10,000.00, other cases are murkier. Further, in Canada, unlike the US or the UK, reporting entities need not identify on the STR a predicate offence. In addition, these *threshold transactions*, where the dollar value of the transaction provides a clear rule for reporting, any transaction—regardless of its value—must be reported if the employee processing it thinks the transaction is in some way suspicious.

The PCMLTFA's responsibilization[11] of banks and bank employees to report suspicious financial transactions is in keeping with an important trend in governance: the state is interested in 'harnessing private control activities for public regulatory purposes', particularly as 'regulatory organisations can be relieved of much of the economic and epistemic burden of detailed rule-making, and can focus on overseeing the design and functioning of local systems'.[12] While this is common to various areas of regulation, including health and safety, teaching, and other areas of public life,[13] using private control activities to control risks to the state can create interesting spaces where regulated entities can take hold of or use the law in ways that may not be precisely what lawmakers intended. What is new, here, is that under the PCMLTFA, and as presented by the bank, the risks of the institution are reoriented and reconfigured into risks borne by employees.

Bank employees receive extensive education regarding AML protocols and initiatives. Initially conducted after hiring, AML training is repeated annually, and 'refresher training' is conducted throughout the year, when employees watch videos, discuss events, and engage in other activities. Part of the annual training involves studying a series of computer modules and passing a test on money laundering, which requires 80% accuracy. In this training, employees learn about the risks posed by money laundering to the bank, to the industry, to global financial networks, and to themselves. These risks are to be taken into account when an employee is evaluating a transaction and determining whether it appears suspicious or unusual, or in other terms indicative of illegal financial activity. This chapter examines how bank tellers, teller supervisors, and customer service managers evaluate the legitimacy of a transaction, specifically by relying upon risk factors outlined by the institution and upon experience acquired in the branch. Though there is no identification of it in the legislation, in the regulations, or in internal training manuals, the opportunity for employees to use their discretion creates the opportunity for idiosyncratic decisions to be made based not necessarily on ideas of risk (as conceived of by law, regulation, or best practice), but rather based on individualized ideas of suspicion.

Risk, AML/CTF, and Suspicious Funds

The sociology of risk and the sociology of money inform the analysis in this chapter. While best practices, red flags, and regulatory requirements provide indicators to employees that transactions should be more closely scrutinized, risk indicators are not used in a vacuum: they are deeply social and their use entwines with personal attitudes towards, and understandings of, currency and other financial instruments. This chapter examines how risk-based analyses of financial transactions can be influenced by personally held beliefs and ideas about how money ought to be used, and how constructions of suspicion in the context of AML/CTF reporting can become conflated with simply odd or unusual, but not necessarily illicit, financial transactions.

The literature on risk is useful in this task, not least because risk discourse permeates AML and CTF discourse. The sociology of risk has documented an increasing social preoccupation with the prevention of averse or negative outcomes,[14] as well as the more positive or productive historical changes brought about by embracing risk.[15] These broader social and historical preoccupations with risk have entrenched themselves in late-modern institutions and have given rise to taken-for-granted practices of risk management such as the audit,[16] and a proliferation of surveillance technologies governing public life.[17] The reality of government and industry dataveillance of private individuals, and the murky possibilities for information in private-sector databases to be accessed for public purposes[18] is evident in late-modern life. This reality is particularly clear in the context of STR activities, wherein data collected by financial institutions are shared with government regulators like FINTRAC, or can be compelled by warrant.[19]

Risk logic now permeates the social world: academics have examined its salience in, inter alia, the 'War on Terror',[20] the insurance industry,[21] and welfare fraud.[22] In particular, analyses of the risks posed by employees, whether by malfeasance, such as through theft or shrinkage[23] or through moral hazard,[24] are instructive for understanding how risk is regulated in other areas, and in particular in the context of terrorism or money laundering. There is a growing literature that critically examines risk-based approaches to AML/CTF activities undertaken in the private sector on behalf of the state;[25] this chapter's contribution is to examine the outcomes of these approaches in the context of generating reports of suspicion. The preoccupation of banks with anticipating, calculating, preventing, minimizing, and controlling risks resonates with the practices of other risk-minded industries.[26] Like other industries that embed risk management features into their operations, banks rely on routinized techniques of risk management to ensure that the overarching goal of profit-building continues with minimal interruption. While it is likely impossible to completely eradicate risk from daily operations, banks mobilize proactive technologies such as scripts, which detail protocol for employees to follow in a particular risk situation,[27] more abstract technologies of risk management, such as CCTV and computer databases and communication systems,[28] and reactive apparatuses such as shaming and bonus forfeiture to recuperate losses that employees allow to occur.

Like other powerful institutions in late-modern society, financial institutions are 'increasingly preoccupied with the future (and also with safety), which generates the notion of risk'.[29] In the current climate, failures of risk management can lead to fines and administrative monetary penalties,[30] so the legal, social, and economic consequences of uncontrolled risks—here, of financing terrorists or laundering money—can be serious. In AML, as in other contexts, banks embed security functions in their day-to-day operations. To that end, institutions that are concerned with managing activities or events that they perceive to be risky invest in risk communication systems, which include technologies and rules identified as best able to identify and manage those threats to their security. Interestingly, these systems of expert knowledge are not only critical to managing risks, as they enable employees to proactively prevent the worst before it happens,[31] but they are also responsible for manufacturing new risks. The logics of risk communication systems thus create new crises by identifying new risks and providing agents of risk management with the foundation upon which to act,[32] creating an endless cycle of proliferating risk types and profiles to examine.

Some scholarship on risk suggests that risk management practices are largely abstract, depersonalized, and draw from expert knowledge on risk classification or categorization.[33] The abstract nature of risk therefore suggests that, relative to one's placement in a risk matrix or other classification instrument, an individual's risk will be governed not according to his or her personal position, risk factors, or identity, but rather in a pool with other similarly ranked individuals. High-risk, low-risk, at-risk: all these categorizations represent the de-individualization of the subject.[34] Yet, in places where discretion can be deployed, institutional or expert categorizations of risk may be circumvented.

The sociology of money can be instructive in this regard. At first glance, financial services such as banks appear to embody the calculating, expert-knowledge-driven nature of late-modern institutions. For example, employees follow set scripts that dictate how much discretion they are able to use when conducting a transaction and are structurally prevented from deviating in any way from the parameters set by corporate security. Employees are formally trained to treat money as an abstraction, trustworthy only insofar as the funds presented can be verified for negotiation.[35] In economic contexts, money is often regarded as a leveller that 'measures all objects with merciless objectivity'.[36] In this view, 'within money transactions all persons are of equal value, not because all but because none is valuable except money'.[37] Best practices in financial services reinforce this understanding of money, as it is 'not only the final purpose but the raw material of [the banker's] activity'.[38] As such, an industry in which money is both the form and the substance of the industry should be the ultimate in 'objectivity in exchange activities[…]since it is free of all the specific qualities of the individual things exchanged and thus *per se* has no biased relationship to any subjective common element'.[39] However, and especially in the context of AML and CTF activities, all funds and sums are not created equal. Financial transactions become moral transactions, and financial risks become moral risks. An analysis of money laundering and terrorism financing detection presents an opportunity to examine how this comes to be in the context of financial services, as the PCMLTFA provides bank employees with significant latitude in identifying potentially suspicious financial transactions.

Employees are largely dependent on expert knowledge, and formal processes to identify and manage the risks of customer impersonations, cheque fraud, and other risks posed by would-be fraudsters, or bank robbers. Internally, there exist a series of checks and controls designed to minimize the risk of successful frauds perpetrated against the institutions. There is no preventive equivalent in financial institutions to keep employees from inadvertently or purposively allowing money laundering or terrorism financing to occur.[40] Employees are obligated under the legislation to use their industry-related expertise, which is a combination of industry best practices and employment experience; the decision, in the end, to start the process of reporting money laundering or terrorist financing is up to the individual conducting the transaction, unless the transaction is within mandatory reporting parameters. In this way, determinations of money laundering or terrorism financing are highly contextual and individualized, based on a small body of expert knowledge provided by the financial institution, and largely informed by the impressions of the individual(s) conducting the transaction. They differ from the problems of fraud or robbery that have traditionally plagued banks and other financial institutions.

Banking is a site where risk takes on new social dimensions. This chapter examines how individual employees understand and manage the risks posed by money laundering and terrorism financing. This chapter looks at how bank employees, whose jobs have built-in risk prevention functions, manage risks when afforded discretion in determining what is risky transaction, and how their personally held ideas about suspicion mix with the best practices of the institution to reduce risky transactions.

A specific strain of the sociology of money—that which focuses on the social meanings of money[41]—is particularly instructive. This literature examines the ways in which money is ascribed value in interpersonal relations and relationships. Money has an exchange value, but its exchange/economic value differs from the social meaning that money takes on in interpersonal relationships. This social meaning of money is particularly relevant in the context of money laundering and terrorism financing: the '*proximate* source, its *ultimate* source, and its *future direction*'[42] influence its social value in ways that the provenance of birthday funds, wedding gifts, or Hanukkah gelt cannot. Indeed, scholarship speaks of dirty dollars,[43] black markets,[44] and grey money.[45] In banking, money can be tainted as the proceeds of crime, and the process of uncovering this taint is likewise the process of uncovering a particular risk. These social dimensions fuse with risk, transforming funds into the dirty money.

While some literature on money and meaning has tended to focus on domestic relations and intimate relationships,[46] banking offers an excellent site for examining interpersonal relations in a related context. One of the central components of a successful relationship in banking is 'know your customer' (KYC).[47] KYC stipulates that bank employees should try to cultivate as much of a relationship with their clients as possible, as having not only bank-related but personal knowledge of a client's regular activities and lifestyle represent opportunities for both furthering the economic relationship the client has with the bank, and preventing fraudulent or illegal activities from occurring against the client's account, or by a client's misuse of banking services. KYC seeks to enable deep personal knowledge about the lifestyle and habits of bank clients. In having access to transactions in a client's recent history, information about the kinds of activities, events, purchases, and food consumption a client enjoys can be made known to the individual conducting a transaction. This kind of access to information leads to a different kind of intimate knowledge of the client by the bank teller, particularly in the context of assessing risk, and an understanding of clean or dirty money is imperative for understanding how employees come to view what kinds of transactions are unusual, and thus worth reporting. Examining valuations of money in retail banking can offer insight into the ways in which notions of 'clean' and 'dirty' money are constructed in the context of assessing risk. How tellers and their supervisors make decisions about the moral meaning of money has much to contribute to both the study of risk and the literature on moral and social meanings of money, as well as the literature on AML.

Methodology

The data used in this chapter was collected as part of a broader study on the detection and prevention of money laundering under the PCMLTFA. This data was collected during a month of participant-observation in the Financial

Intelligence Unit (FIU) of one of Canada's largest financial institutions. During this time, I was allowed access to several sources of data: bank manuals,[48] training materials including modules and tests for the bank's internal online, topic-based AML/CTF program, which employees must complete yearly, and 40 UTRs randomly selected by the bank. Data also include conversations held with individuals working in the AML FIU, including the FIU manager, investigators working in the FIU, and people who were responsible for ensuring regulatory compliance. Finally, the participating FIU provided a sample of 40 UTRs, although the AML FIU could not disclose to me whether they had been converted to STRs.[49]

This chapter also uses semi-structured interviews, relying mostly on vignettes to prompt participants into describing how they might react to a particular client request. Interviews took place with employees working in one of Canada's largest financial institutions. A total of 40 employees—a mix of bank managers, branch supervisors, and bank tellers—were interviewed across 11 randomly selected branches in the City of Toronto. While this data is not representative of bank employees, they make several important contributions to the literature on AML and banks. Retail employees are an understudied population, in Canada as elsewhere, and little is known generally about how security actors make decisions about suspicious financial transactions, though with some notable exceptions in the AML/CTF complex.[50]

As client confidentiality and privacy, as well as the offence of tipping off under s.8[51] of the PCMLTFA, precluded observations of actual client-teller or client-manager interactions, this research used vignettes describing deposit, withdrawal, and wire transfer transactions to provide employees with a framework for describing their thoughts and actions in potentially unusual situations. Interviews were semi-structured and in-depth; questions were posed to interviewees in three phases. First, employees were asked to respond to questions regarding their employment history, including how long they had held their current position within the bank, and how long their banking career had been to that point. Second, they were asked to respond to vignettes, which were constructed so as to determine what aspects of a deposit, withdrawal, and wire transfer would be considered 'unusual', and thus lead a teller to file a UTR. The scenarios described the components of a typical transaction and asked the interviewee to describe how she/he would proceed to complete that transaction, and whether they would submit a UTR. Third, employees were asked to discuss instances in which they made decisions whether or not to submit a UTR, so as to understand how, in practice, employees made determinations of 'unusual' in the context of money laundering and terrorism financing. All questions were focused on the practice of unusual transaction reporting. This research therefore focuses on the first step in the reporting process—the point at which reports are generated by front-line employees and passed on to corporate security, and more specifically on wicket transactions,[52] so as to maximize the likelihood that participants would have familiarity with and have submitted UTRs.

The vignettes posed scenarios that prompted employees to discuss typical transactions. Through the framework of these vignettes, employees were asked to describe how they would act if presented with client transaction requests that might constitute unusual transactions according to banking best practices. The vignettes were intended to prompt employees to discuss their perspectives on conducting such transactions. For example, bank employees were asked to describe how they might proceed if a client presented different amounts of money for deposit or requested to wire funds overseas. These vignettes were used as a means of inquiry into the ways employees who are not normally responsible for crime detection or investigation in the course of their employment discharge that duty. There are real concerns with offloading policing functions, particularly to individuals who are not normally tasked with investigative functions.[53] The combination of vignettes and internal bank documents provides important background information regarding motivations that underlie decisions to report.

Money Laundering, Terrorist Financing, and Risk Management

Bank employees who work with money, in any capacity, are expected to undergo extensive training that meshes the bank's obligations under Canada's AML regulations and legislation with the best practices of the bank. Already having been trained in fraud prevention measures, employees are made to understand through this training how money laundering and terrorism financing are distinct from fraud, and how the bank's 'best practices' are to be used in detecting these activities.

What makes the detection of money laundering and terrorism financing so different from detecting fraud is that where fraud detection practices are very formulaic and include preventative safeguards that can literally prevent employees from completing fraudulent transactions, the guidelines for detecting possible money laundering or terrorism financing are much more elastic and contextual. Employment experience and discretion play a far larger role in detecting these activities than they do in detecting fraudulent ones.

Bank employees play a key role in identifying transactions that might be potentially suspect. As *Global AML/CTF Policy* states:

> Any [bank] employee might encounter a transaction or activity that is unusual. If you do, you must report your concerns by completing an Unusual Transaction Report (UTR).

That manual goes on to say that a transaction might be considered unusual if it is inconsistent with information held about the customer and her normal business practices, if it is not in keeping with the behaviour of an average customer, or if it is not in keeping with how a specific type of account normally operates. Red flags for fraudulent transactions are more specific and include specific scripts that employees must follow and electronic alerts that can prevent employees from withdrawing large sums from a client's account. What the triggering behaviour of an average customer is depends largely on the experience and discretion of the employee processing what may (or may not) be an unusual financial transaction within the context of the branch. Indeed, employees themselves highlighted the individualized nature of detecting money laundering or the financing of terror:

Manager F: The thing is, even though they [tellers] have to report transactions, it's not that all unusual transactions are going to be the same. That wouldn't be very unusual, would it? [laughs] They have to look at the client individually, they have to ask themselves each time if this is something that is normal for this person. That is something they get used to the more they do it, though, and we are always available to help them if they're not sure. If they're not sure, I'll go through it with them and say, 'Why did you think that was unusual?' And they'll tell me, and if I know the client I'll say, 'This is okay', and I'll explain why. But every time, it's a different kind of unusual. That's what makes it unusual.

Manager A: The UTR isn't a cookie cutter kind of thing. You have to measure each individual situation on its own; something that may seem unusual in one person's account may not seem unusual in another person's account. Experience has something to do with it, part of an effect on what you perceive as unusual, experience helps a [teller] to ask the proper questions, get the proper information. [Reporting is] case by case, basically.

For tellers, who as a group have the least autonomy in performing financial transactions,[54] basic or low-risk transactions can be performed autonomously. However, institutional training and compliance culture in the branch—as modelled by the managers above—demonstrate the importance of ensuring that transactions that break the cookie-cutter mould are given extra examination. Employees may be inexperienced or careless, and neglect their reporting duties; they might also be overzealous and report things that are on their face reasonable. Proper training and proper oversight are envisioned as checks against such problems.

The process of generating UTRs is based more on experience as a best practice of risk management than on the expert knowledge of corporate security. This process has particular implications for the ways in which financial transactions are subject to moral classifications and risk assessments. Through the process of generating a UTR, the amount of funds presented for negotiation and the form in which they are presented are transformed from economic abstractions into technologies of risk. Once transformed into technologies of risk, bank tellers evaluate the transaction, producing moral judgements about both the transaction itself, and about the client requesting it. In this way, money, morality, and risk fuse, producing morally risky clients and transactions.

Financial Instruments and the Production of Risk

This section discusses the ways in which funds are differentiated as legitimate or unusual. Specifically, the focus is on how bank employees understand monetary media such as cash or cheques as 'clean' or 'dirty' money, and how monetary media[55] combined with moral valuations of money suggest to an employee that a transaction is institutionally risky and socially wrong.

Bank tellers are taught in training that, all things being equal, cash, cheques, and money orders are to be treated differently from each other, representing a normative earmarking not uncommon in social relations.[56] However, there is very little analysis of the actual forms that money can take. To the possessor, a pay cheque is different from birthday money, but how does it differ from other kinds of cheques or financial mediums at the teller counter? In an arena where there may be no way to immediately verify if the money presented is a gift, a tip, a loan repayment, or the proceeds of drug selling, the actual type of financial instrument presented does matter to those receiving it and depositing it into an account. The notion of monetary media highlights the symbolic value of the medium that money held for those with an interest in controlling the use of US greenbacks. The moral value that currency holds for bank employees is different: cash, cheques, bank drafts, and other ways of presenting money are not merely good or bad, but they can be more or less risky to negotiate. This classification depends on whether the funds are *guaranteed*, whether the instrument presented is *known*, and whether they are *verifiable*.

The issue of guarantee arose in many interviews, suggesting that '[d]ifferent kinds of money, like tools, can look superficially alike, although they do and mean very different things'.[57] Many tellers would immediately ask, 'It's cash, right?' For tellers in particular, but for all employees, the presentation of the money—cash, cheque, or bank draft[58]—made a difference in their comfort with the transaction. Every participant, when discussing vignettes, either spontaneously clarified that they were discussing cash or asked the interviewer for confirmation of the type of financial instrument discussed in the hypothetical vignettes, and independently discussed the difference between types, which indicates that the instrument itself is used as an indicator of risk.[59] Although their comfort with a transaction could be influenced by other factors, including the amount, participants outlined differences between types of financial instruments. Financial instruments were far from mere social abstractions,[60] and the aesthetic format of the funds presented a kind of cue as to the riskiness of the transaction.

Cash was in some ways easier for employees to deal with than any other kind of instrument because, unless counterfeit, cash is negotiable upon receipt. Both *Global AML/CTF* Policy and *Global Anti-Fraud Policy* stipulate that if it is not possible to verify the authenticity of an instrument or the availability of the funds for which it is to be negotiated, the money is to be placed on hold. While this policy is somewhat elastic, in that the client's own cash reserves or 'good relationship' with the bank or branch could ease the hold restrictions somewhat, when transacting with cash there was no need to consider the hold policy. Cash itself was always available to be put in the account and could therefore be taken at face value, whereas cheques and drafts were potentially subject to a 'hold' until the funds cleared from the bank on which they were drawn:

Interviewer: So, is the UTR for cash transactions only?

Manager E: No. We get a lot of cheque fraud here so we always have to be careful with that. Putting the right hold, the right amount of hold, whether it should be on hold or not, the proper amount of days….If it can be verified right away, if it's certified funds or a draft, it's easier to verify.

Cash never gets held because there are rarely questions as to its authenticity or verifiability. Employees could easily spot counterfeit funds, but counterfeit cheques were far more difficult to uncover. In this way, cheques have issues of trust similar to credit, posing a moral risk of fraudulence that cash does not: 'If cash is used to consummate the transaction, the seller/creditor only has to know if the money is trustworthy, and she can forget about the other party. If the money is 'green', so to speak, then it does not matter who the other person is'.[61] Regular pay cheques that have been authorized are treated similarly, and direct electronic fund transfers are also treated with such ease. While cash is immediately negotiable, that can also present a problem related to verification. There is no way to ensure that the cash, while legal tender, was legally earned. In this study, employees immediately highlighted the hazards indicated by cash deposits. Even if the money is 'green', employees were instructed to examine the cash itself, because the individual notes could help confirm wrongful financial dealings: the value of the bills and the condition in which they are presented can reveal their illicit provenance:

Manager D: I'd also just tell them to verify the money, make sure it's authentic. And it also depends on the denominations, if I had a customer come in a couple days in a row and they brought in 5's, 10's, and 20's for a thousand—like, mostly 5's and 10's and a few 20's for a thousand, I'd wonder what was going on. Is it drug money?

In another instance, one particularly vigilant employee filed a UTR because the money 'smelled like marijuana' (UTR report). As cash is immediately negotiable, even low sums of money tendered for deposit can signify moral hazard such as the laundering of drug money. And, once deposited, such money could easily be transacted with and successfully reintegrated into legal financial markets. Concerns regarding funds derived from illegal activities are particularly salient within the bank, especially with regard to money laundering and terrorism financing. Much training is done to ensure that employees recognize the signs and symptoms of money that comes from illegal sources. For example, all employees must pass a test on money laundering detection that includes discussion of the illegal drug economy—their results on this test are retained, providing a record of their successful responsibilization regarding AML and CTF resources. Informally, employees learn of 'markers of suspicion', such as the denominations used by drug dealers, and make note of them, thus transforming denominations of cash into red flags. The actual presentation of money not only signifies risk in terms of money laundering or terrorism financing but also imbues a moral dimension to that risk. This intimate intertwining of 'risk management and moral categorization' relies on the 'moral imaginings'[62] of the employee conducting the transaction. In this way, money produces, identifies, and manufactures further risks to be managed.[63]

While cash may be risky in some senses, it is unproblematic in other respects because it is negotiable upon receipt. By contrast, with financial instruments, the bank distinguishes between *verifiable* and *unverifiable* instruments. Those that are 'verifiable' include cheques drawn on the bank that is negotiating them (because the signature can be authenticated, and it can be determined whether the funds are available) and certified cheques, money orders, and bank drafts (because—unless forged—the funds have been set aside for these cheques, and, again, unless forged, there is no issue of authenticity to sort out prior to cashing or depositing the cheque). Regular cheques, whether drawn on business or personal accounts, are more problematic in this regard, as it cannot clearly be determined in many instances whether the cheque will be returned for insufficient funds, or whether the signature on the cheque is, in fact, that of the account holder. It is not that the instrument itself is bad or risky per se, but that it becomes difficult to put one's trust in the validity of the instrument, for fear of incurring the consequences of failing to successfully manage risk. Branches therefore look to other markers to ensure that a transaction is legitimate, including relying on the regularity of a particular kind of deposit to show that the funds have been available before, and that the cheque depositing *should* be 'good money', just like the money that has come before. Money that is regular and reliable is perceived to be risk-free, because it has previously been proven to be legitimate and should therefore continue to be so:

Teller D2:   Basically, like if he brings always a work cheque every week, it's always the same cheque coming in, maybe off by a few dollars, but it's always the same.[…]It's usually frequent transactions that are always the same.

Manager D: Basically, if you have a customer coming in every week, making regular pay deposits—that's not unusual. But if the same customer comes in making pay deposits and then comes with large amounts of cash all of a sudden, then I'd consider that unusual, or if you have a customer—same thing, like, the same kind of pay, and then comes with large cheques, then I'd want them sent to be verified, and there'd be a five day hold.

Consistency and regularity increased the comfort employees felt with a transaction, because a history or pattern of activity, even if it was not possible to know what specific instrument was negotiated last week, meant that the client was more than likely conducting legitimate financial business. Again, it is noteworthy that, while participants were asked only to respond to instances in which clients brought cash, they felt it necessary to explain that distinction between different kinds of money. Employees highlighted the different valuations of the kinds of moneys that they received, illustrating that different types of money represent a kind of manufactured risk to the bank and to clients alike. In this way, the paper trail it leaves behind as well as its immediate negotiation can produce new risks to be identified, calculated, and prevented.[64]

Sums of Money and the Production of Moral Risk

The amount of the transaction can impact on whether an employee perceives the money to be risky and likely related to money laundering or the financing of terror. In the eyes of a bank teller, the amount of money presented can turn good cash into 'bad', or what is presented as a regular pay cheque into something that is not only socially unacceptable but illegal.

In the context of AML/CTF detection, cash presents unique problems.[65] Interestingly, and ironically, it is possible for a person to have too much money, especially if that money is cash. That cash can be suspect is counterintuitive: too much real cash can indicate that a transaction, and by extension the client, is engaged in financial wrongdoing, and is a particular risk for money laundering or terrorist financing. Specific dollar amounts represent a clear red flag.[66] Any deposit of US$10,000.00 or more must be reported to FINTRAC via the Large Cash Transaction Report (LCTR), a legislative requirement that serves as an alert that a significant amount of cash has been deposited, and the business dealings of the individual or entity depositing this money must be examined further. The LCTR applies to cash, but employees who suspect financial instruments should also submit an STR.[67]

The mandatory LCTR represents a clear instance in which one can have too much cash, and in which the money itself becomes suspect, regardless of the instrument presented. But what of transactions under US$10,000.00? Transactions slightly under this amount are viewed with a different kind of suspicion: anyone who brings in US$9999.99, for example, is almost immediately suspected of smurfing, which is 'the practice of lodging amounts of cash into bank accounts in sums too small to attract attention and disclosure to the authorities'.[68] Such amounts are invariably viewed with suspicion because it is presumed that that individual is depositing smaller amounts of money to circumvent detection. Indeed, the bank AML manual, *Global AML/*

CTF Policy, specifically identifies, inter alia, smurfing as a potential red flag for unusual activity: structuring amounts, conducting large cash transactions, or sending wire payments, in particular for students, or 'inconsistent or unknown source of funds', per the *Global AML/CTF Policy*, could all indicate money laundering or terrorist financing. For such transactions, employees should submit a UTR, because, as *Global AML/CTF Policy* sets out, this particular kind of activity is unusual, regardless of the nature of the actual funds themselves (cash, cheque, wire payment), or how well the client is known to the bank. These concerns seem to be exacerbated in the case of cash. Large amounts of cash constitute at the very minimum indication of illegal activities, and mandatory reporting schemes represent an attempt to prevent employees from failing to recognize situations indicative of ill intent on the part of clients who would launder funds through the branch. In this way, mandatory reporting requirements produce morally suspect clients from simple cash transactions.

Money laundering and avoiding taxes were the activities of particular concern in this context, and even lesser amounts could prompt an employee to submit a UTR:

Interviewer: Does the amount affect your perception of the transaction?

Teller I1:   That does affect it, just because I can see somebody using two thousand maybe to pay a construction worker, or some people spend that much—maybe somebody's buying a sofa and they don't want to pay tax. So I can understand that, but something like six thousand, what do you need this money for? Then I'd start to…and not only that, but why would somebody feel comfortable taking out six thousand in cash when we have other options available? Cheques, money orders—its risky to take out six thousand, unless it's a business that you know regularly does this.

Manager F: [C]ash always gets me going, large amounts of cash, and large meaning—it doesn't have to be ten, twenty thousand, I'd consider three or four thousand as large amounts of cash.

While $2000 or $1000 wasn't necessarily suspicious in and of itself, the higher the amount of money presented or requested, especially in the context of cash, the more a transaction should be inspected for abnormalities. As one teller stated, '$1000 in cash as opposed to $6000 is less suspicious'. That teller continued:

Teller G2:   I would usually get a second opinion—I know they say that UTRs have no monetary limit, but usually it's a large amount that's gonna make you suspicious, you're not gonna put it through if its $50 or $100.

The issue of large amounts of money, especially cash, is important regardless of the size of the denominations used, and 'smaller bills'—5-, 10-, and 20-dollar bills—were the subject of particular suspicion. As discussed above, 'small' bills and amounts seemed to be associated with lower-level drug dealing or other 'unsavoury' activities.

Manager D: Usually, they'll [the tellers] come down and say, 'This client deposited $8000 in 5's, 10's and 20's,' and I'll say, 'Did you put through a UTR?' And I'd insist that they'd bring up the profile and put one through. It could be anything.

Lesser amounts of money, too, could prompt employees to have doubts about the legitimacy of the transaction, particularly if, as discussed above, that particular kind of transaction was not regular for the client.

Manager E: Like I said, two thousand doesn't get you very far, but are they on welfare and social assistance goes in every month? Is this drug money? You have to question that. For an affluent customer I wouldn't, but....Again, it's banking habits, he's on social assistance, he lives pay cheque to pay cheque, and suddenly he brings in $3000 in cash, that'd be unusual for me.

Teller J1   We had a customer, she's young, around 25, she's not working, she has a black boyfriend, I think she's a stripper, and every time she comes she comes with that much [$2500] cash in US or Canadian, that's unusual, too. How did you get that money? Every time you come just with cash? There's something wrong. We have nannies here, they work and get cheques, but when you come with cash in US or Canadian, and she has a brand new car and a Louis Vuitton purse, it's like that, too.

The young woman described above was presented as enjoying a lifestyle of lavish spending, illustrating that in some ways social expectations of appropriate spending by certain kinds of people may remain unchanged. In this way, a client who seems to have too much money may be identified as a moral risk by employees, particularly if the client does not regularly transact with that much money. Employees read into a client's appearance and behaviour morally and socially questionable kinds of employment, such as drug dealing or exotic dancing, from sums as small as $1000. Employees readily made moral judgements about transactions that, in light of their training regarding structuring illegal funds, should not necessarily have provoked any suspicion. Certainly, sporadic deposits of $2500 would make the young woman described above a poorly skilled money launderer. That her transaction was singled out for discussion, and her personal tastes and spending habits called into question, illustrates not only that determinations of risk in this context are highly discretionary, but that even small amounts when negotiated by certain kinds of clients (alleged strippers and drug dealers) transform otherwise normal transactions into AML risks. In this way, cultural notions of appropriate purchasing power and spending behaviour[69] become discretionary tools that may also be relied upon by employees to assess whether a client's transaction is illegitimate.

This is not to suggest that smaller sums of money can never present a risk of terrorist financing. Indeed, serious acts of terrorism can be carried out with small sums of cash: the bombs detonated at the Boston Marathon in 2013 were estimated to have cost less than $100 per bomb,[70] and the attack on Ottawa by Michael Zehaf-Bibeau in 2014 may have been funded by money earned in the Alberta oil patch.[71] These attacks may have been funded in part or in whole with legally earned income. In cases like these, it is difficult to determine the extent to which anyone charged with the task of scrutinizing financial transactions would be able to accurately identify terrorist intent from a regularly earned pay cheque. Even the FATF acknowledges the low cost relative to impact of terrorist attacks: the direct attack costs of the London transit system bombings of 2005 are estimated at £8000; the Madrid train bombings of 2004 were estimated to have cost $10,000 USD.[72] These two attacks crippled transportation systems and killed hundreds of people; yet, given the small amounts they might have reasonably been explained away as proceeds from the sale of furniture or a car, or gone undetected as legally earned income. For financial instruments, especially regular pay cheques, deviations from the regular deposit could be the hallmark of a fraudulent or altered cheque. A bigger pay cheque could be altered from the regular amount, and a draft for a lot of money could be altered or altogether forged.[73]

| Teller B1: | Because say a person has a pay cheque every two weeks, we know they're at that job and we trust them that they're at that job still. But if they quit and they forged that cheque, we're gonna trust them because that's something familiar—we're gonna cash that, we're gonna take a risk on that. |
| Interviewer: | Do you mean that cheques are risky? |

Teller B1:   The bank is always taking a risk when they're doing a cheque; they don't have the money right away. If we're unsure we put a hold—a cheque isn't cash, it's an agreement saying we're gonna give you this money, and once the money clears, the bank's gonna give you this money.

It appears that on some levels *who* is doing the lavish spending, or presenting large or different amounts of money for negotiation, is important to the teller, as it can reveal something that is odd about the situation. As in the case of the woman described above, the issue may be gendered. It may also be related to age, as employees demonstrated a willingness to submit reports for small cash deposits on both teenage and elderly clients. Lesser sums of money may be large in terms of a client's perceived station in life, and the combination of these factors may lead to money being flagged for further AML investigation.

Teller J2:   There's one girl that comes in here with US, lots of US. Personally, we think that she's a stripper, I don't know, we don't know. But on her occupation—when you question her, she's belligerent, rude. And I haven't seen her in quite some time, and once I was doing something, her account popped up, and her account was held, and we were like, she's gonna be peeved. There was a point where she was bringing in a few thousand US many times a month. That's questionable. And last check, it said 'student' on the account. But I think someone's checking that out. It stands out in my mind, particularly 'cause it's US, more so than Canadian. And it wasn't just 2200 in hundreds; it was in a variety, 20, 10, 5. Maybe they're tips [laughs].

Manager E: Like I said, two thousand doesn't get you very far, but are they on welfare and social assistance goes in every month? Is this drug money? You have to question that. For an affluent customer, I wouldn't but....Again, it's banking habits, he's on social assistance...and suddenly he brings in $3000 in cash, that'd be unusual for me.

One UTR for $1000, deposited in $20 denominations, read 'RETIRED DEPOSITING CASH REGULARLY', suggesting that the elderly shouldn't be able to deposit cash, but instead should be living off their pension and savings. This is not to suggest that there is necessarily purposive discrimination against all students, retirees, the poor, foreign students, or women who readily spend money (or their black boyfriends). For tellers, managers, and supervisors, a particular normative or conception of what these kinds of people should be doing exists, and when one or more aspects of the transaction break that standard, the money is more likely to be viewed with suspicion, even though these individuals are not likely those most obviously targeted by the legislation. It may be that, in expecting consistency and regularity from a customer's transactions, implicit ideas about social roles are at play. Perhaps bank tellers expect that construction workers would be paid in cash, but a young woman (ostensibly a student) should not have access to 'that much money'. Individuals who break those social roles, be they retirees who win at bingo or young women who are not employed in a service job can all be conceived of as risks under the current AML/CTF reporting framework.

Discussion

Money, morality, and risk are fused in retail banking. The UTR, meant to generate information regarding potential money laundering or terrorist financing, is not only used by tellers to identify for the internal anti-money laundering unit those transactions they deem unusual. The UTR also highlights the individualized and contextual nature of moral risk management and illustrates that financial transactions are not abstractions in any sense. The amount of money, and the kind of money presented, not only have moral connotations and value akin, but money itself is both an object and signifier of risk, transformed into a moral risk at least in part by its financial value and the kind of financial instrument presented. Contrary to Simmel's contention,[74] and consistent with research on the social meaning of money, money is not simply worth its exchange value. Different financial instruments—currency, cheques, and bank drafts—have different moral and social value beyond their market worth, and the actual financial value of an instrument has implications for the moral meaning of the transaction as well. In light of these different factors, employees were willing to examine transactions in more detail to determine whether, in their opinion, transactions were in fact risky to the financial institution, submitting UTRs based on these initial risk signifiers.

When it is not possible to determine with any degree of certainty where a client earned her money, employees readily imputed from the transaction the source of origin of the funds, based again on the amount and kind of financial instrument presented. This enabled employees to 'justify' their conclusions regarding the legitimacy of a transaction, transforming money of indeterminate origin into *drug money* or *stripper money*, and by extension into a sign of AML risk on the part of the client. In the context of AML/CTF detection, money has meaning, and meanings matter greatly: what kinds of money are presented for negotiation and how much money there is affect employee perceptions of the riskiness of a transaction. This intersection of risk, money, and morality is largely fuelled by discretion. As illustrated above, what is risky or unusual to one employee is not necessarily the same for another. The case-by-case and contextual nature of the decision-making process, informed by employee experience, can vary widely not only within branches but also across branches of a financial institution. This variation itself can present a moral risk to the institution: if bank policies and procedures are such that individual discretion drives the reporting process, individual discretion can result in inconsistent and unwarranted investigation and reporting. As discussed above, clients who do not conform to preconceived social roles may be viewed with increased suspicion, and subject to further risk analysis and scrutiny, whether or not their transactions are legitimate. The fact that a retired client might be depositing $1000 cash is unusual insofar as it may not be a regular transaction for the client, but it does not necessarily indicate money laundering or the financing of terror.

The discretion afforded to employees can erroneously bring the morally innocent under further investigation and divert resources from investigating more objectively suspect transactions. The influence of the structure and culture of an institution can influence employees in ways that may benefit the institution, but they have adverse consequences for clients. Employees are made well aware of the penalties for failing to report suspicious transactions, which under section 76 of the Act include imprisonment and substantial fines. Employees are implicitly encouraged to over-report, reassured by manuals, training programmes, and videos that they suffer no adverse consequences for reporting transactions that are later revealed to be legitimate. Indeed, defensive reporting[75] is a strategy of risk management that can be attractive to financial institutions, as it ensures that however many false-positives may be reported to regulators, the risk of not reporting actual risky transactions can leave the bank open to fines, adverse publicity, and sanctions. While encouraging employee over-reporting and affording significant discretion to them in the reporting process minimizes these risks, the inefficiencies promoted by defensive reporting, and the unfairness to private individuals of having their personal financial dealings scrutinized bear genuine consideration. Private individuals may never know that their transactions, out of the ordinary for them but otherwise legitimate, have been subjected to increased investigation and in many cases disclosure to government agencies. Financial institutions can and do use algorithms that examine patterns of account activity, volumes, and movement of capital flows, and so on: investment in these areas might prove more effective than reports generated by opinions, speculation, and conjecture.

Conclusion

This chapter has sought to address the intersection of morality and risk by examining how money is understood by employees of retail financial services in the context of making decisions about risk. Money in this context clearly possesses a moral dimension derived in part from the amount of money presented for transaction and also from the kind of financial instrument presented. In this way, the social contexts from which money may come, as understood by the teller conducting the transaction, is indicative of AML/CTF risk on the part of the client requesting the transaction. The client's lifestyle, presentation of self, perceived employment, or attitude, may present the tipping point at which a transaction becomes suspicious to the individual conducting it, whatever the objective reality. The legally mandated process of reporting unusual transactions, in conjunction with the best practices of the financial institution, creates structural conditions conducive to over-reporting by bank employees and gives rise to moral risk within the bank. The ways in which financial instruments and transactions are understood to be indicative of moral hazard, in the context of UTR, leaves open the possibility for moral hazard on the part of employees and illustrates the possibility of moral risk to the institution enabled by structural requirements that are part of the reporting process. The subjective nature of the reporting process can create moral hazards where none exist, creating financial risks for the bank's profit-building aims. What is immoral is risky—in the context of money laundering and terrorism financing detection in retail banking, morality and risk cannot be separated.

Notes

1. Daniel Murphy, "Canada's Laws on Money Laundering and Proceeds of Crime: The International Context" (2004) 7(1) Journal of Money Laundering Control 50.
2. Proceeds of Crime (Money Laundering) and Terrorist Financing Act (SC 2000, c 17) (CA), s 7 and s 9(1) clarified by Financial Transactions and Reports Analysis Centre (FINTRAC), "Guideline 2: Suspicious Transactions"

(2016) <www.fintrac-canafe.gc.ca/publications/guide/Guide2/2-eng.asp#s7> 1 March 2017. This Guideline also provides clarification for Proceeds of Crime (Money Laundering) and Terrorist Financing Regulations (SOR/2002–184), in particular clarification regarding industry-specific and general guidelines for reporting entities.

3. Ibid.
4. Canadian Bankers Association, "How Canadians Bank' (2012) <www.cba.ca/en/media-room/50-backgrounders-on-banking-issues/125-technology-and-banking> 10 April 2017.
5. s 7 and s 9(1) (n 2).
6. All sums in this Chapter refer to Canadian dollars unless otherwise stated.
7. For a thorough accounting of the evolution of Canada's legislation, see Margaret E Beare and Stephen Schneider, *Money Laundering in Canada: Chasing Dirty and Dangerous Dollars* (University of Toronto Press 2007).
8. These include a wide range of industries and businesses, such as casinos, life insurance companies, credit unions and caisses populaires, notaries public, dealers in precious metals and stones, and real estate brokers and real estate agents. For a complete list, see FINTRAC, "Who Must Report" <www.fintrac-anafe.gc.ca/reporting-declaration/Info/re-ed-eng.asp> 23 April 2017.
9. Much of what is discussed in this chapter pertains to cash transactions; other financial instruments such as cheques, electronic fund transfers, or money orders are also covered under the legislation. This chapter focuses mostly on cash as that was the chief concern of interviewees.
10. Proceeds of Crime (Money Laundering) and Terrorist Financing Act, s 7.
11. Pat O'Malley, "Risk, Power and Crime Prevention" (1992) 21(3) Economy and Society 252; Pat O'Malley and Darren Palmer, "Post-Keynesian Policing" (1996) 25(2) Economy and Society 137. Responsibilization refers to the practice of removing the responsibility for preventing risks from the auspices of government to private individuals or private enterprise. This situation is different from where individuals are responsible for governing their *own* risks. As will be shown, individuals are made responsible for the state's and their employers' risks, and indeed encouraged to view these risks as their own.
12. Michael Power, *The Risk Management of Everything: Rethinking the Politics of Uncertainty* (Demos 2004).
13. Ibid.
14. Anthony Giddens, "Risk and Responsibility" (1999) 9(1) Modern Law Review 1; Ulrich Beck, *Risk Society: Towards a New Modernity* (Sage 1992).
15. Peter Bernstein, *Against the Gods: The Remarkable Story of Risk* (Wiley 1996).
16. Power (n 12).
17. Kevin Haggerty and Richard Ericson, "The Surveillant Assemblage" (2000) 51(4) British Journal of Criminology 605; Clive Norris and Gary Armstrong, *CCTV and the Rise of Mass Surveillance Society* (Macmillan Press 1999).

18. Reg Whittaker, "A Faustian Bargain? America and the Dream of Total Information Awareness" in Kevin Haggerty and Richard Ericson (eds), *The New Politics of Surveillance and Visibility* (University of Toronto Press 2006).

19. FINTRAC, "FINTRAC, Law Enforcement, and Intelligence Partners: Sharing intelligence, Making the Links" (updated 01 March 2016) <www.fintrac-canafe.gc.ca/publications/brochure/2011-02/1-eng.asp> accessed 10 April 2017; Beare and Schneider (n 7).

20. Louise Amoore and Marieke de Goede (eds), *Risk and the War on Terror* (Routledge 2008).

21. Richard Ericson and Aaron Doyle, "Catastrophe Risk, Insurance, and Terrorism" (2004) 33(2) Economy and Society 135; Richard Ericson and Aaron Doyle, "The Institutionalization of Deceptive Sales in Life Insurance Five Sources of Moral Risk" (2006) 46(6) British Journal of Criminology 993.

22. Dorothy E Chunn and Shelley AM Gavigan, "Welfare Law, Welfare Fraud, and the Moral Regulation of the 'Never Deserving' Poor" (2004) 13(2) Social and Legal Studies 219.

23. Stuart H Traub, "Battling Employee Crime: A Review of Corporate Strategies and Programs" (1996) 42(2) Crime & Delinquency 244.

24. Ericson and Doyle (n 20).

25. Marieke De Goede, *Speculative Security: The Politics of Pursuing Terrorist Monies* (University of Minnesota Press 2012); Anthony Amicelle, "Towards a 'New' Political Anatomy of Financial Surveillance" (2011) 42(2) Security dialogue 161; Gilles Favarel-Garrigues, Thierry Godefroy, and Pierre Lascoumes, "Sentinels in the Banking Industry: Private Actors and the Fight against Money Laundering in France" (2008) 48(1) British Journal of Criminology 1; Martin Gill and Geoff Taylor, 'Preventing Money Laundering or Obstructing Business? Financial Companies' Perspectives on "Know Your Customer" Procedures (2004) 44(4) British Journal of Criminology 582. In this collection, see Chap. 15 (van Duyne, Harvey, and Gelemerova).

26. Les Johnson, *Policing Britain: Risk, Security and Governance* (Pearson Education Ltd. 2000).

27. Richard Ericson and Kevin D Haggerty, *Policing the Risk Society* (University of Toronto Press 1997).

28. Gordon Hughes, *Understanding Crime Prevention: Social Control, Risk, and Late Modern Society* (Open University Press 1998).

29. Anthony Giddens, "Risk and Responsibility" (1999) 62(1) Modern Law Review 1, 3.

30. Marco Chown Oved, Robert Cribb, and Riley Sparks, "Manulife Admits It Was the Bank Fined $1.2 Million by Canada's Money-Laundering Watchdog" *Toronto Star* (Toronto, 27 February 2017) <www.thestar.com/news/world/2017/02/27/manulife-admits-it-was-bank-fined-12-million-by-canadas-money-laundering-watchdog.html> accessed 7 May 2017.

31. Hughes (n 28).

32. Hughes (n 28); Ericson and Haggerty (n 27).
33. Ericson and Haggerty (n 27).
34. For further discussion, see Chap. 12 (Levi) in this collection.
35. Vanessa Iafolla, "Policing Money Laundering and Terrorist Financing: The Reporting of Suspicious Transactions" (2012) 3 Annual Review of Interdisciplinary Justice Research 62.
36. Georg Simmel, *The Philosophy of Money* (first published 1900, Routledge 2004) 431.
37. Ibid. 432.
38. Ibid. 433.
39. Ibid. 436.
40. This is partly because if funds are not traced through a series of accounts, mapping the path of illicit flows can be very complicated.
41. Vivana Zelizer, *The Social Meaning of Money: Pin Money, Pay Checks, Poor Relief, & Other Currencies* (Harper Collins 1994); Bruce Carruthers and Wendy Espeland, "Money, Meaning, and Morality" (1998) 41(10) The American Behavioural Scientist 1384.
42. Carruthers and Espeland (n 41).
43. Beare and Schneider (n 7).
44. RT Naylor, *Satanic Purses: Money, Myth, and Misinformation in the War on Terror* (McGill-Queen's Press 2006); RT Naylor, *Wages of Crime: Black Markets, Illegal Finance, and the Underworld Economy* (Cornell University Press 2005).
45. Kris Hinterseer, *Criminal Finance: The Political Economy of Money Laundering in a Comparative Legal Context* (Kluwer Law International 2002).
46. Gry Mette Haugen, "Relations Between Money and Love in Postdivorce Families: Children's perspectives" 12(4) Childhood 507; Charlott Nyman, "The Social Nature of Money: Meanings of Money in Swedish Families" (2004) 26(1) Women's Studies International Forum 79.
47. Gill and Taylor (n 25).
48. These manuals included the (anonymized) *Global AML/CTF Policy, Global Anti-Fraud Policy,* a series of internal circulars outlining current issues in money laundering, distilled information regarding FINTRAC obligations for branch employees, and other internal manuals regarding anti-money laundering typologies and practices.
49. Sharing this information with me could be a possible violation of 8 of the Proceeds of Crime (Money Laundering) and Terrorism Financing Act (PCMLTFA), which prohibits tipping-off (i.e. the disclosure of a report having been made).
50. Anthony Amicelle and Gilles Favarel-Garrigues, "Financial Surveillance: Who Cares?" (2012) 5(1) Journal of Cultural Economy 105; Amicelle (n 25); Antoinette Verhage, "Between the Hammer and the Anvil? The Anti-Money Laundering-Complex and Its Interactions with the Compliance Industry"

(2009) 52(1) Crime, Law and Social Change 9; Antoinette Verhage, "Compliance and AML in Belgium": A Booming Sector with Growing Pains (2009) 12(2) Journal of Money Laundering Control 113.

51. Of course, the goal of this research was not to impede a current or future criminal investigation; however, the bank was concerned that observing client interactions from behind the teller wicket might somehow alert money launderers or financiers of terrorism that a report of suspicion might be submitted about their particular financial transaction.

52. During the process of obtaining access, retail branch employees—and particularly front-line employees—were identified as those most likely to transact with cash, and those most likely to encounter a wide variety of transactions. Other employees who might process transactions, such as those working in call centres, would not encounter cash transactions; others who process cash transactions but who do not deal directly with the public for most transactions, such as those who work in currency cages processing overnight deposits, would not encounter the same variety of transactions as those working in retail. Subsequent discussions with Financial Intelligence Unit (FIU) employees suggest that of Unusual Transaction Reporting (UTR) submissions, retail branch employees are the largest group by volume of submissions and so are an appropriate group for this study.

53. Julie Ayling and Peter Grabosky, "Policing By Command: Enhancing Law Enforcement Capacity Through Coercion" (2006) 28(4) Law and Policy 420.

54. Tellers have signing limits, which are dollar thresholds under which they can act autonomously. As a person gains experience, her signing limit will increase as well. Above those limits, supervisors must authorize transactions. Anti-money laundering/counter-terrorist financing (AML/CTF) transactions represent a kind of risk that may require a secondary check, particularly if the transactions are for dollar amounts in the thousands.

55. Carruthers and Espeland (n 41).

56. Zelizer (n 41).

57. Carruthers and Espeland (n 41).

58. Although there are slight technical differences between them, a *bank draft, money order*, and *cashier's cheque* are treated synonymously in this chapter, as all three are pre-paid by the client and drawn on the bank's account. A *certified cheque* differs from these three in that the instrument itself is drawn from the client's account directly, and guaranteed by the bank—it is a personal cheque for which the funds have been certified.

59. The first two vignettes did not specify the type of financial instrument, and so employees, prior to proceeding to discuss, clarified for themselves or through the interviewer, what kind of financial instrument they were discussing (cash, cheque, etc.).

60. Simmel (n 36).

61. Carruthers and Espeland (n 41) 1393.

62. Randy Lippert, "Policing Property and Moral Risk Through Promotions, Anonymization and Rewards: Crime Stoppers Revisited" (2002) 11(4) Social and Legal Studies 475, 480.
63. Ericson and Doyle (n 21).
64. Ericson and Haggerty (n 27).
65. For further discussion of cash and AML, see Chap. 7 (Riccardi and Levi) in this collection.
66. Global AML/CTF Policy.
67. Global AML/CTF Policy; AML/CTF Training Programme.
68. Stuart Bell, *Cold Terror: How Canada Nurtures and Exports Terrorism Around the World* (John Wiley and Sons 2008) 289.
69. Zelizer (n 41).
70. Scott Neuman, 'Why Use a Pressure Cooker to Build a Bomb?' *NPR* (17 April 2013) <www.npr.org/blogs/thetwo-way/2013/04/17/177605063/why-use-a-pressure-cooker-to-build-a-bomb> accessed 10 April 2017.
71. Geoffrey Morgan, "How Did Ottawa Shooter Michael Zehaf-Bibeau Get Work in the Oil Patch? Blame the Labour Crunch" *National Post* (Toronto, 28 October 2014) <http://business.financialpost.com/news/energy/how-did-ottawa-shooter-michael-zehaf-bibeau-get-work-in-the-oil-patch-blame-the-labour-crunch> accessed 7 May 2017.
72. Financial Action Task Force, "Terrorist Financing" (FATF/OECD 2008) <www.fatf-gafi.org/media/fatf/documents/reports/FATF%20Terrorist%20Financing%20Typologies%20Report.pdf> accessed 10 April 2017.
73. Global Anti-Fraud Policy.
74. Simmel (n 36).
75. Power (n 12).

Vanessa Iafolla is a Lecturer in Sociology and Legal Studies at the University of Waterloo, Canada. Vanessa received her doctorate from the Centre for Criminology and Sociolegal Studies, University of Toronto. Her areas of research include money laundering and terrorist financing, retail banking and real estate regulation, and finance.

6

Money Laundering, Anti-Money Laundering and the Legal Profession

Katie Benson

Introduction

One of the most notable features of the global anti-money laundering regime, which has evolved over the last three decades into an extensive range of legislative, regulatory and policy frameworks, guidelines, standards and institutions, is the conscription of private, non-state actors into the fight against 'dirty' money. This has involved a number of obligations being imposed on those believed to be in a position to prevent the movement of illicit funds into the legitimate financial system and has been described as a clear example of Garland's 'responsibilisation strategy',[1] whereby responsibility for the prevention and control of money laundering is passed to private entities.[2] Banks and other financial institutions were the first to be assigned a role in the prevention of money laundering, with expectations of improved customer due diligence, identification procedures and record keeping forming a key objective of the Financial Action Task Force's (FATF) original Recommendations. The introduction of the first EU Money Laundering Directive in 1991[3]—which brought the FATF's standards to the European sphere—introduced a series of obligations for financial and credit institutions to implement adequate money laundering procedures, policies and training programmes; to carry out appropriate customer due diligence measures; to refrain from transactions they

K. Benson
School of Law, University of Manchester,
Manchester, UK

© The Author(s) 2018
C. King et al. (eds.), *The Palgrave Handbook of Criminal and Terrorism Financing Law*,
https://doi.org/10.1007/978-3-319-64498-1_6

knew or suspected to be associated with money laundering; and to report suspicious transactions to the relevant national authorities. The obligations imposed by the Directive constituted 'unprecedented changes' in the commercial relationship of financial institutions and their clients.[4] Subsequent Money Laundering Directives[5] have extended these preventative obligations beyond the financial sector to encompass a wide range of actors including art dealers, estate agents, auditors, accountants and tax advisers, and legal professionals, due to a growing concern that institutions and professionals outside of the financial sector were increasingly being exploited by individuals wishing to launder criminal proceeds. The extension of the preventative obligations to the legal profession has been particularly controversial, with the potential implications for the lawyer-client relationship and duty of confidentiality causing considerable concern within the profession. In the UK, the focus on legal (and other regulated) professionals' role in the facilitation or prevention of money laundering has resulted in an anti-money laundering legislative framework that enables the criminal prosecution of such professionals for failing to fulfil their preventative obligations. Money laundering legislation in the UK, therefore, has significant implications for those working in the legal profession.

This chapter considers the relationship between money laundering, the anti-money laundering framework and the legal profession, focusing on three main areas. First, it examines the growing concern about the role that professionals, such as lawyers and accountants, play in the facilitation of money laundering. Recent years have seen an emerging narrative from bodies such as the FATF, policymakers and law enforcement organisations, which suggests that criminals have become increasingly reliant on the services of professionals to manage their criminal proceeds. However, there remains little understanding of the empirical scale and nature of professional facilitation of money laundering. The second part of the chapter considers the designation of legal and other regulated professionals as 'gatekeepers' in the fight against money laundering—a position that has emerged from the view that they are increasingly involved in laundering schemes. The chapter discusses the preventative obligations imposed on professionals, tracking the development of these obligations through international and national frameworks, and highlights the antagonism of including legal professionals in the anti-money laundering regime. Finally, the chapter addresses the implications for lawyers of their designation as 'gatekeepers' in anti-money laundering, and the resultant legislative frameworks, focusing specifically on the UK. This section provides an overview of the offences in UK legislation for which lawyers who are believed to have facilitated money laundering on behalf of a client, or in the process of assisting or providing services to a client, can be prosecuted. Drawing on recent empirical research which analysed cases of solicitors convicted of money laundering offences,[6] the final part of the chapter highlights the far-reaching nature of anti-money laundering legislation in the UK, which allows for the conviction of legal professionals for money laundering offences without criminal intent or actual knowledge or suspicion that money laundering was taking place.

The Facilitation of Money Laundering by Professionals: A Significant Concern?

The Official Narrative

Recent years have seen a growing concern with the role that legal and financial professionals play in the facilitation of money laundering and an emerging official narrative that suggests that this is a significant—and increasing—problem. Intergovernmental bodies, policymakers and law enforcement organisations have highlighted the vulnerability of legal and financial professions to exploitation by those needing to launder criminal proceeds, suggesting that criminals have become increasingly reliant on the services and skills provided by professionals in these sectors to manage the proceeds of their crimes. This increasing reliance, it is suggested, is due to the stringent anti-money laundering controls imposed on financial institutions, making it more difficult to launder criminal proceeds and heightening the risk of detection, and the use of increasingly complex laundering methods. The FATF has been a prominent voice in this argument; for a number of years, its annual *Typologies* reports have drawn attention to the involvement of legal and financial professionals in money laundering, suggesting that this is a growing problem, for example:

> As anti-money laundering regulations have increased in many countries the criminals place increasing reliance on professional money laundering facilitators.[7]

> Accountants, solicitors and company formation agents turn up even more frequently in anti-money laundering investigations. In establishing and administering the foreign legal entities which conceal money laundering schemes, it is these professionals that increasingly provide the apparent sophistication and extra layer of respectability to some laundering operations.[8]

Increasingly, money launderers seek out the advice or services of specialised professionals to help facilitate their financial operations. This trend toward the involvement of various legal and financial experts, or gatekeepers, in money laundering schemes has been documented previously by the FATF and appears to continue today.[9]

In its 2010 *Global Money Laundering and Terrorist Financing Threat Assessment*, the FATF classes 'the abuse of gatekeepers'—defined as professionals who can provide financial expertise or access to functions that could help criminals move or conceal illicit funds—as a significant threat.[10] The *Threat Assessment* suggests that, as a result of the services they provide, members of legal and financial professions have become an increasingly common feature of complex money laundering schemes, particularly those involving organised crime or significant financial frauds.[11] In addition to the risks to the legitimate financial sector associated with its infiltration by criminal funds, the involvement of professionals in laundering activity could cause reputational damage to the individual professionals and businesses involved, and harm the integrity and reputation of these professional sectors as a whole. It may also lead to increased criminal influence in businesses or groups of businesses, affecting decision-making, leading to further exploitation, and distorting the market for the services these professionals provide.[12]

The view that witting or unwitting professionals play a key role in the facilitation of money laundering is shared by others. For example, a report by the *Global Agenda Council on Organized Crime*, published by the World Economic Forum, suggests that professionals can play a critical role in helping criminals manage the proceeds of their crimes, by acting as 'the key doors for facilitating criminal financial transactions and keeping a veil of opacity on criminal assets'.[13] The report admits that the extent to which this, in fact, happens is not known; nonetheless, they argue, it represents a risk that needs to be managed.[14] The increasing engagement of professionals by criminals to 'establish more sophisticated methods to sidestep the financial regulatory environment and law enforcement' has also been noted by the Australian Crime Commission,[15] while Europol has described professional expertise as a key 'crime enabler', suggesting that the skills and services of professionals such as lawyers are sought by organised crime groups for a range of purposes, including the laundering of criminal proceeds.[16]

Within the UK, recent official organised crime threat and strategy documents have highlighted the role of 'professional enablers' in assisting organised criminals, including in the facilitation of money laundering:

Organised crime cannot function without the legitimate economy. Criminals will seek to launder money through the financial sector, or use the services of lawyers or accountants to invest in property or set up front businesses. A small number of complicit or negligent professional enablers, such as bankers, lawyers and accountants can act as gatekeepers between organised criminals and the legitimate economy.[17]

The skills and knowledge of a variety of professionals, such as accountancy service providers, the legal profession, estate agents, and trust and company service providers, are used by [organised crime groups] for sometimes complex money laundering activity. They assist, wittingly or unwittingly, in creating complexity through actions such as setting up networks of corporate structures, acquiring assets to store illicit funds and providing anonymity for the criminal.[18]

In 2014, the National Crime Agency's (NCA) *National Strategic Assessment of Serious and Organised Crime* stated unequivocally that '[c]omplicit, negligent or unwitting professionals in financial, legal and accountancy professions in the UK facilitate money laundering', by compromising the money laundering controls that are in place across the regulated professions.[19] The most recent NCA assessment states that legal professionals assist organised crime groups in complex money laundering activity, primarily through the abuse of client accounts, and purchase of property or assets.[20] This issue also features prominently in the UK's national strategy for serious and organised crime produced by the Home Office, which highlights the critical nature of the role played by financial and legal professionals in the UK who 'facilitate money laundering on behalf of organised criminals'.[21] The subsequent governmental *UK National Risk Assessment of Money Laundering and Terrorist Financing* assesses the money laundering risk within the legal services sector as 'high'.[22] The report suggests that many of the services provided by this sector 'are attractive to criminals seeking to conceal the origins of criminal funds', and that some legal professionals act as 'enablers to money laundering by providing access to these services'.[23]

A Lack of Understanding

A number of commentators in the academic literature have echoed the official narrative that legal and financial professionals play a critical role in the facilitation of money laundering, and are becoming increasingly involved in such activity.[24] However, there is usually little evidence given to support this assertion and a notable lack of understanding of the phenomenon. The nature of professionals' involvement in money laundering has received limited academic attention, and there has been little empirical research in the area. Much of the existing literature considers professionals' involvement in organised crime more generally or in relation to lawyer wrongdoing in various forms. For example, a 2004 special issue of *Crime, Law and Social Change*, based on a study carried out in France, Italy, the Netherlands and the UK, focused on the compromising conduct of legal professionals—including lawyers and, where relevant, notaries—in relation to organised crime.[25] More recently, Soudijn conducted empirical research on what he termed 'financial facilitators', described as 'experts who put criminals in a position to circumvent the anti-money laundering measures'.[26] His research related not just to professionals such as lawyers or accountants but to anyone who assists a criminal in a fundamental way with their money laundering activities, including exchange office cashiers and real estate brokers. In the UK, notable analysis of the role of legal professionals in the facilitation of money laundering has come from Middleton,[27] and Middleton and Levi,[28] who have considered the issue of solicitors involved in various forms of wrongdoing, including fraud, enabling organised crime and involvement in money laundering. In their most recent research, Middleton and Levi concluded that the facilitation of money laundering by lawyers remains under-analysed, its extent and nature is still disputed, and official statements asserting its wide-scale lack of a sound evidential basis.[29]

Published empirical research with a specific focus on professionals' involvement in money laundering is limited in other jurisdictions. In Canada, Schneider used data collected from a sample of Royal Canadian Mounted Police proceeds of crime case files to explore how lawyers may be used to launder criminal proceeds.[30] He found that lawyers 'came into contact with the proceeds of crime' in almost half of the cases examined, and suggested that their involvement in money laundering was primarily due to their role as intermediaries in financial and commercial transactions.[31] Cummings and Stepnowsky analysed a sample of money laundering cases from the US Court of Appeals to examine whether, and to what extent, lawyers are 'involved knowingly or unknowingly in transactions that serve to launder illicit funds'.[32] They found that only a small number of the cases they examined showed evidence of lawyer involvement in laundering transactions and suggested that even in these cases the involvement was primarily unwitting.

Seeking to fill the research gaps, the author's UK study analysed cases of solicitors convicted of money laundering offences alongside interviews with criminal justice practitioners and members of relevant professional and regulatory bodies.[33] This research represents the most in-depth qualitative analysis in this area to date, considering the roles, relationships and decision-making processes of the actors involved. The research highlighted the complex and diverse nature of professional involvement in money laundering, comprising a variety of actions, purposes, actors and relationships, and confirmed the need for greater understanding in this area and for a more accurate assessment of scale. The involvement of professionals in money laundering, therefore, clearly remains an under-researched and poorly understood area. As a result, the construction of professional facilitation of money laundering in official discourse and much of the academic literature—which sees professionals as playing a critical, and increasing, role in the laundering of criminal pro-ceeds—has weak empirical foundations. Despite this, far-reaching legislative and policy measures aimed at preventing professionals becoming involved in money laundering have been implemented, including their own conscription into anti-money laundering efforts through a variety of rules, responsibilities and obligations.

Lawyers as 'Gatekeepers': The Preventative Obligations of Regulated Professionals

In 1999, a meeting of the G8 interior and justice ministers in Moscow adopted what became known as the 'Moscow Communiqué'.[34] This document brought the term 'gatekeeper' to prominence within anti-money laundering discourse, in reference to individuals in the position to provide or deny access to the legitimate financial system for those wishing to launder criminal proceeds. The Communiqué suggested that such actors were often involved in money laundering arrangements, and declared the intention to consider extending suspicious transaction reporting requirements to those categorised as 'gate-keepers' and making the failure to fulfil such requirements a punishable offence:

> We recognize that many money-laundering schemes involve the corruption of financial intermediaries. We will therefore consider requiring or enhancing sus-picious transaction reporting by the 'gatekeepers' to the international financial system, including company formation agents, accountants, auditors and law-yers, as well as making the intentional failure to file the reports a punishable offense, as appropriate.[35]

In response to the Moscow Communiqué, the FATF created a working group to identify those professionals that should be considered as 'gatekeep-ers' with respect to money laundering.[36] In May 2002, the FATF published a

consultation paper reviewing their original 40 Recommendations and suggesting improvements to be made to the anti-money laundering framework.[37]
This paper referred to the growing concern that certain 'gatekeeper professionals', such as lawyers, notaries and accountants, were acting as intermediaries in money laundering schemes or providing advice to criminals to assist
them in the laundering of their illicit funds.[38] The following year, the FATF
issued a revised set of Recommendations, which incorporated the improvements suggested in the consultation paper.[39] The revised Recommendations
extended responsibility for performing customer due diligence, record-
keeping and reporting suspicious activity to those that had been identified as
'gatekeepers' and were now categorised as designated nonfinancial businesses
and professions (DNFBPs). This group included lawyers, notaries and other
independent legal professionals; accountants; trust and company service providers; casinos; real estate agents; and dealers in precious metals and stones.[40]
Therefore, the 2003 revised Recommendations represented the first time that
legal professionals were specifically included in the requirements to undertake
customer due diligence and submit suspicious activity reports.

The inclusion of legal professionals in the preventative measures of the anti-
money laundering regime proved contentious, with considerable debate about
the appropriateness of such a move and challenge from bodies representing
the profession. A number of commentators in the academic literature have
expressed concern over the extension of reporting duties and other anti-money
laundering prevention measures to legal professionals, because of the implications for privacy and the right of lawyer confidentiality, the right to a legal
defence and due process, and the potential risk to professionals who come into
contact with 'dirty' money.[41] Because of their integral role in the legal system
and duty to their clients, the public and 'the mechanism of law that organizes
society', the co-opting of lawyers into money laundering prevention was said
to present 'strains that are more pronounced than in the regulation of other
professions, industries or sectors'.[42] The primary concerns expressed by the
profession related to the independence of lawyers, legal professional privilege
and the duty of confidentiality.[43] The potential for conflict between duty to a
client and the duty to report suspicious activity, and the possible erosion of the
'tenuous relationship' between lawyer and client caused particular unease.[44]

In response to the revised FATF Recommendations, legal professional associations from the European Union (EU), Canada, United States, Switzerland
and Japan signed a 'Joint Statement by the International Legal Profession to
the FATF' in 2003. The purpose of this statement was to draw attention to the
profession's concerns about the implications of the inclusion of 'gatekeepers'
in the Recommendations for the rule of law and access to justice.[45] The

American Bar Association (ABA) expressed considerable concern about the possible threat to attorney-client privilege and independence of the Bar as a result of the obligations for legal practitioners set out in the revised FATF Recommendations.[46] There has been notable resistance to the reporting obligations in Canada, with law societies bringing a series of legal challenges against the 'intrusion upon solicitor-client privilege' in provinces across the country.[47] This objection led to lawyers in Canada being exempted from reporting obligations (and thus Canada being non-compliant with the FATF Recommendations). The Council of Bars and Law Societies of Europe (CCBE) declared that the duty to report would lead to the 'breach of the independence of a lawyer and the irrevocable violation of the principle of client confidentiality'.[48] There were legal challenges against the reporting obligations in both Belgium and France, and by the Law Society of England and Wales.[49]

The extension of the preventative obligations to DNFBPs was incorporated into the EU anti-money laundering framework through the second Money Laundering Directive, introduced in 2001.[50] Provisions introduced by this and later Money Laundering Directives were transposed to the UK through successive Money Laundering Regulations (2003, 2007, 2017) and the Proceeds of Crime Act 2002. The Money Laundering Regulations ('the Regulations') implement the main preventative measures of the EU Directives and apply to those sectors categorised as DNFBPs, including legal professionals.[51] The Regulations require that members of these sectors undertake customer due diligence measures, involving verifying the identity of customers or beneficial owners, and obtaining information on the nature and purpose of the customer's business,[52] and monitoring this relationship on an ongoing basis.[53] They must also keep a record of the information obtained on the customer's identity and business, along with supporting documentation, for a period of five years.[54] Further requirements include the establishment and maintenance of appropriate policies and procedures relating to their money laundering obligations[55] and ensuring that all relevant employees are aware of the law relating to money laundering and terrorist financing and are appropriately trained.[56] Under Regulation 20, organisations within the regulated sector must have a 'nominated officer' responsible for receiving disclosures of suspicious activity from members of the organisation and making disclosures to the relevant authorities (as required by Part 7 of the Proceeds of Crime Act and Part 3 of the Terrorism Act 2000).[57] At the present time, the relevant authority for making disclosures to is the NCA. The Proceeds of Crime Act established the primary money laundering offences in UK legislation. Details of the offences contained in this Act, and their implications for legal professionals, are considered in the remainder of this chapter.

Prosecution of Lawyers Involved in Money Laundering in the UK

Within the UK, legal professionals who are believed to have facilitated money laundering on behalf of a client, or in the process of assisting or providing services to a client, may be prosecuted under various sections of the Proceeds of Crime Act. Sections 327, 328 and 329 of the Act set out the principal money laundering offences, which can be applied to any individual. Section 330 provides for the offence of 'failure to disclose: regulated sector'; this part of the legislation applies only to individuals working in the regulated sector, including legal professionals. This section of the chapter provides an overview of these offences, and discusses their relevance to, and implications for, the legal profession. It does not aim to provide a detailed analysis of the legislation, as this has been done extensively elsewhere.[58]

Proceeds of Crime Act 2002: Sections 327, 328 and 329

The three principal money laundering offences in UK legislation are set out in sections 327, 328 and 329 of Part 7 of the Proceeds of Crime Act. Section 327 covers the offence of concealing, disguising, converting or transferring criminal property, or removing criminal property from England and Wales, Scotland or Northern Ireland.[59] The references to concealing and disguising criminal property also include concealing or disguising its 'nature, source, location, disposition, movement or ownership or any rights with respect to it'.[60] Section 328 focuses on involvement in arrangements known or suspected to facilitate money laundering, stating that a person commits an offence if he

> enters into or becomes concerned in an arrangement which he knows or suspects facilitates (by whatever means) the acquisition, retention, use or control of criminal property by or on behalf of another person.[61]

Section 329 of the Act provides the third principal money laundering offence and relates to the acquisition, possession or use of criminal property.[62] For all three sections, an offence is not committed if the person makes an 'authorised disclosure'[63] or intended to make such a disclosure but had a reasonable excuse for not doing so,[64] or if the actions involved are related to the enforcement of a provision of the Act or any other enactment relating to criminal conduct or its benefit.[65] A person convicted of an offence under any of these parts of the legislation is liable to imprisonment for 14 years, a fine or both.

An offence of money laundering can be charged on its own or included on an indictment containing the underlying predicate offence. In both of these cases, there are two sub-categories:

1. 'own-proceeds' or 'self-laundering', in which the person charged with money laundering also committed the predicate crime
2. laundering by a person or persons other than that who committed the predicate crime[66]

The section 327 offence would be the most relevant for cases of 'self-laundering', where the person who committed the predicate crime is prosecuted for laundering the proceeds of that crime. The section 328 offence, on the other hand, covers situations where a third party handles funds derived from criminal activity. Section 328 would, therefore, be more appropriate if the individual prosecuted for the laundering offence was not involved in the proceeds-generating predicate offence.[67] The Crown Prosecution Service (CPS) guidance on the money laundering legislation highlights the utility of the section 328 offence for the prosecution of professionals who 'launder on behalf of others', suggesting that it can 'catch' individuals working within professional roles who 'in the course of their work facilitate money laundering by or on behalf of other persons'.[68] Therefore, this part of the legislation is of particular relevance to legal professionals, and it has been suggested that this particular component of the Act should be 'of considerable concern to those who handle or advise third parties in connection with money and other types of property'.[69]

For all three principal money laundering offences, 'criminal property' is defined as property that constitutes or represents a person's benefit from criminal conduct, where the alleged offender *knows or suspects* that it constitutes such benefit.[70] This part of the legislation, therefore, provides the *mens rea* requirement across all three offences, based on 'knowledge' and 'suspicion'. There is a further *mens rea* requirement in the section 328 offence, which specifies that the person 'knows or suspects' that the arrangement they have become concerned with facilitates money laundering.[71] The notion of 'knowledge' is relatively straightforward, and its interpretation in the context of these offences unproblematic.[72] However, actual knowledge is not required for a conviction, and the concept of 'suspicion' is more ambiguous and has proved contentious.[73] Guidance on the meaning of 'suspicion' in money laundering offences is provided for the legal profession by the Law Society of England and Wales' *Anti-Money Laundering Practice Note*, which advises its members that:

[t]here is no requirement for the suspicion to be clearly or firmly grounded on specific facts, but there must be a degree of satisfaction, not necessarily amounting to belief, but at least extending beyond speculation.

The test for whether you hold a suspicion is a subjective one.

If you think a transaction is suspicious, you are not expected to know the exact nature of the criminal offence or that particular funds were definitely those arising from the crime. You may have noticed something unusual or unexpected and after making enquiries, the facts do not seem normal or make commercial sense. You do not have to have evidence that money laundering is taking place to have suspicion.[74]

Therefore, although suspicion requires a level of satisfaction greater than mere speculation, it does not require a clear factual basis. Lawyers can be prosecuted under the money laundering legislation for acting in a transaction involving the proceeds of crime if they were considered to have had suspicion that money laundering was taking place, even if they did not have specific facts or evidence to support their suspicion, or knowledge of the nature of the criminal offence or that the funds definitely represented the proceeds of crime.

The *mens rea* requirements for these offences differ markedly from the international frameworks from which the Proceeds of Crime Act derived. As such, the UK has exceeded the obligations contained in relevant treaties and successive EU Money Laundering Directives, which had a much greater focus on intent and knowledge, and were directed towards those deliberately laundering criminal proceeds. The use of 'suspicion' as the basis for criminal liability cannot be found in either the 1998 United Nations Convention Against Illicit Traffic in Narcotic Drugs and Psychotropic Substances (the 'Vienna Convention'), or the 1990 Council of Europe Convention on Laundering, Search, Seizure and Confiscation of the Proceeds from Crime (the 'Strasbourg Convention'). In addition, both Conventions require states to create criminal offences related to money laundering under domestic law only 'when committed intentionally'.[75] All EU Money Laundering Directives to date have defined money laundering as conduct that is 'committed intentionally'. For example, Article 1 of the Fourth Directive, introduced in May 2015, states that:

1. This Directive aims to prevent the use of the Union's financial system for the purposes of money laundering and terrorist financing.
2. Member States shall ensure that money laundering and terrorist financing are prohibited.

3. For the purposes of this Directive, the following conduct, *when committed intentionally*, shall be regarded as money laundering:

(a) The conversion or transfer of property, *knowing* that such property is derived from criminal activity or from an act of participation in such activity, for the purpose of concealing or disguising the illicit origin of the property or of assisting any person who is involved in the commission of such an activity to evade the legal consequences of that person's action.

(b) The concealment or disguise of the true nature, source, location, disposition, movement, rights with respect to, or ownership of property, *knowing* that such property is derived from criminal activity or from an act of participation in such activity.

(c) The acquisition, possession or use of property, *knowing*, at the time of receipt, that such property was derived from criminal activity or from an act of participation in such activity.

(d) Participation in, association to commit, attempts to commit and aiding, abetting, facilitating and counselling the commission of any of the actions referred to in points (a), (b) and (c).[76]

The wording in this Article echoes that of the previous three Directives. It is clear, therefore, that money laundering legislation in the UK goes well beyond what is required by international standards, with no requirement for criminal intent and the mental element being satisfied by suspicion. The legislation is not aimed solely at those deliberately laundering criminal proceeds; its scope is much broader, allowing for the inclusion of a wider range of acts (and omissions) and of those who are less directly—and unintentionally—involved in money laundering.

Section 330: 'Failure to Disclose: Regulated Sector'

Section 330 of the Proceeds of Crime Act contains the offence of 'failure to disclose: regulated sector', which creates the obligation to inform the authorities of suspicions of money laundering. It enforces the disclosure of suspicious transactions to a nominated officer, for example, the designated Money Laundering Reporting Officer (MLRO) within the individual's firm.[77] This offence applies only to members of the regulated sector, when the information relating to the suspicious activity is received 'in the course of a business in the regulated sector'.[78] The Proceeds of Crime Act provided an initial list of activities that, if engaged in by a business, defined the business as being part of the regulated sector.[79] However, the following year, the definition was expanded by various statutory instruments,[80] which resulted in all parties covered by the Second EU Money Laundering Directive being considered as part of the regulated sector.[81] This offence, therefore, applies to a range of business sectors,[82] including the legal profession when involved in financial or property transactions.

According to section 330 of the Act, if an individual working in the regulated sector knows or suspects, or has reasonable grounds for knowing or suspecting, that another individual is engaged in money laundering, and the information has come to them in the course of their business, they must make a report to the relevant nominated officer.[83] It is a criminal offence under this part of the legislation not to do so as soon as is practicable, unless there is a reasonable excuse for not making the required disclosure, sufficient training has not been provided by the relevant employer in relation to these requirements, or, in the case of professional legal advisers, the information is received in privileged circumstances.[84] This section of the Proceeds of Crime Act thus creates positive obligations for individuals working in the regulated sector, making an *omission* (failing to carry out a duty) rather than an *act* the criminal offence.

The mental element of this part of the legislation differs from that of the section 327, 328 and 329 offences, by introducing the objective test of having 'reasonable grounds' for knowledge or suspicion. Also known as the 'negligence test', the objective test asks whether there were

> …factual circumstances from which an honest and reasonable person, engaged in a business in the regulated sector, should have inferred knowledge or formed the suspicion that another was engaged in money laundering.[85]

This means that those working in the regulated sector can be found guilty of an offence of failing to report, under section 330, if they *should have* known or suspected another person was engaged in money laundering, even if they lacked *actual* knowledge of such conduct. As such, acting negligently in the performance of their obligation to report knowledge or suspicion of money laundering is treated as a criminal offence in the same way as deliberate money laundering, albeit with a lesser sentence attached for conviction (a maximum of five years' imprisonment and/or a fine). Further provisions in the Act relate to the disclosure of suspicious transactions in non-regulated sectors. However, the requirements for those in the regulated sector are more stringent than for those in the non-regulated sector, with *actual* knowledge or suspicion being required for a conviction for failing to disclose offences in the non-regulated sector.[86] The introduction of the 'reasonable grounds' component of the offence was justified by two key arguments. First, there were concerns about the difficulties of proving actual knowledge or suspicion and the possibility that those who 'turn a blind eye' to money laundering could avoid prosecution, and that individuals in the regulated sector may choose not to report suspicions because they were aware of these difficulties.[87] Second, it was considered that those working in the regulated sector should be expected to bear the extra responsibility because of their role, as shown by the rationale for the inclusion of the test in the explanatory notes for the Proceeds of Crime Act:

> [P]ersons who are carrying out activities in the regulated sector should be expected to exercise a higher level of diligence in handling transactions than those employed in other businesses.[88]

This position reflects the characterisation of professionals in the regulated sector as 'gatekeepers', and their associated obligations in the prevention of money laundering, highlighted in the previous section. The section 330 offence in the Proceeds of Crime Act, therefore, has its origins in the view of professionals as 'gatekeepers' and concern about their involvement in money laundering. However, once again, UK legislation goes further than international requirements, with the Moscow Communiqué referring only to 'making the *intentional* failure to file [suspicious transaction] reports a punishable offence'.[89] The result is a far-reaching anti-money laundering framework, under which legal professionals can face criminal prosecution without criminal intent, and without actual knowledge or even suspicion that criminal activity was taking place, creating significant implications for legal professionals working in the UK.

Implications for Legal Professionals: Considering Cases of Convicted Solicitors

A recent study by the author on the role of legal and financial professionals in the facilitation of money laundering identified 20 cases of solicitors who had been convicted in the UK between 2002 and 2013, for involvement (related to their professional role) in the laundering of criminal proceeds generated by others.[90] Cases were primarily identified by searching transcripts from relevant professional disciplinary tribunals and the Westlaw UK legal database, as well as media reports and an FATF report which identified examples of legal professionals involved in money laundering in Member States.[91] The criteria for inclusion of cases in the final sample were: solicitors or chartered accountants who have been convicted of money laundering offences (under Proceeds of Crime Act 2002 (POCA), Drug Trafficking Act 1994 (DTA) or Criminal Justice Act 1993 (CJA)) between 2002 and 2013, where the offences committed were related to their professional positions or roles, and involved facilitating the laundering of the proceeds of crimes committed by others. Data is not routinely collected on professionals involved in money laundering in any systematic way by either law enforcement, the criminal justice system, or the professional or regulatory bodies, leading to considerable challenges in the identification of relevant cases. For example, the Solicitors Disciplinary Tribunal in England and Wales provides a full transcript for all tribunal hearings from 2002 on their website. These judgments cannot be searched for cases specifically relating to money laundering, so all 1426 transcripts available at the time were searched individually using the PDF word search function for cases referencing 'money laundering' or 'proceeds of crime'. The 159 cases identified through this process were then read thoroughly to identify those that fit the inclusion criteria. The challenges associated with identifying cases of convicted professionals mean that the 20 cases analysed cannot be considered as an exhaustive sample.[92]

Data collected on the cases from a range of sources[93] demonstrated considerable variation in the actions and behaviours of solicitors that can be considered to facilitate money laundering, and for which professionals can be convicted under the money laundering legislation, as well as in the purpose of the transactions involved, the level of financial benefit gained by the solicitor, and the nature of their relationship with the predicate offender. For example, while acting in the purchase or sale of residential property and moving money through their firm's client account were the most common means by which solicitors in the cases were involved with criminal funds, the cases also included solicitors who had written to a bank to try and have an account unfrozen, paid bail for a client using what was considered to be the proceeds of crime, transferred ownership of hotels belonging to a client, written a series of profit and loss figures on the back of a letter, witnessed an email, allowed the use of headed stationery and provided legal advice for a mortgage fraudster. Although four of the solicitors appeared to directly financially benefit from their involvement in the transactions, the others appeared to acquire no direct financial gain. They may have received the relevant fees for the transaction involved, but this would have represented no more than the normal fee they would have received had the transaction involved non-criminal funds. Notable variation was also seen in the degree of intent involved, and the extent to which the solicitors were aware that they were facilitating money laundering. In four of the cases examined, the data suggested that the solicitor was knowingly and intentionally involved and could be considered as a complicit, active participant in the laundering activity. However, in the majority of cases identified, there appeared to be no intent or active involvement in the laundering; there was not a deliberate decision to offend or actual dishonesty on the part of the solicitor. The facilitation of money laundering by professionals, therefore, is clearly not a homogenous phenomenon; it is complex and diverse, and involves multi-layered relationships. It also cannot be neatly categorised, as the boundaries between levels of awareness and intent, and between categorisations of means of facilitation, are blurred.[94]

The solicitors in the cases analysed had been convicted under a variety of offences. While those whose offence had occurred prior to 2002 were prosecuted under either the Drug Trafficking Act 1994 ($n = 1$) or the Criminal Justice Act 1998 ($n = 5$), the majority ($n = 14$) of the sample were convicted of one of the offences contained in the Proceeds of Crime Act.[95] Perhaps unsurprisingly, the most common offence seen was that set out in section 328 of the Proceeds of Crime Act (entering into or becoming concerned in an arrangement facilitating the acquisition, retention, use or control of criminal property). In eight of the cases, the solicitor was convicted on at least one count under section 328. As was highlighted earlier, this offence is the most appropriate of the three primary money laundering offences if the individual prosecuted was not involved in the predicate offence. In four of the cases, the solicitor was considered to have had *actual knowledge* that the transactions they were involved in facilitated the laundering of criminal proceeds. These solicitors received prison sentences and were usually struck off the roll of solicitors at their subsequent disciplinary hearings. However, in another four cases, convictions were based on the assumption of *suspicion* rather than actual knowledge. In these cases, reference was made during sentencing and disciplinary proceedings to the lower level of *mens rea* and, therefore, culpability of the solicitor, and this was reflected in the sentences and sanctions received. For example, in one such case, the solicitor received a fine of £5000 rather than a custodial sentence, and in another, the solicitor involved was sentenced to 39 weeks imprisonment suspended for 18 months, 200 hours community work and a £5015 fine. Neither of these solicitors were struck off when they subsequently appeared in front of the Solicitors Disciplinary Tribunal.

Seven of the solicitors in the cases were convicted under section 330 of the Proceeds of Crime Act, the offence of failing to report suspicions of money laundering for those working in the regulated sector. Four of these were also convicted of other substantive money laundering offences, but three were convicted solely of one or more counts of the section 330 offence. The solicitors in these cases received, respectively, a custodial sentence of six months (reduced by the Court of Appeal from 15 months), four-month suspended sentence and a fine of £2515. One of the solicitors was struck off the roll of solicitors, but the others received only a fine or suspension. In one of these cases, it was made clear by the Judge in the criminal trial, and the disciplinary tribunal that heard the case, that it was accepted that the solicitor had not known or suspected his client was engaged in money laundering, but that he had reasonable grounds to suspect he was. The data illustrate, therefore, the range of offences that legal professionals who are believed to have facilitated money laundering on behalf of a client, or in the process of assisting or providing services to a client, can be prosecuted under. It demonstrates the potential for conviction if solicitors are considered to have had suspicions that transactions they progress involved the proceeds of criminal activity, even if they did not have actual knowledge or criminal intent, and were not actively engaged in the laundering. Furthermore, the cases show that, under section 330 of the Proceeds of Crime Act, a criminal conviction can be secured without having to show that there was even suspicion of money laundering, if there were reasonable grounds for such suspicion and this was not reported. The implications of the money laundering offences contained within the Proceeds of Crime Act for legal professionals, therefore, are significant.

Conclusion

This chapter has drawn attention to the complex and contentious relationship between the legal profession and the fight against criminal finance. Concern that legal and other professionals involved in financial transactions are playing an increasing role in the facilitation of money laundering has led to such actors being designated as 'gatekeepers', and subjected to various preventative obligations. This follows a trend seen in anti-money laundering policy (as in other aspects of crime control) towards the enlisting of private, non-state actors into a role in the 'policing' of financial transactions, to prevent the flow of illicit funds into the legitimate financial system. The preventative obligations, focused on requirements to undertake customer due diligence and submit suspicious activity reports, are implemented through national legislation (e.g. the Proceeds of Crime Act 2002 and the Money Laundering Regulations in the UK), but they have their foundations in international frameworks. The inclusion of legal professionals in the preventative obligations of the anti-money laundering regime has been contentious, with significant concern raised about the implications for principles of confidentiality and the lawyer-client relationship, and fears about the potential risks for legal professionals.

The implications for legal professionals of their characterisation as 'gatekeepers', and the resultant anti-money laundering legislation and policy measures, are significant. Cases of solicitors convicted of money laundering offences in the UK show that legal professionals can be convicted for facilitating money laundering on behalf of a client, or in the process of assisting or providing services to a client, without having actual knowledge or criminal intent, or being actively engaged in the laundering, if they were shown to have had suspicions that money laundering was taking place or, even, if there were reasonable grounds for suspicion, but no actual suspicion. This is due to the far-reaching nature of money laundering legislation in the UK, which goes far beyond what is required by international standards, with no requirement for criminal intent and *mens rea* requirements being satisfied by suspicion or, for those working in the regulated sector, reasonable grounds for suspicion. Unlike international anti-money laundering frameworks, including UN and Council of Europe Conventions and EU Money Laundering Directives, the legislation is not aimed solely at those deliberately laundering criminal proceeds. Its scope is much broader, allowing for the inclusion of a wider range of acts and omissions, and for those who are less directly—and unintentionally—involved in money laundering.

These aspects of the anti-money laundering policy and legislative frameworks in the UK stem from the concern that professionals play a critical role in the facilitation of money laundering, and the resultant designation of such professionals as 'gatekeepers'. However, this concern does not have a solid evidential basis. The role of professionals in money laundering is under-researched and poorly understood, and there remains no clear picture of the scale or nature of professionals' involvement in money laundering activity. This has not stopped the far-reaching legislation and policy measures aimed at preventing professional facilitation of money laundering described in this chapter being implemented. It is clear, therefore, that there is a need for further research into the involvement of professionals in the facilitation of money laundering, and greater consideration of the obligations of professionals in the prevention of money laundering and the legislative framework which underpins these obligations.

Notes

1. David Garland, 'The Limits of the Sovereign State: Strategies of Crime Control in Contemporary Society' (1996) 36(4) British Journal of Criminology 445, 452.
2. Valsamis Mitsilegas, 'Countering the Chameleon Threat of Dirty Money: 'Hard' and 'Soft' Law in the Emergence of a Global Regime Against Money Laundering and Terrorist Financing' in Adam Edwards and Peter Gill (eds), *Transnational Organised Crime: Perspectives on Global Security* (Routledge 2006).
3. Council Directive 91/308/EEC of 10 June 1991 on prevention of the use of the financial system for the purpose of money laundering (First Money Laundering Directive) [1991] OJ L166/77.
4. Mitsilegas (n 2) 199.
5. European Parliament and Council Directive 2001/97/EC of 4 December 2001 amending Council Directive 91/308/EEC on prevention of the use of the financial system for the purpose of money laundering (Second Money Laundering Directive) [2001] OJ L344/76; European Parliament and Council Directive 2005/60/EC of 26 October 2005 on the prevention and use of the financial system for the purpose of money laundering and terrorist financing (Third Money Laundering Directive) [2005] OJ L309/15.
6. Katie Benson, 'The Facilitation of Money Laundering by Legal and Financial Professionals: Roles, Relationships and Response' (PhD thesis, University of Manchester 2016).
7. Financial Action Task Force, *Report on Money Laundering Typologies 1996–1997* (FATF 1997) para 30.
8. Ibid. para 16.
9. Financial Action Task Force, *Report on Money Laundering Typologies 2003–2004* (FATF 2004) para 86.
10. Financial Action Task Force, *Global Money Laundering and Terrorist Financing Threat Assessment* (FATF 2010) para 44.
11. Ibid.
12. FATF 1997 (n 7); Financial Action Task Force, *Risk-Based Approach: Guidance for Legal Professionals* (FATF 2008); FATF 2010 (n 10); Financial Action Task Force, *Money Laundering and Terrorist Financing Vulnerabilities of Legal Professionals* (FATF 2013).
13. World Economic Forum, *Organized Crime Enablers: A Report for the Global Agenda on Organized Crime* (World Economic Forum 2012) 4.
14. Ibid. 5.
15. Australian Crime Commission, *Key Crime Enablers* (Australian Crime Commission 2013) 2.
16. Europol, *EU Organised Crime Threat Assessment: OCTA 2013* (Europol 2013) 14.

17. Home Office, *Serious and Organised Crime Strategy: October 2013* (Home Office 2013) 48.
18. National Crime Agency (NCA), *National Strategic Assessment* (NCA) *of Serious and Organised Crime 2016* (National Crime Agency 2016) 29.
19. NCA, *National Strategic Assessment of Serious and Organised Crime 2014* (National Crime Agency 2014) 12.
20. NCA (n 18) 29.
21. Home Office (n 17) 19.
22. HM Treasury, *UK National Risk Assessment of Money Laundering and Terrorist Financing* (HM Treasury/Home Office 2015) 41–46.
23. Ibid. 42.
24. For example, Ping He, 'Lawyers, Notaries, Accountants and Money Laundering' (2005) 9(1) Journal of Money Laundering Control 62; Olatunde Julius Otusanya, Solabomi Omobola Ajiboldae and Eddy Olajide Omolehinwa, 'The Role of Financial Intermediaries in Elite Money Laundering Practices: Evidence from Nigeria' (2012) 15(1) Journal of Money Laundering Control 58.
25. Including, Andrea Di Nicola and Paola Zoffi, 'Italian Lawyers and Criminal Clients. Risks and Countermeasures' (2005) 42(2) Crime, Law and Social Change 201; Michael Levi, Hans Nelen and Francien Lankhorst, 'Lawyers as Crime Facilitators in Europe: An Introduction and Overview' (2005) 42(2) Crime, Law and Social Change 117; David Middleton and Michael Levi, 'The Role of Solicitors in Facilitating 'Organized Crime': Situational Crime Opportunities and their Regulation' (2005) 42(2) Crime, Law and Social Change 123.
26. Melvin Soudijn, 'Removing Excuses in Money Laundering' (2012) 15(2) Trends in Organized Crime 146, 147.
27. David Middleton, 'The Legal and Regulatory Response to Solicitors Involved in Serious Fraud: Is Regulatory Action More Effective than Criminal Prosecution?' (2005) 45(6) British Journal of Criminology 810; David Middleton, 'Lawyers and Client Accounts: Sand Through a Colander' (2008) 11(1) Journal of Money Laundering Control 34.
28. Middleton and Levi (n 25); David Middleton and Michael Levi, 'Let Sleeping Lawyers Lie: Organized Crime, Lawyers and the Regulation of Legal Services' (2015) 55(4) British Journal of Criminology 647.
29. Middleton and Levi (n 28).
30. Stephen Schneider, 'Testing the Limits of Solicitor-Client Privilege: Lawyers, Money Laundering and Suspicious Transaction Reporting' (2005) 9(1) Journal of Money Laundering Control 27, 27.
31. Ibid.
32. Lawton Cummings and Paul Stepnowsky, 'My Brother's Keeper: An Empirical Study of Attorney Facilitation of Money Laundering through Commercial Transactions' [2011](1) Journal of the Professional Lawyer 1, 1.

33. Benson (n 6).
34. Ministerial Conference of the G-8 Countries on Combating Transnational Organized Crime (Moscow, 19–20 October 1999), *Communiqué* (Moscow Communiqué) <www.g8.utoronto.ca/adhoc/crime99.htm> accessed 24 July 2017.
35. Ibid. para 32.
36. Kevin Shepherd, 'Guardians at the Gate: The Gatekeeper Initiative and the Risk-Based Approach for Transactional Lawyers' (2009) 43(4) Real Property, Trust and Estate Law Journal 607; Kevin Shepherd, 'The Gatekeeper Initiative and the Risk-Based Approach to Client Due Diligence: The Imperative for Voluntary Good Practices Guidance for U.S. Lawyers' [2010] Journal of The Professional Lawyer 83.
37. Financial Action Task Force, *Review of the FATF Forty Recommendations: Consultation Paper* (FATF 2002).
38. Shepherd (n 36).
39. Financial Action Task Force, *FATF 40 Recommendations October 2003* (FATF 2003).
40. Ibid. Recommendation 12.
41. For example, Helen Xanthaki, 'Lawyers' Duties under the Draft EU Money Laundering Directive: Is Confidentiality a Thing of the Past?' (2001) 5(2) Journal of Money Laundering Control 103; Mitsilegas (n 2); Michelle Gallant, 'Lawyers and Money Laundering Regulation: Testing the Limits of Secrecy in Canada' (3rd Global Conference on Transparency Research, Paris, October 2013).
42. Gallant (n 41) 1.
43. Zaiton Hamin and others, 'Reporting Obligations of Lawyers under the AML/ATF Law in Malaysia' (2015) 170 Social and Behavioral Sciences 409.
44. Ibid. 413.
45. Laurel Terry, 'An Introduction to the Financial Action Task Force and its 2008 Lawyer Guidance' [2010] Journal of the Professional Lawyer 3, 68.
46. Hamin and others (n 43).
47. Gallant (n 41) 9.
48. Danielle Kirby, 'The European Union's Gatekeeper Initiative: The European Union Enlists Lawyers in the Fight Against Money Laundering and Terrorist Financing' (2008) 37(1) Hofstra Law Review 261, 265.
49. Colin Tyre, 'Anti-Money Laundering Legislation: Implementation of the FATF Forty Recommendations in the European Union' [2010] Journal of the Professional Lawyer 69.
50. Second Money Laundering Directive (n 5).
51. The Money Laundering Regulations 2007 (MLR 2007), SI 2007/2157, reg 3(1).
52. Ibid. reg 5.
53. Ibid. reg 8.

54. Ibid. reg 19.

55. Ibid. reg 20.

56. Ibid. reg 21.

57. Ibid. reg 20.

58. See, for example, Peter Alldridge, *Money Laundering Law: Forfeiture, Confiscation, Civil Recovery, Criminal Laundering and Taxation of the Proceeds of Crime* (Hart Publishing 2003); Robin Booth and others, *Money Laundering Law and Regulation: A Practical Guide* (Oxford University Press 2011); Karen Harrison and Nicholas Ryder, *The Law Relating to Financial Crime in the United Kingdom* (Ashgate Publishing 2013).

59. Proceeds of Crime Act 2002 (POCA 2002), s 327(1).

60. Ibid. s 327(3).

61. Ibid. s 328(1).

62. Ibid. s 329(1).

63. Ibid. s 327(2)(a); s 328(2)(a); s 329(2)(a). For details on making an autho-rised disclosure, see s 338.

64. Ibid. s 327(2)(b); s 328(2)(b); s 329(2)(b).

65. Ibid. s 327(2)(c); s 328(2)(c); s 329(2)(c).

66. CPS, *Proceeds of Crime Act 2002 Part 7—Money Laundering Offences: Legal Guidance* (CPS 2010) <www.cps.gov.uk/legal/p_to_r/proceeds_of_crime_money_laundering/> accessed 24 July 2017.

67. For further discussion, see Harrison and Ryder (n 58) 13–15.

68. CPS (n 66).

69. Rudi Fortson, 'Money Laundering Offences under POCA 2002' in William Blair and Richard Brent (eds), *Banks and Financial Crime—The International Law of Tainted Money* (Oxford University Press 2010) 181.

70. POCA 2002 (n 59) s 340(3) (emphasis added).

71. Ibid. s 328(1).

72. Alldridge (n 58) 182. See also Stephen Shute, 'Knowledge and Belief in the Criminal Law' in Stephen Shute and Andrew Simester (eds), *Criminal Law Theory: Doctrines of the General Part* (Oxford University Press 2002); and G.R. Sullivan, 'Knowledge, Belief and Culpability' in Stephen Shute and Andrew Simester (eds), *Criminal Law Theory: Doctrines of the General Part* (Oxford University Press 2002).

73. Alldridge (n 58) 182; Harrison and Ryder (n 58) 13–14.

74. Law Society, *Anti-Money Laundering Practice Note* (Law Society 2013) 72 <www.lawsociety.org.uk/sup   port-services/advice/practice-notes/aml/> accessed 24 July 2017.

75. Council of Europe Convention on Laundering, Search, Seizure and Confiscation of the Proceeds from Crime (8 November 1990) ETS 141/1990, art 6(1); UN Convention Against Illicit Traffic in Narcotic Drugs and Psychotropic Substances (adopted 20 December 1988, opened for signature 20 December 1988) (1988) 28 ILM 497, art 3(1).

76. European Parliament and Council Directive (EU) 2015/849 of 20 May 2015 of the on the prevention of the use of the financial system for the purposes of money laundering or terrorist financing (Fourth Money Laundering Directive) [2015] OJ L141/73 (emphasis added).
77. POCA 2002 (n 59) s 330(5).
78. Ibid. s 330(3).
79. Ibid. Schedule 9, Part 1.
80. The Money Laundering Regulations 2003 SI 2003/3075; Proceeds of Crime Act 2002 (Business in the Regulated Sector and Supervisory Authorities) Order 2003, SI 2003/3074.
81. Doug Hopton, *Money Laundering: A Concise Guide for All* Businesses (Gower Publishing 2009) 57.
82. Financial and credit institutions, including bureaux de change and money transfer services; providers of services in relation to the formation, management or operation of a company or trust; auditors, insolvency practitioners, accountants and tax advisers; independent legal professionals (in connection with financial or property transactions); estate agents; casinos; and dealers in goods to a value of €15,000 or more.
83. POCA 2002 (n 59) s 330(1–4).
84. Ibid. s 330(6–7).
85. Law Society (n 74) 72.
86. POCA 2002 (n 59) s 332. See CPS (n 66).
87. Alldridge (n 58) 183; Hopton (n 81).
88. POCA 2002 (n 59) *Explanatory Notes* para 479.
89. Moscow Communiqué (n 34) para 32 (emphasis added).
90. Research conducted as part of an ESRC-funded PhD carried out at the University of Manchester between 2012 and 2016. See Benson (n 6).
91. FATF 2013 (n 12).
92. Full details of the research methodology can be found in Benson (n 6).
93. Including Solicitors Disciplinary Tribunal (SDT) hearing transcripts; Court of Appeal hearing transcripts; media reports; fieldwork notes and observations from attendance at SDT hearing.
94. Benson (n 6).
95. Prior to the enactment of the Proceeds of Crime Act, laundering offences were covered by two different Acts: laundering the proceeds of drug trafficking was an offence under the Drug Trafficking Act 1994, and laundering the proceeds of other crimes was covered by the Criminal Justice Act 1998. The previous Acts were used to prosecute solicitors in this sample, where the offence had occurred prior to the enactment of the Proceeds of Crime Act.

Katie Benson is a Research Associate in the Centre for Criminology and Criminal Justice, School of Law, University of Manchester. Her primary research interest is the involvement of legitimate professionals in the facilitation of money laundering, and the criminal justice and regulatory responses to this. She is currently writing a research monograph on 'Lawyers and the Management of Criminal Proceeds', based on her PhD research, to be published by Routledge. Katie's wider research interests include money laundering, illicit markets and white-collar crime, and her recent research activity involves projects on corporate bribery, domestic bribery and the organisation of counterfeit alcohol distribution. Katie previously worked as Knowledge Manager at the Scottish Crime and Drug Enforcement Agency and Intelligence Analyst at Derbyshire Constabulary.

7

Cash, Crime and Anti-Money Laundering

Michele Riccardi and Michael Levi

Introduction

In most countries around the world, cash[1] is the main means of transfer (or 'typology', in official language) identified in money laundering/terrorist financing (ML/TF) reports. In Europe, most suspicious transaction/activity reports (STRs/SARs) are related to cash use or cash smuggling, and most seized assets are in the form of cash and movable goods. Why is 'cash still king'[2] in the recorded component of Anti-Money laundering (AML)?

Cash facilitates the laundering of illicit funds because it is anonymous and cannot normally be traced.[3] It is a bearer negotiable instrument which gives no details either on the origin of the proceeds or on the beneficiary of the exchange. This makes it harder for law enforcement to follow the audit trail—although it is also in principle most readily identified, when deposited in financial institutions, as 'out of character' with persons' 'known' or believed income and wealth. Cash is also a preferred means of payment on the leisure pursuits (including drugs purchases) and the 'bling' that are often one of the motives for crime.

M. Riccardi
Transcrime – Joint Research Centre on Transnational Crime, Università Cattolica del Sacro Cuore, Milan, Italy

M. Levi
School of Social Sciences, Cardiff University, Cardiff, UK

© The Author(s) 2018
C. King et al. (eds.), *The Palgrave Handbook of Criminal and Terrorism Financing Law*,
https://doi.org/10.1007/978-3-319-64498-1_7

This chapter provides a review of the numerous facets of the relationship between cash and AML. First, it presents some statistics of how cash is spread in the legitimate economy. Second, it discusses what criminal activities are more prone to generate cash illicit proceeds. Third, it argues how cash is used in the laundering cycle, namely in terms of cash smuggling and of cash-intensive businesses and assets. Then, it provides a review of the regulatory measures introduced to reduce the use of cash and minimise the risk that banknotes are used for criminal purposes. It also discusses the challenges in seizing illicit cash—and managing it once seized. Finally, it suggests some policy and research implications. The focus of the chapter is Europe, but references to US and other countries are also made.

Measuring Cash: Paradoxes and Surprises

As hard to trace, cash is also hard to measure routinely. Because cash payments are not usually recorded (see below), there are no direct proxies of how (for which purpose, how often, in which form) it is used by individuals and businesses.[4] Only indirect measures exist and are briefly discussed below. This is the first paradox: despite being one of the oldest means of payment, cash is still the one we least know about—both in relation to the legal and the illegal economy. The knowledge gap is particularly evident if compared to electronic transactions: data on credit or debit card use are largely available, and are also widely exploited for marketing purposes by companies and banks.

The Increasing Value of Banknotes in Circulation

The first indirect measure of cash is represented by the volume and value of banknotes in circulation. These statistics provide a general indication of the magnitude of the demand of cash across time and space, but do not inform on what printed notes are then used for. The statistics of the two main central banks in Europe—the European Central Bank (ECB) and Bank of England—show that the issuance of new banknotes has constantly grown in the last 15 years. In the EU, it has increased, in terms of value, by five times since 2002, while in the UK by about two times since 2004 (see Fig. 7.1). In both cases, banknotes have grown at a much higher rate than GDP and inflation, and despite the diffusion of alternative payment methods.

Looking at the different denominations, in the EU, the highest increase (in terms of value) has been of 500, 100 and 50 euro banknotes. In particular,

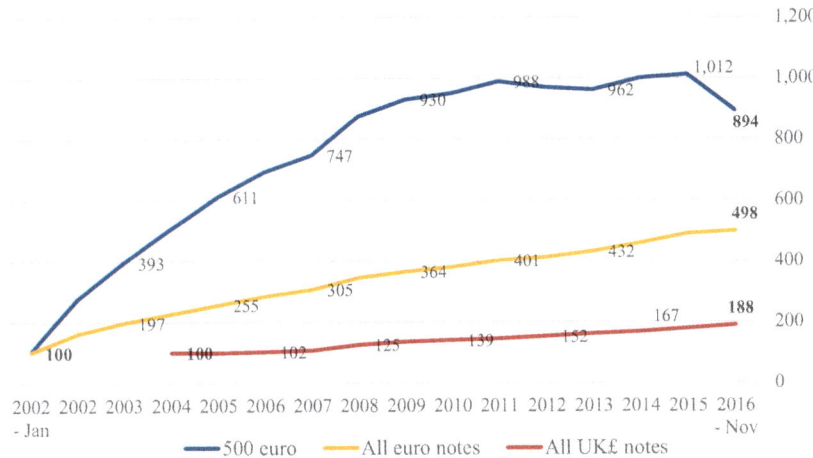

1,200

1,012   1,000

988   962

930   894

800

747   600

611   498

393   400

305   364   401   432

255   188   200
197   167
100   102   125   139   152

100

0

2002 2002 2003 2004 2005 2006 2007 2008 2009 2010 2011 2012 2013 2014 2015 2016
- Jan   - Nov

────500 euro   ────All euro notes   ────All UK£ notes

Fig. 7.1 Value of Euro and UK£ banknotes in circulation. Source: Authors' elaboration on ECB and BOE data. Note: All December values, except when specified. For euro notes, index 2002 = 100. For UK£, index 2004 = 100

the 500 euro note (which will be discontinued by the end of 2018—see below) has increased by nine times, almost twice the growth of other euro notes (though from a lower base rate). In November 2016, these three denominations represent respectively 25%, 22% and 40% of the total value of the outstanding euro notes. In the UK, the highest denomination note (the £50 banknote) increased most in terms of value (+230%), though the £20 note still represents most of the value of notes in circulation in the UK (roughly 60%).

In the euro area, despite the European Monetary Union, wide differences in issuing banknotes exist across different states. While Germany represents, by far, the main issuer, Luxembourg is the outlier when comparing the value of issued banknotes to its GDP (about 200%), while France, Italy and Germany range between 4% and 16%. On average, in the euro area, the value of banknotes rose from 5% of GDP to more than 10% since 2002[5] (Fig. 7.2).

In the United States 'cash remains a unique, resilient, and heavily used consumer payment instrument'.[6] According to Fed data, the amount of currency in circulation has increased steadily over time—and that of higher denominations has accelerated after the 2008 financial crisis. However, the value of cash on GDP (about 7.5%) remains lower than in the euro area.[7]

How can we explain the growth of banknotes, especially of high-denomination notes—500 euro above all? And why are some countries printing more bills than others?

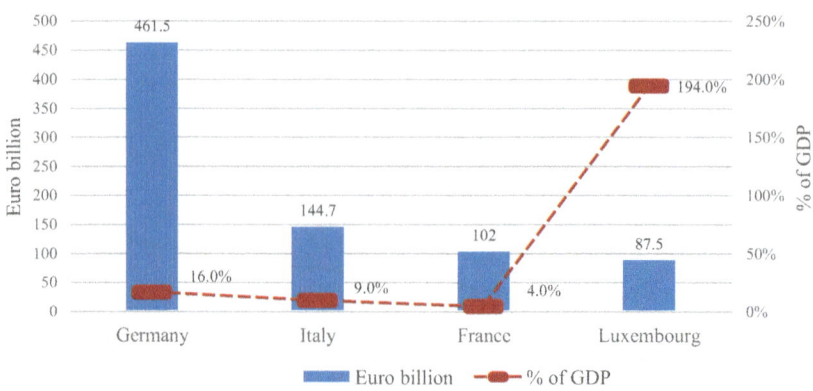

Fig. 7.2 Euro banknote issuers in 2013. Selected EU countries

Only Part of Circulating Cash Is Used for Transactions

Some of these questions can be answered looking at the results of surveys on the use of cash conducted among individuals and businesses—a second indirect measure of cash diffusion. An ECB survey conducted in 2011 (with 2008 data) in eight member states (Belgium, Germany, Spain, France, Italy, Luxembourg, the Netherlands and Austria) revealed that only one-third of the euro banknotes in circulation are used for transaction purposes.[8]

The same 2011 ECB survey pointed out the different attitude in using cash for purchases across different EU countries (Table 7.1). France, the Netherlands and Luxembourg emerge as the most cash-averse countries (i.e. those with the lowest percentage of respondents using cash, whatever the value of the transaction), while Italy and Spain, followed by Austria, are the most 'cash-enthusiastic'. On average, while one-fifth of the population in these eight EU MS use cash for purchases between €200 and 1,000—the percentage reduces to 4% for assets of more than 10,000 euro. These figures have been confirmed by a more recent ECB report (based on national payment diary surveys).[9]

Percentages are similar in the United States, where cash is used in about one-third (32%) of all transactions (50% of those below 25 dollars). According to a latest survey by the Federal Reserve Bank of San Francisco, cash is widely used even when other options are available, and is the preferred means of payment in six out of nine merchant categories, by very young (18–24 years) and elderly (65 and more) people and the poorest ones.[10] In our view, this is likely to be the product of financial exclusion, habituation, convenience and a range of other factors.

Table 7.1 Percentage of respondents always or often using cash by value of purchase

	<20 euro (%)	30–100 euro (%)	200–1000 euro (%)	>10,000 euro (%)
Belgium	84	48	18	5
Germany	91	69	21	4
Spain	90	64	30	6
France	80	15	3	0
Italy	91	77	31	4
Luxembourg	77	27	10	3
The Netherlands	65	20	8	4
Austria	82	60	29	10
AVERAGE (8 EU MS)	**87**	**55**	**20**	**4**

Source: ECB, 2011

Cash-Ratio: South-Eastern Europe on Top

The results at the European level are confirmed by the analysis of cash-ratio. It is another indirect measure, calculated as the ratio between the amount of ATM withdrawals (proxy of cash use) and the sum of total payments, including those through point-of-sale (POS).[11] On average (2011–2015) in the EU, about 42% of payments are made in cash, but large differences exist across countries: if in Finland, the UK, France and Sweden the cash-ratio is below 30%, in Greece, Bulgaria and Romania banknotes and coins are used for more than 80% of payments. Among big countries, Germany and Italy also record high values (65% and 53.2%, respectively) (Table 7.2).

These differences across countries may be driven by different factors, including maximum thresholds on the use of cash posed by regulation (discussed below), financial culture, ageing of the population and availability of alternative payment instruments, first of all POS among merchants.[12] As regards the latter, Table 7.3 presents the first ten countries in the European Union (and UK) by number of POS per capita. Luxembourg ranks first, representing an outlier, followed by Italy, UK and Spain. It has to be noted that much depends on the nature of the local economy, as POS diffusion varies across economic sectors, with hotels, restaurants and retail trade on top.

How to Explain the Gap? The Illegal Economy

The figures presented above help to get a broad overview of how cash is spread in the economy of Europe and other major countries. But they raise also a number of questions. First, despite the diffusion of alternative payment methods, cash still appears as the most preferred means of payment, especially in

Table 7.2 Cash-ratio across European countries. First and last five countries

Country	Cash-ratio (%) (average 2011–2015)
1. Greece	88.8
2. Bulgaria	86.8
3. Romania	84.8
4. Slovakia	73.6
5. Latvia	70.9
[...]	
24. The Netherlands	33.8
25. Finland	28.7
26. UK	27.0
27. France	25.3
28. Sweden	23.4
Euro Area	**46.8**
European Union	**41.9**

Source: Authors' elaboration on ECB data

Table 7.3 First ten EU countries with highest POS rate

EU countries	POS terminals per million inhabitants
Luxembourg	260,596
Italy	32,596
UK	30,077
Spain	29,841
Finland	27,985
Portugal	27,645
Cyprus	26,931
The Netherlands	26,273
Denmark	24,639
Croatia	24,551
EU (median)	**18,758**

Source: Savona and Riccardi, 2017

certain countries and sectors. But (at most) only one-third of banknotes in circulation are estimated to be used for legitimate transaction purposes. Nevertheless, in the same period, cash has been increasing at a higher rate than GDP and inflation, and high-denomination notes like 500 euro (the least likely to be used for small purchases—and also the hardest to get accepted in ordinary retail establishments) have been growing even more. Among the countries issuing more banknotes in Europe is Luxembourg—one of the most cash-averse populations and the one with the highest ratio of POS per capita.

How can we explain these paradoxes? And how can we fill the gap between cash in circulation and the actual demand for legal transactions? Hoarding could be part of an answer, as despite the risk of theft, loss or fire, banknotes are a cheap store of value, especially in an era of low inflation and almost negative interest rates.[13] The demand for cash as a store of value has also increased as a consequence of the financial crisis and especially of the failure of Lehman Brothers in 2008, which led to massive cash withdrawals (most often in high denominations) from deposits as a precautionary measure against the risk of bank failures above the European compensation level.[14] Also banknotes held abroad represent a significant share. But a key role in explaining this gap is certainly played by illegal transactions.

Indeed, several studies have pointed out a correlation between cash diffusion and the level of illicit activities. At European level, the countries with highest cash-ratio (Greece, Romania, Bulgaria) have also very high estimated levels of shadow economy.[15] In Italy, the areas with higher cash-ratios are also those with higher organised crime, tax evasion, irregular labour and money laundering STRs.[16] And in the US, a recent study found that a reduction in cash circulation reduced the overall predatory recorded crime rate, as well as larceny, burglary and assault statistics.[17] This is the first element to consider: the diffusion of cash in legal markets cannot be fully understood without taking into account illegal markets (including—as in the Wright study—opportunities for theft and robbery). While some criminal activities generate cash, most benefit from a cash-intensive economy.

Cash-Generating Illicit Activities

But what are the most cash-generating predicate offences? The cash nature of illicit proceeds depends on a variety of factors, such as the nature of the target and the victim, and the nature and price of the illicit commodity to be exchanged (if any).

Drugs are usually considered as a cash-intensive market. Though this may largely reflect the nature of typical money-laundering investigations, in a Europol survey in 2015, most European AML units reported drug-trafficking as the predicate offence most closely linked to the use of cash in ML schemes.[18] Drug dealers usually receive multiple cash payments, likely in smaller bills, which then require aggregation, often through exchange in higher denomination notes, and laundering.[19] There is wide evidence that this happens, for example, in both the trafficking of drugs by Mexican cartels in the United States[20] and the trade of cocaine from Colombia to Europe.[21] In both cases, smaller denominations of cash are collected in central counting houses, converted into high-denomination notes (like 500 euro or 100 US$) before being smuggled (see below) or stored elsewhere. But cash is also the preferred means for purchase of drugs at the wholesale level: according to some estimates, about 80% of the money generated by Mexican drug trafficking cartels is used to buy new shipments of cocaine and is dispatched directly from destination markets (e.g. the US) to Colombia without passing through Mexico.[22] One question is how this pattern may change in the aftermath of the diffusion of online drug markets where virtual currencies, bitcoins overall, are increasingly adopted: though 'cashing out' may be required at some stage in some place, at least until e-currencies command general acceptance.[23]

Other 'traditional' criminal activities, such as extortion, sexual exploitation and smuggling of migrants, are likely to generate cash proceeds too. In Italy and Mexico, most businesses victims of extortion racketeering pay protection money in cash,[24] although other forms of payment (e.g. imposition of suppliers or raw materials) may be adopted. Though the methods of payment for grand corruption may differ, corruption is the second predicate offence most frequently reported by law enforcement agencies (LEAs) in relation to cash.[25] Indeed, domestic bribes are traditionally paid in cash, as demonstrated by numerous victimisation surveys,[26] although both petty and grand corruption may take other forms.

Similar patterns characterise tax crimes. While large tax evasion schemes may be cash-less, and rather involve complex corporate schemes set up in offshore jurisdictions, 'petty' tax evasion carried out by individuals and businesses is mainly based on under-declaration and on informal payments made in cash. Undeclared revenues are then used to carry out informal cash-payments to suppliers and workers thus pumping, with a flywheel effect, the size of the underground economy.

On the other side, all the variety of cybercrimes (e.g. phishing, ransomwares) appear as the least cash-generating crimes, as they can remain often confined to virtual environments: hackers can attack a victim's account and move the money to another mule's account; or in the case of ransomware can block the victim's computer, demanding bitcoins or some other non-cash form in exchange for cyber-freedom. However, the proceeds generated by these activities may need, at a certain point, some cashing-out activity, as shown in Fig. 7.3.

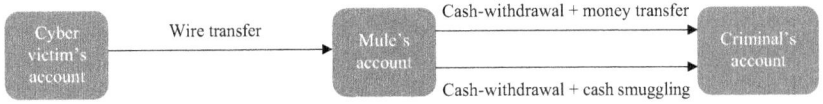

Fig. 7.3   From cyber to cash. Source: Authors' elaboration on Europol, 2015

Cash Smuggling

Smuggling or Laundering?

Cash smuggling can arise because of the need to move the generated illicit cash elsewhere. This is particularly true for those criminal activities with a transnational nature, such as drug trafficking or migrant smuggling, where criminals may wish to move the proceeds to their country of family origin for laundering purposes (e.g. investing in the domestic real estate market), for hoarding, to purchase further illicit commodities or to improve their life-styles. The transfer of cash across the border in violation of currency reporting requirements, that is, above the permitted maximum threshold and without justification, is usually referred to as 'bulk cash smuggling'.[27]

Some authors note that cash smuggling is not strictly money laundering, in the sense that it does not necessarily disguise the criminal origin of the funds: on the contrary, it may 'increase the conspicuousness of its questionable origins since the money is converted into high denomination bills'.[28] However, moving illicit proceeds across borders can be an effective way to distance this money from the predicate offence which originated it, at least unless intelligence or enforcement agencies are tracking it at the time.[29] But the (judicial) relationship between cash smuggling and money laundering is certainly a debated issue, as demonstrated also by the case of *Cuellar v United States*.[30] Humberto Cuellar was convicted in the US for international money laundering after officers in 2004 found more than $80,000, presumed to be proceeds of drug trafficking, hidden in a vehicle he was driving from Texas across the US border into Mexico. Cuellar appealed, arguing that his conviction for money laundering should not stand because he did not attempt to create the appearance of legitimate funds. Instead, according to Cuellar, bulk cash smuggling characterised his actions better than money laundering. In 2008, the US Supreme Court supported Cuellar, quashing the conviction for money laundering: the applicable section of the Money Laundering Control Act of 1986[31] required that Mr. Cuellar knew that the purpose—not merely the effect—of his transporting the money was to conceal or disguise its illicit nature.

Notwithstanding these judicial arguments and any difficulties in spending large-denomination notes or depositing them directly, bulk cash smuggling is widely used by several criminal organisations, in particular those involved in international drug trafficking. A US National Drug Threat Assessment confirmed that, despite the 2008 Merida Initiative, 'bulk cash is a prominent method' for Mexican drug cartels to move their cash back to Mexico,[32] especially with the increased AML controls on the financial sector and on money service businesses.[33] Transportation of cash appears to be the preferred method also for Colombian drug traders to transfer the cocaine revenues generated in Europe to the home country.[34]

Most cash-smuggling methods have, as a pre-condition, the aggregation of the cash proceeds into higher denomination banknotes in order to minimise volume and weight, and ease transportation (see also below): £250,000 in 500 euro notes weighs 0.6 kilos and fits in a medium-size envelope, whereas they weigh 15–20 kilos in £20 notes.[35] Another important issue is the conversion into usable currencies. This could be done in the country of receipt or destination. However, there may be a decision not to exchange, especially if originally denominated in US$ or in euro: should the beneficial owners wish to keep cash for hoarding purposes, then strong currencies could be preferred because they are more stable over time. Moreover, the 'dollarisation' of some central or southern American countries' economies (first of all Mexico and Ecuador, where it is legal tender) make US dollars widely accepted by merchants and banks. According to a 2015 FATF survey, US dollars and euro represents about 70% of the currencies in suspected criminal cash transport cases.[36]

Cash Smuggling Methods

As stated, cash smuggling techniques are various. Cash carried through vehicles and by air passengers appear as the most frequent typologies, according to LEAs and customs agencies worldwide.[37] They are followed by cash moved through mail post and through cargo, either air or maritime freight. When money is moved through motor vehicles, it is usually vacuum sealed in plastic bags and then concealed in wheel wells, panels and spare tire compartments. Sometimes the same cars and lorries used for transporting the drugs (e.g. tractor-trailer trucks used by Mexican cartels to carry cocaine north to the US) are used to move the illicit cash back. According to Farah, who interviewed a number of US and Mexican law enforcement officers, cash is 'smurfed' in smaller shipments ranging from US$150,000–500,000, through multiple vehicles, and often with rotating drivers in order to minimise the risk of large-scale seizures by guards.[38]

Cash mules seem to be the preferred method by drug trafficking organisations to move back illicit cash from Europe to their countries of origins. A recent study by Soudijn and Reuter analysed six cases of smuggling of cash, generated by cocaine trade, from the Netherlands to Colombia and other Latin American countries between 2003 and 2011. The investigation revealed the wide network of couriers employed—about 181 people, hired ad-hoc—all well monitored by drug dealers through a detailed accounting system.[39] Money mules generally carried 300,000 euro each, packed in 500 euro bills. The cost of cash-smuggling through money mules is estimated by the authors between 4.4% and 9.2% of the total value—of which about 3% related to the conversion in higher denomination notes—without taking into account the costs resulting from cash seized and those related to brokers' or coordinators' fees.[40]

Cash-Intensive Businesses and Assets

Once moved to the desired location, if there is a need to launder the illicit cash (rather than simply store or spend it, or re-invest it directly in criminal enterprises), then cash-intensive businesses and assets may play a crucial role.[41]

Cash-Intensive Businesses

A business could be considered highly cash-intensive if (a) it operates mainly on cash-transaction basis; (b) its assets consist mostly of cash or liquid (current) assets.[42] Bars, restaurants, retail trade shops, supermarkets, car washes and betting/gambling businesses (such as casinos) usually receive most payments by clients in cash, and this could be helpful for laundering purposes. It would be easier to justify extra (illicit) proceeds as legitimate revenues and it would be possible to deposit large volumes of cash as daily earnings on companies' bank accounts, thus easing the placement of illicit funds into the financial circuit.[43]

Not surprisingly, recent studies show that cash-intensive sectors are usually preferred by organised crime infiltrating legal businesses. For example, in Italy, wholesale and retail trade, bars, restaurants, hotels and construction represent more than 70% of the approximately 2,000 companies confiscated from mafia groups in the last 30 years (chart below). Confiscated betting agencies and video-lottery/slot machine businesses, despite being low in number, weigh relatively high when compared to their numbers in the legal economy.[44]

A more recent report concludes that these sectors are associated with the highest estimated money laundering risk in the country.[45] Clients seldom pay cash for construction contracts but, at least in Italy, construction is the sector with the most liquid assets (about 70% of average total assets of Italian building companies is held in cash, inventory, receivables and other current assets). It would be rational for criminals to want their businesses to stay liquid in order to ease a quick selling-off should they feel themselves to be under investigation or at risk of seizure and confiscation. In any case, the construction industry—along with bars, restaurants and agriculture—is also the sector with the highest prevalence of irregular workers, who may become another way to launder illicit proceeds—through the distribution of black salaries paid in cash and further spent by workers in the legitimate economy (Fig. 7.4).

The same economic activities—bars, restaurants, retail trade, construction—often appear in relation to firms controlled by organised crime groups in other European (and non-European) countries, for example, in Spain, Sweden, Slovenia, France, the Netherlands, UK, but also in the US and in Canada.[46] In the Netherlands, a recent report finds that cash-intensiveness is a key component of the ML risk of sectors such as hotels, catering and entertainment (which includes gambling, gaming but also legalised prostitution).[47] In order to prevent criminal infiltration, most of these activities (and other cash

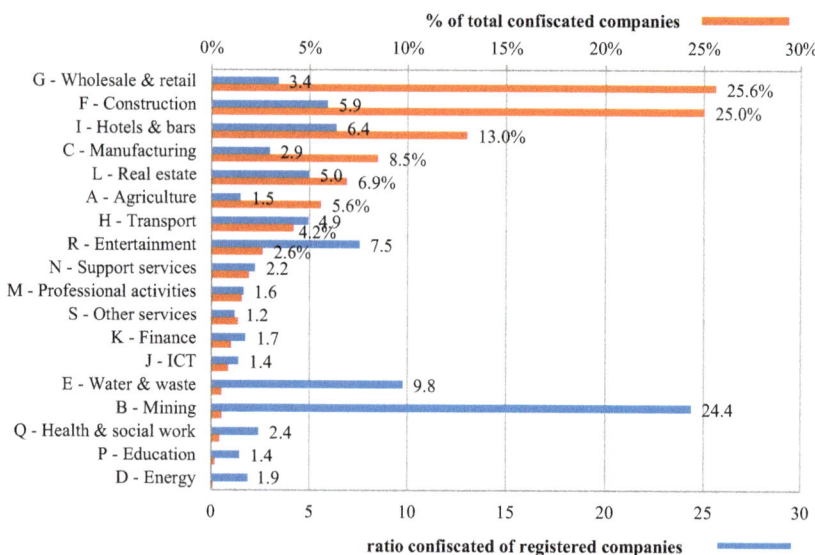

Fig. 7.4 Confiscated companies across business sectors in Italy (1984–2012): Percentages of the total and ratio of registered companies. Source: Riccardi, Soriani and Giampietri (2016)

businesses) are also subject in the Netherlands to the so-called BIBOB law (public administration probity screening act) which provides that companies' or persons' records may be required to be examined before a permit or a subsidy is granted, though this does not mean that they will be examined or examined efficiently.[48]

Cash-Intensive Assets

But companies are not the only method criminals may have at their disposal to place illicit cash in the legitimate economy. They may directly acquire assets in cash—and then trade on the legal market. This much depends on the maximum threshold for cash use foreseen by the local regulation (discussed below) and their enforcement in practice (e.g. vendors may sell for cash and hide this from the tax authorities and/or their partners). Although it appears to be a safe and common place for investment or laundering, real estate is a less cash-intensive market than others. In most European countries it is difficult to buy properties for cash, also because property transactions are often certified by notaries or other professionals subject to AML legislation, if enforced or expected to be enforced. The extent to which this happens, or the mechanisms by which corrupt Chinese or Russian people purchase property in major Western cities, is not well understood.

More likely is the purchase in cash of high-value assets such as cars, boats or jewels which are a quite common consumption pattern for organised criminals and corrupt officers. In various countries, it is still possible to buy a car entirely in cash. In some, car shops should be registered as high-value dealers. But in most they should not. In Germany, for example, according to a survey published by the association of untied (multi-brand) car dealers (BVfK), 67% of car transactions are done in cash.[49] And car shops often apply a discount in case of cash-payments (the so-called *Barzahler-Rabatt*—cash payers' discount).

Reducing Cash Use

Given the analysis so far, it is not surprising that one of the first measures implemented by governments to minimise the ML/TF risk is to reduce the use of cash in the legitimate economy. This means putting rules and thresholds on cash use and fostering the adoption of alternative (and more traceable) means of payments. Three types of threshold on cash-use can be identified in those countries that have controls:

- On purchases, that is, maximum amounts which could be purchased through cash
- On cross-border transfers, that is, maximum amounts of cash which could be brought into/outside a country
- On banknotes denomination, that is, what is the highest denomination note in circulation

Limits on Cash Purchases

The set of rules on cash purchase limits largely vary worldwide—and even within the EU (see below). The different practices range from cash thresholds on all types of goods to thresholds on certain types of goods; from maximum limits per day/month and per person to different thresholds depending on the type of consumer (e.g. resident versus non-resident, legal person vs natural person). Some countries have no thresholds at all, while others require businesses accepting large amounts of cash to report these transactions to the public authority or respond to the same AML obligations pending on banks or professionals.

In the European Union, all these scenarios can be found (see chart and map below). Italy, France, Belgium, Spain, Poland and other member states all have maximum thresholds for cash purchases, which range between 1,000 (e.g. in France, for French residents) and 15,000 euro (e.g. in Poland for all consumers or in Spain for non-residents). In Romania, cash payments are limited to 10,000 RON (about 2,300 euro) per person per day. In Germany, Austria, Slovenia and in some Baltic countries no limitations exist, while in Hungary they apply only if the transaction is made by legal persons.[50] However, it must be noted that in the whole EU, all traders in goods which receive payment in cash above 10,000 euro are subject to AML obligations (Directive 849/2015, Art. 2). But the number of STRs issued by this category is very low (Table 7.4).

In the UK, there is no limit for cash purchases. However, all merchants accepting cash payments of 15,000 euro or more (in single transaction or several linked instalments) should register as High-Value Dealers with HM Revenue and Customs, which has a light-touch regulatory regime.[51] In the United States, all trade or businesses who receive more than US$10,000 in cash in a single or related transactions must report to the Internal Revenue Service by filling the so-called IRS/FinCEN Form 8300. The obligation applies to a wide array of situations, including sale of goods, services, properties, rentals and loan payments. Only persons engaged in trade or

Table 7.4 Cash purchase limits across selected EU countries

Country	Cash limit (euro)	Note
Austria	No limit	
Belgium	3,000	
Bulgaria	5,000 (approx.)	Limit of 9,999 LEV
France	1,000	10,000 euro for non-residents
Germany	No limit	
Hungary	No limit	Limit of about 5,000 euro (1.5 million HUF) for legal persons
Italy	3,000	
The Netherlands	No limit	
Poland	15,000 (approx.)	Limit of 62,220 PLN
Romania	2,250 (approx.)	Limit of 10,000 RON per person per day
Slovenia	No limit	
Spain	2,500	15,000 euro for non-residents

Source: Authors' elaboration based on European Consumer Centre data

businesses should fill the 8300 form, while transactions among private individuals (e.g. the sale of a second-hand car to a private buyer) do not fall under this requirement.[52]

Cash limits also may change over time, following political or socio-economic pressure. For example, in France the maximum threshold for cash-purchase was lowered from 3,000 to 1,000 euro (for French residents) and from 15,000 to 10,000 euro (for non-residents like tourists) in March 2015, after the February attack to Charlie Hebdo, in a way to 'combat low-cost terrorists'.[53] Following the same *zeitgeist,* Germany has also attempted in early 2016 to introduce a limit on cash payments above 5000 euro. However, the proposal has met strong resistance by a wide variety of stakeholders including varied political parties, the German Bundesbank, academics and numerous trade associations—first of all, car dealers and the automotive industry.[54] The main reason argued by opponents was that reducing cash could also reduce data protection and privacy: as mentioned by a German MP 'Cash allows us to remain anonymous during day-to-day transactions. In a constitutional democracy, that is a freedom that has to be defended'.[55] In an opposite direction, in 2016 Italy has raised the maximum limit for cash-use from 1,000 euro (at that moment the lowest in the European Union) to 3,000 euro. This increase, which some authors condemned because of the risk it posed to fostering the underground economy and money laundering, was justified by the government as a 'Keynesian' measure to incentivise demand and spur consumption. Nevertheless, this measure has been accompanied with an obligation on merchants to adopt POS terminals in an attempt to increase the use of more traceable payments such as credit or debit cards.

Limits on Cash Transfers

In most jurisdictions, limitations exist in terms of maximum cash amounts which could be brought in and outside the country. When the value transferred is higher than this threshold, it usually has to be reported to the customs authority—and likely justified. If cash is not declared, it may be seized, and individuals can incur various sanctions including fines or detention. These requirements respond to FATF Recommendation 32 (*Cash couriers*), which was developed with the aim to prevent the physical cross-border transportation of currency by terrorists and other criminals.[56]

In the European Union, the limit is set by Regulation 1889/2005 and corresponds to €10,000, above which any natural person should declare this amount when entering or leaving the area. In December 2016, the Commission proposed also to extend currency reporting requirements to unaccompanied cash such as that sent in postal or freight consignments and to precious commodities such as gold, which often serve as 'quasi-cash'.[57] Since Regulation 1889/2005 adopts a minimum harmonisation approach, some EU member states (such as Belgium, France, Germany, Italy) go beyond what is required and apply the duty to declare also when leaving towards (or entering from) another EU country. On the opposite side, in other member states (such as Austria, Romania, the Netherlands) and in the UK, the obligation holds only for movements across the EU border.[58]

In the United States, as mentioned previously, the limit is set at 10,000 dollars by Title 31 section 5332 of the US Code. Whoever evades the currency reporting requirement can be prosecuted for a cash-smuggling offence.[59] To make prosecutions easier, it has to be proven only that the suspect intended to cross the border with the undeclared cash.

Limits on Banknote Denominations

The third limit which can be identified is that on notes' denominations—that is, the highest allowed banknote value. As mentioned, high-value notes are preferred by criminal organisations and terrorists as they ease the transportation and hoarding of illicit cash proceeds. Table 7.5 presents the highest denominations in selected major and widely accepted currencies.

Among most common currencies, the largest value note is the 1,000 Swiss franc bill, followed by the 500 euro note.[60] However, there are other banknotes in circulation with higher denominations, although most of them have been withdrawn (but are still legal tender). For example, the 1,000, 5,000 and

Table 7.5 Highest denomination banknotes in selected currencies

Country/Area	Currency	Highest denomination banknote	Value in Euro[a]
Euro area	Euro (€)	500[b]	500
UK	Pound (£)	50[c]	57.9
Switzerland	Swiss franc (Fr.)	1000	932.2
United States	US Dollar ($)	100	93.9
Japan	Yen (¥)	10,000	87
China	Yuan (¥)	100	13.7
Canada	Canadian Dollar ($)	100	70.5
Australia	Australian Dollar ($)	100	70.9
India	Rupee (₹)	1000[d]	13.8
Mexico	Peso ($)	1000	42,8
Russia	Ruble (₹)	5000	78.5

Source: Authors' elaboration on various sources
[a]Exchange rate of 19 January 2017
[b]Discontinued by the end of 2018. Next highest denomination is the 200 euro bill
[c]Some banks in Scotland and Northern Ireland produce 100-pound banknotes that
  are not technically legal tender but are nonetheless widely accepted
[d]Discontinued since November, 2016 by the Indian Government (see below)

10,000 US dollar bills (discontinued in 1969, and almost disappeared) and the Canadian 1,000 dollar (equivalent to about 700 euro, not printed since 2000). The Singapore 10,000 dollar bill (about 6,580 euro at current rate) was discontinued in 2014 for AML reasons, but can still be found, while the 1,000 dollar note (658 euro) is still printed. This means that the largest bill in circulation is the Brunei 10,000 dollar (US 6,570 dollars) bill—although that seems to be restricted to the shopping habits of the super-rich.

The Anomaly of the 500 Euro Banknote

In May 2016, the ECB decided to permanently discontinue the production and issuance of €500 banknote by the end of 2018. The measure responded to 'concerns that the banknote could facilitate illicit activities'[61]and followed various studies and reports, already mentioned in this chapter.[62] The 500 euro note means much value in a single banknote of a reliable (and easily exchangeable) currency: the perfect bill to be exploited for cash smuggling purposes by drug trafficking organisations, or as a store of value for large cash illicit proceeds, both in Europe and abroad. According to a 2009 estimate by the UK Serious Organised Crime Agency (now National Crime Agency), 90% of 500 euro notes in circulation in the UK was held by criminal organisations or was used for criminal purposes.[63] And numerous are the cases of 500 euro notes seized in police operations in Latin America or the US.

The withdrawal of this banknote will partially address the problem. But at the moment of the ECB decision, 280 billion euros (equivalent to almost 25% of all outstanding euro value) were still in circulation in this denomination. Therefore the ECB made clear that the 500 banknote will remain indefinitely legal tender. The question then is whether criminals will really feel that they need to exchange their holdings into smaller bills, or whether they could keep the 500 euro for their illegal transactions (e.g. to buy drug shipments or firearms) or as stores of value.

Seizing Cash

Due to the absence of harmonised and centralised data, it is difficult to determine how many assets, and of what types, are seized in Europe and abroad. A recent exploratory analysis produced by Transcrime in 2015 on several EU MS revealed that cash (and other movable assets such as bank deposits) represents the greatest part of seized and confiscated goods in Finland (62.9%), France (96.2%), Ireland (72.4%) and Spain (49.9%). In Italy they represent up to 33%, but real estate properties are more numerous.[64] In the UK, no updated figures are available, although according to the analysis of a Joint Asset Recovery Database sample, cash seems to be a fairly commonly recovered asset.[65]

In addition to any hypothetical impact of AML measures themselves making it more difficult to deposit and move cash, the reason behind these figures could be related to the key role played by cash in the illicit economy: it is more frequently seized because some criminals may prefer to keep dirty proceeds in banknotes than laundering it via real estate or through businesses. But this can be only part of the story. It could be argued that cash is easier to seize than other goods: the research evidence does not tell us how much of it is simply found during a police search of a suspect's house or of a vehicle. For example, though this may reflect long-term surveillance, in March 2007 Mexican police seized approximately US $207 million in cash from the house of a drug trafficker—held in various currencies including US and Canadian dollars, euro, Mexican pesos, yen, Chinese yuan and Traveller's cheques—one of the biggest cash seizures in history.[66] If this value had been held in other type of assets, it would have been harder to trace and recover it.

The third reason is that cash is easier to manage once seized, and in many countries, the authorities may not be geared up for the costs and difficulties of non-cash asset management.[67] Forfeited real estate has substantial management expenses (including maintenance and surveillance) and may involve third-party claims; the same for vehicles while even higher are the costs of managing seized businesses (e.g. judicial administrators' fees, workers' salaries, interest on business debts). Instead, seized cash could be easily placed in a bank account or—depending on the national legislation—kept by the police (as part of the 'gain') or transferred to special public funds used for various purposes.[68]

These practices may bolster the 'policing for profit' debate, raising the suspicion that police investigations and seizures could be cash rather than harm oriented—because the former is easier, cheaper and thus more profitable.[69] But we raise another question: what would happen to asset recovery if criminals shift from cash to other goods and laundering methods?

Policy and Research Implications

In Summary

Cash is appreciated by criminals for ML/TF purposes—and not only for that. Evidence suggests that, especially for very cash-intensive criminal activities such as drug trafficking, or for low-cost terrorists, it is the preferred method for moving illicit funds from one place to another (through cash-couriers). In cash smuggling, large-denomination bills like 500 euro play a key role. Cash is also very common for hoarding purposes, especially if there is no need (or possibility) to launder all the dirty money in other assets such as properties or companies. In this case, especially in an era of low interest rates and almost deflation, it would be convenient to store proceeds in cash—the only costs being the risk of theft, loss, fire, other physical degradation and police seizure.[70]

But data shows that cash is successful also in the legal economy. Despite the increasing use of alternative payment methods, such as credit cards, mobile payments or virtual currencies, banknotes still represent the preferred means of payment both in Europe and abroad, including the United States. This is particularly true for small-scale purchases, in certain sectors (e.g. food or retail), for certain age classes (very young or elderly people) and in certain areas—usually the poorest ones. However, it is also true of some of the seldom-arrested mega-rich who appear to enjoy 'flashing the cash': a problem for the luxury business if cash sales are restricted. In London and some other large cities, there is heavy demand for large amounts of cash from visiting or episodically domiciled Arabs, Russians, Kazakhs, and so on, which in theory can be awkward for salespeople when it exceeds the €15,000 cash reporting threshold.[71]

Implications for Criminals

What then would be the effect on money laundering if cash was legally restricted? And that on crime? This depends on actual and perceived enforcement levels. The impact would be heavier on 'petty' money laundering schemes, like those related to small-scale tax evasion which heavily relies on cash. Also affected would be traditional criminal organisations (including Italian mafias) which, according to wide evidence, seem to prefer to launder their money in cash-intensive businesses. A cash-less economy would make it harder to stay underground, despite some recent estimates arguing that abolishing banknotes would reduce the shadow economy only by 2–3%.[72] The impact of cash reduction on higher level ML schemes, such as those related to grand corruption, involving the use of complex corporate structures and off-shore jurisdictions, would be likely to be less significant—despite the fact these typologies also require, at some stage, some cashing out or cash smuggling.

There has been a trend in some Scandinavian countries towards a cash-less society, but this is a very small proportion of the international crime scene and even if it was to become a more general trend, it is implausible that, without cash, profit-driven crime will disappear. Displacement effects will occur at various levels. For example, the termination of 500 euro banknotes could lead criminals to adopt, for cash-smuggling or hoarding purposes, alternative high-value notes such as the 1,000 Swiss franc or the 200 euro bill. Or they may switch to smaller notes, just changing smuggling habits and techniques—which could become more costly because, for example, a higher number of couriers should be employed to transfer the same value, generating some social redistribution of the proceeds of crime. It cannot even be excluded that criminals decide to keep the 'old' 500 euro bills for their own illegal transactions (e.g. on the wholesale drug market) or as stores of value—at the end these banknotes will remain legal tender and they would keep their value, though use in the licit economy might generate even more suspicion than at present.[73]

Cash restriction would modify the nature of illegal markets, increasing barter, for example, exchanging drugs for firearms or other assets. And this could reshape criminal networks and partnerships. The trend towards virtual marketplaces, such as the dark-web, and virtual currencies, would accelerate. And companies could be used more frequently for 'laundering the product' and for providing a legitimate façade to (certain) illicit goods which could be then sold on legal markets.

Finally, as already noted by some authors, the reduction of cash could lead criminal groups, following new opportunities, to displace from traditional (and cash-intensive) criminal activities to cybercrimes, including 'old crimes in new bottles'.[74]

Implications for Policymakers

Considering its success in the legal economy, any cash restrictions would heavily affect not only criminals' but also consumers' behaviour. Due to a lack of good data, it would be difficult to assess the extent of this impact. Looking at consumer survey statistics, it can be hypothesised that the most affected categories would be those which cannot have ready access to alternative payment instruments—therefore the very young, the elderly and the people in poorest and less-developed areas, notwithstanding regulations which guarantee minimum access.

But the opposition in some EU countries against the proposal to introduce cash purchase limits suggests that cash-oriented interventions would somehow affect everybody's life—and personal freedom. Also when not handling the proceeds of drug trafficking or tax evasion, and even in the perimeter of a perfectly legitimate transaction, consumers would like to keep private what they buy or whom they pay. When paying, everybody has somebody to hide from—including targeted ads, customer profiling agencies and marketing crawlers. The anonymity of cash is still considered the best way to defend this freedom, especially if state and/or corporate personal data protection systems and rules are either inadequate or perceived to be so.

All these issues should be taken into account by policymakers before calling for the abolition or heavier restriction of cash for AML/CFT purposes. Not the least of these is that there would have to be some very good reasons to believe that these cash controls would have a greater impact than others, whose effectiveness in crime reduction have been heavily critiqued.[75] A set of reasonable and very specific measures could be the following:

(1) The discontinuation of 'unnecessarily' high-denomination notes: but are 200 euro banknotes really necessary? The de facto maximum note in the UK is £50.
(2) The reduction of cash purchase limits could make both purchasing drugs and laundering harder, but it seems odd that there is no *harmonisation* of these limits, especially in the European Union where they range from 1,000 euro to no upper limits at all. There is no evidence that there has been a displacement effect of ML/TF activities across countries—but unless the subsidiary principle is applied, current variations are merely an expression of historical preferences.
(3) A better enforcement of already existing instruments—for example, in the EU the AML obligations which apply to all traders in goods above the €10,000 cash payment threshold (Directive 849/2015, Art. 2).

(4) The introduction of incentives, for both consumers and merchants, to abandon cash in favour of alternative (and more traceable) payment instruments. For example, the rate of POS diffusion could much increase if POS fees and commissions paid by merchants were lowered—but this would mean banks and other financial intermediaries being ready to accept a significant reduction of their intermediation profits. More favourable conditions for buyers could help, like the introduction of discounts for those using non-cash instruments (while now instead *Barzahler-Rabatt* discounts favouring those who pay cash are more frequent).

(5) The shift to electronic payments should be accompanied by stricter rules on personal data protection, in order that consumers could keep their freedom and privacy also when using credit cards or other traceable payments.

None of these measures is easy to implement. Even the cut of high-denomination notes, if not adequately planned, could provoke unexpected negative consequences on the economy. On 8 November 2016, the Indian Government suddenly announced the withdrawal of 500 and 1,000 Rupee banknotes in an attempt to combat corruption, underground economy and terrorism. Fifty days were left for people to exchange the bills of this denomination in their possession in other banknotes. However, the measure resulted in a severe shortage of cash which had a significant short-term negative impact on GDP and consumption (without taking into account the problems related to the long queues outside banks and currency exchange agencies). Are government willing to pay such a price for combating crime and money laundering?

Implications for Researchers

A more realistic assessment of the future impact of a cash restriction on consumers and criminals would require a better understanding of contemporary cash habits. Too little is known about how, by whom, for what purpose is cash currently used in Europe and abroad. Surveys should be updated and expanded.[76] And alternative measurement methods—such as the tracking and tracing of banknote samples—should be explored.

Also the knowledge of what criminals do with cash could be improved. Money laundering research could much benefit from a better understanding of criminals' 'numismatic' preferences—what denominations and currencies they prefer, where do they exchange bills, how they store and transfer them. Most criminological studies addressing the cash-issue focus on drug trafficking: what about other offences, such as human smuggling which has received even less systematic attention? As regards the awareness of AML obligations by traders in goods (receiving cash-payments): what is their level of customer due diligence? And what do we know about their efforts in identifying 'suspicious behaviour' and reporting suspicious transactions? Cash is one of the oldest means of payment, but it is one of those about which our knowledge remains poorest.

Notes

1. Intended here to denote the amount of banknotes and coins in circulation: one of the two components, with bank sight deposits, of the narrow money supply (M1).
2. Europol, 'Why is Cash Still King? A Strategic Report on the Use of Cash by Criminal Groups as a Facilitator for Money Laundering' (2015) <www.europol.europa.eu/publications-documents/why-cash-still-king-strategic-report-use-of-cash-criminal-groups-facilitator-for-money-laundering> accessed 21 March 2017.
3. Obviously, there have been experiments in marking notes as part of under-cover operations, and following the £26.5 million robbery from the (Irish) Northern Bank, the bank went as far as changing the design of the Northern Irish notes to prevent them from helping the terrorist cause. See Darwin Templeton, 'The Provos Got So Much Cash From Northern Bank Heist They Could Not Handle It' *Belfast Telegraph* (Belfast, 15 December 2014) <www.belfasttelegraph.co.uk/news/northern-ireland/the-provos-got-so-much-cash-from-northern-bank-heist-they-could-not-handle-it-30833641.html> accessed 21 March 2017.
4. European Central Bank, 'The Use of Euro Banknotes. Results of Two Surveys Among Households and Firms' (2011) 82 <www.ecb.europa.eu/pub/pdf/other/art2_mb201104en_pp79-90en.pdf> accessed 21 March 2017.
5. Heike Mai, 'Cash, Freedom and Crime: Use and Impact of Cash in a World Going Digital' (2016) Deutsche Bank Research <www.dbresearch.com/PROD/DBR_INTERNET_EN-PROD/PROD0000000000427044/Cash,_freedom_and _crime%3 A_Use_and_impact_of_cash_in.pdf> accessed 21 March 2017; Alessia Cassetta, Alberto Di Filippo, and Valeria Roversi, *L'Utilizzo delle Banconote di Taglio Elevato Come Potenziale Strumento di Riciclaggio: Lo Studio del 2011 con una Nota di Aggiornamento* (Banca d'Italia Quaderni dell'Antiriciclaggio 2016).

6. Federal Reserve Bank of San Francisco, 'The State of Cash: Preliminary Findings from the 2015 Diary of Consumer Payment Choice' Fednotes (2016) 2 <www.frbsf.org/cash/publications/fed-notes/2016/november/state-of-cash-2015-diary-consumer-payment-choice> accessed 15 January 2017.
7. Cassetta, Di Filippo, and Roversi (n 5) 23.
8. European Central Bank (n 4). According to another survey carried out in Germany, this share can be even lower, around 5%. See Deutsche Bundesbank, 'Where Does the Cash in Your Wallet Come From?' (2010) <www.bundesbank.de/Redaktion/EN/Downloads/Publications/Studies/cash_management_2010_where_does_the_cash_in_your_wallet_come_from.html> accessed 9 January 2017.
9. European Central Bank, 'Consumer Cash Usage. A Cross-Country Comparison With Payment Diary Survey Data' (2014) ECB Working Paper Series, no 1685 <www.ecb.europa.eu/pub/pdf/scpwps/ecbwp1685.pdf> accessed 28 February 2017.
10. Federal Reserve Bank of San Francisco (n 6).
11. Guerino Ardizzi and others, 'Measuring the Underground Economy with the Currency Demand Approach: A Reinterpretation of the Methodology, With an Application to Italy' (2014) 60(4) Review of Income and Wealth 747; Michele Riccardi, Riccardo Milani, and Diana Camerini, 'Assessing the Risk of Money Laundering in Italy' in Ernesto Savona and Michele Riccardi (eds), *Assessing the Risk of Money Laundering in Europe: Final Report of Project IARM* (Transcrime-Università Cattolica Sacro Cuore 2017).
12. European Central Bank (n 9).
13. European Central Bank (n 4) 89.
14. Cassetta, Di Filippo, and Roversi (n 5). This might be viewed as an irrational reaction and/or fear of systemic bank failure.
15. Friedrich Schneider, Konrad Raczkowski, and Bogdan Mróz, 'Shadow Economy and Tax Evasion in the EU' (2015) 18(1) Journal of Money Laundering Control 34.
16. Riccardi, Milani, and Camerini (n 11).
17. Richard Wright and others, 'Less Cash, Less Crime: Evidence from the Electronic Benefit Transfer Program' (2014) IZA Discussion Paper Series <http://ftp.iza.org/dp8402.pdf> accessed 20 January 2017. We note that it reduces the expected reward per mugging, and so on.
18. Europol (n 2) 11.
19. Ibid.; Melvin Soudijn and Peter Reuter, 'Cash and Carry: The High Cost of Currency Smuggling in the Drug Trade' (2016) 66(3) Crime, Law and Social Change 271.
20. Douglas Farah, 'Money Laundering and Bulk Cash Smuggling: Challenges for the Merida Initiative' (2011) 158 <www.wilsoncenter.org/publication/money-laundering-and-bulk-cash-smuggling-challenges-for-the-us-mexico-border> accessed 28 February 2017.

21. Soudijn and Reuter (n 19); Petrus C van Duyne and Michael Levi, *Drugs and Money: Managing the Drug Trade and Crime-Money in Europe* (Routledge 2005).

22. Farah (n 20) 155.

23. UNODC, *World Drug Report 2016* (United Nations 2016); Stijn Hoorens and David Décary Hétu, 'Dark Web Likely Isn't Fuelling International Drug Sales' *The RAND Blog* <www.rand.org/blog/2016/09/dark-web-likely-isnt-fuelling-international-drug-sales.html> accessed 21 March 2017. For discussion of ML and virtual currencies, see Chap. 8 (Chambers-Jones), and for the regulation of virtual currencies see Chap. 9 (Egan) in this collection.

24. Maurizio Lisciandra, 'Proceeds From Extortions: The Case of Italian Organised Crime Groups' (2014) 15 Global Crime 93; Patricio Rodrigo Estevez-Soto, 'Factors Associated With Extortion Compliance in Mexico: Who Pays and Why?' American Society of Criminology Conference (New Orleans, November 2016).

25. European Central Bank (n 4) 89.

26. For example UNODC, *Corruption in the Western Balkans* (United Nations 2011); Giang Ly Isenring, Giulia Mugellini, and Martin Killias, 'Assessing the Areas of Vulnerability for Swiss Firms in International Business Activities: The Swiss International Corruption Survey' (Universität St. Gallen and KRC 2016).

27. In the European Union, threshold is set at 10,000 euro <http://ec.europa.eu/taxation_customs/individuals/cash-controls_en> accessed 28 February 2017; as regards the United States, threshold is set at US$10,000 <www.ice.gov/bulk-cash-smuggling-center/faq> accessed 28 February 2017. See below for more details.

28. Soudijn and Reuter (n 19) 3.

29. Financial Acion Task Force, *Money Laundering Through the Physical Transportation of Cash* (2015) 39.

30. *Regalado Cuellar v United States* 553 US 550 (2008). See also David Stout, 'Court Rules on Money Laundering' *The New York Times* (Washington, 3 June 2008) <www.nytimes.com/2008/06/03/washington/02cnd-scotus.html> accessed 21 March 2017.

31. 18 USC s 1956.

32. Cited in Farah (n 20) 45.

33. Ibid. 160.

34. Soudijn and Reuter (n 19).

35. FATF (n 29) 56.

36. Ibid. 54.

37. Ibid. 61.

38. Farah (n 20) 158.

39. Soudijn and Reuter (n 19).

40. Ibid. 9.

41. For a review on the issue of criminal infiltration/investment in legal businesses see Ernesto Savona, Michele Riccardi and Giulia Berlusconi, *Organised Crime in European Businesses* (Routledge 2016); Michael Levi, 'Money for Crime and Money from Crime: Financing Crime and Laundering Crime Proceeds' (2015) 21(2) European Journal on Criminal Policy and Research 275.

42. Riccardi, Milani, and Camerini (n 11).

43. Nicholas Gilmour and Nick Ridley, 'Everyday Vulnerabilities. Money Laundering Through Cash Intensive Businesses' (2015) 18(3) Journal of Money Laundering Control 293; Transcrime, *Gli Investimenti delle Mafie* (Transcrime—Università degli Studi di Trento 2013) <www.transcrime.it/pub-blicazioni/progetto-pon-sicurezza-2007-2013/> accessed 28 February 2017.

44. Michele Riccardi, Cristina Soriani, and Valentina Giampietri, 'Mafia Infiltration in Legitimate Companies in Italy' in Ernesto Savona, Michele Riccardi, and Giulia Berlusconi (eds), *Organised Crime in European Businesses* (Routledge 2016) 119; Michele Riccardi, 'When Criminals Invest in Businesses: Are We Looking in the Right Direction? An Exploratory Analysis of Companies Controlled by Mafias' in Stefano Caneppele and Francesco Calderoni (eds), *Organised Crime, Corruption and Crime Prevention* (Springer 2014).

45. Riccardi, Milani, and Camerini (n 11): the ML risk is estimated by author combining a variety of risk factors, all operationalised into proxies, such as connections with offshore jurisdictions, opacity of business structure, level of organised crime infiltration and of tax evasion and, indeed, cash intensity.

46. See for a review Savona, Riccardi, and Berlusconi (n 44) and Levi (n 41).

47. Joras Ferwerda and Edward Kleemans, 'Assessing the Risk of Money Laundering in the Netherlands' in Ernesto Savona and Michele Riccardi (eds), *Assessing the Risk of Money Laundering in Europe: Final Report of Project IARM* (Transcrime-Università Cattolica Sacro Cuore 2017).

48. See <www.government.nl/latest/news/2011/02/21/public-administration-act-bibob-will-be-extended-to-intensify-the-fight-against-organized-crime> accessed 28 February 2017.

49. BVfK, 'Position Paper to the German Ministry of Finance' (2016) <www.bvfk.de/wp-content/uploads/2016/02/Positionspapier-des-BVfK-zur-Bargeldobergrenze-2016-02-151.pdf> accessed 21 March 2017. Unfortunately no details are available on how this figure—which is very surprising—is calculated. However, it likely applies to the segment of used or re-imported cars sold from businesses to consumers by multi-brand car dealers.

50. European Consumer Centre, 'Cash Payment Limitations' (2017) <www.evz.de/en/consumer-topics/buying-goods-and-services/shopping-in-the-eu/cash-payment-limitations/> accessed 28 February 2017.

51. UK Government, 'Guidance—Money Laundering Regulations: High Value Dealer Registration' (2013) <www.gov.uk/guidance/money-laundering-regu-lations-high-value-dealer-registration> accessed 28 February 2017.

52. See <http://www.irs.gov/businesses/small-businesses-self-employed/irs-form-8300-reference-guide#required> accessed 28 February 2017; <www.irs.gov/pub/irs-pdf/f8300.pdf> accessed 28 February 2017.

53. Interview to France's Finance Minister Michel Sapin, cited in Ingrid Melander, 'France Steps Up Monitoring of Cash Payments to Fight 'Low-Cost Terrorism'' *Reuters* (18 March 2015) <www.reuters.com/article/us-france-security-financing-idUSKBN0ME14720150318> accessed 28 February 2017.

54. Philip Oltermann, 'German Plan to Impose Limit on Cash Transactions Met with Fierce Resistance' *The Guardian* (London, 8 February 2016); BVfK (n 49).

55. "Bargeld ist die Möglichkeit zur Anonymität bei Alltagsgeschäften und diese Freiheit muss in einem Rechtsstaat verteidigt warden" from a Tweet on 5 February 2016 by Konstantin Von Notz, MP of the German Bundestag for the green party.

56. Financial Action Task Force, 'International Standards on Combating Money Laundering and the Financing of Terrorism & Proliferation: The FATF Recommendations (2012)' <www.fatf-gafi.org/media/fatf/documents/recommendations/pdfs/FATF_Recommendations.pdf> accessed 21 March 2017.

57. See European Commission, 'What Are the Rules?' <http://ec.europa.eu/taxation_customs/individuals/cash-controls/what-are-rules_en> accessed 28 February 2017.

58. European Consumer Centre (n 50).

59. See US Immigration and Customs Enforcement, 'FAQ: Bulk Cash Smuggling' <www.ice.gov/bulk-cash-smuggling-center/faq> accessed 28 February 2017.

60. To be noted that when the 500 euro bill was issued, only two EU member states had higher denominations in their own currencies: Germany (with the 500 Deutsche Mark bill) and Latvia.

61. European Central Bank, 'ECB Ends Production and Issuance of €500 Banknote' *ECB Press Releases* (4 May 2016) <www.ecb.europa.eu/press/pr/date/2016/html/pr160504.en.html> accessed 28 February 2017.

62. Among them, the already mentioned Cassetta, Di Filippo, and Roversi (n 5); Europol (n 2); Soudijn and Reuter (n 19); Farah (n 20); FATF (n 29).

63. Dominic Casciani, 'Organised Crime Fears Cause Ban on 500 Euro Sales' *BBC News* (London, 13 May 2010) <http://news.bbc.co.uk/1/hi/uk/8678886.stm> accessed 21 March 2017. Mentioned also in Cassetta, Di Filippo, and Roversi (n 5).

64. These percentages refer to the number of movable assets (including cash seizures) out of the total number of confiscated goods. Obviously in terms of value these figures may be lower, as a single property could be worth several millions euro. But data on assets' values in most countries are lacking or are questionable. Depending on the country, they refer to different stages of the asset recovery process, since there are variations in asset recovery processes and

predicate offences. For more details, see Priscilla Standridge and Michele Riccardi, 'A Comparative Analysis Among the Seven OCP Countries' in Ernesto Savona and Michele Riccardi (eds), *From Illegal Markets to Legitimate Businesses: The Portfolio of Organised Crime in Europe. Final Report of Project OCP* (Transcrime—Università degli Studi di Trento 2015) 249.

65. Richard Dubourg and Stephen Prichard (eds), 'Organised Crime: Revenues, Economic and Social Costs, and Criminal Assets Available for Seizure' (2008) 74   <www.gov.uk/government/uploads/system/uploads/attachment_data/file/99094/9886.pdf> accessed 28 February 2017; David Wall and Yulia Chistyakova, 'United Kingdom' in Ernesto Savona and Michele Riccardi (eds), *From Illegal Markets to Legitimate Businesses: The Portfolio of Organised Crime in Europe. Final Report of Project OCP* (Transcrime—Università degli Studi di Trento 2015) 282.

66. Farah (n 20).

67. Standridge and Riccardi (n 64).

68. For example in Italy cash is transferred to FUG—Fondo Unico Giustizia, which 50% is held as bank deposit, and the other 50% is used for social purposes or to finance LEAs activities. In the UK, money recovered from criminals' assets is shared among different public authorities as part of the 'Asset Recovery Incentivisation Scheme'. For a review of management practices of seized cash in Europe see EU ARO (Asset Recovery Office) Platform Subgroup on Asset Management, 'Draft Internal Report' (2015). For further discussion, see Chap. 29 (Vettori) in this collection.

69. On this debate see the recent article 'Police in Britain Want to Keep More of the Loot They Confiscate' *The Economist* (London, 19 January 2017) <www.economist.com/news/britain/21715069-others-worry-it-would-tempt-them-pursue-rich-crooks-not-harmful-ones-police-britain> accessed 21 March 2017.

70. According to Roberto Escobar, Pablo's brother, the Medellin Cartel was losing about 10% of the generated cash each year due to physical degradation. See Roberto Escobar and David Fisher, *The Accountant's Story* (Grand Central Publishing 2009) 5.

71. Interviews with second author.

72. Heike Mai (n 5).

73. Bankers inform the second author that unless there is a good business reason, they regard the deposit of €500 notes with considerable suspicion and would be inclined to make a SAR.

74. Michael Levi 'Assessing the Trends, Scale and Nature of Economic Cybercrimes' (2017) 67(1) Crime, Law and Social Change 3.

75. Terrence Halliday, Michael Levi, and Peter Reuter, 'Global Surveillance of Dirty Money: Assessing Assessments of Regimes To Control Money-

Laundering and Combat the Financing of Terrorism' (2014) <www.lexglobal. org/files/Report_Global%20Surveillance%20of%20Dirty%20Money%20 1.30.2014.pdf> accessed 28 February 2017.

76. The last survey at EU level is dated 2011 (but on 2008 data). A 2014 ECB report (n 9) compared payment diary surveys of seven countries (Canada, Australia, US, Austria, France, Germany and the Netherlands) but based on data from 2009 to 2012. Cash payment surveys in Eastern European countries are almost absent.

Michele Riccardi [MSc Accounting & Financial Economics, University of Essex (UK) and MA International Relations, Università Cattolica Sacro Cuore (Italy)] is senior researcher at Transcrime and Adjunct Professor of Business Economics at the Università Cattolica in Milan. His research focuses on organised crime, financial crime, money laundering, management of confiscated assets and manipulation of corporate information. He has contributed to several international projects, including project IARM (http://www.transcrime.it/iarm), OCP (http://www.transcrime.it/ocportfolio), EBOCS (http://www.ebocs.eu) and BOWNET. He is an expert member of the Asset Recovery Offices Platform of the European Commission and of the EU CEPOL money laundering working group. He has been involved by the Italian Financial Security Committee in the money laundering/terrorist financing national risk assessment in Italy, in the EU Supranational Risk Assessment and for the latest FATF mutual evaluation of Italy.

Michael Levi has been Professor of Criminology at Cardiff University since 1991. He has been conducting international research on the control of white-collar and organised crime, corruption and money laundering/financing of terrorism since 1972. He is an Associate Fellow of RUSI and a Senior Fellow at RAND Europe. He advises Europol on the Serious and Organised Crime Threat Assessment and on the internet-enabled Organised Crime Threat Assessment, and other public positions include membership of the European Commission's Group of Experts on Corruption. In 2013, he was given the Distinguished Scholar Award by the International Association for the Study of Organised Crime, and in 2014 he was awarded the Sellin-Glueck prize for international and comparative criminology by the American Society of Criminology.

8

Money Laundering in a Virtual World

Clare Chambers-Jones

Introduction

Virtual currencies are a key aspect of anti-money laundering (AML) regulation. This chapter investigates the UK's approach to virtual worlds and their virtual currencies, determining whether this currency system is included in national and international money laundering definitions and regulations. Virtual worlds can be a safe haven for criminal activity, such as money laundering, and the lack of sufficient regulation in the UK is one of the pivotal points currently being discussed at regulatory and governmental levels. The chapter is divided into several parts. First, it looks at virtual worlds, their definitions and identifies how virtual currencies are considered to be a money laundering risk. The chapter moves on to provide evidence that money laundering does take place within virtual worlds and, as such, these should be included in the virtual currency definition and regulations. The chapter then considers the approaches taken to prevent virtual currency money laundering and explores the UK's approach to money laundering regulations. The chapter further considers approaches of other countries compared to the UK, and concludes with an analysis and reflection of the UK's approach to regulating virtual worlds and money laundering.

C. Chambers-Jones
University of the West of England (UWE), Bristol, UK

© The Author(s) 2018
C. King et al. (eds.), *The Palgrave Handbook of Criminal and Terrorism Financing Law*,
https://doi.org/10.1007/978-3-319-64498-1_8

Virtual Worlds

Virtual worlds and their economies are not the same as virtual currencies, like Bitcoins, which are cryptocurrencies, but they are both forms of virtual currency.[1] Virtual worlds are computer-based platforms where environments are created and people simulate real or fantasy lives. Within these virtual worlds, economies, societies and personal relationships develop. Therefore, virtual worlds are a type of microcosm of life that is lived in digital pixels and spans a multitude of different jurisdictions. Virtual worlds in this context are discussed as a possible location for money laundering to take place. This is not the same as using digital or cryptocurrencies as a means of money laundering because this takes place in the real world, even if the currency is a virtual currency. The process of the two is different. One uses the virtual environment as a location of criminal activity, whereas virtual currency money laundering uses the internet or other electronic payment systems to disguise or hide the proceeds of crime. However, the two are connected and should be considered as akin to each other.

A useful definition of virtual currencies comes from the European Banking Authority (EBA) which states that virtual currencies are 'defined as a digital representation of value that is neither issued by a central bank or a public authority nor necessarily attached to a Fiat Currency, but is used by natural or legal persons as a means of exchange and can be transferred, stored or traded electronically'.[2] Therefore, virtual currencies that are used within virtual worlds—such as Linden Dollars in Second Life—are considered to be the same as other digital currencies such as Bitcoins. Second Life is a 3D immersive platform-based environment game/world which has developed a culture and economy of its own. Its economy is based on the in world currency, the Linden Dollar, named after Linden Labs, the technical development company which owns the platform. This form of virtual world is popular amongst gamers but also academics and health care professionals who can use the environment as a base for learning and education. It can also be used by criminals as a means of conducting illegal activity.[3] A virtual world according to Castronova is a computer programme with three defining features: interactivity, physicality and persistence.[4] Bell defines virtual worlds as 'a spatially based depiction of a persistent virtual environment, which can be experienced by numerous participants at once who are represented within the space by avatars'.[5]

This chapter focuses on these virtual world currencies and how the existing UK AML laws do not apply to them. Policymakers in the UK are only just beginning to discuss and consult on the necessary guidelines for safeguarding virtual currencies such as Bitcoins, but it is unclear as to how these regulations apply to virtual worlds such as Second Life, World of Warcraft or to Facebook credits, which all fall under the EBA definition of virtual currencies. These forms of virtual currencies are different from where money is exchanged over the internet or mobile phone such as PayPal due to the type of currency which is used. PayPal uses fiat currency whereas virtual currencies need to be exchanged into fiat currency before they can be used in the real world.

Before defining virtual money laundering, it is prudent to determine what cybercrime is, as virtual money laundering falls under this umbrella term and has seen more legislative provisions.[6] Cybercrime 'is one of the fastest growing areas of crime, as more and more criminals exploit the speech, convenience and anonymity that modern technologies offer in order to commit a diverse range of crimes'.[7] One of the earliest detected virtual crimes was that of the virtual rape,[8] which took place in the LambdaMOO Multi-User Dungeon (MUD).[9] The rapist, known as Mr Bungle, described the rape of another MUD user. However, his actions were insufficient for a successful prosecution. There is an academic bifurcation as to whether Mr Bungle's actions amounted to an actual rape capable of prosecution or whether it was insufficient because it lacked real world consequences. Brenner referred to the rape as a 'true virtual crime',[10] whereas Dibble said that he 'was fascinated by the concept of a virtual rape, but I was even more so by the notion that anyone could take it altogether seriously'.[11]

Brenner explored what would enable a virtual crime to be successfully prosecuted, and she determined that the virtual crime would need to have real world elements.[12] Lessig opined that there could be a valuable link between actual rape and the LambdaMOO rape in cyberspace,[13] but this opinion was criticised by Kerr who stated that the link 'is tenuous at best. It is a link between a brutal rape and a fictional story of a brutal rape. Surely the difference is more striking than any similarity'.[14] Although this argument can be considered credible, if there are real world effects stemming from in world action and crime then it is a real world crime and should be met with the same real world consequences. In this sense, virtual money laundering is a crime which takes place in the virtual world but has a true and real effect on the real world whenever dirty money is laundered via the virtual world environment.

Given the interest from law enforcement agencies as to whether crimes committed on the internet are real or not, there is a growing body of literature on the subject. Interpol, acting to combat virtual financial crime, states that, 'the global nature of the Internet allows criminals to commit almost any illegal activity anywhere in the world, which makes it essential for all countries to adopt their domestic offline controls to cover crimes committed in cyber-space'.[15] Therefore, Interpol is contending that to combat this new wave of criminal activity domestic governments should tailor their domestic real world laws to fit the crimes that are being carried out in cyberspace. To be able to commit virtual world money laundering, real money must pass into the virtual world as virtual money and then be able to be extracted once laundered. Interpol has stated that virtual money is 'money value represented by a claim on the issuers which is stored on an electronic device and accepted as a means of payment by others persons other than the issuer'.[16] This definition allows virtual money to be treated as real money for money laundering purposes in law because the money can be used as fiat currency.

There are two types of virtual money—identified virtual money and anonymous virtual money.[17] Identified virtual money can be identified as belonging to someone and is linked to a withdrawal from a banking institution. In other words, it is traceable. Anonymous virtual money (or what is known as virtual cash) is untraceable. Once it is withdrawn, it leaves no discernible trace. There are plentiful criminal activities which can then take place with this money. For example, Interpol states that the main areas are: unauthorised creation, transfer or redemption of virtual money; criminal access to computer systems being used to change illicitly the attribution of funds within the system; criminal attacks on virtual money systems leading to a loss of virtual money value or loss of function on the virtual money system; criminal misuse of virtual money systems for financial crimes or as a tool to subvert or misuse other financial systems; and criminals may use virtual money to reduce the likelihood of capture, for example, the cases of blackmail, kidnapping or extortion, where in the past collection of money has been problematic for perpetrators. This is particularly significant for anonymous virtual money.[18]

The Fraud Advisory Panel describe virtual money laundering as where '[A] fraudster converts the proceeds of illegal activities into online currency, which is then used to purchase goods and/or services from you before being exchanged into real world currency'.[19]

There are three traditional stages of laundering money: placing, layering and integration.[20] The first stage, placing, is to put the money (which is normally cash) into a place such as a bank. In the case of virtual money laundering, this could be a PayPal account as well. The second stage, layering, is to ensure that the money does not raise suspicions. The criminal needs to carry out as many complicated and intricate transactions with the money so that any traces are hard to follow. The final stage, integration, is where the criminal combines the so-called dirty money with legitimate money, making the whole appearance of the money to be clean. From this very brief description, it is clear how virtual worlds, the virtual economy and virtual money transfers lend themselves to the money laundering process. The dirty money can enter the virtual world through a pre-paid card, such as PayPal, where little identification is required. The money can be used to buy in world goods, through numerous accounts and then the criminal can sell these goods in world. The money from these investments in the virtual world can then be withdrawn from the world via an automated teller machine (ATM) or money account and the money appears to be from a legitimate source. It is therefore laundered.[21] In 2006, the Financial Action Task Force (FATF) highlighted concerns about the new method of electronic monetary transfers with a view to this being a new financial crime.[22] However, since this report by the FATF, little has been put in place to provide deterrence, nor any regulations to ensure successful prosecutions within the UK.

Virtual Currencies and Money Laundering

To be able to launder money through the internet, there needs to be a method by which to do so. Money is therefore converted into virtual money, used within a virtual game, which has now converted the real money into a virtual in world currency, and so the means by which a criminal can launder the proceeds of crime is complete. There are various methods of using electronic money to facilitate money laundering; these are through an electronic purse, mobile payments, internet payment services and digital precious metals. An electronic purse is a pre-paid card, which looks like a credit or debit card. There is an electronic chip within the card which stores data as to how much money has been loaded onto the card. Money can be put on these cards at various tellers and shop stores. The cards can then be used to pay for goods and services, where accepted, which is to another electronic purse, but they leave no transaction record. Recently the major credit card companies are also providing these a means of new payment methods.[23]

The second method of payment is through mobile and wireless telecommunications. These mobile payments mostly require financial institutions as part of the transaction. However, this can be avoided should the mobile payment go through a broker account. The broker accounts are normally prepaid with cash and operate in the same way as an electronic purse. This will then lend itself open for money laundering because of the lack of verification of identification and lack of traceability. The third method is through internet payment, which 'rely on an associated bank account and use the internet as a means of moving funds to and from the associated bank account or they operate entirely on the Internet and are indirectly associated with a bank account'.[24] When the payments are not associated with a bank account then there is again a lack of identification and traceability required for the process to occur. Furthermore, most providers will accept cash and may not want to participate in money laundering regulations because of the red tape that will be required to be completed before the completion of a transaction.

The final method is through digital precious metals whereby digital precious metal brokers allow customers to purchase digital precious metal on the world commodity market at market prices. By using a broker, there is again another level of anonymity and lack of traceability for the transaction. As Desguin states, 'the basis for using digital precious metals is to make online transactions possible without regard for underlying currencies or access to foreign exchange'.[25] The result is to enable the laundering of the proceeds of crime.

Why is virtual money an effective mechanism to launder the proceeds of crime? One of the main reasons advocated is that 'digital currencies provide an ideal money laundering instrument because they facilitate international payments without the transmittal services of traditional financial institutions'.[26] Many 'digital currencies are privately owned online payment systems that allow international payments'.[27] Furthermore, an additional feature of virtual world money is where digital currency is used to buy real world metals, which can then be traded. The people that buy the metals with digital cash are allegedly linked to the real commodities stock market. These digital currencies are as bespoke as any real world currency. As the US Department of Justice National Drug Intelligence Centre states 'each digital currency functions as a transnational currency however none are recognised as currencies by the US government'.[28]

Another problem of digital currencies is anonymity, which is 'a heavily marketed characteristic of the digital currency industry'.[29] This allows the cybercriminal an extra layer of protection when laundering money. Some issuers of digital currency do require some form of identification, but because this is facilitated via the Internet, the documents can be scanned or e-mailed or faxed, allowing for easy doctoring. The means of putting real money into digital money is plentiful and each allows the criminal a chance of an easy method of laundering. For example, the money launderer can deposit cash to the issuers exchange bank account, thus the money is not traceable. Secondly, exchanges also accept wire transfers or postal money orders also allowing another layer of difficulty in determining the source of the original money.

Thirdly, money can be transferred via electronic money orders, cheques and online banking transfers, all of which again are hard to determine the true source of the money. Fourthly, money can be transferred into the exchanges via pre-paid cards, and money can be withdrawn.[30]

The use of advanced technology allows the cybercriminal further anonymity and networking ability.[31] The use of Internet Protocol (IP) addresses identifies the user to their computer and therefore their actions allow identification of cyber criminals. However, there are various ways around this identification such as using mobile devices including mobile phones that are internet enabled; hijacking wireless networks, encrypted chat rooms and using public internet access points. It is reported that 'because digital currency is increasingly misused to purchase drugs and other illicit materials that are sold online, the proceeds of that activity are essentially pre-laundered'.[32] Additionally, some digital exchanges allow for transactions to be unlimited in value, which allow drug trafficking to occur in ready abundance.[33] The criminals can launder larger amounts, with total anonymity using fewer transactions.[34] The US government acknowledges that there are regulatory loopholes which must be closed in relation to digital currencies and money laundering.[35] However, regulatory action from one nation is currently insufficient. There must be a joined up multi-national regulatory position that is devised to prevent further cyber financial crimes and money laundering.

One other major problem is the confusion of terms as indicated at the start of the chapter. Virtual money and digital money are not the same thing, but governments use the terms interchangeably and as such cause confusion over the legal status of the crime. Digital currencies such as Bitcoins are being encompassed into AML strategies, whereas virtual worlds are not being discussed as an environment where money laundering can take place, at least outside the academic arena.[36] This is because of a lack of detailed knowledge of virtual worlds and also digital currencies.

There are several major problems associated with regulating virtual money laundering: the issues of anonymity of transactions and digital and real world account details through online transactions; the lack of jurisdiction surrounding these transactions and how they interact with the real world; that there is a trading feature associated with the real world, namely that of digital cash, which too interacts with the real world; and the issue of payment methods from the real world to the virtual world causes a link and relationship between the two worlds. These four issues link the virtual to the real, and vice versa, allowing the continuum of the real into the virtual which will be discussed in detail now.

Analysis of Money Laundering Cases in the Virtual World

Many virtual worlds such as Second Life have their own economy. They have their own monetary exchanges, and real world money can be inputted into the virtual world and used to buy commodities such as clothes, building and experiences. Therefore, these virtual worlds can be used by criminals as an environment in which to commit virtual financial crimes, including money laundering. The next section provides a review of several cases where virtual money laundering has occurred. The section does not cover digital cryptocurrencies where money laundering has taken place, for example Liberty Reserve, as this is outside the scope of this chapter.

Gold Farming

Gold farming is a form of online employment which is popular in China and other Asian countries as the fastest form of new occupation. Heeks purports that 'it employs hundreds of people and earns hundreds of millions of dollars annually'.[37] Gold farming is said to be the production of virtual goods and services for players of online games, and it is this production and selling of goods which can be open to abuse by money launderers and financial criminals. Gold farmers are usually employed as part of a group and controlled by a conglomerate of people. The gold farmers make hundreds and thousands of different virtual goods and services which are then sold within the online game. The selling of these goods produces an income of online currency. With many online worlds now having their own currency (e.g. Linden Dollars in Second Life) and currency exchanges, money can then be exchanged for real world money. Gold farming is now such a large enterprise, it has been determined as its own economic sub-sector. However, there has been little academic research into the phenomenon and very little legislative discussion.

Gold farming can be traced back to 1997 and the introduction of 'real money trading' (RMT) where it can be seen that the first trades for real money were undertaken for goods and services within the virtual worlds. RMT was something of a northern hemisphere phenomenon and did not really penetrate China and Asia until 2001/2, when it has been suggested that US traders saw the opportunity to outsource trading to lower income venues such as Mexico and Asia. Gold farmers make money by sitting and playing online games, making and selling online goods and services, and this is done in three ways. First, they sell in game currency. This is very much the same as the real world currency exchange where it is possible to buy and sell virtual money at different rates and if done correctly can result in profits on the exchanges. Secondly, gold farming can be what is known as 'power levelling', which is where the gold farming firm is given the user name and password of the player who wants to achieve a certain level in the game but does not want to do it themselves. Money is then paid to the gold farmer who plays as the user and attains an agreed level or status within the game. The third way is by selling in game items for virtual money. The gold farmer buys or creates goods and services which are then sold for a profit in game. The money is then exchanged for real world money.

Within the above three scenarios, there is the obvious potential to launder money through the gold farming mechanisms. For example, the gold farming firm which employs these outsourced lower paid employees could be using criminal money to fund the gold farming activities. Once the money has gone through the virtual game and been exchanged back into the real world through a bank or PayPal then it appears to be legitimate. There is little control and monitoring over gold farming, though South Korea has in theory[38] banned virtual currency trading.[39] Conversely, it is reported that the Chinese government has invested heavily in gold farming as it appears to be the new trend of online employment enabling more people to earn a living, albeit in modest proportions.[40] Gold farming can benefit many in society where employment is hard to come by; gold farming however can also, as iterated above, be exploited by fraudsters and criminals. There is little that can be done in terms of a response. For example, if there is fraudulent or criminal activity, the activities can be reported to the game developers. In some cases, where gold farmers are found to be making money, they can be downgraded to lesser roles within the game, this is called nerfing. Accounts can be banned; the game developers can patch the hole in the game which allows this activity. In more serious cases, the IP address of the gold farmer can be banned and blocked. Similarly, channels used for marketing and sales can be blocked. Finally, legal action can be taken against gold farmers if sufficient evidence can be found and jurisdiction established.[41]

Therefore, gold farming is not a legal activity, nor one which is condoned within the gaming industry, and it contravenes the terms and conditions which the massively multi-player online role-playing game (MMORPG) developers have set out. The users must sign and agree to End User Licence Agreements (EULA) and also the Terms of Service (TOS) and Terms of User (TOU). These agreements typically set out the prohibition of conducting activities such as gold farming or those similar to gold farming. Governments are divided in their attitudes to the legality of gold farming. The Chinese government has clearly defended the rights of the gold farmers to make money and to earn a living in employment, yet the USA is strongly against the use of gold farming specifically because it opens up yet another avenue for money laundering and financial crime.

Virtual Money Inc.

In 2008, the owner of Virtual Money Inc. was indicted, convicted and sentenced to 45 months in prison for drug trafficking and money laundering.[42] Robert Hodgins is the owner and chief executive officer (CEO) of the virtual pre-paid cards[43] which have come under scrutiny in the USA over the lack of regulation surrounding the fledgling industry. Hodgins is currently on the run from the police,[44] and the case remains open. However, he is said to have laundered drug money through Virtual Money Inc. on pre-paid cards from Colombia. In 2010, federal prosecutors announced five convictions of drug-related money laundering in relation to the Virtual Money Inc. case, known as VM. VM is said to have been part of the AdSurfDaily and other auto surf companies. One of those convicted, Juan Merlano Salazar, of Medellin, Colombia, pleaded guilty in US District Court in Connecticut to 11 counts of money laundering and one count of conspiracy to commit money laundering. He is facing a 240-year prison sentence and a $6 million maximum fine.

Attorney Turned Launderer

Ken Rijock is an attorney turned launderer but who now works with law enforcement agencies in advising policy on catching virtual money launderers. He described virtual money laundering as 'the perfect crime'.[45] He cautioned that, 'there is no way law enforcement can even enforce the laws, because they don't apply'.[46] One of the main reasons he believed that virtual money laundering is a crime of the future is because of the ease of laundering the money without detection or repercussions. He gave an example as to how virtual money laundering works:

> A drug dealer using fake IDs opens numerous virtual bank accounts through online games. He deposits money into those virtual accounts through ATMs. The criminal's online persona buys, say, virtual real estate from a co-conspirator— or even from one of his other accounts—and transfers payment to the seller's virtual account. The seller can then convert the virtual currency into real money through a virtual money exchange and withdraw it from an ATM or a bank.[47]

Rijock further stated that it is impossible to police and counter the criminal act because there is a total lack of clarity over the legal position of virtual worlds. Greg Short, director of Web presence for San Diego, California-based Sony Online entertainment, agreed: 'The legal system doesn't extend here, there really aren't any laws that govern what happens in them.'[48]

The above examples of virtual money laundering cases demonstrate that the crimes are in fact real and have impact in the real world. They also show how poorly existing legislation works with these virtual crimes, and how complex it is for law enforcement agencies to manage them. International cooperation and more joined up bespoke legislation is needed to combat this developing crime.

Legal Perspective

The main regulatory body for financial services in the UK is the Financial Conduct Authority (FCA).[49] Their *Handbook* for regulatory and compliance guidance provides information for financial institutions on proactive AML procedures. This falls under the Systems and Controls[50] part of the *Handbook*, in particular in section 6.3.[51] Virtual currencies are not yet covered by the FCA guidance and compliance, and, as such, the UK AML framework also does not apply to virtual currencies. In comparison to other countries, the UK is in a state of flux as to how to regulate virtual currencies. In contrast, the USA is starting to adopt various regulations which are aimed at preventing money laundering. These are based around monetary exchanges, know your customer provisions and taxation rules.

The FCA published information on virtual currencies in its AML report 2013/14.[52] The report stated that presently virtual currencies are not regulated by the UK or European Union (EU),[53] but that the FCA and government will monitor the situation closely due to high-profile cases such as Liberty Reserve where virtual currencies had been used as a means of money laundering.[54] Once again virtual currencies are only seen by governments in terms of cryptocurrencies rather than encompassing all virtual currencies—such as Linden Dollars or other virtual world currencies—where money laundering has taken place over a number of years. The FCA report highlighted that the EBA and the FATF had published reports providing some guidance in terms of definitions and potential money laundering and terrorist financing risks, as well as a risk-based guidance approach for firms.[55]

The FATF has acknowledged that virtual currencies such as Bitcoins are an important emergent payment system as well as posing a money laundering and terrorist financing threat to the world.[56] The purpose of the 2014 FATF report was to provide a common definition from which legislators and regulators can work to combat money laundering and terrorist financing risks. The definition of virtual currencies proposed by the FATF ignored the currencies used by virtual worlds and concentrated on whether it is a medium of exchange, a unit of account and a store of value.[57] The EBA, however, does encompass virtual worlds as coming under the definition of virtual currencies.[58]

The FSA has noted some potential risks of virtual currencies, namely the anonymity issue of virtual currencies where transactions take place over the internet where little AML controls can take place, such as know your customer due diligence.[59] Further potential issues relate to the jurisdictional reach of transactions involving complex infrastructures which make it very difficult for AML and terrorist financing compliance and supervision.[60] Additionally the FATF report notes that the rapidly changing nature of decentralised currencies makes it very difficult for regulation to keep pace with the technology and infrastructure.[61]

The FATF reported in 2015 that only convertible virtual currencies—ones which can be converted into real world currencies—pose a money laundering threat.[62] This definition thereby excludes virtual world currencies which cannot be exchanged from the virtual world to the real world. However, it does encompass some virtual world currencies such as Linden Dollars.

The EBA's report in 2014 provides the most comprehensive and inclusive definitions and risks associated with virtual currencies. This is because it does not exclude virtual world currencies and also provides a list of over 70 potential risks that the currencies exhibit.[63] The EBA directly comments on the money laundering and terrorist financing risks posed by virtual currencies.[64] The report notes that, as virtual currencies do not require personal identification and take place peer-to-peer, the risk is high that money laundering could occur. They also note that, due to the lack of a third-party intermediary, there are no reporting mechanisms available. The report also notes that due to the transactions being based online, there are jurisdictional issues related to the lack of borders within the internet. As such the risk that money launderers and terrorists could use these currencies as a means of financing criminal activity is high.[65]

The potential risks have been clearly outlined and countries are working towards applying AML and counter-terrorist financing regulations to virtual currencies.

Different countries have dealt with regulating virtual currencies in different ways. For example, Australia is in a transition to encompass virtual currencies into their AML legislation, the Anti-Money Laundering and Counter Terrorism Financing Act 2006.[66] The UK is somewhat lagging behind others though, historically, their progressive and forward-thinking regulation has demonstrated the government's knowledge of criminal activity in this area. In 2015, the UK Government stated that it intends to apply AML regulations to virtual currency exchanges.[67] Canada is taking a risk-based approach to dealing with virtual currencies and in 2014 amended its AML /counter-terrorist financing regulations to treat those engaged in dealing with virtual currencies as money service businesses.[68] China requires any business involved in virtual currencies to comply fully with AML and counter-terrorist financing regulations.[69] Hong Kong has taken a very cautious approach and not conceded that virtual currencies fall under AML or terrorist financing regulations but has reminded its citizens of the criminal dangers that virtual currencies may pose.[70] Italy has taken a very strict approach and has specified that virtual currencies are not legal tender and warned financial intuitions against dealing in any form of virtual currencies. A reminder of AML regulations was also given to financial intuitions.[71] Russia too has taken a strict approach issuing guidance which states that any transactions involving virtual currencies will be viewed as a potential engagement in illegal activity. To prevent money laundering from occurring in virtual currencies, the Russian government has drawn up a Bill banning electronic monetary surrogates and electronic money surrogate's transactions.[72] Singapore has dealt with the issue of mitigating money laundering risks in virtual currencies differently again, as they have decided to regulate virtual currencies intermediaries and pass laws which are aimed at preventing the risks. These new regulations have not yet been implemented.[73] Switzerland has also issued guidance on encompassing virtual currencies transactions within existing money laundering regulations.[74] This is in contrast to South Africa, where there are currently no laws or regulations governing virtual currencies and their use, and as such virtual currencies are not legal tender which offers users degrees of safety when using them.[75]

From the above survey, it is clear that different jurisdictions deal with virtual currencies and the implications for AML regulations differently. Given the cross-border nature and money laundering disdain for jurisdictional lines of virtual currencies, these variances of approaches pose huge problems for international regulators. International cooperation and regulations are needed to ensure money laundering risks are mitigated and consumers are safe in their monetary transactions where virtual currencies are being used legitimately. This can only be achieved when there are benchmark standards globally on how virtual currencies are treated.

Analysis and Reflection

The UK's position is tenuous at best in terms of understanding, monitoring and regulating virtual money laundering. This diffidence arises for several reasons. There are no precise and delimitative definitions of what constitutes a virtual currency. The EBA, FATF and FCA all see virtual currencies as composing of different things. The most comprehensive is the EBA which does include currencies emanating from virtual worlds as long as they can be exchanged for real world currencies. The FATF and FCA neither provide guidance for this distinction nor include virtual world currencies as being part of virtual currencies. Governments, domestically and internationally, need to agree on a uniform definition in order to provide clear and comprehensive regulation. Without such, there are black holes and confusion. There is enough confusion and bifurcation of opinions as to whether virtual currencies should be regulated or not, without a lack of a suitable definition as to whether they include virtual world currencies.

A further issue stemming from the above is that without including virtual world currencies within the virtual currencies definition, a vast array of different environments are being ignored by the AML regulatory landscape and as such pose a potential and real threat to AML and terrorism financing laws. Virtual worlds can and do have criminal activities taking place within them, and the lack of regulation allows criminals a safe harbour for their illegal transactions. In short, virtual world environments are being ignored because of the lack of understanding of what they are and how they work. The monetary exchanges are also not being included within virtual currencies monetary exchanges because of virtual worlds being excluded from the definition of virtual currencies.

The piecemeal approach to legislation is not just confined to the UK but applies internationally as well. There is a lack of international agreement as to how to tackle and regulate virtual currencies. In some instances, monetary exchanges are being encompassed under the AML regulations, some countries tackle the taxation issues, but none include virtual worlds within their definition of virtual currencies and potential regulations for AML issues.

Therefore, although virtual currencies are coming to be seen as a potential money laundering risk, including virtual world currencies, the very definition of virtual currencies is ad hoc at best. The EBA does include virtual worlds within its definition and this is to be welcomed, but countries such as the UK need to make a definitive statement that virtual world currencies fall under the virtual currencies definition and as such become subject to relevant AML regulations. Without a clear and precise statement, domestically and internationally, virtual worlds will continue to be a safe haven for money laundering and terrorist financing.

Notes

1. For discussion of Bitcoin, see Chap. 9 (Egan) in this collection.
2. European Banking Authority, Opinion on Virtual Currencies, EBA/Op/2014/08, 4 July 2014, 11.
3. Clare Chambers-Jones, *Virtual Economies and Financial Crime: Money Laundering in Cyberspace* (Edward Elgar Publishing 2012).
4. Edward Castronova, 'Virtual Worlds: A First-Hand Account of Market and Society on the Cyberian Frontier' (2001) 618 CESifo Working Papers; Edward Castronova, 'On Virtual Economies' (2002) 752 CESifo Working Papers.
5. Mark Bell, 'Towards a Definition of Virtual Worlds' (2008) 1(1) *Journal of Virtual World Research* 1, 2.
6. See Council of Europe, Convention on Cybercrime (2001) ETS 185; Commonwealth Model Law on Cybercrime (2002).
7. Interpol, *Cybercrime Fact Sheet* (2008) COM/FS/2008-07/FHT-02.
8. Julian Dibbell, 'A Rape in Cyberspace' *The Village Voice* (New York, 23 December 1993) <www.villagevoic e.com/news/a-rape-in-cyberspace-6401665> accessed 28 July 17.
9. MUDs are text-based virtual worlds. For a discussion on this, see Richard Bartle, *Designing Virtual Worlds* (New Riders 2003) 3–21; Julian Dibbell, *My Tiny Life: Crime and Passion in a Virtual World* (Henry Holt and Company 1998) 51–65; Gregory Lastowka and Dan Hunter, 'Virtual Crimes' (2004) 49(1) *New York Law School Review* 293.
10. Susan Brenner, 'Is There Such a Thing as a Virtual Crime' (2001) 4(1) *California Criminal Law Review* 3, paras 105–11.
11. Dibbell (n 9) 21.
12. Brenner (n 10).
13. Lawrence Lessig, *Code and Other Laws of Cyberspace* (Basic Books 1999) 74–78.
14. Orin Kerr, 'The Problem of Perspective in Internet Law' (2003) 91(2) *Georgetown Law Journal* 357, 372–377.
15. ibid. 372–373.
16. Interpol, 'Virtual Money' (2010) <www.interpol.int/Crime-areas/Financial-crime/Money-laundering> accessed 28 July 17.
17. ibid.
18. Kerr (n 14) 372–373.

19. Fraud Advisory Panel, 'Cyber Crime—Social Networks and Virtual Worlds' (2009) 4 Fraud Facts; Clarke Kiernan Solicitors LLP, 'Second Life' <http://clarkekiernan.com/second-life> accessed 28 July 17.

20. For a comprehensive review of money laundering, see Nicholas Ryder, *Money Laundering—An Endless Cycle? A Comparative Analysis of the Anti-Money Laundering Policies in the United States of America, the United Kingdom, Australia and Canada* (Routledge 2012).

21. Nicholas Ryder, 'The Financial Services Authority, the Reduction of Financial Crime and the Money Launderer—A Game of Cat and Mouse' (2008) 67(3) *Cambridge Law Journal* 635.

22. Financial Action Task Force, *Report on New Payment Methods* (FATF/OECD 2006).

23. For more information on electronic purses, see Susan Stepney, David Cooper and Jim Woodcock, *An Electronic Purse: Specification, Refinement and Proof* (Oxford University Computer Laboratory 2000).

24. Heather Desguin, 'Money Laundering Through Virtual Games' (2008) Strategic Assessment, Florida Department of Law Enforcement, Office of Statewide Intelligence 17.

25. ibid. 18.

26. US Department of Justice, National Drug Intelligence Centre, *Money Laundering in Digital Currencies* (2008) 1.

27. ibid. 1.

28. ibid.

29. ibid. 3.

30. US Department of Justice, National Drug Intelligence Centre, *Prepaid Stored Value Cards: A Potential Alternative to Traditional Money Laundering Methods* (2006).

31. US DoJ (n 26) 4.

32. ibid.

33. ibid. 6.

34. ibid.

35. ibid.

36. See Chambers-Jones (n 3); Robert Stokes, 'Virtual Money Laundering: The Case of Bitcoin and the Linden Dollar' (2012) 21(3) Information and Communications Technology Law 221.

37. Richard Heeks, 'Current Analysis and Future Research Agenda on 'Gold Farming': Real World Production in Developing Countries for the Virtual Economies of Online Games' (2008) 32 Working Paper (Development Informatics Groups, Institute for Development Policy and Management, University of Manchester).

38. ibid.

39. Ung-Gi Yoon, 'Real Money Trading in MMORPG Items from a Legal and Policy Perspectives' (2008) 1 *Journal of Korean Judicature* 418.

40. Jin Ge, 'Chinese Gold Farmers in the Game World' (2006) 7(2) Consumers, Commodities & Consumption <http://csrn.camden.rutgers.edu/newsletters/7-2/jin.htm> accessed 28 July 17.

41. Heeks (n 37).

42. *United States v Real Property et al.* [2011] US CoA 11-6064.

43. For a good discussion on prepaid cards, see Courtney Linn, 'Regulating the Cross-Border Movement of Prepaid Cards' (2008) 11(2) *Journal of Money Laundering Control* 146.

44. See PatrickPetty.com, 'Update: Robert Hodgins is Still Wanted by Interpol; Co-defendant in Narcotics Probe with Link to AdSurfDaily Case Sentence to Prison; Colombian Drug Business Used Dame Debit Card as ASD' *PatrickPetty.com* (15 August 2010) <http://patrickpretty.com/2010/08/15/update-robert-hodgins-still-wanted-by-interpol-co-defendant-in-narcotics-probe-with-link-to-adsurfdaily-case-sentenced-to-prison-colombian-drug-business-used-same-debit-card-as-asd/> accessed 28 July 17.

45. Brian Monroe, 'Virtual Worlds Clear and Present Danger for Money Laundering' *Fortent* (26 April 2007) <www.world-check.com/media/d/content_pressarticle_reference/Virtual_Worlds_Clear_and_Present_Danger_for_Money_Laundering.pdf> accessed 28 July 17.

46. ibid.

47. ibid.

48. ibid.

49. See Financial Conduct Authority, *Financial Crime: A Guide for Firms. Part 1: A Firms Guide to Preventing Financial Crime* (FCA 2015). For more on money laundering and the FCA, see Financial Conduct Authority, *Money Laundering and Terrorist Financing* (FCA 2015).

50. Financial Conduct Authority, *Handbook* (FCA 2013), SYSC 3 Systems and Controls.

51. See ibid. SYSC 6.3.

52. Financial Conduct Authority, *Anti-Money Laundering Annual Report 2013/14* (FCA 2014).

53. For discussion in the context of Bitcoin, see Chap. 9 (Egan) in this collection.

54. FCA (n 52) 12.

55. FATF, *Virtual Currencies: Key Definitions and Potential AML/CFT Risks* (FATF/OECD 2014); FATF, *Guidance for a Risk Based Approach. Virtual Currencies* (FATF/OECD 2015); European Banking Authority, 'EBA Opinion on Virtual Currencies' EBA/Op/2014/08, 4 July 2014.

56. FATF (n 55) 3.

57. ibid. 4.

58. European Banking Authority (n 55) 10.

59. Financial Services Authority, *Reducing Money Laundering Risk* (FSA 2003), Discussion paper 22; UK Government, *Money Laundering Regulations*, Money Laundering Regulations. Your Responsibilities (2013).
60. FATF (n 55) 10.
61. ibid.
62. FATF, *Guidance for a Risk Based Approach. Virtual Currencies* (FATF/OECD 2015) 6.
63. European Banking Authority (n 55).
64. ibid. 32.
65. ibid. 32–33.
66. Anti-Money Laundering and Counter Terrorism Financing Act 2006 (Australia). For discussion of the Australian AML framework, see Chap. 13 (Chaikin) in this collection.
67. FATF (n 62) 21.
68. FATF (n 55) 15.
69. ibid.
70. ibid. 18.
71. ibid. 19.
72. ibid.
73. ibid.
74. ibid. 20.
75. ibid.

Clare Chambers-Jones is Associate Professor of Law at University of the West of England (UWE) whose expertise is in cyber law and banking and finance. She has written prolifically in these areas and has spoken internationally on virtual world cybercrime. Chambers-Jones spent her early career in industry working for Grant Thornton and Morgan Stanley. She returned to academia working at Bournemouth University and then moved to UWE in 2008. Chambers-Jones has also been involved with the Commonwealth Legal Education Association and has devoted her time to developing cyber law regulations within the commonwealth.

9

A Bit(Coin) of a Problem for the EU AML Framework

Mo Egan

Introduction

Virtual currency has been defined relatively recently by the European Central Bank (ECB) as 'a digital representation of value, not issued by a central bank, credit institution or e-money institution, which in some circumstances can be used as an alternative to money' whereas cryptocurrencies form a subset of virtual currency that is reliant on cryptography.[1] However, arriving at this fairly succinct description follows several years of academic and practitioner debate. Indeed, the careful phrasing 'can be used as an alternative to money' is telling in that it implies virtual currency is not money. If not money, then there is a question mark hovering over the manner in which it can and should be controlled. In fact, there are those who argue for regulatory restraint or against regulation altogether.[2] The motivation to develop mechanisms of control for these currencies is founded initially in their association with criminality, but over time focus has shifted to their commercial potential.

The European Banking Authority (EBA)[3] that was established in 2011 'to protect the public interest by contributing to [...] the effectiveness of the financial system, for the Union economy'[4] has grappled with the regulation (or lack thereof) of cryptocurrency. As part of their remit, they have an obligation to monitor financial innovation and consider whether there is a need for regulatory or supervisory action. In December 2013, they issued a warning to

M. Egan
Division of Law and Philosophy, School of Arts and Humanities,
University of Stirling, Stirling, UK

© The Author(s) 2018
C. King et al. (eds.), *The Palgrave Handbook of Criminal and Terrorism Financing Law*,
https://doi.org/10.1007/978-3-319-64498-1_9

consumers that cryptocurrencies were unsafe, on the grounds that they may be stolen, that the means of payment is vulnerable and that consumers may be holding cryptocurrency which is subject to tax liabilities. In July 2014, the EBA issued a further opinion on virtual currencies, forming the view that 'Virtual currency schemes do not respect jurisdictional boundaries and may therefore undermine financial sanctions and seizure of assets; and that market participants lack sound corporate governance arrangements'.[5] Moreover, it was suggested that bitcoins specifically presented such risks that domestic supervisors should dissuade regulated institutions from providing any services relating to participants in the Bitcoin system.[6] However, in 2016, the European Parliament's Committee on the Internal Market and Consumer Protection provided a more favourable view of benefits associated with virtual currencies and virtual currency technologies. They argued such benefits would include 'greater speed and efficiency and reduced costs in making payments and transfers … across borders'.[7] In addition, they asserted that the market is likely to expand as virtual currencies have the potential to promote 'financial inclusion and facilitate access to funding and financial resources for the business sector and SMEs'.[8] Nevertheless, they maintain that while there is little evidence to support the claims that virtual currencies have been used as a payment vehicle for criminal activities, virtual currencies present a risk of being used for a wide range of illegal activities including 'financing terrorism, money laundering, tax evasion, tax fraud'.[9]

It is these asserted threats that have gradually gained momentum, demanding that continued consideration be given to whether regulation is necessary and, if so, how this can be designed. The committee's opinion is that where virtual currencies are used as an alternative to fiat currency (defined here as legal tender and issued by a central authority) but are not a national or foreign currency, then they present further risks to the financial system as they sit uncomfortably with currency provisions determining regulation, market surveillance and security in the European Union (EU). They suggest that the solution is to focus on the inclusion of virtual currency exchangers within the pre-existing Anti-Money Laundering and Counter Terrorist Financing framework because those exchangers are the key actors that sit between virtual currencies and access to the fiat system. However, such regulation would result in, as is tradition in the field of policing financial crime, a variety of actors being furnished with policing responsibilities, where the construction of shared meanings will be important in ensuring cooperation between those actors.[10]

In making these statements, the Committee has captured the tension between the virtues and vulnerability of the use and expansion of virtual currencies as well as the problematic evidence base on which regulatory and policing frameworks can be designed. Although there is an appetite at the EU level for approaches to regulation to be founded on appropriate evidence, virtual currency markets present a practical challenge. In a relatively unregulated space, it is difficult to provide a meaningful evaluation of, for example, the size of the market and the characteristics of the actors within it. Following on from this point, it is argued in this chapter that developing a system of regulation that has the potential to be effective in the prevention of exploitation of virtual currency for criminal purposes requires coherent and harmonised conceptual understandings of those currencies transcending jurisdictional boundaries, that are embedded in appropriate legal frameworks, supporting policy and embraced by practitioners as they make operational choices. Indeed, the European Commission agree that 'increasingly cross border and cross sectorial' threats such as those presented by exploitation of virtual currencies demand a 'coordinated response at the EU level'.[11] However, as will become clear, the coordination of such an approach to virtual currencies and their vulnerabilities is just beginning.

Accordingly, this chapter will set out the development of the legal regulation of cryptocurrencies, how policy has evolved to straddle the legal quagmire and provide a first mapping of the paradigm of policing that has been adopted by the EU. It will focus on the case of bitcoin—being the dominant cryptocurrency at the time of this writing.[12] In doing so, the chapter highlights that the recent extension of the anti-money laundering framework may on the one hand create a useful framework of supervision for some actors within the Bitcoin system but that the inclusion of tax offences will present additional challenges to the incorporation of cryptocurrency because of the lack of harmonised conceptual understanding. Therefore, this chapter concludes that this will be detrimental to the ability of law enforcement professionals and those in the regulated sector to deliver an effective coordinated response to the exploitation of cryptocurrencies for criminal purposes.

The Bitcoin Phenomena

The Bitcoin system was proposed in 2008 by Satoshi Nakamoto as he attempted to challenge traditional fiat currency, with cryptocurrency.[13] Stimulated by a loss of faith in this financial system, Nakamoto designed the bitcoin platform to sit outwith the state-controlled banking system through decentralisation, the use of cryptography and facilitating direct peer-to-peer transactions, where this design was subsequently implemented by others.[14] Nakamoto's reasoning was that the use of cryptographic proof negated the need for third-party involvement in transactions laying down the gauntlet to the payment services industry. In doing so, he speculated this would lead to reduced transaction costs.

In practical terms, a bitcoin (small 'b') is a line of code that is produced by solving a mathematical problem. Bitcoin (capital 'B') is the platform where the public ledger is maintained. In order to participate in the creation, purchase or sale of bitcoins one has to download open source software. Then you must obtain an electronic wallet in which bitcoins can be stored. This can either be a wallet stored on a computer in 'cold storage' or one hosted online.[15] Bitcoins can be obtained either by purchasing them with traditional fiat currency or by accepting them as payment for goods or services. Alternatively, you can be rewarded bitcoins for your participation in the process of verification of other transactions, known as mining. However, to participate in the process of mining you require significant computational power, which will incur 'non-trivial' expenditure on the required equipment and power supply.[16] Thus, it is not considered to be a particularly lucrative occupation for the entrepreneurially spirited. Indeed, where miners are established as a business enterprise, it is likely that they will charge a commission on transactions that they are working on. In this way, the evolution of the Bitcoin system is challenging the ethos on which it was originally established.

Still, mining is crucial to the security of the system. Miners verify transactions checking that the code going from one user to the other is the correct code and it is this 'block chain' of code that has provenance. This process ensures that ownership can be established and protects against double spending, where someone attempts to transfer the same code twice. Once verified, the transaction will be recorded in the public ledger that is visible online along with a timestamp.[17] This public ledger presents the illusion that the system is transparent since it allows each transaction to be followed from seller to purchaser. However, the practical implementation of such identification is difficult.

Consequently, the process is said to be pseudonymous because although the block chain is public, allowing anyone to watch a transaction go from one party to another online, the transaction does not require personal identifiers in the same way a traditional transaction would. Individuals have a private key and a public key that allow them to control transfers of their coins. They can share the public key to allow someone to transfer bitcoins to them, where the address is produced by the wallet (automatically). In this way, the public key is connected to a particular wallet without revealing the identity of the owner. While it is possible that the wallet host would be able to identify the associated Internet Protocol (IP) address, individuals commonly also use privacy software such as Tor, which can be used to mask IP addresses.

Research has been carried out to test to what extent it is possible to identify an individual from the Bitcoin 'block chain'. In 2011, Reid and Harrigan attempted to examine whether it was possible to de-anonymise bitcoin transactions by contextualising the 'block chain' within publicly available data sets.[18] They successfully mined the internet for information connected to individual transactions where they were able to map transactions between public wallet addresses and attempted to trace email addresses associated with particular wallets or usernames. Navigating the ethical issues with research of this nature, where it is clear an individual has elected to participate in an pseudonymous system, they highlighted that there is a distinct line between what is public and what is private, specifically that the complete history of bitcoin transactions is public, but the private keys and associated IPs are not generally publicly accessible. Reid and Harrigan were adamant that the ability to identify individuals from the public data alone was limited. Accordingly, such a pseudonymous system remains likely to be exploited for criminal purposes. Indeed as Martin explains in his examination of purchasing drugs on the dark net, 'without a radical breakthrough in defeating TOR encryption or cryptocurrency technologies, cryptomarkets will likely continue on current trends towards further growth and diversification'.[19]

Nevertheless, the number of bitcoins that can be produced is finite, and so the availability of bitcoins is limited. Although it must be acknowledged that each bitcoin can be subdivided into 100 million units, the software creating bitcoin will stop generating bitcoins when it reaches 21 million.[20] Writing in 2013, Plassaras estimated that all bitcoins will have been issued within the next ten years.[21] Yet, the system is designed to increase the difficulty of the computation in order that the production of bitcoins is gradually slowed. This means it could be considerably longer before the last bitcoin is issued. The consequence of this is that the value of bitcoin is likely to increase as we approach that limit (and indeed beyond it) and could potentially have a deflationary impact on the virtual currency economy. Alternatively, it could result in people retaining bitcoins as a savings strategy resulting in fewer bitcoins circulating.

Initial Regulation

Initial regulation of the Bitcoin system has proved problematic because of difficulties in agreeing how bitcoin should be defined. Largely, it appears from Nakamoto's original design that it would be an alternative to traditional forms of money such as fiat currency. This means a constructive starting point is to consider what constitutes 'money'; to establish whether bitcoins are money or whether bitcoins are to be distinguished from these traditional forms of money. If it is established that bitcoins are money, its regulation and control can be determined by the same framework. The theoretical touchstone for an assessment as to whether a payment mechanism constitutes money is to consider the attributes afforded to it or in its 'function'.[22] This means considering to what extent bitcoin is used as a medium of exchange (ultimately being accepted and trusted by another), is capable of storing value and has a stable unit of account. Still, as highlighted by Eder, 'the law of money evidences a constant struggle between the customs of trade and the doctrine of freedom of contract, on the one hand, and on the other, the exercise of the political power for the needs of the government or the relief of private debtors'.[23]

The middle ground between these two vying sides is reflected in the EU legislative framework. As a 'newly' created entity, Bitcoin had to be considered in light of the available legal framework when the genesis block was mined. In 2009, the main pillars of regulation encompassed the regulation of money laundering, payment services providers and e-money. The framework established which institutions were required to perform particular policing functions, required a licence to provide their service, how certain services were to be provided in order that the single market did not become distorted, and that where (certain forms of) criminality is suspected, information was communicated to law enforcement.[24] However, a number of academics formed the view that bitcoin was not captured within existing measures of regulation when the genesis block was created—neither within the EU legal framework[25] nor implementing member states.[26] Still, to make such an assessment tangible, it is necessary to remind ourselves by setting out the operation of bitcoin creation and use.

If we start from the point of entering the system, the first step is to download the relevant software and to obtain a wallet. In doing so, you will be seeking the services of a wallet provider. The software creating the file can be held on your hardware or alternatively, you could elect an ongoing service from a cloud-based wallet host. Thereafter, to procure bitcoins you can purchase them from a bitcoin exchange, receive them in payment for goods or services or be rewarded them for verifying transactions.[27] In any single transaction from peer-to-peer, the only third-party involvement is that of the miner, where they are not responsible for processing the transaction moving bitcoin from one location to another, but rather, are simply responsible for verifying that the details contained in the ledger accurately reflect the transaction that has taken place. On this basis then, it is necessary to consider whether wallet providers, bitcoin exchanges and miners are captured within the scope of the legal provisions as at the establishment of the Bitcoin system.

When bitcoin was initially established, it would have been considered that regulation, if available, would be contained within the 3rd Anti-Money Laundering Directive of 2005 (3MLD),[28] the Payment Services Directive of 2007[29] and the E-money Directive of 2009.[30] The 3MLD set out to refine the regulatory framework criminalising the laundering of the proceeds of crime. To do this, it required that credit institutions, financial institutions and professional services, such as accountants and legal professionals, undertake a variety of training, recording, monitoring and reporting responsibilities.[31] It is fairly clear that wallet providers and miners were not listed within the 3MLD as regulated professionals. It would appear impracticable for them to join this list without further amendments as there was no form of professional accreditation, licencing or supervisory architecture that would support the provision of their services. Equally, it was evident that neither role involved the provisions of credit services which would entail receiving deposits from the public or granting credit.[32] Nor was the work of wallet providers and miners characterised by attributes of financial institutions. However, it was less clear as to the position of bitcoin exchanges in that currency exchanges were expressly included within the definition of 'financial institution'.[33] The ambiguity then arose from the consideration of whether the transaction seeking to exchange bitcoins was in fact one of 'currency' exchange. If so, this would trigger compliance with the Directive being required and consequently member states would have to ensure that bitcoin exchanges situated within their state were supervised appropriately. However, the first bitcoin exchanges were based outwith the EU and, consequently, it was not considered high on the European agenda as a regulatory concern.

The Payment Services Directive complimented the architecture of the EUs regulation of the financial market seeking to harmonise payment services across the member states on the premise that this would facilitate free movement of goods, services, people and capital.[34] Its terms provided that payment service providers were required to be authorised by their member state and that in doing so would be subject to a system of controls associated with that authorisation.[35] However, the problem in the context of bitcoin was to identify the type of the payment services provider and whether they were captured by one of the six categories of provider set out by the Directive.[36] Again, this was likely to be a matter of concern when examining the role of the bitcoin exchange as opposed the role of the wallet providers or miners. Three categories can be dismissed with little controversy, namely: post office giro institutions, Central Banks and Local Authorities acting in a private capacity. However, credit institutions, electronic money providers and payment institutions demand closer attention. Yet, when unpacked, they too fall short of capturing bitcoin exchanges since—as with the anti-money laundering provisions—'credit institution' is defined as '(a) an undertaking whose business is to receive deposits or other repayable funds from the public and to grant credits for its own account; or (b) an electronic money institution' and an 'electronic money provider' being defined as 'an undertaking or any other legal person [...] which issues means of payment in the form of electronic money' and a 'payment institution' being 'a legal person that has been granted authorisation [...] to provide and execute payment services throughout the Community'.[37] Moving away from the institutional exclusion of bitcoin exchange from regulation, in each case only those institutions engaged in the transfer of funds (with funds defined as 'banknotes and coins, scriptural money and electronic money') were captured. Thus, the applicability to bitcoin was clearly limited.[38] Accordingly, the Bitcoin system and its operation could not be superimposed onto the definitions as they stood at that time.

The lack of regulation has been the subject of critical comment from the legal academy and policymakers alike. For example, Vandezande explored the definition of electronic money contained in the E-money Directive and, as noted above, argued that it does not apply in the bitcoin case since bitcoins are automatically generated by the system as opposed to being 'issued upon receipt of funds'.[39] The same issue was highlighted in 2012 by Michel Barnier who, on behalf of the European Commission, noted that bitcoins fell outwith the scope of the E-money Directive and Payment Services Directive because bitcoins 'are not centrally issued by any organisation'.[40] However, Vandezande goes further in his analysis, beyond the issue of creation, and suggests, while this may be true in relation to the original creation of bitcoins, where bitcoins are exchanged for traditional currency, it is possible that the exchange will be subject to the terms of the Directive.[41] Despite this observation, the Commission's view was that bitcoin regulation was simply not considered a threat to the market at that time as 'the total value of Bitcoins currently in circulation [was] estimated at around EUR 35 million at global level'.[42] Consequently, if we consider that in June 2016 the value of US dollars in circulation is $1.46 trillion, 'the amounts of [virtual] currencies in circulation are relatively marginal and do not seem to pose a risk in monetary terms'.[43]

Therefore, in the early stages the position of the Bitcoin system was relatively clear in that bitcoins were not captured by the principal regulatory measures but also were not a policy priority for the EU Institutions. However, it should be noted that it was possible for individual member states to regulate a wider group of entities should they choose to do so within their individual member state and so a level of ambiguity remained in that the Bitcoin system was likely to involve a cross-border dimension where member states may require cooperation from other jurisdictions.

Bitcoin and Crime

It is clear that bitcoin has grown in popularity with over one-quarter of a million transactions taking place per day.[44] As the use of bitcoin has expanded, questions have been raised concerning its stability, security and integrity. Such considerations have become all the more pressing as bitcoins have become linked to a variety of criminal conduct. For example, in 2013, US Authorities shut down the online marketplace Silk Road, where purchases of largely illegal goods and services were made with bitcoin. Later, in 2014, bitcoins became the subject of further attention when some 850,000 bitcoins were claimed to have been stolen from Tokyo-based Mt. Gox, which was at that time the largest bitcoin exchange.[45] However, it later transpired that these claims had been part of a fraudulent enterprise by insiders of the Mt. Gox Exchange highlighting the limited regulatory capture of the industry.[46] In 2015, there were a number of media reports of extortions requiring payment of a ransom by way of bitcoins.[47] And, in 2016, within the European Union, Europol has reported dismantling an organised crime group based in Spain which was involved in laundering the proceeds of crime through the bitcoin mining system as part of Operation FAKE and further afield Bitfinex (a Hong Kong–based exchange) stopped trading following the theft of 119,756 bitcoins.[48] While these cases are only illustrations of the relationship between bitcoins and criminality, there is a significant opportunity for reflection on virtual currencies' criminal potential and appropriate regulation.

The emergence of criminal activity such as that noted above demonstrates bitcoins as yet do not introduce, nor are subject of, 'new' types of crime. Rather, it is necessary to unpack the manner in which bitcoin is being used to determine whether that use is regulated by EU law and associated criminal offences, focussing as they do on preserving the single market, and latterly, as they place greater emphasis on securing an Area of Freedom, Security and Justice.[49] Designation of activities within the regulatory framework of EU law will result in the collation of intelligence and evidence that can be used for the purposes of criminal investigation.

As with any asset, there is the potential for bitcoin to be the subject of theft or fraud exemplified by the Mt. Gox charade noted above. If viewed as a 'currency' it could be subject to counterfeiting but with the role of cryptographic proof being to make such counterfeiting practically improbable this is unlikely to be a concern that merits the attention of EU law. As it stands, the Directive that requires that member states criminalise counterfeiting adopts a definition of currency as 'notes and coins, the circulation of which is legally authorised' which, being so narrow, excludes cryptocurrencies such as bitcoin.[50] This means there may be offences of counterfeiting at the domestic level that are expressed broadly enough to include cryptocurrency but that there is no requirement for member states to do so at the EU level. In any case, such a scenario would require material assistance from the mining community to approve any transactions involving the counterfeit bitcoin. This means that the risk of counterfeiting currency being created is limited since once created it would prove difficult to transfer.

If bitcoins are to be seen as a commodity, their transfer could be subject to market manipulation.[51] The EU Commission's view of the commodities market is that it encompasses energy, agricultural products and raw materials including various metal and minerals and therefore it can be inferred that bitcoin is not captured within its ambit.[52] Indeed, 'commodity' is undefined by the EU legal framework leaving room for it to be defined differently within individual member states. While there has been a recent review and expansion of the scope of the EU measures seeking to address market abuse resulting in the revised Market Abuse Regulation and Market Abuse Directive the provisions do not currently encompass the transfer of bitcoin. Yet, member states cannot ignore its potential to be regulated as a commodity since the very essence of the bitcoin system is its ability to be transferred in a complex jurisdictional space that is not limited to the frontiers of the EU. Indeed, the approach adopted by other states outwith the EU creates the potential for conflict and the need for cooperation in a policing context. In September 2015, the US Commodities and Futures Trading Commission (CFTC) was presented with the opportunity to consider whether bitcoin transfers fell within the scope of their remit. This opportunity arose because an action was raised against Coinflip, a company that was accused of having violated the terms of the Commodity Exchange Act by facilitating the exchange of bitcoins by connecting parties who wished to trade bitcoin options. The issue was that it was illegal to facilitate such exchanges where they concerned unregulated options. To address the issue, the Commission gave their view on the 'regulatory characterisation' of bitcoin and with very little analysis found that the definition given to commodities within the Commodity Exchange Act was sufficiently broad to encompass bitcoins.[53] The significance of such determination is that it will dictate the regulatory offences that may be committed in transactions involving bitcoin. Moreover, where such an offence has been committed, the terms of the US provisions allow the CFTC to claim jurisdiction in relation to interstate transactions, which extend the definition of state to include foreign nations.[54] Although the EU has entered into an agreement with the US securing mutual legal assistance in relation to the investigation and prosecution of criminal offences, there would be grounds for refusal where the offence did not pass the dual criminality test.[55]

As a medium of exchange, bitcoin could be used to launder the proceeds of crime or fund terrorism. If this is the case, it would be captured by the criminal provisions of the EU anti-money laundering framework focusing as they do on criminal property. However, there is a regulatory gap here in that this framework has (until relatively recently) failed to capture actors involved in the Bitcoin system meaning there are few furnished with obligations to identify their clients, to monitor transactions and to report suspicious activity. This results in limited information and evidence that can be drawn upon should an action be raised against a suspected criminal.

However, even after the criminal conduct has been identified—be it theft, fraud, market abuse, money laundering or something else—the pseudonymous, decentralised, cryptographic characteristics of bitcoin, present law enforcement with an investigatory challenge. Specifically, their ability to investigate bitcoin is hampered by limited expertise, the inherent technological challenge of interrogating cryptographic data, and restrictions on their ability to undertake surveillance and evidence gathering, in a multi-jurisdictional space that is exacerbated by legal ambiguity caused by regulatory gaps.

Policy as a Transitional Tool

As cryptocurrencies have evolved and criminal activity identified there has been a proliferation of policy recommendations and guidance issued by organisations with varying geographical and sector-specific interests. Largely, these policies have been attempting to bridge the gaps between currently available legal frameworks in a multi-jurisdictional context but also seeking to influence the direction of future regulation. The Financial Action Task Force (FATF), as the leading international organisation founded expressly to develop efforts to tackle money laundering and latterly to include tackling the financing of terrorism has taken a keen interest in evaluating to what extent virtual currencies are open to exploitation and have led the charge in the demand for their regulation.

The FATF revised its recommendations on what measures are required to prevent money laundering and terrorism financing in 2012. The significance of their revisions was that they recommended that where situations were identified that presented a higher risk of money laundering or terrorist financing it was appropriate for more extensive customer due diligence to be undertaken. Similarly, where lower risk situations were presented, a simplified procedure could be more appropriate. In theory, this would reduce the compliance burden on those who fell within the regulated sector.[56] While this 'risk-based' approach to regulation has been hailed as favourable, in the context of the Bitcoin system it remains problematic. The problem is to what extent participation in the Bitcoin system is linked to criminality and therefore whether there is an increased risk requiring that regulated institutions carry out more extensive due diligence. However, as noted earlier a core component of the Bitcoin systems ethos is its pseudonymous nature which means that the practicality of undertaking enhanced due diligence checks is questionable. The result is—as the EBA suggested in 2014, and as occurred in Australia in 2015—that financial institutions, credit institutions and payment services providers refuse service or de-bank those they known to be involved in the Bitcoin system.[57]

The FATF demonstrates that it has a desire for the web of regulation to cover as wide a range of activities and institutions as possible as they argue that if particular 'types of institutions, activities, businesses or professions that are at risk of abuse from money laundering and terrorist financing' but are not captured by the definitions given to the regulated institutions, countries should elect to apply AML and CTF measures to them in any case.[58] Consequently, although it has been acknowledged by Unger that these Recommendations are only 'soft law' in nature, meaning they have no binding legal effect, the position appears to be when in doubt anti-money laundering measures are required in order to comply with international standards.[59]

As the EBA voiced its concerns in relation to virtual currencies, the FATF adopted definitions and identified risks in an attempt to develop a common language to enable regulated institutions and law enforcement to communicate more effectively.[60] The difficulty was that along with the Recommendations, such definitions were non-binding and so while they may achieve a desire by those in the regulated sector to cooperate with law enforcement or other central authorities, it does not determine whether the EU or individual states will have implemented legislation ensuring that they can be compelled to do so.

In June 2015, the FATF built on these definitions and identified risks by providing guidance that set out how a risk-based approach can be applied to virtual currencies.[61] It focused on precisely the intersection between exchangers and the regulated sector, seeking to help those in the regulated sector apply the FATF recommendations to virtual currencies, acknowledging that the Recommendations were not originally drafted with this in mind.[62] Significantly, they explain that the FATF Recommendations require all jurisdictions to impose AML/CTF requirements on financial institutions where they provide particular services such as money or value transfer services or trading in foreign exchange. Therefore, depending into which of these categories the virtual currency business model falls, they may consequently require regulation. The FATF argues that regulation should be implemented where virtual currencies intersect with the regulated fiat currency system. Having formed this view, it recommends that enhanced due diligence measures are appropriate.[63]

Moving forward, the FATF speculates that should virtual currencies become a 'meaningful part of the financial sector'[64] countries will have to consider examining the relationship between virtual currency AML/CTF regulation and supervision, and other forms of regulation and supervision such as consumer protection or tax compliance.

Extending AML to Actors in the Bitcoin System

A new Money Laundering Directive was proposed in 2013, and, as a result, the scope of the EU money laundering framework was expanded with the adoption of the Directive in 2015. During this time—as can be seen from the views expressed by FATF, ECB and EBA noted earlier—concerns regarding the stability and security of bitcoin had been raised. Consequently, there was ample opportunity for the position of virtual currencies to be addressed by the Directive. Still, the resulting 4th Money Laundering Directive (4MLD) made no binding assertions concerning virtual currencies. As with previous Directives, it provides a definition of electronic money, and electronic money products which does not encompass cryptocurrencies.[65] Consequently, it appears all actors in the Bitcoin system would not be regulated institutions for the purposes of the Directive. However, as the definition of financial institution has been expanded to encompass currency exchange offices, it could be argued that this would cover bitcoin exchanges.[66]

In its Internet Organised Crime Threat Assessment of 2015, Europol acknowledged that the continuation of perceived anonymity attracts criminals to the Bitcoin system; it was also argued that, while virtual currencies may be designed for legitimate use, they are also exploited by a criminal element. At the time of reporting, bitcoin exchanges were highlighted as a crucial link in the chain between dirty money and the legitimate economy. It can be hypothesised that the problem has been exacerbated by the fact that the regulatory framework applying to these exchanges was varied between member states, meaning it was possible to exploit those exchangers who are not required to implement 'know your customer' checks.[67] On this basis, extending AML to bitcoin exchanges is the logical first step in controlling crime orchestrated through the Bitcoin system.

Yet, even if bitcoin exchanges are subject to the 4MLD, this does not solve the problem of policing bitcoins. It simply responsibilises these institutions to retain information on customers, and establish beneficial owners. In each case since these obligations are diametrically in opposition to the ethos of bitcoin creation, the bitcoin exchange is likely to see a reduction in those trying to cashout, or alternatively, denying service to those who cannot, or will not, meet the identification requirements. If anonymity is sacrificed then bitcoins may become less attractive. However, it may also simply displace bitcoin cashing out through the exchange route, to alternative purchases of goods or services (that are not monitored in the same way).

Still, some progress has potentially been achieved through the inclusion of FATF's work in the recitals of the Directive. While this chapter began by arguing that the conceptual confusion and lack of flexibility in legal terminology and scope of regulation had led to the exclusion of the Bitcoin system from effective regulation, conceptual certainty can evolve through the inclusion of definitions adopted by the FATF as the Directive recommends that Union action should take into account FATF recommendations and 'public statements, mutual evaluations or detailed assessment reports'.[68] Indeed, it appears that FATF's statements as to the future regulatory issues surrounding bitcoin were prophetical as this most recent EU Money Laundering Directive renews the relationship between AML and tax offences. While the inclusion of tax offences as a predicate offence for money laundering may secure information and evidence sharing mechanisms for the purposes of tackling tax offences, it is particularly problematic in the context of bitcoins.[69] Operationalising an effective AML system relies on the reporting of suspicious activity by regulated institutions. Their ability to do this is determined by, first, their ability to identify their client and, secondly, their ability to identify the risk associated to that client or their actions.[70] The difficulty in the context of bitcoin is that even if bitcoin exchanges are considered to be regulated institutions, they will have a limited ability to identify their clients and even if they can there remains considerable unregulated space where direct peer-to-peer transactions can facilitate criminal activity. In addition, specifically in relation to taxation, there have been diverse approaches to the tax treatment of bitcoins in different jurisdictions leading to difficulties in determining tax liabilities and consequently attaching administrative or criminal sanctions.

In 2001, Alldridge highlighted that there was an increasing emphasis on tax evasion as a predicate offence for money laundering.[71] He mapped the international and European commitment from the G7 Finance Ministers meeting in 1998 to the FATF Directive in 1999 and the conclusions of the Tampere European Council meeting that same year. Each was in agreement, that the AML regulatory framework can be leveraged to support authorities in their investigation of tax offences.

It is unsurprising, with the Single Market forming the core foundation on which the EU is built, that taxation forms an important economic battle ground for member states as they try to increase their public finances. Member states are able to set their own tax rates in relation to direct taxation, with the EU performing a monitoring role to ensure that those decisions do not conflict with other EU policies. However, the EU coordinates and harmonises indirect taxation on goods and services across the EU member states, with the EU's relationship with member states in the field of taxation being set out in the Treaty of the Function of the European Union.[72]

In 2012, the European Commission set out its intention to tackle tax fraud and tax evasion.[73] In doing so, they wished to promote a 'more joined up approach between direct and indirect taxation'.[74] However, they also highlighted those pre-existing measures that were available to facilitate cooperation between member states' administrative authorities were not being used as well as they might.[75] Of particular concern in the Commission's Action Plan, is the relationship between the EU and third states. The plan itself includes a number of proposed measures designed to improve the good governance standards of third countries and to encourage cooperation in the pursuit of tax administration. In particular, they argue that where member states allow businesses to structure themselves between member states and jurisdictions considered to be tax havens there is a threat to 'fair competitive conditions for business' and 'distortion of the internal market'.[76] To address the issue, they propose the possibility of blacklisting jurisdictions that do not comply with a sufficient standard of good governance. Moving forward, the Commission acknowledge the need to develop measures that specifically address the 'complexities of taxing electronic commerce'[77] and offer to work with the Organisation for Economic Co-operation and Development (OECD) to develop international standards. Moreover, that it is necessary to harness cooperation between law enforcement bodies and anti-money laundering authorities because 'inter-agency cooperation is essential to ensure an efficient fight against tax fraud, tax evasion and tax related crimes'.[78]

In 2015, that commitment came to fruition with the 4MLD. In terms of Article 3 (4)(f) of the directive, tax offences are expressly included within the definition of 'criminal activity' although it is acknowledged that the specific tax offence may diverge between member states as there is no harmonised definition. Despite this disparity, the directive encourages the exchange of information between Financial Intelligence Units to the maximum extent possible and should complement other EU measures directed at cooperation in tax matters.[79]

However, the policing of tax offences and subsequent laundering of assets prove all the more challenging in the context of cryptocurrencies. Indeed Omri has argued that cryptocurrencies have features that are characteristic of traditional tax havens. In particular, the location of a wallet 'online' means that individuals are able to escape tax rules because those rules are oriented towards traditional concepts of geographical territory. In addition, an individual can own multiple wallets and are able to retain (relative) anonymity creating further tax evasion potential.[80] However, there are much more simplistic difficulties with cryptocurrencies in that establishing the tax treatment of cryptocurrency has itself proved problematic. For example, in relation to our specific case of the bitcoin, bitcoin has been categorised differently by different member states, resulting in differing tax liabilities. The knock-on effect of this is that there will be a conflict between jurisdictions' tax offences where the rules differ.

In examining the issue of taxation, Bal focuses on the tax consequences of mining and trading.[81] Bal claims that people who receive bitcoins that from part of their income and is taxable do not pay tax on those sums either because they do not know that the income is taxable or they deliberately choose to avoid paying tax.[82] She emphasises in the first case that this arises because of the lack of clear guidance on the tax treatment of digital currency. However, since publication the position has moved on slightly in that many jurisdictions now issue guidance but the difficulty has become that new guidance is at times conflicting. Bal argues that the propensity to deliberately avoid taxation comes from the ease with which it can be achieved since the bitcoin exchange tends to occur in a multi-jurisdictional setting with limited identification requirements. By and large, since bitcoin is peer to peer with no intermediary and that near anonymity attaches to the sending and receiving to wallets, there is little scope for tax authorities to be aware that the transactions has occurred and to monitor it in an effective way. They are reliant on self-reporting.

Bal goes on to argue that anti-tax evasion measures are unlikely to be useful in these matters as they rely on sovereign jurisdictions who are able to provide information and that this will not work in relation to decentralised cryptocurrencies since no information is recorded. While this may have held water at the time of this writing, there have been some progressive measures taken at the EU level to attempt to facilitate the sharing of information in relation to tax offences specifically, and serious and organised crime generally. It is possible that the most recent directive on network security will open the door to the identification of the 'information holder' and consequently facilitate the appropriate specificity for investigatory and evidentiary tools to be used.[83]

In 2014, Estonia acknowledged that, for the purposes of income tax, bitcoins should be treated as capital gain, and gains from transfer of bitcoins should be subject to income tax. However, they did not recognise it as a financial instrument, e-currency or security, meaning it was not subject to a value-added tax (VAT) exemption for financial services.[84] In March 2015, the General Directorate of Taxes in Spain, formed the view that bitcoins are a form of payment akin to money, and therefore should not be exempt from VAT.[85] In October 2015, the Court of Justice of the EU was afforded the opportunity to consider the issue on the application of Directive 2006/112/EC (common system of VAT) specifically to bitcoin exchanges.[86] This followed a reference for a preliminary ruling from a Swedish court concerning whether exchange from traditional currency to bitcoin and vice versa was subject to VAT. The judgment of the court concluded that such exchanges should fall within the exemption from VAT on the basis that bitcoins are not tangible property in the context of these transactions, and serve no other purpose than as a means of payment. The exchange was to be viewed as the supply of services for a consideration, but that it should be subject to an exemption since it would be difficult to calculate the amount taxable, and therefore the amount deductible.

This decision may create a degree of harmony in the application of the VAT Directive exemption, however it highlights the difficulty of categorising bitcoin and subsequent tax offences. Even if EU VAT harmonisation is achieved, it is necessary to consider third countries as well. Since bitcoins are 'transferred' in a borderless space, from peer to peer, to exchange and back again, the bitcoin itself may have become tainted by tax liability. The block chain will retain the record of the transaction subject to such liability, but it may now be under the control of an innocent third party. Still, the practical problems remain with the identification of those originally involved in the tainted transaction. While the OECD Convention on Mutual Administrative Assistance in Tax Matters facilitates cooperation between a wider range of states, it is also limited in that states should not seek to recover tax claims where the liability is contested; consequently, clarity on tax treatment is desirable.[87]

As the number of alternative cryptocurrencies increases and their circulation grows, it is necessary to consider how a coherent approach to taxation and regulation can best be achieved. In late 2015, the OECD produced a report on how to improve cooperation between tax and anti-money laundering authorities.[88] To do this, they surveyed 28 OECD member states and modelled their current practice of sharing suspicious transaction reports. They categorised the relationships into (1) 'unfettered independent tax administration access', (2) 'Joint access by Financial Intelligence Units (FIU) and tax administrations', and (3) an 'FIU decision-making model'. In the first model, both have direct access to the reports and are able to take appropriate investigation or enforcement action. In the second model, there is a panel drawn from tax administrations and FIUs who come together and decide which action to take. In the third model, the FIU decides how suspicious transaction reports should be disseminated. Given the difficulty in assessing taxation relating to bitcoins, it would seem member states should consider the first two models as preferable to the third. However, given that the AML framework is intended to adopt an all crimes approach, it would seem that the second model has the greatest potential. This allows consideration to be given to operational concerns relating to connected criminality as opposed to each prioritising their own concerns resulting in, at best, duplication of effort and wasted resources and, at worst, jeopardising an ongoing criminal investigation.

Policing in Shifting Regulatory Space

Following a spate of terror attacks in continental Europe in early 2016, the European Commission announced their Action Plan for Strengthening the Fight Against Terrorist Financing. To date, the link between the financing of terrorism and bitcoin has not been the subject of analysis but nevertheless, as with other forms of criminal finance, the Bitcoin system is an attractive option for terrorists since current regulation is piecemeal. The Commission expressly identifies that 'virtual currencies create new challenges in terms of combatting terrorist financing [because] highly versatile criminals are quick to switch to new channels if existing ones become too risky' and 'there is a risk that virtual currency transfers may be used by terrorist organisations to conceal transfers, [because] there is no reporting mechanism equivalent to that found in the mainstream banking system to identify suspicious activity'.[89] Consequently, the Commission proposed a number of amendments to the 4MLD including specifically that virtual currency exchange platforms be encompassed within its scope.[90] The Commission also proposed that it may be appropriate for the Payment Services Directive to be amended to provide for licencing and supervisory architecture and that, in the longer term, consideration should be given to the inclusion of Wallet providers in the regulatory framework. In the interim, the Commission called upon member states to agree to move forward implementation of the 4th Monday Laundering Directive to the end of 2016.

Drafting with a sense of urgency, these suggestions provided the foundation for a further Directive proposed in July 2016.[91] The critical provisions are providing a definition of virtual currency, the extension of the framework to 'providers engaged primarily and professionally in exchange services between virtual currencies and fiat currencies' and 'wallet providers offering custodial services of credentials necessary to access virtual currencies' making them obliged entities, and introducing a licencing requirement to those entities.[92] Accordingly, it appears that the Directive as amended would not capture those who provide exchange services that are auxiliary in nature nor does it address the position of miners in the system.

While acknowledging that national laws provide different definitions of tax crimes, the proposal states that this *shall* not limit the exchange of information, dissemination or use between FIUs. Nor shall member states prevent the exchange of information, the provision of assistance or place unduly restrictive conditions on such information and assistance. This is important in that it indicates a weaker commitment to the obligations placed on member to cooperate.[93]

Conclusion

It has been a turbulent time for those engaged in the bitcoin system—wallet providers, miners and bitcoin exchanges alike. The lack of regulatory clarity between jurisdictions has exacerbated the recognised vulnerabilities of the bitcoin system. The link between the anonymity and criminal exploitation has left ambiguity as to which actors are responsible for identifying suspicious activity and, once identified, what information can be retrieved by Law Enforcement and from whom. The practical challenges of investigating and prosecuting offences connected to bitcoin has gradually evolved. However, law enforcement continues to be inhibited by the technological challenges, dearth of expertise and resources required for effective policing. Still, a body of work has developed such that it is possible to give greater attention to the typologies of bitcoin exploitation.

With the introduction of the 4MLD (as amended), we see the first steps being taken to regulate the Bitcoin system with the inclusion of bitcoin exchanges and wallet service providers. It remains to be seen what impact this extension will have on engagement in a system that was expressly designed as an alternative to state-controlled medium of exchanges. Still, it is hoped that such regulatory inclusion will result in an increase in trust in the system and potentially improve the market potential of virtual currencies while simultaneously deterring criminal exploitation.

However, the extension of the anti-money laundering framework to include tax offences remains problematic. The lack of clarity on tax treatment of bitcoin within and between member states makes effective risk assessment, investigation, prosecution and cooperation difficult. It has been argued here that building on the work of the OECD, member states should consider adopting a joint FIU and tax administration model on the allocation of suspicious activity reports so that issues of tax evasion, avoidance and fraud can be identified with certainty without jeopardising competing operation matters.

Significantly, with the proposed Directive moving forward the period of implementation for the amended Directive to 1 January 2017, we can anticipate an avalanche of domestic steps being taken that will place obliged entities and law enforcement under a great deal of pressure. In terms of future proofing, the development of virtual currency regulation and its effective operation, the proposed Directive requires that the Commission report on the implementation of the directive in 2019 and that they should consider whether at that time there is a need to establish a central register of user identities and wallet addresses that will be accessible to FIUs. It will be interesting to see whether such a proposal is made, and, if so, whether that information will also be available for the administration of taxation.

Notes

1. European Central Bank, *Virtual Currencies Scheme—A Further Analysis* (ECB 2015) 4.
2. See Nikolei Kaplanov, 'Nerdy Money: Bitcoin, the Private Digital Currency, and the Case Against its Regulation' (2012) 25(1) *Loyola Consumer Law Review* 111; Jonathan Turpin, 'Bitcoin: The Economic Case for a Global, Virtual Currency Operating in an Unexplored Legal Framework' (2014) 21(1) *Indiana Journal of Global Legal Studies* 335.
3. Established by European Parliament and Council Regulation (EC) 1093/2010 of 24 November 2010 establishing a European Supervisory Authority (European Banking Authority), amending Decision No 716/2009/EC and repealing Commission Decision 2009/78/EC [2010] OJ L331/80, art 1(5) (f) it is an independent authority accountable to the EU Parliament and Council governed by its Boards of Supervisors being the 28 Heads of National Authorities.
4. See ibid.
5. European Banking Authority, *Opinion on Virtual Currencies* (2014) EBA/Op/2014/08.
6. ibid.
7. European Parliament, *Opinion of the Committee on the Internal Market and Consumer Protection on Virtual Currencies* (2016/2007(INI)).

8. ibid.

9. ibid.

10. See Mo Egan, 'Seeing is Believing: Police Practitioners as an Epistemic Community' in Maria O'Neill and Ken Swinton (eds), *Challenges and Critiques of the EU Internal Security Strategy: Rights, power and security* (Cambridge Scholars Publishing, forthcoming).

11. European Commission, *The European Agenda on Security* COM (2015) 185 final.

12. The research underpinning this chapter concluded in July 2016 and therefore readers should be alert to the temporal sensitivity of the subject matter.

13. See Satoshi Nakamoto, 'Bitcoin a Peer-to-Peer Cash System' (2008) <www.coindesk.com/bitcoin-peer-to-peer-electronic-cash-system/> accessed 28 July 17.

14. See Aleksandra Bal, 'How to Tax Bitcoin' in David Lee Kuo Chuen (ed), *Handbook of Digital Currency: Bitcoin, Innovation, Financial Instruments, and Big Data* (1st edn, Academic Press 2015).

15. See Sarah Gruber, 'Trust, Identity, And Disclosure: Are Bitcoin Exchanges The Next Virtual Havens For Money Laundering and Tax Evasion?' (2013) 32(1) *Quinnipiac Law Review* 135, fn 150.

16. See Robby Houben, 'Bitcoin: There are Two Sides to Every Coin' (2015) 26(5) *International Company and Commercial Law Review* 155.

17. For an extensive analysis of the bitcoin process, see Isaac Pflaum and Emmeline Hateley, 'A Bit of A Problem: National and Extraterritorial Regulation of Virtual Currency in the Age of Financial Disintermediation' (2014) 45(4) *Georgetown Journal of International Law* 1169.

18. See Fergal Reid and Martin Harrigan, 'An Analysis of Anonymity in the Bitcoin System' in Yaniv Altshuler and others (eds), *Security and Privacy in Social Networks* (Springer 2013).

19. James Martin, *Drugs on the Dark Net: How Cryptomarkets are Transforming the Global Trade in Illicit Drugs* (Palgrave Macmillan 2014).

20. See Sergii Shcherbak, 'How Should Bitcoin be Regulated?' (2014) 17(1) *European Journal of Legal Studies* 5.

21. See Nicholas Plassaras, 'Regulating Digital Currencies: Bringing Bitcoin Within the Reach of the IMF' (2013) 14(1) *Chicago Journal of International Law* 377.

22. Phanor Eder, 'The Legal Theories of Money' (1934) 20(1) Cornell Law Review 52, 55. See also Éric Tymoigne, 'An Inquiry into the Nature of Money: An Alternative to the Functional Approach. Or Have Tobacco, Cowry Shells, and the Like ever been Monetary Instruments?' (2006) Working Paper 481 The Levy Economics Institute of Bard College.

23. Eder (n 22) 53.

24. It should be noted that in some jurisdictions it is an administrative authority who is furnished with the responsibility of collecting and disseminating reports of suspicious activity in other member states, it is reported directly to

a law enforcement authority as per Council Decision 2000/642/JHA of 17 October 2000 concerning arrangements for cooperation between financial intelligence units of the Member States in respect of exchanging information [2000] OJ L 271/4, art 3.

25. Examining the position in the EU, see Niels Vandezande, 'Between Bitcoins and Mobile Payments: Will the European Commission's New Proposal Provide More Legal Certainty' (2014) 22(3) *International Journal of Law and Information Technology* 295.

26. Examining the position in the UK implementation of EU measures, see Robert Stokes, 'Virtual Money Laundering: The Case of Bitcoin and the Linden Dollar' (2012) 21(3) Information and Communications Technology Law 221; and examining the scope of the IMFs ability to regulate Bitcoin, see Plassaras (n 21).

27. It is notable that the computational power required is such that an individual is unlikely to be rewarded bitcoins but rather that a group of miners working together may.

28. European Parliament and Council Directive 2005/60/EC of 26 October 2005 on the prevention of the use of the financial system for the purpose of money laundering and terrorist financing [2005] OJ L 309/15.

29. European Parliament and Council Directive 2007/64/EC of 13 November 2007 on payment services in the internal market amending Directives 97/7/EC, 2002/65/EC and 2006/48/EC and repealing Directive 97/5/EC [2007] OJ L319/1.

30. European Parliament and Council Directive 2009/110/EC of 16 September 2009 on the taking up, pursuit and prudential supervision of the business of electronic money institutions amending Directives 2005/60/EC and 2006/48/EC and repealing Directive 2000/46/EC [2009] OJ L267/7.

31. Directive 2005/60/EC (n 28) arts 2 and 3.

32. European Parliament and Council Directive 2000/12/EC of relating to the taking up and pursuit of the business of credit institutions [2000] OJ L126/1, art 1(1).

33. Directive 2005/60/EC (n 28) art 3(2)(a).

34. Directive 2007/64/EC (n 29) rec 1.

35. Vandezande (n 25).

36. Directive 2007/64/EC (n 29) art 1.

37. With 'credit institution' relying on European Parliament and Council Directive 2006/48/EC of 14 June 2006 relating to the taking up and pursuit of the business of credit institutions (recast) [2006] OJ L177/1, art 4(1); with 'electronic money providers' defined in European Parliament and Council Directive 2000/46/EC of 18 September 2000 on the taking up, pursuit of and prudential supervision of the business of electronic money institutions [2000] OJ L275/39, art 3(a); and 'payment institution' being in terms of art 4(4).

38. Directive 2007/64/EC (n 29) art 4(15).

39. Vandezande (n 25) 300.
40. Michel Barnier, 'Response to Question for written answer E-003920/12 to the Commission Sergio Paolo Frances Silvestris (PPE)' (16 April 2012) OJ C247E.
41. See Vandezande (n 25) fn 42 citing Edwin Jacobs, 'Bitcoin: A Bit Too Far?' (2011) 16(2) Journal of Internet Banking and Commerce 1.
42. Barnier (n 40).
43. Board of Governors of the Federal Reserve System <www.federalreserve.gov/faqs/currency_12773.htm> accessed 28 July 17; Barnier (n 40).
44. For some figures, see Blockchain.info <https://blockchain.info/charts/n-transactions> accessed 28 July 17.
45. See Judith Lee and others, 'Bitcoin Basics: A Primer on Virtual Currencies' (2015) 16(1) Business Law International 21; James Guthrie, Decker Jochen Seidel and Roger Wattenhofer, 'Making Bitcoin Exchanges Transparent' in Gunther Pernul, Peter Ryan and Edgar Weippl (eds), *ESORICS 2015. Part II. LNCS 9327* (Springer 2015) who reports 650,000 bitcoins.
46. See Michael Malloy, 'There are No Bitcoins, Only Bit Payers: Law, Policy and Socio-Economics of Virtual Currencies' (2015) 1 *Athens Journal of Law* 21.
47. For example, Dennis Fisher, 'Dutch Police Arrest Alleged Coinvault Ransomware Authors' *Threat Post* (Woburn, 17 September 2015) <https://threatpost.com/dutch-police-arrest-alleged-coinvault-ransomware-aut hors/114707/> accessed 28 July 17; BBC, 'Scottish Hairdressing Firm Warns of Cyber Attack Threat' (27 October 2015) <www.bbc.co.uk/news/uk-scot-land-scotland-business-34647780> accessed 28 July 17.
48. See Europol, 'Spanish Network Behind the Illegal Distribution of Pay-TV Dismantled' Press Release (25 May 2016) <www.europol.europa.eu/content/spanish-network-behind-illegal-distribution-pay-tv-channels-dismant led> accessed 28 July 17; Andrew Quentson, 'Update: Bitcoin Price Plummets with Bitfinex Theft of 119,756 Bitcoins' *Crypocoins News* (2 August 2016) <www.cryptocoinsnews.com/bitcoins-price-plummets-125k-bitcoins-may-stolen-bitfinex/> accessed 28 July 17.
49. See Valsamis Mitsilegas, *EU Criminal Law* (Bloomsbury Publishing 2009), Chapter 1; Estella Baker and Christopher Harding, 'From Past Imperfect to Future Perfect? A Longitudinal Study of the Third Pillar' (2009) 34(1) European Law Review 25; Consolidated Version of the Treaty on European Union [2012] OJ C326/13, art 3(2).
50. European Parliament and Council Directive 2014/62/EU of 15 May 2014 on the protection of the euro and other currencies against counterfeiting by criminal law, and replacing Council Framework Decision 2000/383/JHA [2014] OJ L151/1, art 2(a).
51. With markets requiring supervision seeking to prevent regulatory arbitrage, and market abuse requiring criminalisation within member states, as a result of the European Parliament and Council Regulation (EU)596/2014 of 16

April 2014 on market abuse (market abuse regulation) and repealing Directive 2003/6/EC of the European Parliament and of the Council and Commission Directives 2003/124/EC, 2003/125/EC and 2004/72/EC [2014] OJ L173/1; and European Parliament and Council Directive 2014/57/EU of 16 April 2014 on criminal sanctions for market abuse (market abuse directive) [2014] OJ L173/179.

52. European Commission, *Communication from the Commission to the European Parliament, the Council, the European Economic and Social Committee and the Committee of Regions Tackling the Challenges in Commodity Markets and on Raw Materials* COM/2011/0025/FINAL, para 2(1).

53. See Edward Murphy, Maureen Murphy and Michael Seitzinger, 'Bitcoins: Questions, Answers and Analysis of Legal Issues' (2015) 7-5700 Congressional Research Service R43339.

54. 7 US Code §2(b) Transaction in Interstate Commerce.

55. Agreement on Mutual Legal Assistance Between the European Union and the United States of America [2003] OJ L181/34, art 13.

56. FATF, *The FATF Recommendations: International Standards on Combatting Money Laundering and the Financing of Terrorism and Proliferation* (FAFT/OECD 2012).

57. See Joseph Young, 'Australian Startups Close Down as Banks End Support for Bitcoin' *Bitcoin Magazine* (Nashville, 1 October 2015) <https://bitcoinmagazine.com/articles/australian-startups-close-down-as-banks-end-support-for-bitcoin-1443714795> accessed 28 July 17.

58. FATF (n 56) 31.

59. See Brigitte Unger, 'Money Laundering Regulation: From Al Capone to Al Qaeda' in Brigitte Unger and Daan van der Linde (eds), *Research Handbook on Money Laundering* (Edward Elgar Publishing 2013).

60. FATF, *Virtual Currencies Key Definitions and Potential AML CFT Risks* (FAFT/OECD 2014).

61. FATF, *Guidance for a Risk Based Approach to Virtual Currencies* (FAFT/OECD 2015) 3. They explain that all decentralised virtual currency is by definition convertible since there is no central authority that has established requirements for redemption.

62. ibid. 4.

63. ibid. 8.

64. ibid. 9.

65. Article 3(16) narrates that the definition for the purposes of the Directive is to be taken from European Parliament and Council Directive 2009/110/EC of 16 September 2009 on the taking up, pursuit and prudential supervision of the business of electronic money institutions amending Directives 2005/60/EC and 2006/48/EC and repealing Directive 2000/46/EC [2009] OJ L267/7, wherein it is defined as meaning 'electronically, including magnetically, stored monetary value as represented by a claim on the issuer which is

issued on receipt of funds for the purpose of making payment transactions as defined in point 5 of Article 4 of Directive 2007/64/EC, and which is accepted by a natural or legal person other than the electronic money issuer'.

66. European Parliament and Council Directive (EU) 2015/849 of 20 May 2015 on the prevention of the use of the financial system for the purposes of money laundering or terrorist financing amending Regulation (EU) No 648/2012 of the European Parliament and of the Council, and repealing Directive 2005/60/EC of the European Parliament and of the Council and Commission Directive 2006/70/EC (Text with EEA relevance) [2015] OJ L141/73, art 3(2) (4th Money Laundering Directive).

67. Europol, *The Internet Organised Crime Threat Assessment. IOCTA 2015 Report* (2015) 30.

68. Fourth Money Laundering Directive (n 66) recs 4 and 28.

69. ibid. rec 11 and art 3(4)(f).

70. See Margaret Beare, 'Searching for Wayward Dollars: Money Laundering of Tax Evasion—Which Dollars are We Really After?' (2002) 9(3) *Journal of Financial Crime* 259.

71. See Peter Alldridge, 'Are Tax Offences Predicate Offences for Money Laundering Offences?' (2001) 4(4) *Journal of Money Laundering Control* 350.

72. Consolidated Version of the Treaty on the Functioning of the European Union [2012] OJ C326/47, Title VII.

73. European Commission, *Communication from the Commission to the European Parliament and Council An Action Plan to Strengthen the Fight Against Tax Fraud and Tax Evasion*, COM (2012) 722 final.

74. ibid. 3.

75. Council Directive 2010/24/EU of 16 March 2010 concerning mutual assistance for the recovery of claims relating to taxes, duties and other measures [2010] OJ L84/1; Council Regulation 904/2010/EU of 7 October 2010 on administrative cooperation and combating fraud in the field of value added tax [2010] OJ L268/1; Council Directive 2011/16/EU of 15 February 2011 on administrative cooperation in the field of taxation and repealing Directive 77/799/EEC [2011] OJ L64/1 (Administrative Cooperation in Taxation Directive); Council Regulation 389/2012/EU of 2 May 2012 on administrative cooperation in the field of excise duties and repealing Regulation (EC) N° 2073/2004 [2012] OJ L121/1.

76. European Commission (n 73) 5.

77. ibid. 7.

78. ibid. 10.

79. See Council Directive 2011/16/EU of 15 February 2011 on administrative cooperation in the field of taxation and repealing Directive 77/799/EEC (Administrative Cooperation in Taxation Directive) [2011] OJ L64/1; Council Directive 2014/107/EU of 9 December 2014 amending Directive 2011/16/EU as regards mandatory automatic exchange of information in the field of taxation [2014] OJ L359/29, art 57.

80. See Marian Omri, 'A Conceptual Framework for the Regulation of Cryptocurrencies' (2015) 82 *The University of Chicago Law Review Dialogue* 53.
81. Bal (n 14).
82. ibid. 272.
83. European Central Bank, *Opinion on a Proposal for a Directive of the European Parliament and of the Council Concerning Measures to Ensure a High Level of Network and Information Security Across the Union* [2014] OJ C352/4.
84. See Margus Reiland, 'Recent Tax Developments in Estonia' (2014) paper presented at the Annual International Bar Association Conference (Tokyo, Japan).
85. Alejandro Gomez De La Cruz, 'Bitcoin is Exempt from VAT in Spain' *Law & Bitcoin* (16 April 2015) <http://lawandbitcoin.com/en/bitcoin-is-vat-exempt-in-spain/> accessed 28 July 17.
86. Case C-264/14 *Skatteverket v David Hedqvist* [2015] ECR I-718.
87. OECD, *Convention on Mutual Assistance in Tax Matters (amended by the provisions of the Protocol amending the Convention on Mutual Administrative Assistance in tax Matters)* (2011).
88. OECD, *Improving Cooperation Between Tax and Anti-Money Laundering Authorities: Access By Tax Administrations to Information Held By Financial Intelligence Units for Criminal and Civil Purposes* (2015).
89. European Commission, *Communication from the Commission to the European Parliament and the Council on an Action Plan for strengthening the fight against terrorist financing* COM (2016) 50/2,3.
90. ibid. 5.
91. European Commission, *Proposal for a Directive of the European Parliament and of the Council amending Directive (EU) 2015/849 on the prevention of the use of the financial system for the purposes of money laundering or terrorist financing and amending Directive 2009/101/EC* COM (2016) 450, 223 Final.
92. ibid. art 1.
93. Paul Cooper, 'Is There a Case for the Abolition of the Word "Shall" from EU Law?' (2011) 1 RGSL Research Papers 1.

Mo Egan is Lecturer in Criminal Law and Human Rights at the University of Stirling. She was admitted as a solicitor in 2007, and after a short period in commercial practice, she began her doctoral research in 2009. Funded by the Scottish Institute for Policing Research, she examined the policing of money laundering in a cross-jurisdictional context. In 2014, she was appointed to the Law Society of Scotland Anti-Money Laundering Panel as the academic expert. Egan continues to research in the field of justice and home affairs focusing on police cooperation, and the interplay between state and non-state agencies in the delivery of criminal justice.

10

'Fake Passports': What Is to Be Done About Trade-Based Money Laundering?

Kenneth Murray

Introduction

Trade-based money laundering ('TBML') is a problem that is relatively straightforward to describe but, from a law enforcement perspective, one that is very difficult to tackle. This chapter considers, inter alia, what might be put in place instead of traditional anti-money laundering (AML) tenets as a framework for tackling TBML, in order to at least offer the possibility that the law enforcement response to it can be materially improved. This chapter thus attempts to formulate a platform for developing ideas in this sphere that will provide practical suggestions rather than the usual counsels of despair.[1]

TBML has been defined as: '…the use of trade to move value with the intent of obscuring the true origin of funds'.[2] Another definition is: 'Simply put, this method of money laundering uses trade goods in ways that facilitate illicit value transfer'.[3] There would seem to be two different emphases here, and this chapter will proceed on the basis that one is more useful for its purpose than the other. So which is better? Is it best described as a means of disguising illicit source? Or is it better to consider it as a form of facilitating value transfer? The former is consistent with considering the question within the context of

---

The views expressed in this chapter are those of the author and should not be read as being the views of Police Scotland.

K. Murray
Police Scotland, Glasgow, UK

C. King et al. (eds.), *The Palgrave Handbook of Criminal and Terrorism Financing Law*,
https://doi.org/10.1007/978-3-319-64498-1_10

the traditional money laundering framework established by the Financial Action Task Force (FATF),[4] which emphasises the centrality of predicate offence and relies for exposition on the 'placement-layering-integration' paradigm. However, even the most cursory contemplation of what TBML is, and how it is achieved, indicates that these concept tools—already in some eyes somewhat discredited[5]—really do not serve very well at all when it comes to formulating an approach to TBML that has any chance of making meaningful impact on its incidence. For the purpose of this chapter, therefore, preference is given to the second definition of TBML above: to consider TBML as a phenomenon that is primarily to do with trade. Thus, TBML manifests as a transfer of value through the means of trade, primarily through some falsification of the paperwork. In this chapter, therefore, TBML is considered as an offence in its own right—one that is best tackled in terms of its incidence rather than in terms of its provenance.

What Is TBML?

The essence of TBML can be quickly grasped through the use of the following simplified example in Fig. 10.1.

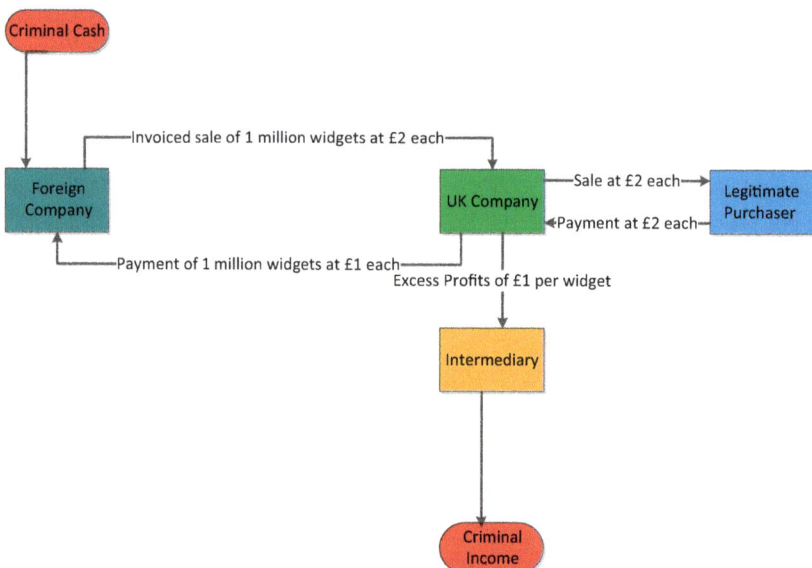

Fig. 10.1 A hypothetical TBML scenario

The criminal cash is paid to the foreign company, which then invoices the UK company for a value which is twice the money it actually receives. The criminal value is thus effectively transferred under the 'false passport' of the invoice. The UK company has effectively received the goods for half the invoiced value and is able to realise the profit arising from this difference by selling the goods for the invoiced value to a legitimate purchaser—essentially realising the criminal value through normal trading at normal prices. The realised criminal value can then be distributed by way of dividends or loans or other transfers to another vehicle in the UK, which in turn enables access for the intended recipients of the criminal value to the laundered funds—or more precisely funds *representing* the laundered funds—in the UK.

There are many variations on this theme. For example, it may be that the quantities of the commodity are falsified rather than the values relating to it. The key defining characteristic is the existence of some form of deceit in the invoicing—the 'passport' for the goods has been falsified to conceal the transfer of illicit value. It follows that any evidence of such a falsified 'passport' in the context of commercial trading is, or at least ought to be considered, strong prima facie evidence of a TBML mechanism being in place.

An admirably minimalist description of TBML was suggested in *The Economist* as follows:

> The basic technique is mis-invoicing. To slip money into a country, undervalue imports or overvalue exports: do the reverse to get it out.[6]

In other words, mis-invoicing enables the transfer of criminal value through trading channels. The criminal value essentially travels under a fake passport. It would therefore appear to make sense to focus on the *incidence* of fake passports in considering how to design combative action within the context of international trade.

The Size and Incidence of TBML

The nature and extent of TBML makes systematic analysis of incidence difficult. It is a form of money laundering that relates to the transfer of *value* rather than money, usually through some form of mis-invoicing.[7] The scope of international trade, when matched against the available resources to check the relevant paperwork, makes it an attractive route for launderers with very low rates of detection. It is also a practice, until recently, that was 'under the radar' in terms of law enforcement awareness and response.

A recent TBML report from the private sector commented, 'though essentially unquantifiable, the scope of the problem is enormous by all indications'.[8] Disparities in trading figures between source and destination nations can, however, provide a guide to the size of the TBML problem. *The Economist*[9] in 2014 cited official trade figures sourced by the International Monetary Fund (IMF) and Global Financial Integrity (GFI) showing that the value of Mexican exports to the USA between 1994 and 2014 was significantly higher than US imports from Mexico—to an extent that it could not be plausibly accounted for by accounting or data errors. The explanation, attributed to Brian Le Blanc of GFI, was that Mexican groups were using TBML to bring dollars into Mexico.

The most recent authoritative guide providing a reliable gauge on size and incidence is that provided in the GFI report on *Illicit Financial Flows from Developing Countries* between 2004 and 2013.[10] That report calculates that the value of such flows in that period breached the $1 trillion mark in 2013. It also noted that this threshold, in the light of improved data analysis, had actually been reached in 2011[11] and had increased at a rate of 6.5% per annum.[12] That GFI report emphasised the scale of the problem posed for developing countries by TBML, identifying trade mis-invoicing[13] as the principal means used for illicit exporting of wealth from developing countries. Over the ten-year period of the study, the fraudulent mis-invoicing of trade was responsible for 83% of illicit financial outflows.

The problem is clearly global in scope and massive in size. The breaching of the $1 trillion watermark suggests a problem that is roughly equivalent in size to the GDP of Australia, the 20th largest economy in the world.[14] Whereas it has been difficult in the past to assess the size of the problem by reference to reliable empirical data, the advent and rapid development of big data analytical methods—producing statistics based on anomalies between the goods transported through trade channels and their invoiced value—is starting to address this and thereby make the issue of TBML more difficult to ignore. The major accountancy and professional service firms already sense this and are seizing the opportunity to sell their big data analytical services on the basis that 'TBML may finally be poised to see action by regulators and trade finance businesses commensurate with its global scope and impact'.[15]

It follows, therefore, that TBML is a problem that is too big an issue for law enforcement and regulatory authorities to ignore. What it represents, essentially, is the big door left open after international AML efforts in the financial sector—implemented under the guidance of FATF—have shut, or attempted to shut, those doors available through abuse of the financial and banking systems.[16]

Current Responses to TBML

Given the apparent scale of the problem, why has so little action been taken thus far? In a seminal article on the subject of TBML, John Zdanowicz argued, in 2009, that: 'International trade as a means of laundering money is a technique generally ignored by most law enforcement agencies'.[17] In the intervening years, it seems that little has changed. A 2015 UK 'National Risk Assessment' of money laundering and terrorist financing does not say a great deal about TBML and appears to confine its consideration of the issue to money laundering conducted through abuse of trade finance, thus bringing it into the compass of the onerous AML compliance regimes applying to the financial sector.[18] The Risk Assessment briefly mentions a thematic review conducted by the Financial Conduct Authority (FCA) in 2013,[19] claiming that 'this work [*ie the FCA review*], alongside that by law enforcement agencies on MSBs, has brought trade based money laundering to the forefront of the UK banks' risk agenda'.

However, if we turn to the FCA thematic review itself, we see instead that it concluded that the majority of banks sampled, including major UK banks, were not taking adequate measures to mitigate the risk of money laundering and terrorist financing in their trade finance business.[20] The FCA review commented: 'More work is required at most banks to ensure high-risk customers and transactions are identified and appropriate action is taken by senior management'.[21]

The impression from the National Risk Assessment is that the UK government clearly wishes to be seen to acknowledge TBML as a threat, but one to be considered primarily within the context of the existing AML compliance regime. This would suggest that the primary responsibility for stopping TBML again rests with the financial sector and even might imply that any growing preponderance of it as a phenomenon might be considered a result of inadequate application of compliance procedures relating to trade finance by the banks.

The scope of TBML, however, cannot be adequately addressed by confining attention to trade finance compliance measures. A number of misinvoicing methods identified in the 2006 FATF report would slip by such compliance measures without too much difficulty.[22] The problem therefore appears to be too broad to be adequately tackled by established approaches.

This might mean that, for the time being, it is in the 'too difficult' box to be confined there for as long as it continues to fall under the radar as an issue requiring urgent attention.

The Difficulties of Applying Financial Sector-Based Responses to International Trade

The difficulties in trying to adapt an institutional response to money laundering issues arising in the context of trade, based on existing initiatives derived from the financial sector, are summed up by McSkimming:

> …. there are legitimate questions about whether the FATF's mandate extends to the trade system and whether it is the best forum to propagate reform, given the existence of international organisations devoted specifically to trade security and border control. It may be, for instance, that the FATF's financial sector expertise is of little practical benefit in the trade sector. … given their preponderant focus on the financial sector, it is questionable whether these organisations are well placed to pursue a TBML/TF agenda. There is also, conceivably, a question about whether the expertise of these organisations extends to perennially delicate trade negotiations.[23]

Writing in 2010, McSkimming concluded that without reliable data, the best thing to do about TBML was nothing.[24] He identified a number of characteristics of international trade which made the monitoring, or policing, of it particularly onerous: the sheer amount of it[25]; the huge variation in commodities; a high incidence of misleading and incomplete documentation; the use of tradable instruments such as Bills of Lading which served to disassociate ownership; and the fact that the various layers of documentation tended to mitigate against transparency rather than enhancing it. In McSkimming's view, the difficulties arising from concerted attempts to deal with TBML through regulation were so fraught with obstacles, that it was questionable whether anything could be done at all:

> Given how little is known about the economic effects of TBML/TF, there are good reasons to be prudent in formulating a policy response…In the present circumstances, in the absence of any reliable data on the scale of TBML/TF and the extent to which it is distorting otherwise well functioning markets, there is scope for the remedy to be worse than the disease. Increased TBML/TF regulation would increase the cost of international trade, with an obvious effect on prices. Further, it would act as a trade barrier—with consequently profound

effects on domestic competitiveness and productivity. Given this, further research is needed before extensive new regulation is adopted.[26]

Implications of the 'Do Nothing' Response

The 'do nothing' response is an attractive argument. It could be argued that the inability to form a coherent institutional response to TBML is a function of an unspoken consensus: TBML is a subject for the moment best treated by mere description of the threat[27] as an inchoate awareness-raising exercise, allied to an implication that the particular risks it poses can be accommodated somehow within the AML framework built around financial institutions.[28]

Describing the problem is one thing, doing something about it is another. Until there is some consensus as to the form such action should take, McSkimming's counsel is likely to be influential, although to an extent unlikely to be officially acknowledged. But it is not likely to prove a sustainable position, however, if a growing appreciation develops that TBML is, as Zdanowicz describes it, the 'back door'[29] for dirty money in those jurisdictions where the compliance regimes of banks have done their job and the banking system has become less easy to penetrate. That is a perception that would potentially do much damage to the reputation and credibility of the entire AML endeavour. Indeed, banks might reasonably ask why they should commit so much time and resources to blocking money laundering routes, when there is so little being done to block money laundering through international trade.

There is persuasive research indicating that the threat of trade routes taking the place of banking routes for illicit funds is not fanciful. There has been extensive research on the applicability of gravity-based trade models to TBML,[30] in particular with the publication of a paper published by De Nederlandsche Bank (DNB) in 2011.[31] This DNB paper builds upon the ground work of Zdanowicz,[32] refined by Bikker[33] and then Unger and Den Hertog.[34] The DNB paper applied gravity-type equations (based on the Walker gravity model)[35] to empirical data in a bid to determine whether this analysis was able to explain bilateral money laundering flows.

The essence of the gravity model is that it describes the geographical allocation of the proceeds of crime by explaining the key factors governing the flow between them. These factors include those that make a country an attractive repository for criminal funds, relative to the country from which they were sourced, thus setting up the equivalent of a gravitational pull on criminal funds exerted by the destination company on the source country. The other explanatory variables of significance identified in the DNB research included the physical distance between the source and destination country, the existence of a common border and the size of the economy of the destination country.

Application of the model to the empirical data appeared to confirm intuitive impressions about the nature of the incidence of TBML. Its incidence is closely correlated to the extent of licit trade—the more trade there is in a certain trading channel between two companies, the less likely TBML will be noticed. As would also be expected, the destination country is likely to have a less exacting AML regime than the source country—the essence of the exercise after all is to transfer the criminal proceeds to a place where they can be more easily 'enjoyed' or at least more easily integrated into the legitimate economy.[36] The researchers concluded that their empirical results sustained the intention of the gravity model in this context—to explain the flow of criminal monies via TBML between a source and destination country.[37] The DNB work, therefore, provides a rare empirical foundation on the subject, which appears to confirm findings which, for the most part, correlate with those that might have been predicted on the basis of intuition.

It is also worth drawing attention to another particularly noteworthy conclusion of the researchers, concerning the relationship between AML efforts and the prevalence of TBML:

> One might expect that governments which agree to fight money laundering experience less TBML. However, our results suggest the opposite: countries which have strict anti-money laundering regulation, experience more trade based money laundering. This may indicate that criminals have discovered a new way of laundering by using TBML to escape stricter anti-money laundering regulation of the financial sector.[38]

The Impact of TBML on the Credibility of AML Efforts as a Whole

The sheer volume of TBML that is now implied by trade data analysis[39] suggests it is more than a displacement effect. TBML is a well-established practice involving the application of a high degree of experience and expertise using an amalgam of methods ranging from the tried and tested to the highly imaginative.[40] The findings of the DNB research appear resilient to serious challenges and have significant implications not just for the integrity of the trading channels affected but for the credibility of AML efforts worldwide.

The tendency of governments to continue to pin responsibility for AML on the financial sector—imposing a significant layer of cost on the sector in the process[41]—is to an extent a function of the enforced acquiescence of banks and financial institutions in the post-2008 financial crash climate. As that sector slowly recovers its reputation, however, it is increasingly likely that it will seek to draw attention to the clearer and more distinct messages now being made available by big data analysis regarding the incidence of TBML. Whereas banks have some exposure to TBML through the provision of trade finance and other trade-related financial products to international trade, they are bound to point out that a serious onslaught against TBML will require a good portion of the AML burden to fall on others' shoulders, such as those of law enforcement and customs officials.

The TBML challenges that McSkimming[42] considered too difficult to confront in 2010 are therefore likely to be increasingly perceived as too important to ignore. In addition to greater visibility afforded by big data analytics, another reason TBML may not be ignored for much longer is the existence of more acute and plausible international terrorist threats and a more sharply developed focus on how these threats are funded.

TBML and Terrorist Financing

The existence of channels enabling significant flows of terrorist enabling finance now regularly commands political and media attention. It is now more widely understood that the movement of criminal monies across borders is not a subject which concerns only banks and financial institutions. The ability of ISIS to fund itself through oil sales, for example, involved the willingness of middlemen to buy that oil from ISIS and the willingness of purchasers in domestic and international markets to buy that oil from the middlemen, even when the source of that oil was known and the purchasers were ISIS enemies.[43]

Exposures arising from links between TBML and terrorist financing were identified in the original FATF paper of 2006.[44] In 2009, John Zdanowicz published a paper entitled 'Trade Based Money Laundering and Terrorist Financing'[45] which discussed the use of interquartile range price analysis ('IQRP analysis') to determine trade risk in the context of tackling terrorist financing. Indices determined in respect of country profile, product profile and custom district profile were based on calculating the dollar amounts of money moved out of the USA as a percentage of total trade for a country, product or customs district. The application of IQRP analysis to expose abnormal trade weights was of particular relevance, quoting examples such as razors from Egypt at 15 kg per unit, footwear from France at 46 kg a pair and towels from Pakistan at 2 kg per unit.[46] Zdanowicz acknowledged that profiling trade for security purposes would never be a universally popular practice, but he argued that it was vital to combat both money laundering and trade financing and that there should be efforts made to internationalise the practice.

The *New York Times* outlined an example of the nexus between terrorist financing and international trade in an article published in 2011.[47] This involved the use of a Lebanese bank in Canada to launder drug money as well as divert funds to Hezbollah as shown in Fig. 10.2.

The TBML in this process was based around the use of used motor cars as transportable stores of value. They were bought into the USA using money from an account at the Lebanese Canadian Bank ('LCB') and shipped to the west coast of Africa. The purpose of this trade was to generate legitimate-looking trading profits which could act as a mixer or diluting agent for the criminal profits earned from cocaine exported to West Africa from South America and then transmitted to the LCB through exchange houses.

The TBML element in this process was extended to the purchase of trade goods from China which were then sold in the South American countries that supplied the cocaine, thereby funding a scheme to recompense the relevant producers. As part of this process, money was also siphoned off to fund Hezbollah in Lebanon. The process therefore represented a template showing how international terrorist organisations could exploit international trading channels in a way that brought financial independence.

As reported by Reuters,[48] LCB was subsequently sued in 2013 by the US authorities[49] and agreed to pay a $102 million settlement. This compared with the $230 million originally sought in a lawsuit that accused LCB of using the US banking system to launder drug-trafficking profits through West Africa back to Lebanon. The US Attorney General for the Southern District of New York, Preet Bharara, hailed this result, claiming: 'Today's settlement shows that bank's laundering money for terrorists and narco-traffickers will face consequences for their actions, wherever they may be located'.[50]

TBML and the Law

Given that TBML is capable of being used to finance international terrorism, it has been argued that the logic of prevention requires that the AML regime applying to banks should apply to all parties in 'the international supply

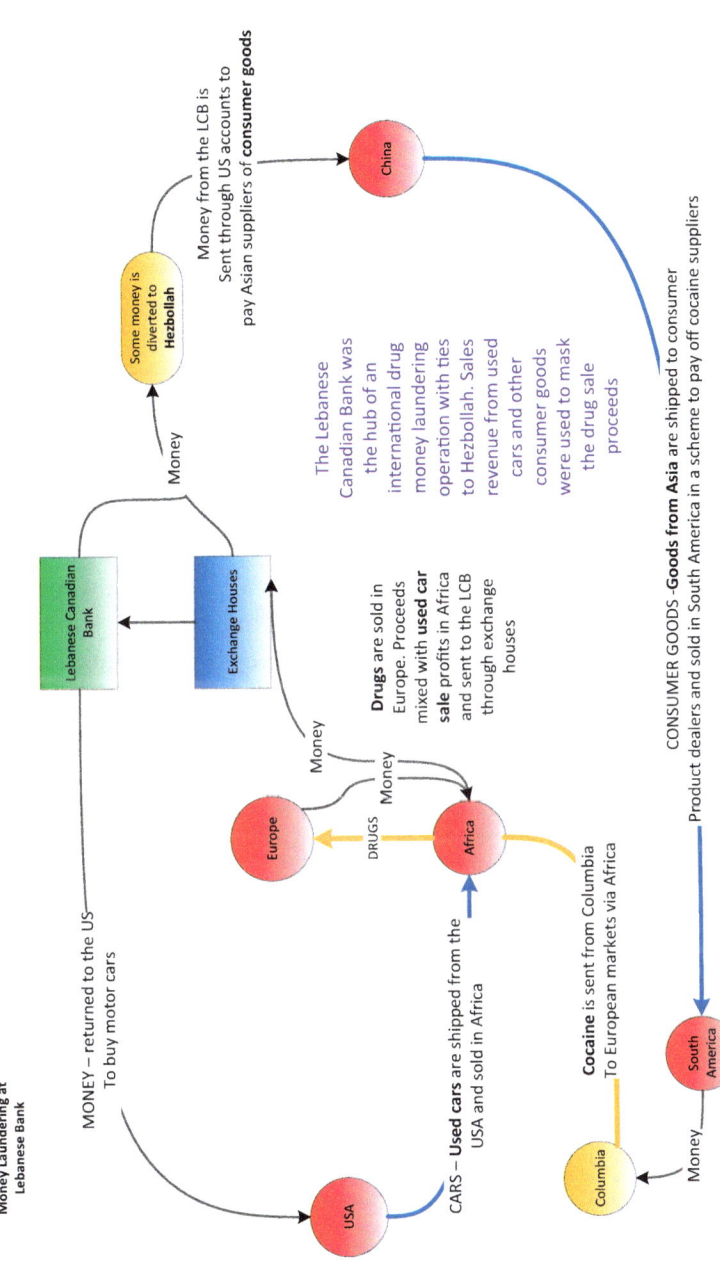

Fig. 10.2 Money Laundering at Lebanese Bank diagram. Source: 'Money Laundering at Lebanese Bank' *New York Times*, December 13, 2011

chain'.[51] This suggestion clearly runs into McSkimming's objections (discussed earlier),[52] but Delston and Walls provide a penetrating analysis of the relationship between TBML and the criminal law, which identifies TBML as a serious crime, but one of a nature that makes it unlikely to be treated as such.

Delston and Walls highlight the difference between the concept of *lex ferenda* (the law as it should be, which they characterise as 'soft law') and *lex lata* (the law as it is, which they characterise as 'hard law'). They make the point that the development of common policies in the international sphere is always more likely to be based on soft law measures because they can deliver with the necessary speed, flexibility and simplicity what can be defended as progress in matters requiring international co-operation.

Soft law measures do not contain explicit and binding mechanisms featuring the imposition of specific sanctions for provision violation. For Delston and Walls, this lack of specific sanctions offers particular attractions for endeavours such as the international response to money laundering. Recourse to litigation is avoided in favour of penalties for non-compliance, which may amount only to broadcasting the fact of non-compliance. This enables the overall object of criminalisation to be recognised internationally, while allowing the methods by which this is achieved to remain open, thus emphasising the modern taste for nudge effects through improving compliance with a view to 'increasing opportunities to engage in desirable behaviour'.[53]

The FATF recommendations of 2006[54] represent a code developed in accordance with these principles, and the essential point of Delston and Walls' paper is that the characteristics of TBML are particularly suited to the same treatment. The recommendations identify a list of red flags which can be used to devise a suitable compliance programme based on Suspicious Activity Reporting for participants in the international trading chain, in the same way as applies to the current AML regime affecting financial institutions and others in the regulated sector.

Another point about the distinction between soft and hard law, however, is that the benefits of using soft law measures—as outlined by Delston and Walls—come at a cost. Whereas the intention and commitment to find and punish money launderers is frequently delivered by law makers—with much apparent resolution and sincerity (*pace* Preet Bharara above)—the extent to which such intentions are deliverable is frequently brought into question.[55] The price of relying on soft law is the perception that it constitutes a soft form of enforcement. The prevailing impression—on the part of both criminals and law enforcers—could well be that the system is not really capable of punishing the crime or making examples of the perpetrators.

The implied hope in soft law measures is that the deterrent effect of oner-ous compliance regimes will replace the traditional jobs of law enforcement, in particular investigation and prosecution. The attraction to governments is the implied shift of the burden and cost of policing the respective channels. The incidence of any enforcement measures would fall on the shoulders of the financial institutions—and the *legitimate* participants in international trading channels—if ever the Delston and Walls recommendations were to come into force.

Tackling TBML Through Compliance 'Red Flags'

In the financial world there has been a mushrooming of compliance schools and service companies[56] set up to exploit the considerable revenue stream that carrying this soft law burden generates. These have been funded, of course, by the banks, meaning ultimately the banks' customers. The extension of this approach to international trade might well generate another specialised com-pliance industry, perhaps based around the following red flags suggested by Delston and Walls[57] (the inverted commas are added by the author of this chapter):

- Items shipped that are 'inconsistent' with the nature of the customer's business;
- Customers conducting business in 'high-risk' jurisdictions
- Customers involved in 'high-risk' activities
- 'Obvious' over- or under-pricing of goods and services
- 'Obvious' misrepresentation of the quantity or type of goods imported and exported
- Transactions that are 'unnecessarily complex'
- Transactions which do not make 'economic sense'
- Transactions involving 'front or shell' companies

With the possible exception of the last item, the words enclosed in inverted commas in these 'red flag' examples would all appear to require the making of some kind of subjective assessment as to whether a red flag should be actioned or not. It may not be overly cynical to suggest that, in respect of these red flag criteria, there would be a profusion of reporting by legitimate players keen to protect their reputations. Reminiscent of ongoing difficulties with the SARs regime, such over-reporting would likely pose its own difficulties in terms of establishing a monitoring regime of sufficient capacity to deal with it, never mind one which had the requisite skillsets on board to competently make the value judgments required.

The extension of Trade Transparency Units ('TTUs'—bilateral agreements between countries committed to the principles of transparent trade as established by the USA in 2004)[58] might, however, provide a suitable model upon which efforts designed to effect a renewed impetus in this area could be based. The essence of TTUs is that they enable both countries to see both sides of a trade transaction so that trade anomalies indicative of TBML can be identified. At the very least, their extended use might shine a light on incidence and practice that would focus attention on how dissident practices redolent of TBML could be countered.

Seasoned TBML practitioners can be expected to adjust their practices to ensure that their value transfers are documented in such a way that they do not trigger red flags. That is not a reason for failing to engage suitable compliance measures but a reminder of the limitations such approaches can achieve on their own. Ultimately, criminal sanctions that can be shown to be effective are likely to remain important deterrents.

TBML and Prosecutions

The further issue to consider, in terms of obtaining the consensus necessary to implement a compliance regime based on the red flags identified, is demonstrating what would be actually done with the genuine positives (disregarding for now the probably very onerous problem of false positives). How would the information made available from a trade-based SAR be rendered capable of being translated into a money laundering investigation that had a better-than-average chance of obtaining a conviction?

Given the experience of financially based SARs, interest groups whose members are being asked to implement such a regime imposed on their international trading activities may prove resistant. There might be significant penalties to pay for non-compliance, but that is not the same as punishing the perpetrators of the actual crime.

Will there be a satisfactory incidence of prosecutions? The problems of prosecuting money laundering in general will also apply to TBML-based cases too. At the heart of these problems are what might be considered fundamental flaws inherent in how the crime of money laundering is defined in international jurisdictions, which make it in practice extremely difficult to prosecute. If there is no deterrent quite as effective as publicised prosecution, the converse point might well be made whereby a lack of prosecutions is likely to undermine the basis for the consent required in the relevant soft law compliance regimes.[59]

What, then, are these fundamental flaws in how money laundering is defined, and is it possible to do anything about them, especially in the context of the considerable challenge that TBML presents?

The difficulty can be traced to the adoption by the FATF, in 2006,[60] of a definition of money laundering that relies on the identification of a 'predicate offence'. The logic derives from the notion that the offence of money laundering requires that the money in question be derived from some form of prior action constituting a crime. It becomes a derived offence in other words, and the natural channel of defence open to those accused of it is to cast doubt on the integrity of the evidential link between the 'predicate' crime and the action held to constitute a money laundering offence. The scope for this process of deflection is nowhere more evident than with TBML.

The reality of modern money laundering is that arrangements are made precisely so there is no continuity of linkage between predicate crime and the visible channels used to launder the proceeds. Breaks will be engineered and other funds substituted to make sure that a classic 'follow the money' back to the crime investigation will meet a cul-de-sac in terms of an apparently genuine legitimate source or an obscure labyrinth of interconnected transactions with an ultimate source that is untraceable.[61]

It is not uncommon in practice for irregular fund flows to be uncovered by law enforcement agencies, where the characteristics of the trading flows are such that it is virtually inconceivable that TBML is not involved. Yet the law agency can be powerless to do anything with the information because it cannot specify anything about the original source of the funds.

A recent example experienced by the author involved a communication from a US agency concerning a US-based jeweller that was receiving significant transfers of funds relating to industrial goods that had no connection with the jewellery business. The funds were being wired from Latvia. The address provided for the shippers, as personally vouched by the author,[62] was a modest semi-detached personal residence in a housing scheme in Rosyth, a naval port in Fife, Scotland.

The brief details provided here with respect to this referral would be sufficient to action red flags in accordance with the Delston and Walls list. Assuming an expanded reporting regime was in place to cover the trading parties concerned, however, and even if the requisite reports were filed, it seems clear, on current interpretations of US money laundering law, that the prosecuting authorities would not be able to do much with these reports unless they had evidence of criminality relating to the source funds being sent from Latvia (which in this case they did not).

In the UK, money laundering offences enacted in the Proceeds of Crime Act 2002 (POCA)[63] appeared (at least initially)[64] to provide an alternative means of establishing the requisite criminality. One respected authority heralded the

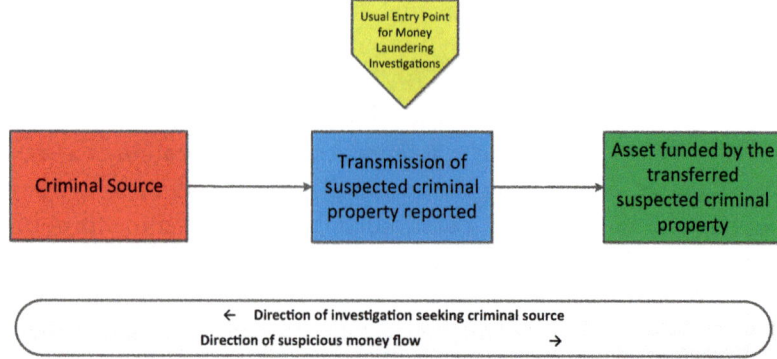

Fig. 10.3   Proceeds of crime timeline. Source: Author

introduction of this legislation as a development that consigned the imported US concept of predicate offence 'to the jurisprudential dustbin'.[65]

As Fig. 10.3 illustrates, proving the money is criminal by reference to the predicate offence would imply a retrospective trace of the funds to the criminal source. As already noted, however, this is a process that an organised crime group does not, typically, find difficult to thwart.

POCA was actually designed in such a way as to recognise this. The Crown Prosecution Service website set out the position as follows:

> Prosecutors are **not** required to prove that the property in question is the benefit of a **particular** or **specific** act of criminal conduct, as such an interpretation would restrict the operation of the legislation. The prosecution need to be in a position, as a minimum, to be able to produce sufficient circumstantial evidence or other evidence from which inferences can be drawn to the required criminal standard that the property in question has a criminal origin (*emphasis in original*).[66]

This guidance, therefore, appears to recognise that the design of money laundering methods, where there is little or no prospect of obtaining an evidential link to a predicate offence (as will usually be the case with TBML), requires an ability, or an option, to prosecute the crime without reference to what is commonly referred to as predicate offence.

TBML and Proving Criminality

The ability to prove criminality through circumstantial evidence is also explicitly recognised in the relevant case law, specifically the case of *R v Anwoir*[67] (the key findings of which were endorsed for Scottish purposes in the appeal hearing in *HMA v Ahmed*)[68]:

...there are two ways in which the Crown can prove the property derives from crime, a) by showing that it derives from conduct of a specific kind or kinds and that conduct of that kind or kinds is unlawful, or b) by evidence of the circumstances in which the property is handled which are such as to give rise the irresistible inference that it can only be derived from crime.[69]

Even though the *'irresistible inference'* test is now established, there is still ground to cover in terms of achieving a necessary consensus as to how the required standard of criminality can be proved. Some recent judgments appear to embody the intended effect of reestablishing the concept of predicate offence as an essential tenet of how the POCA money laundering offences are to be conceived. The key initial judgment of this type was given in the *Geary* case,[70] and the findings of this case have been further endorsed recently in *R v GH*.[71]

These judgments say that section 328 offences relating to arrangements have to apply to property that can be identified as criminal at the time the arrangement begins to operate on it:

In our view the natural and ordinary meaning of section 328(1) is that the arrangement to which it refers must be one which relates to property which is criminal property at the time when the arrangement begins to operate on it. To say that it extends to property which was originally legitimate but became criminal only as a result of carrying out the arrangement is to stretch the language of the section beyond its proper limits.[72]

R v GH clarified the issue as follows: 'criminal property for the purposes of sections 327, 328 and 329 means property obtained as a result of or in connection with criminal activity separate from that which is the subject of the charge itself'.[73]

So the property must be criminal at the outset. But how can that be proved? 'Criminal property' is defined in section 340 as follows: 'a) it constitutes a person's benefit from criminal conduct or it represents such a benefit (in whole or in part and whether directly or indirectly) and b) the alleged offender knows or suspects that it constitutes or represents such a benefit'.[74] Because criminal property is defined in POCA in terms of knowledge, it could be construed that what the *Geary* and *GH* judgments are saying is that there is a requirement to prove that the accused knew the property was criminal when he first came into contact with it. A difficulty arises, however, if this proposition can be interpreted as meaning that the method of treatment by the accused cannot be founded on as a basis for determining his knowledge of its criminality prior to receiving it.

This line of judgments leaves it uncertain as to when the property becomes criminal in terms of proof. Criminal awareness is clearly connected to the nature of the arrangements that the accused participates in. That awareness may well develop and become clear when he is able to properly appraise the true nature of these arrangements. It is not clear from the text of the relevant POCA provisions that this has to be at the start of his involvement in these arrangements. This is a matter of considerable practical significance since it is often the case that the proof of awareness in these circumstances can only be established by the manner in which the accused treats the relevant funds.

The implication of the *Geary* and *GH* judgments is that there are two distinct parts of the criminal property definition that have to be separately proven, and that the criminality of the property has to be proven at the outset of the arrangement, before the action that constitutes the money laundering offence commences. In other words, these judgments appear to take away the possibility of establishing cases where the relevant criminal knowledge is revealed by means of the way in which the money is treated.

The *GH* judgment appears to confirm this through its discussion of the drafting of section 340 as follows:

> As a matter of strict English, the way in which the section has been drafted may be criticised for condensing the separate ingredients of actus reus and mens rea into one. But it places no undue strain on the language to read the section as providing that a person commits an offence if a) he enters into or becomes concerned in an arrangement (relating to criminal property), and b) he knows or suspects that it does so.[75]

The judgment then follows this with a sentence which has profound significance:

> It has to be sensibly read in that way or else a party might be guilty by reason of having the necessary mens rea even if it transpired that the property was not criminal.[76]

What this last sentence might imply is that a catch-all defence is available to all organised crime groups using money laundering schemes which show the most basic levels of sophistication. No matter how compelling the evidence might be relating to the accused's treatment of the money concerned, the lack of any direct evidence proving its criminality at the outset of his engagement with it means he cannot be found guilty—in case it turns out that it is not. It is not easy to reconcile this with the 'irresistible inference' doctrine unless it is subsequently made clear by the courts that actions of deceit in treatment can qualify as evidence of criminality in cases where, as is often going to be the case, there is a lack of evidence of criminal source.

There have been recent cases in Scotland[77] settled by plea where it has been possible to achieve 'irresistible inference' convictions on the basis of evidence that principally related to how the criminal property was accounted for. If legal agents acting for money launderers were encouraged, however, to consider that *de facto* proof of predicate offence is a requirement for successful prosecution, then clearly the plea bargaining dynamic would be materially altered. The signals taken from judicial interpretation of the legislation will have arguably gone some way to neutering its effectiveness. The most progressive money laundering offences on any statute book in the world would have been corralled into the same box as those jurisdictions still requiring a predicate or specified offence, with the same attendant constraints against effectiveness.

It is not clear in this context how TBML can be effectively prosecuted at all if the insistence of predicate offence evidence is adhered to, since it is likely to be, routinely, almost impossible to secure evidential links to the source of the property in TBML trading transactions. The difficulty with the reasoning of the judgments quoted in this area is that interpretations which are secure in terms of their internal reasoning can fail in terms of forming a basis for dealing with the characteristics that manifest in reality of the criminal activity the legislation seeks to tackle.

It may be that there is a sense within relevant legal opinion that the apparent confinements imposed on the scope of the UK money laundering legislation by the *GH* judgment represents a 'best answer' compromise in respect of an offence with which the judiciary have perhaps never been comfortable.[78] The use of money laundering offences as optional add-ons to other charges was criticised by Lord Toulson in the *GH* judgment,[79] but in practice, it may become difficult to use the offences for anything else given the apparent reluctance to offer a secure and accepted understanding of the circumstances under which the 'irresistible inference' doctrine may be applied.

New Tools to Tackle TBML: Alternative Methods of Combat

The lack of any consensus upon which to base an internationally recognised charge of money laundering, where the circumstances are such that a trace back to the root source is impossible, makes the prospect of achieving effective international policing of this activity an ever-remote possibility. If that is the case it is perhaps incumbent on law makers to consider whether the legislative tools currently at their disposal are up to the job. If they are not, what additional or new tools would make a difference?

In order to be effective, these new tools would need to command a degree of acceptance across a broad international canvas. What would the characteristics of such measures be, such that they might be able to secure the necessary consensus? Providing persuasive answers to these questions may require taking a step back to examine the usefulness of the everyday terminology used in this field and consider whether it may be getting in the way of reaching solutions.

Levi[80] has suggested that many of the difficulties of this field are possibly caused by the term 'money laundering'. Some of the set notions around money laundering do seem much less useful now compared to when they were originally devised. Aside from the problems associated with the legacy of 'predicate offence', even the 'placement-layering-integration' model—still routinely used to explain what it is[81]—has significant limitations when it comes to understanding forms of money laundering which originate within the financial system itself.[82]

Is 'money laundering' therefore the best way to describe the criminal activity we are seeking to tackle when we talk of TBML? If this problem was to be considered anew with a clean sheet of paper, it would likely be that we would consider different approaches to solving it. The purpose of the TBML crime is to enable the transmission of criminal value. Proving criminality is problematic, as discussed above. Proving criminality through the actual *actus reus* is also not straightforward within the context of 'money laundering'. However, where it can be shown that money or value has been transported from one location to another under what amounts to a fake passport in the form of some form or other of mis-invoicing, there would appear to be a workable basis for establishing culpability that could be exploited.

McSkimming[83] identified the practical difficulties of casting effective policing supervision over the mammoth volumes involved in international trading channels. That is a problem for the effectiveness of approaches based exclusively on soft law compliance and suspicious reporting regimes. There needs to be another tool brought out of the box—a complementary backup based on tenets more associated with hard law. Well-defined rules need to be established which, if broken, lead to tangible adverse consequences for the rule breakers.

One of the successes of the FATF approach has been its ability, as commented upon by Delston and Wells,[84] to obtain international compliance in respect of its recommendations. Essentially this was achieved by means of a 'name and shame' approach. No nation wanted to be identified as a pariah because they all understood this would have adverse consequences for economic well-being, not to mention international reputation. There should also therefore be a common interest among all nations to tackle TBML, on the basis that it undermines legitimate trade and hampers long-term economic growth. If there was a consensus that could be reached whereby all international shipments were made subject to an internationally recognised virtual licensing arrangement which permitted passage *so long as it was not taken away,* that would establish a basis for punitive deprivation—a tangible punishment in other words for enabling a transfer of value using 'fake passports'. This again might be based on an extension of the American-type TTU, so that it had multilateral rather than bilateral effects.[85]

The possibility of prosecution may well be considered too remote to represent a meaningful deterrent, but the imposition of a credible threat to the ability to trade might obtain a more compliant response. International trading already operates through various processes of consent in terms of whom you can trade with, where you can dock and what you can ship. If you are found to have accommodated a process of TBML, an internationally recognised blackmark could be applied in such a way as to restrict the ability to trade. The possibility of such a mark being applied would be sufficient to change the atmosphere in relevant trading relationships, so that a tangible disincentive would be created to becoming involved with partners whose paperwork was unsatisfactory. The climate so created would also tend to encourage self-policing, with low-risk compliant players likely to disassociate themselves from high-risk players.

Any further process of prosecution could involve establishing offences and sanctions within an FATF framework in the manner already successfully achieved in respect of traditional money laundering offences. If the offences devised were to be constructed along traditional lines, however, certain difficulties would be easy to foresee. The nature of international trading documentation would give rise to proof problems based around who was responsible for what and the extent to which 'mistakes' could in any sense be criminalised. The adjustment required to address this problem is still possible, however, for it has already been introduced in respect of the response to another international economic crime problem formerly considered intractable, namely bribery.

The UK Bribery Act: Transferable Lessons?

The UK Bribery Act 2010 crossed a threshold in a manner which has the potential as a precedent to transform the landscape of a major economic crime. That Act introduced the innovative offence of the failure of commercial organisations to prevent bribery. The section 7[86] offence does not require proof of intent or positive action, instead being one of strict liability. Moreover, it is also an offence of vicarious liability—the organisations carry the guilt irrespective of which party acting on its behalf was responsible for the actions forming the crime. Section 7(2) offers a defence to such circumstances through the demonstration that the accused organisation had in place 'adequate procedures designed to prevent persons associated with the organisation from undertaking such conduct'.[87] The Act's explanatory notes make clear that, although section 7 is concerned with a *criminal* offence, the burden of proof in making this defence is on the organisation to show it had adequate procedures in place, with the relevant standard of proof applied in respect of this defence being the balance of probabilities.[88]

The guidance issued by the government[89] covered a broad range of practical forms of what might constitute 'adequate procedures', including due diligence, training, monitoring and review, sampling procedures and models of top-level managerial commitment. The intention was clearly to establish a sea change in attitudes across the commercial spectrum with regard to the crime of bribery. Whereas the practice of offering and accepting bribes was identified by many as the 'cost of doing business' in many countries, it was clear that the international consensus that 'something had to be done' about this form of corruption had provided the UK government with sufficient resolution to consider that such a fundamental change was indeed practically possible—if the onus on prevention was squarely placed and aligned with the incidence of the crime.

This was indeed the intention of the guidance: to prepare participants for a new playing field; to send an unequivocal message that it was in the interest of every commercial organisation liable to the workings of this legislation to establish codes of conduct that ensured day-to-day practice was compliant with its requirements; and to ensure there was adequate training for all employees to make sure they knew what the rules were—and how it was their duty to protect their employer from any actions that could be construed as being outside of them.

The penalty for the crime of failing to prevent bribery under the Act is an unlimited fine, with any organisation or individual convicted also subject to a confiscation order under POCA[90] and any director subject to disqualification under the Company Directors Disqualification Act 1986. The 'failure to prevent' approach is accepted now as a necessary, workable and general effective piece of legislation in relation to bribery, and the current Director of the UK Serious Fraud Office, David Green, considers this approach should also be used in respect of other forms of economic crime.[91]

The adoption of such an approach to TBML seems compelling. It might offer a number of practical advantages, principally that of showing how participants could be encouraged to police themselves in a trading arena. Compliance could be expected to become a natural constraint as participants were made aware that the penalties for *not* complying were not just the sanctions but also the threat of future participation being impaired through reputational damage. That degree of compliance in turn might be expected to become a function of the legislation being formed in a way that is capable of being enforced.

TBML: Redefining the Offence

Legislation perceived to be difficult to enforce is often a consequence of a political need to be seen to be doing something, rather than a realistic expectation that it will generate prosecutions. But it is not enough to have rules in the book: as discussed earlier, to achieve their aims they need the credibility that comes with prosecutions. This is a test that the UK Bribery Act appears to have passed, according to the director of the SFO.[92] It might be argued, of course, that the concept of a bribe is relatively easy to understand. TBML is typically perceived as a technical offence and therefore somewhat more difficult to understand or explain.

A possible answer is to sidestep the difficulty by making the core offence the transmission of value through mis-invoicing. A key feature of the legislative design of the Bribery Act is strict liability: proving intent is not required. The same approach could apply wherever there is shown to be abuse of invoicing to achieve an illegitimate value transfer. It might be a matter of debate where the materiality limits are set, but the incidence of TBML is such that these should be at a low enough level to encourage compliance, rather than a higher level arising out of estimated proportionality. In addition, as with the Bribery Act, it is developing countries who suffer most from the underlying criminality[93]: this ought to provide a basis for developing the political consensus necessary to establishing workable levels of international compliance.

TBML: A Difficult Problem Maybe, But It Won't Go Away

The corruption of international trading channels through TBML is a difficult problem, but it is wrong to consider it incorrigible. Continued global tolerance is borne of shortsighted convenience and a willingness to ignore its adverse consequences so long as these consequences are not immediately apparent to governments in ways that hurt them. As with bribery, however, the ability of governments to ignore the problem is likely to become less acceptable over time—with or without any dramatic future terrorist events being exposed as having been funded through TBML channels.

It may be that, in the short term, action through the civil courts becomes a driver for change.[94] The need for action is, in any case, likely to become more acute and the challenge is to make such action effective over a multi-faceted international platform. A measured and well-founded route would appear to be available through the natural extension of the innovative legislative approach embodied in the UK Bribery Act. Tackling mis-invoicing directly through the use of sanctions based on what would amount to strict liability, and setting the relevant legislation within the context of an enforced compliance regime which places the burden of preventing its occurrence on the operators, may provide the necessary foundation for establishing a more restrictive trading environment for money launderers and a more open and safer international trading environment for everyone else.

Notes

1. See, for example, Anonymous, 'Uncontained—Trade is the Weakest Link in the Fight Against Dirty Money' *The Economist* (London, 3 May 2014) <www.economist.com/news/international/21601537-trade-weakest-link-fight-against-dirty-money-uncontained> accessed 28 July 17.
2. Clare Sullivan and Evan Smith, *Trade-Based Money Laundering: Risks and Regulatory Responses* (Australian Institute of Criminology 2011), 19–20.
3. United States Senate Caucus on International Narcotics Control, *The Buck Stops Here: Improving U.S. Anti-Money Laundering Practices* (113th Congress 1st session, 2013) 19 <www.drugcaucus.senate.gov/sites/default/fi les/Money%20Laundering%20Report%20-%20Final.pdf> accessed 28 July 17.
4. See the FATF webpage on money laundering <www.fatf-gafi.org/faq/moneylaundering/#d.en.11223> accessed 28 July 17.

5. Stephen Platt, *Criminal Capital: How the Finance Industry Facilitates Crime* (Palgrave Macmillan 2015) Ch. 2.
6. Anonymous (n 1). A survey of core TBML techniques is provided in FATF, *Trade Based Money Laundering* (FAFT/OECD 2006).
7. Asia/Pacific Group on Money Laundering, *APG Typology Report on Trade Based Money Laundering* (APG 2012).
8. PwC, *Goods Gone Bad: Addressing Money Laundering Risk in the Trade Finance System* (PwC 2015) 3 <www.pwc.com/us/en/risk-assurance-services/publications/assets/pwc-trade-finance-aml.pdf> accessed 28 July 17.
9. Anonymous (n 1).
10. Dev Kar and Joseph Spanjers, *Illicit Financial Flows from Developing Countries: 2004–2013* (Global Financial Integrity 2015).
11. ibid. vii.
12. ibid. Chart 2.
13. ibid. para 17, Chart 7.
14. International Monetary Fund, *World Economic Outlook Database April 2015* (IMF 2015); World Bank, *World Development Indicators* (WB 2014).
15. PwC (n 8) 18.
16. For the latest assessment of the resilience of cash smuggling as a money laundering method, however, see the joint report FATF/MENA-FATF, *Money Laundering Through the Physical Transportation of Cash* (FAFT/OECD 2015).
17. John Zdanowicz, 'Trade-Based Money Laundering and Terrorist Financing' (2009) 5(2) Review of Law and Economics 855.
18. HM Treasury and Home Office, *UK National Risk Assessment of Money Laundering and Terrorist Financing* (2015) paras 6(16)–6(19).
19. Financial Conduct Authority, *Banks Control of Financial Crime Risks in Trade Finance* (Thematic Review TR13/3 2013).
20. ibid. para 8.
21. ibid. para 10.
22. FATF (n 6).
23. Samuel McSkimming, 'Trade Based Money Laundering: Responding to an Emerging Threat' (2010) 15(1) Deakin Law Review 37, 50–51.
24. ibid.
25. PwC quote a UN value for global merchandise export trade of $18.3 trillion in 2012: PwC (n 8) 8.
26. McSkimming (n 23) 61.
27. FATF (n 6).
28. HM Treasury and Home Office (n 18).
29. John Zdanowicz, 'Who's Watching Our Back Door?' (2004) 1(1) Business Accents, College of Business Administration magazine, Florida International University 26.
30. For the core application of gravity models to trade, see Jacob Bikker, 'An Extended Gravity Model with Substitution Applied to International Trade' in

Steven Brahman and Peter Van Bergeijk (eds), *The Gravity Model in International Trade: Advances and Applications* (Cambridge 2010). For consideration of gravity models relating to money laundering, see John Walker and Brigitte Unger, 'Measuring Global Money Laundering: "The Walker Gravity Model"' (2009) 5(2) Review of Law and Economics 822.

31. Joras Ferwerda and others, 'Gravity Models of Trade Based Money Laundering' (2011) De Nederlandsche Bank ('DNB') Working Paper 318.
32. Zdanowicz (n 17) 878.
33. Bikker (n 30).
34. Brigitte Unger and Johan den Hertog, 'Water Always Finds Its Way—Identifying New Forms of Money Laundering' (2012) 57(3) Crime Law and Social Change 287.
35. Walker and Unger (n 30).
36. Ferwerda and others (n 31).
37. ibid.
38. ibid. 15.
39. PwC (n 8).
40. Asia/Pacific Group (n 7).
41. Mark Yeandle and others, *Anti-Money Laundering Requirements: Costs, Benefits and Perceptions* (Z/Yen, 2005); British Bankers' Association, *BBA Response to Cutting Red Tape Review: The Effectiveness of the UK's AML Regime* (BBA 2015).
42. McSkimming (n 23).
43. Erika Solomon, Guy Chazan and Sam Jones, 'Isis Inc.: How Oil Fuels the Jihadi Terrorists' *Financial Times* (London, 15 November 2015) <www.ft.com/content/b8234932-719b-11e5-ad6d-f4ed76f0900a> accessed 28 July 17. See also FATF, *Financing of the Terrorist Organisation Islamic State in Iraq and the Levant* (FAFT/OECD 2015).
44. FATF (n 6).
45. Zdanowicz (n 17).
46. ibid.
47. Jo Becker, 'Beirut Bank Seen as a Hub of Hezbollah's Financing' *New York Times* (New York, 13 December 2011) <www.nytimes.com/2011/12/14/world/middleeast/beirut-bank-seen-as-a-hub-of-hezbollahs-financing.ht ml> accessed 28 July 17.
48. Nate Raymond, 'Lebanese Bank to Pay US $102 Million in Money Laundering Case' *Reuters Business News* (London, 25 June 2013) <www.reuters.com/article/us-lebanesebank-settlement-idUS-BRE95O17P20130625> accessed 28 July 17.
49. *US v Lebanese Canadian Bank SAL et al.* [2012] U.S. District Court 11–9186.
50. Raymond (n 48).
51. Ross Delston and Stephen Walls, 'Reaching Beyond Banks: How to Target Trade-Based Money Laundering and Terrorist Financing Outside the

Financial Sector' (2009) 41(1) Case Western Reserve Journal of International Law 85.

52. McSkimming (n 23).
53. Dinah Shelton, 'Law, Non-law and the Problem of Soft Law' in Dinah Shelton (ed), *Commitment and Compliance: The Role of Non-Binding Norms in the International Legal System* (OUP 2003) 15.
54. FATF (n 6).
55. See Jackie Harvey, 'Asset Recovery—Substantive or Symbolic' in Colin King and Clive Walker (eds), *Dirty Assets: Emerging Issues in the Regulation of Criminal and Terrorist Assets* (Ashgate 2014).
56. See, for example, the Association of Certified Anti-Money Laundering Specialists <www.acams.org> accessed 28 July 17.
57. Delston and Walls (n 51).
58. Asia/Pacific Group (n 7).
59. Criticisms of the SARs regime were acknowledged in HM Treasury and Home Office (n 18), 5–6.
60. FATF (n 6).
61. ibid.; Platt (n 5) in particular 29.
62. Personal experience of the author in 2015.
63. Proceeds of Crime Act 2002, ss 327–329.
64. In the next section, we discuss how recent judgments appear to have the intended effect of reestablishing the concept of a predicate offence under the POCA offences.
65. Robert Bell, 'Abolishing the Concept of Predicate Offence' (2002) 6(2) Journal of Money Laundering Control 137.
66. Proceeds of Crime Act 2002 (n 63) Part 7—Money Laundering Offences.
67. *R v Anwoir* [2008] EWCA Crim 1354.
68. *HMA v Ahmed* [2009] HCJAC 60.
69. *R v Anwoir* (n 67) para 21.
70. *R v Geary* [2010] EWCA Crim 1925, para 19.
71. *R v GH* [2015] UKSC 24.
72. *R v Geary* (n 70) quoted in *R v GH* (n 71) para 26.
73. *R v GH* (n 71) para 20.
74. Proceeds of Crime Act (n 63) s 340 (3)F.
75. *R v GH* (n 71) para 39.
76. ibid.
77. For example, *HMA v Michael Handley* [2013] Sentencing statements.
78. Vivian Walters, 'Prosecuting Money Launderers: Do the Prosecution Have to Prove the Predicate Offence?' [2009] Criminal Law Review 571.
79. *R v GH* (n 71).
80. Michael Levi, *Drug Law Enforcement and Financial Investigation Strategies: Modernising Drug Law Enforcement Report 5* (International Drug Policy Consortium 2013).

81. Not least by FATF (n 6).
82. Platt (n 5).
83. McSkimming (n 23).
84. Delston and Walls (n 51).
85. Peter Calvocoressi, Guy Wint and John Pritchard, *Total War: Causes and Courses of The Second World War* (2nd edn, Penguin 1989) 461.
86. The Bribery Act 2010, s 7.
87. ibid. s 7(2).
88. The Ministry of Justice, *The Bribery Act 2010: 'Quick Start Guide'* <www.justice.gov.uk/downloads/legislati   on/bribery-act-2010-quick-start-guide.pdf> accessed 28 July 17.
89. Ministry of Justice, *The Bribery Act 2010: Guidance About Procedures Which Relevant Commercial Organisations Can Put into Place to Prevent Persons Associated with Them From Bribing* <www.justice.gov.uk /downloads/legislation/bribery-act-2010-guidance.pdf> accessed 28 July 17.
90. Proceeds of Crime Act 2002 (n 63). For further discussion, see Chap. 26 (Lord and Levi) in this collection.
91. David Green CB QC, SFO Director, Speech at the Cambridge Symposium on Economic Crime 2016, Jesus College, Cambridge.
92. ibid.
93. Kar and Spanjers (n 10).
94. See *Credit Agricole Corporation and Investment Bank v Papadimitriou* [2015] UK PC 13. In this appeal from the Court of Appeal of Gibraltar, the Court of the UK Privy Council held that the bank was liable for losses arising from laundering activity that it ought to have been in a position to be aware of and to prevent.

Kenneth Murray is a chartered accountant who has been engaged in forensic accountancy work within Scottish law enforcement for the past decade, having previously worked in corporate finance and venture capital. He has extensive experience in the investigation of economic crime as well as presenting evidence in high-profile cases as an expert witness. He has provided strategic advice throughout his career and is managing a long-term project, Project Jackal, which he instigated and designed to transform the law enforcement response in Scotland to the business and financial aspects of organised crime. He has published a number of papers on economic crime in the academic press and is accredited as a forensic accountant by the Institute of Chartered Accountants of England and Wales.

11

De-risking: An Unintended Negative Consequence of AML/CFT Regulation

Vijaya Ramachandran, Matthew Collin, and Matt Juden

Introduction

Other chapters in this handbook explore the complexities of anti-money laundering, counter-financing of terror and sanctions violations regulations (hereafter AML/CFT). This body of regulation has emerged as states attempt to collaborate to frustrate money launderers and those who would finance terror or undermine sanctions programmes. The regime has been constructed in an attempt to protect citizens from exploitation at the hands of organized crime and from the horror of terrorism. Where this system targets sanctions violations, it supports a non-violent approach to the enforcement of international norms. Given these noble aims, it is understandable that the costs of this body of regulation are not often assessed.

However, any attempt to influence a system as complex as the global financial system is certain to have unintended consequences. This chapter

---

This chapter makes extensive use of material in the Center for Global Development Working Group Report, 'Unintended Consequences of Anti-Money Laundering Policies for Poor Countries' (CGD 2015) <www.cgdev.org/sites/default/files/CGD-WG-Report-Unintended-Consequences-AML-Policies-2015.pdf> accessed 27 November 2016.

V. Ramachandran • M. Collin
Center for Global Development, Washington, DC, USA

M. Juden
Center for Global Development, London, UK

© The Author(s) 2018
C. King et al. (eds.), *The Palgrave Handbook of Criminal and Terrorism Financing Law*,
https://doi.org/10.1007/978-3-319-64498-1_11

contends that there may be serious unintended negative consequences of AML/CFT as it is currently implemented. We detail extensive suggestive evidence of such unintended consequences, namely negative impacts on the money transfer and correspondent banking sectors.

The paper is structured as follows. The next section explores the unintended consequences of AML/CFT for money transfer organizations. The following section looks at correspondent banking and other crossborder transactions. The penultimate section looks at the constraints imposed by the lack of data and the final section concludes with recommendations for policy and for future research.

This chapter makes extensive use of two contested terms: 'de-risking' and 'de-banking'. For our purposes, 'de-risking' refers to a general phenomenon where an organization seeks to limit its exposure to risk by ceasing activities in a wholesale rather than a case-by-case fashion. For example, an international organization could de-risk by ceasing to operate in the Middle East as a whole or a given country or sector. It would not qualify as de-risking if the organization assessed each of its operations in turn and stopped those it considered to pass some risk threshold, even if many of these happened to fall in the same region or sector. 'De-risking' is sometimes used in this way, and sometimes in a more general sense, to refer broadly to the process of reducing exposure to risk. We employ the more restrictive definition of 'de-risking' for clarity, in order to avoid confusion between 'good' and 'bad' de-risking. We use 'de-banking' to refer to a bank unilaterally closing the account of an individual or institution. This could happen as a result of de-risking.

The Great De-banking of Money Transfer Organizations

Evidence of Account Closures

In the spring of 2013, over 140 UK-based remittance companies were surprised to receive a notice from Barclays Bank indicating that their accounts would be closed within 60 days. Barclays had announced that these clients had been reviewed according to its new risk-based eligibility criteria and, as a result, the bank would no longer be doing business with them. The local money transfer industry erupted in protest as a number of non-governmental organizations (NGOs) and development professionals expressed concern over the possible disruption of remittance flows.[1] Many MTOs managed to secure a one- or two-month reprieve and, following a High Court injunction, the Somali remitter, Dahabshiil, maintained its bank account until the following year.[2] But by the autumn of 2014, Barclays had completely withdrawn from the remittance sector.

The Barclays incident was not an isolated case, as many banks around the world have decided to stop doing business with the remittance sector. In 2012, following a series of 'strategic assessments' initiated in the wake of financial settlements with US and UK authorities, HSBC decided to close the accounts of a number of MTOs in several jurisdictions.[3] While it is unknown precisely how many accounts were closed, multiple sources report that HSBC completely withdrew from the remittance sector at this time.[4]

In the USA, account closures have hounded remittance companies for several years. In 2011, Sunrise Community Banks, the largest provider of banking services to the US-Somali remittance corridor, decided to close all accounts in order to better comply with US CFT regulation.[5] Similarly, in early 2014, the North Dakotan Bell State Bank closed several money transmitter accounts.[6] The stability of the Somali corridor became even more tenuous when Merchants Bank of California decided to close all its remaining MTO accounts following a cease-and-desist order from the Office of Comptroller of Currency (OCC).[7] While these recent episodes have heightened the focus on Somalia, evidence from a recent report by the Global Remittances Working (GRW) group suggests that many MTOs across the USA are struggling to open or maintain accounts with banks.[8]

The situation has become similarly dire in Australia, the predominant source of remittances for most Pacific Island nations. In spring of 2015, Westpac, one of Australia's largest banks, terminated all accounts held by remittance firms. Anecdotal reports suggest that the rest of the country's 'Big Four' banks have all either closed a large number of accounts or fully withdrawn their support for the remittance sector.[9] While the mass de-banking of remittance providers has received the most attention in the USA, UK and Australia, examples of this behaviour can also be found across Europe.[10] Banks in the Middle East and North Africa surveyed by the International Monetary Fund (IMF) and Union of Arab Banks also reported the debanking of MTOs.[11]

Regulators have repeatedly noted MTOs' decreasing access to banking services. For example, as early as 2005 a joint statement by US regulators Financial Crimes Enforcement Network (FinCEN), the Governors of the Federal Reserve System, the OCC, the Federal Deposit Insurance Corporation

(FDIC), the Office of Thrift Supervision and the National Credit Union Administration noted that '[m]oney services businesses are losing access to banking services as a result of concerns about regulatory scrutiny, the risks presented by money services business accounts, and the costs and burdens associated with maintaining such accounts'. [12] The statement goes on to specify that '[c]oncerns may stem, in part, from a misperception of the requirements of the Bank Secrecy Act, and the erroneous view that money services businesses present a uniform and unacceptably high risk of money laundering or other illicit activity'. [13]

The de-banking of MTOs appears to be a global problem, and it appears to be getting worse. That picture emerges from the World Bank's 2015 Report on the G20 survey in de-risking activities in the remittance market. [14] This survey was sent to a large number of governments, banks and MTOs. In response, 54% of the MTOs reported that they had at least one bank account closed last year. The 45% of responding banks reported that they had closed at least one MTO account that year. Forty-six per cent of responding governments indicated that they had received complaints from MTOs about access to bank accounts. As Fig. 11.1 illustrates, 54% of MTOs reported having lost at least one bank account in 2014. Respondents from the USA, UK and Australia appear to be the worst hit: between 55%

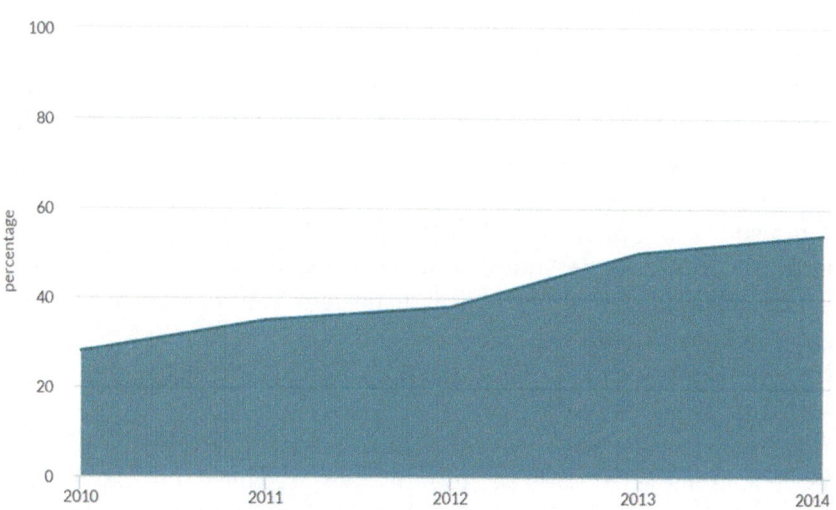

Fig. 11.1 The percentage of remittance companies reporting at least one bank account closure is rising. Source: World Bank [15]

and 82% of MTOs report that they lost at least one bank account in 2014, although these results might be partially driven by differences in response rates across countries.

Drivers of De-banking

Background Increase in Regulatory Pressure

Since 2000, the regulatory pressure on financial institutions relating to AML compliance has increased. This is reflected in the number and value of AML-related fines imposed by regulators in the USA, as Figs. 11.2 and 11.3 demonstrate.[16] Figure 11.2 shows that the number of AML-related fines issued by US regulators has been following a sharp upward trend over the past 15 years, a significant drop after the financial crisis in 2008 and 2009 and a slight drop in 2013 and 2014 notwithstanding. Figure 11.2 also shows that there are regulators with overlapping mandates; this may increase regulatory uncertainty. Perhaps more significantly, the value of fines has soared over the same period, with a very sharp increase over the past five years, as

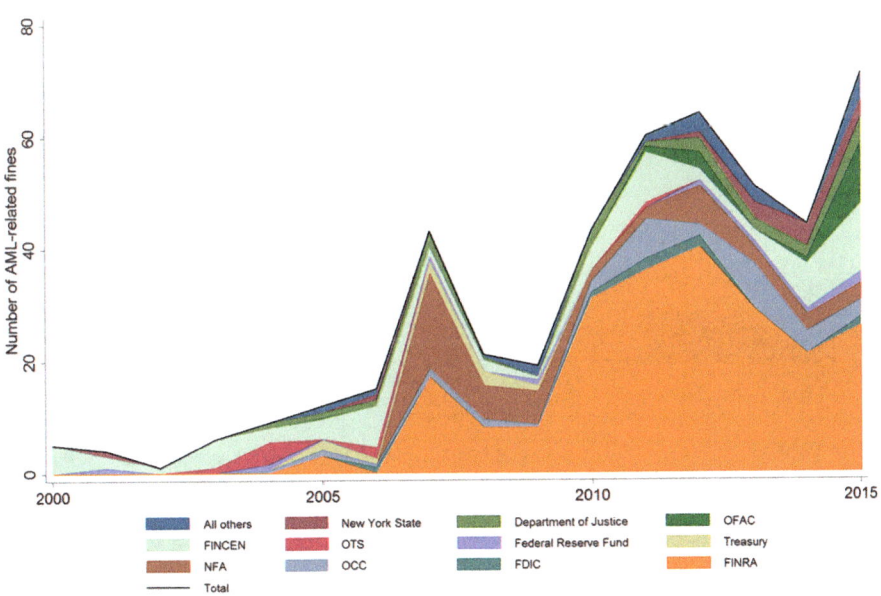

Fig. 11.2 AML-related fines by US regulators (2000–2015). Source: Data compiled from ACAMS reports of enforcement actions[19]

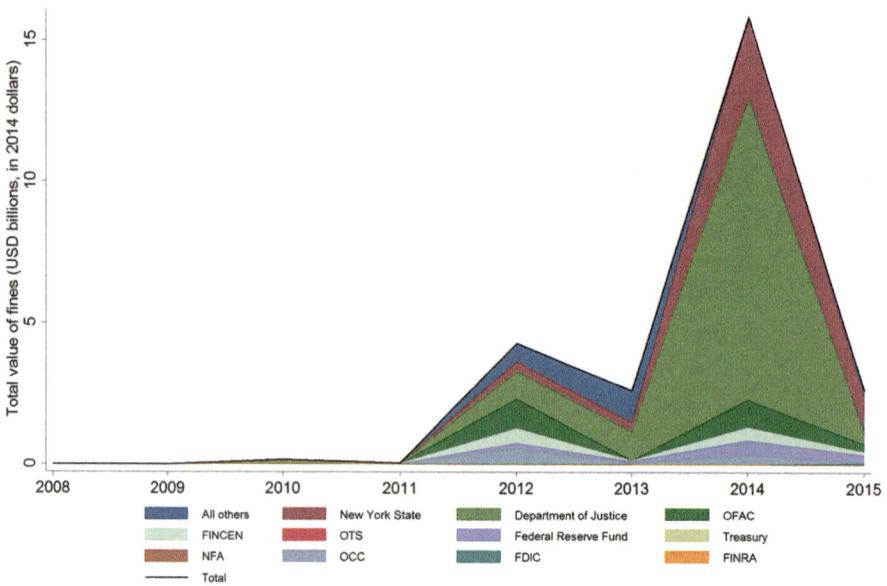

Fig. 11.3 AML-related fines by US regulators (2008–2015). Source: Data compiled from ACAMS reports of enforcement actions

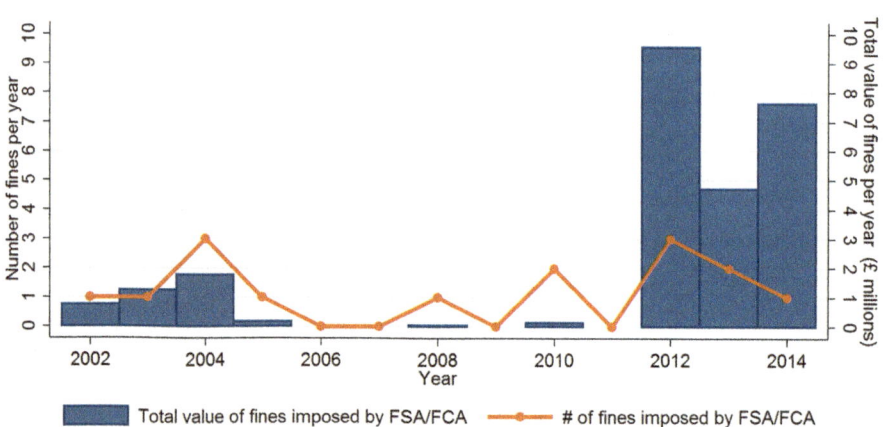

Fig. 11.4 AML-related fines by the UK Financial Services Authority/Financial Conduct Authority (2002–2014). Source: Data compiled from FSA/FCA reports of enforcement actions

Fig. 11.3 shows. Also, newsworthy AML-related fines have become more and more common.[17] A similar picture is evident in the UK (although on a significantly smaller scale)—as illustrated in Fig. 11.4. In the UK, while the number of fines has been relatively low, there has been an increase in the value of fines issued over the past five years.[18] The fines analysed include fines related to all of the constituent offences captured by our use of 'AML'. However, fines related to sanctions violations account for the majority of the value of fines.

Perceptions within the compliance industry align with this analysis. In a 2015 survey of AML professionals conducted by the Association of Certified Anti-Money Laundering Specialists and Dow Jones, 62% of respondents see 'increased regulatory expectations' as the greatest AML compliance challenge faced by their organization.[20] The impact on compliance officer behaviour is likely compounded by an increasing focus on the personal liability of the compliance officer in the USA. Financial regulators have recently begun to hold individual compliance officers (as well as their employers) accountable in cases of non-compliance. High-profile examples include Harold Crawford, former Global AML Compliance Officer for Brown Brothers Harriman, who was held accountable by Financial Industry Regulatory Authority (FINRA) in February 2014,[21] and Thomas Haider, former Chief Compliance Officer for MoneyGram, held accountable by FinCEN in December 2014.[22] The move towards increasing personal liability for compliance officers and other senior managers in financial services is also manifest in the UK, and its potential effects on individual and firm behaviour are not yet well understood.[23]

In addition to (a) regulatory risk—the risk of being punished by a regulator—financial institutions are also concerned with (b) reputational risk, that is: the risk of damage to one's brand resultant from public attention to perceived wrongdoing. Levels of these risks are not necessarily pegged to levels of (c) risk of ML/TF abuse of the institution. Ideally levels of (a), (b) and (c) should correlate for a given institution. In the following sections, it is argued that the risk-based approach has not been well enough implemented to align these risks appropriately, and that this is leading to unnecessarily conservative compliance practices. It is further argued that minimizing (c) at the level of formal financial institutions does not necessarily minimize (c) at the level of the economic system, as undesirable transactions may be pushed into informal institutions. This process of 'sweeping under the rug' would result in a misleading impression of minimized risk if only the formal financial system were analysed.

MTOs as High-Risk Clients

In the world of AML/CFT compliance, money transmitters are often considered to be high-risk clients for two reasons. First, a significant share of world remittances now flows to countries that are deemed to be high risk by regulators. Nearly one in every three dollars remitted in 2013 was sent to a country currently listed as a high-risk or non-cooperative jurisdiction by the Financial Action Task Force (FATF). Thirteen per cent went to countries in the top 25% riskiest countries as measured by the Basel Institute's index of money laundering risk, and 6% went to countries actively covered by an Office of Foreign Assets Control (OFAC) sanctions programme.[24] Many MTOs service regions where the perceived risk of remittances being diverted is so high that even in the face of careful AML/CFT practices and procedures, there remain substantial worries about risk. While much of the media coverage of de-risking has focused on Somalia, this situation is an extreme case and somewhat of an outlier. However, the problem extends beyond Somalia. For example, the Barclay's de-banking episode affected most small- to medium-size MTOs in the UK, regardless of the corridor they served.

Second, remittance companies have also garnered a reputation for being inherently risky no matter what compliance procedures they have in place. While some MTOs operate compliance procedures 'that would terrify any bank manager who happened to pay a visit', others operate comparatively very strong compliance systems, and it is not clear that levels of compliance are systematically lower than in other business sectors.[25] Nevertheless, MTOs are seen to be inherently risky. This is partially due to statements and signals by national and international regulators and standard-setters.

For example, in their UK Treasury-approved guidelines for money service businesses (MSBs, a category which includes MTOs) which use banking services, the Joint Money Laundering Steering Group (JMLSG) refers to a risk of money laundering or terrorist finance which is 'inherent in the MSB sector' and describes characteristics of the sector which 'make it an attractive vehicle through which criminal and terrorist funds can enter the financial system'.[26] While this guidance identifies indicators that an MSB is likely to be lower risk, these indicators specifically exclude MTOs. The UK's latest national risk assessment judges terrorist financing risk in the MSB sector to be 'high'.[27] In its statement originally intended to placate worries about de-risking, AUSTRAC described the remittance sector as a whole as being 'vulnerable to abuse'.[28] In the USA, the FDIC published a list in 2011 comprising merchant categories that were considered to be 'high risk'. This list included money transfer networks; it was later rescinded following complaints.[29]

Risk perceptions by rich world regulators appear to reflect a bias against cross-border transactions (since they imply additional challenges in tracing), even though there is no particular evidence that cross-border transactions are more likely to involve criminal behaviour. Further, compliance with FATF's Recommendation 16 (formerly Special Recommendation VII) should ensure that originator and beneficiary information is present at every point on the payment chain for cross-border transactions just as it is for national-level transactions. The US National Money Laundering Risk Assessment states that it is 'difficult and potentially misleading to attempt to rank order financial services or sectors on the basis of money laundering risk' but it also notes that 'banks … are at the center of the global financial system and as such are at greatest risk for criminal abuse'.[30]

Banks now consider MTOs to be particularly risky in an environment where there is more regulatory pressure on doing business with high-risk customers than ever before. In evidence given at the UK's High Court, representatives from Barclays described the recent spectre of large fines and potential bad publicity of ML failures as impetus for their decision to review their support of the MTO sector.[31] Similarly, HSBC cited the $1.9 billion settlement with US authorities as a driver for its review and subsequent termination of MTO accounts.[32] Bell State Bank specifically cited federal government restrictions and potential fines as a driver of its decision to close accounts.[33] These concerns are also reflected in industry surveys on risk compliance: the 2015 Dow Jones/ACAMS AML survey reveals that 30% of respondents had left a particular business line or segment of business in the past 12 months due to concerns over regulatory risk.[34]

Banks could partially mitigate the risk of regulatory action through more painstaking due diligence work, transaction monitoring and customer screening. However, the costs of these actions for the MTO sector appear to be substantial enough that this sector has become a marginal source of business for banks.[35] The British Bankers Association (BBA) notes that banks lack access to the 'authoritative information' needed to make careful risk assessments.[36] Even when they are privy to information that would allow banks to better screen their customers, regulators have not historically been willing to share it, though this is now changing in some jurisdictions. In the UK, HM Revenue and Customs (HMRC) is solely responsible for regulating MTOs from an AML standpoint, yet until May 2016 shared no information with banks on which firms have been relatively compliant. This situation has been improved through the creation of the Joint Money Laundering Intelligence Taskforce (JMLIT), which is a forum for regulators including HM Revenue and Customs (HMRC) to exchange information with each other, with law enforcement, and with vetted staff from major financial services firms.[37]

When a bank terminates the accounts of MTOs, the burden of compliance falls on the remaining banks that are offering services to the MTO sector. This not only makes it more likely that subsequent banks will exit the sector, but also amplifies the impact of each decision to exit.[38] In this way, regulatory costs may lessen the degree of competition in the banking sector.

Of course, de-risking is one of many sources of the de-banking trend, and there may be a degree of discordance in the reasons banks have given for withdrawing from the remittance sector and their actual reasons. The FATF states that 'drivers for "de-risking" go beyond anti-money laundering /terrorist financing'[39] and specify that 'concerns about profitability, prudential requirements, anxiety after the global financial crisis' might also be driving de-risking.[40] They rightly point out that statements and survey results outlined above are 'anecdotal' evidence but nevertheless recognize the need for an improvement in the evidence base regarding the causes and effects of de-risking. Others have accused banks of using de-banking as an excuse to shoulder their way into the remittance business, with evidence suggesting that banks who have continued to offer their own money transfers services have increased their own prices following the termination of MTO accounts.[41] While the drivers behind de-banking may be myriad, the statements of compliance offices and banks themselves suggest that concerns relating to regulatory and reputational risk from AML/CFT and sanctions compliance have played a large role in the decisions that banks have made.

Scale of De-banking and the Impact on Industry

Estimating the actual number of MTOs that have lost their accounts is difficult, as most banks do not publicly reveal which accounts have been terminated. We also do not know how many MTOs have been forced to open lower quality accounts that are more expensive or less convenient. Unrepresentative sampling and low response rates hamper existing surveys of MTOs, but do give some indication as to the scale of the problem. A 2013 survey of 26 Australian MTOs revealed that over 70% either had their accounts closed or had received a threat of closure.[42] The Association of UK Payment Institutions (AUKPI) estimates that Barclay's termination of services affected up to 90% of the market, although these numbers have been questioned.[43] The World Bank Survey on the impacts of de-risking around the world revealed that 45% of responding MTOs had had at least one account closed in 2014.[44]

Remittance costs are declining overall. But de-banking has the potential to affect the remittance industry in two ways: by exerting upward pressure on costs and by reducing competition in the remittance market over the medium to long term. Banks are an essential part of business for MTOs, which need an account to handle cross-border transactions, usually at the point of settlement. In lieu of that arrangement, MTOs must form relationships with firms that already have access to banking services, such as bulk foreign exchange providers, or become an agent of a larger MTO.[45] Because money transmitters will always choose settlement methods which minimize costs, losing access to their preferred bank could lead to a rise in costs.[46] What is less clear is whether, in the medium term, these costs will translate into higher remittance prices. In considering the possible effects of upward pressure on prices and reduced competition, it is important to distinguish between corridors. While the remittance market as a whole is a site of innovation, the potentially negative effects discussed in this section will apply mostly to corridors and types of transactions that are not well served by innovative new entrants to the remittance market such as 'fintech' start-ups. Completely digital services like TransferWise or BitPesa only have the potential to reduce costs for payments between connected individuals and the success of such services will do nothing to reduce costs for the cash-to-cash customers who are currently paying the highest prices for remittance services.[47]

De-banking also threatens to make remittance markets less competitive. In many cases, the burden of financial exclusion appears to fall mainly on smaller firms: for example, Barclays only closed the accounts of MTOs with less than £10 million in net tangible assets, favouring larger, more established companies such as MoneyGram and Western Union.[48] The higher costs associated with lack of financial access have the potential to drive smaller operators out of the market. In some jurisdictions, such as the UK, bank account access is a prerequisite to maintaining legal status as an MTO, resulting in reports that some firms have been forced to cease operating for fear of running afoul of regulators.[49] Previous research has already indicated that less competitive remittance markets are, on average, more expensive for senders.[50]

To date, there is no definitive data that might enable us to shed light on the impact of de-banking on the structure of the remittance market. In an attempt to gain insight into whether or not the Barclay's incident actually led to any large-scale shifts in the UK remittance industry, we gathered data on the registration of firms from the Financial Conduct Authority's (FCA) online database of authorized payment institutions (APIs) (MSBs which handle more than £3m per month), small payment institutions (SPIs) (smaller MSBs) and the agents which provide geographic coverage of these services. Figure 11.5 shows the number of APIs and small payment institutions (SPIs) active in the UK over the period of the Barclays de-banking. It does not appear that the trend has shifted substantially following the de-banking episode. A similar result can be found if we examine the number of agents operating in the UK in Fig. 11.6.

To examine changes in competition, we created an index of competition based on the share of agents controlled by each firm in a given month, which is equivalent to the probability that any two randomly chosen agents serve a different remittance firm.[51] We only observed a very slight decline in competition immediately following the Barclays de-banking. However, the data presented here are not enough to make definitive statements about the impact of de-risking on the UK remittance industry, and more precise data on which firms lost their accounts would be necessary to establish such a causal impact.

Negative Impacts on Remittance Flows and Transparency

The effects of de-banking on the remittance industry discussed above may potentially lead to changes in the health of the MTO market as well as a rise in remittance prices in some corridors in the long run. There is high-level interest in seeing the price of remittances fall. Driven by the World Bank-chaired GRW group, in 2009 the G8 (and later the G20) adopted a resolution to reduce the costs of remittances by five percentage points to 5% within five years.[52] There are of course inherent difficulties in translating policy targets

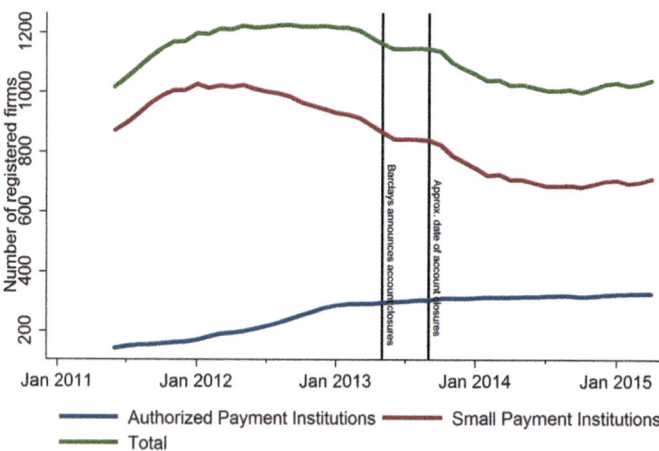

Fig. 11.5 Number of payment institutions operating in the UK (2011–2015). Source: Data compiled from FCA Financial Services Register

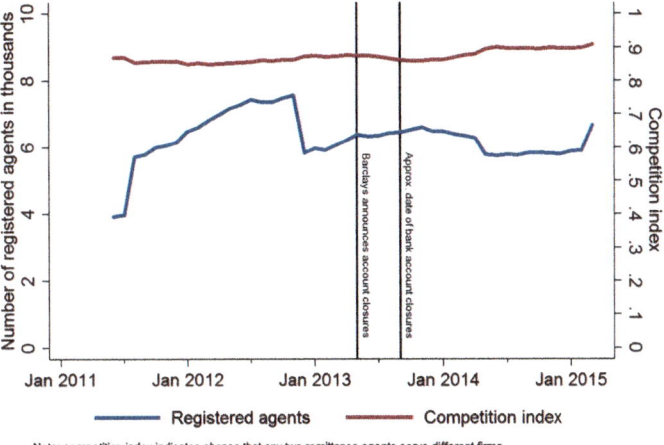

Fig. 11.6 Remittance agents and competition in the UK (2011–2015). Source: Data compiled from FCA Financial Services Register

into market-driven reality. Nonetheless, a high-level policy drive to reduce costs combined with rapid advances in payments technology has lowered the average price of remittances across the globe by less than two percentage points over the past four years. Figure 11.7 highlights this decline, using data provided by the World Bank's online database of remittance prices Remittance Prices Worldwide.

In a brief on migration and development, the World Bank notes '[c]oncerns over money laundering are keeping costs high by increasing compliance costs for commercial banks and money transfer operators, and delaying the entry of new players and the use of mobile technology'.[53] As can be seen in Fig. 11.7, the cost of sending money to countries which score above the 75th percentile in the Basel AML Index has remained more than a percentage point higher than 'low risk' countries throughout the past four years. There are many reasons why high-risk corridors might be more expensive which are not due to AML regulation, so these differences should not be seen as causal. Yet the divide in remittance costs highlights that places which are likely to be negatively affected by de-risking already deal with higher prices.

We cannot infer whether de-risking has had a net effect on remittance prices merely by examining Fig. 11.7. Despite the general downward trend in remittance prices, even for high-risk countries, in order to assess the effect of de-risking, we would have to know what the situation without de-risking. For example, prices might have fallen further without de-risking or they might not have deviated from the observed trend at all. A causal assessment would

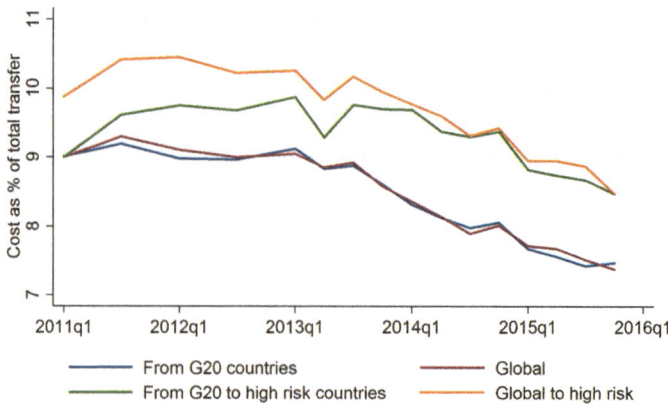

Fig. 11.7 The average cost of remitting $200 (2011–2016). Source: Remittance Prices Worldwide Database (prices calculated using WB methodology)

require knowing with more precision exactly which firms or corridors were affected and when. It would also require a comprehensive picture of remittance prices for affected remittance corridors, which at present is not provided by the Remittance Prices Worldwide database.[54]

If de-risking leads to stagnation and potential future price rises across certain corridors, this will have serious implications for both how much money is sent overseas and how money is sent overseas.

Lower Flows of Remittances to Developing Countries

The bulk of research on the effects of remittance prices on volumes suggest that higher prices lead to lower amounts being sent in aggregate. In a survey of Tongan migrants to New Zealand, Gibson et al. find that in aggregate, remitters would hypothetically send more if the fixed-fee portion of the transfer cost was halved.[55] Freund and Spatafora show that recorded remittance flows are negatively associated with transaction fees.[56] Two separate randomized experiments in which Latin Americans were given discounts to send money home both found that lowering prices increased the total amount remitted.[57] In extreme cases, increases in prices mask a more fundamental threat to remittance flows: when de-banked MTOs lose their ability to handle large volumes of transfers. This concern is perhaps particular to contexts such as the US-Somali corridor, where anecdotal evidence suggests that remitters are having difficulty transferring money.[58]

There are risks that need to be managed in many countries or within conflict zones inside particular countries. But overall, an abatement of remittance flows would have serious negative consequences for poverty alleviation. Today, remittances are one of the most critical sources of finance for developing countries. As of 2014, worldwide remittances were worth more than three times that of overseas development aid.[59] Nearly every academic study on remittances uncovers overwhelmingly positive impacts on those receiving them. Research shows that remittances have the potential to improve household welfare, increase spending on education and raise self-employment.[60] Ultimately, remittances act as extra cash in the hands of poor households, and a large literature shows that cash transfers significantly improve the lives of those that receive them.[61]

Remittances are also a crucial source of income when disaster strikes. Research shows that remittances form a safety net in many contexts, such as supporting those suffering from natural disasters, macroeconomic shocks and even terrorist attacks.[62] There is also evidence that remittances promote financial development and inclusion, by generating financial links within the local banking sector and encouraging recipients to obtain formal accounts.[63] These developments are not only good for economic development, but also pull more transactions into the more transparent formal sector.

In light of these substantial benefits, there are concerns over both the price paid by remitters and the overall health of the market. If it leads to an increase in prices in the short or long run, the de-banking trend undermines these objectives.

Remittance Flows Become Less Transparent

In addition to reducing remittance flows, the changes in the MTO market described above also threaten to make remittance flows less transparent. Anecdotal evidence suggests that many remittance firms are using third parties, including bulk currency exchange providers to settle accounts. As these transactions are aggregated at a high level, they inevitably make due diligence work more difficult. MTOs may also be seeking banking services at lower tier banks with less robust compliance procedures. In extreme cases, such as Somalia, there are reports that some remitters are resorting to moving cash physically across borders, leading to transparency concerns.[64] Industry bodies report that some MTOs may even disguise the true nature of their operations from banks in order to remain banked, further reducing transparency.[65]

In addition to the change in MTO behaviour, there is a tangential concern that more remittance customers will use informal methods of sending money home if formal methods become more expensive. There is already ample evidence that remitters use informal methods to send money home. Freund and Spatafora document a multitude of surveys indicating that a large share of households received remittances through informal channels.[66] The UK Somali Remittance Survey indicated that 21% of those interviewed used informal methods of transferring cash.[67] Amjad et al. describe data from Pakistan indicating that at least one half of households receive overseas remittances through informal 'Hundi' or directly by returning migrants.[68]

When the relative price of formal remittance transfers goes up, informal methods begin to look more attractive. In a survey of 77 central banks in remittance-receiving countries, cost was the most commonly cited barrier for entry into the formal remittance system.[69] In a survey of migrants in the Netherlands, Kosse and Vermuelen find the low relative cost of informal channels to be a strong driver of remittance behaviour.[70] Because of the very nature of informality, it is difficult to determine the extent to which high prices drive remittances to informal channels. But macro-level studies that show that prices depress officially recorded remittances are consistent with the possibility that shifts to informal remittances will no longer be recorded.[71]

The objective of AML/CFT policy is ultimately to reduce the risk of laundered funds and terrorist financing across the entire financial system. Yet remittance flows that are driven through less transparent methods become substantially more difficult to track and secure from diversion. This is true whether the channel is informal, like the *hawala* system,[72] or formal like the use of bulk currency exchanges by cash-intensive MTOs. The possibility that industry de-risking might be driving more money into less transparent channels should be of immediate concern.

Correspondent Banking and Other Cross-Border Transactions Under Threat

The Decline of Correspondent Banking Relationships and Trade Finance in Some Corridors

Banks frequently need to move money across borders. Every day trillions of dollars of cross-border transactions take place in order to facilitate ordinary economic activity such as remittances, foreign exchange trading and trade finance. When a bank needs to conduct payments in a particular country where it does not have a physical presence to transact in that country's local currency, a common solution is for that bank to open an account with another bank located in that country. Such arrangements are often referred to as *correspondent banking* relationships (CBRs).

These relationships are considered crucial for many cross-border transactions. Imagine an IT firm in Kenya wishes to import computer parts from the USA as part of their business, but the US manufacturer requires payment in USD. Unless that IT firm has an account with a US bank, such a transaction would be difficult to make, as its local banks are limited to transactions in Kenyan Shillings. However, if the IT firm is banked with a local bank which has a correspondent account with a larger bank in the USA, the larger bank would be able to process the USD payment on behalf of the local Kenyan bank. Without that direct correspondent relationship, the Kenyan firm would have to make the payment through a longer chain of intermediaries, driving up the cost of the transaction.

Despite the obvious value of CBRs, a number of industry and government surveys of banks have suggested that a substantial number of links between banks have been severed in recent years.

In the 2014 International Chamber of Commerce (ICC) Global Trade and Finance Survey, 30% of respondents indicated they had recently dropped correspondent relationships.[73] In an unpublished report prepared for the October FATF plenary, the BBA surveyed 17 international clearing banks and found that they had severed, on average, 7.5% of their correspondent relationships since 2011.[74] The Society for Worldwide Interbank Finance Telecommunications (SWIFT) is an industry cooperative which manages payment messages between banks around the world.[75] Using data obtained from SWIFT, the BBA report noted that the number of reported counterparty relationships between international clearing houses and countries deemed 'high risk' had declined by 6% over the past two years. SWIFT's own white paper on correspondent banking documents reported a significant decline in correspondent relationships between the top 80 payments banks and the American, Europe, Middle East and African regions since 2005 (SWIFT 3.0).[76] In a network analysis of SWIFT single customer credit transactions, Cook and Soramäki note that the majority of links lost in the payments network since 2007 have been to offshore banking sectors, often considered to be high risk.[77] The 9th European Central Bank Survey on correspondent banking shows a consistent decline among Eurozone bank relationships over the past five years.[78] A survey carried out by the IMF and the Union of Arab Banks failed to find a wholesale de-risking effect except in sanctions-affected countries, but found evidence of increased compliance costs for respondent banks associated with correspondent banking.[79]

A later survey by the World Bank focused on whether large international banks are severing correspondent relationships.[80] The responses from regulators, large international banks, and smaller local and regional banks indicate that a significant number of banks are terminating correspondent accounts. Of the 20 international banks surveyed, 15 reported they had seen a decline in correspondent accounts in the past two and half years.

Certain regions appear to be worse hit than others. The majority of large banks responding to the survey indicated that they have completely withdrawn correspondent banking services from certain jurisdictions. Banking authorities (regulators) in some regions reported that they had noticed some decline or a significant decline in their banks' access to correspondent accounts. As shown in Fig. 11.8, taken directly from the report, regulators in Latin America/Caribbean and Africa are most likely to a report a significant decline in correspondent connections.

Drivers of the Reduction in Correspondent Accounts

As with the de-banking of MTOs, a desire by banks to reduce compliance costs and regulatory risk appears to be one of the drivers of the reduction in the numbers of correspondent banking accounts. Similar to the MTO sector, correspondent banking links have garnered a reputation for being potential avenues for money laundering and so many regulators ask that banks give these accounts special scrutiny. In the USA, the enhanced regulatory focus on correspondent banking began with the introduction of the USA PATRIOT Act of 2001, in which section 312[82] requires banks to perform special due

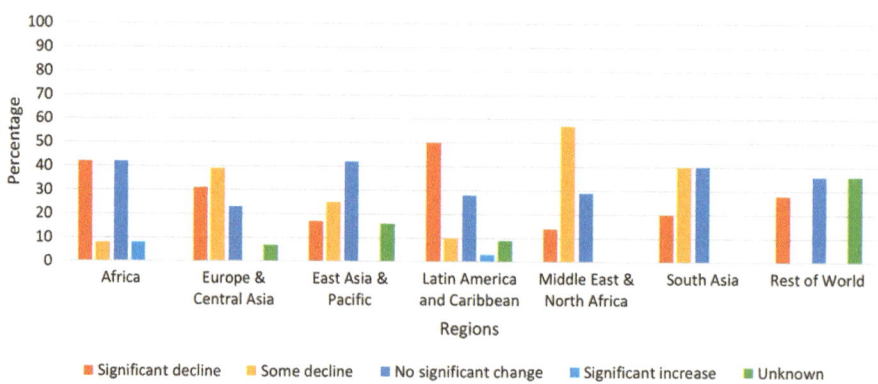

Fig. 11.8 Banking authorities: trend in foreign CBRs-nostro accounts: regional breakdown (%). Source: World Bank[81]

diligence for foreign correspondent accounts. In Australia, similar provisions took effect after the introduction of the AML/CFT Act of 2006. In the UK, the 2007 Money Laundering Regulations specifically call for enhanced due diligence on non-European Economic Area (EEA) respondents.[83]

Similarly, JMLSG guidance indicates that correspondent relationships are inherently less transparent and thus open to abuse, recommending that banks make efforts to know their respondent customer's customers (known in the industry as KYC squared, or 'KYCC'). While recent FATF comments have, to some extent, made it known that KYCC is not always necessary,[84] a large number of banks and other institutions continue to make efforts—perhaps in order to avoid heavy fines or maintain correspondent relationships.[85] SWIFT's new KYC Registry, more specifically, is geared towards facilitating data sharing and making the KYCC concept less expensive and more manageable.[86]

With FATF guidelines recommending both that respondent accounts and a respondent's customers be subject to enhanced due diligence, these efforts are now seen as part of global best practice.[87] From FATF's meeting in Brussels in March 2015, the following guidance was issued:

> When establishing correspondent banking relationships, banks are required to perform normal customer due diligence on the respondent bank. Additionally, banks are required to gather sufficient information about the respondent bank to understand the respondent bank's business, reputation and the quality of its supervision, including whether it has been subject to a money laundering or terrorist financing investigation or regulatory action, and to assess the respondent bank's AML/CFT controls. Although there will be exceptions in high risk scenarios, the FATF Recommendations do not require banks to perform, as a matter of course, normal customer due diligence on the customers of their respondent banks when establishing and maintaining correspondent banking relationships.[88]

KYCC is not *always* seen as best practice, although it is not entirely clear what is considered 'sufficient information' on the respondent's 'business, reputation, and quality of its supervision' given that these directly relate to their customers.

As the onus on banks to do enhanced due diligence on correspondent links has increased, so have the costs of getting it wrong. In the UK, the FSA's thematic review in 2011 of the banking sector revealed that, in the regulator's eyes, banks were not doing enough to monitor CBRs.[89] Since then, the FCA has fined a number of UK-resident banks, including the Bank of Beirut and Turkish Bank, for maintaining correspondent links with 'high-risk' areas without sufficient due diligence. In the USA, a number of the large fines handed down to banks have been due to specific failings in AML procedures covering correspondent banking. In January 2014, the OCC fined JP Morgan Chase $350 million for not implementing an 'adequate BSA/AML program for correspondent banking'.[90] The New York-based Oppenheimer and Co. was fined $20 million by FinCEN in part for deficiencies in monitoring correspondent accounts.[91]

Finally, more jurisdictions are being labelled as 'high risk' than ever before. Three times a year, the FATF adds or removes countries from its High Risk and Non-Cooperative Jurisdictions (HRNC) list.[92] Figure 11.9 graphs the number of countries sitting on the HRNC list in a given quarter, highlighting the surge of FATF activity in the past five years. While FATF only recommends active counter-measures in the most extreme cases, addition to the list is seen as a signal of high risk to both banks and regulators. FinCEN has noted before that the movement of funds through a listed country could be a sign of terrorist financing activity.[93] In its 2011 AML Review, the FSA noted that banks should update their risk assessments to consider countries on the list.[94]

Are these factors actually a determinant in the severing of correspondent banking links? Evidence from industry surveys suggests that this might be the case. The ICC Global Trade and Finance survey reveals that 68% of correspondents have had to decline transactions due to AML concerns, with 31% reporting having to terminate whole relationships due to compliance costs in the past year.[95]

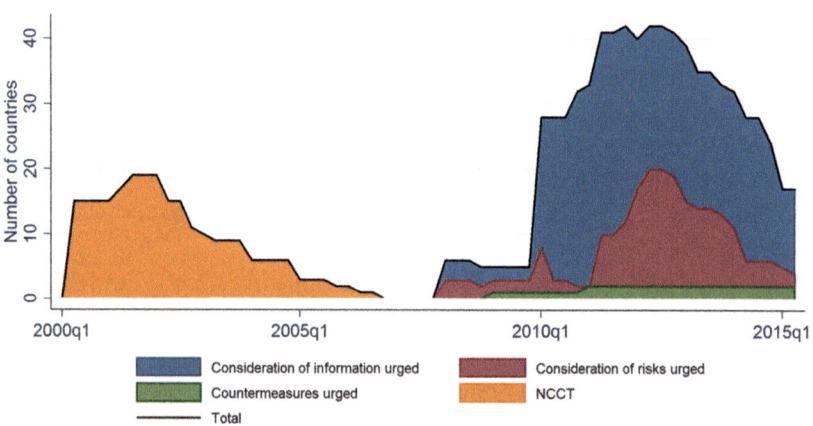

Fig. 11.9 FATF grey and blacklisting (2000–2015). Source: Data compiled from FATF statements

However, to date there has been no rigorous causal evidence linking regulatory concerns to deterioration in the correspondent banking network. While the World Bank survey of correspondent banking is a step in the right direction, follow up surveys (generating 'time series' data) are needed to fully understand what is going on.[96]

Potential Consequences

For many banks, correspondent relationships are crucial for their provision of cross-border services, including payments, foreign exchange and international trade. Furthermore, if a bank wants to settle a transaction in US dollars, they are required to either be domicile in a country hosting one of the few USD clearing-houses in the world or need to bank with a correspondent in that country.[97]

If banks lose access to their primary correspondent account and are unable to establish a new one through another bank domiciled in their target country, the terminated bank must rely on a third party who does have access to a correspondent account to process cross-border transactions. These 'nested' relationships are inherently less transparent, as they force correspondent banks to know detailed information about their respondents' clients in order to detect suspicious transactions. The BBA report highlights several examples of banks clearing transactions through a third party in another jurisdiction.[98] These alternate arrangements are also invariably more expensive, as banks are required to go through intermediaries who can then charge a higher premium for their services.

Aside from the immediate effects on the transparency and cost of financial flows, the degradation of the correspondent banking network has the potential to hamper global trade, as trade finance often uses correspondent accounts for the processing of letters of credit (L/Cs). Over 40% of respondents to the ICC Global Trade Finance survey noted that AML/KYC requirements were a 'very significant' impediment to trade finance specifically in the Africa region.[99] The BBA report describes several anonymous cases of banks losing their ability to process L/Cs due to the termination of their correspondent account, which was necessary for both advising and confirming the letter.[100] Trade L/Cs are a critical enabler for exports.[101] This has the potential to hurt trade both in rich and poor countries: if heavily regulated countries are unable to issue L/Cs due to KYC concerns or lack of correspondent connections, then exports from these countries will invariably suffer. Conversely, if banks in these countries are unable to confirm L/Cs issued by banks in 'high-risk' importing countries for the same reasons, exports from poor, high-risk countries will also be affected.

Responses are Hamstrung by Poor Data Availability

Responses to Date

For some years, and especially since late 2014, regulators and standards setters have been issuing statements that attempt to persuade banks to manage rather than eliminate risks, and to assess customers on a 'case-by-case basis'.[102] In 2016, a US Treasury and Federal Banking Agencies joint fact sheet was issued that stressed the unlikelihood of an astronomical fine for any given compliance deficiency, going so far as to stress that '[t]he vast majority (about 95%) of BSA/OFAC compliance deficiencies identified by the FBAs, FinCEN, and OFAC are corrected by the institution's management without the need for any enforcement action or penalty'.[103] However, it is unclear whether these statements have had any effect.

There have also been attempts by industry to reduce de-risking by reducing the costs of compliance. These range from low-tech process fixes such as better messaging standards and the more rapid adoption of the Legal Entity Identifier scheme through to high-tech so-called FinTech solutions. There is some hope that the leveraging of technological solutions, especially those built on blockchain technology might reduce costs to the point at which nuanced, case-by-case analysis of individual clients based on rich datasets is affordable.

The most promising development so far is the leadership shown by the Financial Stability Board (FSB), which presented to G20 Leaders in November 2015 an action plan to assess and address the decline in correspondent banking.[104] Significant progress has been made since the FSB began working in this area, though this has mostly been limited to persuading governments and multilateral institutions to take unintended consequences of AML/CFT seriously. Most notable is the major report from the IMF, *The Withdrawal of Correspondent Banking Relationships: A Case for Policy Action*.[105] Another positive sign was the FCA's commissioning of a careful study into the drivers and impacts of de-risking, though this chapter relies on expert interviews rather than a quantitative assessment of causality due to a lack of available data.[106]

All of these developments are encouraging, but they fall well short of a systematic attempt to understand and mitigate the unintended consequences of AML/CFT. Tellingly, the FSB has talked about the need for systematic data collection and sharing between governments of information relating to the number of CBRs between jurisdictions and the types of further customers served by these relationships, like MTOs. So far, there has been no sign of that sort of systematic data collection and sharing. The emphasis, rather, has been on one-off surveys and qualitative assessments that are useful right now, but do not create a system for assessing the effect of AML enforcement on payment flows going forward. The next subsection expands on the poverty of the existing data and makes suggestions for how to improve this situation.

Towards Adequate Data

There are two ways that the current data situation can be improved: by better data generation, and by enhanced data sharing by entities that already hold information.

Data Generation

Describing the extent of the various problems identified in the foregoing sections of this chapter requires a representative survey and/or the correct administrative information. Previous and current survey efforts will not be sufficient because of their low response rates. To date, the World Bank surveys are the best available evidence we have on the effects of de-risking around the globe. However, the results are hampered by some limitations which prevent us from fully understanding the scale of the problem. For one, the response rates by banks and MTOs to the remittances survey are very low, as can be seen in Table 11.1.

This can skew the results in unpredictable ways, and the World Bank has itself cautioned against over-interpreting the results. For example, MTOs which have lost bank accounts might be much more likely to fill out a survey on de-risking, making the problem look worse than it really is. The response rates are significantly better in the correspondent banking survey, but a lack of consistency in bank responses means that, while it is possible to know how many banks have cut correspondent relationships in recent years, it is hard to know precisely what the net effect has been.

To really understand de-risking, representative surveys would be required of MTOs and banks. Reasonable sample frames can be constructed using registries of approved MTOs maintained in a number of countries.

Table 11.1 Survey response rate by respondent category

	Governments	Banks	MTOs
Participated	13	25	82
Invited to participate	19	3000	501
Response rate	68.4%	0.8%	16.4%

Source: World Bank[107]

Low response rates or 'survey fatigue' could be mitigated through increased involvement of government and MTO trade organizations. Additionally, those government agencies that keep detailed registries of regulated MTOs, such as FinCEN, FINTRAC, the FCA and AUSTRAC, could make headline statistics public in an easily accessible machine-readable format, including information as far back in time as possible.

Additional data could be generated through government agencies using their powers to collect and disseminate market information. For example, the Egmont Group of Financial Intelligence Units (FIUs) comprises 139 member FIUs that serve as a central repository and analysis centre for information related to money laundering, associated predicate offences and the financing of terrorism. This group serves as a forum for the exchange and analysis of sensitive financial, law enforcement and regulatory information from covered financial institutions (reporting entities) within members' jurisdictions. Integration is even deeper on the EU's FIU.net platform.[108] FATF recommendations 27 and 40 ensure that FIUs are well positioned to collect, analyse and share data on remittances and money services businesses, including from/to regions considered 'high risk'. National FIUs could query financial institutions for data regarding the volume, amounts and types of transactions associated with MTOs and banking correspondents. They could share this data with each other and parties wishing to conduct analyses that are demonstrably in the public interest.

Data Sharing

To better examine the relationship between regulatory enforcement and risk-rating, and the closure of correspondent accounts, bilateral data on payment flows and on correspondent links is crucial. SWIFT, the Clearing House Interbank Payments System (CHIPS), the Clearing House Automated Payment System (CHAPS), the Bank of International Settlements (BIS), and other entities tasked with managing and collecting data on cross-border transactions and relationships could make available data on bilateral payment flows and the number of CBRs between countries. More specific data could be anonymized to protect these entities clients, and only released to parties intending to conduct an analysis in the public interest. The SWIFT Institute currently provides some access to data to researchers though this is limited to a very small number of projects approved by SWIFT.

In order to assist lower capacity jurisdictions and to develop a set of best practices, national governments could make the data that they are using for risk analyses and regulatory impact assessments available to other jurisdictions and to parties conducting analyses that are demonstrably in the public interest. FATF recommendation 40 requires countries to 'ensure that their competent authorities can rapidly, constructively and effectively provide the widest range of international cooperation in relation to money laundering, associated predicate offenses and terrorist financing'.[109] This could be interpreted to include the sharing of risk assessment and regulatory impact assessment data and methodologies.

Conclusion

Money laundering, terrorism financing and sanctions violations by individuals, banks and other financial entities are serious offences with significant negative consequences for rich and poor countries alike. Governments have taken important steps to address these offences. Efforts by the USA, UK and others to combat money laundering and curb illicit financial flows are a necessary step to increase the safety of the financial system and improve security, both domestically and around the world. But, as this chapter has shown, the policies that have been put in place to counter financial crimes may also have unintentional and costly consequences, in particular for people in low and lower-middle income countries. Those most affected are likely to include the families of migrant workers and small businesses that need to access working capital or trade finance. And sometimes, current policies may be self-defeating to the extent that they reduce the transparency of financial flows. It is therefore imperative that better data is generated and shared in order to allow researchers and policymakers to work together to reform the AML/CFT system to be as effective and efficient as possible. This should be seen as both a security and a sustainable development priority.

Notes

1. Grace Cahill, 'Oxfam Reaction to Barclays Closing Last Remittance Accounts to Somalia' (*Oxfam*, 30 September 2013) <www.oxfam.org.uk/media-centre/press-releases/2013/09/closure-of-final-soma li-remittance-accounts/> accessed 20 December 2016.
2. Dahabshiil, 'Dahabshiil Wins Injunction Against Barclays' (*Dahabshiil*, 5 November 2013) <www.dahabshiil.com/ 2013/11/dahabshiil-wins-injunction-against-barclays.html> accessed 14 January 2016.

3. Douglas Flint, 'Evidence Submitted By Douglas Flint, Group Chairman, HSBC, About Access to Banking Services' Official HSBC Letter to the Treasury Committee (February 2015).

4. *Dahabshiil Transfer Services Ltd v Barclays Bank Plc* [2013] EWHC 3379 (Ch).

5. BBC, 'Somalia Fears as US Sunrise Banks Stop Money Transfers' *BBC News* (London, 30 December 2011) <www.bbc.co.uk/news/world-africa-16365619> accessed 14 January 2017.

6. Jamila Trindle, 'Terror Money Crackdown Also Complicates Life for Ordinary Somali-Americans' *The Foreign Policy Magazine* (Washington, 23 April 2014) <http://foreignpolicy.com/2014/04/23/terror -money-crack-down-also-complicates-life-for-ordinary-somali-americans/> accessed 14 January 2017.

7. OCC, 'Consent Order AA-WE-14-07: In the Matter of Merchants Bank of California, N.A., Carson, California' (23 June 2014) <www.occ.gov/static/ enforcement-actions/ea2014-084.pdf> accessed 14 January 2017.

8. A recent (non-random, low response) survey by the World Bank revealed nearly 80% of responding MTOs in the USA had difficulty opening a bank account. Global Remittances Working Group, 'Barriers to Access to Payment Systems in Sending Countries and Proposed Solutions' Special-Purpose Note (WBG 2013) <http://siteresources.worldbank.org/FINANCIALSECTOR/ Resources/28   2044-1359488786791/barriers_web.pdf/> accessed 20 December 2016.

9. Ross Buckley and Ken Ooi, 'Pacific Injustice and Instability: Bank Account Closures of Australian Money Transfer Operators' (2014) 25(4) *Journal of Banking and Finance Law and Practice* 243.

10. The European Payments Institutions Federation (EPIF) notes that members in at least 13 European countries have had difficulty accessing bank accounts: EPIF, "EPIF Position Paper on Access to Bank Services for Payment Institutions" (EPIF 2014) <www.paymentinstitutions.eu/documents/d ownload/51/attachement/epif-position-paper-on-access-to-bankservices-related-to-psd2-final.pdf/> accessed 20 December 2016. See also Global Remittances Working Group (n 8).

11. IMF and Union of Arab Banks, 'Joint Survey by the Union of Arab Banks (UAB) and the International Monetary Fund (IMF)' (IMF 2015) <www. nmta.us/assets/docs/DOBS/the%20impact   %20of%20de-risking%20 on%20the%20mena%20region.pdf> accessed 20 December 2016.

12. FinCEN, 'FinCEN Joint Statement on Providing Banking Services to Money Services Businesses' (*FinCEN*, 30 March 2005) <www.fincen.gov/ news_room/nr/html/20050330.html> accessed 20 December 2016.

13. ibid.

14. World Bank, 'Report on the G20 Survey on De-Risking Activities in the Remittance Market' (WBG 2015) <http://documents.worldbank.org/

curated/en/679881467993185572/pdf/101071-WP-PUB   LIC-GPFI-DWG-Remittances-De-risking-Report-2015-Final-2.pdf> accessed 20 December 2016.

15. ibid.

16. For the purposes of this section 'AML' is used as an umbrella term, in its broadest possible sense.

17. For the two most famous examples, see Nate Raymond, 'BNP Paribas Sentenced in $8.9 Billion Accord Over Sanctions Violations' *Reuters* (New York, 1 May 2015) <www.reuters.com/article/us-bnp-paribas-settlement-sentencing-idUSKBN0NM41K20150501> accessed 14 January 2017; BBC, 'HSBC to Pay $1.9bn in US Money Laundering Penalties' *BBC News* (London, 11 December 2012) <www.bbc.co.uk/news/business-20673466> accessed 14 January 2017.

18. UK fines are in millions of GBP, whereas US fines are in billions of USD.

19. Although not a branch of government, Financial Industry Regulatory Authority (FINRA) fulfils a regulatory function. It is a self-regulatory organization overseen by the Securities Exchange Commission that writes and enforces rules governing the activities of more than 4000 securities firms.

20. Dow Jones, '2015 Global Anti-Money Laundering Survey Results: Detailed Report' Presentation (March 2015) <http://images.dowjones.com/company/wp-content/uploads/sites/15/2015/03/Do   w-Jones-ACAMS-AML-Survey-2015.pdf/> accessed 20 December 2016.

21. FINRA, 'FINRA Fines Brown Brothers Harriman a Record $8 Million for Substantial Anti-Money Laundering Compliance Failures' *FINRA* (Washington, 5 February 2014) <www.finra.org/newsroom/2014/finra-fines-brown-brothers-harriman-record-8-million-sub stantial-anti-money-laundering/> accessed 20 December 2016.

22. FinCEN, 'FinCEN Assesses $1 Million Penalty and Seeks to Bar Former Money Gram Executive from Financial Industry: Individual Accountability Emphasized in Civil Actions' (*FinCEN*, 18 December 2014) <www.fincen.gov/news_room/nr/html/20141218.html/> accessed 20 December 2016.

23. Julia Black and David Kershaw, 'Criminalising Bank Managers' (2013) Law and Financial Markets Project Briefing 1/13 <www.lse.ac.uk/collections/law/projects/lfm/LFMP%201%20%E2%80%93   %20Criminalising%20Bank%20Managers%20[final].pdf> accessed 20 December 2016.

24. Authors' own calculations based on World Bank bilateral remittance flows matrix.

25. Tom Keatinge, 'Breaking the Banks: The Financial Consequences of Counterterrorism' *Foreign Affairs* (26 June 2014) <www.foreignaffairs.com/articles/united-states/2014-06-26/breaking-banks/> accessed 20 December 2016.

26. JMLSG, 'Guidance in Respect of Money Service Businesses' (2014), 2–3 <www.jmlsg.org.uk/downlo ad/9752/> accessed 20 December 2016.

27. HM Treasury and Home Office, 'UK National Risk Assessment of Money Laundering and Terrorist Financing' (October 2015), para 6 (128) <www.gov.uk/government/uploads/system/uploads/attach ment_data/file/468210/UK_NRA_October_2015_final_web.pdf> accessed 14 January 2017.

28. Australian Transactions Reports and Analysis Centre, 'AUSTRAC Statement' (25 November 2014) <www.austrac.gov.au/news/austrac-statement> accessed 28 November 2016.

29. Rob Blackwell, 'FDIC Withdraws Alleged 'Hit List' of High-Risk Merchants' *American Banker: Law and Regulation* (Washington, 28 July 2014) <www.americanbanker.com/issues/179_144/fdic-withdraws-alleged-hit-list-of-high-risk-merchants-1069031-1.html> accessed 20 December 2016.

30. US Department of the Treasury, 'National Money Laundering Risk Assessment 2015' (2015), 51 <www.treasury.gov/resource-center/terrorist-illicit-finance/Documents/National%20Money%20La   undering%20Risk%20Assessment%20–%2006-12-2015.pdf> accessed 14 January 2017.

31. *Dahabshiil Transfer Services Ltd* (n 4).

32. Flint (n 3).

33. Dave Kolpack, 'North Dakota Bank Dumps Money Service Businesses' *The Washington Times* (Washington, 5 March 2014) <www.washingtontimes.com/news/2014/mar/5/north-dakota-bank-dumps-money-service-businesses/> accessed 14 January 2017.

34. Jones (n 20).

35. Martin Arnold and Sam Fleming, 'Regulation: Banks Count the Risks and Rewards' *Financial Times* (New York, 13 November 2014) <www.ft.com/content/9df378a2-66bb-11e4-91ab-00144feabdc0> accessed 14 January 2017.

36. Matt Allen, 'BBA Response to FCA Guidance Consultation: Examples of Good and Poor Practice in "Banks" Financial Crime Controls in Trade Finance' Official letter from the BBA to the FCA (4 October 2013).

37. NCA, 'Joint Money Laundering Intelligence Taskforce (JMLIT)' <www.nationalcrimeagency.gov.uk/a   bout-us/what-we-do/economic-crime/joint-money-laundering-intelligence-taskforce-jmlit> accessed 20 December 2016.

38. The UN International Fund for Agricultural Development discusses how the 'concentration' of MTO accounts in one location generates more risk for the remittance industry. IFAD, 'Sending Money Home: European flows and markets' (IFAD 2015) <www.ifad.org/remittances/pub/money_europe.pdf/> accessed 20 December 2016.

39. FATF, 'Drivers for "De-Risking" Go Beyond Anti-Money Laundering/Terrorist Financing' (*FATF*, 26 June 2015) <www.fatf-gafi.org/documents/news/derisking-goes-beyond-amlcft.html/> accessed 20 December 2016.

40. FATF, 'FATF Clarifies Risk-Based Approach: Case-by-Case, Not Wholesale De-Risking' (*FATF*, 23 October 2014) <www.fatf-gafi.org/documents/news/rba-and-de-risking.html/> accessed 20 December 2016.

41. The World Bank documents an increase in money transfer fees charged by Australia's largest bank after a spate of de-banking. See also Sonia Plaza, 'Remittance Markets: More Court Cases and Higher Costs Due to Anti-Money Laundering and Countering Financing of Terrorism (AML/CFT) Regulations' (*The World Bank*, 14 December 2014) <http://blogs.worldbank. org/peoplemove/remittance-markets   -more-court-cases-and-higher-costs-due-anti-money-laundering-and-countering/> accessed 20 December 2016.

42. Jonathan Capel, 'What Next for Remittances and Money Transfers in the Pacific?' (*CGAP*, 12 June 2014) <www.cgap.org/blog/what-next-remittances-and-money-transfers-pacific/> accessed 20 December 2016.

43. *Dahabshiil Transfer Services Ltd* (n 4).

44. World Bank (n 14).

45. HM Government and Beechwood International, 'Safer Corridors: Rapid Assessment, Case Study: Somalia and UK banking' (September 2013) <www.gov.uk/government/uploads/system/uploads/at   tachment_data/ file/283826/SAFER_CORRIDORS_RAPID_ASSESSMENT__2013__ SOMALIA___UK_BANKING.PDF/> accessed 20 December 2016. See further Chap. 42 (Cooper) in this collection.

46. While specific to the plight of Somali remittance providers, Orozco and Yansura document the cost burden of transferring money without access to a bank account and time spent looking for alternative means. Manuel Orozco and Julia Yansura, 'Keeping the Lifeline Open: Remittances and Markets in Somalia' (*Oxfam America Inc.*, 2013) <www.oxfamamerica.org/ static/media/files/somalia   -remittance-report-web.pdf/>   accessed   20 December 2016.

47. Matt Juden, 'Bitcoins for Everyone? Cryptocurrencies Are Not a Magic Bullet for the Unintended Consequences of Anti-Money Laundering Policies' (*CGD*, 20 March 2015) <www.cgdev.org/blog/bitc oins-everyone-cryptocurrencies-are-not-magic-bullet-unintended-consequences-anti-money> accessed 3 January 2017.

48. *Dahabshiil Transfer Services Ltd* (n 4).

49. In the UK, MTOs which transact more than EUR 3m per month are legally required to be registered as APIs and all such firms must hold a bank account for those transactions. In evidence submitted to the UK Treasury Select Committee on the treatment of financial services consumers, the Association of UK Payment Institutions claimed that a number of MTOs had lost their status due to a lack of bank account access: Dominic Thorncroft and Jawwad Riaz, 'Evidence Submitted by the Association of UK Payments Institutions About Access to Banking Services' Official Letter from AUKPI to the Treasury Committee (January 2015).

50. Thorsten Beck and Maria Soledad Martínez Pería, 'What Explains the Price of Remittances? An Examination Across 119 Country Corridors' (2011) 25(1) *World Bank Economic Review* 105; Kevin Watkins and Maria Quattri,

'Lost in Intermediation: How Excessive Charges Undermine the Benefits of Remittances for Africa' (*ODI*, 2014) <www.odi.org/sites/odi.org.uk/files/odi-assets/publications-opinion-files/8901.pdf> accessed 20 December 2016.

51. This index is equivalent to (1—the Herfindahl index).

52. G8, 'G8 Declaration' (2009) <www.g8italia2009.it/static/G8_Allegato/G8_Declaration_08_07_09_fi nal,0.pdf> accessed 20 December 2016.

53. World Bank, 'Migration and Development Brief 24' (*World Bank*, 13 April 2015), 1 <https://siteresources.worldbank.org/INTPROSPECTS/Resources/334934-1288990760745/Migrat ionandDevelopmentBrief24.pdf.> accessed 20 December 2016.

54. The correlation between de-risking and remittance prices cannot be assessed for some corridors due to data limitations. One important example is the US-Somalia corridor, as the World Bank has only collected price data for this corridor since the second quarter of 2015.

55. John Gibson, David McKenzie, and Halahingano Rohorua, 'How Cost Elastic are Remittances? Evidence from Tongan Migrants in New Zealand' (2006) 21(1) *Pacific Economic Bulletin* 112.

56. Caroline Freund and Nikola Spatafora, 'Remittances, Transaction Costs, and Informality' (2008) 86(2) *Journal of Development Economics* 356.

57. Diego Aycinena, Claudia Martinez, and Dean Yang, 'The Impact of Transaction Fees on Migrant Remittances: Evidence from a Field Experiment Among Migrants from El Salvador' (2010) University of Michigan <http://sites.lsa.umich.edu/deanyang/wp-content/uploads/sites/205/2014/12/aycine na-martinez-yang-remittances.pdf/> accessed 20 December 2016; Kate Ambler, Diego Aycinena, and Dean Yang, 'Remittance Responses to Temporary Discounts: A Field Experiment Among Central American Migrants' (2014) NBER Working Paper 20522.

58. Jamila Trindle, 'Money Keeps Moving Towards Somalia, Sometimes in Suitcases: Some financial Companies in the U.S. Resort to Carrying Cash on Airplanes to Keep Remittances Flowing to Needy Somalis' *The Foreign Policy Magazine* (Washington, 15 May 2015) <http://foreignpolicy.com/2015/0 5/15/money-keeps-moving-toward-somalia-sometimes-in-suitcases/> accessed 14 January 2017.

59. Clemens and McKenzie argue that much of the perceived growth in remittances over the past 25 years is due to better measurement. This makes it difficult to compare the difference in size of remittances in ODA over this period. Michael Clemens and David McKenzie, 'Why Don't Remittances Appear to Affect Growth?' (2014) World Bank Policy Research Working Paper 6856 <www-wds.worldbank.org/external/default/WDSContentServer/WDSP/IB/2014/05/06/000158349_20140506090632/Rendered/PDF/WPS6856.pdf/> accessed 20 December 2016.

60. Dean Yang, 'International Migration, Remittances and Household Investment: Evidence from Philippine Migrants' Exchange Rate Shocks'

(2008) 118(528) *The Economic Journal* 591; Amar Iqbal Anwar and Mazhar Yaseen Mughal, 'Motives to Remit: Some Microeconomic Evidence from Pakistan' (2012) 32(1) *Economics Bulletin* 574; Richard Adams Junior and Alfredo Cuecuecha, 'The Impact of Remittances on Investment and Poverty in Ghana' (2013) 50 *World Development* 24.

61. Ariel Fiszbein and others, 'Conditional Cash Transfers: Reducing Present and Future Poverty' (The World Bank 2009); Sarah Baird, Craig McIntosh, and Berk Özler, 'Cash or Condition? Evidence from a Cash Transfer Experiment' (2011) 126(4) *The Quarterly Journal of Economics* 1709; BBA and others, 'De-Risking: Global Impact and Unintended Consequences for Exclusion and Stability' (2014) <https://classic.regonline.com/custImages/340000/341739/G24%20AFI/G24_2015/De-risking_Re port.pdf> accessed 20 December 2016; Johannes Haushofer and Jeremy Shapiro, 'Household Response to Income Changes: Evidence from an Unconditional Cash Transfer Program in Kenya' (2013) Working paper <www.princeton. edu/~joha/publications/Haushofer_Shapiro_UCT_2013.pdf > accessed 14 January 2017.

62. Dean Yang and Hwajung Choi, 'Are Remittances Insurance? Evidence From Rainfall Shocks in the Philippines' (2007) 21(2) *World Bank Economic Review* 219; Sanket Mohapatra, George Joseph, and Dilip Ratha, 'Remittances and Natural Disasters: Ex-Post Response and Contribution to Ex-Ante Preparedness' (2012) 14(3) *Environment, Development and Sustainability* 365; Giulia Bettin, Andrea Presbitero, and Nikola Spatafora, 'Remittances and Vulnerability in Developing Countries' (2014) IMF Working Paper 14/13 <www.knomad.org/powerpoints/remittances/Remittances_ Vulnerability _in_Developing_Countries.pdf> accessed 14 January 2017; Junaid Ahmed and Mazhar Yaseen Mughal, 'Great Expectations? Remittances and Asset Accumulation in Pakistan' (2015) Centre d'Analyse Théorique et de Traitement de Données économiques Working Paper 6 <http://catt.univ-pau.fr/live/digitalAssets/140/140147_2014_2015_6docWCATT_Great_ Expectations_Remittances_Asset_Accumulation_Pakistan_JAhmed_ MYMughal.pdf> accessed 28 November 2016.

63. Reena Aggarwal, Asli Demirgüç-Kunt, and Maria Soledad Martínez Pería, 'Do Remittances Promote Financial Development?' (2011) 96(2) *Journal of Development Economics* 255; Diego Anzoategui, Asli Demirgüç-Kunt, and Maria Soledad Martínez Pería, 'Remittances and Financial Inclusion: Evidence from El Salvador' (2011) 54 *World Development* 338.

64. Trindle (n 58).

65. Thorncroft and Riaz (n 49).

66. Freund and Spatafora (n 56).

67. Caitlin Chalmers and Mohamed Aden Hassan, 'UK Somali Remittances Survey' (2008) Department for International Development <www. diaspora-centre.org/DOCS/UK_Somali_Remittan.pdf> accessed 20 December 2016.

68. Rashid Amjad and others, 'How to Increase Informal Flows of Remittances: An Analysis of the Remittance Market in Pakistan' (2013) IGC Working Paper <www.theigc.org/wp-content/uploads/2014/09/Amjad-Et-Al-2013-Working-Paper.pdf> accessed 28 November 2016.

69. Jacqueline Irving, Sanket Mohapatra, and Dilip Ratha, 'Migrant Remittance Flows: Findings from a Global Survey of Central Banks' (2010) WB Working Paper 194 <https://openknowledge.worldbank.org/bitstream/handle/1098 6/5929/538840PUB0Migr101Official0Use0Only1.pdf?sequence=1/> accessed 20 December 2016.

70. Anneke Kosse and Robert Vermeulen, 'Migrants' Choice of Remittance Channel: Do General Payment Habits Play a Role?' (2014) 62 *World Development* 213.

71. Freund and Spatafora (n 56).

72. For consideration of *hawala*, see Chap. 42 (Cooper) in this collection.

73. ICC, '2014: Rethinking Trade and Finance, An ICC Private Sector Development Perspective' (ICC 2014), 39 <www.iccwbo.org/Data/Documents/Banking/General-PDFs/ICC-Global-Trade-and-Finance-Survey-2014/> accessed 20 December 2016.

74. BBA and others (n 61) 10.

75. SWIFT is an independent, member-owned cooperative society that facilitates secure transactions and information sharing between more than 10,800 financial institutions, including banks, securities institutions and corporations. The messaging network constructed by SWIFT employs a unified framework composed of Business Identifier Codes (BICs, or SWIFT codes). The use of these codes allows SWIFT to streamline financial messages, increasing their speed, accuracy, and security relative to alternate services. Rather than actually holding funds or securities, and then transferring payments to a different account (electronic fund transfers), SWIFT uses its messaging network to send payment orders from one party to another. These payments are settled by the correspondent accounts that institutions hold with each other, either by virtue of a direct banking relationship, or by being affiliated to one such bank.

76. SWIFT, 'Correspondent Banking 3.0: The Compelling Need to Evolve Towards a Customer-Centric 'Experience Banking' Model' (2011) SWIFT Institute White Paper, 3 <www.swift.com/resources/documents/SWIFT_white_paper_correspondent_banking.pdf> accessed 20 December 2016.

77. Samantha Cook and Kimmo Soramaki, 'The Global Network of Payment Flows' (2014) SWIFT Institute Working Paper 2012–006 <http://ssrn.com/abstract=2503774/> accessed 20 December 2016. The paper also documents a decline in links to sanctions listed countries, such as Sudan, Cuba and Iran.

78. ECB, 'Ninth Survey on Correspondent Banking in Euro' (ECB 2015), 17 <www.ecb.europa.eu/pub/pdf/other/surveycorrespondentbankingineuro201502.en.pdf> accessed 20 December 2016.

79. IMF and Union of Arab Banks, 'Joint Survey by the Union of Arab Banks (UAB) and the International Monetary Fund (IMF)' (IMF 2015) <www. nmta.us/assets/docs/DOBS/the%20impact   %20of%20de-risking%20 on%20the%20mena%2 0region.pdf> accessed 20 December 2016.

80. World Bank, 'Survey on De-Risking' (WBG 2015) <https://remittanceprices. worldbank.org/en/sur vey-on-de-risking/> accessed 12 August 2015.

81. ibid.

82. Section 312 amends the Banking Secrecy Act 1970.

83. Money Laundering Regulations 2007, SI 2007/2157.

84. FATF later clarified that it did not feel that a Know Your Customer's Customer (KYCC) approach was necessary. FATF, 'Dialogue With the Private Sector' (FATF 2015) <www.fatf-gafi.org/documents /news/private-sector-forum-march-2015.html> accessed 20 December 2016.

85. Juan Pedro Schmid, 'How Much Anti-Money Laundering Effort is Enough? The Jamaican Experience' (2015) IADB Policy Brief 242 <http://publications. iadb.org/handle/11319/6904/> accessed 20 December 2016.

86. SWIFT, 'SWIFT Addresses the Know Your Customer's Customer Compliance Challenge' Press Release (*SWIFT*, 12 November 2014) <www. swift.com/about_swift/shownews?param_dcr=news.dat   a/en/s   wift_ com/2014/PR_KYC_new_profile.xml> accessed 20 December 2016; SWIFT, 'The KYC Registry: An Introductory Guide' Presentation <http:// complianceservices.swift.com/sites/complian ceservices/files/the_kyc_registry_ an_introduction.pdf/> accessed 16 August 2015.

87. FATF, 'International Standards on Combating Money Laundering and the Financing of Terrorism and Proliferation: The FATF Recommendations' (FATF/OECD 2012).

88. FATF (n 39).

89. FSA, 'Banks' Management of High Money-Laundering Risk Situations: How Banks Deal with High-Risk Customers (Including Politically Exposed Persons), Correspondent Banking Relationships and Wire Transfers' (FSA 2011) <www.fsa.gov.uk/pubs/other/aml_final_report.pdf/> accessed 20 December 2016.

90. OCC, 'OCC Assesses a $350 Million Civil Money Penalty Against JPMorgan Chase for Bank Secrecy Act Violations' (*OCC*, 7 January 2014) <www.occ.treas.gov/news-issuances/news-releases/2014/nr-occ-2014-1. html/> accessed 20 December 2016.

91. FinCEN, 'FinCEN Fines Oppenheimer & Co. Inc. $20 Million for Continued Anti-Money Laundering Shortfalls' (*FinCEN*, 27 January 2015) <www.fincen.gov/news_room/nr/pdf/20150127.pdf/> accessed 20 December 2016.

92. The HRNC process has replaced the NCCT Initiative, which started in 2000 and listed countries deemed to have significant deficiencies and to be 'non-cooperative' in the context of FATF recommendations. The last country

was de-listed in October 2006. The HRNC process is more discriminatory/specific in its classification of jurisdictions' strategic deficiencies, distinguishing between jurisdictions to which counter-measures apply, jurisdictions which have not made sufficient progress or committed to an action plan, and jurisdictions that have made a 'high-level political commitment' and action plan to address their issues. The International Cooperation Review Group (ICRG) monitors and reviews these countries. See the dynamic list on FATF's web page <www.fatf-gafi.org/publications/high-riskandnon-coop erativejurisdictions/?hf=10&b=0&s=desc(fatf_releaseda te)> accessed 20 December 2016.

93. FinCEN, 'Aspects of Financial Transactions Indicative of Terrorist Funding' (2002) 4 SAR Bulletin <www.sec.gov/about/offices/ocie/aml2007/sarbull0102.pdf/> accessed 20 December 2016.
94. FSA (n 89).
95. ICC (n 73).
96. World Bank, 'Withdrawal From Correspondent Banking: Where, Why, and What to Do About It' (WBG 2015) <http://documents.worldbank.org/curated/en/113021467990964789/pdf/101098-revised-PUBLIC-CBR-Report-November-2015.pdf> accessed 19 December 2016.
97. This includes the USA, Tokyo, Hong Kong, Singapore and Manila.
98. BBA and others (n 61).
99. ICC (n 73) 97. AML/CFT requirements can also restrict trade finance directly by leading banks to deny L/Cs for which they cannot due sufficient due diligence on the listed beneficiary, an issue also covered in the ICC trade survey.
100. BBA and others (n 61).
101. Friederike Neipmann and Tim Schmidt-Eisenlohr, 'No Guarantees, No Trade: How Banks Affect Export Patterns' (2013) CESifo Working Paper 4650 <www.cesifo-group.de/portal/page/portal/Doc Base_Content/WP/WP-CESifo_Working_Papers/wp-cesifo-2014/wp-cesifo-2014-02/cesifo1_wp465 0.pdf/> accessed 20 December 2016.
102. FATF (n 40). See also FinCEN, 'FinCEN Statement on Providing Banking Services to Money Services Businesses' (*FinCEN*, 10 November 2014) <http://optimacompass.com/fincen-statement-on-providing-banking-services-to-money-services-businesses/> accessed 27 November 2016; FDIC, 'Statement on Providing Banking Services' (*FDIC*, 28 January 2015) <www.fdic.gov/news/news/financial/2015/fil15005.pdf/> accessed 20 December 2016. Also, FCA, 'Derisking: Banks' Management of Money Laundering Risk—FCA Expectations' (*FCA*, 27 April 2015) <www.fca.org.uk/about/what/enforcing/money-laundering/derisking/> accessed 20 December 2016.
103. US Department of the Treasury and Federal Banking Agencies, 'Joint Fact Sheet on Foreign Correspondent Banking: Approach to BSA/AML and OFAC Sanctions Supervision and Enforcement' (2016), 1 <www.treasury.

gov/press-center/press-releases/Documents/Foreign%20Correspondent
%20Banking%20Fact%20Sheet.pdf> accessed 20 September 2016.
104. FSB, 'Progress Report to G20 on the FSB Action Plan to Assess and Address
the Decline in Correspondent Banking' (FSB 2016) <www.fsb.org/wp-content/
uploads/Correspondent-Banking-progress-report.pdf> accessed 20 December
2016.
105. IMF, 'The Withdrawal of Correspondent Banking Relationships: A Case for
Policy Action' (IMF 2016) <www.imf.org/external/pubs/ft/sdn/2016/
sdn1606.pdf> accessed 20 December 2016.
106. David Artingstall and others, *Drivers & Impacts of Derisking: A Study of
Representative Views and Data in the UK, by John Howell & Co. Ltd. for the
Financial Conduct Authority* (John Howell & Co. Ltd. 2016) <www.fca.org.
uk/publication/research/drivers-impacts-of-derisking.pdf> accessed 19
December 2016.
107. World Bank (n 14).
108. Clare Ellis and Ines Sofia de Oliveira, 'Tackling Money Laundering: Towards a
New Model for Information Sharing' (RUSI 2015) <www.rusi.org/publications/
occasionalpapers/ref:O56016E6618 244/> accessed 20 December 2016.
109. FATF (n 87) 29.

Vijaya Ramachandran is a senior fellow at the Center for Global Development
(CGD). She works on private sector development and financial inclusion, including
the unintended consequences of rich countries' anti-money laundering policies in
poor countries. Her research has been published in *World Development, Development
Policy Review, Governance, Prism,* and *AIDS* and the *Oxford Handbook of Africa and
Economics*. Prior to joining CGD, Ramachandran worked at the World Bank and in
the Executive Office of the Secretary-General of the United Nations. She also served
on the faculties of Georgetown University and Duke University. Her work has
appeared in *The Economist, Financial Times, The Guardian, Washington Post, The
New York Times, National Public Radio* and *Vox*. Ramachandran holds a PhD in
Business Economics from Harvard University.

Matthew Collin joined the Center for Global Development in January 2014. His
research focuses on illicit financial flows, the adoption and impact of property rights
in developing countries and the role of property rights in large-scale land consolidation. His work includes investigating the impact of ethnic sorting on formalization
behaviour, the effort of neighbour decisions on land title adoption and the impact of
conditional subsidies on gender equity in land ownership. Collin holds a DPhil in
Economics from the University of Oxford and previously worked at the Centre for
the Study of African Economies and as an Overseas Development Institute Fellow in
the Ministry of Finance, Malawi.

Matt Juden is an independent consultant currently working on the potential and limitations of technological innovation in financial systems, or 'fintech', to address development problems. He previously worked on anti-money laundering and terrorist financing regulation for the Center for Global Development for two years. He holds a BA in Philosophy from the University of Cambridge and an MSc in Research for International Development from the School of Oriental and African Studies, where he is a PhD candidate.

12

Punishing Banks, Their Clients and Their Clients' Clients

Michael Levi

Introduction

A major shift in measures to control serious and organised crime occurred during the late 1980s when—starting with drugs trafficking—financial institutions came to be seen as an important line of defence in becoming aware of and reporting the suspected acts of their clients to national financial intelligence units. These were given the name 'suspicious activity reports', which gave them a spurious objective quality when in fact they were *suspected* activities, including all the stereotypes of what criminal activity and 'criminal types' looked like. Gradually, the types of crimes that banks and an increasing number of other bodies were expected to spot and report on has grown, ranging from elite crime like Grand Corruption and tax evasion to petty crimes. Meanwhile, the empirical evidence on how money is laundered and how terrorism is financed has remained relatively primitive, though improving. So apart from the active

The author has been involved significantly in two major reviews of de-risking: a Center for Global Development working group, which looked at the issues quite globally, and a conceptual and empirical review of the UK evidence for the Financial Conduct Authority (FCA). See CGD, *Unintended Consequences of Anti–Money Laundering Policies for Poor Countries A CGD Working Group Report* (2016) <www.cgdev.org/sites/default/files/CGD-WG-Report-Unintended-Consequences-AML-Policies-2015.pdf> accessed 10 March 2017; David Artingstall and others, *Drivers & Impacts of Derisking* (2016) <www.fca.org.uk/publication/research/drivers-impacts-of-derisking.pdf> accessed 10 March 2017.

M. Levi
School of Social Sciences, Cardiff University, Cardiff, UK

© The Author(s) 2018
C. King et al. (eds.), *The Palgrave Handbook of Criminal and Terrorism Financing Law*,
https://doi.org/10.1007/978-3-319-64498-1_12

connivance of banks and other professionals with people they know or suspect to be offenders, it is seldom clear what banks should be looking out for, and the temptation is to look for 'out-of-context' behaviour or behaviour that is not readily explicable. Some banks have taken the initiative and begun to develop highly sophisticated ways of modelling potentially criminal behaviour. Others have not, including the national branches of expanding banks. As some banks have been penalised for various types of risky behaviour, including money laundering (ML), and other regulatory costs have increased, their risk appetites have changed, and one way of dealing with the new risk environment is to get rid of clients—direct clients and/or correspondent banks (often from poorer countries) whose own client activities are not transparent—who pose or appear to pose risks that might lead to the bank itself being penalised.

ML, terrorism financing (TF) and sanctions violations have potentially serious negative consequences for both rich and poor countries and people. The policies that have been put in place to counter financial crimes may also have unintentional and costly consequences for people in poor countries, not just offenders but also especially the families of migrant workers, small businesses that need to access working capital or trade finance, and aid recipients. There is also a risk of counter-productive regulation by reducing the transparency of financial flows and, to the extent that the policies have the effect of making remittances harder, generating greater hostility towards the West.

The crucial problematic term here is 'policy', a word that has caused difficulties in many foreign and domestic contexts. When does a practice that may be a shared or common one become a 'policy'? Early 'law in context' conceptualisations by Packer[1] divided approaches to crime control into a binary category of 'crime control' and 'due process', crudely represented by cops and defence lawyers, respectively. This model has been critiqued thoroughly since,[2] but it remains a useful gestalt against which to locate cultural approaches to repressive measures. It is the argument in this chapter that inasmuch as it is guided by more than a rough instinct, the approach taken by the anti-money laundering/counter-terrorist financing (AML/CTF) community has been a crime control approach, taking little account—except when forced to—either of due process/human rights considerations or of the unintended costs of policies and practices to which the controls give rise. 'Unintended' here includes impacts simply not considered, in the absence of a sophisticated consideration of the costs and benefits of controls apart from the politics of rule-making and rule-implementation.

One of these alleged impacts goes under the title of de-risking, an issue that is currently receiving attention from all intergovernmental organisations (IGOs; such as the International Monetary Fund—IMF—and World Bank) and many non-governmental organisations (NGOs) in the field, as well as the Group of seven (G7), Group of twenty (G20) and the Financial Stability Board (FSB) and several national governments in North and South. This level of attention accelerated during 2015 and 2016, representing the first significant challenge to the rhetorical hegemony of AML/CTF. Of course, experts in regulation studies are wearily familiar with what Grabosky nicely termed 'counter-productive regulation',[3] and so too are foreign policy advisers. But in an era of sound bites, wisdom is often a hard commodity to pursue. What lies behind this rising sense of crisis?

A Demos report notes that, following in the wake of accusations of charities being used to channel funds to Islamic State and other terrorist groups, users of the banking system deemed to be 'high risk' found it ever harder to receive, send and store their money.[4] In the worst cases, charities have had their bank accounts closed, losing financial access, without evidence of wrong-doing. At the heart of these closures is the desire of banks to 'de-risk': to rid themselves of business that might expose them to sanctions in relation to the financing of terrorism or Weapons of Mass Destruction (or other aspects of AML). These decisions take place behind closed doors, and the possible negative consequences of this de-risking have so far been left unexplored. The report argues that banks need to look beyond their innate profit motive and take into consideration the 'reputational return' from working with NGOs to find solutions to these challenges. The banks' answer to this might be:

> well it's all right for you to criticise, but you are not facing multi-billion dollar fines and the threat of *individual* as well as *corporate* prosecution under the fresh 2015 guidelines, nor being banned from occupying a CF11 approved compliance position anywhere in the UK and perhaps overseas financial services sector.

How has this situation come about, in the 'Brave New World' of Risk-Based AML-CTF that was supposedly ushered in by the Financial Action Task Force (FATF)?

What this controversy over categories of 'risky' business does is to expose the intellectual and institutional fault lines in both the policy and the practice of the soi-disant international community's approach to assets that (echoing the title of these 'conversations') arise from dirty behaviour and/or were intended to fund dirty behaviour. Banks speak the language of risk but effectively feel pressurised to practise zero tolerance to anything that might be identified as terrorist finance or sanctions violations,[5] on pain of (1) prosecution from any applicable jurisdiction, (2) regulatory penalties (such as from the US Federal or State regulators) and (3) civil action most likely in the US by direct or indirect 'victims of terrorism' (along the lines of cases such as *Arab Bank*[8]). But analytically, it is not that simple.

First, are the claims of harm valid, and who is being harmed? Second, is bank conduct solely the result of an increase in what the UK Financial Conduct Authority (FCA) would call 'credible deterrence'[7]—which many on the political Left and populist governments have been calling for more of ? And third, what realistically can international bodies do to reign in the decisions of supposedly independent regulators and prosecutors, and should they even try to do so as a matter of policy? This raises the spectre of global market failure in national and transnational policies. This chapter seeks to deal with the first two issues together, and then conclude with the final one.

Who Is Harmed by De-risking?

It may be useful upfront to note what has not properly been discussed upfront in many public policy debates: that the real question is not just who is harmed but who is harmed *unjustifiably*. If banks or money service bureaux who are supportive or even tolerant of crime and/or terrorist finance lose their banking facilities, many might regard that as justifiable—at least if they were satisfied that the evidence on which the decision was based was correct or in any event defensible[8] or procedurally fair.[9] Beyond this, de-risking can lead to a thinning or outright elimination of correspondent banking (banks processing the dollar or other transactions for other banks not licensed to trade in those currencies in exchange for fees)[10] for a country rightly or wrongly deemed high risk—often by a political consensus process rather than via some defensible analytics—and to a thinning of the market for money service bureaux and other financial intermediaries, raising the price of money transfers in the formal market. If the AML/CTF controls are successful and universal, this outcome can choke off remittances and local entrepreneurs; if de-risking is evaded, it can stimulate informal value transfers/*hawala* banking[11] which negates the objectives of the tighter control from the perspective of the richer countries of the Global North, though it still alleviates the regulatory and criminal justice risks from the perspective of the banks who exercise the controls in the formal economy. Unless the controls are tightly targeted against criminal and terrorist transfers, this stance may increase anti-Western sentiment in local populations and may be counter-productive in counter-terrorist terms, also by failing to meet the anti-poverty agenda which can be a competing policy goal.[12]

The evidence on the harms of de-risking is not as clear-cut as might be expected. Up to mid-2016, World Bank survey data on the cost of remittances do not show a significant rise: on the other hand, the counterfactual might be a substantial fall in the price of remittances and strong stimulation to local enterprises and financial services in de-risked jurisdictions, so this would mean that there had been *relative* harm. There is certainly significant political protest. Individual entrepreneurs have been harmed, at various levels, including politically exposed persons (PEPs) like Embassy staff from 'high-risk' jurisdictions post the Riggs Bank scandal[13]—which led to significantly greater caution among banks about retaining or opening accounts for Embassies or embassy staff. Other individuals affected include wealthy entrepreneur Wafic Said (personally and corporately de-risked by Barclays, and publicly complaining in the media about it[14]). Major enterprises affected include the money service bureau, Dahabshiil, (corporately de-risked by Barclays).[15] But to state that they have been harmed is not to show that they have been *unjustifiably* harmed: justifiable net harm reduction is the goal.

As an illustration of changing practices, in March 2014, JP Morgan Chase changed its policies so customers making cash deposits into a consumer account must provide identification or be an authorised signer for cash deposits, to combat misuse of accounts to include ML. In February 2015, JP Morgan announced that it had closed some 114,000 customer accounts through its AML screening and monitoring process. The bank also closed about 4500 business relationships based outside the US because of difficulties in satisfying regulatory requirements.[16]

The dependence of many small states on just one or no international banks allowing correspondent banking in the area has been the subject of substantial alarm,[17] responded to by warm words from the FATF as well as national regulators and IGOs, that currently leave tensions unresolved. The issue of how humanitarian aid from the Global North or IGOs is to be legally distributed in countries under sanctions is merely one significant difficulty. Hence, there is a challenge to the legitimacy of the AML/CTF process from many jurisdictions, and pressure on the Commonwealth Secretariat, IMF, UN and World Bank to resolve it. This problem is described at the end of the chapter.

Bank Policies and Practices

A 2016 study on de-risking, commissioned by the FCA and co-authored by the author of this chapter,[18] found that banks are dealing with fallout from the financial crisis by realigning their businesses, disposing of 'non-core' operations in response to higher prudential capital requirements, liquidity thresholds and compliance costs. Institutions examined are working towards a risk-based approach (RBA) for AML/CTF that they believe mitigates their financial crime exposure. On occasion, this means they eject customers, regardless of the costs of compliance, but sometimes their view of client risk will be coloured by regulators' and prosecutors' actions and their expectations about the future reactions of such government officials.

This phenomenon raises some complex issues of principle and practicality. Currently, in most jurisdictions, banks have the right to service or refuse service to whomever they like: though the granting of account facilities may be accompanied by the making of Suspicious Activity Reports, banks are free to set their own risk appetites.[19] However, whereas sophisticated modelling exists for credit risk and fraud, there is, as yet, no generally agreed quantitative assessment methodology for assessing financial crime risk (or indeed a clear agreement on what 'financial crime' denotes: many banks do not include customer or third-party fraud within their financial crime departments). Risk appetites indicate broad definitions, and reputational risk is open to wide interpretation. Customer risk assessment models, with set categories—at the simplest, 'high, medium, low'—can also foster identification of customers by common factors, like sector, business type and country affiliations, which can amount to a wholesale process. Consistency itself is likely to produce de-risking, even if it is not intended to: it is an unintended outcome of common judgements using shared criteria. Once categorised, it can be difficult, even impossible, for a customer to show that they should be seen as lower risk, as it is difficult to establish clear criteria for how this might be done. Banks are working on an RBA around enhanced due diligence requirements for PEPs, and though these may otherwise be desirable clients, it should be possible in principle to sort the 'good' from the 'bad' in other sectors of the client base.

Larger banks' attitudes to risk—some supply lists of customer types they do not want to handle—can and often do cascade through to smaller institutions within the same jurisdiction and elsewhere, which feel unable to push back without imperilling the correspondent relationship and risking losing it. Since 2014, there is evidence from account turnover of non-banks and interbank relationships that high ML/TF risk customers have been disproportionately impacted through a mixture of focus on strategic reviews, thinly stretched compliance capacity and reduced risk appetite. The FCA report[20] cites two major UK banks which, together, are closing around 1000 personal and 600 business/corporate accounts each month in line with their risk appetite.

Although de-risking is not applied universally, in sectors where it occurs, it tends to be frequent. Correspondent banking and money service business (MSB) accounts have been hardest hit, with some banks with foreign parents shedding large numbers of clients, making it difficult for some foreign nationals and businesses to utilise the UK financial system.[21]

Small and medium enterprises (SMEs) are more likely to be de-risked than larger firms in a sector, which raises competition and concentration issues, with ramifications for financial exclusion. Thus, pawnbrokers and MSBs provide up to £5bn in finance in the UK, but they are facing difficulties obtaining or maintaining banking relationships. The National Pawnbrokers Association surveyed members in September 2015 and found that over 40% had experienced account closure.[22]

Larger charities are not at serious risk of losing their accounts (due to their efforts at compliance), but the Charities Aid Foundation (CAF) and Charities Finance Group (CFG) both worry that an 'avalanche' of de-risking may hit smaller operations.[23]

The defence sector, especially at SME level, has often found it hard to deal with banks (e.g., to secure letters of credit), to the extent of some firms relocating abroad. However, through dialogue between the industry and the British Bankers' Association (BBA), some progress has been made, though many banks' risk appetite for the defence sector is low because of both transnational bribery risks (which in principle can transfer from vendors and middlemen to their bankers under the Bribery Act 2010) and general reputational risk issues.

The Fintech sector has not found it easy to cope. Electronic money institutions and payment institutions (EMI/PIs) can be judged high risk and refused accounts, often by letter with no explanation. The UK National Risk Assessment 2016[24] rated e-money as 'medium' risk and digital currencies 'low' risk for ML: but this offers no legal comfort. The EU's Revised Directive on Payment Services 2015, which must be implemented by 12 January 2018, guarantees firms' access to credit institutions' payment account services on an objective, non-discriminatory and proportionate basis. But as we shall see, proportionality can be an elusive concept. Proportionate to what defined category?

Compliance costs are expensive and have been ratcheted up by increased risks for individuals. The BBA estimates that its members spend at least £5bn collectively each year on financial crime compliance.[25] One large UK bank, when staff turnover rose followed by business expansion, had to cut clients to fit its stretched compliance resource. The 2016 FCA report concluded that to a 'victim' of this process, who may have been with a bank for many years, such a decision would seem inherently unreasonable and unfair.[26]

Changes to Reduce the Counter-Productive Effects

The financial and commercial sectors' responses to de-risking have led to some evolution of the authorities' position. This includes the revised position of the US Federal regulator, the Office of Comptroller of Currency

(OCC): in October 2016, the OCC issued Risk Management Guidance on Periodic Re-evaluation of Foreign Correspondent Banking[27] enunciating the key principle that banks should consider not only the level of AML/CTF risks posed, but their own ability to manage them. Banks need to review if continuing these relationships might breach AML/CTF rules, such as those contained in the (US) Bank Secrecy Act (BSA) 1970. The OCC Guidance stressed that such risk management 'should be an ongoing process, not a one-time exercise, and each bank's risk assessment should be periodically updated to identify changes in the bank's risk profile'. Banks should establish systems so that any concerns revealed during such assessments can be referred up to sufficiently senior decision-makers. Similarly, banks need to create permanent assessment structures charged with regularly assessing correspondent banking relationships, such as an oversight committee. The Guidance recommended that banks considering ending a correspondent relationship should consult the correspondent about their concerns and allow it to offer specific mitigating information—unless the risk is so clear that even this offer might breach US AML laws. If the American bank decided to go ahead with the closure, it 'should provide sufficient time for the foreign financial institution to establish an alternative banking relationship with other US banks', and it should log 'a clear audit trail of the reasons and method used for account closure'. Senior management needs to be kept in the loop so that they can consider the extent to which account closures restrict access to financial services 'for an entire group of customers or potential customers, or an entire geographic location'. The likely effect of this is to increase the costs of closure and put pressure on banks not to close down correspondent accounts or sectors without significantly helping the banks with the judgement about riskiness, including mitigating the risk that independent state regulators or prosecutors will take action should they be deemed to fail or indeed launder money, while waiting for a correspondent to find another bank to take the account!

British and other banks appear to be reluctant to engage in differential pricing based on customers' individual ML/TF risk ratings. Though it might be embarrassing to do so, not to do so might probably be viewed as a form of market failure which, if corrected, might result in less de-risking. Specific guidance from regulators on how to manage high-risk relationships that would otherwise be exited might persuade banks to think again but comments on how significant fines, principally by US authorities, have targeted their corporate failures of conduct, rather than their choice of clients, tend to fall on deaf ears.

Punishing the Banks and Individuals

The 'failure' to de-risk is of course only one among many sources of potential legal sanctions for financial institutions. Separating out the sanctioning of individuals and banks for different 'predicate offences'—such as frauds by clients and by staff, or ML and sanctions violations—is not easy, whether nationally or internationally. Some commercial studies fail to make this distinction,[28] which may be acceptable if one is discussing trends in corporate and individual punishment for market misconduct but is unhelpful if the focus is on ML. What is plain is that fluctuations in regulatory sanctions are considerable, and the setting of temporal cut-off points makes a huge difference to the trends in penalty levels. Thus, the spate of high-profile foreign exchange or other rate manipulation cases (like London Interbank Offered Rate—LIBOR) tend to be cyclical: they generate time-lagged spikes on sanctioning in either national or—more commonly these days—multi-national regulatory action, usually with the US taking the lead, as they share out the settlements/fines over a range of countries in a way that is seldom appropriate to the wrongdoing. This is a radically different way of thinking about punishment than the normal approach in penological or even in regulatory studies, which look at sanctions within nation states, and sometimes compare national data separately for comparative purposes.[29] Of particular relevance for de-risking is the fact that banks may be subject to criminal prosecution federally or at state/local level (such as in New York), to federal or state regulatory penalties, and also to civil action, for example, for contributing to terrorist violence abroad.[30] In the absence of clear and consistent policies in all of these spheres, risk aversion is understandable.

Almost all criminal prosecutions for ML involve self-laundering by predicate offenders or by their confederates and families, or less often professional intermediaries such as bankers and lawyers who are in difficulties and/or become enmeshed in crime networks.[31] Very seldom is there any criminal action against large intermediary firms and banks—and, when there is, the fear of collateral damage hitherto has led to Deferred Prosecution Agreements (DPAs) or similar outcomes.[32] Even regulatory action is rare for failure to report or to take appropriate action against laundering. The few high-profile corporate ML cases such as that against HSBC[33] are (like transnational bribery ones) sometimes taken as emblematic of the amorality or immorality of business conduct: but as in HSBC and BNP Paribas, inter alia, the fear of harming customers and investors, and generating systemic risk normally deters condign punishment and leads to large monetary penalties which may not be seen as proportionate to the gravity of the offences or to the means of the corporate offenders. Indeed, it is very difficult to envisage how we might scale these appropriately or consistently. As regards conventional approaches to dangerousness, corporate recidivism in this arena is difficult to measure and to scale: if a firm that employs hundreds of thousands of people all around the globe in a huge variety of sectors, how do we rank a few hundred or even thousand offences in relation to an individual committing more than one offence? This complicated question is one that has not been satisfactorily addressed and seldom really asked in the literature on sentencing corporate offenders. It is certainly not addressed in the UK sentencing guidelines on ML, discussed below.

Sentencing Council Guidelines for England and Wales

The Sentencing Council Guidelines—published in 2014—set out the processes that criminal courts should follow in corporate cases of fraud, bribery and ML.[34] Of these, ML may have been viewed as the least important because there have been no prosecutions, and therefore no cases that have generated concern. These guidelines involve separating out culpability and harm—as with sentencing generally. Understandably, given how recent these developments in English criminal law have been, it is not clear how they apply in DPAs, especially not multi-state infractions involving both the US and the UK, and sometimes other jurisdictions too, as in the Rolls-Royce transnational bribery DPA 2017.[35] These constructs are very difficult to operationalise in the context of major financial institutions, but there have been no such prosecutions in the UK yet and they have not been litigated in practice.

Sentencers should weigh up all the factors of the case to determine culpability and balance these characteristics to reach a fair assessment of the offender's culpability. However, fairness is left implicitly as an objective professional judgement rather than one that takes into account the diverse professional and popular audiences that may need to be 'satisfied' if a sentence is to be seen as legitimate.[36]

For the guidelines, though attributing culpability to legal persons is anathema in some jurisdictions, culpability is demonstrated by the offending corporation's (perceived) role and motivation—or in jurisprudential practice that of its directing minds—by one or more of the following non-exhaustive characteristics. (The sections relevant to ML have been highlighted in bold.)

A—High culpability
Corporation plays a leading role in organised, planned unlawful activity (whether acting alone or with others)
Wilful obstruction of detection (e.g., destruction of evidence, misleading investigators, suborning employees)
Involving others through pressure or coercion (e.g., employees or suppliers)
Targeting of vulnerable victims or a large number of victims
Corruption of local or national government officials or ministers
Corruption of officials performing a law enforcement role
Abuse of dominant market position or position of trust or responsibility
Offending committed over a sustained period of time
Culture of wilful disregard of commission of offences by employees or agents with no effort to put effective systems in place (section 7 Bribery Act only)

B—Medium culpability
Corporation plays a significant role in unlawful activity organised by others.
Activity not unlawful from the outset.
Corporation reckless in making false statement (section 72 VAT Act 1994)
All other cases where characteristics for categories A or C are not present.

C—Lesser culpability
Corporation plays a minor, peripheral role in unlawful activity organised by others.
Some effort made to put bribery prevention measures in place but insufficient to amount to a defence (section 7 Bribery Act only)
Involvement through coercion, intimidation or exploitation

High culpability is to be evidenced principally through Involving others through pressure or coercion (e.g., employees or suppliers); targeting of vulnerable victims or a large number of victims; abuse of dominant market position, or position of trust or responsibility; and culture of wilful disregard of commission of offences by employees or agents with no effort to put effective systems in place (section 7 Bribery Act only). However, in the absence of a credible corporate criminal liability regime, this remains theoretical to date for ML, though in principle there are ML components of transnational bribery cases such as *Rolls Royce*.[37]

The other key dimension in the guidelines is harm, and they state that 'For offences of money laundering the appropriate figure will normally be the amount laundered or, alternatively, the likely cost avoided by failing to put in place an effective anti-money laundering programme if this is higher'. This might well be a matter for considerable dispute, for example, where there is a mixing of licit and illicit business and where the transactions occur over some time.

Regulatory Penalties in the UK

If there is to be a focus on factors that may influence corporate efforts to control the active commission and facilitation of crime, the policy needs to move away from the exclusive focus on the criminal law and consider the messages sent out also by regulators. The principles behind the setting of penalties are elaborated by the FCA, and broadly follow the kinds of factors one might expect in criminal penalties, except for the focus on the 'conduct of the person after the breach', which is more akin to a restorative justice or a lifetime offender management approach.[38] In the particular case of ML breaches, '[t]he FCA, when considering whether to take action for a financial penalty or censure in respect of a breach of those rules, will have regard to whether a firm has followed relevant provisions in the Guidance for the UK financial sector issued by the Joint Money Laundering Steering Group'.[39]

There is no doubt that regulators have become more active over time in the financial crime space, though the FCA appears to have eased off since the departure in 2015 of Martin Wheatley, allegedly for being too active for the then Chancellor of the Exchequer's taste.[40] We need again to distinguish between the identification and regulation of ML 'failures', and that of other forms of misconduct, especially conspiracies to fix market prices, which are included in the data in the Center for Global Development (CGD) report (Table 12.1).[41]

In the final event in the Table above, the FCA stated that Smith's fine was raised by 10%, because he was aware of the feedback given by the Financial Services Authority (FSA) following its visit to Sonali Bank in 2010, and that the FSA and FCA had both issued guidance (including via other enforcement cases) about AML systems and controls. He was also prohibited from performing the CF10 (compliance oversight) and CF11 (ML reporting) controlled functions on the basis that he had 'demonstrated a serious lack of competence and capability'.[42] The FCA expressly stated that this prohibition extended to his carrying out the equivalent functions under the senior managers' regime (SMR). Sonali Bank also was subject to further controls on the sort of business it could do.[43]

By comparison, the US General Accounting Office found that from January 2009 to December 2015, federal agencies assessed some $5.2 billion for BSA/AML violations and about $6.8 billion for violations of US sanctions programme requirements (plus $27 million for Foreign Corrupt Practices Act (FCPA) violations, which technically are not AML-related cases). Of the $12 billion, federal agencies have collected all but about $100 million from these assessments.[44] This reflects both the agreed nature of such trade-offs and

Table 12.1 Corporate and Individual MLRO Regulatory Fines in the UK, 2002–2016

Year	Organisation	Fine
2002	Royal Bank of Scotland Plc	£750,000
2003	Abbey National Plc	£2,320,000
2003	Northern Bank	£1,250,000
2004	Bank of Ireland	£375,000
2004	Bank of Scotland	£1,250,000
2004	Carr Sheppards Crosthwaite	£500,000
2005	Investment Services UK Limited	£175,000
2005	Investment Services UK Limited—Managing Director—Ram Melwani	£30,000
2008	Sindicatum Holdings Limited (SHL)	£49,000
2008	Sindicatum Holdings Limited (SHL) MLRO Michael Wheelhouse	£17,500
2010	Alpari (UK) Limited	£140,000
2010	Alpari (UK) Limited Sudipto Chattopadhyay (MLRO)	£14,000
2012	Habib Bank AG Zurich (Habib)	£525,000
2012	Habib Bank AG Zurich (Habib) former MLRO Syed Itrat Hussain	£17,500
2012	Coutts	£8,750,000
2013	EFG Private Bank Ltd	£4,200,000
2013	Guaranty Trust Bank (UK) Limited	£525,000
2014	Standard Bank PLC	£7,640,400
2015	Barclays	£72,069,400
2016	Sonali Bank	£3,250,600 (after a 30% early settlement discount)
2016	Sonali Bank MLRO, Steven Smith	£17,900 (after a 30% early settlement discount)

the fact that ongoing businesses have the resources to pay: this differs from the patterns of asset recovery from 'normal' criminal defendants, even in in rem jurisdictions such as the US

In keeping with the American trend of targeting individuals as well as corporations, the number of enforcement cases concluded against compliance professionals has been rising (from a low base rate). Since 2008, the FSA and FCA have concluded 14 enforcement cases against compliance officers, four of whom were Money Laundering Reporting Officers (MLRO). Six of these have been concluded from 2015 to end of 2016, reflecting investigations some time in process. The message is intended to be clear. Compliance professionals or 'gatekeepers' are expected to show both skill and integrity when faced with firms who do not take AML compliance seriously enough (though it is not clear how much is 'enough'). If the firm resists, the MLRO can blow the whistle to the FCA or the Prudential Regulatory Authority, or alternatively resign or take some intermediary measure 'on the record' to protect themselves. Whether this will work and whether they will find another job remains uncertain, since formal rules about whistle-blower protection do not eliminate socio-economic stigmatization or ensure re-employment elsewhere. The Bank of England and Financial Services Act 2016 may make these tensions on the MLROs greater.

Conclusions

This review has shown the ways in which AML efforts have had unintended but largely uncosted consequences for licit firms and individuals in the Global North and South. Of course, the certainty and clarity with which we can categorise people and businesses as *either* licit *or* illicit is open to question, and the underpinnings of those judgements are not usually justiciable or open. Hard decisions have to be made, and there is no point in blaming banks for making defensive decisions to get rid of existing clients or not to take on others if the probability is above zero of suffering serious consequences for making a false-negative judgement about the riskiness of a client (including a correspondent bank). This is true whether those *potential* consequences are severe for the institution or for the MLRO personally. The 'solution' to this wiki problem remains unresolved, both at a nation state and international level. It is difficult to envisage what process might be developed to protect international bankers against criminal, regulatory and civil action in the US (or to a lesser extent elsewhere) for exercising the judgement that a correspondent bank, financial intermediary or client posed an 'acceptable' (or for that matter, an 'unacceptable') risk of committing a predicate crime. This has consequences for the viability in some circumstances of the RBA to ML, which currently lacks an articulation in practice which commands universal acceptance in the courts or in the court of 'public opinion'. Concepts that may be attractive among professionals in a regulatory environment may not translate readily into an ambience of penal populism, leading to divergence in reactions in different venues. The complexities of harm and risk in contemporary financial services risk management may be less sympathetically appreciated by the media, politicians, prosecutors and even regulators under pressure to react to events.

In practice, it seems likely that regulatory processes and penalties will continue to be more salient than criminal sentencing to financial services firms, especially in the UK where corporate criminal liability remains difficult to prosecute.[45] A Report for The Clearing House calls (principally in a US context) for better acknowledgement by bank examiners of broader national and international policy interests when they supervise AML/CTF, and better integration of regulatory and law enforcement concerns, including the development of 'no-action' letters reassuring institutions.[46] Though this would have no international remit, it is the sort of action that may be needed, preferably in concert, to stem the tide of de-risking. In turn, this comprises part of a general conversation about the benefits and costs of AML measures that needs to take place, buttressed by better conceptual and empirical grounding than is currently available.[47]

Notes

1. Herbert L Packer, 'Two Models of the Criminal Process' (1964) 113(1) University of Pennsylvania Law Review 1.
2. See, for instance, Kent Roach, 'Four Models of the Criminal Process' (1999) 89(2) The Journal of Criminal Law and Criminology 671.
3. Peter Grabosky, 'Counterproductive Regulation' (1995) 23(4) International Journal of the Sociology of Law 347. See also Robert Baldwin, Martin Cave and Martin Lodge, *Understanding Regulation: Theory, Strategy, and Practice* (OUP 2012); Julia Black, 'Paradoxes and Failures: 'New Governance' Techniques and the Financial Crisis' (2012) 75(6) Modern Law Review 1037.
4. Tom Keatinge, *Uncharitable Behavior: Counter-Terrorist Regulation Restricts Charity Banking Worldwide* (DEMOS 2014). For further consideration, see Chap. 11 (Ramachandran, Collin, and Juden), Chap. 44 (Walker) and Chap. 45 (Hamin) in this collection.
5. The cynical might add 'unless the financing comes from our major allies'.
6. *In Re: Arab Bank* 808 F 3d 144 (2016). See further Jimmy Gurule, 'Plaintiffs Carry Heavy Burden in Terror Suits Against Banks' (2015) 253(41) New York Law Journal 1; Jimmy Gurule, 'Holding Banks Liable Under the Anti-Terrorism Act for Providing Financial Services to Terrorists: An Ineffective Legal Remedy in Need of Reform' (2014) 41(2) Journal of Legislation 184; Peter Budoff, 'How Far Is Too Far?: The Proper Framework for Civil Remedies Against Facilitators of Terrorism' (2015) 80(3) Brooklyn Law Review 1057.
7. Tracey McDermott, 'Enforcement and Credible Deterrence in the FCA' Presented at the Compliance and Risk Summit' (London, 18 June 2013) <www.fca.org.uk/publication/news/enforcement-credible-deterrence-speech.pdf> accessed 30 January 2017.
8. Heretical though this may be to some lawyers, this is a highly contested issue. Scholars have shown that many people filter evidence through a cognitive lens based on heuristics or 'story models': so what is convincing to us may not be convincing to, for example, Somali traders and general population. See Amos Tversky and Daniel Kahneman, 'Judgment Under Uncertainty: Heuristics

and Biases' (1974) 185(4157) Science 1124; Kara MacKillop and Neil Vidmar, 'Decision-Making in the Dark: How Pre-Trial Errors Change the Narrative in Criminal Jury Trials' (2015) 90(3) Chicago-Kent Law Review 957.

9. See Justice Tankebe and Alison Liebling (eds), *Legitimacy and Criminal Justice: An International Exploration* (OUP 2013).

10. See The World Bank, 'Remittance Prices Worldwide' <https://remittance-prices.worldbank.org/en/countrycorr idors> accessed 29 January 2017.

11. For consideration of informal value transfer systems, see Chap. 42 (Cooper) in this collection.

12. Though we have very little idea of what an Islamic State economic welfare development programme would look like, left to itself: nor does it look likely that we will in the foreseeable future. In areas of the world where there is so much ongoing political intervention, agreed counterfactuals are very hard to come by.

13. See Nora Boustany and Terence O'Hara, 'After Riggs, Embassy Accounts Can't Find a Home' *Washington Post* (Washington, 10 June 2014) <www.washingtonpost.com/wp-dyn/articles/A29674-2004Jun9.html> accessed 10 March 2017; World-Check, 'Reputation Damage: The Price Riggs Paid' (2006) <www.world-check.com/media/d/content_whitepaper_reference/whitepaper-3.pdf> accessed 27 December 2016.

14. See Martin Arnold and Caroline Binham, 'Wafic Said Considers Legal Action Against Barclays After It Cut Ties' *Financial Times* (London, 18 March 2016) <www.ft.com/content/4706d382-ecf6-11e5-bb79-2303682345c8> accessed 10 March 2017.

15. *Dahabshiil v Barclays* [2013] EWHC 3379 (Ch).

16. JP Morgan, 'Chase Annual Report 2014' <www.wsj.com/articles/account-closed-how-bank-de-risking-hurts-legitimate-customers-1439419093> accessed 29 January 2017.

17. For further discussion, see Chap. 11 (Ramachandran, Collin, and Juden) in this collection. For some discussion of this in a broader compliance context, see The Clearing House, 'A New Paradigm: Redesigning the US anti-money laundering/combatting the financing of terrorism (AML/CFT) Framework to Protect National Security and Aid Law Enforcement' (2017) <www.theclearinghouse.org/~/media/TCH/Documents/TCH%20WEEKLY/2017/20170216_TCH_Report_AML_CFT_Framework_Redesign.pdf> accessed 29 January 2017.

18. David Artingstall and others, *Drivers & Impacts of Derisking* (2016) <www.fca.org.uk/publication/research/drivers-impacts-of-derisking.pdf> accessed 10 March 2017.

19. After 18 September 2016, the Payment Accounts Regulations 2015 SI 2038 have obliged some banks to offer basic accounts to EU customers.

20. Artingstall and others (n 18).

21. ibid.

22. ibid.

23. ibid.

24. HM Treasury and Home Office, *UK National Risk Assessment of Money Laundering and Terrorist Financing* (2015).

25. See Artingstall and others (n 18).

26. ibid.

27. OCC, 'Risk Management Guidance on Periodic Risk Re-evaluation of Foreign Correspondent Banking' (2016) <www.occ.gov/news-issuances/bulletins/2016/bulletin-2016-32.html> accessed 29 January 2017.

28. Stacey English and Susannah Hammond, *Cost of Compliance* (Thomson Reuters 2016); Robert Patton and others, 'Trends in Regulatory Enforcement in UK Financial Markets 2015/16 Year-End Report' (2016) <www.nera.com/content/dam/nera/publications/2016/PUB_UK_Regulatory_Trends_0716%20YE%20FCA.pdf> accessed 10 March 2017.

29. This is an issue not restricted to sentencing and regulatory sanctions: the long-running KPMG UK Fraud Barometer produces periodic data on the costs of frauds appearing in court, without the media picking up that these are based on cases that have highly variable lags between the dates of fraud commission and court cases even for those few cases that are prosecuted, and thus it is a fraud prosecution barometer rather than an actual fraud barometer.

30. For further discussion, see Chap. 41 (Gurulé and Danek) in this collection.

31. See David Middleton and Michael Levi, 'Let Sleeping Lawyers Lie: Organized Crime, Lawyers and the Regulation of Legal Services' (2015) 55(4) British Journal of Criminology 647. See also Chap. 6 (Benson) in this collection.

32. See Eric Jensen and others, *National Security Law: Principles and Policy* (Walters Kluwer 2015) 368 for a list of sanctioned foreign banks. For practice in England and Wales, see SFO, 'Deferred Prosecution Agreements' <www.sfo.gov.uk/publications/guidance-policy-and-protocols/deferred-prosecution-agreements/> accessed 29 January 2017.

33. For the Deferred Prosecution Agreements (DPA) against HSBC <www.sec.gov/Archives/edgar/data/83246/000119312512499980/d453978dex101.htm> accessed 31 January 2017; US Department of Justice Press Release, 'HSBC Holdings Plc. and HSBC Bank SA N.A. Admit to Anti-Money Laundering and Sanctions Violations, Forfeit $1.256 Billion in Deferred Prosecution Agreement' (11 December 2012) <www.justice.gov/opa/pr/hsbc-holdings-plc-and-hsbc-bank-usa-na-admit-anti-money-laundering-and-sanctions-violations> accessed 31 January 2017.

34. Sentencing Council, *Fraud, Bribery and Money Laundering Offences: Definitive Guideline* (2014).

35. See *Serious Fraud Office v Rolls Royce* [2017] (unreported).

36. Michael Levi, 'Sentencing Respectable Offenders' in Shanna van Slyke, Michael Benson, and Francis Cullen (eds), *Oxford Handbook of White-Collar*

Crime (OUP 2016); Michael Levi, 'Legitimacy, Crimes, and Compliance in "the City": De Maximis non Curat Lex?' in Justice Tankebe and Alison Liebling (eds), *Legitimacy and Criminal Justice: An International Exploration* (OUP 2013).

37. See *Rolls Royce* (n 35).

38. Financial Conduct Authority (FCA), *The Decision Procedure and Penalties Manual* (2017) <www.handbook.fca.org.uk/handbook/DEPP/6.p df> accessed 27 December 2016, S 6(2)(1)(2).

39. ibid. S 6(2)(3).

40. See Larry Elliott, 'FCA Chief's Departure Means It's Back to Business as Usual for the Banks' *The Guardian* (London, 17 July 2015) <www.theguardian.com/business/2015/jul/17/fca-martin-wheatley-quits-business-usual-uk-banks> accessed 10 March 2017.

41. For further discussion, see Chap. 11 (Ramachandran, Collin, and Juden) in this collection.

42. FCA, 'Final Notice to Steven George Smith' (2016) <www.fca.org.uk/publication/final-notices/steven-smith-2016.pdf> accessed 10 March 2017.

43. FCA, 'Final Notice to Sonali Bank (UK) Ltd' (2016) <www.fca.org.uk/publication/final-notices/sonali-bank-uk-limited-2016.pdf> accessed 31 January 2017.

44. General Accounting Office (GAO), 'Financial Institutions: Fines, Penalties, and Forfeitures for Violations of Financial Crimes and Sanctions Requirements' (2016) <www.gao.gov/assets/680/675987.pdf> accessed 21 February 2017.

45. See Ministry of Justice, 'Corporate Liability for Economic Crime: Call for Evidence' <https://consult.justice.gov.uk/digital-communications/corporate-liability-for-economic-crime/> accessed 8 March 2017, for some discussion of reform proposals in the UK, whose political outcome is uncertain.

46. See The Clearing House (n 17).

47. Terrence Halliday, Michael Levi, and Peter Reuter, *Global Surveillance of Dirty Money: Assessing Assessments of Regimes To Control Money-Laundering and Combat the Financing of Terrorism* (American Bar Foundation 2014); Michael Levi, Peter Reuter, and Terrence Halliday, 'Can the AML/CTF System Be Evaluated Without Better Data?' Crime, Law and Social Change (forthcoming).

Michael Levi has been Professor of Criminology at Cardiff University since 1991. He has been conducting international research on the control of white-collar and organised crime, corruption and money laundering/financing of terrorism since 1972. He is an Associate Fellow of Royal United Services Institute (RUSI) and a Senior Fellow at RAND Europe. He advises Europol on the Serious and Organised Crime Threat Assessment and on the internet-enabled Organised Crime Threat Assessment, and other public positions include membership of the European

Unions Group of Experts on Corruption. In 2013, he was given the Distinguished Scholar Award by the International Association for the Study of Organised Crime, and in 2014 he was awarded the Sellin-Glueck prize for international and comparative criminology by the American Society of Criminology.

13

A Critical Analysis of the Effectiveness of Anti-Money Laundering Measures with Reference to Australia

David Chaikin

In this chapter, the effectiveness of anti-money laundering (AML) measures is analysed by first considering the objectives and development of AML at an international level. The expansion of the goals of AML to include combating any threat to international financial stability has meant that it is very difficult to measure whether the goals are achieved. The global AML standards, which have been adopted by more than 190 countries,[1] provide a framework for judging national AML laws and policy. Since 2013, international peer review assessments of countries' AML systems rate effectiveness equally as important as technical compliance. The focus is on a detailed examination of Australia's AML record because Australia is one of the first countries to be assessed under the new criterion of effectiveness.

There is a rich academic literature on the effectiveness of AML laws that consider a wide range of issues, including the size of the money-laundering problem, and the costs and benefits of AML.[2] This chapter does not intend to critique such literature, but it rather focuses on a more narrow issue, namely how the international AML policy-making community judges effectiveness.

D. Chaikin
School of Business, The University of Sydney,
Darlington, NSW, Australia

© The Author(s) 2018
C. King et al. (eds.), *The Palgrave Handbook of Criminal and Terrorism Financing Law*,
https://doi.org/10.1007/978-3-319-64498-1_13

Objectives and Development of AML Systems

A critique of AML systems requires an understanding of the objectives of AML at an international level and how these objectives are implemented at the national level. The Financial Action Task Force (FATF), which is the principal international policy-making authority on money laundering (ML), was originally conceived in 1990 as an intergovernmental initiative to combat the scourge of global drug trafficking.[3] The FATF had limited objectives of encouraging states to implement the United Nations Convention against Illicit Traffic in Narcotic Drugs and Psychotropic Substances 1988 (Vienna Convention), improving national legal and financial systems to combat drug ML, and strengthening international co-operation to prevent and interdict currency/cash laundering.[4] As national and international law enforcement viewed drug ML as the major challenge in the 1980s, there was a singular focus on drug ML. Given this one focus of AML, it was easier for governments and scholars to assess the effectiveness or otherwise of any specific AML strategy. Nevertheless, it is, and continues to be, extremely difficult to judge whether the AML system has been effective even in meeting this single goal. As will be seen below, the expansion of the goals of the AML system has meant that the problem of assessment of the effectiveness of the system is yet more difficult.

The identification of the goals of AML systems is problematic. The reason for this challenge is that the objectives of the FATF have evolved over time, so that in 2012 the FATF stated that:

> The objectives of the FATF are to set standards and to promote effective implementation of legal, regulatory and operational measures for combating money laundering, terrorist financing and other related threats to the integrity of the international financial system.[5]

The underlying aim of the FATF has expanded beyond combating the laundering of drug cash to encompass criminal behaviour that 'threat(ens)… the integrity of the international financial system'.[6] The language used by the FATF reflects a significant expansion of the FATF mandate, in that effective AML systems are ultimately judged by how they positively contribute to the functioning of the international financial system. The focus of the FATF Recommendations is reflected in the new name of the FATF standards—International Standards on Combating ML, and the Financing of Terrorism and Nuclear Proliferation.

The expansion of the global AML system may be linked to three developments. First, after the 9/11 terrorist attacks in the USA, the FATF Recommendations were expanded to include special recommendations that criminalised terrorist financing (TF) and created specific regulations governing non-profit organisations that could be used for terrorist purposes.[7] These counter-terrorist financing (CTF) measures were seen as interlinked with AML, and thereby an essential component of the FATF mandate. But there was an essential flaw in the policy expansion since TF is usually 'ML in reverse', in that it frequently involves small amounts of legal money being used for illicit purposes, that is, terrorism.[8] The difficulty is that CTF regulation was grafted on to AML regulation in circumstances where the nature of the problem was different, in that small amounts of legitimately sourced money could be used to commit terrorist attacks.

Second, the destabilising 'bad behaviour' of states, particularly the Democratic People's Republic of Korea (DPKR) and Iran, has resulted in an additional refinement of the FATF Recommendations to include the financing of proliferation of weapons of mass destruction.[9] This development has resulted in the FATF becoming embroiled in the issue of financial sanctions. The FATF has requested that its members and other jurisdictions which are members of FATF-style regional bodies apply counter-measures to the DPRK and Iran because 'they have not shown sufficient commitment to address their serious AML/CTF deficiencies'.[10]

Third, the Global Financial Crisis (GFC) of 2008/2009 has led international bodies, such as the International Monetary Fund (IMF), to adopt a policy stance that links issues of financial stability to international financial crime. The IMF considers that ML, TF and predicate crimes may undermine national banking and financial systems, complicate national economic policy-making and have 'adverse spillover effects on the stability of other countries'.[11] Conversely, both the IMF and the FATF consider that financial stability may be promoted through effective AML/CTF systems.[12] This has led the IMF to examine AML/CTF issues as part of its modular stability assessments, albeit on a case-by-case basis.[13] Although financial crimes have the potential to undermine financial and political stability, the laundering of illicit monies may provide liquidity to financial systems under stress. For example, it was asserted that during the GFC, more than US$352 billion of organised crime profits were laundered in the financial system as illicit profits were 'the only (available) liquid investment capital'.[14] Even if illicit monies provide short-term liquidity to banks, there is no suggestion or explanation as to how such monies could provide financial stability. The main point here is that regulators should be aware that banks under financial stress are more vulnerable to organised crime and ML, and consequently should heighten surveillance of banks which are under stress.

The FATF Recommendations have moved beyond drug ML to other serious criminal offences and even beyond terrorism as already mentioned. During the 1990s, the global ML regime broadened its focus to include illicit capital flight and the corruption of kleptocrats.[15] The Recommendations now require countries to apply the ML offence to 'all serious offences' including predicate offences within designated categories, such as trafficking in human beings, environmental crimes, tax crimes, bribery and corruption, insider trading and market manipulation.[16] Given the interconnected relationship between ML and its underlying predicate offences, it is not surprising that regulators view effective AML systems as not only combating ML per se but also underlying predicate crimes. For instance, in the UK, the principal regulator of the financial services industry has the specific regulatory objective of reducing financial crime and views AML as an important vehicle to increase the costs of ML to criminals, and thereby reduce the level of financial crime.[17] The implication of this regulatory perspective is that assessing the impact of AML requires an examination of its effectiveness in combating ML behaviour and financial crimes generally.

But these are not the only goals of AML systems. In Australia, one of the stated objectives of the Anti-Money Laundering and Counter-Terrorism Financing Act 2006 (Cth) (the 'AML/CTF Act') is the fulfilment of Australia's international obligations to combat ML and TF.[18] The debate concerning the appropriate objectives of AML laws in Australia has taken a new direction with the 2016 Australian Government statutory review of the AML/CTF Act (the 'Statutory Review'). The Statutory Review recommended an expansion of the objectives of the AML/CTF Act to reflect the following ideas:

- implementing measures to detect, deter and disrupt money laundering, the financing of terrorism, the proliferation of weapons of mass destruction and its financing and other serious crimes
- responding to the threat posed by money laundering, the financing of terrorism, the proliferation of weapons of mass destruction and its financing and other serious crimes by providing regulatory, national security and law enforcement officials with the information they need to detect, deter and disrupt these crimes
- supervision and monitoring of compliance by reporting entities with Australian sanction laws…and
- promoting public confidence in the Australian financial system.[19]

The proposed objectives of the AML/CTF Act set out what may be viewed as the 'primary goals' of AML control systems,[20] such as detecting and disrupting serious predicate crimes, ML and TF, as well as protecting the integrity and reputation of the financial system. The proposed objectives of the AML/CTF Act codify the diverse aims of and reflect the complex and sometimes competing perspectives as to the appropriate goals of AML laws. At the same time, there is some confusion in that objectives are mixed with means, such as providing timely financial intelligence to governmental authorities, and installing adequate supervision of the private sector. Unfortunately, any restated objectives of the AML/CTF Act will do little to improve our understanding of what would be a reasonable expectation of an effective AML/CTF system. There is an additional problem of measuring whether the statutory response to ML and CTF is proportionate and whether any infringements on civil liberties, especially privacy, are justified.

The FATF Standards, Peer Review System and the Concept of Effectiveness

The FATF Recommendations are comprehensive in nature and provide a framework for national AML policy and international co-operation for combating ML. The FATF Recommendations deal with a wide range of matters including substantive criminal law (such as the definition of ML, TF and designated predicate offences); the prevention of ML through customer due diligence and reporting of transactions; the regulation of reporting agencies, not just financial institutions but also Designated Non-Financial Businesses and the Professions (DNFBPs) (such as the legal and accounting professions); as well as international co-operation to share financial intelligence, provide authenticated evidence of crimes and confiscate illicit assets wherever they are located.[21]

Countries are subject to international peer-review assessments concerning whether they have technically complied with the FATF Recommendations. Technical compliance is judged by five ratings: compliant (no shortcomings); largely compliant (minor shortcomings); partially compliant (moderate shortcomings); non-compliant (major shortcomings) and not applicable.[22] Ratings based on compliance are frequently based on minutia, such as whether the wording of a country's legislation appears to cover a prescribed element, rather than any sophisticated legal analysis, for example, nuanced judicial interpretation of legislation.[23] This approach means that a country may be deemed to comply with the FATF Recommendations merely by enacting

legislation which satisfies the international community's demands for technical compliance. This focus on the enactment of AML legislation, rather than
enforcement of such legislation, was a useful first step in understanding how
countries were implementing their international AML obligations.

Approximately every five years, members of the FATF and members of the
nine regional FATF-style bodies (FASBs)[24] are subject to peer review assessments. It is evident that not only has the FATF sought to strengthen its oversight compliance capacity, but that member countries have improved their
performance in technically complying with the FATF Recommendations.
There are nevertheless significant gaps in technical compliance. For example,
the IMF has pointed out that as a general rule compliance with the FATF
Recommendations is low, with full compliance being the exception.[25] The
IMF has noted that, of the 161 peer reviews of jurisdictions between 2004
and April 2011, full compliance with the Recommendation occurred only in
12.3% of the cases.[26]

This raises questions as to why it has taken so long for countries to implement the global AML/CTF standards. Although countries have publicly
acknowledged the importance of the FATF Recommendations, it is doubtful
whether many of the countries have accepted that all the Recommendations
should apply to their national AML systems. For example, the USA has refused
to apply the FATF Recommendations to the legal profession, citing constitutional concerns regarding the reporting of suspicious transactions, while the
European Court of Human Rights has held that such reporting was not in
breach of the European Convention of Human Rights.[27] In the case of developing countries, the FATF Recommendations are frequently viewed with scepticism in that they are ill-suited to their developmental needs, with compliance
imposing an unnecessary and expensive burden which they can ill afford.[28]
Further, the comprehensive and complex nature of the FATF Recommendations
raises questions as to whether any country can fully comply with the
Recommendations without undermining other important national goals.

Compliance with the FATF Recommendations has become more challenging since 2013, when the FATF introduced a new methodology for peer
review assessments, which made effectiveness as 'equally as important' as
technical compliance.[29] The revised methodology provides not only guidance to reviewers so as to assess a jurisdiction's technical compliance with the
2012 FATF Recommendations but also a new template for assessing whether
a country's AML/CTF system is effective. The concept of effectiveness has a
specific meaning, namely the extent to which national efforts have succeeded
in meeting 11 immediate outcomes/key goals, such as 'the prevention, detection and reporting of proceeds of crime in financial and other sectors'.[30]

The notion of effectiveness requires a judgement by assessors as to whether a particular outcome has been achieved and what further measures are required to improve the outcome. Effectiveness is denoted at four levels: high effectiveness (outcome achieved to a very large extent); substantial effectiveness (outcome achieved to a large extent); moderate effectiveness (outcome achieved to some extent) and not effective (outcome not achieved or achieved to a negligible extent).[31] There is a relationship between technical compliance and effectiveness, in that technical compliance is the foundation stone for effectiveness. The assumption is that if a country has a low level of technical compliance with a FATF Recommendation, it is unlikely that there will be an effective outcome relating to that FATF Recommendation.[32] The same cannot be said in reverse: that is high technical compliance does not mean that there will be high effectiveness.

Several countries have been assessed under the new FATF methodology, including Australia, Italy and Belgium. Under the revised methodology, the peer review assessments will cover the following matters dealing with technical compliance and effectiveness[33]:

National AML/CTF Policies and Coordination	Technical Compliance (R1, R2, R33). Effectiveness: Immediate Outcome 1 (Risk, Policy and Coordination)
Legal System and Operational Issues	Technical Compliance (R3, R4, R29–32). Effectiveness: Immediate Outcome 6 (Financial intelligence) Effectiveness: Immediate Outcome 7 (ML investigation and prosecution) Effectiveness: Immediate Outcome 8 (Confiscation)
TF and Financing of Proliferation	Technical Compliance (R5–8) Effectiveness: Immediate Outcome 9 (TF investigation and prosecution) Effectiveness: Immediate Outcome 10 (TF preventive measures and financial sanctions) Effectiveness: Immediate Outcome 11 (TF and financial sanctions)
Preventive Measures	Technical Compliance (R9–23) Effectiveness: Immediate Outcome 4 (Preventive Measures)
Legal Supervision	Technical Compliance (R26–28, R34, R35) Effectiveness: Immediate Outcome 3 (Supervision)
Legal Persons and Arrangements	Technical Compliance (R24, R25) Effectiveness: Immediate Outcome 5 (Legal Persons and Arrangements)
International Co-operation	Technical Compliance (R36–40) Effectiveness: Immediate Outcome 2 (International Cooperation)

In the 2015 FATF/APG's peer review of Australia, which was part of the fourth round of mutual evaluations, Australia received a rating of compliant or largely compliant (a 'pass mark') in regard to 24 of the 40 Recommendations.[34] Australia was rated as non-compliant or partially compliant with regard to 16 of the Recommendations: with non-compliant in respect of Non-Profit Organisations (R 8), Correspondent banking (R 13), DNFBPs-Customer Due Diligence (R 22), DNFBPs-Other Measures (R 23), Transparency and Beneficial Ownership of Legal Arrangements (R 25) and Regulation of Supervision of DNFBPs (R 28).[35] This is a surprisingly modest result, given that Australia is a leading member of the FATF, and that the first mutual evaluation of Australia's AML system took place in 1992. Australia's modest performance shows that the FATF Recommendations are difficult to implement for legal, political or other reasons.

Australia's failings in technical compliance were matched by its lack of effectiveness to meet specific outcomes. Australia was rated as highly effective or substantially effective in less than 50% of the immediate outcomes (5 out of 11): understanding AML/CTF risks and policy co-ordination (Outcome 1), level of international cooperation (Outcome 2), use of financial intelligence (Outcome 6), investigation and prosecution of those involved in TF (Outcome 9) and system of financial sanctions (Outcome 11).[36] Australia was rated as moderate effective in meeting other key goals: supervising the private sector (Outcome 3), preventing ML and TF (Outcome 4), regulating legal persons and arrangements (Outcome 5), investigating and prosecuting ML (Outcome 7) and confiscation of illicit proceeds (Outcome 8). Technical compliances as well as effectiveness of the Australian AML system with respect to some of these issues are discussed in the following sections.

Implementation of AML Systems in Australia

The principal AML legislation in Australia is the AML/CTF Act 2006 (Cth),[37] which is complemented by the AML/CTF Rules Instrument 2007 (No. 1) (AML/CTF Rules), and certain provisions of the predecessor legislation, the Financial Transaction Reports Act 1988 (FTR Act) which continue to apply. The Statutory Review considers that the 'two AML/CTF reporting regimes' are inefficient from a regulatory perspective,[38] and that the FTR Act should be abolished and replaced by new provisions in the AML/CTF Act.[39]

The AML/CTF Act imposes obligations on any person who provides a designated service, which is defined in detail in the Act.[40] Rather than imposing obligations on generic institutions or types of businesses, the AML/CTF

Act uses the criterion of designated services as the basis for creating regulatory obligations. Designated services include 54 types of financial services, together with bullion and gambling services. Individuals and businesses in Australia are required to make an assessment as to whether their activity falls within a designated service, and thus whether they must register with the Australian Transaction Reports and Analysis Centre (AUSTRAC), the Australian AML regulator. This so-called service-based approach to regulation has been criticised by some businesses because it adds a 'significant layer of technical and legal complexity to the AML/CTF regime, generating uncertainty'.[41] This criticism has led to the Australian Attorney-General's Department in a Statutory Review recommending a simplification of the description of designated services through legislative amendment and/or additional supervisory guidance.[42]

Supervisory Capacity and Effectiveness

Unlike Financial Intelligence Units (FIUs) in many jurisdictions, AUSTRAC has a dual role as FIU and supervisor of a regulatory regime. An important development in the AML system in Australia is the expansion of the regulatory sector and AUSTRAC's increased supervisory responsibility. The number of individuals and businesses subject to the AML regime has grown from less than 4000 'cash dealers' under the FTR Act in the late 1980s to more than 14,040 reporting entities enrolled under the AML Act, including 5379 designated remittance service providers, as at 30 June 2015.[43] The implementation of the AML/CTF Act has provided a significant boost to the number of reporting entities under supervision of AUSTRAC. The range of persons subject to the AML/CTF Act encompasses major financial institutions, such as Australia's four major commercial banks, through to one-person remittance service providers. It is estimated that more than 70% of the reporting entities under Australia's AML legislation are small businesses employing fewer than 20 employees.[44] Given the number and diversity of reporting entities, AUSTRAC faces challenges in providing effective supervision of such entities. Although AUSTRAC has received increased funding through government-imposed industry contributions and direct budget allocations, it is questionable whether it has received sufficient resources to carry out its regulatory mandate. Faced with these circumstances, AUSTRAC faces difficult choices in its employment of resources.

AUSTRAC views enforcement as only one of its supervisory functions, with 'education, guidance and compliance assessment' equally as important.[45] Moreover, AUSTRAC has adopted a graduated approach to compliance which means that it views formal enforcement and sanctions as the end of the supervisory process rather than as the beginning process of supervision.[46] AUSTRAC's approach represents an express adoption of Braithwaite and Ayre's regulatory pyramid.[47] Indeed, the regulatory pyramid is referred to in AUSTRAC's enforcement strategy for 2012–2014, whereby supervisory activity may escalate in intensity from 'engagement activities' (e.g. guidance material), to 'heightened activities' (e.g. transaction monitoring), to 'escalated activities' (e.g. on-site assessment).[48]

Although the AML/CTF Act has given AUSTRAC a wide range of enforcement powers, including issuing infringement notices[49] or remedial notices,[50] obtaining enforceable undertakings,[51] and appointing authorised external auditors,[52] the powers are used infrequently. The failure of AUSTRAC to use its extensive arsenal of powers may be explained by its excessive reliance on the regulatory pyramid approach. The FATF in its 2015 review of Australia's AML/CTF system questioned whether AUSTRAC was an effective regulator because the enforcement measures that it had taken did not have a 'demonstrated effect on compliance by individual reporting entities that were not subject to onsite or offsite engagement'.[53] The FATF critique of Australia also pointed out that there has been no financial penalties imposed on reporting entities that have violated AML/CTF obligations,[54] and that this must raise questions as to regulatory effectiveness. Indeed, the FATF was not impressed by AUSTRAC's supervisory policies, including its graduated approach to applying sanctions, and its excessive reliance on self-certification by reporting entities.[55] Underlying the FATF's criticisms of AUSTRAC as a supervisor—although not stated in the report—was the need for AUSTRAC to spend more resources in supervising reporting entities and become a more aggressive regulator.

Regulation of Designated Non-financial Businesses and the Professions

When Australia's AML/CTF Act was enacted in 2006, it was envisaged that it would be applied in two tranches.[56] Tranche 1, which has been implemented, required financial institutions, the gambling sector, bullion dealers, remittance service providers and persons providing 'designated services' to implement the new AML obligations. Under Tranche 2, DNFBPs, including real estate agents, lawyers, accountants and corporate service providers, would be required to comply with their obligations within 12 months of the Act coming into force in December of 2006. However, nearly ten years later, Tranche

2 has not been implemented mainly because of the opposition of the Law Council of Australia to government regulation of lawyers and the concern of successive governments not to impose an additional regulatory burden on the small business sector.[57] Moreover, the government agreed to exempt certain 'legal practitioner services', in particular, the receiving and transferring of client funds through a trust account, from the scope of 'designated services', unless they are given in direct competition with licensed financial service providers.[58] Moreover, even though Tranche 1 states that it does not affect the law relating to legal professional privilege (LPP),[59] the Law Council has expressed concern about the potential impact of the AML/CTF Act on LPP and client confidentiality, particularly with regard to the imposition of any mandatory obligation on a lawyer to make suspicious matters' reports (SMRs) about their clients to an external body.[60] As Tranche 2 of the AML law is not in force in Australia, lawyers are not obliged to externally report activity they suspect may involve ML unless they provide 'designated services'.

The failure of the Australian Government to implement Tranche 2 of the AML/CTF Act has created new opportunities for money launderers in Australia, especially since some sectors such as real estate agents and lawyers are considered to be 'high ML risk in Australia's National Threat Assessment'.[61] Indeed, in the FATF/APG 2015 review of Australia, it was noted that most DNFBPs are not adequately regulated by AML legislation, and that Australia should prioritise action in expanding AML regulation to DNFBPs. A significant weakness is that there is no extensive requirement imposed on DNFBPs to carry out due diligence of their clients, and this omission is compounded because DNFBPs do not have sufficient understanding of the risks of ML or TF.[62]

Reporting Obligations and Effectiveness

Under the AML/CTF Act, a comprehensive system of reporting obligations is created which affects the banking and non-banking community at large rather than any targeted group of criminals.[63] The AML legislation seeks to influence the behaviour of organised crime by imposing a detailed regulatory system on the private sector, thereby making it unattractive to organised crime. The private sector is required to co-operate with law enforcement by providing a wide range of reports, including reports about threshold transactions reports (TTRs), cross-border movements of physical currency reports (CBM-PCRs), international funds transfer instructions reports (IFTIs), SMRs and AML/CTF compliance reports.[64]

Australia's AML reporting regime provides mandatory reporting of transactions which are not required by the FATF Recommendations. The Australian AML reporting system was modelled on the USA by requiring the reporting by financial institutions of currency/TTRs above $10,000[65] and the reporting by all persons of CBM-PCRs above $10,000.[66] Australian law has gone further than the USA and other developed jurisdictions by also creating a comprehensive AML reporting system in relation to international ML, through a requirement that all IFTIs, no matter what their size, be reported to AUSTRAC.[67]

The Australian reporting regime complies with the core FATF requirement of the creation of a suspicious transactions reporting regime. Under the AML/CTF Act, an SMR must be filed by persons who provide designated services to their customers.[68] The SMR obligation is very wide in that it arises when there is a very low threshold of suspicion ('suspects on reasonable grounds'), and it applies to six situations, for example, where a reporting entity has information relevant to the investigation or prosecution of a person for tax evasion or an attempted tax evasion, or any offence against a law of the Commonwealth, State or Territory, or an ML or TF offence, or the enforcement of a Commonwealth, State or Territory proceeds of crime law.[69] Although the SMR obligation does not apply to foreign offences per se, it may apply where the proceeds of a foreign offence are laundered through an Australian reporting entity.[70]

Australia's SMR reporting regime differs from a number of other jurisdictions, in that a failure to file an SMR when required to do so under the Act is not a criminal offence, but it attracts a civil penalty. AUSTRAC has the power to apply to the Federal Court for a civil penalty for a breach of section 41, where a reporting entity fails to submit an SMR report or submits a late SMR report, but to date no court order has imposed a civil penalty for a breach of section 41.[71] Further, unlike other countries, such as the UK, the criminal offence of ML is not necessarily committed in Australia if a reporting entity proceeds with a transaction in circumstances where the transaction is suspicious requiring the filing of a report.[72] This would suggest that Australian reporting entities face lower criminal and regulatory risk for AML compliance failures compared with reporting regimes in other jurisdictions, and that consequently there is an absence of deterrents for such failures.

There is a trend towards increasing reporting of SMRs' volumes, and this is sometimes presented as an indication of the increasing compliance by reporting entities with respect to their obligations. An examination of statistics concerning the number of SMRs filed with AUSTRAC provides some objective data as to the extent to which the AML regime gathers information about suspected crimes of customers. The statistics from AUSTRAC's Annual Report show that in the year 2014–2015, AUSTRAC received 81,074

SMRs,[73] which represented a 21% increase from the previous year.[74] AUSTRAC asserts that the increase in SMRs' reporting is 'largely due to the effectiveness of our intelligence publications, as well as increased media coverage of terrorist activities, leading to awareness of reporting obligations'.[75] This assertion cannot be tested without surveying the reporting sector. One possible explanation for the increased volume of reporting of SMRs is AUSTRAC's targeted enforcement of AML laws against the remittance sector[76] and the deterrent effect of its sanctions, including the withdrawal and suspension of the licenses of a number of remitters. For example, in November 2014, AUSTRAC cancelled the registration of a remittance dealer in circumstances, where the continued registration of the dealer was said to entail a TF risk.[77]

According to AUSTRAC's analysis from its annual report for the period 2014/2015, the major offences that the SMRs related to were ML (25,867), predicate offences at Commonwealth/State/Territory level (36,295), tax evasion (2641), proceeds of crime (1643) and person agent not who they claim to be (695).[78] These statistics demonstrate that the AML legislative framework is not merely concerned about ML per se but also about suspicions concerning financial crime generally. Indeed, these figures would indicate that the AML regime is just as important for the prevention and detection of financial crimes and tax evasion as it is in combating ML. AUSTRAC in the same analysis noted that the major reasons that the private sector filed SMRs were unusual account activity (22,453), country/jurisdiction risk (20,816), avoiding reporting requirements (16,065), inconsistent customer profile (15,855) and unusual large cash transactions (11,740). SMRs relevant to TF amounted to 536 reports with an associated value of US$53 million for the 2014–2015 year.[79] Although this may appear to be a small number, it represented an increase of 300% from the previous 2013–2014 year. One explanation for this increase in TF reports is that the financial institutions are responding to AUSTRAC's targeting of approximately 100 individuals, their families and supporters, who are 'linked to the number of Australians travelling to join terrorist groups in Syria and Iraq'.[80]

The reasons that the private sector filed SMRs may be dissected to increase our understanding of how the reporting agencies are viewing its customers' transactions which are reported as suspicious. One interesting statistic is the large number of reports of SMRs (16,065) that are filed in circumstances, where customers of reporting entities are trying to avoid reporting requirements. The structuring of financial transactions to avoid mandatory reporting obligations, such as threshold transactions reports or cross-border movements of physical currency reports, amounts to 2 criminal offences in Australia.[81] This illustrates one of the advantages of having a mandatory requirement of reporting of transactions, namely that potential criminals will seek to avoid compliance with such a requirement, and that this may lead to suspicious behaviour which is reported to the FIU.

Various reported cases and expert evidence suggest that Australia's reporting regime is superior to the FATF international standards because of the statutory requirement that all IFTIs be reported to AUSTRAC.[82] Australia's international money transfer reporting regime has existed since 1992, and there are hundreds of millions of transactions that have been captured, stored and subject to extensive analysis, especially by Australia's taxation authorities.[83] This type of information has been critical in the investigation of tax offences and other criminal matters. The effectiveness of the regime has been enhanced because of bank practice, in that banks not only report funds moving in and out of Australia but also certain high-value transfers within Australia. For example, Australia's leading banks when requested by customers to make high-value payments from one bank to another bank will treat the transaction as an international money transfer and file a reportable transaction even though the money is not moving in or out of Australia.[84]

Financial Intelligence and Effectiveness

AUSTRAC is considered one of the most efficient compilers and distributors of financial intelligence in the world, and this is recognised by its high rating in terms of both technical compliance with the FATF Recommendations and effectiveness concerning financial intelligence. Under the AML/CTF Act, reports and other forms of financial intelligence may be disseminated to the clients or partner agencies of AUSTRAC. The list of agencies that have access to AUSTRAC financial intelligence has grown and includes all Australian government law enforcement agencies, national security agencies, revenue, regulatory and social justice agencies, together with state and territory law enforcement and revenue agencies.[85] Australian agencies have access to AUSTAC data based on a Memorandum of Understanding between AUSTRAC and the agency concerned;[86] with the Australian Taxation Office (ATO) having access under section 125 of the AML/CTF Act 'for any purpose relating to the administration and enforcement of a taxation law', including online access by designated ATO officers.[87] Australian agencies have benefited from the increase in the number of reports filed with AUSTRAC since the passage of the 2006 legislation, the bulk data policy of AUSTRAC and AUSTRAC's sophisticated use of data analytics to enhance its financial intelligence product. Whereas 18 million transaction reports were filed by reporting bodies under the AML legislation in 2007–2008, by 2012 this had increased to over 84 million reports, with most of the reports being IFTIs. An explanation for the increased reporting of IFTIs is the continuing globalisation of Australian business transactions that manifests itself in the increasing volume of international financial transactions involving Australia.

In 2014–2015, AUSTRAC distributed a large number of financial intelligence reports, including 943 'detailed financial intelligence reports' to Australia agencies.[88] The breakdown of the recipients of such reports were ATO (80,978), Australian Federal Police (AFP) (3298), Australian Customs and Border Protection Service (ACBPS) (1536), Australian Crime Commission (ACC) (1533) and the Department of Human Services (DHS) (1479). The statistics show that the ATO received by far the largest number of reports, even though the private sector identified tax evasion in a mere 2641 cases as the reason for filing SMRs in 2014/2015. This is because other reports filed with AUSTRAC, especially IFTIs, are routinely used by the ATO in its investigation of tax matters, and that the reports may result in the exercise of administrative powers, leading to amended or new tax assessments.[89]

The potential utility of the information gathered by AUSTRAC may also be judged by the enormous size of the AUSTRAC database which has gathered financial sector information under mandatory obligations since 1989. For the period 1989–2014, AUSTRAC (and its predecessors) collected 'more than 350 million reports', receiving in 2014 'on average 280,000 new reports each day'.[90] The AUSTRAC database is a potential gold mine of information which is subject to the most sophisticated data mining tools available not only to AUSTRAC but also key domestic government authorities, such as the ATO.

Statistics produced by AUSTRAC concerning the utility of its financial intelligence are largely confined to tax. For example, AUSTRAC asserts in its 2014/2015 Annual Report that AML financial intelligence has 'directly contributed to' 16,038 tax cases, which has led to $466 million in additional tax assessments, with a 'total contribution to tax assessments and debt collections of nearly $2.5 billion over the past 10 years'.[91] The significance of these statistics is difficult to assess, since the underlying assumptions have not been spelt out. Further, there is no figure produced as to the amount of tax that was actually collected as a result of AUSTRAC's financial intelligence; the mere raising of a tax assessment does not equate to tax collection. Finally, as the Panama Papers indicate, data leaks from financial institutions and corporate service providers may play just an important role in detecting tax evasion and organised crime. For example, the Panama Papers disclosed the identities of 1000 Australian taxpayers with 80 of those persons matched to the Australian Crime Commission's database.[92]

Although AUSTRAC provides some general information concerning how its information supports operations of its partner agencies, such as the AFP and the ACC, the FATF considers that the 'somewhat limited use of AUSTRAC information by law enforcement as a trigger to commence ML/TF investigations presents a weakness in the Australian AML/CTF system'.[93] The suggested weakness is that Australia's SMR filings have not resulted in the commencement of a sufficiently large number of new ML/TF investigations. Although the FATF recognises that the Australian AML system prioritises the detection and disruption of predicate crimes,[94] this is not what the FATF considers to be the prime function of the international and national AML systems. Given the low level of suspicion required to file an SMR, it is not surprisingly that many of the SMR filings are of limited investigatory utility. As has been noted by one expert, Australia's TTRs and IFTIs have been far more useful to law enforcement than SMRs,[95] which undermines the underlying FATF expectation concerning the importance of SMRs.

Money Laundering Prosecutions

One of the criteria for assessing the effectiveness of AML systems[96] is the number of ML prosecutions in a jurisdiction, the range of underlying predicate offences that underline those prosecutions, and the seriousness of the criminality and amount of monies pertaining to prosecutions. The FATF, in its 2015 review, observed that Australia has improved its conviction rate for ML since its last review in 2005 but commented that the 'overall results are lower than they could be relative to the nature and scale of the risks'.[97] The statistics show that under Division 400 of the Criminal Code 1985 (Cth), 256 persons were convicted of a federal ML offence during the period 2010–2014, but that only 58% (149 persons) received a custodial order.[98] A number of explanations may be offered as to why Australia's ML prosecution record is modest, or in FATF parlance, 'moderately effective'.[99] Firstly, the focus of Australia's AML strategy has been the detection, disruption and prosecution of serious predicate crimes, such as drug trafficking rather than ML per se.[100] It would seem that the FATF regards prosecution of serious predicate offences as not as important as the prosecution of ML.[101] Project Wickenby is cited by the FATF and Asia/Pacific Group (APG) review as the 'best example of the successful use of AUSTRAC information' but that it has only led to three successful prosecutions for ML and 44 criminal convictions for serious tax-related crimes. The problem is that the FATF measures performance and enforcement in a very narrow fashion. It is highly questionable that ML prosecutions per se should be given greater importance than underlying serious predicate offences, such as drug trafficking. From a practical perspective, what does it matter what the criminal is prosecuted for, as long as the charges and the sentencing reflect the criminal behaviour. This suggests that the FATF's policy on criminal prosecutions has a dubious bias, which is also found in relation to the FATF's approach to detection and investigations of financial crime.

Secondly, there has been no criminal conviction of a corporation for ML in Australia,[102] which is largely due to the fact that corporate criminal liability is difficult to establish, in contrast to the USA which relies on the concept of vicarious criminal corporate liability. Under section 12.3 of the Criminal Code (Cth), corporate fault may also be proved through the fault of a 'high managerial agent' of the body corporate, instead of the 'directing mind and will' of the corporation,[103] but this has not significantly improved the prospects of criminal convictions of corporations. Thirdly, the FATF notes that 'stand-alone and third party ML offences are regularly prosecuted…(but) legal issues have arisen in relation to the prosecution of self-laundering offences'.[104] Self-laundering means that the person who committed the predicate offence has sought to launder his or her own illicit proceeds derived from the offence. In Australia, the courts have held that Parliament did not intend that ML offences include cases of 'self-laundering', in that the offences were designed to capture 'activity where persons were intimately involved in dealing with money that was the result of *some other person's criminal activity*, so as to hide the source (emphasis added).'[105] Unless it can be shown that a charge of ML reflects a 'separate act of criminality' from the underlying predicate offence, then there is no legal justification for a prosecution of ML.[106] As a result of the legal position in Australia, future prosecutions of ML will be confined to third-party laundering, which will inevitably dampen ML prosecutorial statistics.

International Co-operation

The FATF 2015 review rated Australia very highly in terms of both technical compliance with the FATF Recommendation on international co-operation and in effectiveness in relation to international co-operation.[107] Formal requests for mutual assistance in criminal matters are dealt with under separate legislation, the Mutual Assistance in Criminal Matters Act 1987 (Cth), and are coordinated by the Australian federal Attorney-General's Department. Specific co-operation on the sharing of financial intelligence in AML matters is the responsibility of AUSTRAC, which has entered into exchange of financial intelligence information instruments with 69 foreign FIUs and is negotiating agreements with other jurisdictions of the Egmont Group.[108] Although AUSTRAC is also a regulator, it has only entered into one agreement with a foreign agency for the exchange of regulatory information, as distinct from financial intelligence.[109]

Under section 131 of the AML/CTF Act, AUSTRAC may communicate information to a foreign country if the government of the foreign country gives appropriate undertakings to protect the confidentiality of the information, to control the use that will be made of it and to ensure that the information will be used only for the purpose for which it is communicated. This provides a certain degree of protection over the use of sensitive financial intelligence, in that the intelligence cannot be used by a foreign authority for a non-authorised purpose without the consent of AUSTRAC. Under current arrangements, AUSTRAC may reply to a request from another FIU in relation to an investigation of foreign criminal offences. According to AUSTRAC, the exchange of financial intelligence between AUSTRAC and foreign FIUs has increased so that in 2014/2015, there were 857 exchanges of financial intelligence, a significant increase from 301 exchanges in 2013/2014.[110] It is difficult to measure the importance of the exchange of financial intelligence, as compared to formal mutual legal assistance (MLA) in relation to criminal matters, where typically the Australian Attorney-General's Department deals with about 300–400 MLA requests each year.[111] However, from a law enforcement perspective, one of the advantages of international AML financial intelligence co-operation is that it is carried out through administrative means without resorting to the judicial process. By directly exchanging intelligence from one FIU to another, information is transmitted in a timely manner, which can be compared to the somewhat laborious process of transmitting information under MLA treaties. Further, as such financial intelligence exchanges are secret, it will be nearly impossible to objectively assess their importance.

Conclusions

This chapter has sought to understand how effectiveness is judged under the new FATF methodology of assessment of a country's compliance with the FATF Recommendations. The new methodology represents an ambitious attempt by the FATF to ensure that implementation of the FATF Recommendations is assessed not merely by assessing technical compliance but also enforcement outcomes. It is likely that the new methodology will increase the complexity in AML performance measurement and make the task of peer reviewers more time consuming and difficult. Whether the new methodology will result in countries changing their AML enforcement behaviour is an open question. This chapter has critically analysed the effectiveness of AML policy by using the Australian experience as a guide. Australia is a useful example because it has been presented as a leading jurisdiction in AML compliance and has been one of the first jurisdictions that have been reviewed by the FATF and APG under the new methodology. Australia's record of effectiveness is mixed, in that it has scored high marks for supervisor capacity and effectiveness in regard to financial institutions, but low scores in regard to DNFBPs, which are largely unregulated. The most important achievement of Australia's AML regulator is its effectiveness as a collector and distributor of financial intelligence, but its record is largely dependent on its ability to obtain and utilise a vast reservoir of daily records of international money movements. There is an irony in that the legislative tool which has led to Australia's greatest success in its AML system is not part of the requirements of the FATF, and indeed it is a relatively costless measure, as compared to the ongoing expansion of the FATF requirements.

Notes

1. See the figures published on the Financial Action Task Force (FATF) website <www.fatf-gafi.org/countrics/> accessed 17 July 17.
2. See for example, Peter Reuter and Edwin Truman, *Chasing Dirty Money: The Fight Against Money Laundering* (Institute for International Economics 2004); Michael Levi and Peter Reuter, 'Money Laundering' (2006) 34(1) Crime and Justice 289; Jason Campbell Sharman, *The Money Laundry: Regulating Criminal Finance in the Global Economy* (Cornell University Press 2011); Brigitte Unger and Daan van der Linde (eds), *Research Handbook on Money Laundering* (Edward Elgar Publishing 2013); Brigitte Unger and others, *The Economic and Legal Effectiveness of the European Union's Anti-Money Laundering Policy* (Edward Elgar Publishing 2014).
3. See William Gilmore, *Dirty Money: The Evolution of International Measures to Counter Money Laundering and the Financing of Terrorism* (3rd edn, Council of Europe 2004) 89–91.
4. See FATF, *The Forty Recommendations of the Financial Action Task Force on Money Laundering* (FATF 1990).
5. See FATF, *FATF Mandate 2012–2020* (FATF 2012) 3.
6. ibid.

7. See *FATF, International Standards on Combating Money Laundering and the Financing of Terrorism & Proliferation: The FATF Recommendations* (FAFT 2012) (updated in 2013 and 2015), Recommendations 5, 6 and 8, which were previously denoted as Special Recommendations 11, 111 and VII.

8. See Tim Krieger and Daniel Meierrieks, 'Terrorist Financing and Money Laundering' (2011) paper available at <http://ssrn.com/abstract=1860069> accessed 17 July 17.

9. See FATF (n 7). Recommendation 7 provides for targeted financial sanctions relating to proliferation.

10. See FATF, *Public Statement* (19 February 2016).

11. See International Monetary Fund (IMF), *Anti-Money Laundering and Combating the Financing of Terrorism (AML/CTF)—Report on the Review of the Effectiveness of the Program* (2011) 20.

12. See Abdullahi Yusuf Shehu, 'Promoting financial sector stability through an effective AML/CFT regime' (2010) 13(2) Journal of Money Laundering Control 139.

13. IMF (n 11) 33.

14. Rajeev Syal, 'Drug Money Saved Banks in Global Crisis, Claims UN Advisor' *The Guardian* (London 13 December 2009) <www.theguardian.com/global/2009/dec/13/drug-money-banks-saved-un-cfief-claims> accessed 17 July 17.

15. See Peter Reuter, *Assessing Money Laundering Controls*, Paper presented at AML/CTF Conference (Sydney April 2009) <www.aic.gov.au/media_library/conferences/2009-anti-money_laundering/presentations/reuter_peter.pdf> accessed 17 July 17.

16. FATF (n 5). Recommendation 3 (Money Laundering Offence), the Interpretive Note to Recommendation 3, and the definition of Designated Category of Offences.

17. See Financial Services Authority, *Fighting Financial Crime* (FSA 2012). See now the Financial Conduct Authority, *Financial Crime: A Guide to Firms*, PS11/15 (FCA 2011).

18. Anti-Money Laundering and Counter-Terrorism Financing 2006 Act (AML/CTF Act) (Australia), s 3.

19. Australian Government, *Report of the Statutory Review of the Anti-Money Laundering and Counter-Terrorism Financing Act 2006 and Associated Rules and Regulations* (Attorney-General's Department 2016), Recommendation 3(1).

20. Reuter (n 15). Reuter refers to 'primary goals' as 'reduc(ing) predicate crimes, protect(ing) the integrity of the core financial systems and combat(ing) "global public bads"', 'and secondary goals' as including 'sanction(ing) major felons', administer(ing) 'just desserts' and inconvenienc(ing) felons'.

21. See IMF (n 11) 6.

22. FATF, *Methodology for Assessing Technical Compliance with the FATF Recommendations and the Effectiveness of AML/CFT Systems* (FATF 2013) (updated October 2016) 13.

23. This observation is based on the author's presence at several FATF meetings which have considered peer review assessments of several countries.

24. The FATF-style regional bodies are: Asia/Pacific Group on Money Laundering (APG), Sydney, Australia; Caribbean Financial Action Task Force (CFATF), Port of Spain, Trinidad and Tobago; Eurasian Group (EAG) Moscow, Russia; Eastern and Southern African Anti-Money Laundering Group (ESAAMLG), Dar es Salaam, Tanzania; Central Africa Anti-Money Laundering Group (GABAC), Libreville, Gabon; Latin America Anti-Money Laundering Group (GAFILAT), Buenos Aires, Argentina; West Africa Money Laundering Group (GIABA), Dakar, Senegal; Middle East and North Africa Financial Action Task Force (MENAFATF), Manama, Bahrain; and Council of Europe Anti-Money Laundering Group (MONEYVAL), Strasbourg, France. See <www.apgml. org/fatf-and-fsrb/page.aspx?p=94065425-e6aa-479f-8701-5ca5d07ccfe8> accessed 17 July 17.

25. IMF (n 11) 8.

26. ibid. 42. The 12.3% figure was based on the percentage of full compliance with the 7889 'observations in the data set', which in turn was calculated by multiplying the number of assessments (161) by the number of Recommendations (49).

27. *Michaud v France* ECHR 2012-VI. See David Chaikin, 'Financial Crime Risks and the Professions' in David Chaikin (ed), *Financial Crime Risks, Globalisation and the Professions* (Australian Scholarly Publishing 2013) 12–13.

28. See Jason Campbell Sharman and Percy Shiavak Mistry, *Considering the Consequences: The Development Implications of Initiatives on Taxation, Anti-Money Laundering and Combating the Financing of Terrorism* (Commonwealth Secretariat 2008).

29. FATF (n 22) 15.

30. ibid. 15–17.

31. ibid. 21.

32. ibid. 17.

33. ibid. 132–139.

34. FATF and APG, *Anti-Money Laundering and Counter-Terrorist Financing Measures, Australia, Mutual Evaluation Report* (FATF and APG 2016) 18–25; See also KPMG, *The FATF Mutual Evaluation of Australia: Are there lessons for New Zealand's reporting entities?* (2015), 4.

35. FATF and APG (n 34) 18–25.

36. ibid. 12–17.

37. The AML/CTF Act was enacted in response to the recommendations of the FATF and APG, *Third Mutual Evaluation Report on Anti-Money Laundering and Combating The Financing of Terrorism* (FATF and APG 2005), and after consultation between stakeholders and the Australian Attorney-General's Department from 2004–2006.

38. Australian Government (n 19) 5 and 11.
39. ibid. 158.
40. See AML/CTF Act (n 18) s 6, Tables 1, 2, and 3.
41. Australian Government (n 19) 23.
42. ibid. 23.
43. See Australian Transaction Reports and Analysis Centre (AUSTRAC), *Annual Report 2014–2015*, 38.
44. AUSTRAC, *Productivity Commission Study: Regulator Engagement with Small Business* (2013), 4.
45. AUSTRAC (n 43) 2.
46. ibid. 11–12. For criticisms of AUSTRAC's supervisory approach, see FATF and APG (n 34) 12, 97 and 102.
47. Ian Ayres and John Braithwaite, *Responsive Regulation: Transcending the Deregulation Debate* (OUP 1992) 35.
48. AUSTRAC, *Enforcement Strategy 2012–2014*, 3.
49. AML/CTF Act (n 18) s 184.
50. ibid. s 191.
51. ibid. s 197.
52. ibid. s 162.
53. FATF and APG (n 34) 101.
54. ibid. 12.
55. ibid. 12, 97 and 103.
56. The following discussion is taken from David Chaikin (ed), *Financial Crime Risks, Globalisation and the Professions* (Australian Scholarly Publishing 2013).
57. See Law Council of Australia, Submission to the Statutory Review of the Anti-Money Laundering and Counter-Terrorism Financing Regime, 30 April 2014, 3–9. See also Australian Government (n 19) 138 and 158.
58. See AML/CTF Act (n 18) s 6, Table 1, item 46(b).
59. ibid. s 242.
60. See Law Council of Australia, *Anti-Money Laundering Guide for Legal Practitioners* (2009) (updated January 2016) 20–21.
61. FATF and APG (n 34) 6. For consideration of lawyers and money laundering, see Chap. 6 (Benson) in this collection.
62. FATF and APG (n 34) 6, 81, and 84.
63. See Privacy Commissioner's observations, quoted in Australian Government, *Checking the Cash: A Report of the Effectiveness of the Financial Transaction Reports Act 1988*, Senate Standing Committee on Legal and Constitutional Affairs (Commonwealth of Australia 1993) 57.
64. See Neil Jensen, 'International Funds Transfer Instructions: Australia at the Leading Edge of Financial Transaction Reporting' (1993) 4(2) Journal of Law Information and Society 304.

65. AML/CTF Act (n 18) ss 43 and 44. A breach of this requirement gives rise to a civil penalty.
66. ibid. ss 53–58. See also the requirement under section 59 to report bearer negotiable instruments, when requested by a customs office or police officer. A breach of this requirement gives rise to a civil penalty.
67. ibid. ss 45 and 46.
68. ibid. s 41.
69. ibid. s 41(1).
70. See definition of money laundering, ibid. s 5.
71. FATF and APG (n 34) 12. See, however, AUSTRAC, Record $45 million civil penalty ordered against Tabcorp, *Press Release*, 16 March 2017.
72. See AML/CTF Act (n 18) s 51, that deems information reported under ss 41, 43, 45 or 49 as not in the possession of the reporting entity for the purpose of money laundering offences in Division 400 and Chap. 5 of the Criminal Code 1995 (Cth).
73. This statistic and other statistics concerning SMRs also include Suspicious Transaction Reports (STRs) which are required to be filed under the FTR Act which is still in force.
74. In 2013–2014, there were 64,076 SMRs/STRs filed; in 2012–2013, the total was 44,062.
75. AUSTRAC (n 43) 65.
76. For consideration of AML and the remittance sector, see Chap. 42 (Cooper) in this collection.
77. See AUSTRAC, *AUSTRAC Cancels Registration: Bisotel Rieh Pty Ltd*, Press Release (10 November 2014).
78. See AUSTRAC (n 43) 67.
79. ibid. 61.
80. ibid.
81. See AML/CTF Act (n 18) ss 142 and 143.
82. See John Walker, *Some Thoughts on Assessing Australia's Performance in Response to the FATF 40+ Recommendations,* Submission to the FATF Mutual Evaluation Assessment Team, Canberra, Australia 31 July 2014 (on file with the author).
83. For the background, see Jensen (n 64).
84. See David Chaikin, *Measuring Performance and Australia's Anti-Money Laundering Laws*, Submission to the FATF Mutual Evaluation Assessment Team, Canberra, Australia, 31 July 2014 (on file with the author).
85. See the definition of a designated agency in AML/CTF Act (n 18) s 5.
86. ibid. s 126(1).
87. See *Memorandum between the Director of AUSTRAC and the Commissioner of the ATO on Access to and Use of AUSTRAC Data* (9 December 2003).

88. AUSTRAC, *Submission to the Parliamentary Joint Committee on Law Enforcement Inquiry into Financial Related Crime* (Australian Parliament 2014) 4.
89. AUSTRAC (n 77) 52.
90. ibid. 4.
91. AUSTRAC (n 43) 44.
92. Australia Crime Commission, *Annual Report 2015–2016*, 70–71.
93. FATF and APG (n 34) 5 and 8.
94. ibid. 5.
95. See Walker (n 82).
96. For further discussion of measuring AML systems, see Chap. 14 (Ferwerda) and Chap. 15 (van Duyne et al) in this collection.
97. See FATF and APG (n 34) 8 and 56–60.
98. ibid. 60.
99. ibid.
100. ibid. 41.
101. ibid. 40 and 50.
102. ibid. 59–60.
103. See *Tesco Supermarkets Ltd v Nattras* [1972] AC 153.
104. FATF and APG (n 34) 47.
105. *Thorn v R* (2009) 198 A Crim R 135. See discussion in Chaikin (n 84).
106. *Nahlous v R* [2010] NSWCCA 58 [17].
107. FATF and APG (n 34) 115–120.
108. The Egmont Group of Financial Intelligence Units consists of 151 member FIUs. See <www.egmontgroup.org> accessed 17 July 17.
109. See AUSTRAC (n 43) 4.
110. ibid. 50.
111. FATF and APG (n 34) 115–116.

David A Chaikin   is the Chair of the Discipline of Business Law at the University of Sydney School of Business, and a practising lawyer specialising in transnational litigation. His research focuses on anti-financial crime regulation, offshore financial services laws and asset protection. He has worked as a consultant with the Financial Action Task Force (FATF) and the Asia Pacific Group on Money Laundering, and previously held positions of Senior Assistant Secretary as well as Head of the International Criminal Law Enforcement and Security Branch in the Australian Attorney-General's Department, and Senior Fraud Officer of the Commonwealth Secretariat. He has a PhD in law from the University of Cambridge, an LLM from Yale Law School, and an LLB/B Com (Accounting, Finance and Systems) from UNSW.

14

The Effectiveness of Anti-Money Laundering Policy: A Cost-Benefit Perspective

Joras Ferwerda

Introduction

Basically all countries in the world have an anti-money laundering framework in place based on the 40 recommendations of the Financial Action Task Force (FATF), an intergovernmental body established by the G-7 countries in 1989.[1] Now that all these countries are spending tax money to fight money laundering, a natural question to ask is how effective is this policy. Do taxpayers receive value for the money spent? In this chapter we discuss the effectiveness and efficiency of anti-money laundering policies and perform a measurement for countries in the European Union.

This chapter is based on the research done in the EU-financed project ECOLEF—The Economic and Legal Effectiveness of Anti-Money Laundering and Counter Terrorist Financing—DG Home Affairs JLS/2009/ISEC/AG/087. This is a revised version of Chap. 12 of Brigitte Unger and others, *The Economic and Legal Effectiveness of the European Union's Anti-Money Laundering Policy* (Edward Elgar Publishing 2014); and Chap. 13 of Brigitte Unger and others, 'The Economic and Legal Effectiveness of Anti-Money Laundering and Counter Terrorism Financing Policy in the EU' (2013) Project Report for the European Commission financed by DG Home Affairs <www2.econ.uu.nl/users/unger/ecolef_files/Final%20ECOLEF%20report%20(digital%20version).pdf> accessed 21 March 2017. I thank all researchers and participants of the ECOLEF project, especially Prof Dr Brigitte Unger, Dr Ioana Deleanu and Dr Melissa van den Broek.

J. Ferwerda
Utrecht University School of Economics, Utrecht, The Netherlands

© The Author(s) 2018
C. King et al. (eds.), *The Palgrave Handbook of Criminal and Terrorism Financing Law*,
https://doi.org/10.1007/978-3-319-64498-1_14

Effectiveness of Anti-Money Laundering Policy

Effectiveness is the extent to which an intended result is achieved. This definition brings us to an important question for measuring the effectiveness of anti-money laundering policies: what is the goal of anti-money laundering policy? Although it might seem logical that the goal must be reducing money laundering, in practice the answer seems to be more complicated. When travelling through the European Union (EU) and speaking with policy makers, practitioners and public prosecutors, a whole range of answers is given apart from the obvious 'fighting/reducing money laundering'; other answers include reducing/fighting crime, confiscating criminal assets, fighting drug crimes, fighting tax evasion, preventing money laundering, being compliant with the FATF 40 recommendations, making sure crime does not pay and implementing the EU Anti-Money Laundering (AML) Directives.[2] Some primarily see the international pressure to comply, while others see fighting money laundering more as an intermediate result with the higher goal being to fight or prevent (specific) crime. The goal of anti-money laundering policy, therefore, is not sufficiently clear for accurate measurement of effectiveness.

But even if the simplest answer is adopted—fighting/reducing money laundering—another problem arises. Money laundering is an activity that is shielded from the public eye, which obstructs direct measurement. There are several estimates of money laundering,[3] but this literature is still developing and has not yet reached a reliable consensus. As such, we lack yearly estimations or useful indicators. One can, for instance, look into the amount of suspicious transactions reported by banks and other reporting institutions. The problem with such an indicator is that its message about the amount of money laundering is unclear. If the number of transactions reported increases, this could mean that money laundering is increasing (the phenomenon happens more often and is therefore more often detected) or decreasing (more transactions are detected, reducing the attractiveness of the country leading to less money laundering) or even staying the same (the reporting institutions increased the effectiveness of their detection framework).

Given these problems, this chapter focuses on the efficiency of anti-money laundering policy. It surveys the costs and benefits of the fight against money laundering to assess the net costs, so that policy makers and taxpayers can gain a better understanding of whether this policy is worth its costs.

A Cost-Benefit Analysis of Anti-Money Laundering Policy

Although a cost-benefit analysis is a standard way to evaluate current and proposed policies in almost all fields, for anti-money laundering policy it is extremely rare to find one.[4] Whitehouse concludes that 'The cost of compliance is increasing rapidly but it would be a brave person who steps up to say that it is too high a price to pay for countering terrorism and serious crime'.[5]

This chapter outlines how to set up a cost-benefit analysis for anti-money laundering policy given the current state of information available on the costs and benefits of the fight against money laundering in the European Union.

Before starting to identify the components and its associated data, we should identify what we want to assess exactly. We can calculate how much has been expended to establish anti-money laundering policy and compare that sum with how much benefit was derived from it (called here the 'historical approach'). Alternatively, we can also assess which costs we would save if the current anti-money laundering policy was halted and what consequent benefits would be lost (called here the 'current approach'). Although these two methods both measure the costs and benefits of anti-money laundering policy and although they seem to be much the same, there is one important difference: With the 'historical approach', the set-up costs of the policy should be included, but these costs are not included in the 'current approach'. These set-up costs could be quite substantial, including not only the work of the FATF to devise the international policy, but also costs like setting up a Financial Intelligence Unit (FIU) in every country in the world, implementing new laws into the legal system, training personnel in both law enforcement agencies and reporting institutions, and other work. The 'historical approach' would tell us whether starting AML/CTF policy has been a good idea, while the 'current approach' considers whether we should continue the current efforts. Geiger and Wuensch conclude that AML regulation is unthinkingly extended instead of assessed and ask themselves why a review does not take place.[6] In this light it seems most fruitful to concentrate on the 'current approach' for now, since it is more policy relevant.

Based on a literature research, plus interviews and discussions during regional workshops with stakeholders involved in money laundering,[7] we can identify the most important components at the country level shown in Table 14.1 below:

Table 14.1 The components of a cost-benefit analysis for AML

Costs	Benefits
Ongoing policy making	Fines (preventive and repressive)
Sanction costs (repressive)	Confiscated proceeds
FIU	Reduction in the amount of ML
Supervision	Less predicate crimes
Law enforcement and judiciary	Reduced damage effect on real economy
Duties of the private sector	Less risk for the financial sector
Reduction in privacy	
Efficiency costs for society and the financial system	

Although there is still very little information on the costs and benefits of anti-money laundering policy,[8] each component will be briefly discussed with findings for countries in the EU.[9] Note that this cost-benefit analysis is at the country level and not at the level of the particular institutions involved. It is also interesting to look at the costs and benefits of AML policy for individual institutions, because this might determine their incentive to cooperate.[10]

It turns out to be hard to gather sufficient statistics—or to make reasonable estimates—for all EU member states and all components. For most components, statistics can be gathered only for some countries, and the countries for which statistics exist differ from component to component. Because this variation rules out a comprehensive cost-benefit analysis, we make a cost-benefit analysis for a hypothetical country which combines the information that was gathered for 27 EU Member States. To correct the statistics for size and price level, our hypothetical country has a population of 10 million people and a price level of 100. The average population in the EU-27 is around 18.5 million, but since a number of countries have a population around 10 million (BE, CZ, EL, HU and PT),[11] we choose this nicely rounded number for our hypothetical country. The international price level statistics normally take the level of the US as 100. The simple average in the EU-27 is only about 5% lower. Bulgaria has the lowest price level in the EU with 53, while Denmark is the highest with 146. The price level of Greece is the closest to the price level of our hypothetical country with 98.5.[12] The calculation will involve all the possible statistics available for every component of the cost-benefit analysis and are corrected to match the size and price level of our hypothetical country.[13] Consequently, we take the average of the statistics available as our best estimate and use the lowest and highest statistics to indicate the bandwidth of the estimations. Although such a procedure does not meet the standards for a cost-benefit analysis,[14] it allows us to illustrate the order of magnitude of the different statistics and show the components without available statistics.

The Costs of AML Policy

Ongoing Policy Making

Since the set-up costs are omitted (see discussion above), we only consider the ongoing policy making costs. Normally this consists only of some policy staff at the relevant ministry. Estimations of these costs are often hindered by the fact that the policy staff are not only responsible for anti-money laundering policy, which makes estimation necessary of their time spent on anti-money laundering policy.

To find out the level of these costs in the 27 Member States, we asked the relevant ministries the following question in an online survey and in a personal interview if the online survey was not answered.[15]

What is the overall budget for the year 2010 at your Ministry (and other ministries, if applicable) for AML/CTF[16] policy? (please provide the overall budget which includes personnel and specify the currency, in case you do not have a statistic, please estimate the amount and indicate this with an asterisk (*) behind the number)

What is the number of staff dedicated full time (or full-time equivalent) on money laundering and terrorist financing matters at your Ministry (and other Ministries, if applicable)?

The responses of the countries are shown in Table 14.2 below.[17]

The initial idea was to estimate the budget based on the data on the number of staff for the last couple of countries that were unable to answer this question. Unfortunately, the data we gathered here falls far short of what is necessary to make such estimations. We are left with three relevant answers that can be used to estimate the ongoing policy making costs for our hypothetical country: €75,000 in Estonia, €980,000 in Ireland and €131,194 in Sweden. Hence, when corrected for the price level and size of these countries, our best estimate for ongoing policy costs for our hypothetical country is €896,754 with a bandwidth of €116,762–€1,813,000.[18]

FIU

Each Member State has set up an FIU to receive reports on money laundering and terrorist financing suspicions from banks and other reporting institutes. Since the FIU is focused on AML/CTF, we should count all costs of the FIU

Table 14.2 Budget and staff of the relevant ministry or ministries

	AML/CTF Budget Ministry	AML/CTF Staff Ministry
Austria		
Belgium		
Bulgaria		
Cyprus		
Czech Republic		
Denmark		4
Estonia	75,000	2
Finland		
France		
Germany		
Greece		
Hungary		3
Ireland	980,000*	15
Italy	11,168,506#	128#
Latvia		
Lithuania		
Luxembourg		
Malta		
Netherlands		5
Poland		
Portugal		3
Romania		
Slovakia		
Slovenia		16
Spain		
Sweden	131,194	1.2
UK		6

#The figures for Italy on the budget of and staff in the Ministry are for a department that is also responsible for policy against usury, corruption, financial embargoes and related international cooperation

and can therefore derive a good estimation of these costs from the budget of the FIU. We have data on the budget of the FIU for 11 EU Member States as in Table 14.3.

After correcting for the size and price level in our hypothetical country, our best estimate for FIU costs for our hypothetical country is €2,892,349 with a bandwidth of €685,460–€9,860,636.

Supervision

The supervision costs for AML/CTF policy are rather difficult, because each supervisor has AML/CTF as just one of its supervision tasks. Moreover, the supervision of the AML/CTF duties of the private sector is normally

Table 14.3 Statistics collected on the number of staff and the budget of FIU

Country	Staff (in fte)	Budget (in euros)
Austria	13 (in 2010)	
Belgium	45 (in 2012)	4,257,645
Bulgaria	32 (in 2011)	
Cyprus	21 (in 2011)	
Czech Republic	35 (in 2011)	1,429,473 (without IT)
Denmark	18 (in 2011)	No budget
Estonia	16 (in 2011)	
Finland	24 (in 2011)	1,565,000
France	73 (in 2009)	4,981,688
Germany	17 (in 2010)	
Greece	29 (in 2011)	1,500,000
Hungary	30 (in 2010)	1,000,000###
Ireland	11 (in 2011)	
Italy	104 (in 2011)	207,000 (only expenses)
Latvia	17 (in 2011)	341,490
Lithuania	10 (in 2011)	
Luxembourg	14 (in 2012)	
Malta	10 (in 2011)	330,107
Netherlands	56 (in 2010)	4,800,000
Poland	45 (in 2008)	
Portugal	30 (in 2011)	
Romania	96 (in 2011)	
Slovakia	30 (in 2011)	
Slovenia	18 (in 2010)	691,000
Spain	79 (in 2011)	11,000,000
Sweden	27 (in 2009)#	1,400,000##
UK	60 (in 2012)	

Source: statistics collected by the EU-funded ECOLEF project, via interviews, online questionnaires and regional workshops, except: # – FATF Mutual Evaluation Report Sweden 2009 and ## = FATF Mutual Evaluation Report Sweden 2006. ### = this figure is estimated using the overall budget of the CCIB; representatives of the Hungarian Ministry of Finance and the Hungarian FIU said that it seems to be a reasonable estimation
Fte full time equivalent

fragmented over different supervisory authorities based on the type of the institutions under supervision. This would normally not be a problem if we were able to get data for all the supervisory institutions. Unfortunately this is not the case. We asked all supervisors in all 27 EU Member States the following two questions via an online survey and sometimes also in a face-to-face interview.

What is the annual overall budget at your authority for supervising AML/CTF regulations? (please provide the overall budget which includes personnel and specify the currency, in case you do not have a statistic, please estimate the amount and indicate this with an asterisk (*) behind the number)

How many persons work in your organization in total in full time equivalence (so two half time employees count as one full time employee)?

The responses of the countries are shown in Table 14.4 below.

Because there is not a single country for which we have data for all the supervisors, we have to devise a way to make an estimation for all the supervisors in total. If we had a good way of knowing the size of the different supervisors in each country, then we would be able to estimate the share of a single supervisor for the overall supervision costs. The staff would be a good indicator for this, but this information is also not available for any single country for all supervisors. We therefore assume that all supervisors are of equal size and expect that, because we use an overall average, the extreme values counter each other out. This assumption would also be indicated by an increased bandwidth. After calculating the supervision costs for nine countries corrected for the number of supervisors and the price level and population of our hypothetical country, our best estimate for supervision costs is €14,332,941 with a bandwidth of €291,906–€112,200,000.

Law Enforcement and Judiciary

Although the total budget of law enforcement agencies and the judiciary is often published, separating the specific AML costs is hard. Many investigations and court cases have money laundering as just one of the crimes. The question then is, if money laundering was left out of the package of crimes that are investigated/prosecuted, how much money would be saved? Such a question seems to be impossible to answer. In the hope that some countries collect relevant statistics, we asked the following questions via an online survey and sometimes in face-to-face interviews.

What is the overall budget for the year 2010 for law enforcement in general (public prosecutor, police and other investigating authorities) in your country? *(please provide the overall budget which includes personnel and specify the currency, in case you do not have a statistic, please estimate the amount and indicate this with an asterisk (*) behind the number)*

Which share of the annual overall budget of law enforcement is spent on AML/CTF? *(Please provide us with an estimate of the percentage, and specify for different law enforcement authorities in case you think their share differs)*

What is the number of staff dedicated full time (or full-time equivalent) to money laundering and terrorist financing in law enforcement agencies?

What is the overall budget for the year 2010 for the judiciary in general in your country? *(please provide the overall budget which includes personnel and*

Table 14.4 Statistics collected on the number of employees and the budget of supervisors

Country	Budget supervisor	Staff supervisor	Number of supervisors[19]
Austria			7
Belgium	GC: 12,000,000	GC: 2	11
Bulgaria			4
Cyprus			7
Czech Republic	CTA: 30,000	CTA: <1, FIU: 5*	7
Denmark		BLS: 1	4
Estonia	FSA: 50,000–75,000*	FSA: 3*	4
Finland			9
France	ACP: 2,700,000	ACP: 14 control + 51 monitoring	11
Germany		CPA: <1	5
Greece		BoG: 13, HCMC: 4, PISC: 3	8
Hungary		TLO: <1	8
Ireland			13
Italy		BoI: 348*	7
Latvia	LGSI: 20,500	FCMC: 4, CSA: <1, LGSI: <1, SIHP: 5*	9
Lithuania			9
Luxembourg		CSSF: 5	8
Malta		FIU: 3, MFSA: 38	3
Netherlands	BFT: 2.2 mln, BHM: 1.5 mln	BFT: 15, BHM: 26	4
Poland	FSA: 250,000	FSA: 6, FIU: 7	7
Portugal			11
Romania			7
Slovakia			3
Slovenia		SMA:5	10
Spain		FIU: 10 full time + 17 part-timers	4
Sweden	BSEA: 54,664*	BSEA: <1, GB: <1	6
UK	OFT: 1.4 mln, ICB: 61,896	GC: 0.2, AIA: 0.2	28

Note: In France, the ACP has a designated 14 staff working exclusively on AML/CTF control and another 51 staff supervising and directing the on-site staff.[20] All budgets are (calculated) in euros. All staff measured in full-time equivalence. * indicates an estimation

CTA Chamber of Tax Advisors, *BLS* Bar and Law Society, *FSA* Financial Services Authority, *CPA* Chamber of Patent Attorneys, *TLO* Trade Licensing Office, *FCMC* Financial and Capital Market Commission, *CSA* Council of Sworn Advocates, *LGSI* Lotteries and Gambling Supervisory Inspection, *SIHP* State Inspection for Heritage Protection, *SMA* Securities Market Agency, *BSEA* Board of Supervision of Estate Agents, *GB* Gaming Board, *BoG* Bank of Greece, *HCMC* Hellenic Capital Market Commission, *PISC* Private Insurance Supervision Committee, *BoC* Bank of Cyprus (not to confuse with the Central Bank of Cyprus), *BoI* Bank of Italy, *MFSA* Malta Financial Services Authority, *BFT* Bureau Financieel Toezicht, *GC* Gambling Commission, *AIA* Association International Accountants, *OFT* Office of Fair Trading, *ICB* Institute of Certified Bookkeepers, *CSSF* Commission de Surveillance du Secteur Financier *specify the currency, in case you do not have a statistic, please estimate the amount and indicate this with an asterisk (*) behind the number. In case you have difficulties to estimate this, keep in mind that the percentage of time the staff spends on AML/CTF might be a good benchmark)*

Which share of the annual overall budget of the judiciary is spent on AML/CTF? *(Please provide us with an estimate of the percentage. In case you have difficulties to estimate this, keep in mind that the percentage of time the staff spends on AML/CTF might be a good benchmark)*

What is the number of staff dedicated full time (or full-time equivalent) to money laundering and terrorist financing in the judiciary?

The responses of the countries are shown in Table 14.5 below.

Although we captured the overall budget for law enforcement agencies and judiciary for some countries, the amount spent on AML/CTF was available in none. In Hungary, spending by the police was revealed, but the amount spent by the public prosecutor's office is missing. We therefore assume that the amount spent on AML/CTF is proportional to the overall spending of the police and the public prosecutor. In Hungary, 7.57 times more is spent by the police than by the PPO. Using this proportion, we derived an (very rough) estimate for our hypothetical country on the amount spent by LEAs to fight money laundering of €1,423,565. If we use, with the same reasoning, the fact that the amount spent by the judiciary is about 28% of the spending by LEAs, our estimate for the amount spent by the judiciary on AML/CTF is €400,245.

Sanction Costs (Repressive)

AML policy has two types of sanctioning: preventive and repressive parts of the policy. The sanctions in the preventive part of the policy are the sanctions against banks and other reporting institutions for not performing their AML duties appropriately. Since these are normally imposed by the supervisors of these reporting institutions, these costs are not considered here to prevent double counting. The sanctions in repressive policy are the sanctions against the money launderers. The main costs here are probably the prison costs for locking up the money launderers, but we can also consider costs for going after money launderers to pay their fines for example. We assume that these costs are relatively low.

To have some basis for estimation, we asked the following questions via an online survey and sometimes in face-to-face interviews.

What is the average imprisonment duration regarding sanctions for natural persons for the offence of money laundering in practice? *Please estimate if you do not have statistics and indicate this with an asterisk (*) after the number.*

Table 14.5 Statistics collected on the number of employees and budget for LEAs and judiciary

Country	Budget LEA	AML/CTF budget LEA	Staff LEA	Budget judiciary	AML/CTF budget judiciary	Staff judiciary
Austria						
Belgium						
Bulgaria						
Cyprus						
Czech Republic						
Denmark						
Estonia	194,778,068			25,035,612		
Finland						
France						
Germany						
Greece						
Hungary	880,270,081	ML police: 658,664 TF police: 220,675		247,494,010		
Ireland	1,485,805,000			134,000,000		
Italy						
Latvia						
Lithuania						
Luxembourg						
Malta						
Netherlands	3,616,600,000			315,800,000		
Poland						
Portugal						
Romania						
Slovakia			31			
Slovenia						
Spain						
Sweden	4,162,982,320			578,191,989		
UK						

- Suspended imprisonment
- Unsuspended imprisonment

What is the average imprisonment duration regarding sanctions for natural persons for the offence of terrorist financing in practice? *Please estimate if you do not have statistics and indicate this with an asterisk (*) after the number.*

- Suspended imprisonment
- Unsuspended imprisonment

The responses of the countries are shown in Table 14.6 below.

Only unsuspended imprisonment is taken to be relevant for our estimation of the prison costs. An estimate of the costs for keeping a criminal in prison for a day can be found, but an important proviso here is to consider whether

Table 14.6 Statistics collected on the average imprisonment for money laundering and terrorist financing

Country	Suspended imprisonment ML	Unsuspended imprisonment ML	Suspended imprisonment TF	Unsuspended imprisonment TF
Austria	6 months*	12 months*	0 years*	3 years*
Belgium	2 years*	2 years*		
Bulgaria				
Cyprus				
Czech Republic				
Denmark				
Estonia	3.8 year*	3.8 year*		
Finland				
France				
Germany				
Greece				
Hungary				
Ireland	1 year*	3 year*		
Italy				
Latvia				
Lithuania				
Luxembourg				
Malta				
Netherlands				
Poland				
Portugal				
Romania				
Slovakia				
Slovenia				
Spain				
Sweden				
UK	40 months*	40 months*		

Note: Belgium, Estonia and UK did not differentiate between suspended and unsuspended in their answers

this criminal would also be in prison if not convicted for money laundering? This question seems impossible to answer, because money laundering is often only one of the offences for which the defendant is convicted. In Ireland the representatives of anti-money laundering policies indicated to the researchers that they normally do not add money laundering to a prosecution which also involves the predicate crime because this complicates the case needlessly. Furthermore, in countries where self-laundering is not criminalized, we would expect that money laundering prosecutions and convictions do not include the predicate crime. Unfortunately, none of these countries was able to answer our questions on the average duration of imprisonment. We therefore only have the Irish estimate to work with. According to the Irish Prison

Service[21] the average annual cost to incarcerate a person in a prison in 2009 was €77,222 and since Irish representatives indicated an average unsuspended imprisonment for money laundering of 3 years, a money laundering conviction costs on average an estimated €231,666. The average number of convictions in Ireland is five per year in the period 2005–2010. This means that the annual prison costs for Ireland would be estimated at €1,158,330, which means that, correcting for size and price level, the very rough estimate based on only one observation for our hypothetical country is €2,142,911.

Duties of the Private Sector

This component comprises all the costs incurred by reporting institutions in fulfilling the duties required by the Third EU Money Laundering Directive. These costs seem to receive most attention in the literature. In relation to the private sector, Alexander states that these costs comprise:

> those tangible operational costs that relate to investments that institutions will make in the form of physical and human capital required to carry out the compliance function. This is a task based on the assumption that laundering activity will be evidenced via some unusual account transaction that the banks will be able to detect through their 'inside knowledge' of all financial transactions. It is without a doubt an immense task to pick out the illegal from the multitude of legitimate financial transactions that pass through the system. [22]

Harvey mentions that 'many costs of compliance are not additional but are part of due diligence activity'.[23] A PricewaterhouseCoopers report notes that 'the costs of AML to a firm will vary enormously between different industry sectors'. [24]

We explore three ways to estimate these costs. Our first intuitive approach is in line with how we calculate most of the components for this cost-benefit analysis. We asked a number of reporting institutions in every Member State to answer the following two questions.

> How much does it cost, on average, to file one report to the FIU? *(This figure should include all possible costs related to filing a report, like personnel, material etc. Please specify per type of report, the currency and in case you do not have a statistic, please estimate the amount and indicate this with an asterisk (*) behind the number)*
>
> How much do you spend annually on total training costs (and compliance systems, if applicable) for AML/CTF policy? *(Please specify the currency and in case you do not have a statistic, please estimate the amount and indicate this with an asterisk (*) behind the number)*

The responses of the countries are shown in Table 14.7 below.

There are several reasons why it is hard to use these answers to derive an estimation of these costs. First of all, the response rate is very low.[25] Second, there is a clear incentive to overestimate the amount. Third, it is hard to extrapolate from the costs for one institution to an estimate for the whole sector, and even more complicated to estimate for all reporting entities in a certain country. We therefore explored a second approach which relied on earlier estimates from a cost-benefit analysis in the UK. This cost-benefit analysis was attached to the Money Laundering Regulations 1993 and consisted of only the costs and benefits for the reporting institutions. The results of this cost-benefit analysis are estimates for the total amount of costs for different type of companies: a large building society, a large unit trust and

Table 14.7 Statistics collected on the institutional costs of AML/CTF

	Filing a report, OE	Training costs, OE
AT		
BE		
BG		
CY	450*	BoC: 90,000
CZ		
DE		Warburg: 20,000
DK		
EE		
EL		
ES		
FR		
FI		
HU		
IE		
IT		
LV	50–100*	
LT		Snoras: 110,000*
LU		
MT		
NL		
PL		
PT		
RO		
SK		
SL		
SE		
UK		

Note: BoC = Bank of Cyprus (not to confuse with the Central Bank of Cyprus). All budgets are (calculated) in euros. All staff measured in full-time equivalence. * indicates an estimation

PEP plan management company, a large life assurance/pensions company and a medium sized motor finance house. Unfortunately, these different types of companies do not come even close to covering all reporting entities in the UK or any other EU Member State. Moreover, there is no precise description of the characteristics of these types of companies, which makes it hard to classify companies in a certain country accordingly. We therefore tried to find a reasonable estimate based on literature research and found a report that estimated the total costs for reporting entities in the Netherlands for their reporting and identification duties at €40.1 million in 2007.[26] We then corrected this estimate for our hypothetical country to have an estimate of €22,055,000 for the duties of the private sector.[27]

Reduction in Privacy

The screening of all financial transactions to filter the ones related to money laundering, and the additional customer due diligence that is required from reporting entities, is—at least in theory—a reduction in privacy, which could be seen as a social cost of anti-money laundering policy. Geiger and Wuensch also mention a reduction in privacy as a cost of AML policy.[28] Whether this reduction in privacy is severe and how much it matters is extremely difficult to measure or estimate. We therefore do not explore such costs further.

Efficiency Costs for Society and the Financial System

The AML policy that is executed by banks and other reporting entities is focused on criminals, but also harms legitimate users/customers. The increased customer due diligence, for instance, is needed for all customers. Moreover, the financial transactions of criminals can be delayed for further analysis, but also other people might have their transaction delayed inadvertently. One could argue that the costs of the AML duties of reporting entities are passed onto their customer by higher prices, but this possibility is excluded here to prevent double counting since these costs for reporting entities were mentioned above. The efficiency costs for society due to AML policy can be substantial, but are very hard to measure or estimate. The delay of a financial transaction can have very severe effects (like stopping an important business deal), but can also be completely harmless (as when transferring money from a checking account to a savings account). The same holds for the intensified identification duties. It could for instance, hamper financial inclusion in Africa—because banking with a mobile phone requires an identification—but it could also be completely harmless if identification would be needed anyway (for instance when doing a real estate transaction through a notary). Other scholars mention these costs, but none has been able to estimate it[29]—except the study by Transcrime that estimated such costs for a small part of AML/CTF policy, namely the transparency requirements in the company/corporate field and banking sector.[30]

The Benefits of AML Policy

Fines (Repressive)

There are two types of fines in AML policy. One in the preventive policy, which are fines for reporting entities that do not comply with their duties, and one in the repressive part of the policy, which are fines for money launderers that are prosecuted and convicted. According to Harvey reporting institutions are usually fined for a lack of compliance rather than for complicity in money laundering.[31] The fines are benefits in the AML framework, but they are at the same time costs for reporting entities. Both components are relevant, and it is here assumed that they will always counter each other out, no matter the size and so no estimate is required. Hence, in this section we only consider the fines on money launderers in the repressive part of the AML/CTF policy.

On this aspect, we asked the following questions via an online survey and sometimes in face-to-face interviews.

> What is the average (criminal) fine for natural persons for the offence of money laundering in practice? Please estimate if you do not have statistics and indicate this with an asterisk (*) after the number.
>
> Does there exist corporate criminal liability, that is: the criminal sanctioning of legal persons, with regard to the offences of money laundering? If YES: What are the corresponding minimum and/or maximum of criminal fines?
>
> What is the number of administrative sanctions for money laundering on an annual basis between 2005–2010 (specified per year), and what is the number of natural persons and the value involved? Please estimate if you do not have statistics and indicate this with an asterisk (*) after the number.

The responses of the countries are shown in Table 14.8 below.

For many countries, it is unknown how often criminal fines are imposed, and since no information is available on the (average) amount, insufficient information exists to make an estimate here. For criminal fines for corporate

Table 14.8 Fines for money launderers and terrorist financiers

Country	Average number of criminal fines imposed per year[32]	Average height of criminal fines	Min/max criminal fines for corporate criminal liability	Administrative law sanctions
Austria	0.75	ML: 100 daily rates,[33] TF: 0		
Belgium				
Bulgaria	10			
Cyprus	0			
Czech Republic	7			
Denmark				
Estonia	0.33			
Finland	1.67			
France	6.67			
Germany	288.75			
Greece				
Hungary	1			
Ireland				
Italy				
Latvia	2.75			
Lithuania	0			
Luxembourg				
Malta	2			
Netherlands				
Poland	0.33			
Portugal	0.25			
Romania				
Slovakia	1			
Slovenia	0.5			
Spain				
Sweden	4.25			
UK	81			

criminal liability and administrative law sanctions, our data availability is the worst; not a single statistic for these fines could be obtained. Even if more statistics were available on the amount of the fines imposed, these totals are not necessarily benefits for our analysis, because we do not know whether these fines are actually paid.

Confiscated Proceeds

Once a money launderer is caught, the risk of confiscation arises, which is designed to take away the incentive of the criminal while generating income for the state.

Regarding confiscation, we asked the following questions via an online survey and sometimes in face-to-face interviews.

> What is the average amount of proceeds confiscated for natural persons for the offence of money laundering in practice? Please estimate if you do not have statistics and indicate this with an asterisk (*) after the number.[34]
>
> How many money laundering prosecutions have led to a conviction on an annual basis between 2005–2010 (separated per year), in how many convictions was confiscation of proceeds imposed and what was the total value? Please estimate if you do not have statistics and indicate this with an asterisk (*) after the number

The responses of the countries are shown in Table 14.9 below.

Three countries offered statistics on the amount confiscated from money laundering. These statistics show that the amounts differ greatly from year to year, so an average for the period 2005–2010 was taken to avoid these extreme values. The main question remaining is to what extent the proceeds would be confiscated if there would have been no anti-money laundering policy. Most of the convictions in these three countries are for self-laundering, which means that these proceeds might also be confiscated based on a conviction for the predicate crime. We therefore adjust these statistics to take this possibility into account by multiplying the statistics with the share of convictions for third-party money laundering.[38] After also correcting for the size and price level of our hypothetical country, our best estimate for the annual amount of confiscated proceeds is €474,294 with a bandwidth of €14,715–€1,039,896.

Reduction in the Amount of Money Laundering and Terrorism

Harvey concludes that 'there is presumed to be an inverse relationship between the degree of regulation and the amount of money laundering taking place. While there is theoretical support for this approach, it has not been empirically tested on a wide scale, nor has account been taken of changes in money laundering behavior resulting from changes in regulatory requirements'.[39] Equally, Geiger and Wuensch conclude that 'whilst this deterrence mechanism sounds logically reasonable, its effectiveness and efficiency for fighting predicate crime is doubtful'.[40] We were also unable to estimate to what extent this goal of AML policy is reached.

Table 14.9 Confiscation statistics for ML and TF

Country	Average confiscation ML	Average confiscation TF
Austria		
Belgium		
Bulgaria	2,870,200[35]	0
Cyprus	3,106,267[36]	
Czech Republic		
Denmark		
Estonia		0
Finland		
France		
Germany		
Greece		0
Hungary		
Ireland		0
Italy		
Latvia	2,849,213[37]	0
Lithuania		
Luxembourg		0
Malta		
Netherlands		
Poland		0
Portugal		
Romania		
Slovakia		
Slovenia		
Spain		
Sweden		
UK		

Effects of Money Laundering: Fewer Predicate Crimes, Reduced Damage Effect on Real Economy and Less Risk for the Financial Sector

The literature on money laundering mentions many indirect effects. A comprehensive literature review yields 25 effects of money laundering on the real economy and the financial sector, as indicated in Table 14.10[41]:

Money laundering can affect the real economy by distorting consumption, savings, investment, inflation, competition, trade and employment. Furthermore, money laundering can affect the financial sector with an increased risk to the solvency, liquidity, reputation and integrity of the sector. On the other hand, money laundering could also be good for the economy, because it increases the profits for the financial sector and leads to a greater availability of credit. Overall, the literature remains uncertain whether money laundering would have a net positive or negative effect on the economy in the long run.

Table 14.10 The effects of money laundering as mentioned in the literature

Effect	Source(s)
1. Law enforcement gets a second chance	Levi (2002) p. 182, Levi and Reuter (2006) pp. 292 and 349
2. Distortion of consumption	Bartlett (2002), Mackrell (1997), Walker (1995)
3. Distortion of investment and savings	Aninat et al. (2002), Bartlett (2002) p. 19, Camdessus (1998), Mackrell (1997), McDonell (1998) pp. 10–11, McDowell (2001), Quirk (1997), Tanzi (1997) pp. 95–96, Walker (1995)
4. Artificial increase in prices	Keh (1996) p. 5, Alldridge (2002) p. 314, FATF (2007)
5. Unfair competition	Mackrell (1997), McDowell (2001), Walker (1995)
6. Changes in imports and exports	Baker (1999) p. 33, Baker (2005), Bartlett (2002) pp. 18–20, Walker (1995), Zdanowicz (2004b)
7. More (or less) economic growth	Aninat et al. (2002), Bartlett (2002) pp. 18–20, Camdessus (1998), Ferwerda and Bosma (2005), McDonell (1998) p. 10, McDowell (2001), Quirk (1997), Tanzi (1997) pp. 92–96
8. Change in output income and employment	Bartlett (2002) p. 18, Boorman and Ingves (2001) p. 8, McDowell (2001), Quirk (1997), Tanzi (1997)
9. Lower revenues for the public sector	Alldridge (2002) p. 135, Boorman and Ingves (2001) p. 9, Mackrell (1997), McDonell (1998) p. 10, McDowell (2001), Quirk (1997)
10. Threatens privatization	McDowell (2001), Keh (1996) p. 11
11. Changes in the demand for money, interest and exchange rates	Bartlett (2002), p. 18, Boorman and Ingves (2001), Camdessus (1998), FATF (2002), McDonell (1998) p. 10, McDowell (2001), Quirk (1997), Tanzi (1997) p. 97
12. Increase in the volatility of interest and exchange rates	Tanzi (1997) p. 8, McDonell (1998) p. 10, Camdessus (1998) p. 2, FATF (2002) p. 3, Boorman and Ingves (2001) p. 9
13. Greater availability of credit	Tanzi (1997) p. 6, Levi (2002) pp. 183–184
14. Higher capital inflows	Baker (2005), Gnutzmann et al. (2010), Keh (1996) p. 4, Tanzi (1997) p. 6, Unger and Rawlings (2008), Levi (2002) pp. 183–184
15. Changes in foreign direct investment	Baker (2005), Boorman and Ingves (2001) p. 9, FATF (2002), Walker (1995)
16. Risk for the financial sector, solvability and liquidity	Alldridge (2002) p. 310, Aninat et al. (2002), Boorman and Ingves (2001) pp. 9–11, Camdessus (1998), FATF (2002), McDonell (1998) p. 10, McDowell (2001), Tanzi (1997) p. 98, Levi (2002) pp. 183–184
17. Profits for the financial sector	Alldridge (2002) p. 310, Takáts (2007), Levi (2002) pp. 183–184

(continued)

Table 14.10 (continued)

Effect	Source(s)
18. Reputation of the financial sector	Aninat et al. (2002) p. 19, Bartlett (2002), Boorman and Ingves (2001) pp. 9–11, Camdessus (1998), FATF (2002), Levi (2002) p. 184, McDonell (1998) p. 9, McDowell (2001), Quirk (1997), Tanzi (1997) pp. 92–98, Walker 1995)
19. Illegal business contaminates legal business	Alldridge (2002) p. 315, Camdessus (1998), FATF (2002), Levi (2002) p. 184, McDonell (1998) p. 11, Quirk (1997)
20. Distorting of economic statistics	Alldridge (2002) p. 306, McDonell (1998) p. 10, Quirk (1997), Tanzi (1997) p. 96, Zdanowicz (2004b)
21. Corruption and bribery	Alldridge (2002) p. 308, Bartlett (2002) pp. 18–19, Camdessus (1998), FATF (2002), Keh (1996) p. 11, McDowell (2001), Tanzi (1997) pp. 92–99, Quirk (1997) p. 19, Walker (1995), Levi (2002) pp. 183–184
22. Increase in crime	Bartlett (2002) pp. 18–22, FATF (2002), Ferwerda (2009), Levi (2002) p. 183, Mackrell (1997), Masciandaro (2004) p. 137, McDonell (1998) p. 9, McDowell (2001), Quirk (1997) p. 19, Levi (2002) p. 183
23. Undermines political institutions	Camdessus (1998), FATF (2002), Mackrell (1997), McDonell (1998) p. 9, McDowell (2001), Tanzi (1997) pp. 92–99
24. Undermines foreign policy goals	Baker (1999) pp. 38–39, Baker (2005)
25. Increase in terrorism	Masciandaro (2004) p. 131

Hardly any of the effects claimed in the literature have empirical support. Most of them are theorized, and some even seem to have no traceable source at all. Bartlett provides examples of this approach, with explanations like 'it is clear from available evidence', without ever mentioning this evidence.[42] Empirical research on the effects of money laundering is mainly hampered by the lack of a reliable estimate of the amount of money laundering in every country in every year.[43] Unger et al.[44] conclude that 'most literature on money laundering effects is pure speculation [...] one source refers to the other source, without much of an empirical solid back up'. Geiger and Wuensch[45] conclude—based on research of Baker,[46] Cuellar[47] and Bolle[48]—that the empirical evidence suggests that the relationship between detecting money laundering and an increased chance of detecting the predicate crime is only weak, if verifiable at all. All these effects of money laundering need empirical testing, but at this stage it is impossible to make any reasonable estimate for the size of these effects for our hypothetical country.

Conclusion

Table 14.11 summarizes the estimates for the annual costs and benefits in our hypothetical country. Most of the costs are possible to estimate, but hardly any of the benefits are. Consequently, the cost-benefit dilemma for AML policy is reduced to the question, 'Are we willing to spend almost 44 million euro with a reduction in privacy and efficiency costs for unknown benefits?' To answer with the words of Whitehouse: 'it would be a brave person who steps up to say that it is too high a price to pay for countering terrorism and serious crime'. [49]

Apart from the actual estimation of costs and benefits, this exercise also shows that the principal costs of AML policy seem to be the duties of the reporting sector and its supervision. In our estimation these two components are responsible for 84% of all the costs that could be estimated. Furthermore, we can conclude that the information available for a cost-benefit analysis is very limited (illustrated by the many components that are based on single estimates) and very diverse (illustrated by the wide bandwidths for certain components).

Table 14.11 Estimates for the annual costs and benefits of AML policy

Costs	Best estimate (bandwidth)	Benefits	Best estimate (bandwidth)
Ongoing policy making	896,754 (116,762–1,813,000)	Fines	Unknown
FIU	2,892,349 (685,460–9,860,636)	Confiscated proceeds	474,294 (14,715–1,039,896)
Supervision	14,332,941 (291,906–112,200,000)	Reduction in the amount of ML	Unknown
Law enforcement	1,423,565 (single estimate)	Less predicate crimes	Unknown
Judiciary	400,245 (single estimate)	Reduced damage effect on real economy	Unknown
Sanction costs (repressive)	2,142,911 (single estimate)	Less risk for the financial sector	Unknown
Duties of the private sector	22,055,000 (single estimate)		
Reduction in privacy	Moral cost		
Efficiency costs for society and the financial system	Unknown		
Total cost estimate	44,143,765 + 2 unknown	Total benefit estimate	474,294 + 5 unknown

Note: these are estimations for a hypothetical country with 10 million people and a price level equal to the US. The numbers are for illustration purposes only, since all estimates are very sensible to many possible biases and estimation procedures

Table 14.12 Estimates (in €) for the annual costs and benefits of AML policy for each country and the whole EU

Country	Estimated costs of AML/CTF	Estimated benefits of AML/CTF
Austria	39,331,650 + 2 unknown	422,591 + 5 unknown
Belgium	52,109,975 + 2 unknown	559,885 + 5 unknown
Bulgaria	16,697,035 + 2 unknown	179,398 + 5 unknown
Cyprus	4,749,348 + 2 unknown	51,028 + 5 unknown
Czech Republic	34,239,484 + 2 unknown	367,879 + 5 unknown
Denmark	35,545,389 + 2 unknown	381,910 + 5 unknown
Estonia	4,355,149 + 2 unknown	46,793 + 5 unknown
Finland	28,707,338 + 2 unknown	308,440 + 5 unknown
France	320,821,916 + 2 unknown	3,447,008 + 5 unknown
Germany	378,177,540 + 2 unknown	4,063,254 + 5 unknown
Greece	46,737,736 + 2 unknown	502,164 + 5 unknown
Hungary	30,925,483 + 2 unknown	332,273 + 5 unknown
Ireland	23,870,414 + 2 unknown	256,471 + 5 unknown
Italy	286,270,198 + 2 unknown	3,075,774 + 5 unknown
Latvia	7,480,286 + 2 unknown	80,370 + 5 unknown
Lithuania	10,304,206 + 2 unknown	110,712 + 5 unknown
Luxembourg	2,517,861 + 2 unknown	27,053 + 5 unknown
Malta	1,477,812 + 2 unknown	15,878 + 5 unknown
Netherlands	80,858,428 + 2 unknown	868,767 + 5 unknown
Poland	109,126,093 + 2 unknown	1,172,484 + 5 unknown
Portugal	44,676,164 + 2 unknown	480,014 + 5 unknown
Romania	60,662,875 + 2 unknown	651,780 + 5 unknown
Slovakia	18,516,679 + 2 unknown	198,949 + 5 unknown
Slovenia	7,404,790 + 2 unknown	79,559 + 5 unknown
Spain	201,599,523 + 2 unknown	2,166,046 + 5 unknown
Sweden	49,501,570 + 2 unknown	531,860 + 5 unknown
UK	260,394,648 + 2 unknown	2,797,759 + 5 unknown
EU-27	2,157,059,590 + 2 unknown	23,176,102 + 5 unknown

With the correction factors[50] used to correct the national data to the size and price level of our hypothetical country, it is possible to estimate the costs and benefits for each country in the EU-27 and for the EU as a whole, as shown in Table 14.12 below.

Notes

1. Joras Ferwerda, 'The Multidisciplinary Economics of Money Laundering' (2012) PhD Dissertation Utrecht University. See further Chapter 3 (Bergstrom) in this collection.

2. Personal experience from the EU-financed project ECOLEF in which we travelled to the EU member states to analyse money laundering policies and interview people involved in the fight against money laundering, such as

policy makers at the relevant ministry/ministries, public prosecutors, employees of the FIU, compliance officers and relevant law enforcement agencies. For a list of the formal interviews, see Unger and others 'Report' (see article note).

3. For an overview, see Chap. 2(2) of Ferwerda (n 1).

4. Martin Gill and Geoff Taylor, *Tackling Money Laundering: The Experiences and Perspectives of the UK Financial Sector* (2002) Report by the Scarman Centre, University of Leicester, 44. For similar issues concerning counter-terrorist financing, see Chap. 34 (Anand) in this collection.

5. Antony Whitehouse, 'A Brave New World: The Impact of Domestic and International Regulation on Money Laundering Prevention in the UK' (2003) 11(2) Journal of Financial Regulations and Compliance 138, 144.

6. Hans Geiger and Oliver Wuensch, 'The Fight Against Money Laundering: An Economic Analysis of a Cost-Benefit Paradoxon' (2007) 10(1) Journal of Money Laundering Control 91, 100.

7. These interviews and regional workshops were part of the EU-financed project ECOLEF (n 2).

8. Gill and Taylor (n 4) 44.

9. The data collection presented in this chapter started before Croatia joined the EU. Therefore, only 27 EU Member States are included in the analysis.

10. For such analyses, see Elöd Takáts, 'A Theory of Crying Wolf: The Economics of Money Laundering Enforcement' (2007) IMF Working paper 07/81 <www.imf.org/external/pubs/ft/wp/2007/wp0781.pdf> accessed 21 March 2017; Jackie Harvey, 'Compliance and Reporting Issues Arising for Financial Institutions from Money Laundering Regulations: A Preliminary Cost Benefit Study' (2004) 7(4) Journal of Money Laundering Control 333.

11. Population statistic from 2010 from Alan Heston, Robert Summers, and Bettina Aten, 'Penn World Table Version 7.0' (2011) Center for International Comparisons of Production, Income and Prices at the University of Pennsylvania. The values are also listed in Unger and others 'Report' (see article note) Annex 12(1).

12. Price level statistic (p) from 2010 from Heston, Summers, and Aten (n 11). The values are also listed in Unger and others 'Report' (see article note) Annex 12(1).

13. See Unger and others 'Report' (see article note) Annex 12(1) for these correction factors for each Member State.

14. The results can for instance be biased when certain costs or benefits are not proportional to population (because of fixed costs or economies of scale for example) or when the countries that provided data are not representative for the EU-27.

15. The online surveys and interviews were part of the EU-financed project ECOLEF (n 2).

16. Since the policies against money laundering and terrorist financing have a significant overlap and are often tied together (especially in terms of policy making), the question asked for the overall estimation of both. As a result, the eventual estimations could overestimate the costs of anti-money laundering policy.
17. Throughout this chapter, all values that are not directly derived from statistics but are estimated by the responsible authority are marked with an asterisk (*).
18. Calculation example of how these numbers are calculated: first the three relevant budgets are multiplied by the overall correction factors mentioned in Unger and others 'Report' (see article note) Annex 12(1). This means we have 3 estimates of this budget: 760,500; 1,813,000 and 116,762. The average of these three numbers is 896,754, which is our best estimate. The lowest (116,762) and highest (1,813,000) estimates indicate the bandwidth.
19. The number of supervisors is based on the specifications in the relevant law, inaccuracies can arise because of unspecified, regional and unclear grouped supervisors.
20. Financial Action Task Force, *Third Mutual Evaluation Report on France* (2011) 420 (footnote) <www.fatf-gafi.org/media/fatf/documents/reports/mer/MER%20France%20ful.pdf> accessed 21 March 2017.
21. Irish Prison Service, 'Annual Report' (2010) 4 <www.irishprisons.ie/images/pdf/annualrepo rt2010.pdf> accessed 21 March 2017.
22. Kern Alexander, 'The International Anti-Money Laundering Regime: The Role of the Financial Action Task Force' (2000) 1 Financial Crime Review 9, 11.
23. Harvey (n 10) 341.
24. Price Waterhouse Coopers LLP, 'Anti-Money Laundering Current Customer Review Cost Benefit Analysis' (2003) Report prepared for the FSA, 19 <www.fsa.gov.uk/pubs/other/ml_cost-benefit.pdf> accessed 21 March 2017.
25. To make a similar type of estimate for a cost-benefit analysis as the Annex of UK's Money Laundering Regulations 1993, the HM Treasury sent out 1000 requests, of which only 60 responded and of which only 1 respondent attempted to quantify these costs.
26. Brief van de Algemene Rekenkamer, Bestrijden Witwassen en Terrorismefinanciering, Tweede Kamer der Staten-Generaal, vergaderjaar 2007–2008, 31 477 no 1. This letter reports the estimate and cites another source, namely, Financiën (2007) Vaststelling van de begrotingsstaten van het Ministerie van Financiën (IXB) voor het jaar 2008. Tweede Kamer, vergaderjaar 2007–2008, 31 200 IXB, no 2. Den Haag: Sdu in which we were unable to find the cited estimate.
27. This estimate is probably an underestimation, since Institut der deutschen Wirtschaft Köln, Consult GmbH (2006) Bürokratiekosten in der Kreditwirtschaft, 9 estimates the costs for AML for the financial sector in Germany at €775 million (if we were to use that figure, the estimate for our

hypothetical country would be €93 million). Unfortunately, this report focuses on the financial sector only, and since there is no estimate for the other reporting institutions in Germany, we could not use this report directly for an estimation on our component 'duties of the private sector'.

28. Geiger and Wuensch (n 6) 98.
29. See for example Donato Masciandaro, 'Crime, Money Laundering and Regulation: The Microeconomics' (1998) 8(2) Journal of Financial Crime 103; Geiger and Wuensch (n 6).
30. Ernesto U Savona, Mario A Maggioni, and Barbara Vettori (eds), 'Cost Benefit Analysis of Transparency Requirements in the Company/Corporate Field and Banking Sector Relevant for the Fight Against Money Laundering and Other Financial Crime' (2007) Study financed by the European Commission—DG JLS <www.transcrime.it/wp-content/uploads/2013/11/CBA-Study_Final_Report_revised_version.pdf> accessed 21 March 2017.
31. Harvey (n 10) 338.
32. The average is over the period 2005–2010 for the years for which statistics are available. The statistics for Hungary are the answers from our online survey, the other statistics come from Cynthia Tavares, Geoffrey Thomas and Mickaël Roudaut, *Money Laundering in Europe, Report of Work Carried Out by Eurostat and DG Home Affairs* (2010).
33. The daily rate differs from defendant to defendant and is for natural persons 360th of the yearly proceeds, reduced or augmented up to 30% taking into consideration its overall economic situation. See IMF, 'Detailed Assessment Report on Anti-Money Laundering and Combating the Financing of Terrorism' (2009) Report 9/298 <www.imf.org/external/pubs/ft/scr/2009/cr09298.pdf> accessed 21 March 2017.
34. Initially the idea was to use this statistic in combination with the number of conviction to make a reasonable estimate for the total amount confiscated per year. However, this question was only answered by the countries that had exact and publicly available statistics on confiscation. Since there is no need to make an estimate when exact statistics are available, their answers for this question were not used in our research.
35. The amount changes considerably per year: 350,000 in 2006, 415,000 in 2007, 286,000 in 2008, 5,700,000 in 2009 and 7,600,000 in 2010, retrieved from Moneyval, 'Mutual Evaluation Report Bulgaria' (2011) 77–79 <www.coe.int/t/dghl/monitoring/moneyval/Evaluations/Progress%20reports%202y/MONE YVAL(2011)5_ProgRep2_BLG.pdf> accessed 21 March 2017.
36. The amount changes considerably per year: 5605 in 2005, 2,645,039 in 2006, 7,388,602 in 2007, 34,853 in 2008, 5,457,236 in 2009, the data comes from our online survey.

37. The amount changes considerably per year: 174,000 in 2005, 17,676 in 2006, 3,130,383 in 2007 and 8,074,795 in 2008, retrieved from Moneyval, 'Second Progress Report Latvia' (2009) 67–68 <www.coe.int/t/dghl/monitoring/moneyval/Evaluations/Progress%20reports%202y/MONEYVAL(2009)39-ProgRep2LAT_en.pdf> accessed 21 March 2017.

38. The amount confiscated then becomes for Bulgaria 175,000 in 2006, 207,500 in 2007, 11,400 in 2008, for Cyprus 0 in 2005, 0 in 2006, 0 in 2007, 1584 in 2008 and for Latvia 58,000 in 2005, 4419 in 2006, 0 in 2007 and 0 in 2008. Shares of convictions for third-party money laundering are calculated from Tavares, Thomas and Roudaut (n 32); when it is not possible to distinguish the conviction statistics between self-laundering and third-party laundering, we assume a 50–50 division between self-laundering and third-party laundering.

39. Harvey (n 10) 343.

40. Geiger and Wuensch (n 6) 92.

41. This overview is an updated version of the literature overview that has been published in Brigitte Unger, *The Scale and Impacts of Money Laundering* (Edward Elgar Publishing 2007) 110–113 and Ferwerda (n 1). Not in all sources it is clear whether the effects of money laundering are described, or also (or only) the effect of anti-money laundering policy.

42. Brent L Bartlett, 'The Negative Effects of Money Laundering on Economic Development' (2002) 77 Platypus Magazine 18.

43. Michael Levi and Peter Reuter, 'Money Laundering' (2006) 34 Crime and Justice 289, 294.

44. Brigitte Unger and others, 'The Amounts and Effects of Money Laundering' (2006) Dutch Ministry of Finance Report <https://pdfs.semanticscholar.org/06d7/b2a51b10c96018fd92fa5eec19f389304f52.pdf> accessed 21 March 2017.

45. Geiger and Wuensch (n 6) 94.

46. Raymond W Baker, *Capitalism's Achilles Heel, Dirty Money and How to Renew the Free-Market System* (John Wiley, 2005) 173–74.

47. Mariano-Florentino Cuellar, 'The Tenuous Relationship Between the Fight against Money Laundering and the Disruption of Criminal Finance' (2003) 93(2/3) The Journal of Criminal Law and Criminology 311.

48. Alain Bolle, 'Le Blanchiment des Capitaux de la Criminalite Organisee' in Ludovic Francois, Pascal Chaigneau, and Marc Chesney (eds), *Blanchiment et Financement du Terrorisme* (Sentinel 2004).

49. Whitehouse (n 5) 144.

50. See Unger and others 'Report' (see article note) Annex 12(1) for these correction factors for each Member State.

Joras Ferwerda holds a Bachelor in Economics and Law, a Master in Economics and Social Sciences and a PhD in Economics from the Utrecht University School of Economics in the Netherlands. He is Assistant Professor of the Economics of the Public Sector chair at the Utrecht University School of Economics. He is currently also a visiting scholar at the University of Maryland College Park Department of Criminology and Criminal Justice. He was senior researcher at the section Criminology of VU University Amsterdam for an EU-funded research project on risk models for money laundering.

15

A 'Risky' Risk Approach: Proportionality in ML/TF Regulation

Petrus C. van Duyne, Jackie Harvey,
and Liliya Gelemerova

Introduction: Risk, Protection and Proportionality

Looking back over the past half century, industrialised countries have gone through an interesting transition: from welfare state to a risk control society. One form of risky conduct most worrying to the authorities was the recreational use of psycho-active substances, a concern with long historical roots.[1] Correlated with this development was the stark increase of crime or, at least, deviant and risk-seeking conduct. To manage these risks requires action by the State; however, such intervention should be proportionate to the risks it aims to control.

Proportionality matters in the relationship between the government and the public. Though it is not operationalised, it evolves alongside political and legislative developments. However, in the field of money laundering, it is questionable whether this principle is met. A review of the Regulatory Impact Assessments for UK Money Laundering Regulations in 1993 and 2001 showed costs to be significantly understated and benefits unquantified, merely

P. C. van Duyne
Tilburg University, Tilburg, The Netherlands

J. Harvey
Newcastle Business School, Newcastle upon Tyne, UK

L. Gelemerova
University of Manchester, Manchester, UK

© The Author(s) 2018
C. King et al. (eds.), *The Palgrave Handbook of Criminal and Terrorism Financing Law*,
https://doi.org/10.1007/978-3-319-64498-1_15

promising sweeping protections for society.[2] This way of dealing with proportionality to justify enhanced measures reduces it to an empty formula. We are of the opinion that the proportionality principle is too important to be ignored, especially in the (global) anti-money laundering (AML) policy which since 2001 additionally encompasses the financing of terrorism. This regime has now been made more targeted by the new risk-based approach. The question is whether this approach has achieved the right proportionality.

The Risk Approach/Concept of the FATF

The anti-laundering policy has to address the risks connected with laundering in a commensurate way as formulated by the AML standard-setter, the Financial Action Task Force (FATF), in its guidance of 2007.[3] Earlier, the Third EU Money Laundering Directive of 2005 had introduced the concept of the 'risk-based approach' for the first time in EU criminal law.[4]

Risk management has long been associated with the insurance industry,[5] where it was relatively straightforward to assess the probability of events within a defined period, then to calculate the loss in the event that such incident took place. Apart from its tempting elegance, there were other reasons to adopt a risk-based approach in the AML world. One of the main complaints with the compliance regime was the costs that compliance placed on those subject to the rules. Compliance was carried out as 'rule based' and did not differentiate between levels of risks which was little cost-effective. It was understandable that banks were more receptive to a 'risk-based approach' as this was familiar language,[6] and they formed part of the group developing guidance to foster a common understanding of what the term actually meant. However, the FATF has opted for a 'soft' intuitive formulation of the risk-based approach that 'encompasses recognising the existence of the risk(s), undertaking an assessment of the risk(s) and developing strategies to manage and mitigate the identified risks'.[7]

Within normal banking business, 'risk taking' is the pursuit of profitable opportunity whereby the business risk being taken is assessed, measured and managed. By way of example, based on their prior experience, banks are able to calculate with a high degree of accuracy their loan-default ratio. Extending this approach, banks should be able to assess the probable number of transactions associated with criminal activity. However, two problems immediately present themselves. First, criminal-related transactions will not necessarily be loss making, so will not be observable from any historical loss database. For this reason, indicators and red flags have to be built up in more interpretative ways. Hence the criticism that banks can only truly observe what is *unusual*.[8] Secondly, when 'suspicions' are reported, banks express 'dissatisfaction with feedback on actions resulting from SARs'.[9] Such feedback information is essential for building a database and to accumulate knowledge.

What is evident is that, despite a common vocabulary, the interpretation of 'risk' within AML is fundamentally different. Within this context the phrase 'being at risk' points at some external and indeterminate threats.[10] The 'threat' justification lingers as heavy *ex post* justification for the AML policy. That general threat is now refined to the extent that 'resources should be directed in accordance with priorities so that the greatest risks receive the highest attention'.[11] A risk-based attempt to operationalise proportionality would mean that a high-risk threat would require greater resources and lower risk less resources. This is more than obvious, but unfortunately we are lacking any objective rod of measurement. The problem of the indeterminable delineation of low or high risk was soon recognised.[12] Naturally, this makes the implementation of this approach more complicated[13] or arbitrary. Without proper yardsticks, institutions must attempt to second guess whether their perception of risk will match that of the regulator,[14] resulting in what we might more accurately term *interpretation risk*.

This problem is aggravated by the way in which the two policy subjects are formulated, namely as 'ML/TF' or 'money laundering and financing of terrorism', as two concatenated sentence parts worded in a kind of repeated incantation. That formulation is repeated in follow-up or related policy papers making the expert community talk and write about 'ML/TF' as a kind of inseparable twin-phenomenon. But in every respect they are not co-joined: money launderers do not blow themselves up and if they do their job correctly, their activity goes unnoticed. Terrorists operate differently and do not need sophisticated financial constructions for the, often, small sums of money they consume. A US government report on the profile of the 11 September hijackers stresses that while terrorists can use proceeds from crime (such as fraud) and funds raised through charities, they can also use legitimately earned funds.[15] This lack of differentiation between two very different activities means that talking of 'being at risk from ML/TF' is meaningless.

Despite these caveats, the FATF made an attempt to clarify the concept of risk. For the purpose of ML/TF risk, the FATF proposes the following key concepts and formula: 'Risk is a function of … threat, vulnerability and consequences'.[16] At first sight this looks reasonably clear. However, the details of these three functions are not specified. *Threat* is all about actors or activities 'with the *potential* to cause harm' with 'past, present and future ML or TF activities'.[17] The concept of *vulnerability* 'comprises those things that can be exploited by the threat'[18] which may be any kind of weakness in the defensive system irrespective of the likelihood of its use. Then comes the component, *consequence*, comprising any 'impact or harm of ML/TF', including 'the underlying criminal and terrorist activity on financial systems and institutions, as well as the economy and society more generally […] short term or long term'.[19] Recognising that specifying the consequences of 'past, present and future threats, short or long term', requires sophistication, the report truncates the approach by allowing 'that countries may instead opt to focus primarily on achieving a comprehensive understanding of their threats and vulnerabilities'.[20] But what is the risk where threat is low and vulnerability is high, or vice versa? Despite this ambiguity, the risk-based approach is expected to ensure proportionality: effort commensurate to risk. This must prevent what is called in the next section the 'nut-sledgehammer effect'.

Save the Nut, Restrain the Sledgehammer

Proportionality is a commonplace concept and often applies without being noticed. We realise its absence when the opposite prevails: 'to take a sledgehammer to crack a nut'. So, how much of the present regulatory and law enforcement 'artillery' is justified by the facts and figures? This question is important as much criminal law policy development and enforcement is rather faith than fact driven: the fear of crime phenomenon in a time of decreasing crime figures, fanned by recycled statements and citations.

The Crime-Money Risk: Faith, Facts and Recycling

Obviously, the basis of all AML efforts is the supposed threat of crime-monies to the financial system and as a 'critical enabler of serious and organised crime, grand corruption and terrorism'.[21] The magnitude of the threat of crime-money is the first term of the equation of proportionality to which the measures of intervention must be proportionate. The evidence loaded onto the threat side of the scale was said to be '2.7% of global GDP or $1.6 trillion in 2009'[22]— this is discussed further below. The destabilising influence of crime-money is part of the ideology of the FATF, World Bank, IMF and the UN. According to this ideology, being obtained from crime, these proceeds cannot be accounted for. Without commercial rationale, they may be put into banks or be withdrawn, making the financial market volatile. Lack of rationality implies transactions to be capricious and, therefore, difficult to predict or control.[23] Warnings in no uncertain terms abound: enshrined in the supra-national regulations, we read that money laundering (and terrorist financing) 'shakes the very foundations of our society'.[24] It should be noted that this 'earthquake warning' was issued well before the credit crisis of 2008, which was unrelated to the presence of crime-money.[25] Have these 'earthquake warnings' been substantiated by solid empirical evidence? Attempts to put 'empirical building blocks' on the scale of the threat are anything but convincing: the methodology used is questionable, while the 'outcomes' from various assessments obtain their weight rather by the social mechanism of quoting and re-quoting until assumptions became facts. In this way, 'truth' is established by what is widely believed and not as a result of empirical evidence. For example, the first such 'estimate' was launched by the FATF in 1990. It was based on more or less hypothetical data of the UN Office of Drugs and Crime (UNODC), to which the FATF attached an equally hypothetical clause that 50–70% could be 'available for laundering'.[26] The semantic implication of the term 'available' has never been properly analysed and has always been taken as what *is* being laundered even if it is not the same. 'Available' is rather a synonym for 'in reserve' where nobody knows what will be actualised and when. Still, this formulation is frequently used to denote the volume of the threat of money laundering while it actually concerns what has not been laundered. In the UNODC 2011[27] report on illicit financial flows, we find the 'availability' phrase 168 times and sometimes refined as 'potentially available' or 'actually available' though without further clarification of this differentiation. Whatever their meaning, they do not contribute to a precision of the threat scale. Apparently the 'empirical building blocks' to measure the threat in order to attune a proportionate response are malleable from the start. That does not mean that a threat approach would be wrong per se, as long as one is sufficiently specific of what that threat implies. One can refer to 'harm' as a measurable effect of laundering and then look at the way the insurance industry solves the insurance against harm.[28] Twenty years ago, the IMF determined the crime-money flood was '2–5 percent of global GDP … probably [as] a consensus range'.[29] With that, two 'truths' were born: the 'consensus' and the '2–5% of GDP' range. Consensus between whom? There is no documentary evidence of it, but nevertheless until the present the alleged 'consensus', sometimes referred to as 'IMF consensus',[30] remains. For the crime-money flood the IMF produced its own evidence: Tanzi[31] and Quirke,[32] both from the IMF, hastened to provide some substantiation in the form of assumptions, flexible concepts, data from Interpol and many regression analyses all leading to the inevitable 'consensus range'. No assessment of the data reliability or the all-encompassing laundering definition, which notably includes legal but undeclared (non-taxed) work.[33]

Despite its *deus ex machina* origin, the 'IMF consensus' has led a tenacious life. Even consensus followers, such as Walker and Unger, call the figure a guess and point at the fact that it has not been replicated 'even by academics doing intensive studies within the Fund'.[34] Nevertheless, they also accept the IMF approach and most of its underlying assumptions. Other authors[35] are more critical and point at the inaccurate or flawed data, without much effect not even a debate.

The available meagre evidence is insufficient as a basis for finding a proportional risk-based counter strategy: proportional to what?

Laundered and Unlaundered Money: More Than Semantics

As previously discussed, the phrase, 'available for laundering', appears central notwithstanding its lack of operationalisation. We now look at its further implication: the existence of *un*laundered monies because not every opportunity is actualised. What does that mean and what is its risk or threat? Here we have several problems to solve going beyond semantics.

In the first place, we face an unsolved problem of delineation or defining where mere possessing of proceeds stops and laundering begins. When we look at the practice of law enforcement, we can observe that there is a pressure from the prosecution to stretch the coverage of the verbs 'possess' and 'hide' such that laundering begins from the moment of 'criminal ownership'.[36] Consequently, every profitmaking crime is laundering which negates the concept of 'available for laundering'. Some crimes by their nature contain laundering, and therefore the concept of availability would not apply.

This conclusion has implications for the elements of risk assessment: threat; vulnerabilities; and consequences. Even if we condemn the activity morally, is there a threat to the financial system when the money is laundered, given that it is included in the GDP, taxed and spent on licit VAT-taxed commodities?

Thus far, the threat scale of the balance appears filled with (often recycled) assumptions, unclear concepts and unreliable data.

The Rumbling Pot of Empirical Research

Despite the high political priority of criminal finances, empirical studies in this field are few and far between.[37] We have economic studies usually from the angle of econometric modelling and 'IMF consensus' following to a varying degree.[38] Next to that, we have behavioural research primarily carried out at the micro-level using data from criminal files, law enforcement databases or fieldwork, some of them testing the mainstream assumptions.[39]

By way of illustration of the problems faced, we discuss the studies carried out by Walker because these appear to have gained considerable attention. Beginning in 1995, they are based on a broad definition of laundering, a basic aspect of the methodology. 'Money laundering is the process by which illicit source moneys are introduced into an economy and used for legitimate purposes.'[40] This definition has an enormous range, encompassing also the 'percolation' of crime-money by means of mere spending. That is a choice one can debate or respect if it were not for the restrictive clause of 'used for legitimate purposes'. There are many definitions of money laundering.[41] Yet in many studies, the definition is unclear, and mentioning a definition at the beginning does not guarantee that the authors adhere to it during the rest of their exposé. Back to Walker's definition: spending money on legitimate objects for criminal purposes remains outside the circumference of laundering: for example, buying a smuggling boat or paying illegal migrant workers.[42] A serious flaw is, however, the extremely low response rate to the questionnaire on which Walker based his study: 28 responding agencies of which only eight mentioned a 'total laundered value' ('proceeded against') of which four could mention a conviction. There was no proper account of the competence of the respondents for making more than just hunches. According to Walker, his respondents estimated the percentage laundered per type of crime at mostly 80%, which is empirically unrealistic.[43] Nevertheless, it attained a high following from, amongst others, the FATF, World Bank and IMF, and that figure found its way into the economic model used in the project for the Dutch Ministry of Justice,[44] repeated in research by Walker and Unger[45] and in the ECOLEF project for the European Commission.[46] The model and findings were finally re-used in the UNODC 2011[47] report on criminal finances prepared by Pietschmann (STAS) and John Walker (consultant).[48] Thus methodologically questionable research that supports the previously mentioned 'consensus' becomes recycled and, in the absence of the researchers' original caveats, politically accepted.

The UNODC report did recognise the problem of definition, but did not solve it. Instead we find the earlier mentioned variations of 'availability' ('actual' and 'potential'). Notable is the phenomenon of 'fact framing' by means of what Van Duyne *et al.*[49] have called the 'indicative bias': sliding from the subjunctive modus of 'may', 'might' and 'could' (but also 'available') to the indicative modus of '*it is*'.[50] Once the suggestions have transited to the indicative modus they have become 'facts'. And having been endorsed by authoritative bodies, they are unassailable.

The last attempt to assess the money laundering threat was funded by the European Commission and carried out by Utrecht University.[51] The study is plagued by a lack of comparable international data which forces the research-ers to resort to 'proxy' variables with many unproven assumptions which generate hypothetical statements. Unsurprisingly, the 'availability' phrase slips into the conclusions this time in the form of 'launderable money as % of the GDP' for the EU and a selection of other countries. The foggy basis is again the unvalidated Australian estimation model with the indicative bias of 'may' slipping to 'is'.

Economic models may impress the unobservant, but only 'data on the ground' can clear the fog. That was at last achieved by Ferwerda, who went through the list of laundering's alleged negative effects on the financial system and looked for matching empirical evidence.[52] He found that evidence was lacking. He shared this experience with Reuter[53] who undertook a similar analysis. Worse, Ferwerda noticed that claims about the existence of evidence were untrue. For example, Barlett claimed that it is 'clear from the evidence' laundering distorts a long list of economic aspects (mentioning 12 in total).[54] Ferwerda checked this list and found no supporting evidence. Also this find-ing did not lead to any debate.

Connecting criminal statistics to reality remains difficult. Ferwerda[55] points at the double-counting problem that arises from counting money laundering in addition to the predicate offence in cases of self-laundering. This is confirmed by the authors' own research as well as by researchers coming to similar conclu-sions.[56] Schneider and Windischbauer criticise the over-reliance on 'scientifically doubtful' data[57] (regretfully with little learning effect in terms of valid data).[58]

Should we thus conclude that the whole crime-money scare was just a political mainstream hoax? Despite lacking evidence, there is still a danger of dismissing all warnings as 'crying wolf' while there are stray-wolves around. There are historical indications that investment in the real estate sector has resulted in local inflation.[59] Journalistic investigations indicate that much 'shady money' swarms in the London property market—'findings' that are included in government response documents.[60] However, for singling out money laundering as an endemic phenomenon with an indiscriminately dev-astating effect on the stability of the financial system, there is insufficient empirical evidence. 'Available' crime-money has to be compared with the effects of other money flows, for example, originating from migrant labour savings or financial windfalls from the oil or minerals extraction industry.[61] Macro-economically, these monies may have similar effects: Russia or Venezuela would be a good example in this regard.

Consequently, we are back to the AML regime as wielding a sledgehammer without knowing what nuts to crack. Obviously, if such an essential term is missing that does not contribute to answering the proportionality question.

The Risk-Based Approach and Proportionality

We may have to resign ourselves to the fact that the evidence of the crime-money threat is meagre and the deducted conclusions debatable. While the enforcement efforts are genuinely sizeable, the seriousness of the money laundering threat remains a matter of belief. How big? The total of all laundering has thus far only caused ripples in the water? Nevertheless, the FATF's approach has been like an old-fashioned broadside firing indiscriminately at all that resembles money laundering. Unsurprisingly, such broadsides always hit something, so that the FATF could always claim success, even if efficiency was far away.

As mentioned earlier, in 2006, the FATF established an advisory group (including banking and securities sectors' representatives) to investigate the risk-based approach to money laundering.[62] This group's *RBA-report* was adopted at FATF's June 2007 Plenary. The report detailed the principles for public authorities as well as financial institutions. The *RBA-report* recognises that each country and respective authorities should tailor its anti-laundering/TF regime according to its individual risks. Hence, no single risk-based model for all. The *RBA-report* recognises the need for flexibility, adapting over time and space and the undesirability of a 'tick box' approach just to be safe and to meet regulatory needs. The *RBA-report* even recognises that 'an over-zealous effort to counter the risks could be damaging and counter-productive, placing unreasonable burdens on industry and act against the interests of the public by limiting access to financial services for some segments of the population'.[63] In line with this observation, it admits that not all suspicious fishes can be caught.

The *RBA-report* is quite detailed in its indications of what kinds of risks are to be rated as low or high, in general as well as for various separate Recommendations. The *RBA-report* provides further separate elaborations for the public authorities as well as the financial institutions. It contains the specific elements for a national risk-based approach as well as for the financial sector. An important theme is the efficient allocation of resources proportionate to perceived risks, which goes through all the ranks, from governmental policy making to the individual account manager. The *RBA-report* does not suggest prohibiting institutions from getting involved in high-risk situations, as long as they have the right risk-mitigating strategies in place. Despite all the well-chosen advice and encouragement, it remains unclear what low- and high-risk factors are, and whether this is meant as a dichotomy: how many shades of grey are between low and high risk and how to determine what is a 'commensurate' action to mitigate risks? It remains an exercise in beating about the bush.

A year after the RBA-report, the FATF issued another report on risk assessment strategies: this time with respect to terrorism.[64] The ML/TF Assessment Strategies describes in general terms what risk assessment is and what it considers national threat assessments reports from ten countries plus Interpol and Europol. These are too diverse to summarise by way of abstract. It is unclear whether they are intended as national threat assessments or tokens of annual stock taking for the usual annual report of the national Financial Intelligence Units (FIU) or another public authority. Full of truisms, they add little value to the 2006 *RBA-report*.

Though the literature reveals no opposition to the concept of a risk-based approach, it took four years for it to become official through its integration into the list of new Recommendations (2012) and connected methodology (2013). In addition, in 2013 the FATF issued another guidance document (*National money laundering and terrorist financing risk assessment*).[65] How do we interpret this new methodology from the risk and proportionality angles?

Again, we have the imaginary 'scale' of resources versus risk. While the above discussed FATF documents refer to the RBA as a tool of resource efficiency at executive level (the financial and designated non-financial sectors), it does not consider the supervisory efforts. That is an omission: the risk-based approach must also be applied by supervisors. This is the implication of Recommendation 1: 'countries should identify, assess and understand risks and designate an authority or mechanism to coordinate actions to assess risks'. This means staff input at all levels of policy supervision and execution: national as well as sector-wise. To put it simply: the risk assessment requirement must be implemented at every step of the 'AML ladder', from government downwards to supervisors and further to the individual financial institutions and 'designated non-financial businesses or professions' in the form of notary or art dealer. One can in addition think of nominated coordinators or commissions at the level of ministries, FIU and recognised sector bodies and staff: the bureaucratic outgrowth accompanying every institutional innovation. That does not arise without expenses, all of which must be put on the 'effort scale'. The same applies to how FATF's effort is allocated.

The allocation of effort or resources must be guided by or weighed against risk assessment, which is the principle bringing greater efficiency by targeted actions.[66] The same meaning is repeated in the Guidance notes on the RBA set out in the FATF 2013 methodology.[67] This provides a further elaboration that discretion is extended to the country authorities to determine appropriate measures 'once ML/TF risks are properly understood'.[68] However, the 2013 guidance remained silent on how to achieve that. Instead, reference is made to nine sectoral RBA guidance papers[69] which lack specificity.

This brings us naturally back to the concept of risk. The FATF provides the formula that risk is a 'function of three factors: threat vulnerability and consequence'.[70] We discussed this earlier and concluded that it is not a very helpful formula. The formula is not repeated in the Recommendations or in the Methodology. Neither do we find a statistical approach to ML/TF risks. The Methodology explicitly states a number of times that assessment is not a statistical exercise, pointing to required flexibility and hence subjectivity in approach. We only find mention of 'low(er) risk', 'high risk' and 'risk' in general. Low(er) risk is very restricted and concerns basically mainly transactions with FATF-compliant institutions and countries, or public bodies. If a country decides not to apply (partly) certain FATF Recommendations, it must demonstrate that 'there is a proven low risk of ML/TF' or 'a financial activity (other than the transferring of money or value) is carried out by a natural or legal person on an occasional or very limited basis, such that there is a low risk of ML/TF'.[71] All else is 'high risk' and does not need to be proven.

In conclusion, there is a new approach with 'risk' as a central concept which is not delineated, except when there is a proven 'low risk', that only occurs in FATF-compliant situations or with recognisable insignificant transactions. And upon this accumulation of indeterminable concepts every country must build a national risk approach.

The Fourth Round: Evidence from 13 Mutual Evaluation Reports

There is no recent evidence of the functioning of the new methodology except what the FATF itself produces in the form of Mutual Evaluation Reports (MERs) in the fourth evaluation round. At the time of writing, only 13 countries have been evaluated.[72] In addition, the MERs provide only the opinion of the assessors: they are the spectacles through which we look at how the requirement of national risk assessment (NRA) has been implemented. This is important as we found that many evaluation teams take it upon themselves to challenge rather than support the view of national authorities. It remains unclear how their knowledge of national risk would be more accurate than that of the national authorities.

Of the countries mentioned in Table 15.1, the evaluations took place in 2014 and 2015 and the reports were accepted and endorsed by the FATF Plenary. We will elaborate on some of the findings which are relevant for our search of proportionality and the corresponding meaning of risk.

Table 15.1 Summary of mutual evaluation reports

Country	Year of MER	Pages	Number of evaluators	NRA in place	Application of NRA	'High risk' and vulnerabilities	'Low risk'
Armenia	2015	182	7	Yes	Not at executive level	Real estate and size of shadow economy	Terrorism
Australia	2015	198	10	Yes, but no national policy	Predicate offence priority	Non-financial Sector Drugs, fraud and tax evasion	Discussed, no specific areas. Review questioning of national assessment
Belgium	2015	213	7	Yes, but fragmented	Needs conversion into national policy	Diamond dealers Money transfer service	Consumer credit and finance leasing companies
Costa Rica	2015	169	8	In development	Priority predicate offence drugs.	Real estate, public corporations. Lack of casino supervision	Terrorism
Cuba	2015	186	9	All in place, but no STRs	Not clear	Drugs, embezzlement, bribery and fraud	*not an attractive place for ML/TF'*
Ethiopia	2015	105	7	In progress	Not applied	Corruption, tax evasion. Trafficking, humans and commodities vehicle dealers and real estate	Formal financial sector not attractive
Italy	2016	230	8	In place and general good understanding of ML risk	Applied but could be better!	Tax and excise, drugs and OC activities	Mainly process no sectors identified

Country	Year of MER	Pages	Number of evaluators	NRA in place	Application of NRA	'High risk' and vulnerabilities	'Low risk'
Malaysia	2015	211	7	Integrated RA into policies and priorities	FIs endorse RBA LEA: minimal outcome	Fraud, drugs and corruption	Counterfeiting and piracy
Norway	2014	206	10	Present but incomplete. No overarching policy	Priority predicate offences, not ML	MVTS, shipping, fisheries and labour markets	Report questioning of approach to identified low risk
Samoa	2015	187	8	NRA reasonable understanding, insufficiently shared	Needs resource allocation. No ML investigations	Remittance sector; domestic banking and IBC. Cross-border cash transfers and IFCs	No terrorism
Spain	2014	206	10	Good: identifying, assessing and understanding	In place but not always followed	ETA and terrorism; drugs, OC, real estate; MVTS	Operational— but lawyers criticised for self-perception as low risk
Sri Lanka	2015	170	8	NRA: reasonable understanding not followed by implementation	Sectors do not follow NRA. Predicate offences priority: 1 ML conviction	Drug trafficking Corruption and fraud	Negative— failure to prove low risk, report questioning of accountant's low risk designation

(continued)

Table 15.1 (continued)

Country	Year of MER	Pages	Number of evaluators	NRA in place	Application of NRA	'High risk' and vulnerabilities	'Low risk'
Vanuatu	2015	167	7	No proper understanding	Not yet completed and doesn't cover specific risks	International FIs; the remittance sector; TCSPs, currency exchange; casinos and gaming businesses	Failure to apply or identify and where they can do so, it is questioned

Source: Country Mutual Evaluation Reports can be found on the FATF website <www.fatf-gafi.org/publications/mutualevaluations/?hf=10&b=0&s=desc(fatf_releasedate)> accessed 8 December 2016

In the first place, there is the repeated FATF aim of 'allocating resources proportionate to the risks'. This applies to financial and economic sectors, to types of customers and countries such that most resources go to the highest risks. Does this also apply to the evaluation resources of the FATF: balancing its resources (staff and time) against the levels of risk posed by various countries to be evaluated? If that were the case, can we expect some ordering in the evaluation? For example, starting with the high-risk countries and doing the lower risk countries later?

In the second place, it appears that we have an unresolved meaning issue as soon as such a rank ordering of 'high–low risk' countries is suggested. This is more than semantics. Attempting to apply the FATF's own formula—risk is a function of threat, vulnerability and consequences—appears to be useless for any ordering or other application. The FATF Guidance had already dropped the component 'consequence' which is an essential external criterion. With the two remaining components, we observe that they are used loosely and often interchangeably, which makes their country-wise application most uncertain. These components can be examined as applied to a selection of countries with a small or less developed economy: Armenia, Ethiopia, Samoa and Vanuatu.

What ML risk do countries such as these pose? The first two countries, Armenia and Ethiopia, are described as financially isolated. Samoa and Vanuatu have off-shore services, but on a modest scale. These countries are each for differing reasons, technically vulnerable, even if hardly anything happens. Should these countries be inspected by a platoon of seven to eight experts for about two weeks, producing reports of 105–182 pages? This is a relevant question if we want to understand the nature of the output: for example, the Ethiopian MER of 105 pages drafted by seven evaluators and subsequently reviewed by six reviewers (three reviewers is more usual).[73] Questions like these cannot be answered from the FATF documents, whether from the methodology or the MERs themselves. For an efficient running of the mutual evaluations, these questions are highly relevant. For example, in cases of the conjecture 'vulnerable but no threat', a quick technical 'compliance scan' could be a sufficient evaluation.

The reverse can also apply: much threat of crime-money ('available' for laundering) but low vulnerability because the 'gates are guarded and the bulwarks manned'. According to the MERs, this seems to be the case with Italy and Spain, rated as enthusiastic appliers, a conclusion which required a 16-day on-site visit by respectively eight and ten evaluators. A virtually risk-free country is Cuba: no threat because of lack of economic freedom and a meticulous technical compliance in accordance with the general control intensity in the country. It took nine experts 12 days to reach that obvious conclusion.

Looking at this first batch of MERs, it is difficult to identify any consideration of resource allocation, let alone a proportionality of applied resources set off against risk. The number of evaluators is higher than in the third evaluation round, the reports are about the same length and it is hardly possible to determine any ordering according to the seriousness of ML or TF risk. In short, this collection of evaluated countries looks rather a 'random sample', revisited because it is once again their turn, rather than as a result of assessment of 'risk'.

In the following sections, we shall focus on what evidence of risk and proportionality the MERs bring forward.

Country-Wise Evidence of Risks and Proportionality

As remarked earlier, the proportionality principle applies at every level of the national ML/TF regime: from the highest policy-making body through to the notary, real estate agent or the dealer of high valued goods such as car dealers or antique shops. That means that, on all levels, allocated resources, mainly staff, must be commensurate to the risks they have to mitigate (Recommendations 1 and 2 and their interpretive notes). What do we learn from the 13 MERs?

In the first place, the evaluators must assess whether and to what degree a national authority and the obliged institutions 'identify, assess and understand the risks', whether this is expressed in a national risk-based assessment that is adopted by the authorities, the sector supervisors and obliged entities. This is not a costless undertaking. It requires broad institutional participation to put it in place and a bureaucracy to maintain it. This has to be justified by the 'identified, understood and assessed risks'. But what are the measuring rods? The answer is: there are none. Even if the formula put forward by the FATF was valid, it is decisively crippled by leaving the 'consequence' component out: a third of the gauge is missing and the remainder is badly formulated. Lacking criteria, the evaluators resort to an enumeration of the usual profitable crimes.

A second serious flaw concerns the underlying statistics. The FATF thus has failed to create the statistical instruments for identifying and analysing (part of) the threat. In light of the poor quality of statistics actually accepted (by the Plenary, but delivered by the evaluators and reviewers), we observe that the FATF itself is and has been consistently deficient on this essential point, thereby contravening its Recommendation 33. Consequently, there is no national unified database from which to learn quantified aspects of the assumed laundering threat. In the absence of sufficient data, a truly 'risk-based' approach is impossible.

In light of this observation, we can only look at the fragments of evidence of what is presented as 'threat'—acting like forensic archaeologists. But which fragments? We have: Suspicious Transaction Reports (STRs) and sometimes Suspicious Activity Reports (SARs), containing a number of transactions, then we may have investigations, prosecutions and convictions, possibly accompanied by asset recovery. Deducing any level of threat from these 'evidence fragments' is as speculative as deducing the colour of hair of a Neanderthal from an excavated little toe. Of the STRs we do not know the number of false alarms; of the prosecutions we do not know whether and how many cases were halted or dismissed or added to the main charge without registration. Some numbers concern cases, other prosecuted or convicted persons. So what do such statistical fragments of the studied MERs tell us? Looking across all of the reports contained in Table 15.1 above, we draw attention to the following as examples.

- The prosecution or conviction rates in nine countries were negligible or not available. Only Austria, Belgium, Italy and Spain have prosecution rates exceeding 100 for the latest available year (2013 or 2014[74]).
- Australia had from 2010 to 2013 on average 3658 convictions each year, of which 1444 for *receiving* offences only.
- Italy had 3189 convictions in 2013 of which 2472 (78%) concerned '*not the more serious crime*'; additionally, convictions for tax crime (1641) and corruption (91) not mentioned under the denominator of money laundering.
- Belgium has 268 laundering convictions for the year 2013, but 'a large number of cases are secured in domestic cases for *self-laundering*'.
- Spain, 'with a high level of understanding of its ML/TF risks', mentions that only 111 persons were convicted for money laundering, of whom 33 were for *self-laundering*.

We cannot deduce from these figures any valid interpretation of a ML or TF threat because the database reliability cannot be determined.

What remains of the fundamental requirement of connecting specific resources to identified 'high risks'? When we look at these 'high risks' as mentioned in the MERs, we see mainly the 'usual suspect' crimes: drugs, fraud, tax evasion and corruption for which we do not need highly qualified evaluators. For Belgium, one specific high-risk sector is mentioned by name—the diamond industry—not because a flow of related STRs reached the Belgian FIU but rather because not a single STR has been submitted, while the evaluators clearly thought there *should* be more! That looks like a strange working thesis: the less there is found, the more there should be.

National Risk Assessment and Strategy Evaluated

As mentioned before, developing and maintaining a risk-based national strategy in addition to a NRA is not a complete solution. Nevertheless, the idea of an all-encompassing national strategy may be over-ambitious or detached from the work floor: the prosecution service, the police and the obliged entities and their supervisors. It may also be the case that a national strategy is difficult to convert into the plans and actions tailored to the details of that work floors. Then a gap may develop between the overall, country-wide risk assessment and deducted strategy on the one hand, and what at the executive level is perceived as the 'real' threat on the other hand. Given the fact that strategy designing is demanding, is there valid evidence to justify such an undertaking for ML/TF?

It appears that most evaluation teams are strict about this first Recommendation which reads like a mantra: countries 'should identify, assess and understand' ML/TF risks and develop a risk-based approach or strategy. A mere summing-up of risks is, in the eyes of the evaluators, not enough as Norway learned. That country ordered its economic and environmental crime on a 'probability plus impact' scale, but the evaluators thought this insufficient for a risk-based approach.

So who did fulfil this requirement and who did not? Below we give a short outline of the evaluators' judgement, to which should be added that the MERs do not contain a short abstract or summary of the evaluated NRA or strategy: regarding this recommendation, the evaluators' judgement is far from transparent.

Fully Compliant

Spain was the only country rated as fully compliant. It showed a 'high level of understanding'[75] and used material from several sources, but yet it was not flawless: it had not brought these components into a single NRA. Nevertheless, it has a 'sound' AML/CTF strategy. Measured by output (for the year 2012), it mentioned: 204 individuals prosecuted and 111 convicted (33 self-laundering), which looks modest for such a high rating with so much effort.

Largely Compliant

Three countries were rated as largely compliant: Belgium, Cuba and Italy.

In the case of Belgium, a deficiency was observed concerning a requirement not found in other MERs: proactive spotting of trends and emerging phenomena. Otherwise the approach was judged as fragmented; there was no adequate ranking (also not mentioned in other MERs) of risks; and there are shortcomings at supervisory level. Still, the law enforcement output was considered high for the country: 268 convictions, but with many 'easy' self-laundering cases.

The MER of Cuba contained little comment on the NRA, except unclear prioritisation.[76]

At the time of reporting, Italy had not yet developed a national strategy. But that has no consequence: even without that important requirement Italy operated well and displayed a 'high understanding' (on most other points perfect ratings). Given this positive judgement what added value would a national strategy impart?

Partly Compliant

The rating of partial compliance was attributed to Armenia, Australia, Costa Rica, Norway, Samoa and Sri Lanka.

Armenia has made progress according to the evaluators, but it does not understand its risks sufficiently: for its NRA it uses convictions, which is not a proper basis ('dark' or missing numbers). Prosecution targets mainly domestic self-laundering cases, with no third-party ML involved. With 15 prosecutions in the last 5 years and 10 convictions, the 'turnover' of cases is low, dampening knowledge building: even a doubling would not be encouraging of extra investment in strategy building.

Australia has a 'good understanding' of ML/TF risks, but is inconsistent with FATF Standards as it focuses more on predicate crime than on ML. Australia has no policy setting out what is to be achieved and how to make clear what results from its efforts. Nor is it clear how the National Threat Assessment is used for further decision-making, again, an apparent evaluation team-specific requirement not mentioned elsewhere. Average annual convictions for 2010–2013 were 3658 of which 1444 were for 'receiving'.[77]

Costa Rica has carried out a 'national risk diagnosis' and is in the process of developing a national strategy, also for commensurate resource allocation. It displayed an 'appropriate level of understanding'.[78] However, the authorities have a clear preference for fighting drug trafficking with scant resources left for ML investigation in other profit generating crimes: 12 prosecutions and 9 convictions (3 acquittals).

Norway was another matter: according to the FATF it lacked 'a proper understanding of risk'.[79] Its NRA (February 2014) shows 'significant shortcomings ... and gaps in input and areas covered'.[80] Also, the priorities are not according to the FATF Standard as 'prosecutor and investigators view ML as an ancillary to the predicate offence',[81] which explains the low prosecution and conviction output, respectively seven and four for 2013, mainly for self-laundering.[82] Samoa displays a 'reasonable overall understanding'[83] for its domestic risks, but has not sufficiently understood the international (off-shore) threat. It also has not shared its NRA, undertaken in 2012, with the private sector, nor has it implemented a comprehensive risk-based approach for allocating resources, which are now devoted to predicate offences. Consequently, there have been no ML investigations, prosecutions or convictions.

Sri Lanka has 'a reasonable understanding of its ML risks',[84] which is not manifested in its national strategy, however. While its FIU gets sufficient STRs (718 in 2014), the prosecution thinks it easier and more cost-effective to prosecute the predicate offences. As a result, there are insufficient resources for ML investigations, and convictions are mainly obtained for predicate offences: three against one for ML from 2010 to 2014.

Non-compliant

Vanuatu and Ethiopia were rated as *non-compliant.*

Ethiopia[85] has only recently (2009) adopted a comprehensive law against ML and is still in the process of drafting its NRA and strategy. The emphasis within AML enforcement is on the flow of capital, in particular the outbound flow which is more of a concern than proceeds from other crimes, according to the evaluators' apparent amazement: 98% of the STRs concerned *hawala* banking which resulted in 32 convictions (March 2013–March 2014).[86] In Vanuatu, the preconditions for an effective AML/CFT system were not present: lack of understanding of risks; no political commitments, resources or skills in law enforcement and regulatory authorities. It has no ML/TF investigations, prosecutions and convictions. The drafting of an NRA is in progress. The country has been placed on the serious warning list.

As mentioned before, these 13 MERs are not considered as a representative sample for the MERs still to come. However, they are sufficient to raise questions.

While analysing these evaluations, the authors wondered how these could be interpreted against the FATF's own requirement of proportionality. Does compliance with the risk-based strategy result in more results, for example, more STR reports or 'mitigation' of ML risks? This question is not raised and even if it had been, none of the MERs are able to answer it. The fuzzy concept formulation of risk, its inconsistent and often ritualistic use in the texts, and the lack of budget data does not provide much that is concrete. Measurement by law enforcement output is methodologically not possible—not even by the best evaluated country for Recommendation 33 (statistics): a 'fully met—C' for Malaysia, illustrating rather the lack of statistical knowledge of the evaluators. The many frequency tables Malaysia produced cannot be taken as an integrated database for a systematic and detailed analysis.

Conclusion and Discussion

In the introduction, we raised the question whether and to what extent the (global) AML regime based on the new risk assessment approach is proportionate to the threat it intends to fight: is the balance between target and resources appropriate? This question (besides concerns about FATF accountability) is difficult to answer, in the first place because of concept incoherence. The FATF truncated its own risk definition by cutting out the essential component 'consequences' without explaining how this changed the whole risk concept. But why should we deal with risks if we are told: 'Don't bother about the consequences if such events happen'? It takes the rationality out of the risk approach: to our knowledge there is no insurance company which would operate on this risk basis.

Despite this fundamental flaw, the FATF has persevered with its risk-based approach, which can be considered as politically consistent, but not as a token of coherence. The FATF failed to address essential questions. Since 2006/7, it has demanded NRAs. But is there evidence of its added value? Is it too early to raise this question? That depends on the countries. Most of the industrialised countries have maintained for many years a mature AML system, underpinned by considerable experience. In our sample, these are Australia, Belgium, Italy and Spain. For these countries, the question should be raised: what will the NRA approach add to the way money laundering has been tackled in the years before and in case of proven added value, will it be proportionate to the additional efforts? For each country, this question should have been raised.

Addressing this question exposes a fundamental flaw: there is no valid baseline or zero measurement from where to assess the added value of an 'extra' risk-based performance. Rather, this requirement has not even been mentioned. True, it is no easy task and requires a database building and a subsequent step-by-step cross-breakdown of data. Rather than be considered as some outlandish undertaking, it will create transparency: the evaluators did mention the relevant variables for such an analysis, but without realising their importance. Naturally, all this presupposes data discipline: reliability and a *clean* database. Clean governmental databases are the exception rather than the rule. In this field, there is one variable for which reliability really matters: the *seriousness* rating. If we want to give meaning to the use of the words commensurate or proportionality, we must know the seriousness of the individual laundering case for further aggregation,[87] not of the general phenomenon which is more or less an ideological issue. This precision is not what we found. The MERs mention for various countries that most of their laundering prosecutions concern 'easy' or small cases, mainly of self-laundering. These are interesting observations, but no more than rough indications. In this unspecified wording, they further decrease the explanatory value of the 'seriousness variable' which for measurement purposes can be considered as 'polluted'.

As remarked before and by way of conclusion, we agree that knowing risks and outlining a strategy are valuable features in all policies, but we also observe that there is no evidence that the NRA yields an added value proportionate to all the efforts.

The MERs brought another issue to the fore, which looks like another dimension, but is nevertheless connected: the national sovereignty in designing a national strategy in which priorities are determined according to a rational weighing of national interests. This came to the open with three criminal law policy aspects: the prioritisation of predicate offences, confiscation prospects and self-laundering. Most of the evaluated countries addressed money laundering as an ancillary to the profit making predicate offence that is more often the source of real public concern than laundering itself. Given the sovereignty of criminal law, should countries be criticised for a policy of predicate crime prioritisation? This question has consequences for further priority setting, for example, the preference for cases with 'easy confiscation' with sufficient proceeds, as was expressed by the Belgian public prosecution office. Why should the local authorities be blamed for such a rational policy: get the crime money first? Moreover, is it the business of the FATF to comment on this legitimate choices? Otherwise, with scarce resources it may be rational to process easy cases first, such as self-laundering. (At least it 'feeds statistics'.) This leads to an ironic outcome: the FATF has consistently blamed countries for not criminalising self-laundering (explicitly mentioned in the MER of Italy[88]). Now that most countries have criminalised this built-in form of money laundering, the FATF notices with irritation that police and prosecution have developed quite a taste for these 'easy' cases. On the other hand, the FATF (or its evaluators) would have reason for reproach if the criminalised self-laundering did not lead to more prosecution.

Does this self-laundering and easy cases issue distract us from the NRA and proportionality discussion? No, it is an inherent part of it, because the risk approach should contribute to a 'proportionate allocation of resources': low risks to be addressed with a lighter touch, 'high risks' with the 'heavy artillery'. Given the mentioned FATF pressure for criminalisation with all political force, it cannot be but 'high risk'. Hence, it is inappropriate for the evaluators to complain about the high prevalence of self-laundering unless the FATF repudiated its historical stand on this point.

Directly connected is the point of tax evasion and self-laundering. Tax crime is now a predicate offence for laundering with a 'built-in' self-laundering because of *disguising* (with the tax form) and *possession* (of the results). Proof of the former is at the same time proof of the latter: 'canned laundering' according to Van Duyne *et al.*[89] These are the easy cases preferred by the prosecution while according to the FATF they form a 'high-risk' category. Therefore, applying the FATF rules, there is no ground for criticism. Or should this category rather be reduced to 'low risk' because the system may become clogged by a too enthusiastic prosecution service 'feeding its ML-statistics'? So, what indeed is high and low risk?

Returning to the relationship between risk and proportionality, it looks so simple and it is so easily written down in the FATF guidelines, recommendations and other policy papers. However, as soon as one has to spell out all implications and ramification, it proves to be more complex. The FATF has failed to unravel this complexity, saddling the global AML community with a defectively elaborated and immature approach.

Notes

1. Petrus C van Duyne and Michael Levi, *Drugs and Money. Managing the Drug Trade and Crime Money in Europe* (Routledge 2005); Walter Laqueur, *Europe Since Hitler* (Harmondsworth 1970); Ben Whitaker, *The Global Connection: The Crisis of Drug Addiction* (Jonathan Cape 1987).
2. Jackie Harvey, 'Compliance and Reporting Issues Arising for Financial Institutions from Money Laundering Regulations: A Preliminary Cost benefit study' (2004) 7(4) Journal of Money Laundering Control 333.
3. Financial Action Task Force, 'Guidance on the Risk-Based Approach to Combating Money Laundering and Terrorist Financing' (2007) <www.fatf-gafi.org/media/fatf/documents/reports/High%20Level%20Principles%20and%20Procedures.pdf> accessed 8 March 2017.

4. Ester Herlin-Karnell, *The Constitutional Dimension of European Criminal Law* (Bloomsbury Publishing 2012).

5. Georges Dionne, 'Risk Management: History, Definition, and Critique, HEC Montreal—Department of Finance' (2013) 16(2) Risk Management and Insurance Review 147.

6. This quantitative assessment to risk is familiar territory for the banking sector under the Basel Accords <www.bis.org/bcbs/basel3.htm> accessed 11 August 2016.

7. FATF (n 3) 2.

8. Gilles Favarel-Garrigues, Thierry Godefroy, and Pierre Lascoumes, 'Sentinels in the Banking Industry: Private Actors and the Fight Against Money Laundering in France' (2008) 48(1) British Journal of Criminology 1; Michael Levi and Peter Reuter, 'Money Laundering' (2006) 34(1) Crime and Justice 289; Martin Gill and Geoff Taylor, 'Can Information Technology Help in the Search for Money Laundering? The Views of Financial Companies' (2003) 5(2) Crime Prevention and Community Safety: An International Journal 39.

9. Jackie Harvey, 'Just How Effective is Money Laundering Legislation?' (2008) 21(3) Security Journal 189, 211.

10. Dionysios S Demetis and Ian O Angell, 'The Risk-Based Approach to AML: Representation, Paradox, and the 3rd Directive' (2007) 10(4) Journal of Money Laundering Control 412.

11. FATF (n 3) 2.

12. Amongst others, by Marcus Killick and David Parody, 'Implementing AML/ CFT Measures that Address the Risks and not Tick Boxes' (2007) 15(2) Journal of Financial Regulation and Compliance 210; Louis de Koker, 'Identifying and Managing Low Money Laundering Risk' (2009) 16(4) Journal of Financial Crime 334; Stuart Ross and Michelle Hannan, 'Money Laundering Regulation and Risk-Based Decision-Making' (2007) 10(1) Journal of Money Laundering Control 106.

13. Lishan Ai, John Broome, and Hao Yan, 'Carrying Out a Risk-Based Approach to AML in China: Partial or Full Implementation?' (2016) 13(4) Journal of Money Laundering Control 394; Maria Bergström, Karin Helgesson, and Ulrika Morth, 'A New Role for For-Profit Actors?: The Case of Anti-Money Laundering and Risk Management' (2011) 49(5) Journal of Common Market Studies 1043.

14. Demetis and Angell (n 10); Liliya Gelemerova, 'On the Frontline Against Money-Laundering: The Regulatory Minefield' (2009) 52(1) Crime, Law and Social Change 33.

15. DM Lormel, Chief Financial Crimes Section, FBI Federal Bureau of Investigation before the House Committee on Financial Services, Subcommittee on Oversight and Investigations (2002) <www.fbi.gov/news/testimony/ financing-patterns-associated-with-al-qaeda-and-global-terrorist-networks>

accessed 11 August 2016; also Financial Action Task Force, 'Terrorist Financing. Typologies Report' (2008) <www.fatf-gafi.org/media/fatf/documents/reports/FATF%20Terrorist%20Financing%20Typologies%20Report.pdf> accessed 8 March 2017.

16. Financial Action Task Force, 'Guidance: National Money Laundering and Terrorist Financing Risk Assessment' (2013) 7 <www.fatf-gafi.org/media/fatf/content/images/National_ML_TF_Risk_Assessment.pdf> accessed 8 March 2017.

17. ibid.

18. ibid.

19. ibid.

20. ibid. 8.

21. UK Government Home Office and HM Treasury, *Action Plan for Anti-Money Laundering and Counter-Terrorist Finance*' (2016) 7.

22. UNODC, 'Estimating Illicit Financial Flows Resulting from Drug Trafficking and Other Transnational Organized Crime' Research report (2011) 7 <www.unodc.org/documents/data-and-analysis/Studies/Illicit_financial_flows_2011_web.pdf> accessed 8 March 2017.

23. Vito Tanzi, 'Money Laundering and the International Financial System' (1996) IMF Working Paper 96/55; Peter Quirk, 'Macroeconomic Implications of Money Laundering' (1996) IMF Working Paper 96/66.

24. European Parliament and Council Directive 2005/60/EC of 26 October 2005 on the prevention of the use of the financial system for the purpose of money laundering and terrorist financing' [2005] OJ L309/15. See also UK Government Home Office and HM Treasury (n 21) where ML/TF jointly 'undermine the integrity of our financial institutions and markets'.

25. Nicholas Ryder, *The Financial Crisis and White Collar Crime. The Perfect Storm?* (Edward Elgar Publishing 2014).

26. Financial Action Task Force, 'Annual Report' (1990) 5 <www.fatf-gafi.org/media/fatf/documents/reports/1990%20ENG.pdf> accessed 8 March 2017.

27. UNODC (n 22).

28. For elaboration, see Petrus C van Duyne, Jackie Harvey, and Liliya Gelemerova, 'The Monty Python Flying Circus of Money Laundering and the Question of Proportionality' in Georgios A Antonopolous (ed), *Illegal Entrepreneurship, Organized Crime and Social Control: Essays in Honour of Professor Dick Hobbs* (Springer 2016).

29. Michel Camdessus, 'Money Laundering—The Importance of International Countermeasures' (1998) IMF Address <www.imf.org/external/np/speeches/1998/021098.htm> accessed 11 August 2016.

30. UNODC (n 22).

31. Tanzi (n 23).

32. Quirk (n 23).

33. Liliya Gelemerova, *The Anti-Money Laundering System in the Context of Globalisation: A Panopticon Built on Quicksand?* (Wolf legal Publishers 2011).

34. John Walker and Brigitte Unger, 'Measuring Global Money Laundering: "The Walker Gravity Model"' (2009) 5(2) Review of Law and Economics 820, 823.

35. Raffaella Barone and Donato Masciandaro, 'Organized Crime, Money Laundering and Legal Economy: Theory and Simulations' (2011) 32(1) European Journal of Law and Economics 115; Friedrich Schneider and Ursula Windischbauer, 'Money Laundering: Some Facts' (2008) 26(4) European Journal of Law and Economics 387; Tom Blickman, 'Countering Illicit and Unregulated Money Flows Money Laundering, Tax Evasion and Financial Regulation' (2010) Crime and Globalisation Debate Papers TNI Briefing Series <www.tni.org/files/download/crime3_0.pdf> accessed 8 March 2017.

36. Petrus C van Duyne, Marc S Groenhuijsen, and AAP Schudelaro, 'Balancing Financial Threats and Legal Interests in Money-Laundering Policy' (2005) 43(2–3) Crime, Law and Social Change 117; Gelemerova (n 33).

37. The authors draw on an earlier elaboration of the empirical evidence in van Duyne, Harvey, and Gelemerova (n 28).

38. See, for example, Schneider and Windischbauer (n 35); Barone and Masciandaro (n 35); Brigitte Unger and others, *Project ECOLEF The Economic and Legal Effectiveness of Anti-money Laundering and Combatting Terrorist Financing Policy*, Project funded by the European Commission DG Home Affairs, JLS/2009/SEC/AG/087 (2013).

39. Petrus C van Duyne and Hervy de Miranda, 'The Emperor's Cloths of Disclosure: Hot Money and Suspect Disclosures' (1999) 3 Crime, Law and Social Change 245; Petrus C van Duyne, Melvin van Soudijn, and T Kint, 'Bricks Don't Talk. Searching for Crime Money in Real Estate' in Petrus C van Duyne and others (eds), *Crime, Money and Criminal Mobility in Europe* (Wolf Legal Publishers 2009); Petrus C van Duyne and Melvin van Soudijn, 'Crime-Money in the Financial System: What We Fear and What We Know' in Martine Herzog-Evans (ed), *Transnational Criminology Manual. Vol 2* (Wolf Legal Publishers 2010).

40. John Walker, *Estimates of the Extent of Money Laundering in and Through Australia* (John Walker Consulting Services 1995) 1.

41. Summarised by Elena Madalina Busuioc, 'Defining Money Laundering. Predicate Offences—The Achilles' Heel of Anti-Money Laundering Legislation' in Brigitte Unger (ed), *The Scale and Impacts of Money Laundering* (Edward Elgar Publishing 2007); Brigitte Unger and Greg Rawlings, 'The Amounts and Effects of Money Laundering' Report for the Ministry of Finance (Utrecht School of Economics 2006).

42. Furthering the commission of crime is one of the clauses of the US Anti-Laundering Act of 1986.

43. Walker (n 40); Peter Reuter, 'Are the Estimates of the Volume of Money Laundering Either Feasible or Useful?' in Brigitte Unger and Daan van der Linde (eds), *Research Handbook on Money Laundering* (Edward Elgar Publishing 2013) 227.

44. Brigitte Unger, *The Scale and Impacts of Money Laundering* (Edward Elgar Publishing 2007); Unger and Rawlings (n 41).

45. John Walker and Brigitte Unger, 'Measuring Global Money Laundering: "The Walker Gravity Model"' (2009) 5(2) Review of Law and Economics 820.

46. Unger and others (n 38). For a copy of the final report for this project see <www2.econ.uu.nl/users/unger/ecolef_files/Final%20ECOLEF%20 report%20(digital%20version).pdf> accessed 8 December 2016.

47. UNODC (n 22).

48. The methodology employed by the UN project was reviewed by an 'external reference group' that included Prof Dr Friedrich Schneider from Johannes Kepler University of Linz and Prof. Dr Brigitte Unger from Utrecht University. See UNODC (n 22).

49. van Duyne, Harvey, and Gelemerova (n 28).

50. That indicative bias has been present from the first FATF report of 1990 onwards, as observed by Petrus C van Duyne, 'Money-Laundering: Estimates in Fog' (1994) 19 The Journal of Asset Protection and Financial Crime 103.

51. Unger and others (n 38).

52. Joras Ferwerda, 'The Effects of Money Laundering' in Brigitte Unger and Daan van der Linde (eds), *Research Handbook on Money Laundering* (Edward Elgar Publishing 2013).

53. Peter Reuter, 'Are the Estimates of the Volume of Money Laundering Either Feasible or Useful?' in Brigitte Unger and Daan van der Linde (eds), *Research Handbook on Money Laundering* (Edward Elgar Publishing 2013).

54. Brent Barlett, 'The Negative Effects of Money Laundering on Economic Development, Countering Money Laundering in the Asian and Pacific Region' (2002) Asian Development Bank, Regional Technical Assistance Project No. 5967, 33 <https://waleolusi.files.wordpress.com/2013/05/the-negative-effects-of-money-laundering-on-econom.pdf> accessed 8 March 2017.

55. Ferwerda (n 52) 43.

56. Peter Reuter and Victoria Greenfield, 'Measuring Global Drug Markets: How Good Are the Numbers and Why Should We Care About Them?' (2001) 2(4) World Economics 159.

57. Schneider and Windischbauer (n 35) 117.

58. See also van Duyne and de Miranda (n 39); Peter Reuter and Edwin M Truman, 'Anti-Money Laundering Overkill?: It's Time to Ask How Well the System is Working' (2005) The International Economy 56; Reuter and Greenfield (n 56)

59. In Morocco and Colombia see, respectively, Peter De Mas, 'De Poreuze Noordkust van Marokko' (2001) 5 Justitiële Verkenningen 72; Douglas I Keh, *Drug Money in a Changing World: Economic Reform and Criminal Finance* (UNDCP 1996).
60. UK Government Home Office and HM Treasury (n 21).
61. van Duyne and Levi (n 1).
62. Financial Action Task Force, 'Guidance on the Risk-Based Approach to Combating Money Laundering and Terrorist Financing' (2007) <www.fatf-gafi.org/media/fatf/documents/reports/High%20Level%20Principles%20and%20Procedures.pdf> accessed 8 March 2017.
63. ibid. 16.
64. FATF (n 15).
65. FATF (n 16).
66. FATF (n 62).
67. Financial Action Task Force, 'Methodology For Assessing Technical Compliance With The FATF Recommendations And The Effectiveness Of AML/CFT Systems' (2013) <www.fatf-gafi.org/media/fatf/documents/methodology/FATF%20Methodology%2022%2 0Feb%202013.pdf> accessed 8 March 2017.
68. ibid. 4.
69. The FATF is in the process of reviewing its sectoral specific guidance and the full list of available reports can be accessed from <www.fatf-gafi.org/documents/riskbasedapproach/?hf=10&b=0&s=desc(fatf_releasedate)> accessed 29 January 2017.
70. FATF (n 67) 7.
71. ibid. 23.
72. This has increased to 23 at the time of final editing, December 2016, justifying a follow-up study. At the time of proofing the number of MERs has risen to more than 30. For further analysis see Van Duyne *et al.*, in preparation.
73. We have previously commented on the cost involved in the third round MER process (van Duyne, Harvey, and Gelemerova (n 28)); the fourth round comprises: Incorporation of self-assessment; desk review of technical compliance and visit to assess outcome effectiveness. This is followed up by an assessment for consistency carried out by an independent team.
74. Data reported is for the latest year included within each of the MERs and is frequently two to three years earlier that the date of evaluation.
75. Financial Action Task Force, 'Anti-Money Laundering and Counter-Terrorist Financing Measures' Spain Mutual Evaluation Report (2014) <www.fatf-gafi.org/media/fatf/documents/reports/mer4/Mutual-Evaluation-Report-Spain-2014.pdf> accessed 8 March 2017.
76. Cuba has remained outside of the FATF procedures and was not part of any prior evaluation round. In 2011 it was added to the 'public statement' (24 June) as 'not having committed … nor constructively engaged', although by

June 2014 the authorities had apparently achieved a sufficient amount to be removed from the October 2014 list and subject to inspection.

77. See Table 3.5, 59 of the Australian MER: 'Convictions equivalent to Vienna/Palermo conventions ("knowledge", recklessness)'. Queensland mentioned only 'receiving'. Queensland and Victoria accounted for 92% of the convictions. For further discussion of Australia, see Chap. 13 (Chaikin) in this collection.

78. Financial Action Task Force, Mutual Evaluation of Costa Rica (2015) 7 <www.fatf-gafi.org/media/fatf/documents/reports/mer-fsrb/MER-Costa-Rica-2015-ENG.pdf> accessed 8 December 2016.

79. Financial Action Task Force, Mutual Evaluation of Norway (2014) 7 <www.fatf-gafi.org/media/fatf/documents/reports/mer4/Mutual-Evaluation-Report-Norway-2014.pdf> accessed 8 December 2016.

80. ibid.

81. ibid. 16.

82. ibid. 60.

83. Financial Action Task Force, Mutual evaluation of Samoa (2015) <www.fatf-gafi.org/media/fatf/documents/reports/mer-fsrb/Mutual-Evaluation-Report-Samoa-2015.pdf> accessed 24 February 2017.

84. Financial Action Task Force, Mutual Evaluation of Sri Lanka (2015) <www.fatf-gafi.org/media/fatf/documents/reports/mer-fsrb/APG-Mutual-Evaluation-Report-Sri-Lanka-2015.pdf> accessed 8 December 2016.

85. Financial Action Task Force, Mutual Evaluation of Federal Republic of Ethiopia (2015) <www.fatf-gafi.org/media/fatf/documents/reports/mer-fsrb/WB-ESAAMLG-Mutual-Evaluation-Report-Ethiopia-2015.pdf> accessed 8 December 2016.

86. ibid. 33.

87. Gelemerova (n 33).

88. Italy has now addressed this apparent deficiency.

89. van Duyne, Groenhuijsen, and Schudelaro (n 36).

Petrus C. van Duyne is Emeritus Professor of Criminology at Tilburg University, Netherlands. He is a psychologist and jurist, and has conducted extensive international critical research on organised and economic crime, fraud, money laundering and corruption. He has carried out research projects on money laundering and corruption in Serbia. He is the initiator of the annual Cross-Border Crime Colloquium of which annual publications he is Chief Editor.and He is a visiting professor at Northumbria University and Utrecht University, Netherlands.

Jackie Harvey is Professor of Financial Management at Newcastle Business School. Her research is focused in the area of criminal financial management, in particular money laundering. Harvey has been invited to speak at numerous academic and practitioner conferences in both the UK and Europe. She is on the Editorial Board for the European Cross-Border Crime Colloquium that brings together researchers from across Europe. Her main teaching interests focus on risk and investment management together with financial market regulation. She holds a PhD is in Taxation Policy. Prior to becoming an academic, Harvey had spent ten years working for a major merchant bank, followed by a three-year posting as fiscal policy adviser (under the auspices of the British Government) to the Ministry of Finance in Belize.

Liliya Gelemerova is an honorary senior lecturer at the University of Manchester, a member of the Steering Committee of Finance against Trafficking and Senior Enhanced Due Diligence Manager at the Royal Bank of Canada, London. Formerly Head of International Contacts and Legal Coordination at Bulgaria's Financial Intelligence Unit, Gelemerova has a strong background in financial intelligence that includes many years of training in anti-money laundering practices. Following a role at Transparency International, Berlin, Gelemerova moved to London where she worked for several investigative consultancy firms, managing a wide range of due diligence and financial crime investigation projects for corporations, financial institutions and law firms. Gelemerova holds a PhD in Global Anti-money Laundering Policies from Tilburg University in 2011.

Part III

Asset Recovery

16

Asset Recovery: An Overview

Colin King

In September 1999, in an influential review that shaped aspects of the Proceeds of Crime Act in 2002, the then-UK Prime Minister Tony Blair stated 'we want to ensure that crime doesn't pay. Seizing criminal assets deprives criminals and criminal organisations of their financial lifeblood.'[1] Part of the logic underpinning a focus on criminal assets is summed up as follows:

> ...failing to remove criminal gains from offenders left individuals in a position to fund a life of crime after punishment, or even to continue to control criminal enterprises from inside prison. In the creation of a safe and just society it could not be tolerated that criminals should continue to benefit from the proceeds of their crimes, thereby showing contempt for the rule of law.[2]

Moreover, '[t]he removal of assets from those living off crime is a valuable end in itself in a just society.'[3] Thus, the drive to confiscate criminal assets has increasingly come to the fore of policy efforts to tackle crime. The benefits of targeting such assets are widely said to include: preventing criminal money from being used to finance other criminal activities; preventing such money from corrupting legitimate society; deterring crime by reinforcing the idea that 'crime does not pay'; and removing negative role models from society.[4] While these underlying rationales do have intuitive appeal, the reality does not necessarily match the rhetoric. As Bullock and Lister argue, 'the assumptions of confiscation are, at best, unprovable and, at worst, fundamentally

C. King
University of Sussex, Brighton, UK

© The Author(s) 2018
C. King et al. (eds.), *The Palgrave Handbook of Criminal and Terrorism Financing Law*,
https://doi.org/10.1007/978-3-319-64498-1_16

flawed.'[5] Notwithstanding significant criticisms of the impact or 'success', including the economic returns, of asset recovery,[6] the underlying rationales persist in asset recovery policy discourse.[7]

Alongside mention of the contentious underlying rationales, it is important to consider some difficult definitional points. Practitioners, policymakers, and academics widely speak of terms such as 'confiscation' and 'forfeiture', yet all too often there is a lack of consensus as to the meaning of such terms. The specific meaning often varies depending on the jurisdiction and, at a practical level, the inevitable ambiguity, indeed confusion, that this can give rise to is problematic. For example, one former police officer in the UK spoke of dealings with colleagues in Hungary where they spent three days collaborating on a proceeds of crime case. On the third day, it was realised that the UK police officials were using the term 'confiscation' in one sense, but the Hungarian officials were using the same term to mean something entirely different.[8] Such definitional 'doublespeak' is encapsulated in the following United Nations Office on Drugs and Crime (UNODC) definition: '"Forfeiture" means the permanent deprivation of property by order of a court or other competent authority. The term is often used interchangeably with confiscation.'[9] In contrast, the Hodgson Committee (in the UK) distinguished between these terms, defining 'forfeiture' as 'the power of the Court to take property that is immediately connected with an offence' whereas 'confiscation' was said to be 'the depriving of an offender of the proceeds or the profits of crime.'[10] As Barbara Vettori points out, 'the potential for confusion is high.'[11]

To this, we must also mention the term 'asset recovery.' According to one European Commission Working Paper, asset recovery encompasses the legal proceedings to confiscate or forfeit property, but it is wider than that; it also includes the asset-tracing phase (such as work by national financial intelligence units (FIUs) and by Asset Recovery Offices (AROs)) and the disposal phase (involving the sale of an asset at auction or reuse of property for public purposes).[12] Atkinson *et al.* prefer to use the term 'asset-focused interventions.'[13] Others use the term 'asset recovery' in the specific context of targeting corruption-related assets of politically exposed persons (PEPs).[14] In this regard, a report from the Stolen Asset Recovery Initiative (StAR) states, '"Asset recovery" is defined to include the powers envisaged in article 53–55 of UNCAC and is effectively the process by which proceeds of corruption are recovered and returned to a foreign jurisdiction.'[15] For the purposes of this chapter, 'asset recovery' is given its broader meaning, not confined to corruption-related recovery.

Part III of this book considers what has now been conceptualised as 'asset recovery' in different jurisdictions and contexts. Asset recovery is, however, not only an issue of concern at the national level; rather it is also an issue high on the agenda at the transnational level. As in Part II of this book, we consider EU developments at the outset of Part III,[16] followed by discussion of asset recovery experiences in different national jurisdictions.

Confiscation of criminal assets is now firmly at the heart of EU efforts to tackle crime, particularly organised criminal activity. In the words of the European Commission, 'Confiscation is a strategic priority in the EU's fight against organised crime.'[17] In Chap. 17, Maugeri focuses on issues of judicial cooperation and mutual recognition of confiscation orders within the European Union. She places a great deal of emphasis not only on the legal foundations, but just as importantly on mutual trust. A notable development in this area is Directive 42/2014.[18] Maugeri notes how this is intended to enhance harmonisation both of confiscation and enforcement. One issue covered by the Directive is mutual recognition which, according to Maugeri, is 'essential for efficient implementation of confiscation in the fight against crime.' However, not all is perfect. For example, the Directive is not restricted to organised crime. Moreover, there are concerns as to the applicable standard of proof. Other issues that arise include ensuring proportionality in confiscation proceedings, the use of third-party confiscation, and the introduction of non-conviction-based (NCB) confiscation in limited circumstances.

The latter issue—the introduction of NCB confiscation—has attracted considerable attention for a number of years.[19] Some Member States (MSs) have been vociferous in their support of such powers, particularly Ireland and Italy. Other jurisdictions have been reluctant to adopt such powers, and indeed have been reluctant to recognise orders from other jurisdictions. The provisions in the Directive were themselves a compromise solution to overcome resistance to the use (and mutual recognition) of NCB powers. Of course, as Maugeri points out, MSs do have the option of going further than the requirements in the Directive—the Directive merely sets down minimal standards. The author goes on to consider a number of other key issues in relation to confiscation, including the Strasbourg Convention, the Framework Decision 2006/783/JHA (on mutual recognition), the decision of the ECtHR in *Gogitidze*,[20] prospects for mutual recognition subsequent to Directive 42/2014, as well as unresolved issues relating to mutual recognition of NCB orders. Further developments, then, can be expected at the European level. With this in mind, Maugeri's concluding words are timely—there cannot simply be a 'sword effect,' there must also be respect for individual rights.

The first national survey in Part II is from the United States, which is well known as being active, indeed proactive, on asset forfeiture. In Chap. 18, Cassella—a former federal prosecutor—outlines key issues in the application of forfeiture in the United States. The degree of enforcement varies from state to state. Nonetheless, asset forfeiture is widely seen to be a key element of law enforcement practices, policies, and, indeed, priorities. Cassella notes how, particularly during the past decade or so, 'gross federal forfeiture receipts have generally exceeded $2 billion a year.' An obvious question is 'what can be forfeited?,' but the US answer is not straightforward. Ultimately forfeiture will depend on the particular offence or statutory measures in question. This, Cassella notes, is problematic for judges and practitioners. Forfeiture under US legislation can be applied to different categories of assets stemming from crime, for example, the (direct and indirect) proceeds of crime and property that was used to facilitate criminal activity. Some statutory provisions are broadly framed, whereas others are much more narrowly defined. Thus, 'the prosecutor or law enforcement agent needs to check the applicable statute to see what can be forfeited in a particular case, and may have to make charging decisions based on the need to invoke a particular forfeiture law.'

There are a number of other contentious issues in how forfeiture law is applied, for example: what constitutes 'proceeds'; whether a 'gross' or 'net' approach should be adopted; what happens where there is mixing, or co-mingling, of legitimate and illegitimate assets; how constitutional provisions act as a restraint upon forfeiture proceedings; and how 'equitable sharing' operates. Of course, such questions arise in many other jurisdictions; hence it is useful to consider how the US authorities and courts have tried to find resolutions. Cassella goes on to outline the operation of, and benefits/drawbacks associated with, three different types of forfeiture, namely administrative (non-judicial) forfeiture, civil (NCB) forfeiture, and criminal forfeiture. Ultimately, he concludes that the federal statutes provide 'a robust set of procedures' to target criminal assets, and that these have 'become an essential part of the enforcement of U.S. criminal laws.'

In Chap. 19, Hopmeier and Mills consider the post-conviction confiscation regime in England and Wales. Confiscation powers have attracted a great deal of attention in recent years, with critical reports by, in particular, the National Audit Office[21] and the Public Accounts Committee.[22] Subsequently, the Home Affairs Select Committee held its inquiry into proceeds of crime,[23] and the Law Commission has identified confiscation as a topic that might be included in its Thirteenth Programme for Reform.[24] Against this backdrop, the chapter by Hopmeier and Mills is timely. At the outset, the authors note the prevalent use of confiscation orders. A superficial glance at the figures (in terms of number of orders made and money recovered) would doubtless result in plaudits, however 'the headline numbers mask a process that remains fraught with problems.' Such problems include uncertainty in the application of the law as well as wide-scale avoidance of payment of confiscation orders. There are various other practical problems, including issues relating to third-party rights (including matrimonial rights, property belonging to a company and lifting of the corporate veil), family law matters (such as a competing claim to assets arising during divorce proceedings), difficulties in determining 'benefit' (for instance, with a temporary possession or where legitimate and illegitimate money are mixed to fund a larger purchase), and controversy as to whether benefit relates to the 'proceeds' or the 'profit' of criminal activity. In the words of Hopmeier and Mills, 'The question becomes far more complex, and the scope of the judicial enquiry is far wider than might first be anticipated.' One other aspect of confiscation that has provoked comment by practitioners is the choice of venue—as confiscation matters are now dealt with in the Crown Court, the expectation is that criminal law practitioners will deal with such proceedings. Yet that ignores the reality of confiscation proceedings—which are often dominated by complex civil, equity, or trust issues. This bone of contention is addressed by the authors, though they note that given its relative infancy the 'actual effects still remain to be seen.'

One issue that has attracted a great deal of attention in recent years—right up to the highest court[25]—is the proportionality question. The authors emphasise that 'Whilst proceeds of crime legislation serves the legitimate aim of removing the incentives for committing offences, this aim cannot be a warrant for abandoning completely the need for the court to act fairly in making its determination.' Proportionality clearly has an important role to play. Given developments in this area, the authors outline emergent principles from the case-law, and this issue is picked up again in the next chapter by Young (Chap. 20). Other contentious issues identified in this chapter include the statutory assumptions where a person is deemed to have a 'criminal lifestyle,' difficulties in challenging these statutory assumptions, the meaning of 'benefit,' calculating the amount that must be repaid, concerns as to 'hidden assets,' and payment/enforcement of a confiscation order. Clearly, as the chapter demonstrates, there have been significant developments in the confiscation regime in England and Wales in recent years and they can be expected to continue apace.

As already mentioned, the question of proportionality has been a contentious one in the context of POCA proceedings, and Simon Young considers this issue further in Chap. 20. A deceptively simple example illustrates the difficulties. A person obtains a mortgage for 60% of the value of property being purchased, with the remaining 40% coming from his own untainted money. If that person makes false statements about his employment record or earnings, that is a criminal offence.[26] This was the situation in *R v Waya*,[27] where the appellant had been convicted[28] and sentenced to 80 hours of community punishment. This sentence 'reflected the judge's view of the relatively low level of his culpability. He was not guilty of a serious mortgage fraud involving dishonest overvaluation of property. There was no loss to the mortgage lender. Nevertheless he did, by dishonestly misrepresenting his own financial position, obtain credit on terms which might not otherwise have been available.'[29] Where the property in question has appreciated in value, depriving that person of that capital gain, or a proportionate part thereof, would be appropriate.[30] Thus far, this scenario appears relatively straightforward. Difficulties arise, however, when trying to calculate a fair and proportionate amount for the confiscation order. In *Waya*, the parties acknowledged the need for proportionality:

> It is clear law, and was common ground between the parties, that this [i.e. A1P1, ECHR] imports, via the rule of fair balance, the requirement that there must be a reasonable relationship of proportionality between the means employed by the State in, inter alia, the deprivation of property as a form of penalty, and the legitimate aim which is sought to be realised by the deprivation.[31]

What the parties did not agree on, however, was what would constitute a proportionate amount in the circumstances. In considering proportionality, we must look at the aim of the legislation as well as the means employed to achieve that aim. As was stated in *Waya*, 'The first governs the second, but the second must be proportionate to the first.'[32] In his chapter, Young delivers a thorough examination of proportionality developments in POCA cases in the UK and Hong Kong, with particular emphasis on both the restraint stage and the confiscation stage. He engages with different approaches to proportionality, considering prescription disproportionality, individualised disproportionality, interpretive proportionality, and supervening proportionality. As he notes, the proportionality question is rarely an issue when considering the lawfulness or constitutionality of POCA powers; rather 'Proportionality enters the picture in individual cases or types of cases and becomes apparent when the impact on individuals does not accord with what the law was intended to achieve.' He contends, quite rightly, that proportionality will soon be commonplace in POCA litigation, certainly in the UK and Hong Kong.

The next country to be considered is Italy. The Italian experience is important for a number of reasons. First, Italy has a long history in confiscation law, particularly in the context of anti-Mafia efforts and can claim to be 'a pioneer.'[33] Second, Italian agencies have considerable experience in the practice of targeting criminal assets, offering many lessons (good and bad). Third, given this background, the EU often looks to Italian experience for inspiration.[34] Fourth, EU and Italian agencies work closely together in efforts to tackle crime, particularly financial crime and in the context of corruption related to EU funds.[35] Fifth, it is important for common law scholars to look beyond their own jurisdictions and to consider continental European approaches.[36] In Chap. 21, Panzavolta traces the development, and expansion, of Italian confiscation measures.

The Italian experience has not been static. Prior to the 1980s, confiscation was afforded a marginal role in criminal justice. But with growing concern related to organised crime, confiscation became a central feature of 'hitting back' at criminal activity. One notable development, which has in turn inspired developments in other jurisdictions, is the adoption of a NCB approach in the 1980s. And in the 1990s, confiscation was expanded even further, particularly in the wake of high-profile events (such as the murder of Judge Giovanni Falcone[37]). As with other jurisdictions, the Italian regime has not been immune to criticism and legal challenge, however. Such criticism often relates to, for example, the breadth and reach of the confiscation legislation, human rights concerns relating to the civil/criminal divide (in the context of NCB powers), and the principle of proportionality. Thus, as Panzavolta concludes, confiscation 'has certainly been beneficial in the fight against criminal organizations. In some cases, however, the compatibility of these new instruments with fundamental rights could be questioned.'

Italy is not the only jurisdiction that resorts to NCB approaches to targeting criminal assets. Indeed, such powers are increasingly gaining traction across the globe, and are variously referred to as 'civil forfeiture,' 'NCB asset forfeiture,' 'NCB confiscation,' and 'civil recovery.' In a similar vein, unexplained wealth orders (UWOs)[38] are a further tool that can be used to seize property, without a requirement of proving criminality, so long as there are reasonable grounds to suspect that the person's lawful income would have been insufficient to obtain that property.[39] While UWOs have recently been introduced in the UK,[40] what impact such orders will have in practice is to be determined.

The next three chapters focus on NCB powers in the UK (Chap. 22, Alldridge), Canada (Chap. 23, Gallant) and Ireland (Chap. 24, King). Again here we see another example of definitional confusion. In the UK, the term 'civil recovery' is used—a term that Alldridge dislikes. In his words: 'civil recovery is not taking back or getting back property that had previously been the State's. It is state appropriation of property.' This is not merely a semantic point; the use of the word 'recovery' goes to the heart of the underlying justifications for this controversial power.

An important issue in any 'successful' (more on which shortly) regime targeting proceeds of crime is, of course, the institutional question: is it better to have what Alldridge describes as a 'dedicated agency approach' or should relevant powers be vested more broadly in, say, a policing agency? There are different experiences in this regard across Europe, for example, there is the Criminal Assets Bureau (CAB) in Ireland,[41] Bulgaria has the Commission for Establishing Property Acquired through Illegal Activity (CEPAIA),[42] while Romania has the National Office for Crime Prevention and Cooperation with EU Asset Recovery Offices (ONPCCRCI) and the National Agency for Fiscal Administration.[43] In the UK, the dedicated agency approach was initially adopted with the Assets Recovery Agency (ARA)—which proved to be successful in Northern Ireland but, in the words of Alldridge, 'an unequivocal failure' in England and Wales. The ARA was replaced by the Serious Organised Crime Agency (SOCA) in 2007, which itself was replaced by the National Crime Agency (NCA) in 2013. In fact, the range of institutions vested with authority to seek civil recovery orders is even broader and includes, *inter alia*, the Serious Fraud Office (SFO)[44]—another agency that Alldridge goes on to explore. The SFO has used its special powers to great effect in recent years—for example, in relation to transnational corporate bribery[45] (for more on which see Chap. 26 by Lord and Levi)—though with the advent of Deferred Prosecution Agreements in 2013,[46] it remains to be seen whether civil recovery will retain its place at the heart of the SFO strategy to targeting proceeds of crime.

Returning to the point of 'success' in targeting proceeds of crime—how are we to measure such success? What are the key performance indicators? Is it appropriate to measure success solely by means of money in/out? Is such an approach even possible—especially where proceeds of crime endeavours are only one part of a much wider enterprise? Moreover, is it desirable to simply focus on the 'money' rather than the 'impact,' such as the level of disruption caused to criminal activities? There has been a notable lack of clarity on such questions in the 15 years since the Proceeds of Crime Act 2002 was enacted.[47]

At the same time as the ARA was disbanded, a new approach was adopted in relation to the use of assets obtained under POCA—the Asset Recovery Incentivisation Scheme (ARIS). From now on, assets would be shared with relevant agencies rather than being sent in their entirety to the consolidated fund. This marked a key milestone in the use of civil recovery, which increasingly became more mainstream and more common. There are, however, a number of concerns—not least the potential for 'policing for profit,'[48] more 'deals' by enforcement authorities and consequently a sidelining of judges, a lack of transparency, and offenders seemingly buying their way out of prosecution.

NCB powers have been subjected to important human rights challenges. For the most part, however, courts have rejected arguments that such proceedings ought to be regarded as equivalent to criminal proceedings, thus attracting all of the enhanced procedural protections of the criminal process.[49] Alldridge critically dissects the approach of the UK courts in upholding the civil nature of such proceedings. Similar experiences are evident in other jurisdictions that have also enacted powers akin to civil recovery, including Ireland,[50] Canada,[51] Australia,[52] Italy,[53] and the United States.[54] Not everyone views such powers as problematic, however. Indeed, there are some who laud the advantages of civil proceedings.[55] Much of this literature has tended to be doctrinal analysis of legislation and case-law. There is scant empirical analysis of the NCB approach to targeting criminal assets, and the bulk of that literature has tended to be on debates surrounding 'policing for profit' in the United States.[56] The next two chapters add new insights to these debates on the use of civil proceedings to target criminal assets.

The value of, and indeed need for, empirical research in this area is summed up by Gallant:

> knowledge of the enforcement narrative is scant. What is needed are systematic studies of the enforcement enterprise, studies that would illuminate the context surrounding civil forfeiture actions. Such knowledge would enhance the understanding of implementation and provide information that might inform any rights inquiries, might be relevant to decisions involving policy or might quell, or antagonize, public opinion.

Gallant has written extensively on civil forfeiture.[57] In Chap. 23, she builds upon earlier doctrinal work to now explore the law in practice, in an attempt to move beyond the rhetoric of civil forfeiture debates. In this, she draws upon analysis of 100 cases in Manitoba, Canada, thereby enabling her 'to ground legal, policy and other discourses in a fuller factual setting.' After outlining civil forfeiture in Canada (and specifically the Manitoban law), as well as various controversies associated with this power, Gallant goes on to offer 'a glimpse of context' through her analysis of 100 case files over a five-year period (2009–2014). Her study focused on different types of information common to all civil forfeiture actions, namely the alleged underlying offence; the type and value of property subject to forfeiture; the types of evidence used in support of forfeiture proceedings; and the outcomes of proceedings. Given the historical development of 'follow-the-money' approaches, it is perhaps unsurprising that the vast majority of cases in this study were drug related. Other cases concerned alleged offences with a profit element. In Manitoba, there have been some particularly controversial cases, including a civil forfeiture action against a home on the basis of alleged sexual offences, though Gallant's study shows that such cases are more the exception, rather than the norm. However, 'That said, nothing within the remit of Manitoban law confines its application to profitable criminal activity. It merely appears to have been restricted, in practice, to that context.' One area that has proved problematic is the forfeiture of property subject to rental agreements, where fault lies with the tenant, rather than the property owner. The cases in this study reveal little as to what care or responsibility is required from landlords to avoid such forfeiture. Overall, this study offers important insights into the operation of civil forfeiture in practice. In concluding, Gallant advocates further study to inform developments in this area: 'Further empirical studies need to inform the developing narrative. Assessment of the legitimacy of civil forfeiture laws should be based on evidence.'

In Chap. 24, King adopts a different approach to exploring the operation of civil forfeiture in practice—drawing upon interviews with officials from the Irish Criminal Assets Bureau, leading legal practitioners, and nongovernmental organisations. Given that questions as to the constitutionality of civil forfeiture have long been settled in Ireland,[58] this chapter focuses on what is described as the 'second wave of legal challenges,' meaning challenges to the operation or application of the Irish Proceeds of Crime Act 1996, rather than challenges to the Act itself. While there is an extensive literature on the first wave of legal challenge,[59] much less has been written about the second wave. This chapter focuses on two of the most contentious rules of evidence in the Irish legislation, namely the use of belief evidence and anonymity of State officials, examining the relevant legislative provisions, their application in case-law, and perspectives of practitioners. King is critical of these evidential provisions, lamenting their at-times almost routine use. In relation to belief evidence, concerns include the prominent role of the Chief Bureau Officer of the Criminal Assets Bureau, difficulties in challenging such evidence, the lack of formal requirement of corroborating evidence, claims of informer privilege, and the deferential approach adopted by the judiciary. As for the anonymity provisions, concerns include the undermining of open justice, the lack of transparency, routine requests for anonymity without any assessment as to whether there is a need for anonymity, and judicial deference. Such concerns have provoked interesting discussions with practitioners, which are reflected in the chapter. In concluding, King points out how the Irish proceeds of crime legislation is widely regarded as a model of international best practice. However, the application of controversial evidential rules has the potential to undermine this reputation: 'Not only do the belief evidence and anonymity provisions leave proceedings open to question in the eyes of a respondent, more widely they also undermine confidence in, and the reputation of, the Irish proceeds of crime model.'

The next two chapters focus on the use of asset recovery powers in the context of bribery and corruption. In Chap. 25, Ziouvas examines asset recovery under the United Nations Convention Against Corruption (UNCAC), while in Chap. 26, Lord and Levi examine asset recovery as a tool to tackle transnational corporate bribery.

Speaking at the 2016 global Anti-Corruption Summit, the then-UK Prime Minister David Cameron called for a global movement to tackle illicit financial outflows[60]—the problem of 'people stealing from poor countries and hiding that wealth in rich ones.'[61] He asserted that the UK should 'clean up our property market and show that there is no home for the corrupt in Britain.'[62] He continued that, 'we also need to ensure that when we expose the corrupt, we are able to seize their assets and return them to the countries from which they were stolen.'[63] We have already considered (in Chap. 4, Talani) how global financial centres are seen as a desirable location to launder proceeds of corruption. Increasingly, there are now global counter-efforts in this regard: examples such as Marcos (Philippines), Mobutu (Zaire), Mubarak (Egypt), and Yanukovych (Ukraine) demonstrate how asset recovery powers can be used against grand corruption.[64] In the words of Sharman, the realisation that 'host countries have a duty to take action to block or seize their illicit funds is a new and in many ways remarkable development.'[65]

One of the most notable developments in the use of asset recovery against grand corruption is the UNCAC—the focus of Ziouvas' chapter. He argues that 'corruption-related asset recovery is a prerequisite for global justice and the promotion of the international rule of law as backbones for sustainable development.' Yet, targeting such assets is not always straightforward: there are significant obstacles to effective asset recovery in practice, especially when such assets have been removed to foreign jurisdictions. Ziouvas is particularly concerned with three aspects of targeting corruption-related assets: preventing laundering of assets, recovering assets, and returning assets. While UNCAC is often regarded as a comprehensive framework for asset recovery, an important factor in the success of asset recovery is capacity and willingness on the part of victim states to engage in the process of recovering corruption-related assets. Such engagement may not be present for various reasons, such as a lack of political will, the absence of appropriate institutions and/or law enforcement mechanisms, or problems associated with political transition. This leads Ziouvas to advocate for 'a proactive approach towards asset recovery for the best interest of the people of looted troubled countries and global justice.'

Corruption-related asset recovery is not confined to corrupt politicians. Such powers have also been used, to varying degrees, against 'respectable' companies who have engaged in transnational bribery—the focus of Chap. 26 by Lord and Levi. A focus on the financial benefits arising from bribery is at the heart of the UK government and the SFO response to such crime. A variety of options are open to them including disgorgement of profits, post-conviction confiscation, civil recovery, and compensation orders.

Lord and Levi focus on the UK as a generator and venue for bribery, with particular emphasis on the 'supply side' of bribery. Other studies of 'dirty assets' often concentrate on proceeds of crime in illegal markets (most notably drugs). In the corporate realm, however, the situation is very different as the 'dirty assets' are concealed and/or moved in legitimate markets by otherwise respectable businesses. This then gives rise to peculiar considerations for asset recovery. The UK is an ideal jurisdiction for this study for two reasons: first, it is regarded as an 'active enforcer' of international anti-bribery obligations and, second, the UK experience provides an interesting insight into how proceeds of corporate bribery can be targeted. Of the various options open to the UK authorities, civil recovery has proven to be the most used thus far, though it may be expected that deferred prosecution agreements (DPAs) will overtake it in time. That these non-prosecution options are so prominent in the UK response to bribery, however, is rather telling. A further issue in the context of targeting the benefits arising from corporate bribery is the extent to which the money recovered, confiscated, or disgorged equates to the value secured as a result of bribery.

Thus far, Part II of this book has focused on confiscation/forfeiture of criminal assets. But, as noted earlier, asset recovery is much wider than the legal proceedings to confiscate or forfeit; also included in the term 'asset recovery' is the asset-tracing phase, including work by national FIUs.[66] In Chap. 27, Amicelle and Chaudieu consider the role of FIUs which 'are the critical agencies at the core of the finance-security assemblage which deals with flows of illicit money, widely known as dirty money.' As greater focus came to be placed on 'following the money trail,' it quickly became apparent that law enforcement agencies would require greater access to financial information, that they would need to engage with the financial system, and that there would be a need for a centralised office or agency.[67] Amicelle and Chaudieu outline the development of FIUs, and go on to explore how transnational sharing of financial intelligence operates in practice drawing upon empirical interviews with practitioners in France, UK, Switzerland, and Canada as well as with officials from Europol.

The authors note how FIUs follow the money trail to determine the origin of financial flows, their destination, the economic reasons for the transaction/operation, and the beneficial owner of assets. Unsurprisingly there will often be a need for transnational cooperation. The authors explore different 'communication channels' used by FIUs in this regard and different cooperation channels 'depending on geographic location, legal framework and technical capacity.' Specifically, they consider the role of the Egmont Secure Web (ESW) and FIU.NET. While these two channels 'are based on the same goal of information-sharing between FIUs, there are a number of differences between them.' Amicelle and Chaudieu go on to explore what they call 'information sharing in numbers,' for example, the number of inquiries sent/received by the FIUs under consideration, as well as information exchanged. The value of their empirical study is reinforced when they consider difficulties in cooperation practices: 'These difficulties are often associated to existing differences in the ways that FIUs operate. Nevertheless, the main differences are not where they might be expected to be.' This exposes a significant problem with the International Monetary Fund (IMF) models of FIUs[68]:

> the classic typology is not sufficient to identify the key operational differences between FIUs and it masks numerous critical elements that make a difference in practice, including those between FIUs that fall into the same model. It gives the mistaken impression that every question relates to status problems.

Rather than focus on 'status problems,' the authors suggest that 'tensions in transnational financial intelligence are due either to a lack of capacity to respond to a request, to the low level of spontaneous dissemination, or to "abusive" restrictions on the use of information'—which they go on to explore in greater depth. Ultimately, they conclude that the 'classic distinction between FIUs remains important for identifying and understanding a number of national variations and international tensions, but these are certainly not the only issues at stake.'

While a great deal of emphasis is often placed on powers to confiscate (whether post-conviction or in the absence of conviction) proceeds of crime, a more muted—but if anything more powerful—option to target criminal activity is the tax system. The quintessential example of the use of tax powers to target criminals is the US case of Al Capone.[69] In Chap. 28, Friel and Kilcommins consider the increasing regulation, and control, of criminal activity through the tax realm—which they suggest represents further illustration of the trend towards 'civil-ising' the criminal process and embodies many actuarial tendencies. The authors consider how tax has come to be used as a tool of control in recent decades. In Ireland—the main focus of this chapter—tax powers really came to the fore with the establishment of the Criminal Assets Bureau in 1996.[70] Taxing proceeds of crime, however, poses some dilemmas. Is it appropriate to tax *proceeds of crime*? Does that not amount to the State essentially condoning crime—so long as an appropriate *price* is paid? And is it appropriate for the State to share in the benefits (i.e. that price) of crime? If crime is to be taxed, what expenses are to be allowed? For example, a bank robber might wish to claim the expenses associated with his criminal activity—the cost of a balaclava, petrol for the getaway car, the rented house where he was 'lying low,' the fee paid to his accountant for laundering the proceeds. Are such expenses to be permitted? What if a fine forms part of a criminal sentence—can that fine be an allowable expense?

Any person who *earns* money from illegal activity will face a 'catch 22' situation: making a tax declaration will involve informing the relevant authorities of income during a specific period, which can lead to that person facing further investigation. While there may be a choice whether or not to make a return, the authors suggest that 'Neither choice works in the individual's favour.' Friel and Kilcommins go on to suggest that the use of tax powers—using the vignette of Thomas 'Slab' Murphy in Ireland—'should be seen as a new approach involving more "networked governance" strategies that employ civil, administrative and regulatory mechanisms alongside expressive criminal law instruments.' Moreover, they suggest that the use of tax powers circumvents the due process framework of criminal law; is premised on efficiency; and affords authorities considerably enhanced powers in terms of disclosure requirements, for example. Ultimately, they conclude, taxing crime 'is simply a late modern, pragmatic response to the reality of living in "criminal enterprise" societies.'

The final chapter in Part III considers a crucial issue, albeit one that often does not receive adequate attention, namely what happens post-confiscation (at the disposal phase). Many different options present themselves, such as sending all confiscated property to a central exchequer in its entirety, using those assets for community purposes, or allowing law enforcement agencies to use such property. Significantly, this issue has recently started to attract attention at a policy level.[71] In Chap. 29, Vettori presents key findings from an EU-funded project 'RECAST—Reuse of Confiscated Assets for social purposes'—which maps existing legislation in different jurisdictions as well as considers obstacles and best practices. An important issue here is 'how seized assets are managed, because this may have a great impact on their subsequent disposal, once these assets are finally confiscated.'

While much discussion of confiscation, and how to improve its operation and/or efficiency, focuses on the confiscation itself, it is important also to consider obstacles that can arise beyond the powers of confiscation. For example, even if confiscation powers are strong, there might be problems in implementation of legislation—whether that be due to resourcing issues, lack of experience or expertise, or something else. Or there might be institutional issues, such as a lack of cooperation. Where confiscation powers are weak or ineffective, then law enforcement agencies will be hampered from the outset in efforts to strip criminals of ill-gotten gains. Also, even if a confiscation order has been granted, what if there are competing third-party claims against particular property (such as from a spouse or a mortgagee)? Moreover, assets might well depreciate during confiscation proceedings or any subsequent proceedings. Clearly then there are a number of issues, or obstacles, that can impact upon the confiscation process—even before final disposal. Vettori engages with such obstacles, as well as experiences of what works—or best practices—drawing upon experiences from different EU jurisdictions. She then goes on to consider what she describes as an 'innovative form of disposal that is attracting increasing attention at the EU level: the reuse of confiscated assets for social purposes.' Here she considers key obstacles and best practices from Belgium, France, Hungary, Italy, Luxembourg, Scotland, and Spain. She concludes that social reuse 'can bring about a significant added value,' but recognises that there is some resistance to adopting social reuse across the EU.

In conclusion, while Part III of this book delivers insights into key aspects of 'asset recovery,' inevitably some questions remain unanswered. We still do not know the extent to which asset recovery is an effective or efficient tool against organised crime and/or corruption. As Atkinson et al. note, 'Whilst the absence of robust evidence on the effectiveness of such approaches is not evidence of their ineffectiveness, this remains an important knowledge gap, not least due to the consequences of the impact of such approaches on legislation, human rights and beyond.'[72] Questions also persist in relation to the legitimacy of such powers—if not the powers as a whole, certainly distinct aspects of how those powers operate. While some jurisdictions appear to have devised a strong institutional framework (such as the Irish Criminal Assets Bureau), others are still struggling to find the right institutional approach. Given different approaches to targeting criminal assets, there have been significant difficulties with cross-border cooperation and/or recognition in this area, and efforts continue today—especially at the EU level—to find a resolution in this regard. A recurring issue throughout this book is the need for greater statistics in relation to AML, asset recovery, and CTF—as well as concerns as to the effectiveness of such responses. In the context of asset recovery, this point is summed up by the European Commission as follows:

> There is currently a scarcity of reliable statistical data in the Union of the value of criminal assets currently being identified, being confiscated, and of the value of EU cross-border freezing and confiscation orders. However, it cannot be disputed that the value of criminal assets recovered in the EU can be considered insufficient, especially if compared to the estimated revenues of organised crime groups.[73]

All that can be said with some certainty is that asset recovery is, and will continue to be, a key element of contemporary efforts to tackle organised crime and corruption.

Notes

1. Performance and Innovation Unit, *Recovering the Proceeds of Crime* (Cabinet Office, 2000), p. 13.
2. Performance and Innovation Unit, p. 13.
3. Performance and Innovation Unit, p. 16.
4. European Commission, *Communication from the Commission to the European Parliament and the Council. Proceeds of organised crime. Ensuring that 'crime does not pay.'* COM (2008) 766 final, pp. 3–4.
5. K. Bullock and S. Lister, 'Post-Conviction Confiscation of Assets in England and Wales: Rhetoric and Reality' in C. King and C. Walker (eds) *Dirty Assets: Emerging Issues in the Regulation of Criminal and Terrorist Assets* (Ashgate, 2014), p. 55. Compare R.T. Naylor, 'Wash-out: A critique of follow-the-money methods in crime control policy' (1999) 32 Crime, Law, and Social Change 1; C. Atkinson et al., *A Systematic Review of the Effectiveness of Asset-Focused Interventions Against Organised Crime* (Forthcoming report, prepared for the What Works Centre for Crime Reduction). Copy on file with author.
6. See, *inter alia*, Committee of Public Accounts, *Confiscation Orders* (HC 942, 2013–2014); National Audit Office, *Confiscation Orders* (HC 738, 2013–2014).

7. See, for example, Criminal Finances Bill, Second Reading, HC Hansard, October 25, 2016, vol. 616, col. 194 et seq.

8. Discussion with author, 2017.

9. UNODC, *Manual on International Cooperation for the Purposes of Confiscation of Proceeds of Crime* (United Nations, 2012), p. 2.

10. Howard League for Penal Reform, *Profits of Crime and Their Recovery: Report of a Committee Chaired by Sir Derek Hodgson* (Heinemann, 1984), pp. 4–5.

11. B. Vettori, *Tough on Criminal Wealth* (Springer, 2006), p. 2.

12. European Commission, *Commission Staff Working Paper. Accompanying Document to the Proposal for a Directive of the European Parliament and the Council on the Freezing and Confiscation of Proceeds of Crime in the European Union Impact Assessment* (Brussels, 12.3.2012. SWD (2012) final) para.2.1.1.

13. C. Atkinson et al., *A Systematic Review of the Effectiveness of Asset-Focused Interventions Against Organised Crime* (Forthcoming report, prepared for the What Works Centre for Crime Reduction). Copy on file with author, p. 7.

14. For example, R. Adam, 'Innovation in Asset Recovery: The Swiss Perspective' (2012) World Bank Legal Review 253–264.

15. L. Gray and others, *Few and Far: The Hard Facts on Stolen Asset Recovery* (StAR, 2014), p. 9.

16. Other institutions that play an important role in asset recovery law, policy and practice include the FATF, MONEYVAL, the European Criminal Assets Bureau, and CARIN.

17. European Commission, 'Confiscation and Asset Recovery.' Available at: https://ec.europa.eu/home-affairs/what-we-do/policies/organized-crime-and-human-trafficking/confiscation-and-asset-recovery_en (last accessed May 30, 2017). See also Michael Fernandez-Bertier, 'The confiscation and recovery of criminal property: a European Union state of the art' (2016) 17(3) ERA Forum 323–342.

18. Directive 2014/42/EU of the European Parliament and of the Council of 3 April 2014 on the freezing and confiscation of instrumentalities and proceeds of crime in the European Union.

19. M. Simonato, 'Directive 2014/42/EU and non-conviction based confiscation: a step forward on asset recovery?' (2015) 6(2) New Journal of European Criminal Law 213–228.

20. *Gogitidze v Georgia* [2015] ECHR 475, App No. 36862/05, May 12, 2015.

21. National Audit Office, *Confiscation Orders* (HC 738, 2013–2014).

22. Committee of Public Accounts, *Confiscation Orders* (HC 942, 2013–2014).

23. Home Affairs Select Committee, *Proceeds of Crime* (HC 25, 2016–2017).

24. Law Commission, Confiscation. Available at: http://www.lawcom.gov.uk/confiscation/ (last accessed May 10, 2017); J. Croft, 'Criminal Asset Confiscation Laws Under Scrutiny' Financial Times (August 22, 2016).

25. *R v Waya* [2012] UKSC 51; *R v Ahmad* [2014] UKSC 36.

26. See, for example, Fraud Act 2006, s.2.

27. The full facts are set out in *R v Waya* [2012] UKSC 51, para.36 et seq.
28. Theft Act 1968, s.15A.
29. *R v Waya* [2012] UKSC 51, para.2.
30. *R v Waya* [2012] UKSC 51, para.42.
31. *R v Waya* [2012] UKSC 51, para.12.
32. *R v Waya* [2012] UKSC 51, para.20.
33. B. Vettori and M. Zanella, 'Going beyond the confiscation of proceeds from organised crime activities: Stripping away ill-gotten gains from corruption in the enlarged Europe' in G. Antonopoulos and others, *Usual and unusual organising criminals in Europe and beyond: Profitable crimes, from underworld to upper world* (Maklu, 2011), p. 283.
34. See Chap. 17 (Maugeri) in this collection for consideration of EU developments.
35. See, for example, European Anti-Fraud Office, 'OLAF and ANAC team up to tackle corruption in Italy and beyond' OLAF Press Release, April 20, 2016.
36. One interesting point is that Italian confiscation is not neatly divided between conviction-based and non-conviction-based approaches: G. Fraschini and C. Putaturo, *Illicit Assets Recovery in Italy: Enhancing Integrity and Effectiveness of Illegal Asset Confiscation* (Transparency International Italia, 2013), p. 6.
37. 'Giovanni Falcone,' *The Telegraph*, May 25, 1992.
38. See Booz Allen Hamilton, *Comparative Evaluation of Unexplained Wealth Orders: Prepared for the US Department of Justice* (Washington DC, National Institute of Justice, 2011); L. Bartels, 'Unexplained wealth laws in Australia,' Trends and Issues in Crime and Criminal Justice No. 395 (Australian Institute of Criminology, 2010).
39. The adoption of UWOs in the UK was influenced by research produced by Transparency International-UK: see *Empowering the UK to Recover Corrupt Assets: Unexplained Wealth Orders and other new approaches to illicit enrichment and asset recovery* (March 2016).
40. Criminal Finances Act, 2017, Part 1.
41. C. King, 'Follow the Money Trail: "Civil" Forfeiture of "Criminal" Assets in Ireland' in P. van Duyne et al. (eds) *Human Dimensions in Organised Crime, Money Laundering, and Corruption* (Wolf Legal, 2013).
42. R. Dzhekova, 'Civil Forfeiture of Criminal Assets in Bulgaria' in C. King and C. Walker (eds) *Dirty Assets: Emerging Issues in the Regulation of Criminal and Terrorist Assets* (Ashgate, 2014).
43. R. Nicolae et al., 'Corruption, Confiscation and Asset Recovery in Romania—the assessment of an ongoing process.' Centrul Resurse Juridice Draft report available at: http://www.crj.ro/userfiles/editor/files/Raport%20CRJ%20-%20 Recuperarea%20produselor%20infractiunilor%20de%20coruptie.pdf (last accessed May 29, 2017).
44. See Criminal Justice Act 1987.

45. Serious Fraud Office, 'Oxford Publishing Ltd to pay almost £1.9 million as settlement after admitting unlawful conduct in its East African operations' (Press Release, July 3, 2012).

46. See Crime and Courts Act 2013.

47. See, for example, National Audit Office, *Confiscation Orders* (HC 738, 2013–2014).

48. See, for example, E. Blumenson and E. Nilsen, 'Policing for Profit: The Drug War's Hidden Economic Agenda' (1998) 65 University of Chicago Law Review 35–114; L. Levy, *A License to Steal: The Forfeiture of Property* (University of North Carolina Press, 1996).

49. In the UK, for example, see *Walsh v Director of the Assets Recovery Agency* [2005] NICA 6; *Gale v Serious Organised Crime Agency* [2011] UKSC 49.

50. C. King, 'Civil Forfeiture in Ireland—Two Decades of the Proceeds of Crime Act and the Criminal Assets Bureau' in K. Ligeti and M. Simonato (eds), *Chasing Criminal Money: Challenges and Perspectives on Asset Recovery in the EU* (Hart Publishing, 2017).

51. M. Gallant, 'Civil Processes and Tainted Assets: Exploring Canadian Models of Forfeiture' in C. King and C. Walker (eds) *Dirty Assets: Emerging Issues in the Regulation of Criminal and Terrorist Assets* (Ashgate, 2014).

52. A. Gray, 'Forfeiture Provisions and the Criminal/Civil Divide' (2012) 15(1) New Criminal Law Review 32.

53. Michele Panzavolta and Roberto Flor, 'A Necessary Evil? The Italian 'Non-Criminal System' of Asset Forfeiture' in Jon Petter Rui and Ulrich Sieber (eds), *Non-Conviction-Based Confiscation in Europe. Possibilities and Limitations on Rules Enabling Confiscation without a Criminal Conviction* (Duncker and Humblot GmbH 2016).

54. M. van den Berg, 'Proposing a Transactional Approach to Civil Forfeiture Reform' (2015) 163 University of Pennsylvania Law Review 867–926.

55. For example, S. Cassella, 'Civil Asset Recovery: The American Experience' (2013) 3 EUCrim: The European Criminal Law Associations' Forum 98–104; J. Simser, 'Perspectives on Civil Forfeiture' in S. Young (ed) *Civil Forfeiture of Criminal Property: Legal Measures for Targeting the Proceeds of Crime* (Edward Elgar, 2009); F. Cassidy, 'Targeting the Proceeds of Crime: An Irish Perspective' in T. Greenberg et al. (eds) *Stolen Asset Recovery: A Good Practices Guide for Non-Conviction Based Asset Forfeiture* (World Bank, 2009).

56. Interesting examples include D. Carpenter et al., Policing for Profit: The Abuse of Civil Asset Forfeiture (2nd ed, Institute for Justice, 2015); John Worrall, 'Addicted to the Drug War: The Role of Civil Asset Forfeiture as a Budgetary Necessity in Contemporary Law Enforcement' (2001) 29(3) Journal of Criminal Justice 171–187; K. Baicker and M. Jacobson, 'Finders keepers: Forfeiture laws, policing incentives, and local budgets' (2007) Journal of Public Economics 2113–2136;

57. For example, M. Gallant, *Money Laundering and the Proceeds of Crime: Economic Crime and Civil Remedies* (Edward Elgar, 2005); M. Gallant, 'Chaterjee v Ontario: Property, Crime and Civil Proceedings' (2010) 56 Criminal Law Quarterly 164–174; M. Gallant, 'Alberta and Ontario: Civilizing the Money Centred Model of Crime Control' (2004) 4 Asper Journal of International Business and Trade 13–33; M Gallant and C King, 'The Seizure of Illicit Assets: Patterns of Civil Forfeiture in Canada and Ireland' (2013) 42 Common Law World Review 91.

58. *Murphy v GM, PB, PC Ltd, GH; and Gilligan v CAB* [2001] 4 IR 113.

59. For example, Colin King, 'Civil Forfeiture in Ireland—Two Decades of the Proceeds of Crime Act and the Criminal Assets Bureau' in Katalin Ligeti and Michele Simonato, *Chasing Criminal Money: Challenges and Perspectives on Asset Recovery in the EU* (Hart Publishing 2017); Liz Campbell, 'Theorising Asset Forfeiture in Ireland' (2007) 71(5) Journal of Criminal Law 441; Francis Cassidy, 'Targeting the Proceeds of Crime: An Irish Perspective' in Theodore Greenberg and others, *Stolen Asset Recovery: A Good Practices Guide for Non-Conviction Based Asset Forfeiture* (World Bank 2009).

60. For consideration of such illicit financial outflows, see Global Financial Integrity, *Illicit Financial Flows to and from Developing Countries: 2005–2014* (April 2017).

61. David Cameron, Anti-Corruption Summit 2016: PM's closing remarks (May 12, 2016) <https://www.gov.uk/government/speeches/anti-corruption-summit-2016-pms-closing-remarks> (last accessed June 14, 2017).

62. Ibid.

63. Ibid.

64. For further discussion see I. Carr and R. Jago, 'Corruption, the United Nations Convention against Corruption ("UNCAC") and Asset Recovery' in C. King and C. Walker (eds) *Dirty Assets: Emerging Issues in the Regulation of Criminal and Terrorist Assets* (Ashgate, 2014).

65. J.C. Sharman, *The Despot's Guide to Wealth Management: On the International Campaign against Grand Corruption* (Cornell University Press, 2017), pp. 6–7.

66. European Commission, *Commission Staff Working Paper. Accompanying Document to the Proposal for a Directive of the European Parliament and the Council on the Freezing and Confiscation of Proceeds of Crime in the European Union Impact Assessment* (Brussels, 12.3.2012. SWD (2012) final) para.2.1.1.

67. International Monetary Fund, *Financial Intelligence Units: An Overview* (World Bank 2004) 1.

68. The judicial model, the law enforcement model, the administrative model, and the hybrid model: see International Monetary Fund, *Financial Intelligence Units: An Overview* (World Bank 2004).

69. See *Capone v US* 56 F 2d 927 (1931), cert denied, 286 US 553; (1932); *US v Capone* 93 F 2d 840 (1937), cert denied, 303 US 651 (1938).

70. Though such powers had been in existence prior to that: Finance Act 1983, s.19.
71. For example, European Parliament, Resolution of 25 October 2011 on organised crime in the European Union (2010/2309(INI)) [2013] OJ C131E/08.
72. C. Atkinson et al., *A Systematic Review of the Effectiveness of Asset-Focused Interventions Against Organised Crime* (Forthcoming report, prepared for the What Works Centre for Crime Reduction). Copy on file with author, p. 47.
73. European Commission, *Inception Impact Assessment: Strengthening the mutual recognition of criminal assets' freezing and confiscation orders.* (DG Just B1 2016/JUST/024, 07.11.2016), p. 3. A notable exception in terms of the collection of detailed statistics is the Netherlands. See, for example, E. Kruisbergen and others, 'Explaining attrition: Investigating and confiscating the profits of organized crime' (2016) 13(6) European Journal of Criminology 677.

Colin King is Reader in Law at the University of Sussex and Co-Founder of the Crime Research Centre. He was an Academic Fellow at the Honourable Society of the Inner Temple from 2014–2017. In March 2016, Colin gave oral evidence at the Home Affairs Select Committee Inquiry into the Proceeds of Crime Act. Colin is co-editor of *Dirty Assets: Emerging Issues in the Regulation of Criminal and Terrorist Assets* (King and Walker, Ashgate, 2014). Also with Clive Walker, King led an AHRC-funded research network (2014–2016) entitled 'Dirty Assets: Experiences, Reflections, and Lessons Learnt from a Decade of Legislation on Criminal Money Laundering and Terrorism Financing.' In 2017, he was awarded a prestigious AHRC Leadership Fellowship to conduct empirical research on proceeds of crime legislation.

17

Mutual Recognition and Confiscation of Assets: An EU Perspective

Anna Maria Maugeri

Introduction

In recent years, the confiscation of assets derived from criminal activities has come to represent an essential tool of the European strategy in the fight against organised crime and profit-generating crime in general. One area taxing the European legislator is how to improve judicial cooperation in this sector through the mutual recognition of confiscation orders. The conclusions of the 1999 Tampere European Council established that the principle of mutual recognition should become one of the cornerstones of the space of freedom, security and justice: 'Criminals must find no ways of exploiting differences in the judicial systems of Member States'[1] and 'no hiding place for … the proceeds of crime within the Union'.[2] Mutual recognition should apply both to judgments and to other decisions of judicial authorities. 'The principle of mutual recognition should also apply to pre-trial orders, in particular to those which would enable competent authorities … to seize assets which are easily movable.'[3] To improve the mutual recognition of confiscation orders, the Council adopted Framework Decision 2006/783/JHA.[4] Mutual recognition must be built on the harmonisation of confiscation laws but also, most importantly, on mutual trust, which demands respect for the rule of law.[5]

This chapter is focused on analysing these two connected aspects, as applied to the two types of confiscation that are considered efficient in order to

A. M. Maugeri
Department of Law, University of Catania, Catania, Italy

© The Author(s) 2018
C. King et al. (eds.), *The Palgrave Handbook of Criminal and Terrorism Financing Law*,
https://doi.org/10.1007/978-3-319-64498-1_17

facilitate the demonstration of the illegal origin of the assets to forfeit: extended confiscation and non-conviction-based confiscation.

Harmonisation of the Extended Confiscation: Council Framework Decision 2005/212/JHA

The Council Framework Decision 2005/212/JHA of 24 February 2005 is intended 'to ensure that all Member States have effective rules governing the confiscation of proceeds from crime, *inter alia*, in relation to the onus of proof regarding the source of assets held by a person convicted of an offense related to organized crime'.[6] That Framework Decision proposes three models of extended confiscation, requiring: (i) conviction, proof of illicit origin and temporal connection[7]; (ii) the same elements plus the origin of the suspected proceeds 'from *similar* criminal activities'[8]; and (iii) conviction, proof of illicit origin and disproportionate value of the property.[9] Each Member State (MS) may also consider adopting the necessary measures to enable it to confiscate property acquired by close relations of the person concerned and property transferred to a legal person in respect of which the person concerned—acting either alone or in conjunction with his close relations—has a controlling influence. The same applies if the concerned person receives a significant part of the legal person's income. MSs may use procedures other than criminal procedures to deprive the perpetrator of the property in question.[10]

The wording 'a national court based on specific facts is fully convinced' seems to require a high standard of proof such as the criminal standard[11] or at least clear and convincing evidence. That wording does not appear consistent with the preponderance of evidence standard used in civil cases because 'society has a minimum interest in the outcomes of these private causes'.[12]

Under the Framework Decision, extended confiscation therefore depends on: the respect of individual rights; conviction of the owner for listed serious offences connected to criminal organisation; the demonstration of the illicit origin of the proceeds; high standard of proof (the criminal standard, beyond any reasonable doubt, or, at least, clear and convincing evidence); temporal connection between the proceeds and the criminal activity; the origin from similar criminal activities; and the disproportionate value of the property.

However, the wording 'at least' used in the Framework Decision allows MSs to apply more extended confiscation powers with fewer safeguards. Nevertheless, some of the confiscation models adopted in the MSs go further than the Framework Decision provisions—for example, some apply confiscation without conviction for a crime, temporal connection and the proof of the criminal origin (e.g., in the Italian, English and Irish systems of law). It would have been better if the Framework Decision had imposed some minimum guarantees to improve mutual recognition.

Directive 42/2014

The Commission's implementation report about the Framework Decision 2005/212/JHA showed that the provisions on extended confiscation might be unclear and lead to piecemeal transposition while the alternative options have restricted the scope for mutual recognition of confiscation orders. Thus, the authorities in one MS will execute confiscation orders issued by another MS only if they are based on the same alternative options applied in that MS.[13] To address this problem, the European Parliament and Council adopted Directive n. 42 on 3 April 2014,[14] which MSs had to apply by 4 October 2016.[15]

Among the several policy options representing different degrees of EU-level intervention,[16] MSs preferred the maximal legislative option—that is, one going beyond the aims of the existing EU legal framework. This option would considerably enhance the harmonisation of national rules on confiscation and enforcement inter alia by amending existing provisions on extended confiscation, introducing new provisions on non-conviction-based confiscation and third-party confiscation, and introducing more effective rules on mutual recognition of freezing and confiscation orders.[17] In this regard, the Directive explicitly states that its aim is 'the adoption of minimum rules [which] will approximate the Member States' freezing and confiscation regimes, thus facilitating mutual trust and effective cross-border cooperation'.[18]

The Directive[19] has the final aim of improving, through harmonisation, mutual recognition of confiscation orders,[20] which is essential for efficient implementation of confiscation in the fight against crime. The Directive replaces the Joint Action 98/699/JHA and partially the Framework Decisions 2001/500/JHA and 2005/212/JHA.[21] In the effort to achieve the difficult balance between efficiency and safeguards, it is stated:

> This Directive respects the fundamental rights and observes the principles recognised by the Charter of Fundamental Rights of the European Union ('the Charter') and the European Convention for the Protection of Human Rights and Fundamental Freedoms ('the ECHR'), as interpreted in the case-law of the European Court of Human Rights. This Directive should be implemented in accordance with those rights and principles.[22]

Article 5 of the Directive introduces extended confiscation for the crimes listed in Article 83(1) TFEU as set out in the existing Union legislation[23] and covers other criminal activities not specifically listed in Article 83(1), where those activities are committed by participating in a criminal organisation.[24] This limitation of the field of application would have been very welcome because these are extremely serious crimes connected to organised crime, and the mitigation of safeguards, related to this form of confiscation, is acceptable only to tackle this form of crime. Article 3[25] of the Directive, however, broadens the definition of criminal offences covered by the Directive: 'as well as other legal instruments if those instruments provide specifically that this Directive applies to the criminal offences harmonised therein'.[26]

Notwithstanding that the Directive emphasises the fight against organised crime,[27] it does not limit its application to this sector. Indeed, its provisions can be applied to all crimes listed in Article 3; in addition, the provisions can apply to all offences that are subject to harmonisation under Article 83.2.[28] Moreover, the scope of the Directive extends to the offences committed 'with the intention of generating regular profits from criminal offences'.[29]

The standard of proof adopted is not entirely clear. Unlike Framework Decision 212/2005, Article 4 of the original proposed Directive used the expression 'substantially more probable'; in other words, the proposal did not require the court to be 'fully convinced' or to apply the criminal standard of proof. However, when the Directive was passed it did not demand that standard (i.e., substantially more probable), but instead required that 'a court, on the basis of the circumstances of the case, including the specific facts and available evidence, … is satisfied that the property in question is derived from criminal conduct'.[30] By using the term 'is satisfied', Article 5 demands a lower standard of the proof than 'fully *convinced*' as used in the Framework Decision n.212/2005, Article 3. Similarly, the Directive specifies that 'it could, for example, be sufficient for the court to consider on the balance of probabilities, or to reasonably presume that it *is substantially more probable,* that the property in question has been obtained from criminal conduct than from other activities'[31] (emphasis added).

The question is whether the civil standard of proof based on the preponderance of evidence is sufficient, because Article 4 of the proposal and recital 21 of the Directive added the adverb *substantially.* The civil standard is provided in some common law systems, also for kinds of extended confiscation that follow conviction (such as North-American criminal forfeiture and British post-conviction confiscation). The French versions of the Directive use the expression *nettement plus probable*, which indicates more clearly that illicit origin must be with little doubt, and the Italian translation, *molto più proba-*

bile, supports this construction. In conclusion, Article 5 could be interpreted like the 'clear and convincing evidence' standard, a reinforced civil standard which ensures that the unlawful origin of the proceeds *is certainly more probable than not.*

The civil standard of proof, even if strengthened, will cause an inevitable weakening of criminal procedural safeguards, including the presumption of innocence and the right to defence. The civil standard is acceptable only in civil cases because 'the society has a minimum interest in the outcomes of these private causes'.[32] Furthermore, the Directive permits the use of presumptions by the MS in order to demonstrate the illegal origin of the property to confiscate.[33]

In practice, extended confiscation is based on the presumption of the illegal origin of the assets, which follows the conviction for some crimes; thereupon, the owner must give evidence of the legal origin of his assets. This reversal of the burden of proof is considered reasonable to some legislators—the investigating authorities are relieved of the heavy task of having to prove a direct nexus between the various assets of the accused and the specific criminal activities being investigated. Thus, the presence of circumstances of the unlawful origin becomes 'sufficient proof', that is, the accused has to refute the presumption that his or her wealth is linked to organised crime.

For Article 5 of the Directive, and in the practice of many MSs, the conviction for a specific crime is enough to engage the presumptions (in relation to the illegal origin of the proceeds) and the civil standard of proof. Even a conviction for crimes not connected with organised crime, and not so serious, will suffice.

The Directive seems to express the same opinion, expressed in some Italian Supreme Court judgments, which restrict the application of constitutional safeguards in criminal matters when the sanction affects a property right. The presumptions (in relation to the illegal origin of the proceeds) do not violate the presumption of innocence under Article 27 paragraph 2 of the Italian Constitution, because this principle concerns only the protection of personal freedom (under Article 13),[34] and the right to silence affects only the demonstration of the responsibility of the accused, and after the sentence, it is not relevant.[35]

In the opinion of some judgments and scholars, the rights of the defence are respected because the owner is afforded the opportunity to demonstrate the lawful source of the assets.[36] In this respect, the European Court of Human Rights (ECtHR) held that the right to be presumed innocent under Article 6(2) does not arise in confiscation proceedings, which adopt the civil standard of the proof, because they do not involve criminal charges.[37] Only the fair trial provisions under Article 6(1) are applicable.[38] The problem is that the silence of the accused can become evidence by supporting the presumption of the illicit origin of the assets. Furthermore, as the Italian Supreme Court affirmed, in order to refute the presumption, the owner has to fully demonstrate how accumulation of the assets came about.[39]

In conclusion, in order to apply types of extended confiscations that can affect entire estates on the assumption of an alleged illegal activity, it would be preferable—in terms of respect for the presumption of innocence and the right to silence, as well as the right to property and proportionality—to apply the criminal standard of proof. This does not mean that the accuser has to prove the nexus between each property and a specific crime, but he has to give sufficient evidence on the basis of the criminal standard of unlawful acquisition. In the Italian system, it would be sufficient to use circumstantial evidence under Article 192 of the Italian Criminal Procedure Code ('serious, precise and consistent evidence').[40]

The Directive also provides that '[T]he fact that the property of the person is disproportionate to his lawful income could be among those facts giving rise to a conclusion of the court that the property derives from criminal conduct.'[41] This element is relied on by Article 12 *sexies* of Law Decree 306/1992 (extended confiscation after conviction) of the Italian system[42] and by Article 127 bis of the Spanish Criminal Code (L.O. 1/2015), *decomiso ampliado* (extended confiscation). The Italian Supreme Court imposes on the prosecutor the need to demonstrate that the value of each asset is disproportionate to the lawful income of the convicted person at the moment of acquisition.[43] The generic proof of the disproportionate character of the estate is not enough. In this way, the defendant is required only to prove the legal origin of the goods whose disproportionate character was established and limited to the moment of its acquisition. The Directive also contains another important element to limit the scope of extended confiscation: 'Member States could also determine a requirement for a certain period of time during which the property could be deemed to have originated from criminal conduct.'[44]

These two elements, the disproportionate character of the property and the temporal limitation of the presumption of illegal origin, are demanded in Framework Decision 212/2005, Article 3. In some judgments, the Italian Supreme Court has required the explanation of the temporal connection between the purchase and the suspected criminal activity in order to apply the confiscation preventive measure[45] as well as, as examined before, the demonstration of the disproportionate character of the property for each asset at the moment of the purchase. Likewise, the (UK) Proceeds of Crime Act 2002, section 10, provides for a limit of six years.

In Italy, the Supreme Court has also recently established that the confiscation preventive measure is of a 'preventive nature', and not punitive, only if the confiscation is applied to the property purchased in temporal connection with the 'social dangerousness' of the subject.[46]

Another important limit to the extension of this model of confiscation derives from the definition of the concept of 'proceeds' in the Directive: '… proceeds can include any property … which has been intermingled with property acquired from legitimate sources, up to the assessed value of the intermingled proceeds'.[47] This specification—'up to the assessed value of the intermingled proceeds'—is a very important safeguard against the temptation to apply the extended confiscation[48] or the preventive measure[49] to entire companies when the illicit proceeds were invested in the business, because it would be impossible to separate licit from illicit property. In this way, the extended confiscation becomes a kind of general confiscation, a disproportionate punishment in violation of the legality principle and of the constitutional protection of private property, as well as of the principle of proportionality.[50]

The Directive further suggests the introduction of a clause to ensure compliance with the principle of proportionality in two cases. First, 'the relevant provisions could be applicable where, in view of the particular circumstances of the case at hand, such a measure is proportionate having regard in particular to the value of the instrumentalities concerned'.[51] Second, 'confiscation should not be ordered' in exceptional circumstances, where confiscation would represent undue hardship for the affected person.[52]

This clause ensures respect for the proportionality principle in cases where illegal profits were reinvested, and their removal would result in jeopardising the viability of a business.[53] The respect of this principle hampers the use of confiscation of proceeds as a punitive sanction, but this still happens in the Italian and British legislative systems when the confiscation of the value is applied in full to each accomplice[54] or to the aider who has not received the profits.[55] In a number of recent cases, the English Courts have tried to limit the scope of confiscation due to the proportionality principle,[56] in order to respect Article 1 of Protocol 1 (A1P1) of the European Convention,[57] such as in *Waya*.[58]

The Directive establishes that 'it is … necessary to enable the determination of the precise extent of the property to be confiscated even after a final conviction for a criminal offence, in order to permit the full execution of confiscation orders when no property or insufficient property was initially identified and the confiscation order remains unexecuted'.[59] The European legislator would like to ensure the confiscation of the illicit proceeds, notwithstanding the evasive manoeuvres of suspected or accused persons who conceal property with the hope of benefiting from that property once they have served their sentences. This rule is interesting as it attempts to guarantee the efficiency of confiscation orders, for example, section 22 of the (UK) Proceeds of Crime Act 2002 permits the reconsideration of the available amount (even at the risk of creating problems, such as the risk of confiscating legal earnings with negative effects on the convict's rehabilitation).[60]

Finally, third-party confiscation is allowed only under specific conditions, where the acquiring third party paid an amount lower than market value and should have suspected that the assets are proceeds of crime, and after an assessment showing that confiscation of assets directly from the person who transferred them is unlikely to succeed. This rule introduces two well-balanced criteria to protect the rights of third parties, namely that (i) it protects bona-fide purchasers who (ii) have paid a market value.[61]

Harmonisation: Non-conviction-Based Confiscation

Article 4, paragraph 2,[62] of the Directive introduces non-conviction-based confiscation in limited circumstances with a view to addressing cases where criminal prosecution cannot be exercised because the suspect is permanently ill or when his flight or illness prevents effective prosecution within a reasonable time and poses the risk that it could be barred by statutory limitation. At the proposal stage, Article 5 included also the case of the suspect's death; the Italian and British systems of law provide for this case.

It seems possible to apply without conviction only the confiscation of the property provided by Article 4, paragraph 1 ('Where confiscation on the basis of paragraph 1 is not possible') of the Directive and not also the extended confiscation by Article 5, as it has already been established in several legal systems.[63]

The Directive, therefore, does not accept the common model of *actio in rem*, and non-conviction-based confiscation does not become an alternative to confiscation post-conviction, applied in order to implement the forfeiture of estate with more impact but fewer safeguards.[64] It is very important to stress that neither Article 4(2) nor paragraph 15 of the Directive excludes the possibility that an MS may introduce forms of confiscation without conviction in other situations; both specify that non-conviction-based confiscation has to be guaranteed 'at least in the cases of illness or absconding of the suspected or accused person'. The Directive explicitly states that 'This Directive lays down minimum rules. It does not prevent Member States from providing more extensive powers in their national law, including, for example, in relation to their rules on evidence.'[65] Furthermore, the Directive takes no position on the essential safeguards that must accompany such confiscation. This means that the confiscation preventive measure and the British or Irish civil forfeiture regimes[66] may comply with the Directive, but mutual recognition is not mandatory for corresponding states.

The Directive, in fact, allows MSs to choose the nature of the confiscation: 'Freezing and confiscation under this Directive are autonomous concepts, which should not prevent Member States from implementing this Directive using instruments which, in accordance with national law, would be considered as sanctions or other types of measures.'[67] It is also stated that 'Member States are free to bring confiscation proceedings which are linked to a criminal case before any competent court.'[68] Article 4 concerns confiscation in relation to a criminal offence, but it allows MSs to choose whether confiscation should be imposed by criminal and/or civil/administrative courts.[69]

Cooperation Through the 1990 Council of Europe Strasbourg Convention

The 1990 Council of Europe Strasbourg Convention, which has been ratified by all EU MSs, still remains the cornerstone of judicial cooperation in relation to confiscation without conviction. This is because the 2005 Council of Europe Convention on Laundering, Search, Seizure and Confiscation of the Proceeds from Crime and on the Financing of Terrorism[70] has been ratified by only 15 MSs. The other 13 (including France, Germany, Italy and the UK) have not ratified it but continue to apply the 1990 Council of Europe Convention.

The Convention of 1990 would seem not to have adopted any particular stance on the legal nature of confiscation, defining it indifferently as a 'penalty' or 'measure' under Article 1(d); therefore, proceedings *in rem* are also subject to the Convention.[71] The explanatory report specifies that each type of procedure, regardless of connection with criminal proceedings and the procedural rules applicable, can be the basis for the application of a confiscation order, so long as it is conducted by a judicial authority and has criminal nature, because it concerns the instrumentalities and the proceeds of crime: proceedings *in rem* are said to fall into this category.[72] Article 13 obliges the

Contracting Parties to implement requests made of them by other State Parties. However, the grounds for refusal of cooperation contained in Article 18 are many—especially in relation to safeguarding the fundamental principles of the legal system of the requested party.[73]

Crisafulli-Friolo is an interesting case of judicial cooperation concerning Italian preventive confiscation.[74] The French Court based its decision on the fact that, pursuant to Articles 12 and 14 of the Strasbourg Convention of 1990, mutual assistance was required; the confiscation order was final and enforceable; French law provided for the confiscation of the proceeds of drug trafficking and subsequent money laundering activities (albeit with the confiscation as an accessory punishment); and the French legislation did not require the same legislation.[75]

Mutual Recognition of Confiscation: Framework Decision 2006/783/JHA

The Framework Decision 2006/783/JHA has been introduced to apply the principle of mutual recognition to confiscation orders, and in particular to extended confiscations under Article 3 of Framework Decision 2005/212/JHA, now replaced by Article 5 of the Directive 42/2014.[76]

While this Framework Decision is the leading legal instrument on mutual recognition of judicial decisions on confiscation, the recognition of confiscation issued by a non-criminal court faces significant difficulties, not least because Article 1 (Objective) demands a court competent in criminal matters. This clearly impedes cooperation under this instrument where MSs apply confiscations outside criminal proceedings. We can consider also that Article 2 defines a 'confiscation order' as a final penalty or measure imposed by a court following proceedings in relation to a criminal offence or offences, resulting in the definitive deprivation of property; thus, this requires a judicial proceeding connected with one or more crimes.[77] This, then, would preclude, for example, the procedure under section 289(6)–(7) of the (UK) Proceeds of Crime Act 2002.[78]

On this note, Article 6 of the European Convention of Human Rights (ECHR) accepts a broad definition of 'criminal matter'.[79] Punitive administrative or other proceedings for the enforcement of afflictive sanctions can be regarded as being of a criminal nature, but the Strasbourg Court does not include the confiscation preventive measure in its autonomous concept of criminal matter neither does it regard the English 'civil recovery' or 'cash forfeiture' as 'criminal matters'.[80] It is significant then that the Framework Decision refers to confiscation orders against individual convicted parties, insisting that it concerns forms of criminal confiscation issued as a result of a criminal trial in the strict sense.

The Framework Decision, however, is not restricted to mutual recognition of confiscation orders made on the basis of the power and the extended powers indicated in the previous Framework Decision 2005/212 (Articles 2 and 3)—now the Directive 42/2014 (Articles 4 and 5). The Framework Decision (Article 2(d)(iv)) also permits mutual recognition in relation to measures taken with additional powers of confiscation—permitted by the Framework Decision 212/2005 and by the Directive 42/2014—regardless of the safeguards recognised and the powers implemented; this could potentially conflict with fundamental principles such as the presumption of innocence. In this way, the Framework Decision has chosen not to establish and impose a minimum standard of safeguards on which the principle of mutual recognition should be based. However, it does permit mutual recognition to be refused (Article 8 n. 2, g and n. 3) in relation to forms of extended confiscation applied with these additional powers (the extended powers of confiscation referred to in Article 2(d)(iv), that is, extended powers of confiscation under the law of the issuing State).[81]

In conclusion, the Framework Decision 783/2006 does not hinder the mutual recognition of confiscation orders issued in an *actio in rem*, but in these cases recognition is not mandatory.

The Judgments of the ECHR: The Gogidtize Case and the Nature of Non-conviction-Based Confiscation

According to the ECtHR, the concept of 'penalty' is an autonomous Convention concept under Articles 6 and 7.[82] The Court takes into account that while some proceedings share some of the characteristics of civil proceedings, the reality is often that they are criminal proceedings under another name, and they should therefore attract the same due process and evidential constraints, including the presumption of innocence, that are available to defendants on any other criminal charge.

Notwithstanding this autonomous concept of 'penalty', the ECtHR has always considered some forms of extended confiscation without conviction (variously referred to as *'confisca di prevenzione'*—civil recovery or civil forfeiture), based on rebuttable presumptions, compatible with the 'fair trial' guarantee under Article 6(1) and with the protection of property ensured by A1P1. The Court has not applied either Articles 6(2) (presumption of innocence) or 7 (retrospective criminalisation) because these forms of confiscation are not considered penalties.

In *Gogitidze v Georgia*,[83] the ECtHR confirmed its opinion in relation to civil forfeiture (civil proceeding *in rem*). The Georgian provisions were specifically aimed at recovering wrongfully acquired property and unexplained wealth from a public official, as well as from that person's family members, close relatives and so-called connected persons, even without prior criminal conviction of the official concerned. The Georgian provisions further permitted the burden of proof in the proceedings to be shifted to the respondent. Even in this case, the ECtHR did not consider the confiscation a 'penalty', but stated that 'the forfeiture of property ordered as a result of civil proceedings *in rem*, without involving determination of a criminal charge, is not of a punitive but of a preventive and/or compensatory nature'.[84]

The Court acknowledged that the confiscation order amounted to interference with the right to peaceful enjoyment of possessions under A1P1, ECHR. The Court reiterated that 'where a confiscation measure has been imposed independently of the existence of a criminal conviction but rather as a result of separate "civil" … judicial proceedings … such a measure … constitutes nevertheless control of the use of property within the meaning of the second paragraph of Article 1 of Protocol No. 1',[85] which gives the State the right to adopt 'such laws as it deems necessary to control the use of property in accordance with the general interest'.[86] So In the Court's opinion, this form of confiscation is not a penalty, but only a manifestation of this power of control by the MSs, which has to be prescribed by law, in pursuit of a legitimate public interest and to be proportionate to the legitimate aim pursued, in respect of the principle of proportionality.[87]

The Court, however, did not require conformity with the principle of non-retroactivity (even if respected in this case) because this forfeiture is not considered a penalty.[88]

In relation to the pursuit of a public interest, this form of confiscation without conviction seeks 'to prevent the unlawful use, in a way dangerous to society, of possessions whose lawful origin has not been established. It therefore considers that the aim of the resulting interference serves the general interest.'[89] The Court accepted that the impugned measure forms part of a crime-prevention policy; it considers that in implementing such a policy, the legislature must have a wide margin of appreciation both with regard to the existence of a problem affecting the public interest. In the *Gogitidze* case, the public interest was represented by the fight against the corruption and in other cases by the fight against the 'mafia' or against drug trafficking.

Furthermore, the Court did not sustain a violation of the right to property provided by A1P1 because the purposes of this form of confiscation are considered proportionate to the instrument. In the *Gogitidze* case, the court said that 'any interference' has to 'be reasonably proportionate to the aim sought to be realised. In other words, a "fair balance" must be struck between the demands of the general interest of the community and the requirements of the protection of the individual's fundamental rights.'[90] The court further stated that 'a wide margin of appreciation is usually allowed to the State under the Convention when it comes to general measures of political, economic or social strategy, and the Court generally respects the legislature's policy choice unless it is "manifestly without reasonable foundation"'.[91]

The Court adopted a broad concept of 'proceeds', even in relation to third parties (without prejudicing the rights of bona fide third parties): 'any incomes and other indirect benefits, obtained by converting or transforming the direct proceeds of crime or intermingling them with other, possibly lawful, assets'.[92]

The Court went on to say that the compensatory aspect consists of the obligation to restore the injured party in civil proceedings to the status which had existed prior to the unjust enrichment of the public official in question, by returning wrongfully acquired property either to its previous lawful owner or, in the absence of such, to the State.[93] In this instance, the Court was of the opinion that the forfeiture was in accordance with the general interest in ensuring that the use of property does not procure an advantage for the applicant to the detriment of the community.[94] The Court also emphasised that the deterrent and preventive aims of civil proceedings *in rem* were 'to prevent unjust enrichment through corruption as such, by sending a clear signal to public officials already involved in corruption or considering so doing that their wrongful acts, even if they passed unscaled by the criminal justice system, would nevertheless not procure pecuniary advantage either for them or for their families'.[95]

The Court was unequivocal in relation to the reversal of the burden of the proof: 'there can be nothing arbitrary, for the purposes of the 'civil' limb of Article 6(1) of the Convention, in the reversal of the burden of proof onto the respondents in the forfeiture proceedings *in rem*'.[96] Thus, the Court demanded a substantiated claim against the accused. In this instance, the Court put great emphasis on the numerous supporting documents available in the case file and rejected the applicants' complaints 'that the domestic courts ordered the confiscation of their property on the grounds of a mere, unsubstantiated suspicion put forward by the public prosecutor'.[97] In this way, this position of the

ECtHR, while expressly allowing the reversal of the burden of the proof, appears not far from the position of the Italian Supreme Court, which does not admit a shift of the burden of the proof but instead places a mere allegation burden on those affected by the confiscation preventive measure (even though it gives evidentiary value to silence).

The ECtHR also demands the demonstration of the illicit origin of the proceeds from the accuser, even if it is to a civil standard ('or a high probability of illicit origins'). The Court:

> ...found it legitimate for the relevant domestic authorities to issue confiscation orders on the basis of a preponderance of evidence which suggested that the respondents' lawful incomes could not have sufficed for them to acquire the property in question. Indeed, whenever a confiscation order was the result of civil proceedings *in rem* which related to the proceeds of crime derived from serious offences, the Court did not require proof "beyond reasonable doubt" of the illicit origins of the property in such proceedings. Instead, proof on a balance of probabilities or a high probability of illicit origins, combined with the inability of the owner to prove the contrary, was found to suffice for the purposes of the proportionality test under Article 1 of Protocol No. 1.[98]

It remains very important, however, to guarantee the right of the defence in proceedings conducted in an 'adversarial manner'[99] in accordance with Article 6(1). According to the Court, the respondents in the civil proceedings for confiscation must be afforded 'a reasonable opportunity to put their arguments before the domestic courts'.[100]

In general, the ECtHR has expressed in this case a favourable disposition towards civil forfeiture as a strategy against serious crimes[101]:

> Having regard to such international legal mechanisms as the 2005 United Nations Convention against Corruption, the Financial Action Task Force's (FATF) Recommendations and the two relevant Council of Europe Conventions of 1990 and 2005 concerning confiscation of the proceeds of crime (..), the Court observes that common European and even universal legal standards can be said to exist which encourage, firstly, the confiscation of property linked to serious criminal offences such as corruption, money laundering, drug offences and so on, without the prior existence of a criminal conviction.[102]

In conclusion, while the ECtHR did not regard non-conviction-based forfeiture as a 'penalty', such forfeiture can be regarded as compensatory so long as the illicit nature of the proceeds has been absolutely established—even if only by circumstantial evidence. In other words, using proceeds of crime to purchase property does not legitimise that acquisition. But, the more that forfeiture is based on presumptions and reduced burden of proof, the more likely that a punitive purpose emerges. In such circumstances, the confiscation risks becoming a punishment of the suspect, for offences not proved in court but only suspected. In any case, when it is possible to forfeit an entire company or all the assets of an individual, with the connected stigmatisation for those affected (by being considered a habitual offender or Mafioso or in any case involved in criminal activities) then the confiscation has a punitive impact.[103]

Civil forfeiture, moreover, can often be applied at a step removed from the original illegal activity, even many years after that criminal activity. It will remain possible to start proceedings to forfeit the illicit proceeds, even if they are invested in a legal activity for many years (such as a businessman who has invested in his factory the proceeds of money laundering). In Italy, it is possible that criminal prosecution might become time barred, but it is always possible to apply the confiscation preventive measure. This represents a kind of sword of Damocles hanging indefinitely over freedom of economic initiative.

So, the question remains whether, in light of the autonomous notion of criminal matters adopted by the ECtHR,[104] it is possible to attribute criminal nature to civil forfeiture (non-conviction-based confiscation) in order to apply the safeguards of Articles 6 and 7 of the ECHR. Confiscation is a definitive measure applied in connection with criminal offences (the nature of the infraction); it involves a stigma for those affected and a limitation of the freedom of economic initiative and of property rights, pursuing a deterrent scope (the nature of the sanction); and it can hit all the assets of the affected (the severity of the sanction). A number of authors have expressed similar sentiments, stressing the punitive nature of confiscation without conviction in the autonomous meaning of the ECHR, because this kind of confiscation limits property rights, limits the freedom of economic activity and stigmatises the person affected.[105] The dissenting opinion of Judge Pinto de Albuquerque in the *Varvara* case is very interesting:

…the Court affords weaker safeguards for more serious, indeed more intrusive, confiscation measures, and stronger guarantees for less serious confiscation measures. Some "civil-law" measures and some "crime prevention" measures, which disguise what is in effect action to annihilate the suspect's economic capacities, sometimes on threat of imprisonment should they fail to pay the sum due, are subject to weak, vague supervision, or indeed escape the Court's control, while other intrinsically administrative measures are sometimes treated as equivalent to penalties and made subject to the stricter safeguards of Articles 6 and 7 of the Convention.[106]

The Prospects for the Mutual Recognition of Confiscation Orders

The Directive will require MSs to reform their legislation and so could represent an opportunity for a rationalisation of the rules. For example, Article 2 of the Directive, which provides for a broad definition of 'proceeds', will force the Italian legislator to reform the obsolete Article 240 of the Criminal Procedure Code that still distinguishes between the price and the profit and considers optional the confiscation of proceeds. It will also be necessary for the Italian legislator to work out conflicts in case law (gross or net profit, confiscation of intangible benefits). The concept of proceeds as defined in this Directive should be interpreted in a similar way to the proceeds of criminal offences not covered by this Directive.

In reforming legislation on confiscation, the national legislator has to balance the needs of efficiency and criminal law safeguards, which must be a necessary requirement of mutual recognition. The ECHR, the EU Charter of Fundamental Rights and national constitutional principles will constitute the parameters for assessing the legitimacy of national provisions as well as of the models of confiscations in the Directive. And, of course, there will be a key role for the right to property,[107] the related principle of proportionality,[108] the right to a fair trial,[109] the principle of legality[110] and the principle of *ne bis in idem*.[111]

Once revisions are in place, it will be interesting to analyse whether, and to what extent, the safeguards provided for by the Directive should be considered binding on the national legislator, the mechanisms of adaptation, the consequences for national legal systems, and whether the provisions of the Directive which tend to emphasise efficiency should be considered mandatory. In relation to whether the Directive should be binding on national legislatures, the Directive[112] does contain a proportionality clause—a principle well established in some legal systems[113] but not in the Italian system of law.[114] As for the case of proceeds of crime that are intermingled with property acquired from legitimate sources, the Directive allows, as discussed above, for confiscation only 'up to the assessed value of the intermingled proceeds', avoiding the practice of the Italian Courts to use extended confiscation as a general confiscation of property. On the other hand, the Directive provides for the confiscation of the value of instrumentalities of crime,[115] which assumes an unjustified punitive nature even in the absence of conviction.

The Framework Decision 2006/783 is the basis for mutual recognition of the forms of confiscation provided in the MSs in accordance with the Directive. Some authors, however, affirm the necessity of a new instrument which 'should mirror the new Directive. In other words, the elements in the new Directive should also have a basis in an instrument based on the principle of mutual recognition and execution.'[116]

Furthermore, the question of mutual recognition of non-conviction-based confiscation is still open. In approving the Directive, the European Parliament and the Council issued a Statement which urged the Commission to identify a model of *actio in rem* in respect of shared common traditions:

> …on the confiscation of property deriving from activities of a criminal nature, also in the absence of a conviction of a specific person or persons for these activities.[117]

The European legislator then is aware of the need for further reflection on whether to improve the *actio in rem*.

In the Eighth Meeting of the Consultative Forum of Prosecutors General and Directors of Public Prosecutions of the MSs of the EU,[118] the necessity to improve the recognition and execution of non-conviction-based confiscation orders was emphasised. Additionally, more and more MSs have introduced an *actio in rem* in their system of law[119] and demand the mutual recognition of confiscation without conviction.

Two strategies could be adopted in the future to face this question: either impose harmonisation on all MSs in order to build a shared model of confiscation without conviction or impose the mutual recognition of confiscation without conviction even if the MSs do not adopt this model.[120] This second minimalist approach must be based on mutual trust and confidence among the competent authorities, and its implementation would require a change of approach by the European legislator.

Until now, the European legislator has always applied an approach more concerned with effectiveness than with the respect of safeguards, subject to demanding 'at least' a specific model of confiscation 'minimalist in terms of efficiency', allowing MSs to introduce more extended powers of confiscation but with fewer safeguards,[121] without concern for a minimum of essential respect for constitutional safeguards. The prospect for the future may be represented by the effort to identify minimum safeguards in the presence of which MSs should apply non-conviction-based confiscation, even if they do not adopt this model.

The Stockholm Programme highlights the need to intensify work in order to achieve full cooperation based on the principle of mutual recognition, through harmonisation, not only of the incriminating norms but also of the minimum rights to the extent necessary for mutual recognition, in order to build the mutual trust that is the indispensable basis of cooperation. The Europe of rights must be an area in which the rights of suspected and accused persons are protected.

In any case, it would be appropriate in the future to distinguish cases in which there is a 'pure' non-conviction-based confiscation and cases where the procedure aimed at non-conviction-based confiscation is accessory and parallel to a criminal trial (this often happens in the Italian system of law). In these cases, mutual recognition on the basis of existing instruments could be allowed.

Moreover, further effort is necessary to determine if it is possible to elaborate a broader model of 'actio in rem' reflecting the proposals of the Recommendation of the European Parliament (2011)[122] and the FATF Recommendations[123] and complying with the highest standards of safeguards and judicial control, as proposed by the Committee on Civil Liberties, Justice and Home Affairs (LIBE) Committee.[124] The LIBE Committee proposed a model of confiscation without conviction, to be applied only to the fight against organised crime, to be subject to the ECHR guarantees and in accordance with a high standard of proof of the illicit origin of the proceeds.

Any in rem non-conviction-based model of confiscation must contain sufficient safeguards so as to be compatible with standards in certain systems of law, such as, for example, the German Verfall and Erweiterten Verfall or the Austrian Abschöpfung der Bereicherung or Verfall.[125] In this respect, the implementation of Article 8 of the Directive will be very important in order to provide procedural safeguards for the defence and third parties ensuring, first of all, a proceeding in front of a judicial authority[126] and so the right to an effective remedy and a fair trial which must take the form of an adversarial judicial proceeding, as emphasised by the ECtHR in Gogitidze.[127]

A further issue to briefly mention is the social reuse of confiscated assets[128] (imposed in some countries, such as Italy and Spain). There currently is greater focus on the powers to deprive a person of assets than on what those assets are subsequently used for.[129] In this respect, Article 10.3 of the Directive establishes that MSs shall consider taking measures allowing confiscated property to be used for public interest or social purposes.[130]

In conclusion, the process of Europeanisation of the mechanisms of judicial cooperation cannot only emphasise the sword effect of criminal law but must also ensure the shielding effect of rights:

> [I]f it is true that mutual recognition is a tool that strengthens the area of security, freedom and justice, it is equally true that the protection of human rights and fundamental freedoms is a prius that legitimizes the existence and development of that space.[131]

Notes

1. Tampere European Council, Presidency Conclusions (1999) para 5.
2. Ibid. para 6.
3. Ibid. para 36.
4. In particular, to implement extended confiscations under Article 3 of the Council Framework Decision 2005/212/JHA of 24 February 2005 on Confiscation of Crime-Related Proceeds, Instrumentalities and Property [2005] OJ L68/49, replaced by Directive 2014/42/EU of the European Parliament and of the Council of 3 April 2014 on the freezing and confiscation of instrumentalities and proceeds of crime in the European Union [2014] OJ L127/39.
5. See Valsamis Mitsilegas, 'The Constitutional Implications of Mutual Recognition in Criminal Matters in the EU' (2006) 43(5) Common Market Law Review 1277; Matthias Borgers, 'Mutual Recognition and the European Court of Justice: The Meaning of Consistent Interpretation and Autonomous and Uniform Interpretation of Union Law for the Development of the Principle of Mutual Recognition in Criminal Matters' (2010) 18(2) European Journal of Crime, Criminal Law and Criminal Justice 99.
6. Framework Decision 2005/212/JHA (n 4) para 10.
7. Ibid. art 3(2).
8. Ibid. art 3(2)(b).
9. Ibid. art 3(2)(c). See Anna Maria Maugeri, 'The Criminal Sanctions Against the Illicit Proceeds of Criminal Organisations' (2012) 3(3–4) New Journal of European Criminal Law 257, 280ff.
10. Framework Decision 2005/212/JHA (n 4) art 3(3)–(4).
11. In civil law systems, that standard would be the full belief of the judge, whilst in common law systems, that standard would be 'beyond any reasonable doubt'.
12. *Addington v Texas* 441 US 423 (1979); US Sentencing Commission, *Guidelines Manual* (West 1993) 1; Anna Maria Maugeri, *Le Moderne Sanzioni Tra Funzionalità e Garantismo* (Giuffrè 2001) 876ff.
13. Matthias Borgers, 'Confiscation of the Proceeds of Crime: The European Union Framework' in Colin King and Clive Walker (eds), *Dirty Assets: Emerging Issues in the Regulation of Criminal and Terrorist Assets* (Ashgate Publishing 2014) 48.
14. Directive 2014/42/EU (n 4).
15. See about the Directive, Anna Maria Maugeri, 'La Direttiva 2014/42/UE Relativa alla Confisca degli Strumenti e dei Proventi da Reato nell'Unione Europea tra Garanzie ed Efficienza: Un "Work in Progress"' (2015) 1 Diritto Penale Contemporaneo 300; Nicola Selvaggi, 'On Instruments Adopted in the Area of Freezing and Confiscation' (2015) 7 Diritto Penale Contemporaneo 1.

16. (i) A non-legislative option, (ii) a minimal legislative option (correcting deficiencies in the existing EU legal framework which inhibit it from functioning as intended) and (iii) a maximal legislative option (going beyond the aims of the existing EU legal framework).

17. James Forsaith and others, 'Study for an Impact Assessment on a Proposal for a New Legal Framework on the Confiscation and Recovery of Criminal Assets' (2012) <https://ec.europa.eu/home-affairs/sites/homeaffairs/files/e-library/docs/external_study_used_as_a_basis_for_the_commission_ia_october_2012_en.pdf> accessed 20 March 2017.

18. Recital 5.

19. Based on art 82, s 2 and art 83, s 1 (Directive 2014/42 (n 4) para 5). See Carmela Salazar, 'Commento Art 82' in Carlo Curti Gialdino (ed), *Codice dell'Unione Europea* (Jovene 2012) 896ff; Carmela Salazar, 'Commento art 83' in Carlo Curti Gialdino (ed), *Codice dell'Unione Europea* (Jovene 2012) 914ff.

20. European Criminal Bar Association, 'Statement on the Proposal for a Directive of the European Parliament and of the Council on the Freezing and Confiscation of Proceeds of Crime in the European Union' <www.ecba.org/extdocserv/201210_assetseizureECBA_statement.pdf> accessed 12 July 2016.

21. Directive 2014/42 (n 4) art 14.

22. Ibid. para 38.

23. 'Member *States* shall adopt the necessary measures to enable the *confiscation*, either in whole or in part, of property belonging to a person convicted of a criminal offence *which is liable to give rise, directly or indirectly, to economic benefit, where a court, on the basis of the circumstances of the case, including the specific facts and available evidence, such as that the value of the property is disproportionate to the lawful income of the convicted person, is satisfied that the property in question is derived from criminal conduct*': ibid. art 5 (emphasis added).

24. As defined in Council Framework Decision 2008/841/JHA of 24 October 2008 on the fight against organised crime [2008] OJ L300/42.

25. As amended by LIBE Committee (amendment n 28).

26. Art 83, para 2 TFUE. See Valsamis Mitsilegas, 'European Criminal Law and Resistance to Communautarisation After Lisbon' (2010) 1(4) New Journal of European Criminal Law 463; Johan Boucht, 'Extended Confiscation and the Proposed Directive on Freezing and Confiscation of Criminal Proceeds in the EU' (2013) 21(2) European Journal of Crime, Criminal Law and Criminal Justice 141.

27. Directive 2014/42 (n 4) para 19.

28. Ibid. art 3.

29. Ibid. para 20. See also Boucht (n 26) 144: 'habitual criminality at national level'.

30. Directive 2014/42 (n 4) art 5.
31. Ibid. para 21.
32. *Addington* (n 12) 423; US Sentencing Commission (n 12); Maugeri (n 12) 876 ss.
33. Directive 2014/42 (n 4) para 21.
34. *Montella* Cass SSUU pen (17 December 2003) n 920; Luigi Fornari, *Criminalità del Profitto e Tecniche Sanzionatorie. Confisca e Sanzioni Pecuniarie nel Diritto Penale Moderno* (Cedam 1997) 222; Antonio Gialanella, 'Funzionalità e Limiti Garantisti dell'Ordinamento Penale alla Difficile "Prova" delle Misure di Prevenzione Patrimoniale' (1999) Critica del Diritto 538, 548.
35. *Derouach* Cass SSUU pen (30 May 2001) n 37140. Art 12 sexies law decree 306/1992—extended confiscation—does not 'presume' the guilt of the accused but only the unlawful source of the assets, *Montella* (n 34).
36. See Fornari (n 34) 222; Gialanella (n 34) 548; *Montella* (n 34).
37. *Raimondo v Italy* App no 12954/87 (ECtHR, 22 February 1994); *Prisco v Italy* App no 38662/97 (ECtHR, 15 June 1999); *Madonia v Italy* App no 55927/00 (ECtHR, 25 March 2003); *Andersson v Italy* App no 55504/00 (ECtHR, 20 June 2002); *Arcuri v Italy* App no 52024/99 (ECtHR, 5 July 2001); *Riela v Italy* App no 52439/99 (ECtHR, 4 September 2001); *Bocellari and Rizza v Italy* App no 399/02 (ECtHR, 13 November 2007); *Butler v UK* App no 41661/98 (ECtHR, 26 June 2002).
38. See, for instance, *Phillips v UK* App no 41087/98 (ECtHR, 12 December 2001), para 40; *Salabiaku v France* App no 10519/83 (ECtHR, 7 October 1988), para 28; Peter Alldridge 'Smuggling, Confiscation and Forfeiture' (2002) 65(5) Modern Law Review 781, 791.
39. *Montella* (n 34); Cass pen sez I (30 May 2007) n 21250 para 4; Domenico Potetti, 'Riflessioni in Tema di Confisca di cui alla Legge 501/1994' (1995) Cassazione Penale 1690; Luigi Ferrajoli, *La Normativa Antiriciclaggio* (Giuffrè 1994) 33; Giovanni Fiandaca and Enzo Musco, *Diritto penale—Parte generale* (6th edn, Zanichelli 2010) 848; Gaetano Nanula, 'Le Nuove Norme sul Possesso Ingiustificato di Valori' (1995) Il Fisco 10137.
40. See further Maugeri (n 9) 284ff.
41. Directive 2014/42 (n 4) para 21.
42. *Basco* Corte Costituzionale (1996) n 18. Also, for the confiscation preventive measure, the Italian Supreme Court requires the demonstration of this element for each acquisition at the moment of the purchase *Spinelli* Cass SSUU pen (26 June 2014) n 4880; *TG and others* Cass pen sez VI (31 May 2011) n 29926.
43. *Montella* (n 34); Cass pen sez I (13 May 2008) n 21357; Cass pen sez II (30 October 2008) n 44940.
44. Directive 2014/42 (n 4) para 21.
45. Cass (2008) n 21357 (n 43); Cass pen sez I (4 July 2007) n 33479.

46. *Spinelli* (n 42).
47. Directive 2014/42 (n 4) para 11.
48. Art 12 sexies law decree 306/92.
49. Art 2 ter l 575/65—art 24 preventive measures code.
50. Anna Maria Maugeri, 'Dalla Riforma delle Misure di Prevenzione Patrimoniali alla Confisca Generale dei Beni Contro il Terrorismo' in Oliviero Mazza and Francesco Viganò (eds), *Il "Pacchetto sicurezza" 2009* (Giappichelli 2009) 425; Anna Maria Maugeri, 'Dall' Actio In Rem alla Responsabilità da Reato delle Persone Giuridiche' in Costantino Visconti and Giovanni Fiandaca (eds), *Scenari Attuali di Mafia* (Giappichelli 2010) 297ff.
51. Directive 2014/42 (n 4) para 17.
52. Ibid. specifies that this exceptional circumstance should only be permitted 'in cases where it would put the person concerned in a situation in which it would be very difficult for him to survive'.
53. Thomas Fischer and others, *Strafgesetzbuch und Nebengesetze* (58th edn, Verlag CH Beck 2011) s 73c; Karl Lackner and Kristian Kühl, *Kommentar zum Strafgesetzbuch* (27th edn, Beck 2011) s 73c, ss 1–3; Adolf Schönke, Horst Schröder, and Albin Eser, *Strafgesetzbuch Kommentar* (Verlag CH Beck 2010) s 73 c, s 2, 1130. See Bundesgerichtshof, 17 giugno 2010–2014 StR 126/10; Bundesgerichtshof 10 June 2009, 2 StR 76/09 (2009) Neue Juristische Wochenschrift, 2755; Bundesgerichtshof 28 June 2000—2 StR 213/00 (2000) Neue Zeitschrift für Strafrecht, 590; Bundesgerichtshof 5 April 2000—2 StR 500/99 (2000) Neue Zeitschrift für Strafrecht, 480.
54. *Alloum* Cass pen sez fer (28 July 2009) n 33409; Cass pen sez II (13 May 2010) n 21027; *R v Ahmad and another* [2014] UKSC 36, [46]ff; contra Cour de cassation (2ᵉ ch E) (11 September 2013) P. 13.0505.F, in (2014) Revue de Droit Pénal et de Criminologie 131.
55. See *Fisia Italimpianti* Cass SSUU pen (2 July 2008) n 26654; Cass pen sez II (16 November 2012) n 8740; Cass pen sez II (20 September 2012) n 35999; *Ahmad* (n 54) [54].
56. *R v del Basso* [2011] 1 Cr App R (S); *Waya* [2012] UKSC 51. For further discussion, see Chap. 19 (Hopmeier and Mills) and Chap. 20 (Young) in this collection.
57. See Christopher Badger, 'R v Waya—Proportionality in Confiscation Proceedings' (2013) 28(1) Journal of International Banking and Financial Law 47; Peter Alldridge, 'Proceeds of Crime Law Since 2003: Two Key Areas' [2014] Criminal Law Review 174; Janet Ulph, 'Confiscation Orders, Human Rights, and Penal Measures' (2010) 126(2) Law Quarterly Review 251.
58. *Waya* (n 56); *Ahmad* (n 54); Peter Alldridge, *Money Laundering Law: Forfeiture, Confiscation, Civil Recovery, Criminal Laundering & Taxation of the Proceeds of Crime* (Hart Publishing 2003) 176; Boucht (n 26) 158ff; Maugeri (n 15) 308ff.
59. Directive 2014/42 (n 4) para 30 and art 9.

60. See, for example, *R v Padda (Gurpreet* Singh) [2013] EWCA Crim 2330. For discussion, see Gavin Doig, 'Revisiting the Available Amount—Confiscation of Post-Acquired Legitimate Assets' (2014) 78(2) Journal of Criminal Law 110.

61. Such criteria are already used within some legal systems and in the USA have been introduced by CAFRA 2000. See Maugeri (n 12) 554ff and 308ff.

62. In the proposal for the Directive, this was set out in the then Article 5.

63. See Jon Petter Rui, 'The Civil Asset Forfeiture Approach to Organised Crime: Exploring the Possibilities for an EU Model' (2011) 4 European Criminal Law Associations' Forum 153.

64. See for France, Chantal Cutajar, 'Compte Rendu du Colloque: «Identification, Saisie et Confiscation des Avoirs Criminels»' (2010) 11 Caiers de la Securite 211ff.

65. Directive 2014/42 (n 4) para 22.

66. For consideration of the UK civil recovery regime, see Chap. 22 (Alldridge) in this collection.

67. Directive 2014/42 (n 4) para 13.

68. Ibid. para 10.

69. See Maugeri (n 9) 287ff.

70. Article 49(6).

71. See Council of Europe, *Explanatory Report to the Convention on Laundering, Search, Seizure and Confiscation of the Proceeds from Crime* (1990) ETS 141 paras 19 and 20, 5–6 <https://rm.coe.int/CoERMPublicCommonSearch Services/DisplayDCTMContent?documentId=09000016800cb5de> accessed 20 March 2017; Alastair Brown, *Proceeds of Crime, Money Laundering, Confiscation & Forfeiture* (Sweet and Maxwell 1996) 93; Maugeri (n 12) 603–604.

72. *Explanatory Report* (n 71) art 13, para 43, 13.

73. Giovanni Fiandaca and Costantino Visconti 'Il "Codice delle Leggi Antimafia": Risultati, Omissioni, Prospettive' (2012) Legislazione Penale 181; Maugeri (n 12) 602–603.

74. *Cour de Cassation, Chambre Criminelle, Crisafulli—Friolo* (13 November 2003).

75. See also Senate Judiciary Commission, Rapport n° 328 (2009–2010) de M François Zocchetto (24.02.2010) <www.senat.fr/dossier-legislatif/ppl08-454. html> accessed 20 March 2017.

76. See Maugeri (n 9) 282ff. Case C-123/08 *Dominic Wolzenburg* (2009) ECR I-09621.

77. Todor Kolarov, 'Mutual Recognition of Judicial Decisions on Confiscation: The Way Forward' Contribution to the Seminar on Mutual Recognition of Judicial Decisions and Confiscation 15 Years after Tampere (Siracusa, 22–23 September 2014).

78. Home Office, *Confiscation and Money Laundering: Law and Practise. A Guide for Enforcement Authorities* (Stationery Office 1997) 61.

79. See *Engel v the Netherlands* App no 5101/71, 5354/72, 5102/71, 5370/72, 5100/71, (1976) 1 EHRR 647 (ECtHR, 8 June 1976); *Öztürk v Germany* App no 8544/79 (ECtHR, 21 February 1984) Series A no 73.

80. *Butler* (n 37). See Alldridge (n 58) 223–246; Colin King, 'Civil Forfeiture and Article 6 of the ECHR: Due Process Implications for England and Wales and Ireland' (2014) 34(3) Legal Studies 371.

81. Each MS may deposit a declaration that its competent authorities will not recognise confiscation orders based on the extended powers of confiscation referred to in Article 2(d)(iv), that is, extended powers of confiscation under the law of the issuing State. The declaration may be withdrawn at any time (art 7, n 5 Council Framework Decision 2006/783/JHA of 6 October 2006 on the application of the principle of mutual recognition to confiscation orders [2006] OJ L328/59).

82. *Engel* (n 79); *Öztürk* (n 79).

83. *Gogitidze v Georgia* App no 36862/05 (ECtHR, 12 May 2015).

84. Ibid. para 126.

85. *Air Canada v UK* App no 18465/91 (ECtHR, 5 May 1995), para 34; *Riela and Others v Italy* App no 52439/99 (ECtHR, 4 September 2001); *Veits v Estonia* App no 12951/11 (ECtHR, 15 January 2015), para 70; *Sun v Russia* App no 31004/02 (ECtHR, 5 February 2009), para 25; *Immobiliare Saffi v Italy* [GC] App no 22774/93 (ECtHR, 28 July 1999), para 44.

86. *Agosi v UK* App no 9118/80 (ECtHR, 24 October 1986).

87. Ibid. para 51ff; *Handyside v UK* App no 5493/72 (ECtHR, 7 December 1976), paras 62–63.

88. *Gogitidze* (n 83) para 99. See also *Azienda Agricola Silverfunghi S.a.s. v Italy* App no 48357-52677-52687-52701/07 (ECtHR, 24 June 2014), para 104; *Arras and Others v Italy* App no 17972/07 (ECtHR, 14 February 2012), para 81; *Huitson v UK* App no 50131/12 (ECtHR, 13 January 2015), paras 31–35.

89. See *Raimondo* (n 37) para 30; *Marandino v Italy* App no 12386/86 (ECtHR, 15 April 1991) EHRR 70, 78.

90. *Gogitidze* (n 83) para 97.

91. *Azienda Agricola Silverfunghi* (n 88) paras 76 and 103.

92. See Anna Maria Maugeri, 'La Responsabilità da Reato degli Enti' (2014) Rivista Trimestrale di Diritto Penale dell'Economia 708ff.

93. *Gogitidze* (n 83) para 102.

94. Ibid. para 103. The court referred to *Phillips* (n 38) para 52.

95. *Gogitidze* (n 83) para 102; *Raimondo* (n 37) para 30; *Veits* (n 85) para 71; *Silickienė v Lithuania* App no 20496/02 (ECtHR, 10 April 2012), para 65.

96. *Gogitidze* (n 83) para 122. The court referred to *Phillips* (n 38) para 52.

97. *Gogitidze* (n 83) para 112.

98. Ibid. para 107.
99. Ibid. para 111.
100. Ibid. para 111.
101. Ibid. para 103; *Butler* (n 37) para 8.
102. *Gogitidze* (n 83) para 105.
103. See Colin King, 'Using Civil Processes in Pursuit of Criminal Law Objectives' (2012) 16(4) International Journal of Evidence and Proof 337, about the use of civil processes as a crime control strategy.
104. Even if judgments are not always consistent.
105. See Maugeri (n 9) 294 and authors quoted; Anthony Gray, 'The Compatibility of Unexplained Wealth Provisions and "Civil" Forfeiture Regimes With Kable' (2012) 12(2) QUT Law and Justice Journal 11; Colin King, '"Hitting back" at Organized Crime: The Adoption of Civil Forfeiture in Ireland' in Colin King and Clive Walker (eds), *Dirty Assets: Emerging Issues in the Regulation of Criminal and Terrorist Assets* (Ashgate Publishing 2014) para 168; Susan R Klein 'Civil In Rem Forfeiture and Double Jeopardy' (1996) 82(1) Iowa Law Review 183.
106. *Varvara v Italy* App no 17475/09 (ECtHR, 29 March 2014).
107. Art 17 Charter and I Prot ECHR.
108. Art 49 Charter.
109. Art 6 ECHR and arts. 47 and 48 Charter.
110. Art 7 ECHR and art 49 Charter.
111. Art 4 Prot 7 ECHR.
112. See, for example, paras 17–18.
113. For instance, *Härtevorschrift* s 73 c StGB.
114. Recital n 18: 'When implementing this Directive, Member States may provide that, in exceptional circumstances, confiscation should not be ordered, insofar as it would, in accordance with national law, represent undue hardship for the affected person, on the basis of the circumstances of the respective individual case which should be decisive. Member States should make a very restricted use of this possibility, and should only be allowed to provide that confiscation is not to be ordered in cases where it would put the person concerned in a situation in which it would be very difficult for him to survive.'
115. Art 4.
116. Maurice Kempen, 'The Mutual Recognition and Execution of Freezing and Confiscation Orders', presented at the Seminar Mutual Recognition of Judicial Decisions and Confiscation 15 Years after Tampere (Siracusa, 22–23 September 2014) 12.
117. Council, (OR. en) Interinstitutional File: 2012/0036 (COD) 7329/1/14 REV 1 ADD 1 CODEC 657 DROIPEN 39 COPEN 83, Statement by the European Parliament and the Council on an analysis to be carried out by the Commission (31 March 2014) <http://register.consilium.europa.eu/doc/srv?l=EN&f=ST%207329%202014%20REV%201%20ADD%201> accessed 20 March 2017.

118. Eighth Meeting of the Consultative Forumof Prosecutors General and Directors of Public Prosecutionsof the MSs of the EU (The Hague, 12 December 2014) <www.eurojust.europa.eu/doclibrary/Eurojustframework/consultativeforum/IT%20Presidency%20-%20Conclusions%20of%20CF%20meeting%20of%2012-122014%20(Council%2   0document%20 8552-15)/CF-2014-12-12_ST08552-15_EN.pdf> accessed 20 March 2017.

119. For example, in Spain, the *Ley Orgánica 1/2015,* 30 Marz, has introduced the 'decomiso sin sentencia' in art 127, s 4 Código Penal.

120. On 21 December 2016, a 'Proposal for a Regulation of the European Parliament and of the Council on the mutual recognition of freezing and confiscation orders' was presented, in order to impose the mutual recognition of all types of orders covered by Directive 2014/42/EU (confiscation of the value ex art 4, direct confiscation ex art 4 and extended confiscation ex art 5, and confiscation of assets in the possession of third parties ex art 6), as well as other types of orders issued without final conviction within the framework of criminal proceedings; this regulation should not apply to freezing and confiscation orders issued within the framework of civil or administrative proceedings. The choice of a regulation based on art 288 TFEU on the basis of art 82(1) TFUE is worthwhile in terms of effectiveness, but it is also problematic because of the uncertain boundary between cooperation and harmonisation which falls under art 82(2). Some concern also arises regarding the concept of criminal proceedings mentioned in the regulation; see Anna Maria Maugeri, 'Proposal for a Regulation of the European Parliament and of the Council on the Mutual Recognition of Freezing and Confiscation Orders: Prime Osservazioni' (2017) Diritto Penale Contemporaneo 1.

121. Framework Decision 212/2005 (n 4) art 3; Directive 42/2014 (n 4) artt 4 and 5.

122. European Parliament Resolution of 25 October 2011 on organised crime in the European Union 2010/2309(INI).

123. Financial Action Task Force, 'Recommendations' (2012) <www.fatf-gafi.org/media/fatf/documents/recommendations/pdfs/FATF_Recommendations.pdf> accessed 20 March 2017.

124. European Criminal Bar Association, 'Statement on the Proposal for a Directive of the European Parliament and of the Council on the Freezing and Confiscation of Proceeds of crime in the European Union' (2012) <www.ecba.org/extdocserv/201210_assetseizureEC BA_statement.pdf> accessed 20 March 2017.

125. See Maugeri (n 12) 269ff.

126. Directive 2014/42/EU (n 4) art 8 para 4.

127. *Gogitidze* (n 83) para 111.

128. For further discussion, see Chap. 29 (Vettori) in this collection.

129. Center for the Study of Democracy, *Disposal of Confiscated Assets in the EU Member States Laws and Practices* (2014). See Commission Staff, Working

paper accompanying document to the proposal for a Directive of the European Parliament and the Council on the freezing and confiscation of proceeds of crime in the European Union impact assessment <http://eur-lex.europa.eu/legal-content/it/TXT/?uri=CELEX:52012SC0031> accessed 20 March 2017.

130. Recital 35: 'for law enforcement and crime prevention projects, as well as for other projects of public interest and social utility'. In the proposal, amended by LIBE Committee, the improvement of this scope, the social reuse of the confiscated property, was mandatory.

131. Alessandro Bernardi, 'Politiche di Armonizzazione e Sistema Sanzionatorio Penale' in Tommaso Rafaraci (ed), *L'Area di Libertà, Sicurezza e Giustizia* (Giuffrè 2007) 277.

Anna Maria Maugeri is Full Professor of Criminal Law and Coordinator of the PhD School on 'Law', University of Catania, Italy. She is/was a member of the 'Stati generali della lotta al crimine organizzato' (Ministry of Justice 2016–2017); a restricted expert group on *Improving Mutual Recognition of freezing and confiscation orders*, EU Brussels (2015); Study Commissions to reform the Italian Criminal code (Ministry of Justice, 2016–2017)and the sanction system (2013–2015); Scientific Committee of the International Institute of Higher Studies in Criminal Sciences (ISISC), Siracusa; and the review committee of the Diritto Penale Contemporaneo and the Padova University Press, a peer-review committee of four legal journals. She has taught abroad as part of the Erasmus Exchange Programme at the University Autónoma de Madrid, Castilla La Mancha and University of Heidelberg. She is involved in international research projects. She has written many articles and books on different topics of comparative, European and international criminal law.

18

Asset Forfeiture Law in the United States

Stefan D. Cassella

Introduction

Asset recovery plays a significant role in the enforcement of the criminal laws in the United States. Though the degree of enforcement differs widely from state to state, virtually all states have some form of asset recovery legislation, and the federal government has a robust set of forfeiture provisions that apply to the great majority of serious crimes that may be enforced at the federal level. This chapter will focus exclusively on federal law for three reasons: the case law is well developed at the federal level; federal enforcement is uniform across the country; and it is federal law that foreign courts, legislatures, academics and practitioners generally look to when referencing asset recovery in the United States.

This chapter first discusses the purposes that asset recovery is intended to serve as part of the prosecutor's arsenal of weapons in the enforcement of the criminal laws. Second, it discusses the categories of property that are subject to forfeiture—that is, the proceeds of the crime, facilitating property, and so forth. Third, it compares the alternative ways in which property may be recovered in conviction-based and non-conviction-based proceedings. Finally, the chapter discusses in some detail the procedures that apply in a criminal case when the prosecutor seeks to recover criminally tainted assets as part of the defendant's sentence.[1]

S. D. Cassella
Asset Forfeiture Law, LLC, Laurel, MD, USA

© The Author(s) 2018
C. King et al. (eds.), *The Palgrave Handbook of Criminal and Terrorism Financing Law*,
https://doi.org/10.1007/978-3-319-64498-1_18

Why Make Forfeiture Part of the Criminal Process?

In *Kaley v United States*, Justice Elena Kagan, writing for the Supreme Court, listed the commonly accepted reasons why asset recovery—almost always referred to as 'asset forfeiture' in the United States—is viewed as an important part of criminal law enforcement: 'Forfeiture serves to punish the wrong-doer, to deter future illegality, to lessen the economic power of criminal enterprises, to compensate victims, to improve conditions in crime-damaged communities, and to support law enforcement activities such as police training.'[2] It is worth spending a moment to view each of those reasons in turn.

Prosecutors are often told, 'don't just put the defendant in jail; take away the fruits of the crime.' In a fraud case, it would make no sense to convict the defendant of committing the fraud but allow him to keep the fraud proceeds; in a money laundering case, it would make no sense to convict the defendant of money laundering but allow him to keep the money. In such cases, the confiscation or forfeiture of the criminal proceeds is simply the logical complement to the other aspects of a criminal sentence. Moreover, most prosecutors report that the defendant is often far more concerned about the loss of his property than he is about the temporary loss of his freedom. Having the money or other property available once he is released from incarceration, or available to his family while he is incarcerated, was often the criminal's primary goal in committing the criminal offence. If punishment is the Government's goal, it must include depriving the criminal of that opportunity.

Punishment, of course, serves multiple purposes. One is to force the wrong-doer to face the consequences of his crime, but another is to deter others from following him down the same path. The point of committing crimes involving property is to make money. The criminal who gets to enjoy a lavish and notoriously open lifestyle based on the fruits of his criminal wrongdoing serves as a role model for would-be followers. Conversely, if a given defendant does not get to keep the money he obtained when committing a particular offence, there is less incentive for the next person to commit the same offence.[3]

A third purpose of punishment is incapacitation. Generally, when we speak of incapacitation, we are thinking about protecting society from future harm by keeping the individual defendant locked up behind bars for some period of time. But asset forfeiture is another form of incapacitation. Depriving the criminal of the 'tools of his trade,' and of his economic resources, makes it more difficult for him—or his associates—to perpetrate similar acts while he is incarcerated or on probation or once he is released. We do not want drug dealers to keep the airplane that they used to smuggle drugs, or the armed felon to keep the gun that he used to commit the robbery, because we do not want them to use that property again to commit a similar crime in the future.

If asset forfeiture can disrupt an individual's ability to commit an offence, it can do the same to a large criminal organization. Money is the glue that holds organized criminal enterprises together; they have to recycle their illegally derived money to keep their illicit activities on-going. Take the money or other economic resources away, and the organization must start over.[4] Criminals who become cooperating witnesses in drug cases, for example, routinely report that the law enforcement activity that was most effective in disrupting their operations was not the arrest of a given supplier or courier, or even the seizure of a given load of drugs, but the seizure of the large sum of money that was needed to pay for the next load, and to compensate the organization's employees. For the same reasons, figuring out how terrorism is financed,[5] and taking away the money before it can be used, is a critical part of the anti-terrorism effort.

Next, for a number of reasons, forfeiture is almost always a more effective way of recovering money for victims than ordering the defendant to pay restitution.[6] In the United States, restitution is ordered only at the conclusion of a criminal case, after the defendant has been convicted. Under the restitution laws, however, there is no way to seize, restrain, or otherwise preserve property prior to conviction so that it is available for that purpose. In contrast, the forfeiture laws allow the Government to act affirmatively, prior to trial, and in many cases, prior to indictment, to preserve assets that will ultimately be used to compensate victims. Moreover, as one appellate court has observed, the Government's far greater resources make it more likely that the victims will be compensated if the Government uses its tools to preserve and recover property than if the victims were left to their own private remedies.[7]

A further underlying rationale is to protect the community, which can be seen in different ways. Forfeiture provides law enforcement agencies with the opportunity to demonstrate to the community in a highly visible way that crime does not pay, and that criminals will receive their just desserts. It also provides a vehicle for shutting down a dangerous, on-going operation—a place where young women are held for service in the sex trade or where drugs are openly bought and sold—that threatens the public health and safety. Perhaps most important, forfeiture allows the Government to ensure that the economic playing field is level, so that people trying to run businesses honestly don't have to compete with those whose capital investment is derived, tax-free, from illegal sources. Forfeiting the restaurant that a drug dealer opened with the proceeds of his drug sales allows other would-be entrepreneurs to compete, whereas failing to forfeit the restaurant would convince many that the only way to amass the resources necessary to run a successful restaurant is to be a drug dealer.[8]

Finally, forfeited property can be put to socially desirable uses,[9] whether it be converting a drug-infested motel into a shelter for battered women or refugees, or sharing the money with law enforcement agencies to be used to fund training and other law enforcement programmes. Care must be taken in designing such programmes to ensure that they do not cross the line between putting criminal proceeds to socially desirable uses and causing police agencies to engage in what is called 'policing for profit.' But it can be done.

For all of these reasons, the federal law enforcement agencies in the United States have made asset forfeiture part of the enforcement of most serious federal crimes, ranging from investment fraud and insider trading to drug trafficking, public corruption, and the production of child pornography. In the years since 2008, gross federal forfeiture receipts have generally exceeded $2 billion a year, with the total in some years being much greater due to the influx of money recovered in some of the more notorious cases, such as the fraud committed by Bernie Madoff.

What Can Be Forfeited?

Most countries have enacted asset recovery laws that provide, in fairly simple terms, that the property derived from or used to commit any crime—foreign or domestic—is subject to forfeiture or confiscation. That, unfortunately, is not the case in the United States. In the United States, there is no uniform description of the property subject to forfeiture that applies to all crimes. To the contrary, what property is subject to forfeiture depends on the offence being committed and the statute being violated. What can be forfeited in a fraud case, for example, is different from what can be forfeited in a drug case, or a child pornography case, or a case involving wildlife trafficking. To the regret of judges and practitioners, this is the consequence of different federal statutes being drafted by different committees of Congress at different times over many decades.

For most crimes, federal law enforcement agencies can forfeit the proceeds of the offence. For many crimes, they can forfeit facilitating property, that is, property used to make the crime easier to commit. And for some crimes, they can forfeit much more. In money laundering cases, for example, the Government may forfeit all property 'involved in' the financial transaction;[10]

in racketeering cases (prosecuted under the RICO statute), it can forfeit the defendant's entire interest in the RICO enterprise;[11] and in terrorism cases, it can forfeit virtually everything the terrorist owns, whether it is connected to the offence or not.[12]

On the other hand, for some offences, the Government's forfeiture authority is limited to particular categories of property—such as the vehicles, vessels and aircraft used to smuggle illegal aliens, or the vehicles and equipment used to steal cultural property from federal or Indian land. And for still other offences, there is no federal forfeiture authority at all. Accordingly, the prosecutor or law enforcement agent needs to check the applicable statute to see what can be forfeited in a particular case, and may have to make charging decisions based on the need to invoke a particular forfeiture law.

Unfortunately, the forfeiture provisions are spread all over the US Code. For some crimes, the forfeiture provision is part of the statute setting forth the criminal offence itself.[13] Others appear in list of forfeiture provisions in the general criminal forfeiture statute, 18 U.S.C. s. 982.[14] And others require the Government to rely on the catch-all forfeiture provision in 18 U.S.C. s. 981(a)(1)(C) which authorizes the forfeiture of the proceeds—and only the proceeds—of a list of some 250 crimes incorporated by cross-reference to other statutes.[15] That is, for example, where one would find the forfeiture authority for all of the most common white collar crimes, such as mail and wire fraud, bank fraud, bankruptcy fraud, securities fraud, bribery, embezzlement and theft.[16] It can be tedious to explain to the court how to find the forfeiture authority for a given offence, but fortunately there are a number of cases that explain the nested cross-references.[17]

What Are 'Proceeds'?

What constitute the proceeds of a criminal offence is fairly obvious in most cases: it is whatever the defendant acquired or retained as a result of having committed his particular crime. If he robbed a bank, the money that he took from the bank would be the proceeds of the offence. But experience shows that 'proceeds' is often much broader in scope than that example would suggest.[18] One way to approach this is with a 'but for' test: what property would the defendant not have obtained or retained but for having committed the crime. For example, if the defendant would not have been able to acquire stock, make an investment, or obtain a contract but for having committed extortion, bribery or fraud, the property obtained would be considered the proceeds of the criminal offence.[19] In fact, under the 'but for' test, an entire business and all of its revenue and assets would be subject to forfeiture if the business would not exist but for the investment of criminal proceeds to start the business or to keep it going.[20]

'Proceeds' is not limited to property that is newly acquired but may include 'cost savings' and other property *retained* as a result of an offence. If a person succeeds in having a debt reduced by paying a bribe, the money saved by not paying the full debt would be considered the proceeds of the bribe.[21] Similarly, if someone qualifies for a subsidized rental apartment because she submitted a false application, the money saved on the rent would be the proceeds of the false statement.[22] 'Proceeds' also includes property that was obtained not by the defendant personally, but by others who acted in concert with him, or by a corporation that served as the defendant's *alter ego*. In such cases, the property is said be to proceeds that the defendant obtained 'indirectly.'[23]

When a defendant uses the proceeds of his offence to make a purchase, or converts it to another form, the newly acquired property is considered to be the proceeds of the original crime. Thus, if the defendant buys a boat with his fraud proceeds, the boat constitutes the proceeds of the fraud; and if he later sells the boat, or uses the boat as the security for a loan, the sale or loan proceeds would be the proceeds of the fraud as well.[24] Moreover, if the proceeds of the crime are used to acquire an asset that appreciates in value over time, the appreciation is forfeitable as property traceable to the original offence.[25] A well-known example of this possibility concerns a drug dealer in Texas who invested one dollar of his drug proceeds in a lottery ticket and saw it appreciate greatly in value when he hit the jackpot. Because his good fortune was traceable to the proceeds of his drug offence, it accrued thereafter to the benefit of the Government which became the proud holder of the winning ticket when it was forfeited as drug proceeds.[26]

Finally, while forfeiture in a criminal case is generally limited to the property derived from the offence of conviction, if the crime is charged as a 'scheme' or a 'conspiracy' and not as an isolated event, the Government would be entitled to forfeit the proceeds of the entire course of conduct and would not be limited to the proceeds of the particular execution of the scheme that was alleged in the defendant's indictment.[27]

The Gross Versus Net Controversy

Another issue that arises frequently when the Government seeks to forfeit criminal proceeds is whether the term 'proceeds' means 'gross revenue' or only 'net profits.' Unfortunately, while this issue has generated a great deal of litigation in the United States, it remains unresolved. Depending on the nature of the underlying crime, a court may hold that the defendant is entitled to offset the forfeiture to reflect the costs he incurred in committing the offence—or it may not. In general, the courts apply the no-offset rule to activity that is considered 'inherently illegal'—drug trafficking is the most obvious example—but are inclined to limit the forfeiture to net profits if the defendant committed an illegal act in the course of running an otherwise legal business. The problem is that it is not always clear when something is inherently illegal.

One court might say that an investment fraud scheme was inherently illegal because it was entirely unlawful from the beginning and accordingly require the defendant to forfeit the gross revenue that he obtained in the course of the offence.[28] But another court might say that handling investments or buying and selling securities is not an inherently illegal activity, and thus allow the defendant to take an offset to reflect his costs.[29] This issue arises frequently in Government contracting cases: is it inherently illegal to obtain a contract through bribery, or by misrepresenting one's eligibility to participate in the bidding process? If so, the contractor should be required to forfeit all of the money that he received under the contract. But if being a Government contractor is not inherently illegal activity, the contractor might expect to be given credit for the costs of the goods and services that he did provide.[30]

Facilitating Property

In addition to authorizing the forfeiture of 'proceeds,' some federal statutes authorize the forfeiture of property 'used to commit or to facilitate the commission' of the criminal offence. This is usually referred to as 'facilitating property.'[31]

In cases involving criminal offences for which the forfeiture of facilitating property is authorized, the phrase 'property used … to facilitate the commission of the offense' is interpreted broadly as anything that makes the crime easier to commit or harder to detect. This may include such obvious examples as the gun used to commit a crime of violence, the vehicle used to transport drugs, or the warehouse where contraband items are stored. But it also includes property whose nexus to the crime is not as obvious. The classic example concerns a heroin operation that was being conducted on what was ostensibly a cattle ranch. To create a false aura of legitimacy, the defendant populated his ranch with cows and horses. When the time came to forfeit the property the defendant had used to commit the drug trafficking offence, the defendant objected that these were 'innocent' cows and horses that had played no role in the heroin operation. But the court held that because the defendant used the animals to make his property appear to be an actual ranch and not a heroin operation, they would be forfeited as property that made his offence easier to commit.[32]

The forfeiture of facilitating property is not without its limits, however. When seeking the forfeiture of property under a facilitation theory, the Government is required to show that there was a 'substantial connection' between the property and the offence—that is, that the connection was not 'merely incidental or fortuitous.'[33] Moreover, all forfeitures of facilitating property are limited by the Excessive Fines Clause of the Eighth Amendment, which bars the courts from ordering a forfeiture that would be 'grossly disproportional to the gravity of the offense.'[34]

Money Laundering

As mentioned earlier, forfeiture under the money laundering statutes is broader than it is for most other offences. It includes all property 'involved in' the money laundering transaction, which may include the criminal proceeds being laundered, property used to commit or to facilitate the commission of that transaction, or any other property that is the subject of the illegal transaction, including any 'clean' money that is commingled with the criminal proceeds when the money laundering offence takes place.[35] Again, this is limited by the Excessive Fines Clause of the Eighth Amendment.[36]

Forfeiture Procedure

Federal law in the United States authorizes three ways of forfeiting property that is implicated in a criminal offence: administrative (or non-judicial) forfeiture, civil (or non-conviction-based) forfeiture and criminal forfeiture. We shall look briefly at each of these in turn.

Administrative Forfeiture

As its name implies, administrative forfeitures are handled exclusively by a federal law enforcement agency without the involvement of the court, and in most cases, without the participation of a prosecutor. The administrative forfeiture process begins when the property is seized—generally with a warrant, but without a warrant if there are exigent circumstances. Moreover, the seizure must be based on probable cause to believe that the property is subject to forfeiture—for example, because it is the proceeds of a criminal offence for which forfeiture is authorized, or was used to commit such an offence. The agency is required to send notice of the seizure and of the property owner's right to contest its forfeiture within 60 days, and the property owner—or anyone else with a legal interest in the property—then has 30 days to respond.[37] If no one files a claim to the property, it is forfeited administratively when the agency files a document called a Declaration of Forfeiture that extinguishes all interests in the property and vests title in the United States.[38] The property eligible for administrative forfeiture includes currency in any amount and other personal property up to a value of $500,000. Real property, however, is not eligible for administrative forfeiture.[39]

Which agency seizes the property and processes the administrative forfeiture depends on the nature of the underlying criminal offence: drug cases are handled by the Drug Enforcement Administration (DEA); immigration and customs cases by Immigration and Customs Enforcement (ICE); credit card fraud by the Secret Service; firearms cases by the Bureau of Alcohol, Tobacco and Firearms (ATF); and so forth. Most white collar cases are handled by the Federal Bureau of Investigation (FBI) or the Internal Revenue Service (IRS). These can be purely federal cases that involve only federal law enforcement agencies, task force cases in which federal, state and local agencies participate jointly, or purely state cases that the federal agency adopts from state or local law enforcement so that the forfeiture can be processed under federal law. Most federal forfeitures start out as administrative forfeitures and the vast majority—which, based on government data available to the author when he was a federal prosecutor, are approximately 80 percent—are resolved that way. That is because 80 percent of the time no one files a claim to the seized property, and it is forfeited by default.

Critics cite this statistic as evidence of the unfairness of the administrative forfeiture procedure, but prosecutors and other law enforcement officials disagree. They point out that a great many criminal prosecutions involve a parallel administrative forfeiture of the seized property that the criminal defendant simply chooses not to contest—and with good reason. A notice advising that the Government has seized $65,000 in bundled cash, a kilo of cocaine and a loaded handgun prompts few to come forward to proclaim, 'Yes, that is mine.' As the courts have recognized, administrative forfeiture is a good way for the Government to save time and resources in uncontested cases.[40] If no one is going to contest the forfeiture of the property, there may be no need to involve the court in the process even if there is a pending parallel criminal prosecution. If someone does file a timely claim contesting the forfeiture, however, the administrative forfeiture proceeding must stop, and the case must be referred by the seizing agency to the federal prosecutor's office for forfeiture in a judicial proceeding. When the prosecutor commences that proceeding a claimant who is also the defendant in a parallel criminal case is entitled to a stay of the civil proceeding to avoid having to surrender his Fifth Amendment right against self-incrimination to protect his property interest.[41]

Civil Judicial Forfeiture

When a contested case is referred by a seizing agency, the United States Attorney—the federal prosecutor—has two alternatives: to commence a civil (or non-conviction-based) forfeiture action against the property, to include the property in a criminal indictment or both. The law requires the prosecutor to take at least one of these steps—or seek a judicial extension of time—within 90 days of the date when the person contesting the forfeiture—the 'claimant'—filed his or her claim with the seizing agency.[42]

Civil forfeiture cases are *in rem* actions in which the property itself is named as the defendant, which is why the cases tend to have funny names: for example, *United States v Approximately 600 Sacks of Green Coffee Beans*,[43] *United States v One Etched Ivory Tusk of African Elephant*,[44] or *United States v 160 Cartons of Glass Water Pipes*,[45]—which were cases involving the importation of contraband items such as food, endangered species and drug paraphernalia, respectively.

The concept of *in rem* forfeiture originated in American law in the Eighteenth Century as a means of taking title to contraband items—such as pirate ships and slave-trading vessels—when the owners of those assets were outside the borders of the United States and thus were beyond the reach of its courts and law enforcement agencies.[46] The older cases were based on the legal fiction that the property itself had committed the crime giving rise to the forfeiture, but that is not the contemporary view. Rather, as Justice Anthony Kennedy explained it in *United States v Ursery*, civil forfeiture today is viewed merely as a procedural device that names the property as the defendant so that all persons claiming an interest in the property can make their claims and have them resolved in a single proceeding.[47] The alternative—requiring the Government to file a separate in personam civil action against every person with a potential interest in the property—would be impossibly cumbersome to pursue.

The important thing to know about civil forfeiture is that it does not require a criminal conviction or even a criminal case.[48] Indeed, as discussed below, the primary role of civil forfeiture is to fill the gap that occurs when the Government is not able to bring a criminal case but nevertheless has a legitimate reason to take title to the property. Moreover, civil forfeiture is available whether the property belongs to the wrongdoer or to a third party: the focus is on the nexus between the property and the criminal offence, not the nexus between the property and the criminal offender. So, for example, if someone uses his wife's car to commit a crime, the car would be subject to forfeiture in a civil case even though the wife was not charged with any crime.[49] She would be entitled, by statute, to assert an innocent owner defence, but if she was aware of her husband's illegal use of her property and failed to take all reasonable steps to prevent it, that defence would not succeed.[50]

If civil forfeiture has so many advantages, one may ask why doesn't the Government use civil forfeiture in every case instead of forfeiting the property as part of the defendant's sentence in its criminal cases. First, as a practical matter, filing a civil forfeiture action involves a great deal of unnecessary extra work for something that can be done easily if there is a criminal case. But also, civil forfeiture has a serious limitation: because it is an in rem action against specific property, there are no substitute assets or money judgments in civil forfeiture cases. The forfeiture is limited to property directly traceable to the offence.

Accordingly, the Government typically reserves civil forfeiture for cases where the criminal forfeiture is not possible or is not appropriate, or where a criminal case is not ready to indict. In particular, the prosecutor will choose to file a civil forfeiture action in the following six situations: (1) the defendant is dead, a fugitive or incompetent to stand trial;[51] (2) the crime is a violation of foreign law, but the property is in the United States or is subject to the jurisdiction of a US court;[52] (3) the defendant has already been convicted in a state, foreign or tribal court, making a second criminal prosecution unnecessary;[53] (4) the defendant pleads guilty to a different offence than the one giving rise to the forfeiture; (5) the property subject to forfeiture as facilitating property belongs not to the defendant but to a non-innocent third party (such as his spouse); and (6) the Government could file a criminal case but the interests of justice militate in favour of a lesser punishment.

The last example has proven to be unexpectedly controversial. Critics of law enforcement argue that if the Government really has sufficient evidence to prove a case beyond a reasonable doubt, it should file criminal charges and not seek to forfeit the wrongdoer's property under the lesser preponderance of the evidence standard that applies in civil forfeiture cases. Prosecutors and law enforcement professionals respond, however, that not every violation of the criminal law merits a full-blown criminal prosecution resulting, if the Government is successful, in a criminal conviction and sentence. Sometimes, in the exercise of prosecutorial discretion, it is appropriate for the Government to seek a civil remedy for a criminal act. For example, in *United States v 6 Firearms, Accessories and Ammunition*, an elderly woman violated the federal firearms laws when she purchased guns and ammunition for her son knowing that, as a convicted felon, he was not lawfully permitted to possess them. In that case, the Government had three choices: to do nothing; to file criminal charges against the mother; or to file a civil forfeiture action to confiscate the guns. It chose the latter option.[54]

Civil Forfeiture Procedure

The procedure in civil forfeiture cases is governed by Supplemental Rule G of the Federal Rules of Civil Procedure. Briefly stated, the procedure works like this: The Government files a complaint naming the property as the defendant in rem and setting forth the legal and factual grounds for seeking its forfeiture in terms of the applicable federal statute. It must then send notice of the forfeiture action, including a copy of the complaint, to all persons appearing to have an interest in the property. Persons wishing to contest the forfeiture—'claimants'—have 30 days to intervene in the forfeiture action by filing a claim stating under oath that they have a legal interest in the property and are opposed to its forfeiture. The claimant must then file an answer to the Government's complaint admitting or denying the Government's allegations and setting forth his affirmative defences.

The case then proceeds to litigation, beginning with civil discovery under the rules that apply in all federal civil cases. If the Government suspects that the claimant does not really have a bona fide interest in the property, it may challenge his standing to contest the forfeiture. Otherwise, the Government must establish the forfeitability of the property at trial (which may be a trial by jury if the claimant so elects) by a preponderance of the evidence. If the Government succeeds in meeting its burden, the burden then shifts to the claimant to establish an innocent owner defence, if he wishes to do so.[55] Finally, if the property is found to be subject to forfeiture, the claimant has the option of asking the court nevertheless to mitigate or reduce the forfeiture all together if the forfeiture would be grossly disproportional to the gravity of the underlying offence.[56] At the end of the day, the entry of a civil forfeiture judgment by a federal court extinguishes all property interests that may have existed in the property and gives the Government clear title to it.[57]

Criminal Forfeiture

Criminal forfeiture is part of the defendant's sentence, not an element of the underlying crime, and not a collateral sanction that occurs in a separate proceeding.[58] Many things flow from that, but these are a few of the most important points. First, because criminal forfeiture is part of the defendant's sentence, there is no forfeiture unless the defendant is convicted; and if the conviction is vacated, the forfeiture order is vacated as well. This is one reason why it is useful for the Government to have a parallel civil forfeiture case available as an option.[59]

Second, because criminal forfeiture is part of the defendant's sentence, the forfeiture is limited to the property connected to the particular crime for which the defendant was convicted. If the defendant is convicted of Crime A, the forfeiture is limited to the property connected to Crime A. It doesn't matter that the defendant *could have been convicted* of Crimes B and C.[60] To avoid this problem and to establish a basis for the forfeiture of the property involved in the entire course of conduct, the Government must charge the defendant with a conspiracy or an offence involving a 'scheme to defraud.'[61]

Third, and most important, because criminal forfeiture is part of the defendant's sentence, it is an *in personam* punishment directed against the defendant, not his property. This is why, in criminal cases, the Government is not limited to forfeiting property directly traceable to the offence as it is in civil forfeiture cases. To the contrary, it can obtain a forfeiture order in the form of a money judgment and can enforce it by forfeiting 'substitute assets' that are not connected in any way to the defendant's crime.[62] This last point is what makes criminal forfeiture such a powerful law enforcement tool and is the primary reason why prosecutors favour criminal forfeiture over civil forfeiture.

On the other hand, from the Government's perspective, criminal forfeiture has a serious limitation. The criminal forfeiture statutes allow the court to order the forfeiture of any property derived from or used to commit the offence. Thus, in the forfeiture phase of the criminal case the Government does not have to prove that the property belonged to the defendant; it only has to prove the connection between the property and the offence.[63] But because third parties are excluded from the criminal case, facilitating property that belongs to third parties, or criminal proceeds acquired by a bona fide purchaser for value, cannot be forfeited. Indeed, it would violate the due process rights of a property owner to forfeit his property in a proceeding in which he was not allowed to participate. Accordingly, after a criminal forfeiture order is imposed as part of the defendant's sentence, the Government is required to give notice of the forfeiture to all third parties with a possible interest in the forfeited property and provide them with an opportunity to contest the forfeiture in a post-trial ancillary proceeding.[64] If the third party succeeds in establishing his superior interest in the property in that proceeding, the forfeiture order must be modified to exempt that interest. From the Government's perspective, this is the major *disadvantage* to criminal forfeiture. There is, of course, a procedure for forfeiting the property of third parties who knowingly allowed their property to be used to commit a crime: it is called civil forfeiture.

Obtaining a Criminal Forfeiture Order Step-by-Step

The following is a brief discussion of the steps that a prosecutor in the United States must take to make a forfeiture order part of the defendant's sentence in a criminal case.[65]

First, the indictment or other charging document must give the defendant notice that the Government intends to seek the forfeiture of his property as part of his sentence. The notice, however, does not need to list the specific items to be forfeited nor set forth the amount of the money judgment that the Government will be seeking.[66]

Second, often the property subject to forfeiture will already be in the Government's possession when the indictment is returned, but if it is not, the prosecutor may ask the court to issue a pre-trial restraining order or seizure warrant to preserve the property pending trial.[67] To obtain the restraining order or warrant, the Government simply files an ex parte application stating that an indictment has been returned and that there is probable cause to believe that the property in question will be subject to forfeiture if the defendant is convicted. If the grand jury that returned the indictment did not name the property in the indictment, the application must contain an affidavit setting forth the facts establishing the connection between the property and the offence.[68]

Third, the defendant may agree to the forfeiture as part of a plea agreement, which should be as specific as possible in naming the property the defendant is agreeing to forfeit and/or the amount of the money judgment the defendant is agreeing to pay. It should also say that the defendant is waiving all of his rights to contest the forfeiture under the procedural rules, and provide a factual basis for the forfeiture.[69] Because the forfeiture order will be part of the defendant's sentence, the court must enter a 'preliminary order of forfeiture' as soon as practicable after the entry of the guilty plea—or after the return of a guilty verdict at trial—and provide that the order will become final as to the defendant at sentencing.[70] The idea is that the defendant is entitled to have all aspects of his sentence imposed at one time—that is, as part of a single package.[71] The easiest way for the prosecutor to comply with this requirement is to have the defendant sign a Consent Order of Forfeiture at the time he or she enters a guilty plea.

Fourth, if the defendant no longer has the proceeds of his offence, or any property traceable to it, at the time he is convicted, the court must enter an order of forfeiture in the form of a money judgment.[72] The Government may then move to satisfy the money judgment by forfeiting substitute assets.[73] Like the directly forfeitable property and the money judgment, the forfeiture of substitute assets is mandatory, and can include any property the defendant owns, even though it is not traceable to the offence.[74]

Fifth, if the case goes to trial, the forfeiture does not come up until the jury has returned a guilty verdict, at which point there is a post-verdict forfeiture hearing. There is no constitutional right to a jury in the forfeiture phase of the trial,[75] but there is a statutory right to have the jury determine the forfeiture if the Government is seeking specific assets.[76] In that case, the prosecutor must prepare jury instructions and special verdict forms geared to the particulars of the property the Government is seeking to forfeit and its connection to the offence for which the defendant has been convicted.[77]

Sixth, the forfeiture order must be included in the oral announcement of the sentence and included in the judgment.[78]

Seventh, and finally, as mentioned earlier, the forfeiture order must be entered without regard to the ownership of the property. Determining the ownership of the property is deferred to the post-trial ancillary proceeding and is necessary only if a third party files a claim asserting a legal interest in the property.

Conclusion

The forfeiture statutes in the federal criminal code provide prosecutors with a robust set of procedures that allow them to recover the proceeds of crime and other property involved in the commission of a criminal offence in a variety of ways. What the statutes lack in uniformity and simplicity, they compensate for in terms of scope and enforcement. They have, in all of their forms and applications, become an essential part of the enforcement of US criminal laws.

Notes

1. For a more complete discussion of these issues, see Stefan D Cassella, *Asset Forfeiture Law in the United States* (2nd edn, Juris 2013) and 2016 Supplement.
2. *Kaley v United States* 134 S Ct 1090 (2014).
3. See *United States v Martin* 662 F 3d 301, 309 (4th Cir 2011).
4. Mark Osler, "Asset Forfeiture in a New Market-Reality Narcotics Policy" (2015) 52(1) Harvard Journal on Legislation 221.
5. For a social network approach to examining terrorism finances, see Chap. 39 (Leuprecht and Walther) in this collection.
6. See Courtney J Linn, "What Asset Forfeiture Teaches Us About Providing Restitution in Fraud Cases" (2007) 10(3) Journal of Money Laundering Control 215.
7. *United States v Blackman* 746 F 3d 137, 143 (4th Cir 2014).
8. See Ernesto Savona, Michele Riccardi, and Giulia Berlusconi (eds), *Organised Crime in European Businesses* (Routledge 2016).
9. For further consideration of social re-use, see Chap. 29 (Vettori) in this collection.
10. 18 USC ss 981(a)(1)(A) and 982(a)(1).
11. Ibid. s 1963.
12. Ibid. s 981(a)(1)(G).
13. See, for instance, 7 USC s 2024(f) (forfeiture of property used to commit food stamp fraud); 18 USC s 1028(b)(5) (forfeiture of personal property used to commit identity theft); 18 USC s 1029(c)(1)(C) (forfeiture of personal property used to commit access device fraud); 18 USC s 1030(i) (forfeiture of proceeds of computer fraud, and personal property used to commit computer fraud); 18 USC s 1037 (forfeiture of proceeds of email fraud, or 'equipment, software or other technology' used to commit the offence).
14. See, for instance, 18 USC s 982(a)(2)(A) (forfeiture of proceeds of fraud affecting a financial institution); 18 USC s 982(a)(7) (forfeiture of gross proceeds of health care fraud); 18 USC s 982(a)(8) (forfeiture of proceeds and property used to commit telemarketing fraud).
15. See 18 USC 981(a)(1)(C) incorporating the list of offences that appears in the money laundering statute; 18 USC s 1956(c)(7); the RICO statute; 18 USC s 1961(1); and the terrorism statute 18 USC s 2332b(g)(5)(B).
16. Section 981(a)(1)(C) is a *civil forfeiture statute* but it authorizes *criminal forfeiture* as well through 28 USC s 2461(c). Cases explaining this include *United States v Razmilovic* 419 F 3d 134, 136 (2nd Cir 2005); *United States v Black* 526 F Supp 2d 870, 878 (ND Ill 2007); *United States v Evanson* 2008 WL 3107332, *1 (D Utah 2008); *United States v Rudaj* 2006 WL 1876664, *3–4 (SDNY 2006).

17. See *United States v Taylor* 582 F 3d 558, 565 (5th Cir 2009) (explaining how s 981(a)(1)(C) incorporates the money laundering predicates from ss 1956(c)(7) and 1961(1)); *United States v St Pierre* 809 F Supp 2d 538, 542 n 2 (ED La 2011) (explaining how s 981(a)(1)(C) authorizes forfeiture for violations of ss 666 and 1343).
18. For a full discussion of the forfeiture of criminal proceeds, see Cassella (n 1), Chap. 25.
19. See *United States v Clark* 2016 WL 361560, *4 (SD Fla 2016); *United States v Galemmo* 2015 WL 4450669 (SD Ohio 2015); *United States v Lustyik* 2015 WL 1467260 (D Utah 2015); *United States v Cekosky* 171 Fed Appx 785, 2006 WL 707129 (11th Cir 2006).
20. See *United States v Warshak* 631 F 3d 266, 329–330 (6th Cir 2010); *United States v Smith* 749 F 3d 465, 488–489 (6th Cir 2014); *United States v Daugerdas* 2012 WL 5835203, *3 (SDNY 2012).
21. See *United States v Esquenazi* 752 F 3d 912, 931 (11th Cir 2014).
22. See *United States v Torres* 703 F 3d 194, 204 (2nd Cir 2012). See also *United States v Wong* 2014 WL 6976080, *2 (CD Cal 2014); *United States v Tyson Foods, Inc*, 2003 WL 8118660 (ED Tenn 2003).
23. See *United States v Peters*, 732 F 3d 93, 102 (2nd Cir 2013); *United States v George*, 2010 WL 1740814, *1 (ED Va 2010).
24. See *United States v Swanson* 394 F 3d 520, 529 n 4 (7th Cir 2005); *United States v Schlesinger* 396 F Supp 2d 267, 273 (EDNY 2005); *United States v Miller* 2009 WL 2949784, *7 (D Kan 2009).
25. See *United States v Hill* 46 Fed Appx 838, 839 (6th Cir 2002); *United States v Kalish* 2009 WL 130215, at *5–6 (SDNY 2009); *United States v Vogel* 2010 WL 547344, *4 (ED Tex 2010).
26. *United States v Betancourt* 422 F 3d 240 (5th Cir 2005).
27. See *United States v Venturella* 585 F 3d 1013, 1015, 1016–1017 (7th Cir 2009); *United States v Hailey* 887 F Supp 2d 649 (D Md 2012); *United States v Newman* 659 F 3d 1235, 1244 (9th Cir 2011).
28. See *United States v Sigillito* 899 F Supp 2d 850, 864–865 (ED Mo 2012).
29. See *United States v Contorinis*, 692 F 3d 136, 145 n 3 (2nd Cir 2012).
30. See *United States v Martin* 2014 WL 221956, *5 (D Idaho 2014).
31. For a full discussion of the forfeiture of facilitating property, see Cassella (n 1), Chap. 26.
32. *United States v Rivera* 884 F 2d 544, 546 (11th Cir 1989). See *United States v Schifferli* 895 F 2d 987, 990–991 (4th Cir 1990); *United States v Huber* 404 F 3d 1047 (8th Cir 2005); *United States v Puche* 350 F 3d 1137 (11th Cir 2003); *United States v Thornton* 2012 WL 2866467, *2 (SD Miss 2012).
33. 18 USC s 983(c)(3).
34. *United States v Bajakajian* 524 US 321, 323 (1998); 18 USC s 983(g) (codifying the *Bajakajian* decision for civil forfeiture cases). For a full discussion of

the proportionality issue under the Excessive Fines Clause of the Eighth Amendment see Cassella (n 1), Chap. 28.

35. See *Huber* (n 32) 1056 and 1058; *United States v Coffman* 2014 WL 354632, *3 (ED Ky 2014); *United States v Tencer* 107 F 3d 1120, 1135 (5th Cir 1997).

36. See *United States v Stanford* 2014 WL 7013987, *4–6 (WD La 2014). For a full discussion of forfeiture under the money laundering statutes, see Cassella (n 1), Chap. 27.

37. 18 USC s 983(a)(1) and (2).

38. For a summary of administrative forfeiture procedure, see *Malladi Drugs and Pharmaceuticals, Ltd v Tandy* 552 F3d 885, 887 (DC Cir 2009); *Ramos v United States* 2015 WL 1433549 (DVI 2015); *Pert v United States* 2011 WL 1792767, *5 (D Nev 2011); *VanHorn v Florida* 677 F Supp 2d 1288, 1293 (MD Fla 2009); *United States v $200,255 in US Currency* 2006 WL 1687774, *2–4 (MD Ga 2006); *Rodriguez v United States* 2006 WL 889557, *2 (DNH 2006); *Bermudez v City of New York Police Department* 2008 WL 3397919, *3 (SDNY 2008).

39. 19 USC s 1607.

40. See *Malladi* (n 38); *United States v Ninety-Three (93) Firearms* 330 F 3d 414, 422 (6th Cir 2003); *United States v Miscellaneous Firearms* 376 F 3d 709, 713 (7th Cir 2004); *In re: Application for Warrant to Seize One 1988 Chevrolet Monte Carlo* 861 F 2d 307, 310 (1st Cir 1988).

41. 18 USC s 981(g)(2).

42. 18 USC s 983(a)(3).

43. 381 F Supp 2d 57 (DPR 2005).

44. 871 F Supp 2d 128 (EDNY 2012).

45. 2014 WL 936293 (CD Cal 2014).

46. See Cassella (n 1), Chap. 2 for a history of the development of forfeiture law in the United States.

47. *United States v Ursery* 518 US 267, 295–296 (1996) (J Kennedy concurring).

48. See *United States v One Assortment of 89 Firearms* 465 US 354, 361–362 (1984); *One Lot Emerald Cut Stones v United States* 409 US 232, 234–235 (1972); *Paret-Ruiz v United States* 827 F 3d 167 (1st Cir 2016); *United States v $6,190.00 in U.S. Currency* 581 F 3d 881, 885 (9th Cir 2009).

49. See *Bennis v Michigan* 516 US 442, 446 (1996).

50. 18 USC s 983(d).

51. See *United States v $506,069.09 Seized from First Merit Bank* 2014 WL 7185585, *7 (ND Ohio 2014); *United States v Real Property Known As 7208 East 65th Pl* 185 F. Supp.3d 1288 (ND Okla 2016); *United States v One Gray 2007 Dodge RAM Truck* 2015 WL 8362399 (SD Ind 2015).

52. See *United States v One Gulfstream G-V Jet Aircraft* 941 F Supp 2d 1, 10 (DDC 2013).

53. See *United States v $7,679.00 U.S. Currency* 2015 WL 7571910 (WDNY 2015).
54. *United States v 6 Firearms, Accessories and Ammunition* 2015 WL 4660126 (WD Wash 2015).
55. For a detailed discussion of civil forfeiture procedure, see Cassella (n 1); Chaps. 6, 7, 8, 9, 10, 11, 12, 13, and 14. See also *United States v $133,420.00 in U.S. Currency* 672 F 3d 629, 634–635 (9th Cir 2012) (setting out the procedures for commencing a civil forfeiture action under s 983 and Rule G).
56. 18 USC s 983(g).
57. See *United States v Real Property Located at 475 Martin Lane* 545 F 3d 1134, 1144 (9th Cir 2008); *In re Matthews,* 395 F 3d 477, 481 (4th Cir 2005).
58. See *Libretti v United States* 516 US 29, 39 (1995) (by Rule 32(2)(b)(3) (the order of forfeiture 'shall be made part of the sentence and included in the judgment')); *United States v Christensen* 828 F 3d 763 (9th Cir 2015); *United States v Smith* 770 F 3d 628, 637 (7th Cir 2014).
59. See *United States v Harris* 666 F 3d 905, 910 (5th Cir 2012).
60. See *United States v Capoccia* 503 F 3d 103, 110, 114 (2nd Cir 2007).
61. See *Venturella* (n 27) 1016–1017.
62. See *United States v Vampire Nation* 451 F 3d 189, 202 (3rd Cir 2006); *United States v Lazarenko* 476 F 3d 642, 647 (9th Cir 2007); *United States v Roberts* 696 F Supp 2d 263, 270 (EDNY 2010).
63. See FR Crim P 32.2(b)(2). *De Almeida v United States* 459 F 3d 377, 381 (2nd Cir 2006); *United States v Watts* 477 Fed Appx 816, 817–818 (2nd Cir 2012); *United States v Dupree* 919 F Supp 2d 254, 274–275 (EDNY 2013); *United States v Molina-Sanchez* 298 FRD 311, 312–313 (WDNC 2014).
64. Rule 32.2(c); 21 USC s 853(n). The post—trial ancillary proceeding is explained in detail in Cassella (n 1), Chap. 23.
65. For a complete discussion of criminal forfeiture procedure, see Cassella (n 1); Chaps. 15, 16, 17, 18, 19, 20, 21, 22, 23, and 24.
66. Rule 32.2(a). See *United States v Hampton* 732 F 3d 687, 690 (6th Cir 2013); *United States v Lazarenko* 504 F Supp 2d 791, 796–797 (ND Cal 2007); *United States v Galestro* 2008 WL 2783360, at *10–11 (EDNY 2008); *United States v Woods* 730 F Supp 2d 1354, 1372–1373 (SD Ga 2010); *United States v Clemens* 2011 WL 1540150, *4 (D Mass 2011).
67. 21 USC ss 853(e) and (f).
68. See Kaley (n 2); *United States v Cosme* 796 F 3d 226 (2nd Cir 2015); *United States v Holy Land Foundation for Relief and Development* 493 F 3d 469, 475 (5th Cir 2007).
69. See *United States v Beltramea* 785 F 3d 287 (8th Cir 2015).
70. Rule 32.2(b). See *United States v Marquez* 685 F 3d 501, 510 (5th Cir 2012).
71. See *United States v Yeje-Cabrera* 430 F 3d 1 (1st Cir 2005).
72. See *Vampire Nation* (n 62); *Hampton* (n 66) 691–692; *United States v Viloski* 814 F 3d 104, 110 n 11 (2nd Cir 2016); *Blackman* (n 7).

73. 21 USC s 853(p); Rule 32.2(e).
74. See *United States v Fleet* 498 F 3d 1225, 1231 (11th Cir 2007); *United States v Carroll* 346 F 3d 744, 749 (7th Cir 2003); *United States v Alamoudi* 452 F 3d 310, 314 (4th Cir 2006).
75. See *Libretti* (n 58) 49; *United States v Valdez* 726 F 3d 684, 699 (5th Cir 2013).
76. Rule 32.2(b)(5).
77. See *United States v Armstrong* 2007 WL 809508, *2 (ED La 2007); *United States v Phillips* 704 F 3d 754, 771 (9th Cir 2012).
78. Rule 32.2(b)(4). See *United States v Smith* 656 F 3d 821, 828 (8th Cir 2011); *United States v Holder* 2010 WL 478369, *3 (MD Tenn 2010).

Stefan D. Cassella is the author of *Asset Forfeiture Law in the United States*, a one-volume resource designed to lead the practitioner, prosecutor, judge and policy-maker through the labyrinth of statutes, rules and cases that govern this dynamic area of the law, and of more than 35 law review articles on money laundering and forfeiture. He is also the author and publisher of the *Money Laundering and Forfeiture Digest*, a monthly compendium of the forfeiture and money laundering cases decided by the federal courts. As a federal prosecutor, he was one of the federal government's leading experts on asset forfeiture and money laundering law for over 30 years. He now serves as an expert witness and consultant to law enforcement agencies and the private sector.

19

Post-conviction Confiscation in England and Wales

HHJ Michael Hopmeier and Alexander Mills

The power to make a confiscation order, after the conviction of a defendant, against their proceeds of crime has been available under statute to judges of the Crown Court in England and Wales for nearly 30 years.[1] Statistics demonstrate that such orders are made in the thousands: between 2014 and 2015, 5924 confiscation orders were imposed and a total of £155m was recovered.[2] Such a well-established regime that results in the payment of vast sums of money to the state arguably should be seen as a laudable achievement of the criminal justice system. Nevertheless, the headline numbers mask a process that remains fraught with problems. Between January 2015 and July 2016 there were over 40 reported judgments delivered either by the Court of Appeal or by the Supreme Court on confiscation issues. Whilst some appeals were well founded, approximately 70% were dismissed. In the first 10 months of 2017 there have been well over 20 reported cases in the Court of Appeal or the Supreme Court. This is indicative of some uncertainty in the application of the law and efforts made by defendants in some cases to avoid paying their orders. In the case of *Stannard*[3] the outstanding confiscation order dated back as far as 2003. The comments made by the judge provide an insight into a familiar position:

> [the defendant] has fought tooth and nail to avoid paying anything, and made life as difficult as possible for the Enforcement Receiver, with the result that

HHJ. Michael Hopmeier
Southwark Crown Court, London, UK

A. Mills
City, University of London, London, UK

© The Author(s) 2018
C. King et al. (eds.), *The Palgrave Handbook of Criminal and Terrorism Financing Law*,
https://doi.org/10.1007/978-3-319-64498-1_19

there is still such a substantial amount outstanding ten and a half years after the generous deadline set for payment ... In reality he is still doing his level best to avoid making any further payment, to go behind decisions unfavourable to him that have already been made by the Court and which he has not appealed, to re-run arguments he has already lost, and to put the [prosecution] and the Enforcement Receiver to as much further trouble and expense as possible, presumably in the hope that they will give up and go away[...].[4]

The proceeds of crime legislation in England and Wales 'is under sustained legal challenge from criminals who are constantly seeking new ways to avoid its reach and frustrate asset recovery'.[5] The National Audit Office has reported that for every £100 that represents the proceeds of crime, just 26p has been recovered through the confiscation process,[6] and the system has come under criticism from the press[7] and Members of Parliament[8] for generating orders that either cannot or will not ever be enforced. This has diminished public confidence that the Proceeds of Crime Act (POCA) regime is used appropriately by those in the criminal justice system[9] to deter criminals from offending through the threat of having their ill-gotten gains removed.[10] In July 2016, the Law Commission announced that it is considering a review of the law governing confiscation orders as part of its next law reform programme,[11] despite a suite of reforms having just been brought into force in June 2015[12] through the Serious Crime Act 2015 ('SCA 2015'). It is in light of these difficulties that this chapter examines the nature of the confiscation regime in England and Wales and how that regime is applied in practice.

The Nature of 'Confiscation Orders' in England and Wales

Since 24 March 2003[13] confiscation orders have been made pursuant to the Proceeds of Crime Act 2002 ('POCA 2002'). Confiscation orders follow conviction[14] and are therefore determined before judges in the criminal courts, in particular the Crown Court,[15] which has jurisdiction over indictable offences. At the confiscation hearing, applying the civil standard of proof (the balance of probabilities)[16] the criminal court judge must first determine the defendant's benefit from crime[17] and then order that a sum be repaid that is equivalent to that benefit from crime,[18] unless the amount that can in fact be recovered from the defendant is less.[19] Because the sum to be repaid is 'equivalent to'[20] the defendant's benefit from crime, a confiscation order does not require that he sell any particular asset. Indeed, 'it is open to the defendant to pay off the order [from] whatever assets he or she has available'.[21] It is therefore referred to as an *in personam* order (against the person) rather than an *in rem* order (against a particular 'thing').[22]

Scope of the Enquiry into Benefit

The first stage of confiscation is to determine the defendant's benefit from crime. On the surface, this should be straightforward. If £100,000 is received from drug dealing, then the court should order repayment of £100,000.[23] However, what if that money has been used to partly fund the purchase of the matrimonial home, in which the defendant lives with his unwitting wife? What if the defendant invested the money in a 'legitimate' business which has seen an increase in profits as a result of that investment? The question becomes far more complex, and the scope of the judicial enquiry is far wider than might first be anticipated.

Third-Party Rights

Part of the problem that has beset the confiscation regime is that the issues in the above scenarios fall to be determined in the Crown Court. Judges and practitioners who may have spent their entire careers dealing with criminal matters have been thrust into the position of having to marshal complex arguments about matters that traditionally fall far outside of the ambit of the criminal law, such as trust arrangements and beneficial ownership. When POCA was first enacted Crown Court judges were not required to resolve such matters definitively. Because a confiscation order is made against a defendant personally to pay a sum of money from any assets he or she has available, no specific assets are at stake through the making of the order. It was therefore logical that 'POCA [made] no express provision for the court to deal with … third party interests […] when determining the amount of a confiscation order'.[24] Instead, third-party rights were determined at the enforcement stage, when the prosecution was seeking to realise specific assets, for example, through the appointment of an enforcement receiver. Whilst there was some logic to this approach, it effectively gave defendants another opportunity to challenge a confiscation order through a third party, thereby complicating, lengthening and frustrating[25] the confiscation process. The solution introduced through the SCA 2015 was to permit a judge of the Crown Court to determine the extent of a defendant's interest in property.[26] It was intended that this would expedite the confiscation process, with such determinations being taken at an early stage and having a conclusive and binding effect upon any court or other person involved in the enforcement of a confiscation order.[27] This provision took effect on 1 June 2015[28] and, given its relevant infancy,[29] its actual effects still remain to be seen.[30] However, the pressure that making such 'civil law' determinations places upon the criminal Bar and judges, who may be versed only in criminal law, is self-evident. Practitioners must assist the court thoroughly and precisely. At the outset, a prosecutor's 'statement of information' to the court must 'include any information known to the prosecutor which the prosecutor believes is or would be relevant' to making a third-party determination.[31] Similarly, the defendant can be required to provide information about the nature and extent of an interest held in an asset.[32] Furthermore, the third party themselves may be ordered to provide the court with information.[33] There are sanctions for failing to provide this assistance. For example, if the 'interested person'[34] fails to give the requisite information without a reasonable excuse, then, without prejudice to any other power of the court, the judge may draw such inference as believed to be appropriate to beneficial ownership.[35]

Despite this help from the parties, the pressures upon the Bench in making such civil law determinations remain, and are reflected in two ways. First, the supposedly binding determination of the Crown Court judge in relation to third-party interests may be disregarded at the enforcement stage 'if it appears to the court that there would be a serious risk of injustice'.[36] On its face, it is unlikely that defendants who have 'fought tooth and nail'[37] to avoid paying their confiscation orders will simply ignore this provision. In every case in which a judge is asked to revisit the third-party determination at the enforcement stage, consideration will have to be given to the arguments raised at the confiscation hearing and to how those arguments were dealt with by the judge and by counsel. It is easily imaginable that new counsel with civil law expertise may be instructed for enforcement proceedings, who will then argue that judges at the confiscation stage were not directed to particular authorities or statutes which may have assisted in determining a third-party interest. Whether or not such arguments are successful, there is the potential to delay significantly the conclusion of enforcement proceedings by requiring the judge to reconsider the merits of the third-party determination. Second, the SCA 2015 envisages that determinations of third-party interests will only be made 'in relatively straightforward cases'[38] by judges 'whose experience allows them to do so'.[39] If there is agreement as to the nature and extent of the third-party interest, then it would appear appropriate for a judge of the Crown Court to make the determination.[40] However, in other cases it may be difficult for practitioners to submit to a judge that they may not have the requisite experience. It is therefore suggested that it is incumbent upon the judges themselves to take time to reflect upon this issue in deciding whether it would be appropriate for them to make a third-party determination in light of the information provided by the parties in advance of the hearing.

The third party may, of course, be a company. The courts must also grapple with, and correctly apply, company law principles in confiscation cases.[41] In 2016, there has been a flurry of cases emphasising the need for judges to apply detailed knowledge of, and close scrutiny to, when it may be appropriate to lift the corporate veil.[42]

Family Law Matters

The Crown Courts are also faced with challenges from spouses who bring competing claims to the defendant's assets through proceedings for a divorce and financial remedy. This raises the spectre of 'unseemly competition'[43] between the prosecution and the wife. Accordingly, neither proceedings under POCA nor the Matrimonial Causes Act 1973 have priority over one another.[44] Instead, the court must achieve a fair balance between the competing interests. Generally, this may involve a determination as to whether the spouse was innocent of wrongdoing.[45] If she was, then as a matter of public policy it is inappropriate to adopt a starting point that the wife should suffer the punitive effects of being 'kicked out' of the family home. Accordingly, in such circumstances it is ordinarily the case that the matrimonial financial proceedings take precedence,[46] and the Crown Court judge should adjourn confiscation proceedings pending their resolution. However, even when the wife is 'innocent', there remains a public policy consideration, namely the extent to which a wife should be able to benefit from her husband's criminality.[47] Therefore, the prosecution is permitted to intervene during the matrimonial financial proceedings.[48] Even where such ancillary relief proceedings are not in train, judges have been required to consider the relevance of family law and related trust law principles.[49] Practitioners and judges therefore may need to apply specialist legal knowledge far beyond that normally associated with a criminal trial.

Considerations in Determining 'Benefit'

Even in cases with no such matters requiring specialised knowledge, the court must still grapple with what amounts to a 'benefit'. This is of fundamental importance to the confiscation exercise because without a 'benefit' from crime, there can be no confiscation order.[50] Section 76(4) posits what on its face is a clear test, namely that 'a person benefits from conduct if he obtains property as a result of or in connection with' criminal conduct. However, once again, this ostensibly straightforward test is more nuanced than it first appears. First, what if the defendant only obtains the criminal property temporarily? Second, what is the extent of the defendant's benefit if criminal money is mixed with legitimate money to fund a larger purchase?

Transient Nature of Holding or Possessing Property

There are two fundamental issues relating to the transient nature of property with which the court must grapple in determining benefit. First, what if a defendant merely held the property temporarily in order to pass it on to another? A drug courier may only be a 'middle man' who temporarily obtains property from criminal conduct (namely the money for drugs or the drugs) and holds it simply for as long as is necessary to pass it on to the drug dealer. The English courts apply the test of whether the defendant had a power of control or disposition in relation to the property in question. If so, the defendant has 'obtained' the property within the meaning of the legislation.[51] A courier ordinarily has no power of control or disposition over its delivery. He merely holds property with the permission and under the direction of the person who transferred it to them.[52] Any benefit to the courier is therefore limited ordinarily to what they were paid for assisting in the criminal transaction.[53] Defendants have sought to extend this principle to individuals who hold money temporarily in their bank accounts on behalf of others, for example, money launderers. However, the Court of Appeal has reasoned that there is a difference. Ordinarily, a person who holds funds in their account has a power of control over how those funds are distributed, even though they promised to distribute those funds in a particular way.[54] It is the account holder's choice that they did not realise the full fruits of the criminality because they elected to transfer the funds.[55] Intellectually, it could be said that couriers are precisely the same. They too may decide not to return the illicit drug money or drugs to the drug dealer. Arguably, the distinction drawn by the Court of Appeal could be attributed to the facts of the individual cases.[56] In none of the cases involving bank accounts could the defendant truly be said to be acting as a mere 'nominee' with no real power of control or disposition over the funds therein. If the court was presented with evidence to support the proposition that the holder of the account was acting for a fixed fee and solely under the direction of another, it may be hard to conclude that they truly 'benefited' from the funds in the account.

The second issue surrounding the transient nature of the acquisition or possession of property is the conflation of 'benefit' with 'profit'. Any criminal enterprise will incur expenses, whether it be the cutting agents needed for drugs, or the necessary expenses incurred in a fraudulently run business. Ultimately, a defendant obtains a 'net' profit only after running up these costs. There is a public policy justification for not equating benefit with profit. Normal accounting practice relates to lawful traders conducting lawful business, where transactions are not a sham or designed to obscure criminality.[57] The courts have therefore held a strong line that a criminal should not be able to 'offset' the cost of their criminality by reducing their confiscation order,[58] and that therefore benefit should not be equated with gross profit.

Proportionality

The extent of the finding of benefit and any order which may ultimately be made are also subject to a test of proportionality. Whilst proceeds of crime legislation serves the legitimate aim of removing the incentives for committing offences,[59] this aim cannot be a warrant for abandoning completely the need for the court to act fairly in making its determination. Therefore, any confiscation order must be a proportionate interference with the right to peaceful enjoyment of possessions, as guaranteed by Article 1 of the First Protocol to the European Convention on Human Rights.[60]

A series of principles about when it is proportionate to make a confiscation order are emerging from the appellate case law. First, where a defendant makes a part-purchase using tainted money, it is disproportionate to ignore any legitimate contributions to the purchase price of that asset. Therefore, the finding of benefit may be limited to that part of the property which was obtained through criminal conduct.[61]

Second, it is often contended that benefit accrued to a business through its criminal activities should be limited to a sum well below its entire gross profit. A distinction has been drawn by the courts between undertakings that are entirely unlawful and businesses that are generally legitimate but which are tainted by an act of illegality. In the case of the former it is likely to be proportionate to make an order that the full gross profits of that undertaking are the benefit from crime. However, this is unlikely to be the case for the latter.[62]

Third, when there are multiple defendants in an enterprise where each held the proceeds of crime, it is not disproportionate to make an order that each defendant is jointly and severally liable for the entire sum.[63] Therefore, the court should order that each defendant repay in full a benefit from crime that is jointly obtained. However, the order should provide that it is not to be enforced to the extent that the sum has already been recovered through another defendant.[64] The Supreme Court[65] has recognised that such an order may well produce 'inequity between criminal conspirators'.[66] However, it dismissed this as an 'inherent feature of joint criminality'.[67] For example, a victim of fraud suing the conspirators would be 'entitled to enforce against whichever defendant he most easily could'[68] in a civil law context, and there is no reason why a similar principle should not apply to confiscation.

The final key issue of proportionality addressed by the courts is whether a defendant should still be found to have benefited from crime even where that benefit has been repaid before any order is made. The courts have concluded that where a defendant has voluntarily repaid all of the benefit from crime there is no need to make a confiscation order.[69] Not only is this approach sensible but it also represents an 'obvious policy consideration',[70] namely to encourage defendants to repay their proceeds of crime, and to do so quickly. Once again, however, what is seemingly a straightforward proposition has been subject to challenge and refinement. For example, close scrutiny should be paid to whether the benefit has truly been disgorged *voluntarily*. The payment of proceeds of crime to the tax authorities in settlement of a tax liability has been found to be the equivalent of voluntary repayment because the money had already been passed willingly to the State.[71] However, voluntary repayment of the proceeds of crime must be distinguished from its seizure by the State. Although in both cases a defendant no longer retains their proceeds of crime, it remains proportionate to make a confiscation order after seizure by the State because there is no evidence that the defendant would have voluntarily given up their benefit. Seizure is 'an occupational hazard' for criminals, and they should not be rewarded for it.[72] Furthermore, the mere fact that the court has ordered a defendant to pay compensation in the sum of the benefit from crime is not the equivalent of voluntary repayment because it remains uncertain whether payment will actually be made.[73] If repayment has not been made by the day of the confiscation hearing, proof that payment is guaranteed is necessary to avoid the making of a confiscation order.[74] Expressions of 'well-meaning intentions' on behalf of a defendant which are not backed by assurance of repayment may well not be entertained.[75]

Statutory Assumptions as to Benefit

As the foregoing demonstrates, accurate calculation of the direct benefit from crime can be time consuming. However, it is rarely the end of the matter.

Where a defendant has a 'criminal lifestyle' within the meaning of POCA 2002, the court must also apply the lifestyle 'assumptions',[76] which can dramatically increase the amount to which a defendant will have been deemed to have benefited from criminal conduct. As one might expect, a defendant has a criminal lifestyle if he is engaged in serious organised criminal activity, such as money laundering, people trafficking and arms trafficking.[77] However, a defendant is also deemed to have a criminal lifestyle in less dramatic circumstances. Commission of a single offence over a period of at least six months from which the defendant gained at least £5000 is sufficient. The rationale is clear, a person who commits crime for financial gain over a prolonged period of time and who has managed to hide that criminality from the authorities during that time is likely to have done so with a degree of sophistication and is also likely to have used some of that financial gain to provide for themselves or for others. The broad definition of criminal lifestyle means that many defendants are caught in a consideration of their benefit that extends far beyond the benefit from the 'particular criminal conduct'[78] for which they were convicted.

There are four lifestyle assumptions that apply in order to calculate benefit from 'general criminal conduct',[79] two of which allow the court to enquire back as far as the 'relevant day', namely, the day six years prior to the date upon which proceedings against the defendant were commenced.[80] Although a defendant may have never faced charges for other criminal offences,[81] the court must then assume the following: first, that any property transferred to the defendant at any time after the relevant day was obtained by him as a result of his criminal conduct[82]; second, that any property held by the defendant at any time after the date of conviction was obtained by him as a result of his criminal conduct[83]; third, that any expenditure incurred by the defendant at any time after the relevant day was met from property obtained by him as a result of his criminal conduct[84]; and fourth, that for the purpose of valuing any property obtained by the defendant, such property was obtained free of any other interests in it.[85] The court is therefore required to take an expansive view of benefit. Every household bill over a six-year period will be deemed to have been paid from the proceeds of crime, unless the defendant can show otherwise.[86] Any money passing through his accounts during that period will also be deemed to have been derived from criminal activity.[87] The wide ambit of the lifestyle assumptions is supposedly tempered[88] by the ability to rebut the assumptions if the defendant can satisfy the court on the balance of probabilities that their application would be incorrect.[89] However, this can prove problematic. Defendants are required to produce clear and cogent evidence in order to rebut the assumptions.[90] Obtaining a clear audit trail for transactions over a six-year period may not be easy. Furthermore, some transactions may have been informal, and so it may be impossible for a defendant to account for their legitimacy. Nevertheless, the Court of Appeal has held that this is a risk inherent in such transactions that a defendant has elected to run:

> …if people chose to operate their business dealings only in cash and kept no records of any kind whatsoever they had to take the consequences that might arise for the purposes of the potential application of the Proceeds of Crime Act 2002[…].[91]

A defendant may therefore feel obligated to give evidence at the confiscation hearing in order to rebut the assumptions. This too is problematic.[92] Generally, confiscation hearings are presided over by the judge who heard the trial at which a defendant was convicted.[93] Whilst a trial judge should take particular care when making remarks about the credibility of a defendant prior to the confiscation hearing,[94] the defendant's version of events at trial (if he gave evidence) is likely to have been disbelieved by the jury, and so a defendant may feel that the judge has already formed a negative view about their case. That defendant now has a criminal conviction and is facing the prospect of losing assets. Plainly, a judge must take great care in assessing the facts in relation to the assumptions and must not conclude that merely because the defendant may not have been reliable in evidence at trial that he cannot provide reliable evidence in the confiscation proceedings.[95]

The Amount to Be Repaid

Great care must also be taken at the next stage of the exercise, namely the calculation of the amount that a defendant will in fact have to repay. Whilst it is generally appropriate to order a defendant to repay the entirety of their benefit from crime, if the defendant can establish on the balance of probabilities[96] that they hold insufficient assets to make full repayment, the court may order payment of a lesser sum.[97] This may balance the public interest in recovering the proceeds of crime with the need to make fair, just and enforceable orders. However, by placing the burden of proving that the available assets from which an order could be repaid are worth less than the benefit incurred by the defendant the courts have been obliged to make orders that may seemingly appear to be far from fair, just and enforceable. Orders may be inflated because of a real suspicion (at times well founded) that defendants have 'hidden' their assets and defendants are failing to prove otherwise. There is some merit in the proposition that because criminals work hard to make money from crime, they will also work hard to keep that money from the authorities.[98] Of the 'top ten' outstanding confiscation orders, some £119m of assets are thought to be held overseas.[99] It is self-evident that in cases of sophisticated criminality a defendant may have the acumen to keep their assets at arm's-length. Nevertheless, the principle that a defendant must prove that they do not have hidden assets from which to repay their benefit from crime applies to all levels of criminality.

How does a defendant in a criminal confiscation case demonstrate that they do not have hidden assets? First, as with the application of the lifestyle assumptions, a defendant may feel obligated to give evidence at the confiscation hearing. Judges are at liberty to (and often do) find that if a defendant has been evasive, vague or obstructive, this will support a conclusion in favour of hidden assets.[100] Second, as with the lifestyle assumptions, a defendant must produce cogent evidence to demonstrate the whereabouts of the proceeds of crime. A failure to produce a clear[101] audit trail is often used to justify a finding of hidden assets.[102] This may disregard the fact that a defendant may not have kept a written record of the dissipation of his criminal gains. These two problems are encapsulated neatly by the case of *Sawyer*,[103] in which a defendant was found to have hidden assets despite having no real identifiable assets at all and a large number of clearly evidenced debts. The hidden assets ruling was upheld by the Court of Appeal on the basis that the defendant had the capacity to have secreted the money away at the time that it was obtained, and no evidence had been produced of where the money stolen from the defendant's employer had gone.

Some concessions are made to defendants. If a judge rejects the defendant's account of his/her assets, the court should be clear in articulating its reasoning[104] for the sake of fairness and transparency. This facilitates the appeal process.[105] Judges are also required to have regard to all of the evidence in making a determination about hidden assets.[106] For example, although a judge is not permitted to take into account expenses incurred during the course of a criminal enterprise when calculating the amount which a defendant *obtained* from crime,[107] he may take into account those expenses when determining how much of that amount obtained can in fact be *repaid*. Logically, money expended on a criminal enterprise has not been 'hidden' by a defendant for his/her later use.[108] Nevertheless, these safeguards helped little in the *Sawyer* case, and hidden assets findings continue to be made in many cases. As of March 2016, £1.76bn remained outstanding in respect of unpaid confiscation orders,[109] of which £310 million has been deemed uncollectable by enforcement agencies.[110] It is notable that £206 million (66%) of that uncollectable debt has been attributed to unrealistic hidden assets orders.[111]

The balance between making an enforceable order and an order that reflects the fact that defendants have made unsurmountable efforts to hide their assets is a difficult one to strike. Rather than address this balance, the Home Affairs Select Committee's recommendation was that the *reporting* arrangements be altered, to reflect 'collectable' and 'uncollectable debts'.[112] In fairness to the report, however, it does touch upon a concern in relation to preventing a defendant from hiding their assets in the first place, namely the failure to obtain an order restraining the defendant from disposing of his assets prior to conviction.[113] The court is mandated by section 69(2) POCA 2002 to exercise its powers in connection with such restraint orders to ensure that assets remain available and are not diminished in value so that a confiscation order may be satisfied to best effect.[114] However, the court can only begin to do so upon application by the prosecutor or by an accredited financial investigator.[115] It may be a welcome development that the number of restraint order applications has begun to rise in 2016, which has been attributed to amendments brought about by the SCA 2015 aimed at 'enabling assets to be frozen more quickly and earlier in investigations'.[116] Section 40(2) POCA 2002 as originally drafted allowed a court to grant a restraint order if there was 'reasonable cause to believe' that an alleged offender had benefited from criminal conduct. The SCA 2015 amended the test to one of 'reasonable grounds to suspect' that an alleged offender has benefited from criminal conduct. This has two apparent benefits in strengthening the effectiveness of POCA. First, the threshold to which the court must be satisfied is lower.[117] This will make it easier for a restraint order to be obtained at an early stage of the investigation thus increasing the potential for effective preservation of assets. Second, it aligns the test for restraint with the test for arrest, meaning that restraint orders can be more readily obtained for service at the same time as the initial arrest of the defendant, thereby reducing the opportunities for him to dispose of his assets.[118] The courts should seek to encourage the early use of restraint provisions and a focus on identifiable assets in order to ensure that effective and enforceable confiscation orders are made.

Enforcing the Confiscation Order

The fact that an order may be enforceable does not, however, mean that it will be easy to enforce. The courts have a number of powers at their disposal in order to incentivise payment including the abilities to set tight controls on the time allowed for payment,[119] to impose a period of imprisonment for non-payment,[120] and to make a 'compliance order'[121] with any requirement that the court sees fit in order to render the confiscation order effective. In order to maximise the prospects of successful satisfaction of the confiscation order, the courts must use these powers to best effect. The courts should also emphasise that interest will accrue on any sum that remains unpaid by the set time.[122]

Time to Pay

The SCA 2015 gave effect to the Home Office Serious and Organised Crime Strategy's aim of strengthening POCA by 'significantly reducing the time that the courts can give offenders to pay confiscation orders'.[123] The court previously had a discretion to grant an extension of time to pay of up to a maximum of one year 'if the defendant show[ed] that he need[ed] time to pay the amount ordered to be paid'.[124] This allowed a defendant a lengthy period of time in which to pay and also allowed the defendant to benefit from a 'broad brush' approach to that deadline. If the defendant had particular assets which were not immediately realisable, the deadline to pay the entire sum could be deferred even though some assets could be realised readily. The discretion has now been narrowed in three ways. First, the court can 'stagger' payments.[125] If the defendant has some assets whose value is immediately realisable, the court may order that payment be immediate in relation to those assets. However, the deadline for payment of a sum representing the value of assets which may take longer to realise, such as houses, may be extended. This allows the court to keep much tighter control over the defendant, whose degree of freedom in realising the assets has been narrowed and whose level of accountability to the court has been strengthened. Second, the time to pay period has been reduced from six months to three months.[126] That period may be extended by a further three months, allowing a maximum total period of six months to pay.[127] This has reduced by half the overall maximum period for payment. Third, the wording of the test for granting an extension of time to pay has been altered to permit such an extension only if the court be satisfied 'that, despite having made all reasonable efforts, the defendant is unable to pay the amount'.[128] This new wording emphasises that the onus is on the defendant to do all that he can to realise his assets during the 'time to pay' period. If the court does grant an extension of time it remains open to the court to stagger the payments, granting different extensions (or no extension at all) over particular sums of money. The court and defendants are therefore now required to actively manage the timetable for the realisation of assets. It is hoped that such tighter control will lead to greater success in enforcing confiscation orders, particularly when combined with the consequences of non-payment, namely imprisonment in default and the accrual of interest.

Default Sentences for Non-payment

To further incentivise payment, England and Wales is one of very few jurisdictions in which defendants can be imprisoned for non-payment.[129] That term of imprisonment is to be served consecutively to any sentence of imprisonment imposed for the substantive offence.[130] Despite concerns about whether default terms are an effective means of enforcement,[131] the SCA 2015 gave effect to the Serious and Organised Crime Strategy's aim of 'substantially strengthening the prison sentences for failing to pay confiscation orders'.[132] The maximum period of imprisonment has been increased from 10 to 14 years,[133] and the 'early release' provision generally applicable to sentences of imprisonment no longer applies to confiscation orders made in excess of £10m.[134] The effect of these combined provisions on the maximum sentence to be served in default is dramatic. By way of contrast, under POCA as originally drafted, a defendant with a £10m confiscation order would be given a maximum default sentence for non-payment of ten years, with automatic eligibility for release after five years. That same defendant will now have to serve a full 14 years for non-payment, an increase of 9 years. For any criminal, that penalty is a substantial loss of liberty and should provide a clear incentive to pay their order. The consequences of non-payment should be made clear to any defendant by both counsel and the court, and the Crown Court Compendium Example Direction on confiscation to be given to defendants requires the judge to do so.[135]

Interest

Interest also accrues on unpaid sums under the confiscation order from the expiry of the time to pay period at the rate specified under the Judgments Act 1838,[136] which is currently 8% per annum.[137] This interest must be paid in addition to the sum due under the original confiscation order, and the default sentence can be activated in respect of outstanding interest.[138] Again, this would appear to be a powerful incentive to pay the order, and to do so quickly. However, over half a billion pounds of the outstanding £1.76bn owed on confiscation orders represents unpaid interest.[139] Whether it is an effective incentive to pay or merely a punitive by-product of POCA is, therefore, debatable. In order to use interest as an effective incentive to pay, judges and advocates should reiterate this potential penalty to the defendant.

Compliance Orders

The SCA 2015 has also strengthened enforcement by giving the court the power to make such orders as it considers appropriate for the purposes of ensuring that the confiscation order is effective.[140] Whilst it is in the court's discretion as to whether a 'compliance order'[141] is ultimately made, the court must at least consider making one[142] at the time[143] that the confiscation order is imposed.[144] It is also open to the prosecutor to ask the court to make a compliance order at a later date.[145] The court's discretion as to the nature of the conditions is wide, but it *must* consider 'whether any restriction or prohibition on the defendant's travel outside of the United Kingdom ought to be imposed'.[146] It is hoped that this will reduce access to hidden assets that have been secreted overseas and ultimately disincentivise the moving of assets out of the jurisdiction.[147] Compliance orders, including travel bans, are not limited to defendants, but can extend to any third party.[148] This is not simply a punitive measure to encourage repayment by the defendant. By extending the bans to third parties there is a clear recognition that defendants will use any means at their disposal, including friends and family members, to move assets.

In any event, the power to make such orders over third parties is tempered by a right given to any person affected by the compliance order to apply to the Crown Court to vary or discharge the order.[149] The broad discretion in relation to compliance orders gives the court an invaluable tool in the fight to ensure that confiscation orders are effective and courts should make use of it whenever it is reasonable to do so.

Conclusion

The millions of pounds recovered under the post-conviction confiscation regime in England and Wales referred to at the beginning of this chapter demonstrates that when this regime is used effectively and appropriately it can yield significant results in depriving criminals of their proceeds of crime. However, as this chapter further demonstrates, the court must hold parties robustly to their legal obligations. The parties must comply with their obligations to provide sufficient information upon which a clear determination can be made about the circumstances in which a defendant came to hold criminal assets, and about the nature and extent of the defendant's interest in those assets. All parties, and the court, should be aware of any relevant case law or statute or guidance. Where possible, using that information, issues relating to interests of parties other than the defendant should be resolved quickly at the outset of proceedings. Defendants should be clear about the requirement upon them to provide clear and cogent evidence to the courts in both rebutting the statutory assumptions and in establishing their benefit and should come to a confiscation hearing armed with the evidence that they need, and the knowledge of the consequences of failing to produce that evidence. Prosecutors should perhaps consider carefully whether it is in fact appropriate to seek a finding of 'hidden assets' in a particular case, or whether it will in fact lead to an unenforceable order being made. Furthermore, prosecutors and investigators should, in appropriate cases, apply for restraint orders at an early stage of the investigation to prevent assets from being hidden in the first place. Having made an order, all parties should ensure that a defendant is well aware of the consequences of non-payment, and ensure that the enforcement of the order is robustly monitored.

The House of Commons Home Affairs Committee report on the proceeds of crime, published in June 2016, has recommended that specialist 'confiscation courts' would assist the judiciary to develop the relevant expertise needed to deal effectively and expeditiously with confiscation.[150] On its face the proposal would relieve the pressure on the regular criminal courts, where lengthy hearing time which could be devoted to the resolution of substantive criminal prosecutions is taken up dealing with confiscation. Leaving aside the practical and policy issues of having a specialist confiscation court with 'ticketed' judges, on which the authors of this chapter express no views, there is one key hurdle that must be overcome. Confiscation depends on the calculation of benefit from the crimes for which the defendant has been convicted. Accordingly, the case law has been clear that the trial judge should ordinarily deal with the confiscation proceedings because evidence adduced at trial can be taken into account at the confiscation hearing and the trial judge will have been best placed to evaluate this evidence and the credibility of the defendant.[151] Will a specialist confiscation court judge have to preside over the criminal trial? Alternatively, will time have to be set aside for the confiscation court judge to read a lengthy transcript of the proceedings? These are matters of practicality that will have to be addressed. Nevertheless, the proposal is an interesting one. A possible opportunity to implement the proposal presented itself in the Criminal Finances Bill 2016. However, this Bill enacted in April

2017 as the Criminal Finances Act 2017, focuses on non-conviction based asset forfeiture through the establishment of a new regime in respect of 'unexplained wealth',[152] the expansion of the magistrates courts' non-conviction based forfeiture regime to include certain types of immoveable property such as precious metals and stones,[153] and the amendment of the regime governing the forfeiture of assets connected with terrorism.[154] There will no doubt be further opportunities for the amendment of the conviction-based confiscation regime in due course, at which stage the proposal for confiscation courts may be considered as having potential to further increase effectiveness.

Notes

1. Drug Trafficking Offences Act 1986 (Commencement No. 3) Order 1986, SI 1986/2145.
2. National Audit Office, *Confiscation Orders: Progress Review* (HC 2015–2016, 886).
3. *R v Stannard* [2015] EWHC 1199 (Admin).
4. Ibid. paras 79–80.
5. Home Office, *Serious and Organised Crime Strategy* (Cmd 8175, 2013) para 4(49); *Kelly* [2016] EWCA Crim 1505 para 35.
6. National Audit Office, *Confiscation Orders* (HC 2013–2014, 738).
7. Martin Bentham, 'Criminal 'Mr Bigs' Escape Having to Pay Back Illicit Profits After Prosecutors Give Up on Cases' *Evening Standard* (London, 2 October 2015) <www.standard.co.uk/news/london/criminal-mr-bigs-escape-having-to-pay-back-illicit-profits-after-prosecutors-give-up-on-cases-a3071296.html> accessed 19 July 2017.
8. Home Affairs Committee, *Proceeds of Crime* (HC 2016–2017, 25); Public Accounts Committee, *Confiscation Orders: Progress Review* (HC 2016–2017, 124).
9. Home Affairs Committee (n 8) paras 30–31; Public Accounts Committee (n 8) Conclusions & Recommendations para 1.
10. Helena Wood, *Enforcing Criminal Confiscation Orders—From Policy to Practice* (RUSI Occasional Paper 2016) 2.
11. Law Commission, *Confiscation* <www.lawcom.gov.uk/confiscation/> accessed 19 July 2017.
12. Serious Crime Act 2015 (Commencement No. 1) Regulations 2015, SI 2015/820.
13. Proceeds of Crime Act 2002 (Commencement No. 5, Transitional Provisions, Savings and Amendment) Order 2003, SI 2003/333.
14. Ibid. s 6(2).
15. Ibid. s 6(1).

16. *R v Whittington* [2009] EWCA (Crim) 1641.
17. POCA 2002 (n 13) s 6(4).
18. Ibid. s 7(1).
19. Ibid. ss 6(5) and 7(2).
20. Ibid. s 7(1).
21. Explanatory Notes to the Serious Crime Act 2015 (SCA 2015) para 16.
22. *R v Johnson* [2016] EWCA Crim 10.
23. Although we see the difficulties even in such a simple calculation *R v Smith* [2016] EWCA Crim 240.
24. Explanatory Notes (n 21).
25. Explanatory Notes to the Serious Crime HC Bill (2014–2015) [116] para 21; Home Office (n 5) para 4(4).
26. POCA 2002 (n 13) s 10A.
27. Ibid. s 10A(3); Explanatory Notes (n 21) para 20.
28. SCA 2015 (n 12).
29. Although there has been a published determination as to whether a person fell within s 10A so as to be heard at the confiscation hearing: *R v Hayes*, unreported 14 March 2016, Central Criminal Court.
30. *R v Taylor* Unreported. 9th February 2017 Manchester Crown Court.
31. POCA 2002 (n 13) s 16(6A).
32. Ibid. s 18(2).
33. Ibid. s 18A(2).
34. Ibid. s 18A(1).
35. Ibid. s 18A(5).
36. Ibid. s 51(8B).
37. *R v Stannard* (n 3).
38. Explanatory Notes (n 21) para 21.
39. Ibid.
40. POCA 2002 (n 13) ss 18(6)(b) and 18A(6).
41. *R v Boyle Transport (Northern Ireland) Ltd* [2016] EWCA Crim 19.
42. *R v Boyle Transport* (n 40); *R v Thantrimudali* [2016] EWCA Crim 199; *R v Powell* [2016] EWCA Crim 1043.
43. *Customs & Excise Commissions v A* [2002] EWCA Civ 1039.
44. Ibid.
45. *Crown Prosecution Service v Richards* [2006] EWCA Civ 849.
46. *Customs & Excise Commissions v A* (n 42); *Webber v Webber (Crown Prosecution Service Intervening)* [2006] EWHC 2893 (Fam).
47. *R v Reynolds* [2017] EWCA Crim 57.
48. *Webber v Webber* (n 45).
49. *R v Parkinson* [2015] EWCA Crim 1448; *R v Thompson* [2015] EWCA Crim 1820.
50. *R v Straughan* [2009] EWCA Crim 955.
51. *R v Allpress* [2009] EWCA Crim 8.

52. *R v Sewell* [2009] EWCA Crim 488.
53. *R v Tatham* [2014] EWCA Crim 226.
54. *R v Mehmet* [2015] EWCA Crim 797.
55. *R v Chahal* [2015] EWCA Crim 816.
56. *R v Roper* [2014] EWCA Crim 2476.
57. *R v Chahal* (n 53).
58. *R v Del Basso* [2010] EWCA Crim 1119; *R v Kaif* [2014] EWCA Crim 2441.
59. *R v Sekhon* [2002] EWCA Crim 2954.
60. POCA 2002 (n 13) s 6(5)(b); *R v Waya* [2012] UKSC 51. For further discussion of proportionality, see Chap. 20 (Young) in this collection.
61. *R v Bello* [2015] EWCA Crim 731.
62. *R v Beasley* [2013] EWCA Crim 567; *R v King* [2014] EWCA Crim 621.
63. *R v Evans* [2016] EWCA Crim 671.
64. *R v Ahmad* [2014] UKSC 36.
65. *R v Reynolds* [2017] EWCA Crim 1455.
66. Ibid. para 73.
67. Ibid.
68. Ibid.
69. *R v McGarry* [2014] EWCA Crim 1103.
70. *R v Kakkad* [2015] EWCA Crim 385.
71. *R v Harvey* [2015] UKSC 73.
72. *R v Louca* [2013] EWCA Crim 2090.
73. *R v Davenport* [2015] EWCA Crim 1731.
74. *R v Reynolds* [2017] EWCA Crim 57.
75. *R v Jawad* [2013] EWCA Crim 644 [23].
76. POCA 2002 (n 13) s 10.
77. Ibid. s 75(2)(a).
78. Ibid. s 6(4)(c).
79. Ibid. s 6(4)(b).
80. Ibid. s 10(9).
81. *R v Bagnall* [2012] EWCA Crim 677.
82. POCA 2002 (n 13) s 10(2).
83. Ibid. s 10(3).
84. Ibid. s 10(4).
85. Ibid. s 10(5).
86. *R v Ernest* [2014] EWCA Crim 1312.
87. *R v Bagnall* (n 77).
88. POCA 2002 (n 13) s 10(7).
89. *R v Parveaz* [2017] EWCA Crim 873.
90. *R v O'Shea* [2015] EWCA Crim 1395.
91. *R v Jones* [2006] EWCA Crim 933 para 20.
92. *R v Virk* [2016] EWCA Crim 81.
93. *R v Sudharan* [2012] EWCA Crim 739.

94. *R v Saddiq* [2010] EWCA Crim 1962.
95. *R v McIntosh* [2011] EWCA Crim 1501.
96. *R v Barnham* [2005] EWCA Crim 1049.
97. POCA 2002 (n 13) s 7.
98. *R v Mehta* [2009] EWCA Crim 1601.
99. National Audit Office (n 2).
100. *R v Carnall* [2014] EWCA Crim 287; *R v Omorogieva* [2015] EWCA Crim 382.
101. *R v Lee* [2013] EWCA Crim 657.
102. *R v Carnall* (n 95); *R v Omorogieva* (n 95).
103. *R v Sawyer* [2014] EWCA Crim 2227.
104. *R v McIntosh* [2011] EWCA Crim 1501.
105. *R v Balqis* [2016] EWCA Crim 1726.
106. Ibid.
107. *R v Del Basso* (n 56); *R v Kaif* (n 56).
108. *R v Hartshorne* [2010] EWCA Crim 1283.
109. Her Majesty's Courts and Tribunals Service, *Trust Statement 2015–2016* (HC 472) 14.
110. National Audit Office (n 2) para 2(17).
111. Her Majesty's Courts and Tribunals Service (n 104); Home Affairs Committee (n 8) para 74.
112. Home Affairs Committee (n 8) para 77.
113. Ibid. para 14; POCA 2002 (n 13) s 41.
114. POCA 2002 (n 13) ss 69(1)(a) and 69(2).
115. Ibid. ss 42(1) and 42(2).
116. Home Office (n 5) para 4(49).
117. Explanatory Notes (n 21) para 67.
118. Ibid.
119. POCA 2002 (n 13) s 11.
120. Ibid. s 35.
121. Ibid. s 13A(2).
122. Ibid. s 12.
123. Home Office (n 5) para 4(49).
124. POCA 2002 (n 13) s 11(2).
125. Ibid.
126. Ibid. s 11(3).
127. Ibid. s 11(5).
128. Ibid. s 11(4)(b).
129. Ibid. s 35; see also Criminal Justice Act 1994, s 19 (Ireland).
130. POCA 2002 (n 13) s 38.
131. Home Affairs Committee (n 8) para 72.
132. Home Office (n 5) para 4(49).
133. POCA 2002 (n 13) s 35(2A).

134. Criminal Justice Act 2003, s 258(2B).
135. Judicial College, *Crown Court Compendium Part II—Sentencing* (June 2016) para 7(3).
136. POCA 2002 (n 13) s 12(2).
137. Judgments Act 1838, s 17(1).
138. *R (on the application of Emu) v Westminster Magistrates' Court* [2016] EWHC 2561 (Admin).
139. Her Majesty's Courts and Tribunals Service (n 104) 14.
140. POCA 2002 (n 13) s 13A.
141. Ibid. ss 13A(1) and (2).
142. Ibid. s 13A(3).
143. Ibid. s 13A(3)(a).
144. *R v Pritchard* [2017] EWCA Crim 1267.
145. Ibid. s 13A(3)(b).
146. Ibid. s 13A(4).
147. Home Affairs Committee (n 8) para 73.
148. Explanatory Notes (n 21) para 46.
149. POCA 2002 (n 13) s 13A(5).
150. Home Affairs Committee (n 8) para 32.
151. *R v Sudharan* (n 88).
152. Criminal Finances HC Bill (2016–2017) 75, Pt1 Ch 1.
153. Ibid. Cl 13.
154. Ibid. Cl 34–36.

Michael Hopmeier is a Circuit Judge at Southwark Crown Court, England. He is a Master of the Bench at Middle Temple, a visiting Professor at City University, London, an Honorary Professor at the University of the West Indies in Kingston, Jamaica, and Judicial member of the International Committee of the Judicial College. Since 2008 Michael has been a lecturer and tutor at the Judicial College and continues training judges in confiscation/asset recovery in the UK and overseas. In 2017 Michael was appointed Director of the Long and Complex Trials Course at the Judicial College. In 2015, he was appointed to a restricted expert group on Improving Mutual Recognition of freezing and confiscation orders, EU Brussels. Michael is a joint Editor of *Millington and Sutherland Williams on The Proceeds of Crime* (5th Edition) published by OUP. He is a contributor/reviewer of the chapter on Money Laundering, *Halsbury's Laws of England*, published by Lexisnexis and contributor/reviewer of the chapter on Money Laundering, in *Blackstones Criminal Practice*, published by OUP. He is an author of a *Guide to Restraint and Confiscation* published by the Judicial College, UK, in February 2017. He is a Committee member of the Wadham College (Oxford) Law Society and a Committee member European Criminal Law Association (ECLA UK).

Alexander Mills was called to the Bar of England & Wales in 2004 and has special-ised in the proceeds of crime since 2008. He now works as a Senior Lecturer at City, University of London, where he leads the Fraud and Economic Crime module on the Bar Professional Training Course. He has worked on the Judicial College guide to restraint and confiscation with HHJ Hopmeier since 2009 and has trained judges and practitioners in jurisdictions as diverse as Botswana, Namibia, Zanzibar, the Seychelles and Papua New Guinea. He has also worked as a consultant drafter on proceeds of crime and mutual legal assistance rules of court for Jamaica.

20

Disproportionality in Asset Recovery: Recent Cases in the UK and Hong Kong

Simon N. M. Young

Introduction

Courts and practitioners are paying closer attention to the proportionality of enforcement action that targets the profit element in crime. In *R v Waya*, nine justices of the United Kingdom Supreme Court (UKSC) agreed that judges 'should, if confronted by an application for [a confiscation] order which would be disproportionate, refuse to make it but accede only to an application for such sum as would be proportionate'.[1] In 2015, the UK Proceeds of Crime Act 2002 (POCA) was amended to allow exceptions to making a mandatory confiscation order to the full recoverable amount if it would be 'disproportionate to require the defendant to pay' that amount.[2] Exactly what does it mean to arrive at a proportionate sum? And what does proportionality entail at the restraint pending confiscation stage? This chapter addresses these two issues with reference to recent cases from the UK and Hong Kong. Both jurisdictions share the same essential features in their proceeds of crime legislation and have developed a rich body of human rights law, including legal protections for the right to property, respectively, under article 1 of the First Protocol to the European Convention on Human Rights (A1P1) and article 105 of the Hong Kong Basic Law.[3]

The author thanks Colin King, Peter Alldridge, Clive Walker, Jimmy Gurule and Christopher Michaelson for their helpful comments. The author was counsel for the respondent in *HKSAR v Tsang Wai Lun Wayland* (2014) 17 HKCFAR 319, discussed in this chapter.

S. N. M. Young
Faculty of Law, The University of Hong Kong, Hong Kong, China

© The Author(s) 2018
C. King et al. (eds.), *The Palgrave Handbook of Criminal and Terrorism Financing Law*,
https://doi.org/10.1007/978-3-319-64498-1_20

The chapter begins by outlining a distinctive approach to proportionality in restraint and confiscation cases known as 'individualised proportionality'. The proportionality of a legal measure is a function of the relationship between the measure's objective and its effect on an individual. In general, a legal measure is disproportionate if it is unable to serve its objective, exceeds its objective detrimentally or has effects that are grossly out of proportion to its objective. Two different methodological approaches to judicial application of proportionality—interpretive and supervening—are identified. The chapter reviews the development of the concept of proportionality in UK confiscation law from the 2008 trilogy of House of Lords decisions[4] to the 2012 decision in *Waya* and subsequent cases. It is argued that the two-step approach of supervening proportionality is preferred from the standpoint of simplicity, respect for the intent and natural meaning of legislative words, and coherence in the law. The chapter also reviews three recent cases from Hong Kong that exhibit a cautious approach to disproportionality in restraint and a strong approach to interpretive proportionality in confiscation. It concludes by recommending that English and Hong Kong courts adopt a supervening approach to proportionality to give effect to the natural meaning of legislative terms while affording judicial discretion to correct disproportionate outcomes.

Disproportionality in Asset Recovery

The UK and Hong Kong courts have yet to outline a clear approach to determining proportionality in asset recovery cases. Since asset recovery engages the protected right to property, it is natural to think of proportionality in terms of the commonly applied test for justifying prescribed restrictions on fundamental rights.[5] The test involves an assessment of whether: '(1) the legislative objective is sufficiently important to justify limiting a fundamental right; (2) the measures designed to meet the legislative objective are rationally connected to it; and (3) the means used to impair the right or freedom are no more than is necessary to accomplish the objective'.[6] The origins of the modern test can be traced to approaches adopted by the European Court of Human Rights, the German Constitutional Court (*Bundesverfassungsgericht*), and the Supreme Court of Canada.[7] Lord Reed in *Bank Mellat v Her Majesty's Treasury (No 2)* described the judgment in the Canadian case of *R v Oakes* as providing 'the clearest and most influential judicial analysis of proportionality within the common law tradition of legal reasoning'.[8] Hong Kong has also adopted a similar approach for testing violations of rights protected in the Hong Kong Bill of Rights and Basic Law.[9]

The restrictions test is normally used to assess whether a measure prescribed by law is constitutionally compliant. What if a law in its general effect passes the restrictions test but operates in a disproportionate manner in the circumstances of a particular case? The concept of proportionality should also be able to cater to this form of interference. The restrictions test would require adaptation if used to test whether a measure, although constitutionally compliant, operates in a disproportionate manner in specific circumstances. Thus, a distinction can be made between 'prescription disproportionality' and 'individualised disproportionality'. The former assesses the legal measure as a whole and weighs it against specific governmental policies and aims; the latter assesses the real impact of a measure in the circumstances of a particular person.

In the context of asset recovery, proportionality is rarely concerned with the lawfulness or constitutionality of the relevant power itself.[10] It is generally accepted that judges can be conferred with prescribed powers to confiscate or restrain a person's proceeds of crime. Proportionality enters the picture in individual cases or types of cases and becomes apparent when the impact on individuals does not accord with what the law was intended to achieve. Inspiration for a legal approach to individualised proportionality can be found in the Supreme Court of Canada's decision of *Canada (Attorney General) v Bedford*.[11] This case involved a constitutional challenge to several prostitution-related offences on the ground that they interfered with the prostitutes' right to security of the person in a manner inconsistent with principles of fundamental justice.[12] The court applied three distinct principles, arbitrariness, overbreadth and gross disproportionality, to determine whether laws that threatened the prostitutes' security of the person were consistent with principles of fundamental justice. It is submitted that these principles when properly adapted are useful in fashioning an approach to individualised proportionality, particularly in the asset recovery context.

In *Bedford*, arbitrariness was 'used to describe the situation where there is no connection between the effect and the object of the law'.[13] Overbreadth occurs when 'the law goes too far and interferes with some conduct that bears no connection to its objective'.[14] It 'deals with a law that is so broad in scope that it includes *some* conduct that bears no relation to its purpose. In this sense, the law is arbitrary *in part*'.[15] Gross disproportionality arises when 'the law's effects on life, liberty or security of the person are so grossly disproportionate to its purpose that they cannot rationally be supported'.[16] This principle is usually only engaged in 'extreme cases where the seriousness of the deprivation is totally out of sync with the objective of the measure'.[17] Gross disproportionality 'is not concerned with the number of people who experience grossly disproportionate effects; a grossly disproportionate effect on one person is sufficient to violate the norm'.[18] This signifies a more individualised approach to proportionality than the restrictions test, which assesses prescription proportionality.

In adapting and applying the three *Bedford* principles under a single heading of individualised proportionality, it is necessary first to identify the relevant objective of the measure in question. Proportionality can then be assessed by determining whether the measure is unable to serve its intended objective, exceeds the objective in a systemic and detrimental manner, or has unintended effects that are harsh and grossly out of proportion to the objective. In asset recovery, separate proceedings are brought for the restraint and confiscation of criminal property. Since the objectives of restraint and confiscation are different, the proportionality analysis in respect of each must be considered separately.[19]

Disproportionate Restraint

The object of restraint is to preserve a suspect's property temporarily in order to make it available for confiscation. Restraint serves confiscation, but if the prosecution has no intention to bring confiscation proceedings in respect of the restrained property, then the restraint is indefinite and tantamount to a confiscation. This would be disproportionate, if not also abusive, because the objective of restraint, the temporary preservation of property for confiscation, is not being served. Even if the prosecution intends to seek confiscation, prolonged and systemic delay may result in a disproportionate restraint because the purpose of *temporary* preservation has been exceeded.

In the third form of disproportionality, the social and economic effects of the restraint on individuals and legal persons, especially those who may be innocent of any wrongdoing, are weighed against the importance of maintaining the freeze on property in the circumstances of the case. Indeed, most proceeds of crime legislation allow access to restrained property to pay reasonable legal and living expenses as a way to mitigate potentially harsh consequences.[20]

Judicial oversight of the process is an important safeguard to ensure proportionality, especially if there are disputes concerning access to restrained property. Another safeguard is the availability of compensation where an illegitimate restraint of property has caused foreseeable economic loss.[21] If these safeguards are in place, proportionality will not require that restraint be restricted to property reasonably suspected to be proceeds of crime. Such a restriction would be incompatible with the English and Hong Kong confiscation systems, which allow all of a defendant's property (known as realisable property) to be used to satisfy a confiscation order of a sum representing the benefit from crime.[22] Safeguards capable of mitigating the harsh consequences of restraint and addressing systemic delay and abusive conduct serve to ensure overall proportionality, notwithstanding the restraint of property untainted by crime.

Disproportionate Confiscation

In *Waya*, it was stated that the object of confiscation is to 'recover the financial benefit that the offender has obtained from his criminal conduct', and 'a confiscation order must therefore bear a proportionate relationship to this purpose'.[23] Applying the individualised approach to proportionality, confiscation can be disproportionate in at least three ways: if the confiscation order cannot serve the recovery objective, exceeds that objective in a systemic and detrimental manner, or impacts the offender (and possibly others) in a manner that is grossly out of proportion to the gravity of the criminal conduct from which the financial benefit was obtained. As recognised in *Waya*, if the offender has already repaid the amount of his benefit to the victim, imposing a confiscation order in the same amount would be disproportionate because it would not be serving a recovery purpose, perhaps a punitive purpose.[24] An example of systemically exceeding the objective is if the government imposed a 5 per cent surcharge on all confiscation orders for 'administrative purposes'.

The third form of disproportionality looks to test whether the effects of the confiscation are grossly out of proportion to the benefit obtained from the specific criminal conduct in question. Take the circumstances of a mortgage fraud in which 60 per cent of the home purchase price comes from fraudulently obtained mortgage funds and 40 per cent comes from the defendant's untainted money. It would be wholly disproportionate to hold that since the house was obtained as a result of the fraud, the total current value of the house is liable to be confiscated. In *Waya*, the offender misrepresented his employment history to obtain mortgage funds used to pay for 60 per cent of the flat purchase price.[25] By the time of the confiscation proceedings, the flat had been remortgaged with untainted funds and its value had risen substantially. All the judges agreed that it was incorrect to assess the benefit by taking the current value of the flat less the original untainted contribution or even by taking 60 per cent of the current value. The majority (Lord Walker, Lord Justice Hughes, Lord Judge, Baroness Hale, Lord Kerr, Lord Clarke and Lord Wilson) held that the benefit was 60 per cent of the increased value of the flat, as this represented the chose in action the defendant obtained under the mortgage agreement. The dissenters (Lord Phillips and Lord Reed) held that such an amount would still be disproportionate in this case where the evidence showed that Waya would still have obtained the mortgage if he was honest but perhaps on different terms. The confiscated amount should have been based on the 'real benefit' obtained from having negotiated a mortgage on better terms than he would have received had he been honest, for example, avoided a penalty clause or a higher contribution to the home purchase price from personal funds. It was disproportionate in this case to determine the confiscation order from how the mortgage funds were in fact used. Despite the judges' disagreement, the case highlights the importance that individualised proportionality places on a close examination of the precise benefit obtained by the defendant from the specific criminal conduct.

As recognised by the European Court of Human Rights, judicial review is essential to ensuring proportionality. Courts help to ensure that 'the fair balance which should be struck between the protection of the right of property and the requirement of the general interest' is not upset.[26]

Development of Proportionality in UK Confiscation Law

Most proceeds of crime legislation have in-built mechanisms of proportionality. For example, English and Hong Kong confiscation laws cap the amount to be confiscated at the amount of realisable property that exists at the time of confiscation, even though the total benefit from crime may have been much more.[27] Another example is the availability of compensation where restraint has caused loss and confiscation proceedings were either not instituted or instituted and failed.[28]

More interesting is how courts apply the proportionality principle in the adjudication of cases. There are two possible methodological approaches, and the UKSC judges have yet to agree on the correct approach to follow. One approach is to interpret the words in the legislative scheme restrictively so as to give effect to the principle. Since this approach applies proportionality to inform interpretation of existing doctrine, it can be described as interpretive proportionality. Under POCA, the judge makes a confiscation order in a recoverable amount based on the defendant's 'benefit' from the conduct concerned, and a person 'benefits from conduct' if he 'obtains' property 'as a result of or in connection with the conduct'.[29] Interpretive proportionality would tend to constrict the meaning of terms such as 'benefit' and 'obtains'. This approach potentially goes further than the canon of strict interpretation of criminal legislation because of the importance of the protected right to property. The House of Lords decisions in *R v May* and *Jennings v Crown Prosecution Services* were instances where the Law Lords, though not explicitly, applied interpretive proportionality to narrow the ambit of the concept of 'benefit'.[30] Lord Bingham in *May* held that 'mere couriers or custodians' of criminal property do not 'benefit' from such property, though they have physically received and possessed it.[31] Rewarded by a specific fee, these persons have no interest in the property and are unlikely to be found to have 'obtained' it.[32]

A second way for courts to give effect to the proportionality principle is to apply proportionality as a separate legal doctrine that supervenes or corrects the initial outcomes of the statutory scheme. This can be described as supervening proportionality. As the dissenting judges held in *Waya*, the determination of the confiscation order should involve two stages: 'The provisions of POCA are simple to apply when accorded their natural meaning. Where this produces a disproportionate result, the judge should tailor the confiscation order so as to produce a result which is proportionate'.[33] In this two-stage approach, the terms of the legislative scheme are interpreted and applied at the first stage with reference to the usual common law principles of statutory interpretation; proportionality only comes into the picture at the second stage as a supervening or corrective element in the result. This approach will require courts to develop a new proportionality doctrine consisting of a set of normative principles. But as Peter Alldridge notes, the judges in *Waya* did 'not lay down much guidance on the operation of the proportionality test'.[34]

Both approaches are consistent with the remedial norm of reading and giving effect to legislation in a way compatible with fundament rights, but the difference lies in the selection of provisions to be interpreted.[35] Interpretive proportionality alters the meaning of component words or expressions in the legislative scheme, while supervening proportionality qualifies the exercise of the ultimate powers to ensure a proportionate outcome. In *Waya*, it was said that it is 'plainly possible to read [the confiscation power in section 6(5)(b) of the Proceeds of Crime Act] as subject to the qualification: "except in so far as such an order would be disproportionate and thus a breach of article 1, Protocol 1"'.[36] This suggested an approach of supervening proportionality, but, as discussed below, the majority applied an interpretive proportionality approach to the legislation.

While the approaches of interpretive and supervening proportionality are not mutually exclusive, courts should avoid their concurrent application, whether in the restraint or confiscation contexts. Otherwise, courts run the risk of creating incoherence in the law, doubling the limiting effect of proportionality, and thereby undermining the aims of proceeds of crime legislation.

If given a choice between the two approaches, courts should apply supervening proportionality for the following reasons. First, supervening proportionality's two-step approach ensures that the legislative intent behind the legislative scheme is fully respected in the first instance. Second, the approach obviates the need to draw fine distinctions and invoke complex legal concepts to reach a restrictive interpretation of the words in the legislative scheme. Third, the second step brings greater transparency to the corrective effect of proportionality. A proportionality doctrine can be developed independently of the legislative scheme. Fourth, supervening proportionality confers flexibility and discretion on an otherwise rigid statutory scheme and allows courts to craft individualised outcomes. Interpretive proportionality, on the other hand, changes the law for everyone and pays less attention to individual circumstances. Where the case law has adopted both the interpretive and supervening approaches to proportionality, courts should attempt to shift the law to embrace only supervening proportionality in order to achieve greater coherence.

The 2008 trilogy of cases exhibited an approach of interpretive proportionality to the terms of the confiscation scheme. This was done before the recognition of supervening proportionality in *Waya*. After *Waya*, the UK case law manifests the concurrent application of the two approaches. *May* held that persons who obtain physical possession of the proceeds of crime are deemed not to have obtained a benefit if they are in the class known as mere couriers or custodians. But had supervening proportionality been recognised earlier, the result could have been different. It could have been held that couriers and custodians 'benefit' like anyone else who physically obtains the property, but whether it would be proportionate to make them account for the total value of the property handled given their limited interest in the property should be decided at the second stage of analysis on a case-by-case basis. It would not have been necessary to draw fine distinctions in defining who has or has not obtained a benefit if there was a second stage to correct for proportionality.

Indeed, the holding in *May* is difficult to reconcile with the treatment of the solicitor, Morris, in *R v Allpress*, a case concerned with the laundering of value-added tax (VAT) proceeds cheated from the government.[37] While Morris' role was to receive the proceeds in a client's account and to disburse the funds to other co-conspirators (in the way that money launderers would operate), it was held (correctly in this author's view) that he obtained a benefit, whether or not he retained any property for himself. Yet substantively, his role is no different from that of a courier who transports the proceeds from persons A to B. The difference is only one of form—that Morris had used the bank account in the name of the law firm of which he was a partner 'so that he had a thing in action against the bank, but he also had in fact sole operational control over the account'.[38] As Janet Ulph notes, the distinction turns on a control test, which from 'a policy perspective … is not necessarily satisfactory' since those who assist with the laundering of the proceeds are accessories themselves guilty of criminal offences.[39]

The majority in *Waya* can also be criticised for adopting interpretive proportionality to the statutory terms of 'obtaining' and 'represents', whilst recognising the possibility of supervening proportionality.[40] The decision can be praised for its careful consideration of the precise benefit obtained in the specific circumstances of the offence (thereby reflecting a proportionality to offence gravity), but it was, as the dissenting judges said, unnecessarily complex. As the dissent held, what Waya obtained from his fraud was 'the flat'.[41] This is how criminal lawyers would regard it. On closer examination, one would exclude the contribution to the purchase price made from Waya's personal funds and loan amount—neither of which could be said to be a benefit to Waya from his crime. Only at the second stage, does one assess whether the recoverable amount is disproportionate to the objective of confiscation in the circumstances of Waya's offence. Both the majority and dissenters agreed that confiscating the whole of the increased value of the flat would be disproportionate. Where they disagreed was whether what was fraudulently induced could be traceable to any part of the appreciated value. The majority held it could, tracing into only the portion of the increased value representing the original benefit obtained; the dissenters held it could not, placing emphasis on the fact that even if Waya was honest he would still have obtained the loan though on different terms. In the dissenting judges' opinion, confiscation should be based on a concept of 'real benefit', and in Waya's case, since his crime only contributed to better terms in the loan agreement, the proportionate response was to quantify that marginal benefit, which bore no relationship to the appreciated value of the flat.

While the dissenters' approach is closest to the supervening proportionality approach advocated here, it is not free from criticism. Proportionality as a supervening doctrine should not be confined to an assessment of 'real benefit'. This is only one way of demonstrating that the effects of the confiscation are out of proportion to the gravity of the criminal conduct that generated a benefit. There may be other instances where the impact of confiscation will be out of proportion to its objective in the circumstances of a particular case. The European Court of Human Rights' approach looks to whether the property-owner has had to bear 'an individual and excessive burden', such as to upset a fair balance between protection of the right to property and the requirements of the general interest.[42] As discussed earlier, disproportionality will also be seen if the confiscation fails to serve or exceeds the recovery objective.

The UKSC returned to the issue of proportionality in the two confiscation appeals, *R v Ahmad* and *R v Harvey*.[43] In *Ahmad*, the Court appeared to be shifting the law towards the supervening approach that respects the natural and broad meaning of legislative words at the first step of the analysis. This case concerned the question of how confiscation orders should be assessed where a number of people are involved in a crime that results in property being acquired by them together. It was held that common law principles of joint and several ownership, which had developed in relation to lawfully acquired property, was 'inapposite in relation to criminals with no rights of ownership in the property obtained'.[44] The legislation was concerned not with ownership but with obtaining, and 'joint obtaining' referred to conspirators obtaining property together. The Court held that the 'word "obtain" should be given a broad, normal meaning, and the non-statutory word "joint" … should be understood in the same non-technical way'.[45] Further, it was held that since the interests of accomplices are not taken into account in determining the value of the property obtained by a defendant, there was no basis for apportioning the benefit as between defendants.[46] Up to this point, no regard had been paid to proportionality. The right to property in A1P1 comes into the picture only when the state tries to 'take the same proceeds twice over', such as by enforcing the full confiscation orders made against each of the co-defendants in a case.[47] 'To take the same proceeds twice over would not serve the legitimate aim of the legislation and, even if that were not so, it would be disproportionate'.[48] Consequently, the confiscation order would have to be subject to a condition that would preclude its enforcement if the proceeds had already been paid to the state.[49] The unanimous decision in *Ahmad* appeared to settle the methodological issue by following the two-step approach of supervening proportionality. It also illustrates the third form of disproportionality that if all co-defendants were made to account fully the cumulative sum to the state would be grossly out of proportion to the gravity of the offence reflected in the total benefit obtained.

However, the decision in *R v Harvey* confirms that the judges have yet to agree on the correct methodological approach. This case concerned whether VAT charged to customers but fully accounted for to the government should be deducted from the total income generated from the lease of stolen equipment when determining the benefit from several offences of handling stolen property. The defendant's otherwise legitimate business had earned substantial income from hiring out stolen machinery. The majority (Lord Neuberger, Lord Reed and Lord Mance) held that VAT should be deducted, while the two dissenting judges (Lord Hughes and Lord Toulson) held it should not.

The majority recognised that POCA should first be given an ordinary domestic statutory construction and doing so meant that VAT was 'obtained' by the defendant as part of the income.[50] However, such a construction had an infringing effect on A1P1 because there would be 'double recovery' for the government, once under VAT legislation and again under POCA.[51] For the majority, this meant that the effect of the construction had to be modified 'so that it no longer has that infringing effect'.[52] Essentially, this was following the approach of interpretive proportionality described above as the decision impacted directly the construction of the word 'obtaining'.

In his dissenting opinion, Lord Hughes was critical of the majority's approach and criticised it for deviating from the two-step approach set out in *Waya*:

> It is important to understand that the overriding principle, derived from A1P1, that a confiscation order must be proportionate, does not affect the question of what is obtained. The test of proportionality comes to be applied at the next stage, when one asks what confiscation order is to be made. This was explained in *Waya* at paras 15 and 16. The A1P1 requirement of proportionality is given effect by reading down section 6(5)(b) of POCA. There is no question of reading down section 76(4) or (7), which is where it is provided that a defendant benefits when he obtains property as a result of or in connection with his (criminal) conduct, and to the extent of the value of what he obtains. Nor is there any question of reading down section 80, which is where the rules for valuation of benefit are set out. The section which is read down is section 6(5)(b) which requires the making of an order in the sum of the recoverable amount (defined in section 7(1) as the value of the benefit obtained). Section 6(5)(b) is read down by adding the qualification 'except insofar as such an order would be disproportionate and thus a breach of article 1, Protocol No 1' and the section has now been amended to this effect. This difference is not simply technical. It may matter. Because the focus is on the fairness (proportionality) of the amount of the ultimate order, then if the VAT element *is* to be deducted there might be a difference between a defendant who has paid the VAT element over to the Revenue, and a defendant who, even if he has declared it, has not paid it.[53]

Lord Hughes went on to note that '*Waya* did not purport to lay down any general test for disproportionality', and there was no general principle against 'double recovery'.[54] He concluded that it would not be disproportionate to include the VAT as part of the defendant's benefit. In line with the view of the dissenters, it is difficult to see how any of the three forms of disproportionality outlined in this chapter would be engaged by the inclusion of VAT in the calculation of the recoverable amount.

Recent Developments in Hong Kong

Hong Kong courts have yet to establish a clear approach to proportionality in asset recovery. Hong Kong's confiscation laws were enacted in 1989, for proceeds of drug trafficking, and 1994, for proceeds of serious crimes.[55] Without any substantial reform since enactment, they reflect the terms of the early English confiscation laws. Despite the significant consolidation brought about by POCA, both UK and Hong Kong courts have noted that the early English confiscation law jurisprudence remains relevant to the interpretation of the POCA given the similar structure of the confiscation systems and terminology used.

Hong Kong also has a constitutionally protected right to property, although differently worded than the terms of A1P1.[56] Hong Kong's human rights jurisprudence has developed a general restrictions test that is structured similarly to the proportionality test identified in *Bank Mellat v Her Majesty's Treasury*.[57] While practitioners have already started citing *Waya* in Hong Kong confiscation cases, it awaits to be seen whether and how the courts will apply proportionality in proceeds of crime cases. Three recent cases indicate that Hong Kong will proceed cautiously but still look to UK authorities for inspiration and guidance.

Indefinite Restraint

In *Securities and Futures Commission v C*, the applicants challenged the High Court's statutory power to restrain and prohibit persons from dealing in property believed by the securities authority to be the proceeds of insider dealing.[58] This power, when compared to the restraint powers used against the proceeds of drug trafficking and serious crimes, lacked the same safeguards, for example, no requirement to specify an expiration date for the order or to demonstrate grounds to believe that the substantive proceedings would be initiated. The applicants argued that without these safeguards the use of the power to restrain their assets was 'unreasonable and disproportionate' and violated their right to property protected in article 105 of the Basic Law.[59] The Court rejected the challenge and noted that by the terms of the legislation before an order is made, a court would have to 'satisfy itself, so far as it can reasonably do so, that it is desirable that the order be made, and that the order will not unfairly prejudice any person'.[60] Meeting this requirement was substantively no different from satisfying the court that 'there is reasonable cause to believe' that proceedings would be initiated after further investigation.[61] As for the non-requirement to specify an expiration date, the court noted the availability of applying to the court at any time to 'reverse, vary, discharge or suspend the operation of the order'.[62] The court concluded that the discretion was not unlimited and cited several Australian authorities as providing 'reasonable clarity' on the scope and manner of exercise of the discretion.[63]

C considers A1P1 authorities on the right to property and applies a proportionality test similar to the restrictions test applied by Hong Kong courts in respect of other protected rights.[64] However, it is only a decision of the Court of First Instance, and the right to property issue was not considered again when the matter was appealed to higher courts.[65] Bearing this qualification in mind, *C* holds that statutory restraint powers that require prior judicial authorisation and provide effective access to the courts for review and variation will likely be found proportional even if the orders have no specific expiration dates. This would be an assessment of prescription proportionality, and the issue of individualised proportionality, assessed on a case-by-case basis, would still remain.

What is the position in relation to administrative restraint of property? *Interush Ltd v The Commissioner of Police* was a challenge to the 'no-consent' regime under Hong Kong's money laundering law.[66] Strictly speaking, the regime is not an administrative restraint power, but where a financial institution makes a suspicious transaction report, as required by law, the institution can wait indefinitely for the police to 'consent' to the institution dealing with the property. The institution can deal with the property without police consent, but it runs the risk of committing the money laundering offence, which only requires proof of having reasonable grounds to believe that the property dealt with is proceeds of an indictable offence.[67] Obtaining the consent before dealing, however, is a sure defence to a possible charge.[68] Risk-wary banks in practice suspend accounts until police consent has been obtained. Unlike the UK law, the regime did not impose any time limit to decide whether to consent or deem the expiry of a 'no-consent' decision unless extended.

The judge in *Interush* rejected the challenge and found, surprisingly, that the account holder's right to property under the Basic Law was not engaged and thus the proportionality issue was not reached. The right was not engaged because any restraint on property was entirely a decision of the financial institution, and the police's 'no-consent' letter, relating only to a defence to a possible charge, was immaterial: 'Certainly, it remains for the financial institutions to decide whether to honour the instructions of their customers despite their suspicion and the disclosure'.[69] As for the absence of time limits, the judge found adequate safeguards in the police operational guidelines, which required monthly reviews, and the availability of either judicial review or the right of the property owner to sue the financial institution.

It is submitted that the judge took a myopic view of 'no-consent' letters. Their operation and effects must be viewed in the context of both the suspicious reporting and money laundering offences. It is the combined effect of the legal duty to report suspicious transactions, the low threshold yet serious money laundering offence, and the sure defence of police consent that affects financial institutional decision-making and impacts the freedom of persons to access their property. Using this indirect method, the police are able to achieve the same effects of a restraint order but without complying with all the strictures and safeguards of obtaining a restraint order from a judge.

It is the 'no-consent' legal regime as a whole that engages the rights of persons 'to the acquisition, use, disposal...of property'.[70] This was the view of the Guernsey Court of Appeal in *Chief Officer v Garnet Investments Limited*, which the Hong Kong judge cited but not on this point.[71] In this case, the court found that the Guernsey 'no-consent' scheme, which is similar to Hong Kong's, engaged the right to property in A1P1. The Guernsey Court wrote that the 'temporary seizure of property in criminal proceedings constitutes a control of use for the purposes of the second paragraph of Article 1 of the first protocol', and 'on this matter...the question of proportionality arises'.[72] On the facts of that case, the scheme and its operation was found to be proportional. One might reach the same conclusion in the Hong Kong case, but proportionality needs to be reckoned with and applied as an applicable and essential safeguard in the operation of the no-consent scheme. Disproportionality will be at risk where a no-consent restraint is in place longer than the reasonable time needed to complete the investigation for obtaining a restraint order in the circumstances of the particular case.

Confiscation and the Proceeds of Money Laundering

Hong Kong cases have yet to articulate a clear approach to proportionality in confiscation cases. The Court of Final Appeal's approval of the House of Lords trilogy in *HKSAR v Tsang Wai Lun Wayland* is indicative of an interpretive approach to proportionality, although this was not a confiscation case.[73] It remains to be seen how supervening proportionality, which has already been applied in other right to property contexts, will be incorporated into confiscation law. *Tsang* was concerned with a novel use of the money laundering offence. The narrow question was whether a person's 'proceeds of an indictable offence' included all payments received by the person in connection with the commission of an indictable offence (wide meaning) or only payments in the nature of a reward received in connection with the offence (narrower meaning)? The payment in question was a $32 million bank transfer consisting of clean funds obtained from a lender and paid to Tsang, who was chairman of a listed company known as Grand Field. The transfer was intended to produce payment evidence to deceive the Stock Exchange into believing that Grand Field's interest in a gas pipeline joint venture had been sold. In fact, the joint venture was also false and was used as a means to prop up Grand Field's stock price. The movement of the $32 million had all the trappings of a money laundering funds trail, for example, multiple transfers through numerous accounts in different amounts but ultimately returning (almost in its entirety) to the lender within 24 hours. But it was clear that the funds were being used as an instrument of crime rather than being the fruits derived from crime.

Overturning the lower courts' decisions, the Court of Final Appeal held that there was no money laundering because the $32 million was never a payment received in the nature of a reward for crime. In adopting the narrower meaning, the Court took into account the ordinary meaning of 'proceeds of an indictable offence', the demarcation made in other statutory formulations between proceeds and instruments of crime, and the policy implications of having a money laundering offence 'of great and uncertain width'.[74] The UK case law on confiscation was said to provide 'persuasive and helpful guidance in the purposive construction' of the legislation.[75] The 'central proposition' of the purposive interpretation is that 'property ought not to be held to be a particular defendant's "proceeds" unless that defendant has gained an economic benefit from such property'.[76] Applying this to the facts, the Court reasoned that since the $32 million payment was 'never intended to benefit the appellants but were merely instrumentalities of the conspiracy to defraud' it did not qualify as proceeds of an indictable offence.[77]

As argued above, this 'economic benefit' approach to confiscation limits the reach of the law and introduces uncertainty. *May*, with proportionality in mind, held that mere couriers or custodians of cash proceeds would not be caught by the benefit net. Lord Bingham felt however the approach would be applied differently to money launderers. But the Court of Final Appeal, by applying *May* to bank transfers, has supported the position that money launderers in general do not come within the benefit net because it is rarely intended that they should benefit from the funds they are supposed to hide and dispose of. In a hypothetical example used by the Court to explain its decision, it was suggested that if a professional money launderer was paid a $100,000 fee to launder $3 million of drug proceeds, the convicted launderer could only be subject to a confiscation order of $100,000 even if he was still in possession of the $3 million.[78] The only way to confiscate the $3 million is to convict the original drug trafficker and obtain a confiscation order against him for this sum. In practice, it may not be possible to convict the trafficker (e.g. he is overseas or the offence took place outside the jurisdiction) and, in the absence of civil recovery powers, it will not be possible to confiscate this money, which is clearly the proceeds of drug trafficking. As proceeds of crime, the $3 million should be subject to confiscation, and it should not matter whose hands they are in.

The position adopted in the hypothetical example runs against the grain of English authorities, which have now clearly distinguished between the courier and custodian cases, where there is no benefit other than the fee received, and cases involving money laundering through the banking system, where there is a benefit, such as in the circumstances of Morris in *Allpress*.[79] What the cases look to is whether the person had signing authority and operational control over the account in question. Where this is the case, the person has a relevant interest in the funds that flow in and out of the account. It matters not whether it was intended for the person to benefit from the funds or retain any part of them. Indeed with money launderers it is usually intended that they neither benefit nor retain the funds as the goal is to hide and return them to the criminal who generated the proceeds in the first place.

The Court of Final Appeal tried to distinguish the Hong Kong case on the facts. It reasoned as follows:

> It is of course true that for a very short period of time, as the funds washed around the circular flow of payments, a chose in action arose as a matter of law representing a debt owed by the bank to Tsang. It disappeared once the funds were passed along the chain of payments. The very essence of the Charge 3 conspiracy was that the payments were a sham. It was a conspiracy to defraud the Stock Exchange and the shareholders of Grand Field by dishonestly concealing the absence of any genuine acquisition of an interest in the Mainland joint venture and pretending to have effected a disposal of that interest. *There was no question of the payment conferring upon Tsang a genuine power of disposition or control over the funds which briefly transited his bank account.* It was essential to the conspiracy that the funds belonged to [the lender] and that they would complete the circle and return to [the lender] after having effected the deception.[80] (Emphasis added)

As emphasised, the Court looked to see if the appellant had a 'genuine' power of disposition or control 'over the funds'. The English cases, however, ask whether the person had authority and actual control over the account itself, which Tsang in fact had, rather than over specific funds within the account.

In substance, it is submitted that the Hong Kong court was extending the courier/custodian category to cases where it was never intended for the recipient to benefit or retain any part of the property (other than a small fee) irrespective of the form of the property. This goes beyond the English cases and will severely impair the law's ability to confiscate proceeds of crime in the hands of money launderers. It also illustrates the tendency of interpretive proportionality towards drawing complex and fine distinctions that take the law further from its purpose.

Tsang's implications for confiscation must now be seen through the lens of *Waya* and proportionality. Although *Waya* was cited with approval on the issue of benefit, the court did not address or foresee the implications of supervening proportionality on the issue of interpretation. It probably would have been best if the court had reserved comment on confiscation law as it was unnecessary for purposes of reaching its decision on the narrow interpretation issue concerning the money laundering offence. As the comments are *obiter*, there is still an opportunity in a proper case for the final court to widen the doctrine of 'obtaining a benefit' in accordance with the natural meaning of words in the legislation, while recognising a wide discretion to correct for proportionality.

Conclusion

Proportionality will soon be commonplace as an operative principle in proceeds of crime litigation in the UK and Hong Kong. Its precise role in restraint proceedings remains unclear, and one Hong Kong court has failed even to acknowledge its relevance in the 'no-consent letter' context. While the need for proportionality in confiscation has been recognised in both jurisdictions, the UK is more advanced and progressively working towards a coherent relationship between interpretative and supervening proportionality, although the UKSC judges are still far from unanimous on this methodological point. In *Tsang*, strong interpretive proportionality was seen in the court's decision to circumscribe the doctrine of 'obtaining', perhaps to an unduly restrictive position that will present operational difficulties for law enforcement. The Hong Kong court will likely need to consider in the near future whether to adopt the majority or minority approaches to proportionality in *Waya*. As argued here, the approach of supervening proportionality has merit and hopefully the obiter remarks on confiscation in *Tsang* will be reconsidered in the light of that approach.

What has not been touched upon in this chapter is how the proportionality principle would apply to a power to confiscate or forfeit the instrumentalities of crime. While the objective(s) of the power would be different from that of restraining or confiscating the proceeds of crime, the three-part proportionality approach outlined above would still be a valuable analytical tool to keep the exercise of the power within constitutional limits.

Notes

1. *R v Waya* [2012] UKSC 51, [2013] 1 AC 294 [16].
2. Serious Crime Act 2015 (c 9), Sch. 4 para 19, amending s 6(5) of the Proceeds of Crime Act 2002 (c 29), in force from 1 June 2015, see Serious Crime Act 2015 (Commencement No 1) Regulations 2015, reg. 3.
3. A1P1 provides that 'Every natural or legal person is entitled to the peaceful enjoyment of his possessions. No one shall be deprived of his possessions except in the public interest and subject to the conditions provided for by law and by the general principles of international law. The preceding provisions shall not, however, in any way impair the right of a State to enforce such laws as it deems necessary to control the use of property in accordance with the general interest or to secure the payment of taxes or other contributions or penalties'. Article 105 of the Basic Law provides that 'The Hong Kong Special Administrative Region shall, in accordance with law, protect the right of individuals and legal persons to the acquisition, use, disposal and inheritance of property and their right to compensation for lawful deprivation of their property. Such compensation shall correspond to the real value of the property concerned at the time and shall be freely convertible and paid without undue delay. The ownership of enterprises and the investments from outside the Region shall be protected by law'. In *Hysan Development Co Ltd v Town Planning Board* (2016) 19 HKCFAR 372, FACV21/2015, the Court of Final Appeal outlined its approach to proportionality where planning restrictions laid down by the Town Planning Board engaged private property rights protected by art. 105.
4. *R v May* [2008] UKHL 28, [2008] AC 1028; *Jennings v Crown Prosecution Service* [2008] UKHL 29, [2008] 1 AC 1046; *R v Green* [2008] UKHL 30, [2008] AC 1053.
5. Aharon Barak, *Proportionality: Constitutional Rights and Their Limitations* (Cambridge University Press 2012) 146–147.
6. *de Freitas v Permanent Secretary of Ministry of Agriculture, Fisheries, Lands and Housing* [1998] UKPC 30, [1999] 1 AC 69 [80] (Lord Clyde). Both UK and Hong Kong courts (see *Hysan Development* (n 3) [135]) have accepted a fourth step in the proportionality analysis that weighs the societal benefits of

the encroachment and the detrimental impact on rights to determine if a reasonable balance has been struck.

7. See Eric Allen Engle, 'The History of the General Principle of Proportionality' (2012) 10(1) Dartmouth Law Journal 1; Lady Justice Mary Arden, 'Proportionality: The Way Ahead?' [2013] 7 Public Law 498; Nicola Lacey, 'The Metaphor of Proportionality' (2016) 43(1) Journal of Law and Society 27.

8. *Bank Mellat v Her Majesty's Treasury (No 2)* [2013] UKSC 39, [2014] AC 700 [70], citing *R v Oakes* [1986] 1 SCR 103, [1986] CanLII 46 (SCC).

9. *HKSAR v Lam Kwong Wai* (2006) 9 HKCFAR 574, FACC4/2005; Hong Kong Bill of Rights Ordinance (Cap 383).

10. In *Green* (n 4) Lord Bingham noted that 'challenges to the proportionality of the confiscation regime (as in *Phillips v United Kingdom* [2001] ECHR 437, [2001] 11 BHRC 280; and *R v Rezvi* [2002] UKHL 1, [2003] 1 AC 1099) have not succeeded': [16].

11. *Canada (Attorney General) v Bedford* [2013] SCC 72, [2013] 3 SCR 1101.

12. Section 7 of the Canadian Charter of Rights and Freedoms provides that 'Everyone has the right to life, liberty and security of the person and the right not to be deprived thereof except in accordance with the principles of fundamental justice'.

13. *Bedford* (n 11) [98].

14. Ibid. [101].

15. Ibid. [112] (emphasis in the original).

16. Ibid. [120].

17. Ibid.

18. Ibid. [122].

19. The test would also be different for a confiscation or forfeiture power directed at the instruments of crime, a power that would probably aim more at crime prevention and deterrence.

20. Proceeds of Crime Act 2002, c 29 s 41(3)(a) (POCA); Rules of the High Court (Cap 4, sub leg A), O 117, r 5(1).

21. POCA (n 20) ss 72 and 73; Organized and Serious Crimes Ordinance (Cap 455), s 29 (OSCO).

22. POCA (n 20) s 49(2); OSCO (n 21) s 17(3).

23. *Waya* (n 1) [21], quoting from para 4 of the notes to POCA (n 20), and para 22.

24. *Waya* (n 1) [17]–[18].

25. Ibid. [36]–[37].

26. *Paulet v United Kingdom* (2015) 61 EHRR 39 [65].

27. POCA (n 20) s 7(2); OSCO (n 21) s 11(3).

28. POCA (n 20).

29. Ibid. ss 6–9.

30. *May* (n 4) [15] and [48]; *Jennings* (n 4) [13] and [14].

31. *May* (n 4) [48].

32. Ibid.

33. *Waya* (n 1) [108].
34. Peter Alldridge, 'Proceeds of Crime Law Since 2003—Two Key Areas' [2014] Criminal Law Review 171, 177.
35. Human Rights Act 1998, s 3(1); *Lam Kwong Wai* (n 9) [71]–[73].
36. *Waya* (n 1) [15].
37. *R v Allpress* [2009] EWCA Crim 8, [2009] 2 Cr App Rep (S) 58.
38. Ibid. [153].
39. Janet Ulph, 'Confiscation Orders, Human Rights, and Penal Measures' (2010) 126(2) Law Quarterly Review 251, 259. But Ulph goes on to argue that the approach is 'defensible when one considers common law principles'.
40. *Waya* (n 1) [53], [55], [56], [58] and [70].
41. Ibid. [92], [106] and [109].
42. *Paulet* (n 26) [65].
43. *R v Ahmad* [2014] UKSC 36, [2015] 1 AC 299; *R v Harvey* [2015] UKSC 73, [2016] 2 WLR 37.
44. *Ahmad* (n 43) [62].
45. Ibid. [64].
46. Ibid. [86].
47. Ibid. [96].
48. Ibid. [97].
49. Ibid.
50. *Harvey* (n 43) [30].
51. Ibid. [26].
52. Ibid. [31].
53. Ibid. [69].
54. Ibid. [71].
55. Drug Trafficking (Recovery of Proceeds) Ordinance (Cap 405); OSCO (n 21) (Cap 455).
56. See A1P1 (n 3).
57. See *Lam Kwong Wai* (n 9); *HKSAR v Hung Chan Wa* (2006) 9 HKCFAR 614, FACC1/2006.
58. *Securities and Futures Commission v C*, unreported, HCMP727/2008, 22 October 2008, CFI.
59. Ibid. [103].
60. Ibid. [111].
61. Ibid. [100].
62. Ibid. [112].
63. Ibid. [114].
64. Ibid. [105]–[110].
65. *Securities and Futures Commission v C* [2009] 4 HKLRD 315 (CA), CACV 319/2008.
66. *Interush Ltd v The Commissioner of Police* [2015] 4 HKLRD 706 (CFI), HCAL167/2014.

67. OSCO (n 21) ss 25 and 25A. On the meaning of 'having reasonable grounds to believe', see *HKSAR v Pang Hung Fai* (2014) 17 HKCFAR 778, FACC8/2013; *HKSAR v Yeung Ka Sing, Carson* (2016) 19 HKCFAR 279, FACC5/2015.

68. OSCO (n 21) s 25A(2)(a).

69. *Interush Ltd* (n 66) [52].

70. Basic Law (n 3) art 105.

71. *Chief Officer, Customs & Excise, Immigration & Nationality Service v Garnet Investments Ltd*, unreported judgment 19/2011, 1 August 2011, Guernsey Court of Appeal, leave to appeal to the Privy Council refused 20 November 2012.

72. Ibid. [100].

73. *HKSAR v Tsang Wai Lun Wayland* (2014) 17 HKCFAR 319, FACC4-5-6/2013.

74. Ibid. [83].

75. Ibid. [67].

76. Ibid. [68].

77. Ibid. [44].

78. Ibid. [69(f)].

79. See *Allpress* (n 37) [151]–[154]; *R v Sharma* [2006] EWCA Crim 16, [2006] 2 Cr App Rep (S) 416, approved of in *May* (n 4) [34]; *R v Frost* [2009] EWCA Crim 1737, [2010] 1 Cr App Rep (S) 73; *R v Clark* [2011] EWCA Crim 2516, [2011] 2 Cr App Rep (S) 55; *R v Warwick* [2013] NICA 13.

80. *Tsang Wai Lun Wayland* (n 73) [79].

Simon N. M. Young is Professor and Associate Dean (Research) in the Faculty of Law, The University of Hong Kong, and a practicing Hong Kong barrister at Parkside Chambers. He teaches criminal law and evidence and has led a continuing legal education programme for Hong Kong prosecutors since 2011. He has appeared as junior counsel in Hong Kong's Court of Final Appeal on cases concerned with the money laundering offence and joint criminal enterprise. He is co-editor-in-chief of the *Asia-Pacific Journal on Human Rights and the Law* (Brill).

21

Confiscating Dirty Assets: The Italian Experience

Michele Panzavolta

Introduction

'*Qui confisque le corps confisque les biens*': the State forfeits all the assets of the convict. This was the rule in the period of the *ancien régime* before 1791,[1] and it often made confiscation a harsher punishment than bodily imprisonment. The enlightenment, however, adopted a very critical judgement against this form of general or sweeping confiscation (*confiscation générale*).[2] When the Italian State was founded (in 1861), the rule which made confiscation of all assets an automatic consequence of conviction, alongside imprisonment of the person, was no longer popular in Europe. Thus, the Italian justice system never provided for a similar sweeping form of confiscation. The law does not permit the confiscation of all the property of a person. Although the issue never arose, a measure of sweeping/general confiscation would collide with the Constitution in many respects. It would breach the principle of the rehabilitation of convicts,[3] and it would constitute a disproportionate measure.[4] From the first official code of criminal law until today, Italian legislation only permits forfeiture of some assets, specifically identified around their features or the character of its owner.

Confined within these boundaries, confiscation occupied, for a long time, a marginal role in the context of the system of criminal justice. That changed in the 1980s with the adoption of legislation to fight the worrying (and growing)

M. Panzavolta
KU Leuven (University of Leuven), Leuven, Belgium

© The Author(s) 2018
C. King et al. (eds.), *The Palgrave Handbook of Criminal and Terrorism Financing Law*,
https://doi.org/10.1007/978-3-319-64498-1_21

problem of organized crime and particularly mafia crime. Politicians realized the importance of the economic factor in criminal activities and networks. Criminals often engage in crime to make profits, and they usually need money to pursue their activities. It is an evil spiral: the more profits criminals make, the more money they can invest in new activities, which will in turn further their illicit goals. From the 1980s, lawmakers enacted policies to fight the economic expansion of (mafia-)organized crime and to deprive criminals of their assets. Next to this, politicians also observed that the economic factor was of crucial importance in the detection and investigation of illegal activities. By following the 'money-trail', investigators could find and prosecute criminals more effectively. Economic transactions would often be the first evidence that enabled authorities to uncover illicit connections. Investigating dirty assets came to be seen to be as important as investigating individual personal liability for crimes.

This change in policy resulted in a series of reforms that transformed the role of confiscation within the criminal justice system. From a marginal tool, confiscation became a central part of the modern criminal policy focused on ensuring that 'crime does not pay'. This chapter considers the changes undergone by the Italian system of asset confiscation by looking at three aspects. First, it sketches the traditional system of confiscation provided for by the criminal code. Then, it describes the expansion and development of the confiscation regime with the introduction in the 1980s and 1990s of two new types of confiscation, namely preventative confiscation outside the system of criminal justice and a form of preventative confiscation inserted within criminal proceedings (extended confiscation). To conclude, it outlines the changes undergone in recent years by the traditional system of criminal confiscation and offers a brief final assessment of the current Italian legislation on asset forfeiture.

The Italian Traditional System of Criminal Confiscation

The measure of confiscation of assets is provided for by the criminal code (*Codice Penale* 'CP'). Article 240 CP defines confiscation as a security measure, which can accompany criminal punishment. There are criminal penalties which have a financial nature, such as fines, but these are not really cases of confiscation. Since its inception, confiscation displayed a clearly preventative orientation.

The Italian sentencing system follows a 'double track system', where 'security measures' (*misure di sicurezza*) stand next to penalties (*pene*). The latter have a punitive aim, while the former a preventative one. Penalties punish the convicted offenders for their criminal deed,[5] while security measures want to prevent offenders from committing further harm.[6] If the person is deemed dangerous, the judge can impose a security measure.

What is the difference between these two categories *in concreto*? Unlike criminal penalties (*pene*), security measures do not always require a conviction of the individual. In some cases, they can be applied even in case of acquittal. This is because they are intended to prevent dangerous individuals from committing further crimes. Nonetheless, security measures require at least a finding that criminal conduct took place. An acquittal on the basis of an insanity defence could be sufficient ground for imposing a security measure, but not an acquittal based on the lack of evidence of the criminal conduct (*actus reus*). The underlying logic is that individuals can be restricted in their liberties for preventative purposes only if there was a breach (whether intentional or unintentional) of the criminal law.[7]

Security measures must respect the principle of legality (Article 199 CP), with the sole exception of the possibility of retroactive application. A security measure can be imposed against an individual as long as it is foreseen by the law at the moment of sentencing, regardless of whether the provision predated the commission of the criminal act (Article 200 CP). The application of the principle of proportionality differs even more significantly from penalties (*pene*). Due to their preventative logic, the degree of intensity of a security measure is measured against the danger they seek to prevent.[8]

Despite their preventative aim, security measures (*misure di sicurezza*) fully belong to the realm of criminal justice. Both criminal penalties and security measures can be imposed only at the end of criminal proceedings. Even in the limited amount of cases in which security measures do not require a previous conviction, they can only be imposed within criminal proceedings, that is, with application of all the rights granted by the criminal procedure. Hence, they are characterized by the fact that their preventive rationale remains confined within the boundaries of the strong procedural safeguards offered by the criminal justice system. This point is important because, as we shall see in the next section, some of the later developments of confiscation went in a different direction and detached it—at least in part—from criminal proceedings.

The rules on the confiscation of assets in the criminal code are organized around the different objects that can be forfeited.[9] In this respect, a distinction is drawn between: (a) the instrumentalities of the crime, (b) the product of the crime, (c) the profit gained from the crime and (d) the price of the crime.

The general concept of proceeds of crime, which identifies any legal advantage from the crime,[10] must here be split into different categories. The product of the crime is the object directly produced by criminal activity, such as the drugs obtained in the laboratory or the forged banknotes or credit cards. The price of the crime refers to the compensation or value received for performing the criminal act, such as for instance the bribe paid to public officials. All other advantages are the profits of the crime, that is, the enrichment which the crime has directly brought about through direct and indirect enrichment.[11]

The Code provides that the confiscation of the aforementioned objects is left to the discretion of the judge (Article 240 section 1 CP), except for the price of the crime, where confiscation is legally mandated (Article 240 section 2 n. 1 CP). Another case of mandatory confiscation is the confiscation of 'contraband' items, meaning objects whose use, possession, transportation, production or sale is criminal (Article 240 section 2 n. 2 CP). The case-law clarifies that when confiscation is mandatory, the courts can impose the measure even if the defendant is acquitted, so long as the commission of the crime was proved. In particular, if the defendant is found liable but acquitted on the basis of the statute of limitations, the courts must forfeit the value of the crime,[12] despite different scholarly opinions in this regard.[13]

The logic of this regime is not always straightforward.[14] It seems that it can best be reconstructed around the logic of preventing danger which is the hallmark of security measures. When confiscation is mandated, the lawmaker treats the property as inherently dangerous. In other cases, the property can become dangerous when left in the hands of a person who can be dangerous. Hence, when confiscation is left to the discretion of the courts, they would need to identify whether the person is dangerous and whether deprivation of certain property can reduce or limit such dangerousness.[15] Here the dangerousness of the property is to be seen in its connection with a culprit (the product, the instrumentalities[16] and the profits of a crime); hence, they may be confiscated only when the courts establish the commission of an offence and/or the personal liability of the defendant.

The limits of this traditional system, which remains in force, became rather evident. Confiscation was confined to a marginal area. It was an ancillary consequence of crime, which could only be imposed in limited circumstances. Although it displayed from the beginning preventative features (prevent the commission of crimes), its preventative function would operate only in limited situations. Traditional criminal confiscation was not intended as an autonomous tool to prevent crime, but only as an ancillary one.

When the lawmaker embraced the policy of fighting crime by tackling illegal assets, it immediately identified the shortcomings of the traditional confiscation regime. First, it only tackled property that had a direct connection with an adjudicated crime. Second, it did so only via the application of criminal safeguards, in a way which was necessarily connected to (and therefore did not differ from) the adjudication of individual guilt. Third, it was largely left to the discretion of the courts, after an assessment of dangerousness which was often difficult to carry out.

The last shortcoming has been in the past decades addressed by introducing a mandatory confiscatory regime for certain criminal property.[17] For a number of offences, the lawmaker now foresees that, in case of conviction, all or some of the proceeds of crime must be forfeited.[18] The other two shortcomings were instead addressed with the introduction of two new confiscatory measures, which is discussed below.

The Creation of Non-criminal Confiscation

The first major change in the confiscation regime was the creation of a form of confiscation outside the criminal justice system. This change occurred during the 1980s. The lawmaker did not immediately opt for the creation of a completely autonomous regime of confiscation. The idea had not yet entirely developed that illegal assets could be dangerous in themselves and hence that they could be the object of a separate State action aimed at their removal.

Furthermore, Parliament was at that time focused on fighting mafia assets and not all illegal assets. The lawmaker wanted to tackle mafia associations on economic grounds having realized that mafia clans were increasingly running their groups as a business and were also laundering the proceeds of crime to start and foster legal forms of businesses. The lawmaker considered 'mafia-run enterprises' to be particularly dangerous because they distort the free market by outperforming competitors through the use of criminal monies and/or means.[19] The decision was therefore taken to introduce a new confiscatory regime, which was attached to preventative measures passed against mafia suspects.

Preventative measures (*misure di prevenzione*) are aimed at preventing crimes, just like the already-discussed security measures (*misure di sicurezza*). They are however to be kept distinct from each other. Security measures are *post delictum* measures, applied within criminal proceedings (at the end thereof). Preventative measures are *ante delictum* or *praeter delictum* measures, in that they are applied regardless of the commission of a crime,[20] and are non-criminal measures, in that they are applied outside of the realm of criminal law in a separate set of proceedings, which could roughly be termed administrative proceedings (administrative punitive law). While they fall outside of the formal application of criminal law, preventative proceedings remain fully judicial proceedings. It is only a court that can impose preventive measures; hence, a minimum of safeguards for the defendant is assured.[21]

Preventative measures can be imposed against clearly identified categories of dangerous individuals, including mafia suspects. At the origin, these measures entailed the restriction of the freedom of movement and in some cases of personal liberty. Examples of preventative measures would be placing the individual under a surveillance regime, banning the individual from travelling to certain areas of the country or obliging the individual to remain in a certain place.[22]

In the context of the expansion of the fight against mafia organization, the Italian lawmaker passed the statute (*legge*) n. 646 of 1982 (so-called *Legge La Torre-Rognoni*), which introduced the possibility to confiscate the assets of mafia suspects against whom a preventative measure had been passed.[23] Confiscation thus became a preventative measure applied outside of criminal proceedings. However, in the 1982 Act, confiscation was necessarily attached to another preventative measure. It was initially not possible to forfeit assets without imposing another preventative measure (surveillance, movement restrictions, etc.), neither was it possible to investigate the origin of suspicious patrimonies without starting proceedings for the adoption of another preventative measure. It was only many years later, in 2008–2009,[24] that the lawmaker finally severed the measure of confiscation from the other (personal) preventative measures, making the confiscation of assets an autonomous preventative measure that could be imposed in an independent and separate set of proceedings. Meanwhile, the lawmaker also extended the targets beyond the initial perimeter of mafia suspects and adjusted several aspects of the procedure.

The rules on the confiscation of assets are now contained in the so-called Anti-mafia code (Legislative decree 159 of 2011—AMC),[25] a statute which collated all the provisions on preventative measures which were previously scattered in different statutes.[26] The AMC makes it possible to forfeit all property of a list of dangerous people in two cases (Article 24 AMC). In the first case, the courts can forfeit the property owned or de facto controlled by individuals (a) which proves to be disproportionate to their legitimate income (measured on the basis of either their tax returns or the lawful economic activity that they exercise) and (b) in relation to which the provenance of the ownership or possession cannot be explained. Next to this possibility, the courts can also forfeit property which proves to be the fruit of criminal activities or the reinvestment (i.e. the laundering) of criminal activities.

The aforementioned forfeiture is permitted only with regard to dangerous people, according to the definitions set out by Articles 4 and 16 of AMC.[27] The list of dangerous people against whom the measure can be taken is quite long. The two most relevant groups are individuals suspected of being affiliated to a mafia association (as defined by Article 416-bis of the criminal code)[28] and suspects of other serious organized crime offences, such as criminal associations committing human trafficking, drug trafficking, counterfeiting, contraband and mafia-related crimes.[29] The list also includes individuals involved in preparing terrorist acts, now expressly including foreign fighters,[30] individuals included in the freezing list of the UN Security Committee or another competent international institution,[31] individuals fostering the ideals of the Italian fascist party[32] or of other secret illegal groups,[33] and individuals involved in acts of violence on the occasion of sporting events.[34] Furthermore, confiscation can be imposed against individuals convicted of crimes concerning weapons, if it appears from their behaviour that they are inclined to commit similar crimes.[35] Finally, the measure can target property of individuals whom the courts consider to be dangerous on the basis of a series of legally given criteria.[36]

The measures target the suspicious property of such individuals. Such property can be confiscated if the target owns it or possesses it either directly or indirectly (e.g. through a fictitious person).[37] In the latter case, it is then possible that forfeiture is imposed against a third party, with the exception of bona fide third parties. The forfeited property can be of any kind. It can be movable property but also real property, such as land or buildings. Even businesses, such as stores, farms or factories, can be confiscated.

The lawmaker even offers the possibility to pass a measure of seizure/confiscation against a deceased person.[38] It is not infrequent for people to die when proceedings are underway. The introduction of this possibility was in fact prompted by a strand of case-law,[39] which deemed confiscation legitimate despite the fact that the person had died during the proceedings. According to the law, once the request for seizure/confiscation is filed, the confiscation proceedings carry on after the death of the person against the heirs and successors in title. It is even possible to start proceedings to recover property of a defunct person but only within five years after the person's death.[40] Here too the proceedings are instituted against universal or particular heirs.

The Constitutional Court found this possibility to be in line with constitutional standards in a case in 2012.[41] Some of the intervening heirs had complained about the breach of their right to defence due to the impossibility of giving evidence so as to dispel suspicion against their deceased parent. Third parties, like heirs, may have little knowledge of the deceased's conduct or lifestyle. However, the Constitutional Court found that the heirs have an adequate opportunity to defend themselves, as they are entitled to prove the absence of the required conditions for the taking of the seizure/confiscation. The Court refused to reason on the basis of the fact that in some cases it may be difficult to offer evidence of the lack of a requirement, because it held that this is a normally recurrent problem in litigation.[42] The Supreme Court had already adopted a similar line of reasoning.[43]

In some cases, it might be difficult to reach the identified owners and notify them of the measure (and of the hearing). Criminals (particularly mafia-criminals) may well be at large. The mere fact that the owner cannot be found does not block the taking of the measure. Proceedings for the taking of financial preventative measures can be started or continued even when the individual is absent or lives abroad but only with regard to the property for which there is reason to believe that it is the proceeds (fruits) of illicit activities or their reinvestment.[44] This last limit seems to be grounded on the fact that the absent person cannot bring evidence in his favour. The law thus moves away from the mechanism of the rebuttable presumption (all disproportionate proportionate is unlawful unless there is evidence of the contrary) and leaves only the possibility of the forfeiture of assets for which the prosecutor can offer clear evidence of illicit origin.

Next to the situation of criminals on the run, the law also deals with the possibility of criminals hiding their assets. If the defendants have destroyed, concealed or devalued their property, the tribunal can seize and confiscate other assets of equivalent value.[45] This applies even when the property is sold to bona fide third parties, since, in that case, it would not be possible to confiscate the suspicious property directly. In other words, if the proceeds of crime (such as an apartment obtained by the mafia through racketeering) are sold to a bona fide third party, the prosecuting authorities can forfeit property of the target of equivalent value to the proceeds sold (property of equivalent value to the apartment).

The law also provides for a case of preventative confiscation that does not require connection with a suspected or dangerous owner. When there is a reasonable suspicion that an economic activity is exercised with a view to facilitating the commission of activities related to mafia associations or other serious crimes,[46] or of aiding the activities of a dangerous person, the law empowers the court to place the business under the coerced administration of a person appointed by the court for a period of up to 12 months. At the end of this period, the court can order the forfeiture of the business and all the assets, which reasonably appear as the fruits of a crime or their reinvestment.[47]

The measure of preventative confiscation is applied by a Court which is not formally a criminal court. The competent court is the Tribunal of the place where the person has his/her residence.[48] A panel of three professional judges decides whether the suspicious property is to be seized and confiscated.

Before the assets are forfeited to the State, they must first be seized. The seizure is a provisional measure which blocks the exercise of property rights. It takes the assets away from the owner (or the person who is in possession) but without there being a transfer of property to the State. With the exception of the measure of the coerced administration of businesses, the seizure is a mandatory pre-condition of the confiscation decision and divides the proceedings in two phases. The first phase is the investigative phase. The competent investigating authorities (including the public prosecutor[49]) investigate potential targets and their properties. If they collect sufficient evidence to support confiscation proceedings (see the requirements discussed above), this phase leads to the seizure of the assets. The seizure is ordered by the Court *inaudita altera parte* (without any hearing).[50] The second phase is the hearing phase. The case is discussed in court in the presence of the defendant and their counsel.

As for procedural rules, the proceedings follow a looser, more flexible approach than criminal process. The advantage offered by confiscation as a preventative measure is that such proceedings need not apply to all safeguards of criminal procedure. The procedural rules of preventative proceedings can be looser and less cumbersome. Likewise, the standard of proof is lower, since the beyond reasonable doubt rule need not be followed. Instead, the standard of proof to be applied requires that the Courts are satisfied to a reasonable probability that the person falls in the listed categories and that the property is suspicious, because it might either derive from the crime or it is disproportionate, and there is no evidence of a lawful acquisition. The Courts refuse to speak of proof on a balance of probabilities, which is the test used in civil cases. They prefer to use a somewhat vaguer formula, by which judges should have a reasonable degree of suspicion (that the person committed a crime and that the property is criminal). To put it in other terms, the judges need not be absolutely certain, nor should they establish a high degree of probability.[51] Discussion on the exact level of the standard of proof seems too often to forget that what needs to be proved (the object of proof) is a suspicion. Being convinced beyond doubt that someone is a suspect entails having the reasonable belief that someone committed a crime. Courts should however avoid being satisfied with the reasonable suspicion of a suspicion, which would be a far too low standard of proof. In the daily practice, the Courts seem to follow the former approach more than the latter, but there are cases where the factual assessment of the level of suspicion seems rather cursory.

Next to the standard of proof concerning the identification of the target, there is the standard of proof concerning the property. Here there is clearly no room for the application of the beyond reasonable doubt principle. The fact that the law also relies on a presumption to identify suspicious property—when property is disproportionate to the income or lawful economic activity—shows that the standard of proof is far from being the one normally employed in criminal cases. With regard to the second case of forfeiture, confiscation of property derived from the crime, the courts should have a reasonable belief that the property bears a connection with the crime, but they need not be absolutely certain of such link.[52]

There is a further advantage. The rules on preventative confiscation also set out a very detailed regime for the management/reallocation/sale/use of frozen and then confiscated assets.

Scholars and courts in Italy debate the precise logic and nature of preventative confiscation.[53] The lawmaker categorized the measure as preventative so that it would fall outside the realm of criminal justice. Nonetheless, some assert that the measure goes beyond the goal of mere prevention because it deprives a person of some property and not only temporarily. However, the approach of the Italian lawmaker found support in decisions of the Supreme Court and of the Constitutional Court which defended the possibility to forfeit the assets of the deceased.[54] The Courts held that although a deceased person could no longer be dangerous, the measure could find its justification in the goal of removing illegal assets from the economic market (flow), which makes it a measure of its own (sui generis) which could be assimilated to an administrative penalty.[55] The case-law of the Court of Cassation is now steadily oriented in this direction, thus excluding the criminal nature of the measure.[56] Others argue in a similar vein that the measure no longer aims at tackling dangerous criminals, but it is rather directed at tackling criminal assets, hence remaining within the area of crime prevention. They believe that the measure represents an *actio in rem*, which targets property rather than people.[57]

Several scholars contend that despite its formal classification the measure should be equated to a criminal penalty, with all the consequences which this brings in terms of applicable rights.[58] However, other scholars and the majority of courts reject such criticisms,[59] and this view is supported by the case-law of the European Court of Human Rights (ECtHR).

The ECtHR has repeatedly stated that the *confisca di prevenzione* could not be considered as a form of adjudication upon a criminal charge; thus, criminal procedural protections do not necessarily have to be applied.[60] Although some Italian scholars lament that the measure breaches the presumption of innocence, the ECtHR has in this respect reached a different conclusion, by refusing to test the measure against Article 6(2) ECHR.[61] Therefore, Article 6 ECHR can find application only in its civil tenet, and the ECtHR has in fact found the Italian State to be in breach of its obligations by not granting the defendants a public hearing.[62]

The ECtHR particularly emphasized that preventative measures (in that instance of a preventative seizure) are justified 'by the general interest', and that they are proportionate to the aim pursued 'in view of the extremely dangerous economic power of an "organisation" like the Mafia'.[63] It went on to observe 'the difficulties encountered by the Italian State in the fight against the mafia. As a result of its unlawful activities, in particular drug-trafficking, and its international connections, this "organisation" has an enormous turnover that is subsequently invested, inter alia, in the real property sector. Confiscation, which is designed to block these movements of suspect capital, is an effective and necessary weapon in the combat against this cancer'.[64] Finally, the ECtHR has also found the preventative measure to be in line with the respect of the right to property, since the measure is provided for by the law and pursues a general public interest.[65]

The fact that the measure has so far survived scrutiny by the ECtHR does not necessarily mean that it perfectly complies with the convention standards. The ECtHR seems in its reasoning to accept the measure as a necessary evil, which can be tolerated in light of the extraordinary need to fight powerful criminal connections. This logic of emergency does not appear to be bulletproof for the future and nothing excludes a change in the case-law.

A couple of points in this respect deserve attention. While not all confiscation measures constitute *per se* criminal penalties, which require the application of criminal safeguards, much depends on how the measure is structured. The Italian system is formally labelled as a preventative system, but this label in itself cannot be considered binding in Strasbourg. Its logic is to remove criminal profits from circulation. Nonetheless, this is done not by merely targeting suspicious assets. With one exception, the property is considered suspicious only in connection with the profile of an individual. In other words, the identification of criminal assets is done by looking first at suspicious individual profiles, that is, the categories of people listed in Article 4.[66] The measure cannot therefore be equated to a pure *actio in rem*, such as in the common law construction of civil asset forfeiture schemes.[67] This might be problematic when the law departs from some general principles of criminal law. In other words, the preventative forfeiture of assets for which there is evidence of connection with a criminal activity raises no problems concerning the safeguards of criminal law, because there is sufficient justification to target the property regardless of any link with a suspicious person. In other words, if the property is targeted for its inherent features (because it is dangerous or because it is the means, the product, the profit of criminal activity), then the measure can never be equated to a criminal penalty, and there can be a departure from the standards of criminal law. Instead, some doubts can be raised with regard to the preventative confiscation of all disproportionate assets of a person with the income or the lawful economic activity, particularly if courts do not engage in a careful assessment of the evidence available.

The second issue that deserves attention is the principle of proportionality in the forfeiture of the assets. Formally, the principle is respected because the law does not deprive the person of assets gained in a lawful manner. Nonetheless, if the assessment of proportionality with income is done in too loose a manner, the risk of hardship against individuals cannot be excluded. The absence of any time requirement with regard to the confiscation of disproportionate incomes can be seen as a further example thereof, as it can be difficult for the individual to show the proportionality of some property with the income many years after its acquisition.

The Extension of Criminal Confiscation

Towards the end of the 1980s and at the beginning of the 1990s, mafia clans became more aggressive in their action and challenged the State's powers in many respects. They even perpetrated several terrorist bombings against key institutional targets.[68] Some said that the mafia clans were waging war against the Italian State. The political reaction was to widen the array of tools to fight crime and organized crime in general. This paved the way, among others, for the expansion of confiscation.

Above, we saw that the first move of the lawmaker in the 1980s had been to introduce a new type of confiscation in the field of preventative measures (i.e. measures passed outside the criminal law area). The new regime had proved to be only partially effective for two reasons: (a) confiscation could only be applied together with another measure[69]; and (b) confiscation was initially limited to assets of mafia suspects and did not extend to other criminal assets. One of the Government proposals at the beginning of the 1990s was to expand the application of confiscation as a preventative measure beyond the area of mafia suspects to all those suspected and/or convicted of serious crimes. The proposal encountered resistance because it seemed that the area of punitive preventative measures would expand too much.

At the beginning of 1992, the Italian lawmaker introduced a new offence which made it a crime for suspects (and convicts) of serious crimes to possess property disproportionate to their income or legal economic activity without giving evidence of their lawful acquisition.[70] The Constitutional Court, however, quashed the provision because it breached the presumption of innocence.[71]

The Parliament decided then to react by enacting a form of extended confiscation.[72] Art. 12-sexies decree law of 8 June 1992, n. 306, empowers the criminal courts to grant an order, in relation to specified offences, providing for the confiscation of all assets that are disproportionate to individual income if the convicted person cannot give evidence of their lawful acquisition. This measure survived the scrutiny of the Constitutional Court.[73] In particular the Court held that the measure was fully compatible with the protection of the right to property and that there was no violation of the presumption of innocence. In essence, Article 12-sexies removes the causal link between the forfeited property and the adjudicated crime. The authorities can even confiscate property that bears no direct connection with the prosecuted crime, and prosecutors need not prove any derivation from the prosecuted crime.

The list of crimes, the conviction of which triggers the extended confiscation, has become very lengthy over time, with the lawmaker adding from time to time new offences to the list. It includes several sorts of public briberies; joint criminal enterprises with a view to committing trafficking in human beings, or favouring illegal immigration, or selling counterfeited goods; mafia association and organizing the prostitution of minors. In all these cases, the confiscation of the assets is mandatory.

This confiscatory measure fully belongs to the realm of criminal justice. It expands significantly the scope of the criminal confiscation, in that it allows the forfeiture of assets which, though not directly connected with the adjudicated crime, have been acquired illegally. The measure is passed at the end of criminal proceedings with the conviction of the individual. It is however possible to adopt a temporary freezing measure (*sequestro*), when criminal proceedings (even in the investigation phase) are underway.[74] The temporary measure is adopted in order to avoid that the property be concealed and thus with a view to ensuring that the final confiscation measure can later be enforced.[75]

Scholars have rightly observed that the measure, particularly when applied during the investigation stage, is particularly far-reaching. The problematic issue is not connected to the abolition of a causal link between the property and the adjudicated crime. Many other systems have in fact enacted types of extended confiscation that allow the forfeiture of assets of convicts which are presumed to be of criminal origin.[76] The ECtHR tolerates the use of presumption within schemes of assets confiscation.[77] The problem lies in the fact that the measure does not seem to be entirely in line with the principle of proportionality.

The Courts forfeit assets that are disproportionate to the income (or lawful activity) of the person. Just like with preventative confiscation, the safety valve of the system is given by the possibility to rebut the presumption by giving evidence of a lawful acquisition. The assessment of what is proportionate to one's legal gains is not always straightforward, however. Furthermore, it can be particularly burdensome to offer evidence of a lawful acquisition of some property, particularly where many years have passed since acquisition. Unlike other countries, the Italian confiscation legislation does not contain a time condition by which the forfeiture of disproportionate assets is limited to those acquired in specified recent years. The Supreme Court held that since the measure forfeits property without a direct connection with the crime, it cannot be of any relevance when the property was acquired and whether it was acquired before or after the crime.[78] This seems to stretch the confiscation power beyond the boundary of proportionality and reasonableness.

Another problem is that the temporary measure (sequestro) is normally applied on the basis of a limited compendium of evidence. The case-law considers it enough for the prosecutor to offer evidence of the probability that a crime has been committed and of some link between the individual and the crime. The threshold remains well below the reasonable suspicion that is, for instance, required to place people in pre-trial custody. Likewise, the prosecutor can simply produce some evidence that property appears disproportionate to the income. The Court's reasoning seems to be grounded on the assumption that a temporary freezing measure does limited harm to the individual who, if proved innocent, would obtain the immediate return of the property.

The regime of extended confiscation largely overlaps with that of preventative confiscation, though the perimeter of extended confiscation is wider. Nevertheless, in many cases, both measures could potentially be available to prosecuting authorities. A person suspected of being a mafia associate could face either a freezing for extended confiscation (in the context of criminal proceedings for mafia association) or the application of preventative seizure and confiscation, or even both. The law does not exclude a simultaneous application of both measures, but it does give precedence to the preventative one. Both confiscation orders remain valid, but the rules on the management of the assets to be followed are those of the preventative measure.[79] The reason for this is that the law on preventive confiscation provides for a more efficient management of the forfeited assets (which are devolved to a specific administrative agency).[80]

The most problematic situations are cases when the judges have already denied the application of one of the two measures. Could the prosecuting authorities apply for one measure when the request for another has been turned down due to lack of evidence of the alleged crime or because the property was found proportionate to the income or the lawful economic activity of the person? Briefly put, yes. The courts have held that the judicial rejection of a prosecutorial request of extended confiscation does not preclude the possibility to forfeit the assets under the preventative regime.[81]

The Supreme Court held that the assessment of proportionality (with regard to the income and the lawful economic activities) is different for the two measures. The proportionality test of the preventative measure is more far-reaching than that of the extended criminal confiscation. The Supreme Court case was concerned with the (not infrequent) claim of a defendant alleging that he had, for a long time, carried out a lawful economic activity, though one that was never reported to the tax administration. On this basis the defendant requested the lifting of a measure of preventative confiscation of real estate properties and a number of businesses. In its judgement the Supreme Court distinguished between the two measures—extended confiscation and preventative confiscation—stressing that they have different aims. The goal of extended confiscation is to deprive the criminals convicted for serious crime of assets which they presumptively have acquired by their criminal actions. The goal of the preventative measure is instead to remove all property of any illicit or unlawful origin, thus including profits acquired from tax evasion.[82] In other words, the proportionality test of the preventative measure does not take into account property acquired via tax evasion. The preventative measures remove all sorts of illegal profits regardless of how they were acquired. To this end, the Court also emphasized a difference in the wording of the two forfeiture provisions.[83] The measure of preventative confiscation removes not only property where possession or ownership is disproportionate with the legal income or the lawful activities exercised by the person, but also all property which is derived from any crime or is the reinvestment thereof. This second condition is not spelled out in the extended confiscation provided for by Article 12-*sexies*, which targets only assets disproportionate to the income and lawful economic activities of the person.

Concluding Remarks on the Italian Legislation on Asset Forfeiture

Over the years, Italian legislation on asset forfeiture has significantly changed. It has moved from a very traditional approach, where confiscation was only a possible side-consequence of a conviction, to a modern one, where confiscation is one of the most important—and most frequently used—tools to fight organized crime. The legislation now tackles criminal assets in a very aggressive manner. Alongside mandatory confiscation of criminal profits connected to specific criminal activities, the legislation also provides for preventative confiscation outside of criminal proceedings and extended confiscation within the realm of criminal justice. These last two instruments are particularly aggressive in that they allow the State to forfeit suspicious property which bears connection with criminal activities. This has certainly been beneficial in the fight against criminal organizations. In some cases, however, the compatibility of these new instruments with fundamental rights could be questioned. In this respect, one point seems particularly important, namely the overlap between the preventative measure and the measure of extended confiscation. The lawmaker seems here to follow the logic 'the more the better' (or *quod abundant non vitiat*). But this logic does not seem appropriate in an area which also concerns fundamental rights.

The overlap is also the effect of the incomplete transformation of preventative confiscation. Preventative confiscation started as a measure to tackle dangerous individuals, but over time moved away from this idea and closer to the approach of tackling dangerous assets. Criminal property, that is property connected to serious criminal activities, is certainly dangerous for the economic system and society at large, and on these grounds deserves to be removed. Nonetheless, the system of preventative confiscation has not yet fully implemented this logic and still emphasizes the connection between the property and the dangerous individual. A system which targets the criminal profits of suspicious individuals falls better within the perimeter of criminal justice (as is the case of the measure of extended confiscation). When the lawmaker moves outside of the realm of criminal law, it should focus only on the connection between the property and the crime. It is suggested in this chapter that the Italian lawmaker should move in this direction and should restructure the system of preventative confiscation around a direct connection between assets and criminal endeavours. This would not be just a move back to the old traditional arrangement. In the past, confiscation outside of criminal law was not possible. Preventative confiscation allows in fact the forfeiture of assets without any conviction, whereas in the past no confiscation was permissible without convicting an individual. Preventative confiscation can however be defended only insofar as it does not breach the fundamental rights of individuals. When criminal property is targeted, there is no need to apply the safeguards of criminal law, but when an individual is directly targeted for an alleged inappropriate conduct, those safeguards cannot be circumvented. Thus, if the property is confiscated because of its link with a suspicious or dangerous person, the measure requires that the targeted individual be offered sufficient safeguards as to effectively dispel suspicion and the standard of proof would have to become much higher. Nonetheless, the system of preventative confiscation has been so successful that the lawmaker is more concerned with extending its scope to new targets, such as suspects of bribery and corruption, than to adjust the way in which it functions.[84]

Notes

1. This adage is often attributed to Loisel, but the general confiscation of property was abolished by the Penal Code of 1791 but was then reintroduced by the Decree of 10 March 1793: Senate, *Proposition de Loi Visant à Faciliter la Saisie et la Confiscation en Matière Pénale* 1 <www.senat.fr/rap/l09-328/l09-3281.html, 2017> accessed 5 June 2017.

2. Cesare Beccaria, *An Essay on Crimes and Punishments Translated from the Italian to Which is Added a Commentary by MD Voltaire* (Philip H Nicklin 1819) 87.

3. As stated in art. 27, s 3 of the Italian Constitution.

4. In breach of arts. 3, 25 and 42 of the Italian Constitution.

5. Criminal penalties are imposed against individuals found criminally liable at the end of the criminal proceedings as a just desert for the crime they committed. Criminal penalties have to be proportionate to the gravity of the crime (although the judge may also take into account the personality of the culprit at the sentencing stage) and are determinate in length (save for the remaining cases of crimes punishable with life sentences).

6. Security measures can be of two kinds: some restrict the personal liberty of the individual (i.e. restrictive of personal liberty), others like confiscation affect the property (or financial liberty) of the person.

7. It is only in a few exceptional instances that a security measure can be imposed for facts that do not constitute an offence (see art. 202 CP). This is the case of the so-called quasi-offences: for instance, an attempt to commit a crime that was inherently unable to succeed (art. 49, s 4 CP) or the instigation to commit an offence if not followed by the commission of the crime (art. 115 CP).

8. For this reason, some personal security measures can even be indeterminate in length and their termination depends upon an assessment of the (lack of) actual dangerousness on the part of the offender.

9. This marks the difference from the historical experience of the *confiscation générale*, when confiscation was a penalty that would deprive the culprit of all properties, see Ferrando Mantovani, *Diritto Penale* (Cedam 2015) 841.

10. See for instance art. 1 of the Council Framework Decision 2005/212/JHA of 24 February 2005 on Confiscation of Crime-Related Proceeds, Instrumentalities and Property Framework decision [2005] OJ L68/49.

11. The case-law deems to be profits of crime the assets directly obtained with the commission of the crime, including those which are the product of the

reinvestment of such initial profits, with exception of the gains made with the reinvestment. See *Caruso*, Cassazione (sez Unite) 25 June 2009, rv 244189. On this issue, see Anna Maria Maugeri, 'Confisca', *Enciclopedia del Diritto. Annali VIII* (2015) 195.

12. *Lucci*, Cassazione (sez Unite) 26 June 2015, rv 264434. A different principle had been upheld by the decision of *De Maio*, Cassazione (sez Unite) 10 July 2008, rv 240565. The decision had raised quite some controversy in the case-law (not least so because it had urged the lawmaker to take action in order to allow confiscation to be passed even in case of acquittal). Several courts had departed from that decision, by taking the broader approach, which is now endorsed by the latest decision. *Ciancimino*, Cassazione (sez II) 5 October 2011, rv 251195. The opposite position is taken by *Ferone*, Cassazione (sez VI) 9 February 2011, rv 249590.

13. See Alberto Alessandri, 'Confisca', *Digesto Discipline Penalistiche* (1989) 45 (according to whom the confiscation of assets is not connected to the danger-ousness of the person, as it is proven by the fact that it can/must be imposed even when the execution of the sentence against the defendant has been sus-pended). For a general overview of the cases of confiscation without a previ-ous conviction, see Marco Panzarasa, 'Confisca Senza Condanna? Uno Studio De Lege Lata e De Iure Condendo sui Presupposti Processuali dell'Applicazione della Confisca' (2010) 4 Rivista Italiana di Diritto e Procedura Penale 1672.

14. It is for instance difficult to explain why only confiscation of the price of the crime is mandated, while that of other objects connected to the crime is not.

15. Giuseppe Guarneri, 'Confisca (Diritto Penale)', *Novissimo Digesto Italiano IV* (1968) 42; Mario Trapani, 'Confisca II) Diritto Penale', *Enciclopedia Giuridica Treccani VIII* (1988) 2.

16. The confiscation of the instrumentalities of the crime is not mandatory, exception made for computer systems and tools that were used to commit some specifically identified cyber offences (art 240, s 2, point 1*bis* CP).

17. Michele Panzavolta and Roberto Flor, 'A Necessary Evil? The Italian 'Non-Criminal System' of Asset Forfeiture' in Jon Petter Rui and Ulrich Sieber (eds), *Non-Conviction-Based Confiscation in Europe. Possibilities and Limitations on Rules Enabling Confiscation without a Criminal Conviction* (Duncker and Humblot GmbH 2016).

18. This applies for instance to the price or the profits of corruption (art 322*ter* CP). Likewise, confiscation must be applied on conviction to proceeds of crime committed by public officers against the administration of justice (art 335*bis* CP). A conviction for the crime of mafia association entails the man-datory confiscation of the instrumentalities, the price, the product and the profits of that crime (art 416*bis*, s 7 CP). The profits and the product of laun-dering offences must be confiscated on conviction (art 648*quater* CP). Mandatory cases of confiscation are also specified for sexual offences against

minors (art 600*septies* CP), or exploitation of workers (art 603*bis* CP), and in many other cases, often in special statutes beyond the CP.

19. Stefano Guzzini, 'The "Long Night of the First Republic": Years of Cientelistic Implosion in Italy' (1995) 2(1) Review of International Political Economy 27, 41; Anna Maria Maugeri, 'I Modelli di Sanzione Patrimoniale nel Diritto Comparato' in Anna Maria Maugeri (ed), *Le Sanzioni Patrimoniali Come Moderno Strumento di Lotta Contro il Crimine: Reciproco Riconoscimento e Prospettive di Armonizzazione* (Giuffré 2008) 7ff.

20. Although in some cases the conditions for the applications of a preventative measure are in fact connected to a suspicion against a person of the commission of a crime.

21. On preventative measures in general, see Sandro Furfaro (ed), *Misure di Prevenzione* (Utet 2013).

22. Notable challenges have been made before the European Court of Human Rights; *Guzzardi v Italy*, App no 7367/76, (1980) Series A 39; *Raimondo v Italy*, App no 12954/87, (1994) Series A281-A; *Labita v Italy*, App no 26772/95, ECHR 2000-IV 119; *de Tommaso v Italy* App no 43395/09, ECtHR, 23 February 2017.

23. The first sign of this policy is found in the Act of 1975 (Law n 152 of 1975, so-called *Legge Reale*) which introduced the temporary deprivation of the individual right to administer one's properties, with the exclusion of property related to the professional or business activity of the target (art 22).

24. Art. 10 Decreto Legge (decree law) 23 May 2008, n 92 (*Misure Urgenti in Materia di Sicurezza Pubblica*), convertito in legge (approved by law) 24 July 2008, n 125. The 2008 Act was followed by Law 15 July 2009, n 94, which clarified some interpretative problems. The Acts of 2008 and 2009 had however a major flaw. While declaring that a financial measure could be imposed independently from a personal measure, they did not separate the two proceedings. Hence, the request to seize/confiscate could be filed only on condition that proceedings for the imposition of a personal preventive measure were underway, save for the exceptions expressly provided for by the law. See the criticism raised in Anna Maria Maugeri, 'La Riforma delle Sanzioni Patrimoniali: Verso un Actio In Rem' in Oliviero Mazza and Francesco Viganò (eds), *Misure Urgenti in Materia di Sicurezza Pubblica (Decreto Legge 23 Maggio 2008, n 92 Convertito in Legge 24 Luglio 2008, n 125)* (Giappichelli 2008) 135.

25. Decreto Legislativo, 6 settembre 2011, n 159, *Codice delle Leggi Antimafia e delle Misure di Prevenzione, Nonché Nuove Disposizioni in Materia di Documentazione Antimafia, a Norma degli Articoli 1 e 2 della Legge 13 agosto 2010, n. 136* (AMC).

26. For an overview of the Antimafia code, see Mario Erminio Malagnino (ed), *Il Codice Antimafia* (Giappichelli 2011); Francesco Menditto, *Le Misure di Prevenzione Personali e Patrimoniali. La Confisca ex Art. 12-sexies l. n. 356/1992* (Giuffrè 2012).

27. Respect of the principle of legality in the determination of the suspicious persons who are the potential targets of the measure is a point of debate: see Francesco Menditto, 'Presente e Futuro delle Misure di Prevenzione (Personali e Patrimoniali): Da Misure di Polizia a Prevenzione della Criminalità da Profitto' in AAVV, *La Giustizia Penale Preventiva. Ricordando Giovanni Conso* (Giuffré 2016) 145ff. In the same collection, see also Anna Maria Maugeri, 'I Destinatari delle Misure di Prevenzione tra Irrazionali Scelte Criminogene e il Principio di Proporzionale' 27ff. See also Corte Costituzionale 9 April 2003, n 109.

28. AMC (n 25) art 4, s 1a.

29. Ibid. s 1b.

30. Ibid. s 1d. The addition of foreign terrorist fighters was made by the Legge 17 April 2015, n 43 Recante Conversione in Legge, con Modificazioni, del Decreto-Legge 18 Febbraio 2015, n 7.

31. AMC (n 25) art 16 s 1b.

32. Ibid. art 4, s 1e.

33. Ibid. s 1f.

34. Ibid. s 1i. In this case, however, the scope of confiscation is limited to property which could further other violent acts in relation to sporting events.

35. Ibid. s 1g.

36. Ibid. s 1c and art. 1. Dangerous individuals are either (a) those habitually involved in the commission of criminal activities (career criminals); (b) those habitually living, even in part, on the proceeds of crimes; (c) those whose outward conduct gives good reasons to believe that they have tendencies to commit crimes that harm or put in danger the physical or moral integrity of minors, the public health, the public security or the public tranquillity.

37. Ibid. art. 26, s 2 identifies cases where the sale or donations of items to some family members in the two years prior to the proceedings is presumed to be fictitious unless evidence of the contrary is given.

38. Ibid. art 18, s 2.

39. *De Carlo*, Cassazione (sez V) 20 January 2010, rv 246863.

40. Art. 18, s 3. The reason for the five-year time-limit is grounded in the need to assure some degree of certainty for economic operators, hence, assuring some element of protection to commerce and other economic activities. The proceedings are void if they are instituted after the five-year time-limit: *Abbate*, Cassazione (sez VI) 20 October 2011, rv 251648.

41. Corte Costituzionale 25 January 2012, n 21.

42. Some scholars voice the concern that, if taken rigidly, this approach of the Constitutional Court might breach defence rights and suggest that the confiscation could be imposed only if the heirs could effectively defend themselves: see Menditto (n 27) 178.

43. *Casucci et al.*, Cassazione (sez V) 17 November 2011, rv 251717. The Court held that the proprietary rights of third parties are not unduly restrained by

preventive confiscation in that bona fide third parties are allowed to intervene in the proceedings and given ample possibility to offer evidence to prove their innocent position and their ignorance of any connection between the assets and criminal activities.

44. AMC (n 25) art 18, s 4. See Malagnino (n 26) 58.
45. AMC (n 25) art 25.
46. Listed in letters a and b of AMC (n 25) art 4.
47. Ibid. art 34.
48. Ibid. art 5, s 4.
49. Preventative proceedings can be commenced also upon the initiative of the chief of police of the province (questore), the district public prosecutor (i.e. the chief of the prosecution office established by the tribunal in the cities where the courts of appeal sit), or the Director of the anti-mafia brigade (Direzione Investigativa Antimafia, DIA).
50. AMC (n 25) art 20, s 1.
51. Francesco Caprioli, 'Fatto e Misure di Prevenzione' in AAVV, *Misure Patrimoniali nel Sistema Penale. Effettività e Garanzie* (Giuffré 2016) 54; Maugeri (n 27) 58.
52. Caprioli (n 51) 56.
53. For an overview, see Silvia Astarita, 'Presupposti e Tipologia delle Misure Applicabili' in Sandro Furfaro (ed), *Misure di Prevenzione* (Utet 2013) 341.
54. *Simonelli*, Cassazione (sez Unite) 17 July 1996, rv 205262; Corte Costituzionale 30 September 1996, n 335.
55. Corte Costituzionale (n 54) para 2.1.
56. *Spinelli*, Cassazione (sez Unite) 26 June 2014, rv 260303; *Repaci et al*, Cassazione (sez Unite) 29 May 2014, rv 260244; *Ferrara et al*, Cassazione (sez I) 17 May 2013, rv 256141; *San Carlo Invest S.r.l.*, Cassazione (sez I) 8 October 2013, rv 257605. See also Corte Costituzionale 9 June 2015, n 106.
57. Giusepe Balsamo, 'La Controversa Natura delle Misure di Prevenzione Patrimoniali' in Sandro Furfaro (ed), *Misure di Prevenzione* (Utet 2013) 313; Giuseppe Balsamo, 'Le Misure di Prevenzione Patrimoniali Come Modello di "Processo al Patrimonio". Il Rapporto con le Misure di Prevenzione Personali' in Antonio Balsamo, Vania Contraffatto, and Guglielmo Nicastro (eds), *Le Misure Patrimoniali Contro la Criminalità Organizzata* (Giuffré 2010) 48.
58. Francesco Mazzacuva, 'Le Sezioni Unite sulla Natura della Confisca di Prevenzione: Un'Altra Occasione Persa per un Chiarimento sulle Reali Finalità della Misura' (2015) 4 Diritto Penale Contemporaneo 231, 240; Francesco Mazzacuva, 'The Problematic Nature of Asset Recovery Measures: Recent Developments of the Italian Preventative Confiscation' in Katalin Ligeti and Michele Simonato (eds), *Chasing Criminal Money* (Hart Publishing 2017) 101; Vittorio Manes, 'The Last Imperative of Criminal Policy: Nullum Crimen Sine Confiscatione' (2016) 6(2) European Criminal Law Review 143, 155; Anna Maria Maugeri, 'Una Parola Definitiva sulla Natura della

Confisca di Prevenzione? Dalle Sezioni Unite Spinelli alla Sentenza Gogitidze della Corte EDU sul Civil Forfeiture' (2015) 58(2) Rivista Italiana di Diritto e Procedura Penale 942. Astarita (n 53) 387, 391. Italian scholars often point to the decisions of the European Court of Human Rights (ECtHR) in *Sud Fondi Srl et autres v Italy* App no 75909/01 (ECtHR, 20 January 2009) and *Varvara v Italy* (2013) ECHR 1048, where the Italian state was found to be in breach of art. 7 ECHR in the passing of a confiscation measure. It is to be observed, however, that these last cases dealt with the traditional system of criminal confiscation, not with the preventative system. Others highlight that the case-law of the ECtHR on confiscation is not consistent and, consequently, that it cannot be considered binding at national level; for this position, see Mariano Menna, 'Natura Sanzionatoria della Confisca di Prevenzione, Proporzionalità nell'Applicazione delle Garanzie del Giusto Processo e Sistema di Neutralizzazione dei Patrimoni Illeciti Parallelo a Quello Penale' in AAVV, *La Giustizia Penale Preventiva. Ricordando Giovanni Conso* (Giuffré 2016) 320.

59. Menditto (n 27) 160; Menditto (n 26) 358.
60. *Raimondo v Italy* (n 22); *Arcuri v Italy*, App no 52024/99, ECHR 2001-VII, where the court observed that preventive measures 'do not involve a finding of guilt, but are designed to prevent the commission of offences'; hence, they are 'not comparable to a criminal sanction' and 'the proceedings under these provisions did not involve the determination … of a criminal charge'; *Riela v Italy* App no 52439/99 (ECtHR, 4 September 2001); *Licata v Italy* App no 32221/02 (ECtHR, 27 May 2004); *Leone v Italy* App no 30506/07 (ECtHR, 2 February 2010); *Cacucci et Sabatelli v Italy* App no 29797/09 (ECtHR, 17 June 2014).
61. The Court has not tested the measure against the presumption of innocence, since it rejected the approach of the criminal nature of the proceedings: *Paleari v Italy* App no 55772/08 (ECtHR, 26 July 2011), paras 31–36; *Pozzi v Italy* App no 55743/08 (ECtHR, 26 July 2011), paras 33–38. For further discussion, see Colin King, 'Civil Forfeiture and Article 6 of the ECHR: Due Process Implications for England and Wales and Ireland' (2014) 34(3) Legal Studies 371.
62. *Bocellari et Rizza v Italy* App no 399/02 (ECtHR, 13 November 2007); *Perre v Italy* App no 1905/05 (ECtHR, 8 July 2008); *Capitani et Campanella v Italy* App no 24920/07 (ECtHR, 17 May 2011); *Paleari v Italy* (n 61); *Pozzi v Italy* (n 61) paras 27–30; *Leone v Italy* (n 60).
63. *Raimondo v Italy* (n 22) para 27.
64. Ibid. para 30.
65. *Riela v Italy* (n 60); *Arcuri v Italy* (n 60); *Leone v Italy* (n 60) paras 36–37; *Pozzi v Italy* (n 61) paras 27–30; *Capitani et Campanella v Italy* (n 62) paras 33–35; *Paleari v Italy* (n 61) para 37.
66. Exception made for the power foreseen in AMC (n 25) art. 34.
67. Panzavolta and Flor (n 17) 147; *Spinelli* (n 56).

68. Most notorious were the murders of Judges Giovanni Falcone and Paolo Borsellino: see Alexander Stille, *Excellent Cadavers: The Mafia and the Death of the First Italian Republic* (Vintage 1995); John Follain, *Vendetta: The Mafia, Judge Falcone and the Quest for Justice* (Hodder and Stoughton 2012).

69. See ibid.

70. Decree Law 8 June 1992, n 306, art 12-*quinquies*, s 2.

71. Corte Costituzionale 9 February 1994, n 48.

72. Introduced by Decree Law 20 June 1994, n 399 (as ratified by Law 8 August 1994, n 501), art. 2. The provision introduced art. 12-sexies in the Decree Law 8 June 1992, n 306.

73. Corte Costituzionale 22 January 1996, n 18.

74. On the basis of art. 341 Code of Criminal Procedure (*Codice di Procedura Penale*, CPP).

75. The risk that property be concealed need not be proved by the public prosecutor in order for the judge to pass the temporary measure. It is considered to be inherent in the possession of the suspicious property. The public prosecutor must only (a) produce evidence of reasonable suspicion that a listed crime has been committed, and (b) show that the property is disproportionate to the income of the person.

76. This is for instance the case of the Netherlands (art. 36e and following of the Criminal Code) and Belgium (art 43-*quater* of the Criminal code).

77. See, for instance, *Welch v UK*, App no 17440/90, (1995) Series A 307. More generally, on the possibility use of presumptions in areas related to criminal law, see *Salabiaku v France*, App no 10519/83, (1988) Series A 141A, para 28.

78. *Simoni*, Cassazione (sez II) 23 September 1998, n 5358 in *Cassazione Penale* (1999) 3550.

79. AMC (n 25) art. 30.

80. Agenzia Nazionale per l'amministrazione e la destinazione dei beni sequestrati e confiscati alla criminalità organizzata. For further discussion on the management of forfeited assets, see Chap. 29 (Vettori) in this collection.

81. See *De Masi*, Cassazione (sez V) 19 June 2017, rv 269173, reasoning on the basis of the conclusions reached by *Repaci et al.* (n 56). While a preventative seizure or confiscation might follow the judicial rejection of a request for extended criminal confiscation, the opposite case seems less likely. Although nothing forbids that an order of extended confiscation is passed after the denial of a preventative measure of seizure/confiscation, the evidence available in the latter proceedings normally includes that available in criminal proceedings. Furthermore, the preventative measure is, as mentioned, wider and looser in the assessment, which makes it less likely that after its rejection a criminal judge might grant an order for extended confiscation.

82. *Repaci et al.* (n 56).

83. Ibid.

84. In 2015, the Chamber of Deputies of the Italian Parliament passed a bill which extends the application of the confiscation to new targets including suspects of bribery and corruption offences and introduces changes to improve the efficiency of preventative proceedings. See <www.camera.it/leg17/522?tema=modifiche_al_codice_antimafia#contenut> o-10 accessed 5 June 2017; <www.senato.it/service/PDF/PDFServer/BGT/00947175.pdf> accessed 5 June 2017. As of 1 June 2017, the Bill is still being examined in Senate committee <www.senato.it/leg/17/BGT/Schede/Ddliter/46203.htm> accessed 5 June 2017.

Michele Panzavolta is Associate Professor of Criminal Law at the University of Leuven, where he also is vice dean for international relations. He is visiting professor at the University of Hasselt. He teaches criminal law, criminal procedure and cybercrime. Prior to joining KU Leuven, he worked as lecturer and assistant professor at the University of Maastricht, where he was a Marie-Curie Fellow for a research project on intelligence. He graduated from the University of Bologna (Italy) and obtained his doctorate at the University of Urbino (Italy). He was postdoctoral fellow at the University of Bologna and visiting scholar at the University of Cambridge. He is a qualified attorney at the bar of Bologna (Italy) and has experience as a practicing criminal lawyer in Italy. He is a specialist in European and international criminal law and in comparative studies on criminal law and procedure. His research interests are in intelligence and cybercrime-related topics, financial crimes and asset recovery and, more generally, the protection of individual rights in criminal matters.

22

Civil Recovery in England and Wales: An Appraisal

Peter Alldridge

Introduction

This chapter considers the civil recovery procedure,[1] its relationship to human rights provisions and the other mechanisms available in respect of the proceeds of crime. The first general[2] provisions of English Law on proceeds of crime were put in place by the Proceeds of Crime Act 2002 (POCA). Where there has been a conviction, proceedings with a view to a confiscation order are commonplace. The purpose of this chapter is to assess another specific part of the *régime*—the 'civil recovery' procedure introduced by POCA and intended for the case where there is no criminal conviction. Civil recovery has been in operation from February 2003 and was established to target and acquire the proceeds of crime in whosesoever hands they were. It is a 'specific-property' *régime*,[3] to be differentiated from a 'value-based' system such as confiscation. It confers upon a designated state official a right to bring a proprietary action to acquire property in the hands of a criminal or anyone else,[4] not being a *bona fide* purchaser for value,[5] and to trace it into property that 'represents' the unlawfully acquired property, without any requirement first to obtain a conviction.[6] Since it is a proprietary action, accrued profits are

I am grateful to the editors and to those who made comments at the conference. Errors and omissions remain my responsibility.

P. Alldridge
Department of Law, Queen Mary University of London, London, UK

© The Author(s) 2018
C. King et al. (eds.), *The Palgrave Handbook of Criminal and Terrorism Financing Law*,
https://doi.org/10.1007/978-3-319-64498-1_22

included.[7] Mixed property is divided proportionately according to source, rather than by a 'last in, first out' rule.[8] It is expressly provided that there can be no provision in a recovery order inconsistent with Convention rights.[9] There now is a dual criminality requirement.[10] In order to be subject to the procedure, there must be 'property obtained through unlawful conduct'.[11] It was not the objective to litigate every case. As with any other civil case, a settlement will often be the preferred outcome. Guidance as to its policy in reaching settlements was published, first by the Assets Recovery Agency (ARA), then by its successors in this regard, the Serious and Organised Crime Agency (SOCA) and subsequently the National Crime Agency (NCA). The increased use of settlements of civil recovery proceedings, rather than criminal prosecution, had been, until 2012, part of the Serious Fraud Office's (SFO) policy in the areas under its jurisdiction and is something to which the chapter returns.

'Recovery'? 'Civil'?[12]

There is a legal expression, 'recaption', to describe the common law self-help remedy of taking back one's own property.[13] In a technical expression, lawyers talk of 'recovering' damages. Nonetheless, the use of the expression 'civil recovery' has nothing to do with that. The procedure is not consistent with normal English usage, 'recovery', and it requires considerable casuistry to call it 'civil'. The primary meaning of the word 'recover' is 'get back, or take back'.[14] Here, civil recovery is not taking back or getting back property that had previously been the State's. It is state appropriation of property. It might be property that the possessor should never have had, or only had because he/she acted illegally, but it was never the State's property, so the State is not getting something back: it is *getting* something, and arguments about the legitimacy of the procedure should start from that basis. These semantic observations matter because the justifications that are offered for 'civil recovery' frequently appeal to ordinary language notions of recovery and return. Returning the money, in the case of a drug dealer, would mean giving it back to those who purchased the drugs, in the case of people trafficking to the people who pay to be smuggled, and in the case of other 'victimless' crime to the willing participants. That is not the policy at all. If the crime has an identifiable victim, then usually the victim will be entitled to 'recover' it,[15] so the areas where 'recovery' by the State will operate are drugs, people trafficking, illegal gaming and, increasingly, corruption and market offences without identifiable victims. These areas, and in particular drugs, are at the heart of the money laundering panic.

Rationales[16]

There are three major possible rationales usually advanced for the procedure, and there is support for each of them in the case law. It might be (a) to prevent the criminal having control over the funds to commit further crime[17]; (b) because the criminal had no proper title to it; and/or (c) because of the fact that the property was obtained by crime, the State acquires a proprietary interest in them.

None of these is entirely satisfactory. Possibility (a) would justify very few cases of civil recovery. Where the claim is that by taking property off a person the State *prevents* the commission of crime, the law in this area should be consistent with that relating to the exercise of state power to prevent crime in other contexts, most obviously the use of force to prevent crime. In particular, there should be appropriate restrictions in terms of the degrees of likelihood that the property would be used in crime, the degree of dangerousness of that crime and the continuing appropriateness of the action.[18] The first rationale would also have the curious consequence that if the money is to be used on conspicuous consumption (buying cars, yachts, houses and racehorses) by the criminal rather than the continuation of the crime, then it would not apply (because the money is not being invested in crime), yet it is precisely the houses and racehorses that are targeted by civil recovery proceedings. No such limitation has been suggested for the powers either of confiscation or of civil recovery.

Positions (b) and (c) both have rhetorical support in the cases. For example, in *Director, Assets Recovery Agency v Walsh,* Kerr LCJ said: 'After all, the person who is required to yield up the assets does no more than return what he obtained illegally',[19] and Newman J said in *Ashton*: 'The fact of the matter is that the person who is in possession of the proceeds of crime has, in accordance with the purpose and intention of Parliament, no right to hold that property. It is not a deprivation of anything. Parliament has said that such proceeds are not the entitlement of anyone. That is not to deprive anybody of anything.'[20] The obvious objection to this proposition is that the law does not in general grant the State such a right, and it is difficult to see what the basis would be for a moral right. A criminal does obtain a good title, for example, to the proceeds of drug dealing.[21] A system of property law that automatically made all proceeds of crime the property of state would be quite different from that which obtains, would render Part 5 of POCA unnecessary and would very seriously undermine security of transactions and of property. The argument from priority has no more plausibility. There is no authority for the proposition that the state has priority over the possessor. The fact that there is no single sustainable rationale for civil recovery will necessarily make consistent application of the law difficult and has marred decision-making in this area.

It makes little sense to justify the use of civil recovery on the basis of claims which, if true, would render it redundant. Even though the state makes a proprietary claim, it is not because of any inherent proprietary right. It makes the claim, and the proceedings that follow, part of a crime control strategy directed to deprive criminals and others of the proceeds of crime, notwithstanding that the property is theirs. A far better justification than any of these, for proceeds of crime law in general and civil recovery in particular, would be to say candidly that it is State appropriation of property belonging to the criminal with a view to putting the criminal in the same position or a position no better than he/she would have been in, had he/she not committed the crime. This observation will bear upon the operation of civil recovery and its relationship to Article 1 of the First Protocol (A1P1) to the European Convention on Human Rights (ECHR).

Matters Institutional

Two major preliminary policy questions about the role of civil recovery in law enforcement require resolution. The first is whether obtaining property from criminals or their transferees is best achieved by a separate body established specifically for that purpose and for no other, with performance indicators set overwhelmingly by reference to sums of money brought in, or whether it is better used as one of a range of legal responses available when acting against someone suspected to be the proceeds of crime. The 'dedicated-agency' approach, which did have the advantage that it is easier to isolate the expenditure involved, was tried with the introduction by the POCA of the ARA. Although the ARA is regarded as having succeeded in Northern Ireland, where there was a history of racketeering linked to terrorism, it was, by the criteria then applied to it, an unequivocal failure in England and Wales. It operated until 2007 and was then abruptly abolished. This followed the publication of a report by Grant Shapps MP, which established that in the first four years of its existence the Agency had not been able to acquire enough money to cover its own costs,[22] and a critical Public Accounts Committee report shortly afterwards.[23] With the end of the ARA, the duties and powers of the Director were placed by the Serious Crime Act 2007 in the hands of various directors responsible for prosecutions.[24] The civil recovery and taxation powers of the ARA were given to the SOCA and then to the NCA and also to the major prosecuting bodies.[25] SOCA generated about £11 million in 2011–2012 from civil recovery orders and the SFO generated £6 million.[26] From around 2011, the Crown Prosecution Service (CPS) prioritised POCA powers (including civil recovery powers).[27] The SFO has a team specifically dedicated to the active pursuit of proceeds of crime and clearly sees civil recovery as a significant element in its shift away from the use of criminal prosecutions.[28]

After the publication of the National Audit Office (NAO) report on confiscation orders,[29] and in response to a Home Affairs Committee Report,[30] the NCA published a new account of what it is seeking to achieve when bringing civil recovery proceedings. It turns out that it is not now even trying to use civil recovery primarily to increase revenue. '*We want to deny criminals access to their money whenever we can, but the aim is not to generate revenue. The real value of going after the money comes from its disruptive effect on criminal activity.*'[31]

King and Crewe's *The Blunders of Our Governments* contains a chapter devoted to the ARA and contends that the problem was a lack of clear focus.[32] Subsequent events have indicated that it may be that the abolition of the ARA might have been the mistake, not its establishment. Had the NCA current policy on civil recovery (prioritising disruption not revenue) been articulated, at the time of the collapse of the ARA, as the ARA's policy, it would have provided an excellent reason not to abolish the Agency. But had it been known at the outset that civil recovery was not going to yield large sums, then the ARA probably would not have been established in the first place.

In a significant move contemporaneous to the abolition of ARA, the rules on the allocation of monies obtained by the State in civil recovery actions were changed to provide financial incentives to law enforcement by giving the bodies responsible for investigation and prosecution a share in whatever proceeds were obtained by the State,[33] rather than deploying them for general purposes via the consolidated fund.[34] The First Schedule of POCA, which dealt with the ARA, was repealed.[35] The Home Secretary then put in place the Assets Recovery Incentive Scheme (ARIS). The scheme was not made under powers conferred by statute nor the prerogative. It was apparently an exercise of the 'Ram Doctrine'.[36] Under the most recent version of the scheme, agencies get back 50% of assets they recover by civil recovery, split between the investigation, prosecuting and enforcing agencies (currently) in the ratio: 18.75%: 18.75%: 12.5%.[37]

The second policy question is as to the relationship between the use of criminal justice (prosecution, conviction and sentence) and other approaches to acquisitive crime. Should there be a pre-determined hierarchy, or should prosecutors simply regard civil recovery as one of their options or should there be some intermediate course—a combination of discretion and guidance? As first introduced, civil recovery was not intended to be an alternative to criminal proceedings, where conviction and a subsequent confiscation order were available. During the Parliamentary stages of the POCA, a clear hierarchy seems to have been contemplated in the approach the ARA was to take to someone suspected of being in possession of the proceeds of crime. First preference was for criminal prosecution, followed by civil recovery, then, if appropriate, for the invocation of the tax jurisdiction.[38] That is, civil recovery was a fallback.[39]

Since the end of the ARA, POCA has stated that the directors who have responsibility for civil recovery proceedings must exercise their functions in the way which it considers is best calculated to contribute to the reduction of crime, and in doing that must have regard to guidance from the relevant minister, and that the guidance must indicate that the reduction of crime is in general best secured by means of criminal investigations and criminal proceedings.[40] The requirement for guidance on these lines is, therefore, striking. It is possible to imagine a conference of penologists coming together to discuss whether or not it is indeed correct to say that 'the reduction of crime is in general best secured by means of criminal investigations and criminal proceedings'. In the field of acquisitive crime, it seems that if reduction of crime is really 'in general' secured at all well by means of criminal investigations and criminal proceedings, the POCA would have been unlikely to have been brought forward in the first place. Attempts to deal with crime by 'following the money trail' are a clear result of the failure of criminal investigations and criminal proceedings to secure the reduction of crime.

Civil recovery actions originally concentrated upon a range of cases in which prosecution followed by the imposition of confiscation orders is not available and others in which they are difficult to obtain. There are two major sets of cases where civil recovery is the preferred option. The first is where criminal prosecution followed by a confiscation order is not feasible at all. The principal ones are as follows[41]:

(1) where the person in question is dead.[42] No criminal proceedings can be brought where the respondent is dead, so confiscation orders are not available.[43]
(2) where there is insufficient admissible evidence to secure a criminal conviction, and criminal proceedings are not brought.[44] Cases in which there is insufficient evidence for the criminal courts—either because of the rules

of admissibility[45] or the burden of proof—may still be viable on the basis of proof on the balance of probabilities in a civil action that the property is the proceeds of criminal conduct.

(3) where a prosecution is brought, on the basis that it has a prospect of success such as to satisfy the guidance for the CPS,[46] but in fact the defendant is acquitted, either because of the differing rules of admissibility or the difference in the burden of proof, or error by the prosecutor, or because of any of the other reasons for which juries acquit; it may still be possible to prove on the balance of probabilities in a civil action that the property is the proceeds of criminal conduct.[47]

(4) where the property is, but the respondent is not, and is unlikely to be brought, within the jurisdiction. In this case, it will not be possible to prosecute, but there will be legal mechanisms available to freeze and subsequently to seize the property.[48] Following a decision that where the property is outside the jurisdiction, the high court had no power,[49] POCA was then amended to provide for such orders to be made provided that there was a relevant 'connection' to the jurisdiction.[50]

(5) where there is insufficient evidence admissible at a confiscation hearing[51] to link the proceeds to the crime.

(6) where an English court would not have jurisdiction over the crime.

These cases were always thought of as clear ones for civil recovery. After the ARA was abolished and the Incentive Scheme was in place, a significant shift took place, particularly within the SFO. Civil recovery was brought to the mainstream. Additions were made to the categories of cases against which civil recovery was to be deployed. New guidance was issued by the Home Secretary and the Attorney-General in 2009,[52] which rehearsed the appropriateness of the use of prosecution, but shifted emphasis by giving far greater attention to the use of civil recovery where prosecution would be a plausible option—that is, to the use of civil recovery not because prosecution is not possible, but because it is not thought to present the best possible outcome. This gives rise to a second group of cases, where conviction might be feasible, but civil recovery is now considered a better option. Those cases are as follows:

(1) Using non-conviction-based powers better meets an urgent need to take action to prevent or stop offending which is causing immediate harm to the public, even though this might limit the availability of evidence for a future prosecution.

(2) It is not practicable to investigate all of those with a peripheral involvement in the criminality, and a strategic approach must be taken in order to achieve a manageable and successful prosecution.
(3) Civil recovery represents a better deployment of resources to target someone with significant property which cannot be explained by legitimate income.
(4) The offender is being prosecuted in another jurisdiction and is expected to receive a sentence that reflects the totality of the offending, so the public interest does not require a prosecution in this country.[53]

This guidance applies to all prosecutors, not just the SFO. It was the basis of the increased attention given by the CPS to civil recovery. The introduction of deferred prosecution agreements[54] will not affect this. In the cases now targeted for civil recovery, criminal prosecution and conviction are no longer thought to be the most appropriate ways for the State to proceed because there are other, more financially advantageous avenues available, and negotiated settlements offer greater probability of a return. The SFO was criticised for its low conviction rate in contested trials, and it has been suggested that the length and complexity of financial crime trials is a contributory factor to this low rate. It is happy to avoid long and complex trials if it can and is consequently not averse to making deals. The possibility of some sorts of bargain has long been recognised by the common law[55] and now has statutory expression.[56] Part of the consolidated Practice Direction for prosecutors deals with guilty pleas and discussions prior to them.[57]

The move towards deals is heightened by the introduction, particularly in the case of bribery and corporate fraud, of incentives for self-reporting.[58] The guidance for prosecutors when dealing with alleged corporate offenders[59] contains '[a]dditional public interest factors against prosecution', which include 'A genuinely proactive approach adopted by the corporate management team when the offending is brought to their notice, involving self-reporting and remedial actions, including the compensation of victims'; 'The existence of a genuinely proactive and effective corporate compliance programme'; and the availability of civil or regulatory remedies that are likely to be effective and more proportionate. It is noted that appropriate alternatives to prosecution may include civil recovery orders combined with a range of agreed regulatory measures. The important things to note are that negotiated civil recovery is particularly attractive to a corporate entity because of the opportunity the negotiation offers to control the publicity that is given.[60]

Greater emphasis upon making deals with defendants is also consistent with the possibility of developing 'global settlements' in criminal matters.[61]

This trend was considered, and an attempt was made to restrain it, in the judgment of Thomas LJ (sitting as a Crown Court Judge) in *Innospec*.[62] An agreement had been arrived at between the SFO and the defendants whereby a series of guilty pleas, fines, confiscation orders and civil recovery orders were to be presented to a judge, in effect, for ratification. Thomas LJ was firm in rejecting such a restricted view of the sentencing role of the judge.

> ...the imposition of a sentence is a matter for the judiciary. ...It is in the public interest, particularly in relation to the crime of corruption, that although, in accordance with the Practice Direction, there may be discussion and agreement as to the basis of plea, the court must rigorously scrutinise in open court in the interests of transparency and good governance the basis of that plea and to see whether it reflects the public interest.[63]

The difficulty is that civil recovery orders are not, strictly speaking, part of sentence. In cases of large companies, the defendant is better resourced and has better legal advice available than would a normal defendant but that should not be a reason not to deal. It may be that financial detriments become business expenses. Thomas LJ was correct to emphasise the problems in setting off the financial element of the agreement against any loss of opprobrium, but if corporate criminal liability is defensible at all, it is no more or less of a problem here than elsewhere.

Notwithstanding *Innospec*, we can expect to see greater use of deal-making with corporate defendants, and for those deals to include civil recovery,[64] but deal-making should not take place unconstrained. Thomas LJ in *Innospec* and Bean J in *BAE Systems* each consented to the deal that had been struck between prosecutor and defendant, but neither was happy. If this practice is to continue or increase, then attention to civil recovery will increase and a series of issues will need to be addressed. The first is the general one of the appropriate role of the judge. The existence of civil recovery as a mechanism threatens the power of the judge to give effect to the denunciatory role of the criminal law, because in principle it makes the matter a civil one susceptible to agreement between civil parties. The second factor bearing on decisions to deal with defendants is the nature of the offence. The judiciary has been clear[65] that corruption is a serious offence and should be dealt with by the criminal courts. The same should go for any serious financial crime. The incentive for pleading guilty should be a reduced sentence and not, at least in the first instance, a civil recovery order. Third, there are general considerations of transparency and publicity. It would be unacceptable for the respondent to be able to buy their way out of adverse publicity or convictions of offences of an appropriate gravity to the conduct in question. The advent of the NCA[66] and the reallocation of the powers in relation to civil recovery are unlikely to bear upon their exercise, but there does seem to have been a shift of mood. By early 2017, three deferred prosecution agreements have been entered into,[67] but if this practice is reflected in civil recovery, then it should attract greater emphasis.

Human Rights Challenges to Civil Recovery[68]

From the time of its enactment, POCA was known to risk the possibility of challenges, on various grounds, under the Human Rights Act 1998.[69] Unusually, compliance to the Act was expressly written into the civil recovery procedure.[70] The major human rights claim that has been made against the use of the civil recovery procedure is procedural (in the sense that they do not say that there is anything wrong in principle with the State appropriating property on the basis only that it is, or represents, the proceeds of crime). It is a claim under Articles 6.2 and 6.3, that the civil recovery procedure is in effect a criminal procedure and should be treated as one, with the consequences that the civil burden of proof is inappropriate and that the respondent should be afforded, amongst others, the specific rights conferred by Article 6.3.

Had the Articles 6.2/6.3 claim succeeded, the whole civil recovery edifice would have collapsed at the outset. The civil recovery procedure exists to make things easier for the claimant by setting the standard of proof as the civil one, by admitting evidence that would not otherwise be admissible and by restricting the extent to which the resources of the State have to be called upon to pursue the case. The moral claim of a respondent in civil recovery proceedings, when he/she is the alleged perpetrator of the unlawful conduct, is that they are criminal proceedings by another name. They have the effect, where the action is successful, of publicly labelling the respondent (or where the respondent has acquired the property otherwise than as a bona fide purchaser, his/her source) a criminal and, in consequence, of depriving him/her of property he/she considered his/her own. Whether or not the claim is ultimately successful, the respondent's assets may be frozen pending its resolution, and he/she has to undergo questioning about matters which in other times would have been considered private.

Confiscation proceedings occur after a conviction has already been gained. The defendant has been charged and the prosecution has shown beyond reasonable doubt that he/she is guilty. For that reason, it has been held consistently that proceedings for a *confiscation order* are not covered by Articles 6.2 and 6.3.[71] Similarly, assessments to tax due are not, without more, covered by Articles 6.2 and 6.3, because the collection of tax is not punitive,[72] but assessments to tax *penalties* are covered (because of their penal element).[73] Proceedings for forfeiture are not covered.[74]

After some early decisions in the lower courts,[75] the stem authority on civil recovery is now the decision of the Court of Appeal of Northern Ireland in *Walsh*,[76] holding that someone who was the object of recovery proceedings was not 'charged with a criminal offence' for the purposes of the Convention and consequently did not benefit from the rights in Articles 6.2 and 6.3. The Court in *Walsh* was won over by the supposed analogy with confiscation orders. Kerr LCJ said:

> But Mr McCollum focussed on the statement that the confiscation proceedings did not involve any inquiry into the commission of drug trafficking offences and suggested that, if such an inquiry had been required, the Privy Council would have held that the respondent had been charged with a criminal offence. Again we do not accept that submission. We do not regard the fact that there was no inquiry into drug trafficking offences as pivotal to the decision.[77]

Thus, the Court held that the fact of the conviction is irrelevant to whether or not Article 6 applies. This point has been cited with approval subsequently,[78] but it is by no means clear that this was what was intended by the series of judgments in which the Judicial Committee of the Privy Council, the House of Lords and the European Court of Human Rights held that confiscation proceedings did not involve being charged with a criminal offence, but merely involved the determination of the consequences of a conviction.[79]

The critical judgment on Article 6 in the confiscation cases is that of Lord Bingham in *McIntosh*. In this Scottish appeal, the Judicial Committee of the Privy Council overruled a decision of the High Court of Justiciary,[80] which had held that Article 6.2 did apply to confiscation orders. His starting point was a critical distinction from civil recovery.

> A number of points on the construction of this section are noteworthy. (1) In proceedings on indictment the making of a confiscation order is dependent on conviction of the accused…[81]

Lord Bingham then gave a series of reasons why confiscation proceedings under the (Scottish, but in all relevant particulars identical to the English) legislation preceding POCA were not subject to Article 6:

> There are a number of compelling reasons why he would not be … regarded [as being subject to a criminal charge for the purposes of Article 6]. (1) The application is not initiated by complaint or indictment and is not governed by the

ordinary rules of criminal procedure. (2) The application may only be made if the accused is convicted, and cannot be pursued if he is acquitted.[82] (3) The application forms part of the sentencing procedure. (4) The accused is at no time accused of committing any crime other than that which permits the application to be made. (5) When, as is standard procedure in anything other than the simplest case, the prosecutor lodges a statement under section 9, that statement (usually supported by detailed schedules) is an accounting record and not an accusation. (6) The sum ordered to be confiscated need not be the profit made from the drug trafficking offence of which the accused has been convicted, or any other drug trafficking offence. (7) If the accused fails to pay the sum he is ordered to pay under the order, the term of imprisonment which he will be ordered to serve in default is imposed not for the commission of any drug trafficking offence but on his failure to pay the sum ordered and to procure compliance. (8) The transactions of which account is taken in the confiscation proceedings may be the subject of a later prosecution, which would be repugnant to the rule against double jeopardy if the accused were charged with a criminal offence in the confiscation proceedings. (9) The proceedings do not culminate in a verdict, which would (in proceedings on indictment) be a matter for the jury if the accused were charged with a criminal offence.[83]

In conclusion, confiscation proceedings are proceedings to work out the consequence of a conviction that has already been arrived at and consequently that they do not have the effect of designating anyone, *de novo* a criminal. It is suggested that they did not provide a sufficient reason not to apply Articles 6.2 and 6.3 to civil recovery. Reason (1)—that the ordinary rules of criminal procedure do not apply—is common to all the cases outlined above and clearly does not automatically prove the procedure in question against Article 6.2. Reasons (2), (3), (5), (6) and (7) do not apply to civil recovery, but could be advanced as part of a list of respects in which confiscation differs from civil recovery. Reason (8) does apply equally to civil recovery proceedings and confiscation recovery but is not a reason to afford the protection of either Article 6.2 or 6.3 to defendants. Reason (9) does not differentiate confiscation proceedings from civil recovery proceedings nor uses a jury, which is not, of course, a requirement of Article 6.

In *Phillips v United Kingdom*,[84] the ECtHR held that the pre-2003 English rules on confiscation[85] were not covered by Article 6. In *Rezvi*[86] and *Benjafield*,[87] the House of Lords in England followed *McIntosh*, dealt with the First Protocol argument[88] and held that the statutory assumptions about lifestyle[89] were consistent with the Convention. In all these cases, however, particularly *McIntosh*, it does seem to be critical that there had been a conviction. It is suggested that Kerr LCJ's reading of the confiscation decisions as applying to civil recovery cannot be supported.

Consequently, even if confiscation proceedings are not, without more, criminal charges within the Convention,[90] it need not have followed that the same is true for civil recovery. The significant difference here is that the person in question has not been convicted and punished, so what would be the proceedings to determine consequential upon a conviction in the case where they had is actually a process of a public allegation of serious wrongdoing followed by taking away the goods of the respondent. In this context, what Lord Bingham said about the nature of criminal proceedings is relevant:

> It is in my judgment the general understanding that criminal proceedings involve a formal accusation made on behalf of the state or by a private prosecutor that a defendant has committed a breach of the criminal law, and the state or the private prosecutor has instituted proceedings which may culminate in the conviction and condemnation of the defendant.[91]

In civil recovery, the investigatory structures[92] smack precisely of the use of the power of the State. *Walsh* was decided the way in which it was, for reasons, it is suggested, that do not bear examination. There was no appeal in *Walsh* itself (an application to the House of Lords for leave to appeal was turned down).[93] *Walsh* is now settled law[94] and was followed without serious challenge by the Court of Appeal of England and Wales in *Gale v SOCA*.[95] It has subsequently been emphasised that in all civil recovery proceedings following an acquittal, the court should be astute to ensure that nothing it says or decides is calculated to cast the least doubt upon the correctness of the acquittal.[96]

Other human rights challenges to the procedure have been equally unsuccessful. Article 7 prohibits retrospective criminal legislation. POCA states that the civil recovery power applies whether or not the conduct in question was committed before or after its enactment.[97] When a challenge came before the courts, the Article 7 argument was brushed aside on the grounds that the Article 6 and 7 arguments must stand or fall together.[98] Similarly, it was held that the general rejection of first protocol claims in confiscation proceedings governs civil recovery equally. 'The legislation is a precise, fair and proportionate response to the important need to protect the public. In agreement with the ECtHR in *Phillips v United Kingdom* I would hold that the interference with Article 1 of the First Protocol is justified.'[99] The interest in A1P1 claims created by the 'seismic shift'[100] in *R v Waya*[101] will be less significant in civil recovery. A1P1 restricts confiscation, particularly in areas where the value of the confiscation order(s) exceeds and, under *May*,[102] could be a multiple of the amount obtained by the crime. That could not happen in specific-property proceedings, the nature of which excludes multiple claims. In *Sanam v National Crime Agency*,[103] A1P1 gave no comfort to one who had not given consideration. It did, however, restrict the amount recovered in cash forfeiture proceedings in *Ahmed v Commissioners*.[104]

Proof

The decision that civil recovery proceedings fall outside the protection of Articles 6.2 and 6.3 affects the evidential aspects of civil recovery, from what needs to be proved, the burden and standard of proof, to the evidence that is admissible. So far as concerns *probandum and burden and standard of proof*, POCA section 242(2)(b) states:

> (2) In deciding whether any property was obtained through unlawful conduct … (b) it is not necessary to show that the conduct was of a particular kind if it is shown that the property was obtained through conduct of one of a number of kinds, each of which would have been unlawful conduct.

If the claimant actually has to produce something as specific as an indictment so as to prove a particular offence, then civil recovery will be unavailable in the case of the person suspected of benefitting from crime when the crimes themselves are not able to be described. On the other hand, if the claimant can make baseless claims to place an onus on the respondent, then that will be a serious intrusion. In a detailed judgment in an early case,[105] Sullivan J held that the ARA did not have to specify the precise criminal conduct by which the property was acquired, but did have to set out the matters that were alleged to constitute the particular kind or kinds of unlawful conduct by or in return for which the property had been obtained.[106] So a claim for civil recovery could not be sustained solely upon the basis that a respondent had no identifiable lawful income to support his/her lifestyle. Subsequent judges have leaned further towards the claimant. There was support in *Walsh* for the view that mere possession of unaccounted wealth would be enough, in the absence of other evidence to satisfy this burden. Kerr LCJ said, 'We consider that it would be open to the agency to adduce evidence that the appellant had no legal means of obtaining the assets without necessarily linking the claim to particular crimes.'[107] In *Gale*, Griffith Williams J commented on *Green* in the following terms:

> While a claim for civil recovery may not be sustained solely upon the basis that a respondent has no identifiable lawful income to warrant his lifestyle, the absence of any evidence to explain that lifestyle may provide the answer because

the inference may be drawn from the failure to provide an explanation or from an explanation which was untruthful (and deliberately so) that the source was unlawful. …[W]here civil recovery proceedings are brought, the fact that the property is indeed recoverable as the product of criminal activity must be proved and not assumed. It is not sufficient for a claimant to show that the property was acquired by a person with no known source of legitimate income sufficient to acquire it. At least, the broad class of criminal activity concerned needs to be identified.[108]

It follows that there are two ways in which enforcement agencies can prove that that assets derive from unlawful conduct: either by proving it derived from particular crimes or by evidence of the circumstances in which the property was handled, such as to give rise to the irresistible inference that it could only have been derived from the crime.[109] In *SOCA v Turrall*,[110] the court was able to draw inferences from various factors to conclude that multiple items of property had been purchased with the proceeds of crime and were therefore recoverable under section 266 of the POCA.

The application of this 'unaccounted wealth' doctrine has been most clearly evident with respect to the cash forfeiture power,[111] which exists both in respect of property that would be liable to civil recovery and to property intended for use in crime.[112] Its exercise has come quite close to the criminalisation of possession of large amounts of cash.[113] It is not so important in civil recovery proceedings where there might be other evidence, but even in those proceedings, inferences from failure to respond take on greater significance.

As to the burden and standard of proof, *Walsh* decided that Articles 6.2 and 6.3 do not apply to civil recovery, so the applicable rules of evidence and procedure are the civil ones. This means that relevant evidence is admissible and is not subject to the same constraints as might apply to criminal cases.[114] Even where the 'civil' standard of proof applies, there is a question as to what that exactly means. The standard of proof in civil cases for the proof of criminal behaviour has long been the subject of contention.[115] There were two distinct lines of authority—one held that the standard of proving criminal conduct in civil proceedings is the normal civil standard, of the balance of probabilities, and the other held that when an allegation of crime is made in civil proceedings, sometimes a 'variable civil' standard comes into play—that is, a standard somewhere between the 'plain' civil standard and the criminal standard.[116] The assumption that is made is that criminal behaviour is ipso facto less probable than non-criminal behaviour and that the consequences of losing civil cases in which there is an allegation of criminality can often be extremely serious for the party concerned, so more or higher quality evidence is therefore necessary to establish it on the balance of probabilities. Following a series of decisions dealing with proof, in civil cases, of crime,[117] the leading case on this issue is now *In Re B*, where Lord Hoffmann said quite unequivocally: 'I think that the time has come to say, once and for all, that there is only one civil standard of proof and that is proof that the fact in issue more probably occurred than not.'[118] In the context of civil recovery, this means that:

> The burden of proof is on the claimant and the standard of proof is the balance of probabilities. However, the serious nature of the allegations being made and the serious consequences of such allegations being proved mean that careful and critical consideration has to be given to the evidence for the Court to be satisfied that the allegations have been established.[119]

Types of Evidence

Because the rules of criminal evidence do not apply to civil recovery, a range of types of evidence become admissible in civil recovery proceedings that would not be allowed at a criminal trial.

Inference from Silence

Even outside the area of cash forfeiture, the civil recovery procedure is very difficult for the person who is not prepared to explain the provenance of his/her wealth. It is set up to generate the sort of dialogue that would not usually arise in a criminal case, with heavier obligations imposed upon the respondent and greater possibilities of adverse inference from inaction. In a criminal trial, if a defendant says nothing from the time of arrest to the time of the end of the trial, in the absence of a case to answer, without more, no adverse inference may be drawn.[120] Quite the contrary position obtains in civil proceedings.

> While there is no burden on a respondent to provide answers, clearly, if an answer is not provided to an important question, and the court is satisfied that the respondent had the knowledge to answer the question and chose not to, an inference adverse to that respondent may be drawn but any decision as to a failure to answer must have regard to delay, which must be ruled out as a possible explanation for the failure to answer before any adverse inference may be drawn.[121]

This means that the system of pre-trial procedure in a civil action will expose the respondent, for example, to interrogatories to which he/she must respond or risk the drawing of adverse inferences. It has implications for lifestyle and unaccounted wealth.

Although a civil recovery order cannot be made solely on the basis that a respondent has no identifiable lawful income to warrant a particular lifestyle, the absence of evidence to explain that lifestyle may provide the answer because the inference may be drawn, from the failure to provide an explanation or from an explanation which was untruthful (and deliberately so), that the source of funds was unlawful.[122]

Previous Behaviour

Even after the Criminal Justice Act 2003, there are limits to the extent to which evidence of the defendant's previous conduct is admissible against him/her in a criminal trial.[123] In civil recovery, on the other hand, the position now is that a defendant to civil recovery action may have adduced against him/her the following evidence: his criminal record from his youth until when he was 32 years old together with those of his criminal associates;[124] police intelligence material which reveal that he was suspected of drug trafficking in the United Kingdom on occasions several years earlier; an attempt to breach an Interim Receiving Order within days of service by opening a new bank account in a false name with a substantial transfer from another account; the compromise of proceedings brought in Ireland to restrain funds which were alleged to be the proceeds of crime; and his access to funds, not identified by the interim receiver or disclosed to the interim receiver, which he has used to fund his living expenses from July 2005 to date. All these matters were admitted in *Gale*. Without more, none of this would have been admitted in a criminal trial for drug dealing or money laundering.

Illegally Obtained Evidence and Abuse of Process

In criminal cases, evidence which is obtained in circumstances such that to admit it would have an adverse effect on the fairness of the proceedings may be excluded.[125] In *Olden v SOCA*,[126] evidence had been excluded in criminal trial under section 78 of the Police and Criminal Evidence Act 1984, but it was admitted in subsequent civil recovery proceedings. The judge held that Article 32.1(2) of the Civil Procedure Rules gave the court power to exclude evidence that would otherwise be admissible, but that this power must be exercised in accordance with the overriding objective in Part I of the Rules to deal with cases justly *as between the parties*. The Court of Appeal held that the exercise of its power involves balancing any unlawfulness against the importance of the court reaching the correct decision on the basis of all the evidence available.

Hearsay

There *is* no question of applying the criminal rules of hearsay. SOCA *v Hymans*[127] and *SOCA v Coghlan*[128] reiterate that sections 4(1) and (2) of the Civil Evidence Act 1995 govern and make clear that the issue is weight and not admissibility. Measures (usually during case management, compelling the makers of the statements) are available, where appropriate to challenge statements in documents.[129]

Legal Advice

A matter that would have been resolved neatly by holding the proceedings to be criminal would have been the question of legal aid. Article 6(3)(c) confers the right upon a defendant 'to defend himself in person or through legal assistance of his own choosing or, if he has not sufficient means to pay for legal assistance, to be given it free when the interests of justice so require'. Since Articles 6.2 and 6.3 do not apply to civil recovery proceedings at all, then Article 6(3)(c) does not confer the right to legal assistance in civil recovery proceedings. The policy of POCA is that as far as possible the assets which are the subject matter of the proceedings should not be dissipated in lawyers' fees. Consequently, the Act as enacted clearly prohibited the use of the assets to defend a civil recovery action.[130] This lead to an unwelcome but obvious consequence in the case of *Squirrell Ltd v National Westminster Bank Plc*,[131] a decision of Laddie J to the effect that someone who had no access to any assets (they all having been frozen) just had to put up whatever defence in person he could muster. In fact, there was a perfectly arguable defence that could have been put on his behalf.[132] The response to this ugly spectacle was to put in place (minimal) provision[133] to prevent its recurrence. The amendment sets out conditions under which the Director may consent to the release of assets to defend the action. If the government really thought that civil recovery actions are 'just' civil matters, then it should have stuck to its guns and to section 252(4).[134]

It follows that in civil recovery proceedings the respondent is very significantly less well placed than he/she would be in a criminal trial followed by confiscation proceedings. The standard of proof, the *probandum*, the breadth of the inferences that may be drawn and the range of admissible evidence all make matters relatively easy for the claimant and will conduce towards many settlements. That, of course, was the idea. The question is whether this has been achieved with appropriate regard to the rights of the respondent. In the clearest cases—cash—it might be, but otherwise there may be dangers.

Results and Some Conclusions

This chapter concludes by drawing attention to three major issues: the role of civil recovery within the criminal justice system, the questions surrounding financial privacy, and the ECHR. The plan, set out in the Performance and Innovation Unit (PIU) report that was the foundation of POCA,[135] was that by 2009–2010 the Government would be acquiring £250 million per annum from the proceeds of crime and in due course £1 billion, that includes a significant proportion from civil recovery. Before the abolition of the ARA, there was something to be said for considering the receipts of civil recovery independently of other aspects of the proceeds of crime *regime,* but now that civil recovery is regarded simply as one of a number of tools available to law enforcement, it only makes sense to consider a global figure. The annual average is now about £150 million.[136]

There are two standard responses of criminal justice agencies when results fail to meet targets. The first is to say they do not have enough powers. This was part of the *apologia* of the Director of the ARA when it was disbanded,[137] but, in this instance, it is difficult to sustain. The second is to say that although the results appear disappointing, nonetheless, the powers are being appropriately used for reasons other than those for which they were originally granted. In the case of these data, the increased use of interlocutory mechanisms (freezing by restraint order, without subsequently seizing either by confiscation or by civil recovery proceedings) may indicate one of two things. The first is that more widespread use of these mechanisms will take a couple of years or so to feed through, but that the proportion of sums ultimately seized as a proportion of those frozen will continue to fluctuate around a constant. The other is that the amount of money finally seized by the State, as a proportion of money frozen, is diminishing. If this is the case, then the explanation may be that NCA is now using the powers conferred by the Act in an attempt to fulfil its allocated function of 'disrupting' criminal enterprises.[138] The introduction of 'disruption of criminal enterprises' as a target[139] for law enforcement bodies allows their failings in other regards to be disguised because disruption is very difficult to measure.[140] If the law enforcement agency is busy disrupting, it is no longer critical—as it was for the ARA—that large sums of money are not being seized. Use of pre-conviction powers (arrest, detention, questioning, surveillance) as part of a 'disruptive' strategy against crime is part of NCA's remit. It would, however, be a very significant move to seek to justify powers originally directed specifically to obtaining money and other property as now forming part of an integrated strategy to disrupt crime.

The fundamental constitutional issue underpinning this area of law is the extent to which a person needs to explain him/herself, specifically his/her ownership of and dealings in property, to the State. The older, broadly liberal view was that, apart from when filling in tax returns, or asking to enter a country, or in times of emergency or war, or where there is some trigger that requires an explanation (the mere fact of possession of unexpected amounts of property being no such trigger), it was the right of everyone to tell the state to mind its own business. The arguments are well known in other areas. For instance, there is no general duty to help the police or assist their inquiries.[141] It may be that we have moved on, and that, so far as concerns possession of property, or at the very least certain types of property, we are now prepared to accept a more communitarian view that the citizen is under a duty to explain him/herself. Re-evaluation of the value of financial privacy might be overdue and may well be triggered by the HSBC Suisse (2015) and Panama Papers (2016) affairs, but that should at least be recognised and acknowledged.

Finally, the ECHR ascribes tremendous significance to the criminal/civil boundary, ascribing different sets of rights. This chapter has criticised the application of that distinction in the case of civil recovery. That criticism leads to one or both of two outcomes. First, it might be that the interpretation of Articles 6.2 and 6.3 in the cases under consideration (especially in *Walsh*) is misguided and that a better decision would have been to hold that at least some civil recovery actions are governed by Articles 6.2 and 6.3. In particular, if the prosecution procedure is to be replaced by a bargaining procedure of which fines, confiscation orders and civil recovery orders may all form part, it would be very difficult to defend a system in which the rights of the defendant varied accordingly as to whether the enforcement agency opted for a criminal conviction and confiscation order, on the one hand, or a civil recovery order, on the other.

Attention has been drawn to the way in which Articles 6.2 and 6.3 are being sidestepped in various areas—'civil' and other fixed penalties, regulatory fines and so on.[142] There was much talk at the time of the enactment of the Human Rights Act 1998 about the creation of a 'human rights culture'.[143] The reality is that any legislation directed towards constraints upon the way in which someone might want to behave can have a range of consequences. It can change behaviour and change attitudes. It can also give rise to avoidance or 'creative compliance'. Human rights legislation places constraints upon how the government may behave. One of the responses, therefore, might be to seek out mechanisms to achieve a particular purpose while complying. It ought not to be a surprise that they seek to avoid its effects, and POCA contains a deal of such avoidance.

A broader conclusion might therefore be that Articles 6.2 and 6.3 place too much weight upon the civil/criminal distinction and that unless we have a clearer notion of the reasons for and the significance of this distinction, the binary opposition which seems to be presented by Articles 6.2 and 6.3 might usefully be replaced with an incremental scale.[144] The ECHR was drawn in the 1940s, and the advent since then of an increased range of regulatory bodies with powers to punish, and the use of draconian powers by civil courts, has made the distinction more difficult to sustain. We should question the continuation of the criminal/civil distinction as a human rights axiom. It is suggested that both these responses have much to commend them.

Notes

1. The statutory civil recovery scheme should not be confused with the scheme also (unhelpfully) called 'civil recovery' under which stores sue shoplifters.
2. Previously, there was a bifurcated regime under the Criminal Justice Act 1988 and the Drug Trafficking Act 1994.
3. *In the Matter of Stanford International Bank Ltd and In The Matter Of The Cross Border Insolvency Regulations 2006* [2010] EWCA Civ 137 per Hughes LJ [162]; *R v Waya* [2012] UKSC 5 [2]–[3].
4. Proceeds of Crime Act 2002, s 305 (POCA).
5. On consideration, see *Executive Jet Support Ltd v SOCA* [2012] EWHC 2737 (QB). On notice and good faith, see *SOCA v Coghlan* [2012] EWHC 429 (QB). On claims otherwise than from bona fide purchasers, and their relationship to A1P1, see *Sanam v National Crime Agency* [2015] EWCA Civ 1234.
6. POCA 2002, ss 305–306.
7. Ibid. s 306. This does not, of course, depend upon the money having been invested lawfully. The enforcement authority might therefore benefit from such a windfall: *Foskett v McKeown* [2001] 1 AC 102.
8. POCA 2002, s 306.
9. Ibid. s 266(3)(b).
10. Ibid. s 241 as amended by Serious Organised Crime and Police Act 2005, Sch 6 para 8(a). POCA applied to proceeds in the UK acquired by activity performed elsewhere which would have been unlawful in the UK—such as a Spanish matador living in retirement in Eastbourne. Since domestic acquittals do not provide a defence, neither do overseas ones. *SOCA v Hakki Yaman Namli & Topinvest Holding International Ltd* [2013] EWHC 1200 (QB).
11. See POCA 2002, s 241; *Director of Assets Recovery Agency v John and Lord* [2007] EWHC 360.

12. See George Rainbolt and Alison F Reif, 'Crime, Property, and Justice: The Ethics of Civil Forfeiture' (1997) 11(1) Public Affairs Quarterly 39; George Rainbolt, 'Crime, Property, and Justice Revisited: The Civil Asset Forfeiture Reform Act of 2000' (2003) 17(3) Public Affairs Quarterly 219.

13. CA Branston, 'The Forcible Recaption of Chattels' (1912) 28(3) The Law Quarterly Review 263; Law Reform Committee, *Eighteenth Report: Conversion and Detinue* (1971) (Cmnd 4774) paras 116–126.

14. *Recuperare* from *re* + *capio*—Oxford English Dictionary.

15. By civil action or by compensation order or restitution order under the Powers of Criminal Courts (Sentencing) Act 2000, ss 130ff and ss 148ff, respectively, or under the Police (Property) Act 1897.

16. See also Colin King, 'Civil Forfeiture and Article 6 of the ECHR: Due Process Implications for England and Wales and Ireland' (2014) 34(3) Legal Studies 371, 372ff; Jennifer Hendry and Colin King, 'How Far is Too Far?' Theorising Non-Conviction-Based Asset Forfeiture (2015) 11(4) International Journal of Law in Context 398.

17. 'The purpose of Part 5 proceedings is not to determine or punish for any particular offence; it is to ensure that property derived from criminal conduct is taken out of circulation'. Lord Dyson JSC in *SOCA v Gale* [2011] UKSC 49 [123]. Cash forfeiture under POCA 2002, s 298, which is a hybrid between civil recovery of proceeds and forfeiture of property intended for criminal use, is permissible for this reason but in general civil recovery is not.

18. See Andrew Simester and others, *Simester and Sullivan's Criminal Law: Theory and Doctrine* (4th edn, Hart Publishing 2010) 766ff.

19. *Director, Assets Recovery Agency v Walsh* [2005] NICA 6 [26].

20. *R (Director of the Assets Recovery Agency) v Ashton* [2006] EWHC 1064 [43].

21. *R v Cuthbertson* [1981] AC 470.

22. Grant Shapps, *Report into the Underperformance of the Assets Recovery Agency* (2006).

23. Public Accounts Committee, Session 2006–2007 50th Report (HC 391).

24. Serious Crime Act 2007, s 74 and Schedules 8 & 9.

25. Serious Crime Act 2007, s 74; Courts and Crime Act 2013, Part 1.

26. SOCA, *Annual Report 2011–2012* HC 291, 15.

27. Earlier, there had been less interest in the CPS: HC Debates, 10 Feb 2009: Column 1861W (Vera Baird).

28. And see the discussion of *R v Innospec plc* [2010] EW Misc 7 (EWCC). The numbers of orders obtained by the SFO remain low. See SFO, *Annual Report and Accounts* 2012–2013 (HC 9) 11. For further discussion, see Chap. 26 (Lord and Levi) in this collection.

29. National Audit Office, *Confiscation Orders* (HC 738, 2013–2014).

30. Home Affairs Committee *Evaluating the New Architecture of Policing: The College of Policing and the National Crime Agency* (HC 800, 2014–2015).

31. National Crime Agency Press Release, 'NCA Approach to Criminal Assets' (17 February 2015) <www.nationalcrimeagency.gov.uk/news/news-listings/549-nca-approach-to-criminal-assets> accessed 10 March 2017.

32. Anthony King and Ivor Crewe, *The Blunders of Our Governments* (Oneworld Publications 2013).

33. Mary De Ming Fan, 'Disciplining Criminal Justice: The Peril Amid the Promise of Numbers' (2007) 26(1) Yale Law and Policy Review 1; Jefferson E Holcomba, John L Worrall, and Tomislav V Kovandzic, 'Is Policing for Profit? Answers from Asset Forfeiture' (2008) 7(2) Criminology and Public Policy 151; Tomislav V Kovandzicb and Marian R Williams 'Civil Asset Forfeiture, Equitable Sharing, and Policing for Profit in the United States' (2011) 39(3) Journal of Criminal Justice 273.

34. Compare POCA 2002, Schedule 1 para 5.

35. Serious Crime Act 2007, s 74 and Sched 8 Part 6 para 142.

36. Matthew Weait and Anthony Lester, 'The Use of Ministerial Powers without Parliamentary Authority: The Ram Doctrine' [2003] Public Law 415.

37. HC Deb, 11 June 2012, c86W (James Brokenshire).

38. Peter Alldridge, *Money Laundering Law* (Hart Publishing 2003) 246ff.

39. See *Satnam Singh v Director of the ARA* [2005] EWCA Civ 580 [9]; *SOCA v Olden* [2010] EWCA Civ 143 [17].

40. POCA 2002, s 2A. And see *SOCA v Agidi* [2011] EWHC 175 (QB) [130]ff.

41. See Anthony Kennedy, 'Civil Recovery Proceedings Under the Proceeds of Crime Act 2002: The Experience So Far' (2006) 9(3) Journal of Money Laundering Control 245.

42. For example, *R (Director of Assets Recovery Agency) v Obialo* [2006] EWHC 2876.

43. See *R v Kearley (No 2)* [1994] 2 AC 414. No Article 6(2) or 6(3) argument against the use of civil recovery will arise in such circumstances: *AP, MP and TP v Switzerland* (1998) 26 EHRR 541 [48].

44. CPS Prosecution Guidelines <www.cps.gov.uk/Publications/docs/code_2013_accessible_english.pdf> accessed 8 February 2016.

45. Though the hearsay and bad character provisions of the Criminal Justice Act 2003 have reduced them, there are still significant differences in the rules of evidence.

46. CPS (n 44).

47. Lord Phillips PSC in *Gale* (n 17) [54]; *SOCA v Trevor Hymans et al* [2011] EWHC 3332; for overseas acquittals, *SOCA v Hakki Yaman Namli & Topinvest Holding International Ltd* [2013] EWHC 1200 (QB).

48. Kennedy (n 41) also mentions the case where the ownership of the property is uncertain.

49. *Perry v SOCA (No 2)* [2012] UKSC 35; *Hymans* (n 47).

50. Courts and Crime Act 2013, s 48 and Schedule 7A.

51. This is unlikely to happen. The strict rules of criminal evidence do not apply in a confiscation hearing (*R v Silcock & Levin* [2004] EWCA Crim 408) and the civil standard of proof applies: POCA 2002, s 6(7).

52. A–G's Guidance under POCA 2002, s 2A (2009) <www.attorneygeneral.gov. uk/Publications/Pages/Atto rneyGeneralissuedguidancetoprosectuingbodies ontheirassetrecoverypowersunder.aspx> accessed 15 June 2016.

53. Ibid.

54. Courts and Crime Act 2013, s 45.

55. *R v Turner (FR)* [1970] 2 QB 321; *R v Goodyear (Karl)* [2005] EWCA Crim 888. See the acceptance of plea agreements in the speech of Lord Brown in *McKinnon v Government of the United States* [2008] UKHL 59 [34].

56. Plea agreements with a 'cooperating defendant'—Serious Organised Crime and Police Act 2005, s 73.

57. Ministry of Justice, 'Rules and Practice Directions' (2015) <www.justice.gov. uk/courts/procedure-rules/criminal/rulesmenu-2015#Anchor3> accessed 8 February 2016.

58. SFO, 'Corporate Self-Reporting' <www.sfo.gov.uk/publications/guidance-policy-and-protocols/corporate-self-reporting/> accessed 8 February 2016.

59. See <www.cps.gov.uk/legal/a_to_c/corporate_prosecutions/#a12> accessed 15 June 2016.

60. Making the terms of the consequential press release part of the agreement was criticised by Thomas LJ in *Innospec* (n 28).

61. The global settlement announced by the SFO in respect of its investigation of alleged bribery by BAE in Tanzania is the prime example. The trial judge (Bean J) (reluctantly) accepted the agreement: *R v BAE Systems PLC* [2010] EW Misc 16 (CC).

62. *Innospec* (n 28). See *R v Dougall* [2010] EWCA Crim 1048.

63. *Innospec* (n 28) [27].

64. The decision of the Court of Appeal in *R v Underwood* [2004] EWCA Crim 2256 establishes that, whether or not pleas have been agreed, the judge is not bound by any such agreement. *BAE* (n 61) is an application of this principle.

65. See *Innospec* (n 28); *Dougall* (n 62); *BAE* (n 61).

66. Courts and Crime Act 2013, s 45.

67. *Serious Fraud Office v Standard Bank Plc* [2016] 1 Lloyd's Law Reports FC Plus 121; *Serious Fraud Office v XYZ Ltd* [2016] Lloyd's Law Reports FC Plus 372; *Serious Fraud Office v Rolls Royce* [2017] (unreported). For further discussion, see Chap. 26 (Lord and Levi) in this collection.

68. See Colin King, 'Civil Forfeiture and Article 6 of the ECHR: Due Process Implications for England and Wales and Ireland' (2014) 34(3) Legal Studies 371.

69. Joint Parliamentary Committee on Human Rights, *Third Report, The Proceeds Of Crime Bill* (2002).

70. POCA 2002, s 266(3)(b) requires that no order be inconsistent with the Human Rights Act.

71. *HM Advocate v McIntosh (Sentencing)* [2001] UKPC D1, 2001 SC (PC) 43; *Phillips v United Kingdom* (2001) 11 BHRC 280; *R v Rezvi* [2002] UKHL 1, [2003] 1 AC 1099; *R v Benjafield* [2002] UKHL 2, [2003] 1 AC 1099.

72. *Customs and Excise Commissioners v Han* [2001] EWCA Civ 1040, [2001] STC 1188. See *Khan v Director, Assets Recovery Agency* [2006] STC (SCD) 154. The ECHR jurisprudence on this question is disappointingly unclear. See *AP v Switzerland*, App no 19958/92, (1998) 26 EHRR 541; *Jussila v Finland*, App no 73053/01 (2006), [2009] STC 29; *Glantz v Finland* [2014] STC 2263.

73. *Georgiou (trading as Mario's Chippery) v United Kingdom* [2001] STC 80; *King v Walden (Inspector of Taxes)* [2001] STC 822; *King v United Kingdom* [2004] STC 911.

74. *Goldsmith v Customs and Excise Commissioner* [2001] 1 WLR 1673.

75. *R (Director, Assets Recovery Agency) v He* [2004] EWHC 3021.

76. *Walsh* (n 19).

77. Ibid. [26].

78. In *Ashton* (n 20) [23].

79. *HM Advocate v McIntosh (Sentencing)* [2001] UKPC D1; *Phillips* (n 71); *Rezvi* (n 71); *Benjafield* (n 71).

80. *McIntosh v HM Advocate* 2000 SCCR 1017.

81. Ibid. [6].

82. Emphasis added.

83. Para 14.

84. *Phillips* (n 71).

85. Criminal Justice Act 1988, ss 71ff, which does not differ in relevant particulars from those under POCA.

86. *Rezvi* (n 71).

87. *Benjafield* (n 71).

88. *Rezvi* (n 71) *per* Lord Steyn [17]. The A1P1 argument took off much later, see *Waya* (n 3); *R v Ahmad, R v Fields* [2014] UKSC 36; *R v Harvey* [2015] UKSC 73.

89. These provisions apply in confiscation proceedings to generate the assumption that all property acquired by the defendant in the six years prior to the conviction was acquired by crime.

90. A confiscation order is a 'sentence' for the purposes of Criminal Appeal Act 1968: POCA 2002, s 456 and Schedule 11 para 4(3), amending Criminal Appeal Act 1968, s 50. Before POCA, there were some suggestions that confiscation orders could constitute part of the penalty (*Rezvi* (n 71) per Lord Steyn [10]), but POCA 2002, s 13(2) provides that the appropriate penalty must be arrived at *before* confiscation proceedings begin. Nonetheless, the

doctrine that confiscation orders apply to receipts not profits seems to make confiscation orders punitive.

91. *Custom and Excise Commissioners v City of London Magistrates' Court* [2000] 1 WLR 2020, 2025.
92. That is, the extensive investigatory powers conferred by POCA 2002, Part V Chap. 2.
93. House of Lords minutes 7 July 2005, 17th Report from the Appeal Committee, para 12. An ECtHR appeal also failed: *Walsh v United Kingdom*, App no 43384/05, 21 November 2006.
94. *He* (n 75); *R (Director of the Assets Recovery Agency) v Green* [2005] EWHC 3168.
95. *Gale v SOCA* [2010] EWCA 759, this issue not considered in *Gale* (n 17); and for Scotland, see *Doig* [2009] CSIH 34.
96. See *Gale* (n 17) per Lord Brown [115], and Lord Dyson [138].
97. POCA 2002, s 413(5).
98. *He* (n 75); *Director of Asset Recovery Agency v Charrington* [2005] EWCA Civ 334 per Lord Laws [15]–[18]; *Director, Assets Recovery Agency v Woodstock* [2005] EWHC 2128; *Ashton* (n 20).
99. *R v Rezvi* [2003] 1 AC 1099 per Lord Steyn [17].
100. *R v Harvey* [2013] EWCA Crim 1104 [38].
101. *Waya* (n 3). See also *Ahmad* (n 88); *Harvey* (n 88).
102. *R v May* [2008] UKHL 28 [48(4)]. See also *R v Paulet* [2009] EWCA Crim 1573.
103. *Sanam v National Crime Agency* [2015] EWCA Civ 1234.
104. *Ahmed v Commissioners* [2013] EWHC 1991 (QB).
105. *Green* (n 94).
106. See *R (Bavi) v Snaresbrook Crown Court* [2013] EWHC 4015 (Admin); *National Crime Agency v Perry* [2013] All ER (D) 221 (Nov); *Angus v United Kingdom Border Agency* [2011] EWHC 461 (Admin); *SOCA v Matthews* [2009] EWHC 1544 (Admin).
107. *Walsh* (n 19) [26].
108. *SOCA v Gale* [2009] EWHC 1015 [14].
109. *Coghlan* (n 5) [14].
110. *SOCA v Turrall* [2013] EWHC 2256 (Admin).
111. 'Cash' is defined widely to include notes and coins in any currency, postal orders, cheques, bankers' drafts and bearer bonds. POCA 2002, ss 289(6) and (7).
112. *SOCA v Lundon* [2010] EWHC 353 (QB) per Blake J. The broad class of criminal activity concerned needs to be identified: see *SOCA v Pelikanos* [2009] EWHC 2301 (QB); *Olupitan v Director, Assets Recovery Agency* [2008] EWCA Civ 104 [16]; *Director, Assets Recovery Agency v Szepietwoski* [2007] EWCA Civ 766 [106]–[107].
113. *Green* (n 94) (Sullivan J) [32]–[33].
114. See also *Director, Assets Recovery Agency v Jackson* [2007] EWHC 2553.

115. See, for instance, Paul Roberts and Adrian Zuckerman, *Criminal Evidence* (2nd edn, OUP 2010) 284ff.

116. The Federal Rules of Evidence uses the expression 'the preponderance of the evidence' to designate this intermediate stage.

117. *Clingham (formerly C) (a minor) v Royal Borough of Kensington and Chelsea* [2002] UKHL 39; *Chief Constable of Merseyside v Harrison* [2006] EWHC 1106; *Re U (A Child) (Serious Injury: Standard of Proof)* [2004] EWCA Civ 567.

118. *In Re B (Children) (Sexual Abuse: Standard of Proof)* [2008] UKHL 35 [13]. See Peter Mirfield, 'How Many Standards of Proof Are There?' (2009) 125 Law Quarterly Review 31; *Re D* [2008] UKHL 33.

119. *SOCA v Pelekanos* [2009] EWHC 2307 (QB) per Hamblen J [19]. See also *Revenue and Customs Commissioners v Khawaja* [2008] EWHC 1687 (Ch); *Agidi* (n 40); *SOCA v Kelly* [2010] EWHC 3565 (QB).

120. Criminal Justice and Public Order Act 1994, ss 34–39.

121. *Gale* (n 108) (Griffith Williams J) [10]. See, in an action in the tort of conspiracy, *Revenue & Customs Commissioners v Sunico A/S* & 6 Ors [2013] EWHC 941.

122. *Coghlan* (n 5) (QB) [14] (Simon J).

123. Paul Roberts and Adrian Zuckerman, *Criminal Evidence* (2nd end, OUP 2010) 600ff. Mike Redmayne, *Character in the Criminal Trial* (OUP 2015).

124. See *SOCA v Fielding* [2009] EWHC 2684 (Admin).

125. Police and Criminal Evidence Act 1984, s 78.

126. *Olden v SOCA* [2010] EWCA Civ 143.

127. *Hymans* (n 47).

128. *Coghlan* (n 5).

129. Ibid. [16].

130. POCA 2002, s 252(4).

131. *Squirrell Limited v National Westminster Bank Plc and HM. Customs and Excise* [2005] EWHC 664.

132. That there was no money identifiable as the proceeds of his tax evasion: see Peter Alldridge and Ann Mumford, 'Tax Evasion and the Proceeds of Crime Act 2002' (2005) 25(3) Legal Studies 353.

133. POCA 2002, (Legal Expenses in Civil Recovery Proceedings) Regulations 2005 SI 2005/3382. See now also POCA, (Legal Expenses in Civil Recovery Proceedings) (Amendment) Regulations SI 2008/523; *SOCA v Szepietowski* [2009] EWHC 344 (Ch); *Agidi* (n 40) [107]ff.

134. See *AP and Anor v Crown Prosecution Service and Revenue & Customs Prosecutions Office* [2007] EWCA Crim 3128.

135. Cabinet Office Performance and Innovation Unit, *Recovering the Proceeds of Crime* (2000).

136. CPS, *Proceeds of Crime Strategy* (2014) <www.cps.gov.uk/publications/docs/cps_asset_recovery_strate gy_2014.pdf> accessed 15 June 2016.

137. Jane Earl, Director of the ARA, blamed the limitation period of six years that governed civil recovery actions: BBC News, 'Laws "Let Down" Crime Assets Body' *BBC* (London, 13 February 2007 <http://news.bbc.co.uk/1/hi/uk/6356165.stm> accessed 9 March 2017).

138. The objective of disruption was first set out in legislation in the NCIS (Secretary of State's Objectives) Order 1999 SI 822 and then the National Crime Squad (Secretary of State's Objectives) Order 2002 SI 779. This objective appeared in the Serious Crime Act 2007, Part 3 and Crime and Courts Act 2013, s 3.

139. See SOCA, *Annual Plan 2010/11*; Clive Harfield, 'SOCA: A Paradigm Shift in British Policing' (2006) 46(4) British Journal of Criminology 743.

140. For the ARA, no such 'excuse' was possible.

141. *Rice v Connolly* [1966] 2 QB 414.

142. Robin M White, '"Civil Penalties": Oxymoron, Chimera and Stealth Sanction?' (2010) 126 Law Quarterly Review 593.

143. *Rights Brought Home* (Cm 3782, 1997).

144. To some extent, the jurisprudence under *Engel v Netherlands (No 1)* (1976) 1 EHRR 647 has achieved this end.

Peter Alldridge is Drapers' Professor of Law (since 2003) and was Head of the Department of Law (2008–2012) at Queen Mary, University of London. He was Specialist Adviser to the joint Parliamentary Committees on the draft Corruption Bill (2003) and the draft Bribery Bill (2009); he was made a Fellow of the Academy of Social Sciences in 2014 and in 2017–2018 will be President of the Society of Legal Scholars. He has published widely in the areas of criminal law, evidence, legal education, law and information technology, medical law and law and disability. He is the author of *Relocating Criminal Law* (2000), *Money Laundering Law* (2003), *What Went Wrong with Money Laundering Law?* (Palgrave, 2016) and *Taxation and Criminal Justice* (2017).

23

An Empirical Glimpse of Civil Forfeiture Actions in Canada

Michelle Gallant

Popular media stories of civil forfeiture often relate an unsettling tale. A modern legal tool conceived principally to contend with profitable crimes, notoriously the lucrative trade in illegal drugs, it stands regularly accused of impaling innocent parties, eviscerating long-held rights and illegitimately expropriating property.[1] If these images accurately depict the enforcement narrative of civil forfeiture law, they are profoundly troubling.

But knowledge of the enforcement narrative is scant. What is needed are systematic studies of the enforcement enterprise, studies that would illuminate the context surrounding civil forfeiture actions. Such knowledge would enhance the understanding of implementation and provide information that might inform any rights inquiries, might be relevant to decisions involving policy or might quell, or antagonize, public opinion. In beginning to develop this knowledge, this chapter offers a glimpse of the enforcement context drawn from an examination of 100 randomly selected actions commenced between 2009 and 2014 at the courthouse in Winnipeg, Manitoba, Canada The study originates in a perceived disconnect between popular tales and the

This research was supported by the Legal Research Institute of Manitoba. Jennifer Litchfield, research assistant, Faculty of Law, University of Manitoba, conducted excellent research verifying factual aspects of this work and assisting in the collection of materials. A special thank you to the staff at the Manitoba Courthouse for facilitating access to research materials.

M. Gallant
Faculty of Law, University of Manitoba,
Winnipeg, MB, Canada

C. King et al. (eds.), *The Palgrave Handbook of Criminal and Terrorism Financing Law*,
https://doi.org/10.1007/978-3-319-64498-1_23

actual enforcement context surrounding civil forfeiture. It initiates an exploration and aspires to begin to ground legal, policy and other discourses in a fuller factual setting.

The chapter commences with an introduction to civil forfeiture law and a consideration of the principal themes of controversy provoked by this device. The next segment delineates the chief attributes of the Manitoba civil forfeiture model. The chapter then presents the findings borne out of the examination of the 100 files. It concludes with observations on this tentative portrait of the civil forfeiture enforcement narrative.

Civil Forfeiture Regulation

Civil forfeiture law arises from modern global efforts to cope with crime by tackling its financial underpinnings. It occurs as part of a vast edifice of contemporary laws aimed at tracking, detecting and facilitating the forfeiture, or confiscation, of property tainted by some link to crime. The strategy comprises a set of international legal instruments, the first of which deals with illegal drugs. The edifice is commonly known as global anti-money laundering, anti-terrorist finance, law. In 1990, an organization formed, the Financial Action Task Force (FATF), and assumed the task of overseeing the implementation of the strategy. Drawing on the content of international conventions, the FATF issues a series of recommendations which are widely acknowledged as constituting the minimum global standards regarding anti-money laundering, anti-terrorist finance regulation.[2]

The focus of this strategic modern approach to criminal activity reflects an awareness of the financial magnitude of certain crimes, chiefly the trade in illegal drugs, and a perceived need to implement mechanisms aimed specifically at wealth associated therewith. In part, tackling the underpinnings urges the conceptualization of lucrative crimes as large-scale 'criminal businesses', businesses that might be strategically starved of the resources upon which their prosperity depends.

Core attributes of this modern global edifice include the post-conviction confiscation of assets and, recently, non-conviction-based confiscation, or forfeiture.[3] Post-conviction anticipates the confiscation of property once someone has been convicted for a criminal offence. Non-conviction-based confiscation, often known as civil forfeiture, does not require a criminal conviction. Informed by allegations of criminal activity, forfeiture displaces convictions as a pre-requisite to the taking of property. This casting aside of convictions animates many admonitions of civil forfeiture law.

Within Canada, the bulk of this anti-criminal finance strategy manifests in national law, the remit of the federal state. National law permits the post-conviction forfeiture of property linked to criminal offences.[4] National law also implements another important piece of the global strategy, anti-money laundering regulation.[5] This latter slate of provisions helps to detect and intercept criminal resources including resources that might be linked to terrorist activity. This location of provisions in national law reflects the Canadian constitutional division of powers, that the Federal Parliament has jurisdiction over the criminal law.[6] Non-conviction-based models of forfeiture reside in provincial law. However, provincial legislators rarely, if ever, speak of a connection of the provincial devices to the broader global strategy or to the national schemes. In truth, the provincial models preceded the global call to rely on non-conviction-based approaches to assets tainted by crime. That formal global endorsement happened in 2012, whereas some Canadian provinces entertained reliance on this approach at least a decade earlier.[7]

Rather than speak of the obvious direct fit within the global trend, provincial law-makers usually justify their civil forfeiture apparatus by allusions to the problem posed by criminal organizations, profitable unlawful activity and the need to assist the victims of crime.[8] In addressing these local preoccupations, these laws sometimes have particular applications to criminal organizations, usually the attaching of assumptions that facilitate forfeiture if property is owned, or possessed, by a criminal organization.[9] Such networks benefit from, and sustain themselves with, the profits of unlawful activity. Provincial regulation tends to prefer to the language of profitable 'unlawful activity' as opposed to crime. Federal devices speak more explicitly of 'crime', the proceeds of crime. There is no real distinction between 'unlawful activity' and 'crime'. Initiatives at the provincial level ubiquitously stress the civil, remedial or victim-oriented character. Alberta's civil forfeiture regime, for example, is called the Victim's Restitution and Compensation Payments Act. Ontario's is called the Civil Remedies Act. Provincial regimes typically expressly permit some funnelling of forfeit resources to the victims of crime. Despite the difference in emphasis and semantics, the fit of civil forfeiture regulation with the global trend, and with national law, is palpable. Global undertakings, national law and provincial law all target property derived from, or connected to, criminal conduct.

Since the province of Ontario endorsed a non-conviction-based model in 2001, most Canadian provinces, including Manitoba, have enacted legislation that enables property linked to criminal offences to be forfeited in civil proceedings.[10] The particular ingredients of any regime, whether the provincial models or models introduced in other jurisdictions, differ. The persistent common denominator is that these civil archetypes allow the state to seize and forfeit property within the confines of a civil legal process.[11] It is a classically civil process governed by the conventional legal norms applicable to any civil proceeding. The state's entitlement to property ensues when it demonstrates, to the civil standard of proof, a link between property and some criminal offence. Such mechanisms are referred to as non-conviction based because the obtaining of a conviction has no place in the action. Again, however, this fusing of the civil devices with crime and dispensing with convictions elicits controversy.

One of the most salient, and widely publicized, aspects of these models is the wealth they succeed in capturing. In 2014, Manitoba civil forfeitures realized approximately $3 million.[12] Given that crime control is traditionally a cost-intensive exercise, a few million dollars are significant. In the larger province of British Columbia, forfeitures in 2012 and 2013 totalled $19 million.[13] The statistics available for Ontario indicate that since the commencement of operations in 2003, $37.6 million has been secured under Ontario's civil forfeiture law.[14] Ontario is likewise a larger jurisdiction than Manitoba and was the first to endorse this approach.

Consistent with the global anticipation, much of that wealth appears to be associated with the trade in illegal drugs. Data from British Columbia indicates the principal underlying offence triggering a forfeiture action concerns illegal drugs.[15] This is echoed by evidence from Ontario.[16] With respect to Manitoba, there is no public data to confirm such a connection although the present study suggests the situation resembles that of Ontario and British Columbia. Curiously, although there is some tracking of the resources forfeited and some accounting of the crimes to which those resources relate, there is little understanding of the impact of civil forfeiture on crime. It may be axiomatic that the removal of resources, particularly those extracted from the illegal drugs industry, affects crime. Yet that relationship is rarely examined.[17]

A Controversial Approach

Arming the state with an instrument that couples concepts of the civil law with allegations of criminal activity evokes considerable controversy. Much of the controversy revolves around distinctions between the criminal and the civil law and the legality of using a civil legal process to accomplish putatively criminal law objectives.[18] This is principally due to the fact that allegations of criminal wrongdoing, rather than allegations of some civil wrongdoing, underpin the action. Whether the device is a civil or criminal mechanism, whether it imposes civil or criminal consequences and whether it constitutes an incidence of remedial or punitive justice are recurrent themes of discord. Framed as constitutional, or rights-based challenges, a central argument is whether civil forfeiture is sufficiently criminal in character to attract the more generous set of procedural and substantive safeguards that govern prosecutions rather than the restricted set that ordinarily apply to a civil legal process.

Comparisons to strictly conventional civil actions related to crime illuminate this tension. Criminal and civil liability can derive from the same set of factual circumstances. It is not unusual for criminal allegations to underpin an action for a civil remedy. Civil actions usually concern the mediation of interests between two private parties, with the remedy reflecting compensation for some injury. The civil standard of proof and any substantive or procedural rights or doctrines applicable thereto determines the outcome. Obviously one of those parties can be the state when it seeks to assert some claim to a remedy such as damages for the destruction of state-owned property. Civil forfeiture cannot readily be analogized to a civil action by the state for some injury peculiar to it or to its property. Rather, forfeiture contemplates the imposition of civil liability by the state for criminal conduct. Even in a purely civil context a claim for punitive damages, which is arguably tantamount to an acknowledgement that conduct verges on the criminal sphere, is a rare occurrence.[19] Fundamentally, civil forfeiture involves the same parties as a criminal action and involves allegations of criminal conduct, conduct that fully enters into, rather than verges upon, the criminal sphere. Despite the obvious close resemblance to a criminal prosecution, civil forfeiture draws on the rules of civil justice since it allegedly, or formally, constitutes a civil undertaking.

Judicial decisions related to this tension tend, for the most part, to vindicate the legality of civil forfeiture law. American law holds that a civil forfeiture action subsequent to a criminal prosecution does not violate the protection against double jeopardy.[20] Civil forfeiture does not qualify as a second criminal prosecution. Similarly, the constitutional protection against excessive fines, under American jurisprudence, does govern civil forfeiture but that safeguard regulates both criminal actions and civil actions.[21] Decisions in the United Kingdom and Ireland reflect similar interpretations: civil forfeiture does not necessarily attract rights or other legal protections that apply to criminal actions.[22]

Decisions from the Canadian Supreme Court show a similarly vindicating tilt. An early decision involving civil forfeiture under Canadian customs law held that the action was civil, not criminal.[23] Although the forfeiture in question had serious financial consequences, the action was a civil collection mechanism, designed to deter but not to punish.[24] It did not come within the remit of the criminal law. Later, a decision on Ontario's modern provincial civil forfeiture law held that the instrument was not sufficiently criminal in character to constitute an exercise of the criminal law power, a power that the Canadian constitution confers exclusively on the federal government.[25] In Canada, civil forfeiture is a creature of provincial law. In that decision, the Court held the forfeiture law created a property-based scheme through which to seize money and other tainted property tainted by crime. Moreover, the forfeiture did not occur as part of a sentencing process since no one stood accused of any criminal offence.[26] Therefore, despite the mixing of criminal ingredients with a civil process, jurisprudence on the controversy appears to lean towards the legality of civil forfeiture law.

A further arena of dispute, although one which is now largely banished from civil forfeiture regulation, is reliance on a standard of proof that is less demanding than the civil standard. When American law began to apply forfeiture to financial crimes, in certain circumstances, property could be forfeited by applying the threshold needed to secure a warrant, the standard of probable cause.[27] Most civil regimes acknowledge that that standard is too low and the governing threshold is the civil threshold of a balance of probabilities or a preponderance of the evidence. Still, it is rather astonishing to even entertain the notion of such a low threshold, particularly when the consequence is the permanent deprivation of interests in property.

The polemic that the civil strategy attracts is not strictly confined to divides between criminal and civil proceedings or to issues of thresholds of proof. Broader issues of justice inform the tense narrative. Critics contend forfeiture constitutes a form of incentivized policing and perverts impartiality in the enforcement of law.[28] This is a function, in part, of forfeiture's obvious ability to bring considerable resources under state control. The capture of significant assets suggests that forfeiture's underlying ambition is revenue-generation rather than crime reduction.[29] Given the tendency to collect information on amounts of property forfeited and to ignore, or be unable or unwilling to track, the effect of regulation on crime lends some credence to this complaint. Moreover, there is a tendency, both in popular media and within the machinations of the state, to present these impressive amounts as evidence of the 'success' of civil initiatives. This reinforces the idea that the civil strategy is more concerned with replenishing public coffers than it is with the management of crime.

Criticism is also levied at the way forfeited resources may be allocated.[30] Civil forfeiture apparatuses can be self-funding initiatives. Rather than allocate a portion of a state budget to its operation, the resources forfeited flow to the units dedicated to enforcing the law. When funding for public projects is strained, civil forfeiture is a viable crime control project because it generates its own operational resource. This can invite questions of accountability given its self-perpetuating character. Moreover, sometimes reclaimed criminal property directly enhances policing budgets.[31] This means that policing units have a vested interest in pursuing these actions as opposed to revenue-neutral, or unbiased, law enforcement. Any financial incentives built by law or by policy can distort the presumptively disinterested nature of law.

In addition to these more common controversies, civil forfeiture generates a number of subsidiary tensions. In the main, these result from the peculiar mechanics of any regulatory regime. US schemes, South African and, indeed, Canadian provincial regimes permit the forfeiture of the 'instruments of crime'.[32] This phrase has a rather unusual legal pedigree. Historically, it has secured the forfeiture of things, property, which is malum in se, things whose inherent characteristics link the property to criminal activity.[33] Exemplifying this understanding would historically include the forfeiture of illegal drugs, or instruments used to create counterfeit currency or, during prohibition, items associated with the distillation of alcohol. Under modern civil forfeiture regulation, this 'instruments of crime' extends to any property used in connection with criminal activity, property that is not 'inherently' criminal. The controversy this creates is the potential complete lack of proportionality between property subject to forfeiture and any underlying offence. An expensive house, for instance, in which a series of drugs transactions occurred, becomes liable to forfeiture as the 'instrument of crime'. On such occasions, the scope of the taking may grossly exceed the scale of underlying misdeeds. Such distinct absences of proportionality obviously prompt concern.

In a similar vein, civil forfeiture regimes often contemplate the removal of the 'proceeds of crime'. This phrase entered the lexicon with the arrival of the broader anti-criminal finance strategy. The 'proceeds of crime' is usually defined as property, whether real or personal, derived from criminal activity. It usually receives no other legal definition. A dictionary defines 'proceeds' as 'something that results or accrues' or as 'the profits of a sale or investment'.[34] While the dictionary appears to admit no distinction between 'proceeds' and 'profits', reliance on the term 'proceeds' tends to likewise permit no particular distinction. Controversy sometimes emerges from the failure to adequately distinguish between 'proceeds' of crime and the 'profits' of crime. The former term arguably captures lawfully acquired property since it does not, in the context of profitable criminal businesses, allow for the deduction of expenses.[35] Axiomatically, the scope of a potential forfeiture action increases.

Finally, civil forfeiture regulation can entangle property belonging to innocent third parties. Someone whose personal vehicle is unwittingly borrowed and deployed to transport illegal substances generally falls afoul of the injunction against the 'instruments of crime'.[36] Most modern regimes contain some measure of protection for innocent owners of property assailed by forfeiture. In the absence of these protections, that property is forfeit regardless of any fault lying with the property owner. 'Fault', in this context, usually means that property owners assume some positive obligation to prevent their property's co-optation into criminal pursuits. Law may prescribe the ambit of that obligation. In Ontario, for example, to prevent forfeiture, a property owner must promptly notify law enforcement of any misuse of their property and refuse permission to continue to use that property.[37]

Manitoban Civil Forfeiture Law

Manitoba's civil forfeiture apparatus, the device upon which this study is based, forms part of the Criminal Forfeiture of Property Act.[38] Since its enactment in 2004, the province has brought over a thousand civil forfeiture actions.[39] This study examines 100.

Manitoban civil forfeiture law creates two civil forfeiture powers: the power to forfeit the 'proceeds of unlawful activity' and the power to forfeit the 'instruments of unlawful activity'.[40] 'Unlawful activity' comprises offences defined under federal law and provincial law and includes acts occurring outside of Canada and Manitoba that would, if committed in the province, constitute offences.[41]

'Proceeds of unlawful activity' denotes property acquired as a result of unlawful activity including any increase in the value of property or any decrease consequent upon a debt obligation secured against the property.[42] An 'instrument of unlawful activity' consists of property that has been used, or is likely to be used, to engage in unlawful activity that results in, or is likely to result in, the acquisition of property or has caused, or is likely to cause, serious bodily harm.[43] The language of 'has been used, or likely to be used' contemplates both past use and prospective use of property. The definition of property liable to forfeiture covers real and personal property and specifically includes cash.[44]

Manitoban civil forfeiture law operates in rem, the subject of the action being property, the *res*, rather than particular owners or other legal entities having some interest in that property.[45] Scholars refer to this as the 'guilty property fiction' as it anticipates the descent of liability on property, or limits liability of forfeiture to the value of the property.[46] To a degree, this informs the Supreme Court of Canada decision noted previously: forfeiture does not form part of a sentencing process since no person stood accused of crime.

Manitoban law permits the pre-trial ex parte seizure of property and provides for the filing of notice in provincial registries. The original seizure application issues upon reasonable grounds to believe the property is liable to forfeiture. Pre-trial seizure makes forfeiture a particular effective instrument. It ensures that property is neither dissipated nor removed from the jurisdiction pending completion of the action. The 'defendant' property is captured and held, seized and preserved for eventual forfeiture. Obviously the in rem legal fiction assists in achieving this effectiveness since it is, after all, the property, and not the person, who is the subject of the action.

The perfection of the forfeiture is governed by the civil standard of proof, a standard known in Canadian law as the balance of probabilities standard.[47] Notably, in satisfying that standard, the province needs to demonstrate a connection to some crime, not a specific crime.[48] It need not, for instance, prove that the property is linked to drugs trafficking but, rather, that the property is linked to some crime. Moreover, proof that a person was convicted of an offence, found guilty of an offence or found not criminally responsible on account of mental disorder constitutes proof of the alleged offence.[49] Thus even someone excused from criminal liability by virtue of some mental impediment can lose property to a forfeiture action.

Inherent in the targeting of property is the potential to ensnare property belonging to third parties, commonly described in the literature as 'innocent owners'. This is particularly relevant in the context of potential forfeitures of real estate—houses, fields, gardens or yards—allegedly used as the situs of crime, the 'instrument of unlawful activity'. It would equally entangle personal property—whether boats or cars—that was unwittingly used by another in connection with crime. Like most civil forfeiture devices, Manitoban law provides some protection for third parties—an innocent owner defence. Prior holders of registered interests in property such as institutional lenders are protected by virtue of registration.[50] Private parties such as owners of homes subject to rental agreements are protected if they demonstrate that they did all that they reasonably could to prevent their property from being co-opted into criminal engagements.[51]

The Manitoban structure vests the Court with the residual discretion to refuse forfeiture should a refusal be in 'the interests of justice'.[52] The law contains no formal guidance on the kinds of circumstances that might attract this exception. The Courts appear to be interpreting the 'the interests of justice' as a type of proportionality test.[53] Responding to the disproportionality concerns noted earlier, this feature of Manitoban law tends to mitigate against the otherwise blunt termination of interests in property. While there is no definitive list of criteria to be taken into account in applying this test, the Courts have found that a forfeiture was not in the 'interest of justice' when the property owner was not the perpetrator of the offences and had taken measures, to the extent they were able, to deny the misuse of property.[54] Similarly, in assessing proportionality and fairness of the forfeiture, the Courts have found that an action was not in the interest of justice when the relationship between the misuse of property and an alleged offence was tenuous.[55]

Finally, the law creates a fund for the receipt of forfeit property.[56] The Act prioritizes disbursements from the fund. The first priority is management of assets and the administration of the civil forfeiture law. Any residual amounts may be used to compensate the victims of crime, to remedy the consequences of crime, to create safer communities and to support victim-assistance programmes.[57]

A Glimpse of Context

A contextual investigation of the enforcement cannot provide specific answers to legal and policy debates. It can be instrumental in shaping those debates, or in otherwise ensuring that the developing narrative takes some account of context. This glimpse begins to generate some preliminary knowledge.

This exploration coaxes knowledge from 100 civil forfeiture actions examined at the Manitoba courthouse.[58] The files were randomly selected from the years 2009 through 2014, with each action commencing in a given calendar year.[59] These were all in various stages of processing. Some were complete. Others had discrete matters pending final determination. Some produced thick files, complete with statements of defence, diverse legal motions, and involved multiple parties and multiple properties. Others were relatively thin.

In painting a tentative portrait, this study focuses principally on four kinds of information common to all the civil forfeiture actions.[60] The first category consists of the principal alleged underlying offences. Although the province does not need to prove a link to a specific offence, it typically alleges, or alludes, to the particular crime, or crimes, that precipitate the action. Given the prevalence of drug crimes, the study also takes account of the kinds of drugs involved. The second category inquires into the type and value of property liable to forfeiture. The third category investigates the kinds of evidence marshalled in support of the action. Critics, in contending that forfeiture takes the property of innocent parties, tend to equate innocence with the absence of a criminal conviction. This category provides a window onto what culpability, in the civil sense, means in a forfeiture action with respect to the underlying evidential basis. The fourth category comprises the outcomes, whether the province was successful in its application for forfeiture. Information on this aspect may explain the popularity of civil forfeiture actions. In addition to these categories, the study takes some account of the nature of currency, whether Canadian or foreign, associated with forfeitures. Other information, when determined relevant to illuminating the context of civil forfeiture, is also noted.

The information drawn from the study is related below principally in a quantitative manner. Knowledge of a more qualitative order is reserved for the observations segment that follows.

The Findings

A majority of files involved allegations of offences related to illegal drugs including trafficking offences or the possession of the proceeds of crime related to drugs offences (87).[61] None appeared to exclusively involve possession of drugs for the purposes of personal consumption.[62] Many concerned drugs-related offences together with other alleged offences: the possession of illegal arms, the possession of weapons for a dangerous purpose, the possession of stolen goods, the association with a criminal organization, the unlawful sale of tobacco, credit card fraud and forgery, breach of probation, obstruction of a police officer, and the theft of electricity and water (33).

A modest set did not contain allegations related to drugs offences (11). These involved various species of fraud, forgery, break and enter, trafficking in credit cards and the falsification of credit card data, the possession of property obtained from crime, possession of the proceeds of unlawful activity and the possession of illegal weapons (6). One file concerned alleged offences related to the making and possession of child pornography, forcible confinement and forms of sexual exploitation. Two concerned offences related to the illegal sale of tobacco products; another alleged violations of the Wildlife Act including using lights at night to hunt wildlife (1); another involved allegations of prostitution (1).

In the context of drugs-related forfeitures, the principal illegal substance was cannabis, commonly known as marijuana. The majority of actions concerned marijuana or marijuana together with other illegal substances (67). Some of these concerned marijuana combined with other drugs, including cocaine, psilocybin, heroin, diazepam, steroids, Percocet, ecstasy and methamphetamines (11). Offences related to illegal substances exclusive of marijuana were fewer (21). In one case, the allegations related to drugs offences but the particular type of illegal substances was unclear.

With regard to the second category, the types of property seized as liable to forfeiture included various kinds of personal property—commonly sums of cash and automobiles—and real property, chiefly residential houses. Many involved some mix of forfeitable property, some combination of cash and automobiles, cash and residential properties, cash and other items of personal property.

Almost half of the actions involved the forfeiture of real estate, principally residential homes allegedly used in the production of marijuana (40). One involved the potential forfeiture of multiple pieces of real estate. Sometimes other property was also seized along with real property (8).

Most properties were subject to mortgages. Although the registered property owners were named as respondents to the forfeiture actions, some of the properties appeared to be subject to rental arrangements or the file indicated that registered owner did not reside at the property or did not reside in the province (16). In some cases, ownership of the property liable to forfeiture was not entirely clear (2).

Roughly half of the files examined involved the seizure of cash currency, either on its own or in connection with other property (48). In one case, a significant sum of cash was seized ($7000) although it was not subject to forfeiture. Cash, together with other property, was occasionally seized (8). Cash was exclusively seized on four occasions.

The amounts of cash liable to forfeiture varied widely, from modest amounts (less than $1000) to upwards of $90,000. Only three actions involved in excess of $40,000 in cash, with most ranging anywhere between $5000 and $25,000. Only two involved appreciable amounts of foreign currency, the seizure of $36,000 cash in US dollars and $14,000 in Jamaican currency.

A smattering of actions consisted of the seizure of automobiles together with other property (15), with a few actions concerning exclusively the forfeiture of automobiles (9). One involved the exclusive forfeiture of a motorcycle. A snowmobile and two recreational vehicles formed part of wider seizure efforts (3). Other property seized included bank accounts (2), gold (2) and jewellery (2).

The principal evidence underlying the forfeiture action obviously differed with the alleged offences. Certain patterns of evidence, however, particularly in the context of forfeitures of real estate, did recur. In the context of the forfeitures of real estate related to the trading in cannabis substances, with a singular exception, all residential properties contained marijuana plants.

The quantities of plants seized ranged from a minimum of 200 plants to upwards of 1400. All involved a mix of evidence of stolen electricity, excessive hydro use or tampering with hydro connection and evidence of excessive water use or tampering with water supply. All involved equipment necessary for the interior cultivation of plants, the value of which equipment was estimated at anywhere from $10,000 to $25,000. Also commonly found, or associated with the real property, were scales, notes of figures and initials and plastic bags (some containing illegal drugs). Evidence also regularly included modest or trace amounts of other illegal drugs such as cocaine or methamphetamines. The street value of marijuana operations varied widely, anywhere from $100,000 to over $2 million.

In the context of non-marijuana-related real estate civil actions, one involved 5 kilograms of methamphetamines with an alleged value of 1 million dollars. Stand-alone forfeitures of cash related to alleged drugs offences, with the exception of one action, involved some mix of illegal drugs and evidence linked to drugs transactions. The quantities of illegal drugs ranged from a single gram to upwards of 200 grams. Scales, score sheets and bags also formed part of the evidential mix. Similar evidence accompanied stand-alone forfeitures of automobiles. Notably, in no case was an extremely modest of illegal drugs the sole basis of the forfeiture.

With regard to the few non-drug-related civil forfeiture actions, the forfeiture of $11,000 in cash was linked to one-quarter million cigarettes that had not been stamped, or otherwise marked, for lawful sale in Canada. With regard to the alleged fraud, the action concerned the forfeiture of cash, valuable coins, bank accounts and a vehicle. With regard to forfeiture related to allegations of theft, the evidence underlying the action included the stolen articles and prior convictions for theft. On two occasions, tax records formed part of the evidential mix, probably with a view to revealing discrepancies between the scope of individual's declared income and the scale of resources subject to forfeiture.

With respect to the fourth category of information, the precise outcomes of provincial forfeiture bids were as varied as the evidence underlying the actions. Still, in almost all of the actions that were complete at the time of examination, the province was either partly, or wholly, successful in its forfeiture bid. A significant part of those successes resulted from default judgments (40). Claimants appeared to have failed to respond to the initial notice of the pending forfeiture, or to have otherwise abandoned any claim to property allegedly tainted by some association with crime.

The bulk of those actions to which individuals did respond related to the forfeiture of real estate. Many of these resulted in some portion, usually a very modest portion, of the seized assets being returned to the claimant. Some involved real estate that was subject to a rental arrangement with property owners contending they had no knowledge of the alleged use of the property for the cultivation of illegal drugs. A few of these appeared to result in property owners losing some of their interests in property to forfeiture (4). The relationship between the renters and the property owners was not always clear although a few appeared to involve familial relationships (3).

A significant number of the actions resulted in consent judgments (13), and a number of actions were discontinued (12).

Observations on Contextual Study

Amidst the thousand actions pursued in Canada, a modest sample of 100 actions cannot speak authoritatively of the context within which forfeiture applies. The sample merely begins to fill a small corner of a much larger contextual canvass. Even within the narrow confines of Manitoban law, the portrait may not necessarily be representative. Still, crediting this study with some representative merit, what does it reveal about civil forfeiture law?

The investigation tends to confirm the existing knowledge that this regulatory apparatus applies principally in the context of trafficking in illegal drugs. The bulk of the actions involve allegations related to drug crimes. To a pronounced degree, that is consistent with the overarching strategy of which forfeiture partakes, the idea of severing the link between drugs and money. Arguably, many, if not most, of the other alleged offences possess some profit dimension. Stolen goods, illegal arms, fraud and the possession of illegal cigarettes constitute crimes whose commission typically garners some financial benefit. Again, to the extent that the target of forfeiture is resources tainted by crime, profits derived from crime, the enforcement context appears to be tightly moored to that premise.

Within Manitoba, a civil forfeiture action that achieved some notoriety concerned the alleged taking of a residential home which was underpinned by allegations of sexual violence or sexual offences.[63] The case received extensive media coverage but does not appear to be reflective of the broader context within which forfeiture occurs. The taking of property outside of the context of profitable crime would appear to be somewhat of an aberration.[64] That said, nothing within the remit of Manitoban law confines its application to profitable criminal activity. It merely appears to have been restricted, in practice, to that context.

Property seized pursuant to Manitoban actions ranged from cash and auto-mobiles to bank accounts and residential homes. While cash and bank accounts may constitute the proceeds of crime, residential homes are typically forfeit as constituting the instrument of crime. Many actions concerned the forfeiture of property allegedly used to produce illegal substances, colloquially known as 'grow-ops'. With residential houses, the consistency of the eviden-tial basis is conspicuous. Most involved evidence of the theft of electricity, evidence of cultivation and production equipment, evidence of bundles of cash and hundreds of marijuana plants. Arguably, in these cases ample evidence tied the property to crime. The abundance of evidence sits uneasily with the idea of 'innocent' occupiers of property.

Many forfeitures of real estate were subject to rental agreements. Typically, the property was allegedly used in drug production. This obviously raises the spectre of innocent property owners losing their property to forfeiture because of the acts of tenants. This illustrates the clear tension created when property owned by one party is tainted, or liable to forfeiture, consequent upon its misuse by another. In most cases, the owners of rental property, while alleg-edly not themselves the primary agents of criminal activity, suffered some proprietary loss, a loss attributable to some assumption of responsibility for the property's association with crime. Notably, not a single residential prop-erty was forfeited on the basis of some passing, transient or temporary con-nection to drugs trafficking. Each was substantially devoted to the project of producing illegal substances.

Presumptively, rental properties raise some difficult issues. Under civil for-feiture law, property owners appear to have some positive duty to police the use of their premises. Periodic annual inspections might suffice. While in theory this might afford some promise, it creates a rather tense situation for owners. Confronting suspected traffickers would be unwise. A preferable option might be to encourage owners to immediately report any suspicions to law enforcement by defining such an obligation in law. To prevent co-optation of their property in criminal activity, the owners of rental property would need to periodically seek to inspect their premises and to immediately report any hints of impropriety to the police for possible further investigation and action.

The examination of the 100 files reveals the effectiveness of this apparatus in securing title to assets tainted by crime. For the most part, the province was successful in its forfeiture application, with many actions resulting in default judgments. The proportion of successful outcomes underscores its tremen-dous capacity to fell prodigious amounts of wealth. This underpins its acclaim as a modern device that effectively secures the province title to tainted assets. It does not, however, attest to forfeiture's capacity to control crime.

Finally, the prevalence of marijuana in civil forfeiture actions necessarily invites the question of whether debates over decriminalization should be revisited. Debates typically centre on the decriminalization of marijuana rather than harsher prohibited substances (i.e. cocaine). This is not the place to consider the merits of forms of partial or full legalization. However, it is quite clear that in Manitoba, civil forfeiture is tightly tied to marijuana production. In terms of money, legalization would shift interest from forfeiture to taxation.[65] Taxation of the business income of a lawful industry would generate public revenues as would the imposition of a commodities tax on sales. This is not to propose legalization of marijuana: merely that the investigation of civil forfeiture actions opens a window to its re-examination.

Conclusion

This study reveals that, for the most part, the enforcement of civil forfeiture law remains tethered to its initial ambitions. It is deployed principally in the context of the illegal drugs trade and the trade's financial undercurrents. Unlike the evocative media accounts, in none of the case files examined in this study did the forfeiture appear to be grossly disproportionate to the underlying offence. Many cases engaged multiple offences. In the case of the forfeiture of houses, or real estate, in all instances, the property was quite clearly involved in the production of significant quantities of illegal drugs. The most problematic cases concerned the forfeiture of property subject to rental agreements. Arguably, this is one of the most contentious issues presented by forfeiture as it involves the taking of property when the 'fault' lies more fully with the tenants rather than with the property owners. It seems sensible to require that property owners exercise some degree of care over their property. The cases investigated really say very little about what constitutes the exercise of sufficient care over property by property owner, sufficient in the sense that the exercise of care or responsibility would preclude the forfeiture of their interests in property when the property is misused by tenants. That dimension of civil forfeiture, the potential forfeiture of the property of wholly innocent owners, is certainly something that warrants watching. At a minimum, the study of the 100 cases suggests that the enforcement context of civil forfeiture actions merits scrutiny. Further empirical studies need to inform the developing narrative. Assessment of the legitimacy of civil forfeiture laws should be based on evidence.

Notes

1. Sunny Dhillon, 'B.C. Father Facing Civil Forfeiture Says He Wasn't Living at the Grow-op Site' *The Globe and Mail* (Vancouver, 10 November 2015) <www.theglobeandmail.com/news/british-columbia/bc-father-says-he-was-not-living-in-grow-op-home-when-pot-discovered/article2718425 6> accessed 19 July 2017; Opinion, 'The Unfairness of the Forfeiture Law' *The Globe and Mail* (Toronto, 3 September 2007) <www.theglobeandmail.com/globe-debate/the-unfairness-of-the-forfe iture-law/article1327164> accessed 19 July 2017; Marni Soupcoff, 'Ontario's Civil Forfeiture Racket' *National Post* (Toronto, 21 August 2014) <http://news.nationalpost.com/full-comment/mar ni-soupcoff-ontarios-civil-forfeiture-racket> accessed 19 July 2017; Joseph Quesnel and Kathleen Canjar, 'Civil Forfeiture Erodes Rights' *Winnipeg Free Press* (Winnipeg, 23 March 2014) <www.winnipegfreepress.com/opinion/analysis/Civil-forfeiture-laws-erode-rights-251790591.html> accessed 19 July 2017.

2. See generally, William Gilmore, *Dirty Money: The Evolution of International Measures to Counter Money Laundering and the Financing of Terrorism* (Council of Europe Publishing 2011). For consideration of global developments, see Chap. 3 (Bergstrom) in this collection.

3. Financial Action Task Force, *International Standard on Combatting Money Laundering and the Financing of Terrorism and Proliferation. FAFT Recommendations* (FAFT 2012), Recommendation 4. In 2012 non-conviction-based models of forfeiture, civil forfeiture, were added to the international standards.

4. Criminal Code (Canada) RSC 1985 c C-46, Part XII.2 (Proceeds of Crime s 462(32)—s 462(36)).

5. See, generally, Proceeds of crime (Money Laundering) and Terrorist Financing Act (Canada), SC 2000 c 17.

6. Constitution Act 1982 (Schedule B of the Canada Act 1982 (UK)) s 91(27).

7. FAFT 2012 (n 4) Recommendation 4.

8. See, for example, the Saskatchewan Minister of Justice justified forfeiture as reflecting the government's commitment to creating a hostile environment for organized crime and a device that prevented the use of property in profit-making activity and potentially violent offences: Saskatchewan, Legislative Assembly, Hansard, Mandatory Testing and Disclosure (Bodily Substances) Act (No 102), Second Reading 19 April 2005, 2570 (Hon Frank Quennell); Saskatchewan, Standing Committee on Human Services, Hansard Verbatim Report 20 17 May 2005, 285 (Hon Frank Quennell).

9. For example, Seizure of Criminal Property Act 2005 (Saskatchewan) c S 46.001, s 15. Manitoba law contained similar provision, but these were repealed in 2012; SM 2012, c 13, s 12.

10. Civil Forfeiture Act 2005 (British Columbia); Victims Restitution and Compensation Payment Act 2001 (Alberta); Seizure of Criminal Property Act 2005 (Saskatchewan); Criminal Property Forfeiture Act 2004 (Manitoba); Civil Remedies Act 2001 (Ontario); Act Respecting the Forfeiture Administration and Appropriation of Proceeds and Instruments of Unlawful Activity 2007 (Quebec); Civil Forfeiture Act 2010 (New Brunswick); Civil Forfeiture Act 2007 (Nova Scotia). For discussion, see Michelle Gallant, 'Civil Processes and Tainted Assets: Exploring Canadian Models of Forfeiture' in Colin King and Clive Walker (eds), *Dirty Assets: Emerging Issues in the Regulation of Criminal and Terrorist Assets* (Ashgate Publishing 2014).

11. See, for example, Anthony Kennedy, 'Designing a Civil Forfeiture System: A Issues List for Policymakers and Legislators' (2006) 13(2) Journal of Financial Crime 132; Michelle Gallant and Colin King, 'The Seizure of Illicit Assets: Patterns of Civil Forfeiture in Canada and Ireland' (2013) 42(1) Common Law World Review 91.

12. Manitoba Justice Annual Report 2013–2014, 25. Amounts forfeit south of the border are much more impressive. In 2014, forfeitures pursuant to United States federal law totaled in excess of $4 billion. However, this data is not preclusive to civil actions but includes the forfeitures obtained post-conviction (criminal forfeiture); United States Department of Justice, FY 2014 Total Net Deposits to the Fund by State of Deposit <www.justice.gov/afp/reports-congress/fy-2014-total-net-deposits-fund-state-deposit> accessed 19 July 2017.

13. British Columbia Ministry of Justice, 2012/13 Annual Service Plan Report, 12   <www.bcbudget.gov.bc.ca/Annual_Reports/2012_2013/pdf/ministry/jag.pdf> accessed 19 July 2017.

14. Ontario Ministry of the Attorney General, Civil Forfeiture in Ontario, September 24, 2013 <http://news.ontario.ca/mag/en/2013/09/civil-forfeiture-in-ontario-33.html> accessed 19 July 2017. An additional $24.5 million was held pending completion of forfeiture proceedings.

15. Ministry of Justice, Civil Forfeiture Office, Sum of Unlawful Activities by Region—All Police Referrals (dataset) <http://catalogue.data.gov.bc.ca/dataset/sum-of-unlawful-activities-by-region-all-police-referrals> accessed 19 July 2017.

16. 73% of Ontario civil forfeiture actions are related to drugs offences: Ministry of the Attorney General, Civil Forfeiture in Ontario 2007, An Update on the Civil Remedies Act 2001, 11.

17. Often assessments of the effectiveness of regulation define effectiveness as a function of the amounts forfeit. Effectiveness is a measure of how well regulatory regimes manage to divest property tainted by crime. Potential legislative improvements are predicated on facilitating that divesture: Elaine Koren, *Civil Forfeiture Regimes in Canada and Internationally: Literature Review* (Public Safety Canada 2013).

18. Nkechi Taifa, 'Civil Forfeiture v Civil Liberties' (1994) 39(1/2) New York Law School Review 95; Anthony Gray, 'Forfeiture Provisions and the Criminal/Civil Divide' (2012) 15(1) New Criminal Law Review 32; Colin King, 'Using Civil Processes in Pursuit of Criminal Law Objectives: A Case Study of Non-Conviction Based Asset Forfeiture' (2012) 16(4) International Journal of Evidence and Proof 337.

19. *Whiten v Pilot Insurance Company* [2002] 1 SCR 595.

20. *United States v Ursery* 518 US 267 (1996).

21. *Austin v US* 509 US 602 (1993).

22. *Gale v Serious Organized Crime Agency* [2011] UKSC 49; *Gilligan v CAB* [2001] 4 IR 113; *Phillips v United Kingdom* ECHR 2001-VII; *Butler v United Kingdom* ECHR 2002-VI.

23. *Martineau v MNR* [2004] 3 SCR 737.

24. Ibid. paras 25–39.

25. *Chatterjee v Ontario (Attorney General)* [2009] 1 SCC 264.

26. Ibid. See also Michelle Gallant, 'Ontario (Attorney General) v $29,020 in Canadian Currency: A Comment on Proceeds of Crime and Civil Forfeiture Laws' (2006) 52(1) Criminal Law Quarterly 64.

27. Once the state showed probable cause for forfeiture, the burden shifted to the owner of the property to prove an affirmative defense. This changed with the Civil Asset Forfeiture Reform Act of 2000: Stefan Cassella, 'Establishing Probable Cause for Forfeiture in Federal Money Laundering Cases' (1994) 39(1/2) New York Law School Law Review 163; David Pimentel, 'Forfeitures Revisited: Bringing Principle to Practice in Federal Court' (2012) 13(1) Nevada Law Journal 1, 16–21.

28. David Fried, 'Rationalizing Civil Forfeiture Law' (1988) 79(2) Journal of Criminal Law and Criminology 328, 360 (Fried refers to civil forfeiture as privateering); Eric Blumenson and Eva Nilsen, 'Policing for Profit: The Drug War's Hidden Economic Agenda' (1998) 65(1) University of Chicago Law Review 35; Darpana Sheth, 'Policing for Profit: The Abuse of Forfeiture Laws' (2013) 14(3) Criminal Law & Procedure 24.

29. Ibid. For consideration in the UK context, see Chap. 22 (Alldridge) in this collection.

30. John Worrall, 'Addicted to the Drug War: The Role of Civil Asset Forfeiture as a Budgetary Necessity in Contemporary Law Enforcement' (2001) 29(3) Journal of Criminal Justice 171; Patrick Daley, 'Civil Asset Forfeiture: An Economic Analysis of Ontario and British Columbia' (2014) 5(3) Western Journal of Legal Studies 2.

31. Katherine Baicker and Mireille Jacobson, 'Finders Keepers: Forfeiture Laws, Policing Incentives and Local Budgets' (2004) Working Paper 10484 National Bureau of Economic Research 1.

32. William Carpenter, 'Reforming the Civil Drug Forfeiture Statutes: Analysis and Recommendations' (1994) 67(4) Temple Law Review 1087, 1092;

Vinesh Basdeo, 'The Legal Challenge of Criminal and Civil Asset Forfeiture in South Africa: A Comparative Analysis' (2013) 21(3) African Journal of International and Comparative Law 303, 315–320.

33. See, generally, Michelle Gallant, *Money Laundering and the Proceeds of Crime* (Edward Elgar Publishing 2005) 56–57.

34. 'Proceeds', <dictionary.com, www.dictionary.com/browse/proceeds?s=t> accessed 19 July 2017.

35. In the *United States v Santos*, the United States Supreme Court affirmed that, in the narrow context of a conviction based, in part, on the distinction between proceeds and profits, the word proceeds meant profits: 461 F 3d 886 [2008].

36. See *Bennis v Michigan* 517 US 1163 (1996) wherein the state forfeiture law did not provide an innocent owner defense.

37. Civil Remedies Act (n 11) s 7.

38. Criminal Property Forfeiture Act 2004, CCSM c C 306.

39. Enforcement of the apparatus did not fully begin until 2009. The province awaited the outcome of a constitutional challenge to Ontario's civil forfeiture instrument: *Chatterjee v Ontario* [2009] SCC 19.

40. Criminal Property Forfeiture Act (n 39) s 3(1).

41. Ibid. s 1.

42. Ibid. The definition covers property acquired directly, or indirectly, in whole or in part and includes increases in the value of property or any decreases in debt obligations.

43. Ibid.

44. Ibid.

45. Ibid. s 3(3).

46. James Maxeiner, 'Bane of American Forfeiture Law Banished at Last' (1977) 62(4) Cornell Law Review 768.

47. Criminal Property Forfeiture Act (n 39) s 7 and s 17(12).

48. Ibid. s 17(15)(2). In 2011, the Act was amended to permit 'administrative forfeitures'. When the property liable to forfeiture is less than $75,000, if potential claimants do not respond to notice of the action, forfeiture automatically ensues, eliminating the need for a full trial or any fuller determination of the relationship between the property and the alleged crime; see Ibid. ss 17(1)–17(9).

49. Ibid. s 17(13).

50. Ibid. s 16. Equally, those whose entitlements arose prior to the alleged crime may also be protected: Ibid. s 17(1).

51. Ibid. s 17(2).

52. Ibid. s 14(1). Apart from this exception, the Court is compelled, if it concludes that the property constitutes the proceeds of unlawful activity or an instrument of unlawful activity to order forfeiture.

53. See, for example, *Ontario (Attorney General) v 8477 Darlington Crescent* (2010) ONCA 363; *Mihalyko (Re)* (2012) SKCA 44; *British Columbia (Director of Civil Forfeiture) v Rai* [2011] BCJ No 241.
54. *Ontario (Attorney General) v 20 Strike Avenue* (2014) ONCA 395.
55. *British Columbia (Director of Civil Forfeiture) v Wolff* (2012) BCCA 473.
56. Criminal Property Forfeiture Act (n 39) s 18(1).
57. Ibid. s 19(4).
58. Although 100 actions were identified, information was drawn from 98. One file was eliminated because of its notoriety; another was transferred to a different judicial district. The files were examined in November 2013, April and May 2014 and December 2014.
59. The full list is on file with the author and the editors. 2009 was the first year of operation of civil forfeiture apparatus, in part because of the Supreme Court of Canada decision earlier that year to uphold the constitutional validity of such regimes.
60. A preliminary sampling in November 2013 sought to discern the kinds of recurrent information readily available in the files.
61. Some of these also involved other allegations of criminal activity though the principal basis of the forfeiture action related to illegal drugs.
62. While the possession of illegal substances was listed as an offence in a few cases, it was coupled with charges related to other offences.
63. Gabrielle Giroday, 'Province Targets Alleged Sex Offender's House' *Winnipeg Free Press* (Winnipeg, 30 December 2010) <www.winnipegfreepress.com/local/province-targets-alleged-sex-offenders-ho me-112652209.html> accessed 19 July 2017; CBC News 'Lawsuit Over Manitoba House Spurs Rights Concerns' *CBC News* (Manitoba, 30 December 2010) <www.cbc.ca/news/canada/manitoba/la wsuit-over-man-house-spurs-rights-concerns-1.950034> accessed 19 July 2017; CBC News 'Ex-Soccer Coach Pleads Guilty to Sex Charges' *CBC News* (Winnipeg, 9 July 2012) <www.cbc.ca/news /canada/manitoba/ex-soccer-coach-pleads-guilty-to-sex-charges-1.1183174> accessed 19 July 2017.
64. Civil forfeiture may be beginning to migrate beyond the profitable crime context: Travis Lupick, 'Environment and Wildlife New Areas for BC Civil Forfeitures' *Straight* (Vancouver, 11 March 2015) <www.straight.com/news/407716/environment-and-wildlife-new-areas-bc-civil-forfeitures> accessed 19 July 2017.
65. Income from illegal businesses is subject to taxation: *Regina v Poynton* [1972] 3 OR (Ontario) 727.

Michelle Gallant is a Professor of Law at the University of Manitoba, Commissioner at the Manitoba Law Reform Commission and occasional lecturer in the IALS LL.M Program. Her research, teaching and scholarship is in the areas of tax law, charity law, international law, corporate governance, money laundering regulation and bank secrecy.

24

The Difficulties of Belief Evidence and Anonymity in Practice: Challenges for Asset Recovery

Colin King

Introduction

The first wave of legal challenges to civil forfeiture in Ireland has now passed. Since its enactment in 1996, the Proceeds of Crime Act (POCA) has been unsuccessfully challenged as repugnant to the Constitution. The main two grounds of challenge have been, first, that POCA essentially formed part of the criminal law, not the civil law, and that persons affected by this legislation were deprived of criminal law safeguards such as the presumption of innocence, the standard of proof, trial by jury and the rule against double jeopardy. Second, it has also been contended that POCA violated the guarantee of private property. The Irish courts have rejected such arguments.[1] The second wave of legal challenges involves challenges to the operation or application of the Act, rather than challenges to the Act itself[2]—an area that has received scant attention in the literature to date. This chapter, then, focuses on two of the most controversial evidential provisions, namely the use of belief evidence (whereby a senior police officer or revenue official can testify that they believe that a person is in possession or control of 'proceeds of crime' worth not less than €5000) and anonymous testimony by State officials. For each of these

I would like to thank Jo Bridgeman, Jimmy Gurulé, Saskia Hufnagel, Hannah Quirk, Lindsay Stirton, Clive Walker and Dermot Walsh for their very helpful comments on previous drafts.

C. King
University of Sussex, Brighton, UK

© The Author(s) 2018
C. King et al. (eds.), *The Palgrave Handbook of Criminal and Terrorism Financing Law*,
https://doi.org/10.1007/978-3-319-64498-1_24

evidential provisions, this chapter examines the statutory framework and developments in case law. The doctrinal analysis is then followed by examination of how these evidential provisions are implemented, what safeguards apply (in both the statutory provisions themselves and how they operate in practice) and criticisms of these provisions. Ultimately, the focus of this chapter is on how, if at all, these evidential provisions impact upon the fairness and openness of proceedings, which hitherto have not been explored in the literature on POCA.

The belief evidence and anonymity provisions give rise to serious concerns, which have far wider significance than the Irish asset recovery model.[3] First, by allowing such evidence, there are limitations on open justice and natural justice.[4] How can these fundamental principles be respected when some matters relevant to the proceedings are kept secret on the basis of claims to public interest?[5] Moreover, by denying a respondent access to relevant material, these evidential provisions impact upon the fairness of the proceedings. As van Harten points out, 'The conflict of interest that is inherent in hidden government presents a major concern for adjudication because of the ways in which secrecy tends to undermine truth-seeking.'[6] Second, while the discussion in this chapter focuses on asset recovery in Ireland, it is important to stress that the Irish civil forfeiture regime is widely regarded as a model of best practice, with many jurisdictions taking their precedent from Ireland.[7] Thus, the use of both belief evidence and anonymous testimony in Irish asset recovery cases might well have wider consequences. Indeed, many jurisdictions—both common law[8] and civil law[9]—have by now adopted one form or another of non-conviction-based asset forfeiture, and steps have been taken towards an EU Directive in this regard.[10] It is clear that these evidential provisions merit further examination. As Kutz points out, in the context of secret law, 'it can be worthwhile to tease apart the problems with secret law, not just so we can understand our objections, but because by doing so, we may reveal something about the nature of law and its moral and political qualities'.[11]

There is a burgeoning literature on the first wave of legal challenges to civil forfeiture in Ireland. This literature, in the main, adopts a doctrinal approach to critique both the legislation and subsequent case law. Some commentators are complimentary,[12] others much less so.[13] A similar pattern is evident in other jurisdictions, with civil forfeiture subject to both praise[14] and condemnation.[15] Apart from a small number of notable exceptions, however (mainly in the United States),[16] there is a lack of empirical analysis of the operation of civil forfeiture in action, the 'law in action' rather than the 'law in books'. This chapter, then, explores how civil forfeiture operates in practice, drawing upon insights from experienced practitioners in the field, with particular focus on the evidential provisions under POCA.

Moreover, civil forfeiture can be seen as a further example of 'civil-ising' the criminal process[17] and the expansion of procedural hybrids to deal with different forms of undesirable behaviour[18]—what Mann describes as a 'middle-ground' system of justice.[19] There are, however, significant concerns about this resort to civil processes: in earlier work, I have criticised the circumvention of criminal procedural safeguards,[20] arguing that civil forfeiture undermines due process rights[21] and lacks legitimacy.[22] Similar criticisms have been expressed by others—in Ireland[23] and elsewhere.[24] This chapter expands upon such criticisms of civil forfeiture, going beyond the civil/criminal distinction, by focusing on evidential rules under POCA and how they apply in practice. Here too there are significant concerns as to procedural fairness, due process and a lack of legitimacy. Not only does this chapter provide an in-depth analysis of relevant statutory provisions and subsequent case law, it also delivers the first empirical analysis of the controversial powers of belief evidence and anonymity.

Methods

Semi-structured qualitative 'elite' interviews were conducted with ten practitioners,[25] with considerable expertise in POCA. Interviews lasted on average for 1 hour 40 minutes. The number, and length, of interviews allows deep insight into how POCA operates in practice—in a sense, 'giving a voice' to practitioners.[26] There are less than 30 practitioners at the Irish Bar who are actively practising in this area of law. It is difficult to estimate how many solicitors practise in this area, as POCA work tends to come to them through their expertise as criminal defence solicitors—thus every criminal defence solicitor could potentially work in this area. However, given that the number of POCA cases tends to be limited to, approximately, 10–15 each year, it is unlikely to be a large cohort.

Interviews were conducted with barristers (five), defence solicitors (two), officials from the Criminal Assets Bureau (CAB) (two) and a representative of the Irish Council for Civil Liberties (ICCL) (one). It is worth setting out the expertise of these interviewees: both INT1 and INT8 are criminal defence solicitors; INT3 and INT5 are CAB officials; INT2 is a barrister who, in POCA proceedings, mainly acts against CAB; INT4, INT6, INT7 and INT9 are barristers who, in POCA proceedings, mainly act (or previously acted) on behalf of CAB; and INT10 is an ICCL representative. Given the expert knowledge of interviewees, the interview itself was seen as 'an opportunity to have an informed discussion'.[27] The value of interviews with legal practitioners is that they allow us to explore how law operates in practice, going beyond legislation and case law to gain valuable insights from those who work at the coalface of the legal system.[28]

Belief Evidence: The Law

Perhaps the most controversial evidential provision in POCA is the use of belief evidence (often known as opinion evidence). As a general rule, witnesses are not allowed to express their opinion in criminal matters,[29] but, as Heffernan points out, '[t]he prohibition on opinion evidence is a general norm rather than an absolute, categorical rule'.[30] The Irish parliament has enacted a number of exceptions to this rule—section 8 of POCA being one such statutory exception.[31] Section 8(1) permits a senior police officer or revenue official to state his/her 'belief' that a person is in possession or control of specified property that constitutes or stems from proceeds of crime and that the value of that property is not less than €5000.[32] If the court is satisfied that there are reasonable grounds for that belief, then it shall be admitted as evidence.

In *FJMcK v GWD*,[33] McCracken J helpfully set out a seven-step approach to belief evidence under section 8:

1. The trial judge should consider the position under section 8. This includes consideration of the belief evidence of a member or authorised officer[34] and also any other evidence that might point to reasonable grounds for that belief.
2. If the trial judge is satisfied that there are reasonable grounds for such a belief, then the he judge should make a specific finding that that belief is evidence.
3. Only then should the judge consider the substantive criteria set down in the Act. In this, the he judge should consider the evidence tendered by the plaintiff.
4. The judge should consider whether the evidence establishes a *prima facie* case against the respondent. If it does, the onus then shifts to the respondent.
5. The trial judge must then consider the evidence introduced by the respondent.
6. If the judge is satisfied that the respondent has discharged the onus of proof then the proceedings should be dismissed.
7. If the judge is not so satisfied, the he judge should then proceed to consider whether there would be a serious risk of injustice.

A significant criticism of belief evidence provisions relates to corroboration of such evidence. Strictly speaking, there is no requirement of corroboration before belief evidence can be relied upon. In *Gilligan v CAB*, McGuinness J expressed the view that 'a court should be slow to make orders under s.3 on the basis of such evidence without other corroborating evidence'.[35] The learned judge did not, however, completely rule out such a possibility; she merely opined that a court *should be slow* to do so. Indeed, the wording of section 3 is significant here:

> Where, on application to it in that behalf by a member, an authorised officer or the Criminal Assets Bureau, it appears to the Court, on evidence tendered by the applicant, **which may consist of or include evidence admissible by virtue of section 8**... (Emphasis added)[36]

This statement would appear to suggest that the legislature envisaged the courts granting an order under section 3 even where belief evidence is the sole plank of the applicant's case. Indeed, in *FMcK v TH and JH*,[37] the Supreme Court emphasised that, so long as there are reasonable grounds, belief evidence, in itself, would suffice to ground an order under section 3 if there were no evidence to the contrary or if, as happened in that case, the court rejected the evidence of the respondent.[38] In essence, therefore, on the face of the legislation, a case may be *proved* on the basis of unsubstantiated allegations, often from unidentified or unidentifiable sources, with either a Chief Superintendent of An Garda Síochána (Garda—the Irish police force) or an authorised revenue official effectively acting as a decider of fact.

Where belief evidence is admitted under section 8, it is up to the court to determine what weight ought to be attached to such evidence.[39] It is important, though, that the courts do not simply accept such evidence unquestioningly. The danger is that the courts will too readily accept the belief evidence of a senior police officer or revenue official.[40]

No indication is given in the legislation as to the weight that ought to be attached to belief evidence. That weight will depend on a variety of factors such as, *inter alia*, the person who expressed the opinion, the circumstances in which it was expressed and whether the opinion was challenged or not. If belief evidence is not undermined in cross-examination, that can create a *prima facie* case against the respondent. It will then be up to the respondent to introduce credible evidence as to how the property in question came into his possession or control.[41] The difficulty, though, is that the respondent may be put to proof where the only evidence against him is belief evidence, giving such evidence a higher status than it merits.[42]

This difficulty is exacerbated when belief evidence is based on hearsay. The rationales for the rule against hearsay are well known: it is preferable that witnesses give oral testimony, under oath or affirmation, about events that they directly witnessed. Witnesses can then be cross-examined and their demeanour can be assessed during their testimony.[43] Yet, in *FJMcK v GWD*, it was said that '[e]vidence of belief under section 8 does not have to be direct. The value of belief evidence is not diminished by being based on hearsay'.[44] In *Murphy v GM, PB, PC Ltd.*, O'Higgins J stated '[t]he basis of many beliefs is information gathered from different sources some of which frequently will be based on hearsay. It is illogical to conclude that it is unreasonable to accept such information.'[45] And in *Byrne v Farrell and Farrell,* Feeney J stated '[w]hile s.8 of the 1996 Act permits the introduction of hearsay evidence it is the case that that evidence is not conclusive and is open to challenge by a respondent'.[46] Feeney J did acknowledge, though, that '[t]he real ability of a defendant to challenge hearsay evidence is a significant factor in whether the Court should rely on such evidence'.[47]

In *Murphy,* Peart J said 'the hearsay evidence given on an application under s. 3 of the Act of 1996 is not given as proof of its content but rather in order to demonstrate that there are reasonable grounds for the belief evidence given. It can be rebutted by the defendant if he/she chooses to call evidence in that regard. It can be cross-examined in order to try and dislodge it or at least diminish the weight that the Court should properly attribute to it. But it cannot be said, and no authority has been cited in support of the proposition, that it is inadmissible evidence.'[48] Peart J went on to note that an application for an order under sections 2 or 3 of POCA can consist of or include belief evidence under section 8—so long as there are reasonable grounds for that belief.[49] It was said: 'There is no reason in my view in principle or otherwise why the basis for that belief evidence cannot consist of information that may have come to the applicant officer from a third party, or which is otherwise outside his own direct knowledge, without the necessity of that third party coming to court to give that evidence directly in the normal way.'[50]

The difficulty in challenging belief evidence is further exacerbated where the respondent does not know the source of the belief tendered under section 8. Where a witness tendering belief evidence under section 8 claims privilege as to the source of that belief, it is virtually impossible to challenge that evidence.[51] Such a claim of privilege is often said to be necessary to protect informants.[52] But, as Farrell points out in relation to belief evidence in anti-terrorism legislation, 'The result is that the court is effectively receiving hearsay evidence from anonymous sources and about unknown events and is totally dependent on the Chief Superintendent's assessment of the reliability of those sources.'[53] He goes on to say: 'The accused person cannot defend him or herself against allegations of involvement in unspecified criminal conduct made by persons who cannot be cross-examined and whose character or motives cannot be challenged, despite the obvious dangers of relying on evidence from informants—unreliability, spite, desire to cover their own tracks etc.'[54] It is not unusual for a claim of privilege to be made in relation to belief evidence under section 8 of POCA. While a respondent does, of course, have a right to cross-examine the witness, in practice there can be restrictions on such cross-examination which, it is suggested, significantly impact upon a respondent's ability to challenge belief evidence.

One of the few cases where belief evidence was not accepted in a proceeds of crime application (indeed, the only reported case) is *Byrne v Farrell and Farrell*.[55] Even then, the belief evidence was not admitted simply due to the peculiar circumstances in that case. CAB claimed that specified property and money represented proceeds of crime by the late Patrick Farrell (the deceased husband and father of the defendants). Patrick Farrell was murdered in 1997; it was almost 3 years later that POCA proceedings were commenced, and over 14 years had elapsed between the date of that murder and the current proceedings being heard. Furthermore, a number of the properties in question had been acquired in the 1970s and 1980s. In those circumstances, it would be extremely difficult for the respondents to rebut belief evidence. Inevitably, this judgment might lead proponents of belief evidence to point out that the courts are demonstrably strict in deciding whether or not to admit belief evidence. However, that would be to take this judgment too readily at face value. Rather, the result in *Farrell* is the exception, not the norm: it was only the particular circumstances of the case, and the 'real, special and unique problems'[56] posed, that resulted in the belief evidence being excluded.

The admission of belief evidence is clearly controversial. But, as we have seen with the seeming sole exception of *Farrell*—the courts are generally receptive to such evidence. And, belief evidence has been found to be compatible with the Constitution.[57] In *GM/Gilligan*, section 8(1) was challenged on the ground that there was no equality of arms between the parties given that the applicant (usually the CAB or the Chief Bureau Officer (CBO) of CAB) could rely on such evidence whereas the respondent could not: that argument was unsuccessful. It was held that the respondent 'will normally be the persons in possession or control of the property and should be in a position to give evidence to the court as to its provenance without calling in aid opinion evidence'.[58] The courts have, however, recognised the need to exercise caution as to what has been described as 'the very great potential unfairness'[59] of admitting belief evidence. Indeed, the Supreme Court has stressed that such evidence is 'capable of gross abuse, and capable of undermining the ability of a person against whom they are deployed to defend himself by cross-examination'.[60] That, however, has not stopped the almost routine admission of belief evidence in POCA proceedings.

Belief Evidence in Practice

One of the dangers of belief evidence is that the courts will be overly reliant on law enforcement officials—to justify the use of belief evidence and to present such evidence—and may become conditioned to favour not only the admissibility of such evidence but also its reliability.[61] In light of such concerns, we now consider how belief evidence operates in practice, focusing on, first, the role of the CBO of CAB and, second, difficulties in challenging such evidence.

The CBO is the head of CAB. The CBO is appointed by, and accountable to, the Garda Commissioner. The CBO is appointed from the ranks of Chief Superintendent of An Garda Síochána.[62] Despite not being set out in legislation,[63] in practice it tends to be the CBO who tenders belief evidence (INT2; INT3; INT6; INT7; INT9). The rationale behind this practice is to make the CBO accountable. While some practitioners found it reassuring that accountability was personalised in this way (INT7), others noted that this makes it difficult to challenge belief evidence. As INT2 stated: 'he has a position of high trust and authority and so to challenge that is a very difficult thing to do'. This practice can be contrasted with belief evidence in other types of cases (such as the offence of membership of a criminal organisation or in bail applications) where there are a number of senior Gardai who would tender such evidence.

Given that the CBO tends to be in post for a lengthy period, coupled with the fact that a single judge is usually 'ticketed' to hear POCA cases, there is a danger that such evidence will be accepted all too readily. Indeed—particularly where informer privilege is pleaded—the court (and the respondent) is restricted in looking into the source of the CBO's belief.[64] INT5, however, rejected such criticism stressing that the courts do scrutinise belief evidence to ascertain whether there are reasonable grounds for that belief. Some proponents did recognise potential difficulties with the practice of one person tendering belief evidence but stressed that the belief evidence provisions are used appropriately (INT9). Others, however, disagreed, stressing that the same person regularly tendering belief evidence to the same judge is problematic and that this is not a good procedure (INT10).

A recurring criticism is that it is very difficult to challenge belief evidence. Indeed, INT8 stated: 'It's impossible to challenge.' INT8 described a situation where she represented a person suspected of, but never charged with, drug offences. INT8 took exception to the approach adopted by CAB, where the grounding affidavit for the proceeds of crime application named that person as being the person responsible for at least six murders. However, that person had never even been questioned by the police in relation to drug offences nor murder. INT8 stated that she had no issue with CAB using relevant powers to target illicit assets, in appropriate cases, but: 'I do have a problem with them putting up affidavits to say that they are responsible for murders because it has no relevance to the proceeds of crime application.' She further noted the futility of challenging the CBO's evidence ('a fairly pointless exercise') as the CBO will claim informer privilege.

Before considering informer privilege, however, it is important to consider the issue of corroboration. As seen earlier, there is no requirement of corroboration before belief evidence can be relied upon. And one CAB interviewee (INT5) acknowledged that an application under POCA could succeed on the basis of belief evidence alone. Notwithstanding, it would appear that a more stringent approach is adopted in practice. A number of interviewees stressed the importance of corroborating evidence (INT3; INT4; INT7; INT9).[65] INT7 referred to analogous criminal prosecutions for membership of an illegal organisation, where belief evidence played a significant role, and said that even in those cases—where a conviction can be secured in the absence of corroborating evidence[66]—the practice from prosecutors was to 'almost always insist on corroboration—substantive evidence'. A similar practice, she suggested, developed with POCA cases.[67] Similar sentiments were expressed by INT9:

> So, while on the face of it you can read it and say "oh my God, you can get an order on the back of just a fella's word", in practice the courts, in my experience, were always careful to ensure that there was adequate substantiation for any opinion.

INT4 went so far as to say that 'almost by definition there is corroboration in every proceeds of crime application'. While INT3 stated 'What is also important to say is that it is not available uncorroborated—there are again significant safeguards in that it cannot be used unless corroborated', this statement does not appear consistent with judicial dicta (discussed above). Yet, INT3's statement apparently reflects how the law is applied in practice. It was further emphasised that the court must be satisfied that there are reasonable grounds for the belief (INT5; INT9).[68]

Proponents went further and stressed that belief evidence: should not be over-emphasised (INT3), is there to assist the court (INT3), cannot fill an evidential gap (INT3), cannot prop up a weak case (INT3), maps out CAB's case (INT5), can be ignored by the court (INT5), is of secondary or tertiary importance (INT7), is a confirmation of pre-existing evidence (INT7), and is merely an opinion, backed up with supporting evidence, that then calls for an explanation from a respondent (INT9). There was criticism, however, from defence practitioners interviewed. They contended that belief evidence undermines the presumption of innocence (INT1) and the information relied upon would be inadmissible in a criminal case and would not meet the criminal standard of proof (INT8: 'it's hearsay on hearsay on hearsay'). Thus, it was suggested that it is 'far from a level playing field' (INT8).

The difficulty in challenging belief evidence is most evident where the respondent does not know the source of the belief tendered under section 8. For example, where the belief is based on information provided by an informer,[69] then the respondent will struggle to challenge the informer's reliability without knowing the identity of that person. Moreover, as that informer is not called to testify, it is not possible for the court to observe that person's demeanour during adverse cross-examination.[70] This begs the questions: can a respondent receive a fair hearing when information is kept from that person thereby impacting upon that person's ability to properly challenge the case against him/her?[71]

While some proponents did acknowledge difficulties in challenging belief evidence (INT3: 'I'll accept that, I accept that there's a disadvantage'), it was suggested that difficulties are offset by procedural safeguards. It was noted that the courts approach informer evidence with caution (INT9), that a case will not be brought solely on the basis of belief evidence and a claim of informer privilege (INT4), and that it is possible to challenge such evidence, by cross-examining the CBO, even without knowing the identity of an informer (INT3). Such supposed safeguards, however, are inadequate.

The respondent will be hampered in challenging evidence against him; thus, the court will not hear additional information and arguments that might otherwise have come to light. Indeed, 'without any opportunity for confrontation, individuals subject to proceedings that use secret evidence are forced to prove their innocence in the face of the anonymous slurs of unseen and unsworn informers'.[72] Critics argue that withholding relevant information undermines due process and severely restricts a respondent in challenging evidence against him/her. To say, for example, that a respondent does have the opportunity to cross-examine the person tendering belief evidence fails to recognise the difficulties in undermining belief evidence when privilege is claimed, as INT8 stated:

> That's not a great safeguard. You ask the guy a question and he says I can't answer that because the information is confidential. That's not a great safeguard.

Anonymity: The Law

The CAB Act contains a number of provisions in relation to investigatory powers, including provision for anonymity of non-Garda bureau officers and other members of staff of the Bureau.[73] This includes the granting of anonymity when giving evidence in court. On application by the CBO under the CAB Act, 1996, s.10(7), the court may grant anonymity if satisfied that there are reasonable grounds in the public interest to do so.[74]

The statutory provisions provide that anonymity can include restrictions on the circulation of affidavits or certificates; the deletion from affidavits or certificates of the name and address of the Bureau official; or the giving of evidence in the hearing, but not the sight, of any person. This power was challenged in *CAB v PS*,[75] as being repugnant to the Constitution and the European Convention of Human Rights. More specifically, it was contended that such anonymity offended the guarantee of equality before the law and the administration of justice in public. While *PS* concerned an assessment for tax, the decision equally applies to proceedings under POCA. In that case, the CBO had made an application for anonymity to be granted to a revenue official (as a Bureau Officer). The grounds for this application were summarised as follows:

> his evidence was that if anonymity was not afforded he had a concern for the safety of that Officer. The Defendant in that witness's belief is involved with persons involved in organised crime and if he became aware of the identity of the Officer he could transmit it to other persons. One of the traits of organised crime is that they utilise intimidation of witnesses. Such intimidation would hinder the gathering of evidence against persons involved in organised crime. The Defendant did not lead evidence to contest the existence of the belief. There is a public interest that crime should be investigated and criminals punished: there is a public interest in persons who derive assets from criminal activity being deprived of the benefit of the same.[76]

It was also noted that the defendant could have introduced evidence as to the source of his assets but failed to do so. Further, it was said that the court would have to balance any order for anonymity against the effect that such an order would have on the defendant in presenting his case. In this instance, Finnegan P concluded '[on] the basis of Chief Superintendent McKenna's evidence I am satisfied that it was reasonable to grant anonymity and that there was no impediment to the Defendant presenting his defence resulting from the anonymity and indeed no such impediment was urged upon me'.[77]

However, the granting of anonymity to a State official—on the ground that a respondent is 'involved with persons involved in organised crime'—leaves a distinct sense of unease. That is not to say that anonymity ought never be afforded; to date, however, the courts have been too quick to accede to a request for anonymity. The approach adopted in *PS*—essentially granting anonymity on the basis of a form of guilt by association—runs counter to the principles of open justice and natural justice.

In *PS*, Finnegan P also stated: 'I am satisfied that the provisions of the [Criminal Assets Bureau Act 1996] section 10 operate in special and limited cases within the meaning of the Constitution.'[78] He emphasised the safeguard that the judge must be satisfied that there were reasonable grounds in the public interest before granting anonymity and went on to say:

> It is conceivable that in a particular case the grant of anonymity might work an injustice: however the fact that the operation of the section might work an injustice does not render the provision unconstitutional and a Defendant has the safeguard that in the event that the operation of the section worked an injustice then the operation of the section, although not the section itself, would be unconstitutional. The Court in considering the constitutionality of a statutory provision will assume that the same will be operated in a constitutional manner.[79]

In this instance, it was noted that no evidence was led before the court to suggest that section 10 worked an injustice or operated unfairly against the defendant; thus, it was held that that provision did not infringe Article 40 of the Constitution. Specifically in relation to Article 40.1 of the Constitution ('All citizens shall, as human persons, be held equal before the law'), Finnegan P acknowledged that the granting of anonymity in this instance does result in the defendant being treated differently before the law but that that treatment cannot in any way be related to the defendant's dignity as a human person; thus, section 10 of the CAB Act was held not to infringe Article 40.1.[80]

The anonymity provisions were also applied in *CAB v PMcS*[81] (another revenue case), which concerned anonymity of two revenue officials who had signed a tax assessment on behalf of the CAB.[82] In that instance, the CBO:

> told the Court that it was his belief that in the event of the identity of the two officers becoming known, it would hinder the work of the Bureau in the general sense that other enquiries would be affected if the people in question were known. He said it would be difficult to get suitable applicants to come and work in the Bureau if their identity was not protected. He further gave evidence of his belief that the Defendant was a person suspected of drug dealing in Cork, an

activity which by its very nature was likely to pose safety and security risks to Bureau officials if their identity became known, although he was not aware of any specific threats in the instant case. He based his belief on information supplied to him by Drug Squad Officers from Cork and investigations carried out in the Bureau since 1996.[83]

In granting anonymity, Kearns J based his decision on the opinion that 'the efficient functioning of the Bureau required anonymity for Bureau officers'.[84] Kearns J went on to say:

> I therefore did not need to rely on the separate ground advanced by Chief Superintendent McKenna for granting anonymity, namely, his belief derived from contact with members of the Drug Squad that the Defendant is actively involved in drug dealing, an activity which of its nature suggests safety concerns for Bureau officers whose identity is not protected. I should say, however, and in my ruling so held, that for the limited purpose of S.10(7) of the 1996 Act and bearing in mind that the objectives of the Bureau extend to "suspected" criminal activity, that hearsay would be admissible to establish "reasonable grounds in the public interest" where no evidence to the contrary was led.[85]

Similarly, in *CAB v Craft and McWatt*,[86] an order of anonymity was granted pursuant to section 10(7) 'following evidence from Detective Inspector Byrne that he would be concerned for the safety of and could not rule out threats to the Revenue Officers of the Bureau if their names were disclosed'.[87] Thus, the approach of the courts in deciding whether or not to grant an order of anonymity has echoed discussion of anonymity provisions when POCA was at the Bill stage in the Oireachtas: for example, Deputy Róisin Shortall stated: 'They are ordinary people, many with families, who understandably fear for their safety. In many ways it has been unfair and unrealistic to expect people in the Revenue Commissioners to get involved with these dangerous people.'[88] Minister Quinn stated: 'We cannot expect them to be heroes on behalf of the State. That is not fair. It is not reasonable or practicable. One protection we can give them is anonymity, and it is essential.'[89] There are, however, a number of concerns with this approach, which are explored in the next section.

Anonymity in Practice

Anonymity gives rise to a number of concerns. It is a fundamental feature of the administration of justice that the trial process should be subject to public scrutiny and that witnesses tender evidence in public. This is crucial to maintaining public confidence in the legitimacy of the system. Where the trial process resorts to accepting evidence tendered anonymously:

> confidence in the integrity and impartiality of the judicial fact-finding process is diminished and doubt over whether justice has prevailed in any particular case will inevitably arise and be extremely difficult, if not impossible to dispel.[90]

The courts ought to be on guard to protect against the erosion of a fundamental aspect of the administration of justice,[91] yet it appears that the courts have become rather conditioned to meekly accept applications for anonymous testimony.

Notwithstanding such concern, a number of interviewees did come down heavily in support of the anonymity provisions under the CAB Act due to the nature of crime, and the people, that CAB investigates (INT5), concerns for the safety of Bureau officials (INT7), the capacity of serious criminals to threaten State officials (INT9) and the composition of the Bureau itself, that is a small unit with a relatively small number of people (INT9). It was said that anonymity is 'fundamentally important' (INT5). Others, while being supportive of CAB/POCA, were indifferent: INT4 opined that anonymity should be an operational matter for CAB, while INT6 stated that she did not have any particular view on anonymity or whether it was needed. Other interviewees, however, were critical of the anonymity provisions. It was said that anonymity is 'over the top' (INT1; INT2), on the grounds that the names of other officials (e.g. solicitors, police officers) in CAB proceedings are not withheld, so why is there a need for anonymity for some officials (INT1) and that POCA actions are not confined to serious crime (INT2: 'but the vast majority of cases would be to do with people who are, say, market vendors or, (*trails off*)'). INT8 was particularly scathing about the anonymity provisions: 'I think it's preposterous.'

That a State official need not be identified where he acts in writing, gives evidence in court proceedings or where he swears an affidavit gives rise to significant concerns as to transparency, accountability and equality between the parties.[92] In what types of situation, then, might the courts grant anonymity? As seen in the cases of *PS*, *McS* and *Craft*, discussed above, anonymity has been granted on the basis of concerns for the safety of bureau officials, the efficient functioning of CAB investigations and the people with whom the respondent associates. These reasons have been deemed to be 'reasonable grounds in the public interest' to grant anonymity.[93] However, the approach of the courts—in all too easily acceding to requests for anonymity—leaves a distinct sense of unease. This concern was acknowledged by some proponents

(INT7: 'Certainly at a policy level, you're right to be uneasy about whether that's an appropriate approach'), but it was nonetheless suggested that anonymity represents 'a proportionate balancing of the interests involved' (INT7):

> bring it back to brass tax, what tended to happen was the individual would be in court, the anonymous official would get into the witness box, be visible—not behind a screen or anything like that—be visible to the cross-examining defence counsel and so on, and to the judge, so their demeanour could be observed and all that stuff. So, there was no handicap in terms of, you know, your concern would be if somebody is behind a screen, then you don't know who the hell they are; are they who they say they are; what's their demeanour like. Then you're kind of going, "well, that's a bit Kafkaesque" maybe. But if they're there and all you're doing is saying that their name shouldn't be published in a judgment or in the newspapers because if they do, and word gets back out to potentially dangerous criminals, that could be dangerous for them. It's a balancing of interests. I mean, the case takes place in open court, so it's in public, there are reporting restrictions, there are anonymity restrictions for the purposes of the judgment and court orders, but that's probably a proportionate balancing of the interests involved.

Others (INT4) argued that a respondent will not be disadvantaged by not knowing the identity of a tax official, for example. Indeed, INT5 went further and said that CAB encourages media not to report the names of Garda officials as well—'there's no good reason for doing it'—and that naming of Garda officials 'does cause family difficulties'.

In relation to the safety of non-Garda officials, INT10 expressed the view that anonymity might properly be granted to anyone who might need it in order to make the trial effective, once the defence rights can be upheld with anonymity in place (e.g. effective cross-examination, authority to challenge an application for anonymity). Ultimately for her, whether anonymity should be granted would 'depend on the case'. Her views were heavily influenced on the legislation being used against the serious players of organised crime, what was described as 'the Mr. Big's'. (INT10: 'if you are going after a Mr Big …in certain circumstances it could absolutely be reasonable for a social welfare official to remain anonymous. I don't think they would testify otherwise'.)

Significantly, though, the powers under POCA are not restricted to organised crime-type cases. While the legislation was enacted against a backdrop of concern as to such crime,[94] it can be used against any type of crime so long as the statutory conditions (e.g. the €5000 threshold) are satisfied.[95] Moreover, notwithstanding comments in support of anonymity, affording anonymity to a State official, acting as such, still leaves a sense of unease[96]—as both INT1 and INT2 opined 'It's a bit over the top.' This unease is amplified in the case of an official of what is, essentially, a policing body.[97]

It is not appropriate that anonymity be granted simply on the grounds that a person is suspected of serious criminality. Even less so, is it justifiable on the grounds that a person is 'involved with persons involved in organised crime'?[98] At a minimum, there ought to be an assessment as to the actual threat posed by the person against whom proceedings have been taken.[99] As Andersen states, 'anonymity should be restricted to cases with a manifest aspect of necessity'.[100] According to Costigan and Thomas:

> The granting of anonymity to state agents should be on the basis of necessity, rather than convenience, with the court's decision being made on the provision of evidence as to the level of risk to each individual seeking such protection.[101]

The danger with how the anonymity provisions have been applied is that they can become almost routinised in use. After outlining the rationale underpinning the anonymity provisions, INT9 stated: 'as a matter of policy, I don't think it's necessarily a bad thing but, like all these things, you've just got to be very careful how it applies in practice'. She continued:

> And there probably was an extent to which it became a bit of a default, and it seems to me that you've got be guarded against that; it has to be demonstrated in any given case as to why a particular official needs anonymity. Because, our justice is administered under the constitution, in public and, as a general principle, people shouldn't have the immunity of anonymity if they're going in to give evidence.

INT10 did note that perhaps more stringent requirements are needed before an anonymity order should be granted.

A further issue with the anonymity provisions under the CAB Act is that there are peculiar difficulties when an anonymous witness is actually a State official. Indeed, that official will likely have been involved at the investigative stage in preparing the case against the respondent. In an analogous situation, concerning the tendering of evidence anonymously by police officers, the Strasbourg Court has recognised:

> their position is to some extent different from that of a disinterested witness or a victim. They owe a general duty of obedience to the State's executive authorities and usually have links with the prosecution; for these reasons alone their use as anonymous witnesses should be resorted to only in exceptional circumstances.

In addition, it is in the nature of things that their duties, particularly in the case of arresting officers, may involve giving evidence in open court.[102]

Bureau officers should not fall within the ambit of 'disinterested' witnesses: they are acting as agents of the State, in a law enforcement capacity. It is difficult to see how they could be regarded as a disinterested party to proceedings initiated by CAB, particularly where they have been involved in the investigation leading to such proceedings. Non-Garda bureau officers work alongside Garda officials and they are entrusted with policing powers. As such, they ought to be subject to checks and balances that apply to members of Garda.

Conclusion

It is widely recognised that natural justice is now 'under sustained attack throughout the common law world'.[103] In this chapter, the focus has been on how 'secrecy' (specifically in the context of controversial evidential provisions in POCA) has negative consequences for natural justice. There are many reasons to criticise secrecy[104] or, to put it another way, why openness and transparency is important. Such reasons include those based on historical justifications, catharsis reasons, an educative effect of publicity, the role of the public-as-a-control, enhancing fact-finding, publicity as a form of accountability, enabling a defendant to properly participate in proceedings and ensuring that an adverse judgment can properly be seen as an expression of public condemnation.[105] Indeed, public justice has been described as 'fundamental to the recodifications of political power that established the modern state'.[106]

Looking beyond the proceeds of the crime context, there is a tension between procedural fairness and transparency, on the one hand, and the desire to keep certain matters secret, on the other, in ongoing debates relating to, *inter alia*, secret evidence and closed material procedures,[107] anonymous witnesses (both in terrorism[108] and in non-terrorism cases[109]), warrantless surveillance[110] and special advocates,[111] to name but a few. And as Appleby points out, the greater weight afforded to secrecy is:

> explicable by reference to the fact that the protection of procedural fairness is a fundamentally deontological exercise, where the consequences of breach are not readily apparent and can be more easily dismissed if considered unlikely to change the final result. In contrast, the protection of state secrecy is a fundamentally consequentialist exercise, where the courts can focus on the potentially disastrous consequences of failing to protect national security or police operations for the community.[112]

In the context of civil forfeiture proceedings under POCA, the use of belief evidence ignores the key point that evidence must be capable of withstanding scrutiny from the other side, and the person best placed to challenge such evidence is the respondent. To allow a State official to selectively choose information, and to form a belief on the basis of such information, undermines the notion of an adversarial contest. To permit that to be done without identifying the source of that belief (as where informer privilege is claimed) further undermines ideals of procedural fairness and transparency. The allowing of anonymous testimony reinforces concerns as to secrecy in POCA proceedings. Moreover, resorting to such evidence on grounds of expediency, rather than any demonstrated necessity, runs counter to principles of open justice. Ultimately, the belief evidence and anonymity provisions lead to the view that the scales are firmly weighed in favour of the State and that equality of arms between the parties is conveniently sidelined.

Of course proponents disagree with this assessment; instead they proclaim that such evidence accords with principles of procedural fairness, pointing to the use of similar provisions in other contexts (particularly the anti-terrorism framework) in support of their stance. However, that such evidential rules have been used in other contexts does not necessarily lend support to their use in POCA proceedings. Indeed, such evidential rules have been criticised in terrorism trials.[113] Moreover, in (criminal) terrorism trials, the use of such evidential rules is offset by the higher standard of proof that must be met before a defendant is convicted. In POCA proceedings, the standard of proof is the civil standard. It is no answer to say that a respondent in POCA proceedings does not face a loss of liberty; there are serious consequences of an adverse judgment in POCA proceedings, not least the loss of property and stigma. If anything, the use of such controversial evidential provisions lends support to the argument that a higher standard of proof ought to be required in POCA proceedings.[114]

To prevent any suspicion that the CAB has abused its powers, procedural fairness and open and natural justice are essential to maintain confidence in the system.[115] The Irish proceeds of crime legislation, and the multi-agency CAB, are widely recognised as models of best practice.[116] Many other jurisdictions are influenced and guided by the Irish model.[117] It is essential then that the Irish model should maintain stringent standards in how it operates; however, that has not proved to be the case as regards the belief evidence and anonymity provisions. Moreover, the deferential approach of the courts is problematic, for example, it 'opens the door not simply to intentional abuse but also to unintended error or misrepresentation'.[118] The undermining of procedural fairness and open justice sends out the wrong message. Not only do the belief evidence and anonymity provisions leave proceedings open to question in the eyes of a respondent, more widely they also undermine the confidence in, and the reputation of, the Irish proceeds of crime model.

Notes

1. The leading judgment is *Murphy v GM, PB, PC Ltd., GH; and Gilligan v CAB* [2001] 4 IR 113. This case was an appeal from separate High Court decisions in *Gilligan v CAB* [1998] 3 IR 185 and *Murphy v GM, PB, PC Ltd.* [1999] IEHC 5.
2. I thank Ben O'Floinn BL for this description of 'waves' of legal challenge, when discussing POCA at the conference 'Confiscation and Recovery of Criminal Assets' (Dublin, 12 April 2013).
3. See Greg Martin, Rebecca Scott Bray, and Miiko Kumar (eds), *Secrecy, Law and Society* (Routledge 2015); JUSTICE, 'Secret Evidence: A JUSTICE Report' (2009) <https://2bquk8cdew6192tsu41lay8t-wpengine.netdna-ssl.com/wp-content/uploads/2015/07/Secret-Evidence-10-June-2009.pdf> accessed 10 April 2017.
4. The terms 'open justice' and 'natural justice' are often used interchangeably by some authors; however, there are distinctions between them. These distinctions are teased out in Joseph Jaconelli, *Open Justice: A Critique of the Public Trial* (OUP 2002) 29ff. For further consideration of the value of open justice, see Matthew Simpson, *Open Justice and the English Criminal Process* Unpublished PhD Thesis (University of Nottingham 2008).
5. See Adam Tomkins, 'Justice and Security in the United Kingdom' (2014) 47(3) Israel Law Review 305.
6. Gus Van Harten, 'Weaknesses of Adjudication in the Face of Secret Evidence' (2009) 13(1) International Journal of Evidence and Proof 1, 10.
7. Anthony Kennedy, 'Designing a Civil Forfeiture System: An Issues List for Policymakers and Legislators' (2006) 13(2) Journal of Financial Crime 132.
8. Notable examples include Australia, the United Kingdom and the United States.
9. Notable examples include Bulgaria, Italy and Romania.
10. See Chap. 17 (Maugeri) in this collection.
11. Christopher Kutz, 'Secret Law and the Value of Publicity' (2009) 22(2) Ratio Juris 197, 199.
12. See Francis Cassidy, 'Targeting the Proceeds of Crime: An Irish Perspective' in Theodore Greenberg and others, *Stolen Asset Recovery: A Good Practices Guide for Non-Conviction Based Asset Forfeiture* (World Bank 2009); Shane Murphy, 'Tracing the Proceeds of Crime: Legal and Constitutional Implications' (1999) 9(2) Irish Criminal Law Journal 160.

13. See Colin King, 'Civil Forfeiture in Ireland—Two Decades of the Proceeds of Crime Act and the Criminal Assets Bureau' in Katalin Ligeti and Michele Simonato, *Chasing Criminal Money: Challenges and Perspectives on Asset Recovery in the EU* (Hart Publishing 2017); Liz Campbell, 'Theorising Asset Forfeiture in Ireland' (2007) 71(5) Journal of Criminal Law 441.

14. See Brittany Brooks, 'Misunderstanding Civil Forfeiture: Addressing Misconceptions About Civil Forfeiture with a Focus on the Florida Contraband Forfeiture Act' (2014) 69(1) University of Miami Law Review 321 (United States); Alan Bacarese and Gavin Sellar, 'Civil Asset Forfeiture in Practice' in Jon Petter Rui and Ulrich Sieber (eds), *Non-Conviction-Based Confiscation in Europe* (Duncker & Humblot 2015) 211 (UK). In this collection, see Chap. 18 (Cassella).

15. See Zaiton Hamin and others, 'When Property is the Criminal: Confiscating Proceeds of Money Laundering and Terrorist Financing in Malaysia' (2015) 31 Procedia Economics and Finance 789 (Malaysia); Annemarie Bridy, 'Carpe Omnia: Civil Forfeiture in the War on Drugs and the War on Piracy' (2014) 46(3) Arizona State Law Journal 683 (United States). In this collection, see Chap. 22 (Aldridge).

16. See Dick Carpenter and others, *Policing for Profit: The Abuse of Civil Asset Forfeiture* (2nd edn, Institute for Justice 2015). In this collection, see Chap. 23 (Gallant).

17. Mary Cheh, 'Civil Remedies to Control Crime: Legal Issues and Constitutional Challenges' in Lorraine Green Mazerolle and Jan Roehl (eds), *Civil Remedies and Crime Prevention* (Criminal Justice Press 1998) 45.

18. See, for example, Stuart Hoffman, and Simon MacDonald, 'Should ASBOs be Civilised?' [2010] Criminal Law Review 457; Simon Bronitt and Susan Donkin, 'Australian Responses to 9/11: New World Legal Hybrids?' in Aniceto Masferrer (ed), *Post 9/11 and the State of Permanent Legal Emergency* (Springer 2012) 223.

19. Kenneth Mann, 'Punitive Civil Sanctions: The Middleground between Criminal and Civil Law' (1992) 101(8) Yale Law Journal 1795.

20. Colin King, 'Using Civil Processes in Pursuit of Criminal Law Objectives: A Case Study of Non-Conviction Based Asset Forfeiture' (2012) 16(4) International Journal of Evidence and Proof 337.

21. Colin King, 'Civil Forfeiture and Article 6 of the ECHR: Due Process Implications for England and Wales and Ireland' (2014) 34(3) Legal Studies 371.

22. Jennifer Hendry and Colin King, 'Expediency, Legitimacy, and the Rule of Law: A Systems Perspective on Civil/Criminal Procedural Hybrids' (2016) 9 Criminal Law and Philosophy 1.

23. Liz Campbell, 'The Recovery of "Criminal" Assets in New Zealand, Ireland and England: Fighting Organised and Serious Crime in the Civil Realm' (2010) 41(1) Victoria University of Wellington Law Review 15.

24. Anthony Davidson Gray, 'Forfeiture Provisions and the Criminal/Civil Divide' (2012) 15(1) New Criminal Law Review 32.
25. Robert Mikecz, 'Interviewing Elites: Addressing Methodological Issues' (2012) 18(6) Qualitative Inquiry 482; William Harvey, 'Strategies for Conducting Elite Interviews' (2011) 11(4) Qualitative Research 431.
26. Throughout this article the pronoun 'she' is used when referring to interviewees, to preserve anonymity.
27. Mikecz (n 25) 485.
28. Kate Fitz-Gibbon, 'Overcoming Barriers in the Criminal Court System: Examining the Challenges Faced When Interviewing Legal Stakeholders' in Karen Lumsden and Aaron Winter (eds), *Reflexivity in Criminological Research: Experiences with the Powerless and the Powerful* (Palgrave Macmillan 2014).
29. For discussion of whether civil forfeiture under POCA ought to be regarded as a civil or a criminal matter, see the contrasting views expressed in Cassidy (n 12) and King (n 13).
30. Liz Heffernan, *Evidence in Criminal Trials* (Bloomsbury 2014) 27.
31. Other notable statutory exceptions, also relating to belief evidence, are s 3(2) of the Offences Against the State (Amendment) Act 1972 and s 71(B) of the Criminal Justice Act 2006. See Dermot Walsh, *Walsh on Criminal Procedure* (Roundhall 2016) Chapter 21; Kevin Sweeney, 'The Power of Silence: Using Adverse Inferences to Investigate Terrorism in Ireland' (2016) 26 Irish Criminal Law Journal 38.
32. The Proceeds of Crime (Amendment) Act 2016 reduced the monetary threshold from €13,000 to €5000.
33. *FJMcK v GWD* [2004] 2 IR 470, 491–492; [2004] IESC 31, para 70.
34. POCA, s 1 defines 'member' as 'a member of the Garda Síochána not below the rank of Chief Superintendent' and 'authorised officer' as 'an officer of the Revenue Commissioners authorised in writing by the Revenue Commissioners to perform the functions conferred by this Act on authorised officers'.
35. *Gilligan v CAB* [1998] 3 IR 185, 243.
36. POCA, s 3(1) as amended. See also *CAB v Murphy and Murphy* [2016] IECA 40, para 65.
37. *FMcK v TH and JH* [2007] 4 IR 186, 196.
38. Similarly, see *McK v F*, unreported, High Court, Finnegan J (24 February 2003).
39. *Murphy v GM, PB, PC Ltd., GH; and Gilligan v CAB* [2001] 4 IR 113, 155; *FJMcK v GWD* [2004] 2 IR 470. A long line of authority, in relation to similar evidence under the Offences Against the State legislation, was influential in interpreting s 8 of POCA. See, for example, *Maher v Attorney General* [1973] IR 140; *State (McEldowney) v Kelleher* [1983] IR 289; *O'Leary v Attorney General* [1993] 1 IR 102; *The People (DPP) v Gannon*, unreported, Court of Criminal Appeal (2 April 2003).

40. See the decision of Finnegan J in *McK v D* [2002] IEHC 115 (HC), appealed in *FJMcK v GWD* [2004] 2 IR 470.

41. *FMcK v TH and JH* [2007] 4 IR 186, 195.

42. Commenting on belief evidence under s 3(2) of the Offences Against the State Act 1972, a majority of the Offences Against the State Committee expressed concern 'that the Oireachtas has given evidential status to an expression of opinion which may not merit that status': *Report of the Committee to Review the Offences Against the State Acts, 1939–1998 and Related Matters* (Stationery Office 2002) para 6.90.

43. For further discussion, see Michael Seigel, 'Rationalizing Hearsay: A Proposal for a Best Evidence Hearsay Rule' (1992) 72(5) Boston University Law Review 893; HL Ho, 'A Theory of Hearsay' (1999) 19(3) Oxford Journal of Legal Studies 403.

44. *FJMcK v GWD* [2004] 2 IR 470, 481 (Fennelly J).

45. *Murphy v GM, PB, PC Ltd.* [1999] IEHC 5, para 176. In *FJMcK v SMcD* [2005] IEHC 205 Finnegan P opted to exclude hearsay from his mind when considering whether or not the applicant had established the necessary belief, based on reasonable grounds, under s 8. Too much emphasis should not be placed on this however. The President, applying the best evidence rule, merely preferred to rely on other evidence tendered by the applicant.

46. *Byrne v Farrell and Farrell* [2012] IEHC 428, para 3.6.

47. Ibid.

48. *CAB v Murphy and Murphy* [2016] IECA 40, para 65.

49. Ibid. Whether there were reasonable grounds for the belief in that instance was considered by the court at paras 67ff.

50. *CAB v Murphy and Murphy* [2016] IECA 40, para 66.

51. For consideration of informer privilege and its effects on belief evidence, see Walsh (n 31) Chapter 15. See also Liz Heffernan, 'Evidence and National Security: "Belief Evidence" in the Irish Special Criminal Court' (2009) 15(1) European Public Law 65.

52. See, for instance, *Director of Consumer Affairs and Fair Trade v Sugar Distributors Ltd* [1991] 1 IR 225; *Breathnach v Ireland (no.3)* [1993] 2 IR 458; *DPP v Special Criminal Court* [1999] 1 IR 60. For in-depth consideration of informer privilege, see Henry Mares, 'Balancing Public Interest and A Fair Trial in Police Informer Privilege: A Critical Australian Perspective' (2002) 6(2) International Journal of Evidence and Proof 94.

53. Michael Farrell, 'The Challenge of the ECHR' (2007) 2 Judicial Studies Institute Journal 76, 84.

54. Ibid.

55. *Byrne v Farrell and Farrell* [2012] IEHC 428.

56. Ibid. para 7.1.

57. The use of belief evidence has also been upheld in criminal proceedings: *The People (DPP) v Kelly* [2006] 3 IR 115 (Irish Supreme Court) and *Donohoe v Ireland*, App No 19165/08 (ECtHR, 12 December 2013).
58. *Murphy v GM, PB, PC Ltd., GH; and Gilligan v CAB* [2001] 4 IR 113, 155, as approved *in FMcK v TH and JH* [2007] 4 IR 186, 194; [2006] IESC 63, para 23.
59. *FMcK v TH and JH* [2007] 4 IR 186, 194.
60. Ibid.
61. Van Harten (n 6) 3.
62. Criminal Assets Bureau Act 1996, s 7.
63. The legislation provides that a 'member' or 'authorised officer' can tender such evidence—thus, any Chief Superintendent (or higher) or any authorised revenue official.
64. Farrell (n 53) 84.
65. Interviewees gave examples of what would be used to support belief evidence, including bank statements, bank details, social welfare records for comparison, absence of any visible means of income, level of expenditure, purchases of items, personal and real property, previous criminal convictions, criminal associations and testimony from investigating officials.
66. See *The People (DPP) v Kelly* [2006] 3 IR 115.
67. Other interviewees also referred to the influence of the anti-terrorism framework: as INT3 stated, 'we had the history and considerable experience in the use of [*the anti-terrorism legislation on belief evidence*]'.
68. *FJMcK v GWD* [2004] 2 IR 470.
69. INT5 stated that there are cases where they would rather lose the case rather than give up the name of a confidential informant.
70. See Didier Bigo and others, *National Security and Secret Evidence in Legislation and Before the Courts: Exploring the Challenges* (European Parliament 2014) 26.
71. See Greg Martin, 'Outlaw Motorcycle Gangs and Secret Evidence: Reflections on the Use of Criminal Intelligence in the Control of Serious Organised Crime in Australia' (2014) 36(3) Sydney Law Review 501.
72. Anon, 'Secret Evidence in the War on Terror' (2005) 118(6) Harvard Law Review 1962, 1980, referring to *Jay v Boyd*, 351 US 345, 365.
73. Criminal Assets Bureau Act 1996, s 10. In addition, there are further provisions providing that it is a criminal offence to identify (current or former) non-Garda bureau personnel, to publish the names or addresses of such persons or to identify members of family of current or former bureau officers or members of staff or the address of any such person (s 11). It is also an offence to threaten, intimidate, menace, assault or attempt to assault a bureau officer of a member of staff of the bureau or any member of the family of such a person (ss 13 and 15).
74. Compare Offences Against the State Act 1939, s 41.

75. *CAB v PS* [2009] 3 IR 9; [2004] IEHC 351.
76. Ibid. 32.
77. Ibid. 33.
78. Ibid.
79. Ibid.
80. Ibid. The court had regard to *Quinns Supermarket v Attorney General* [1972] IR 1.
81. *CAB v PMcS* [2001] IEHC 162.
82. Criminal Assets Bureau Act 1996, ss 10(4)–(6).
83. *CAB v PMcS* [2001] IEHC 162 para 14.
84. Ibid. para 80.
85. Ibid.
86. *CAB v Craft and McWatt* [2001] 1 IR 121.
87. Ibid. 124.
88. Dáil Éireann, Criminal Assets Bureau Bill 1996, Second Stage (25 July 1996) vol 468, col 1054.
89. Seanad Éireann, Criminal Assets Bureau Bill 1996, Second Stage (09 October 1996) vol 148, col 1567.
90. David Lusty, 'Anonymous Accusers: An Historical and Comparative Analysis of Secret Witnesses in Criminal Trials' (2002) 24(3) Sydney Law Review 361, 423.
91. See Gilbert Marcus, 'Secret Witnesses' [1990] Public Law 207.
92. Concerns as to anonymity and secrecy are aptly described in Kafka's *The Trial*, where Josef K proclaimed, 'There is no doubt that behind all the utterances of this court, and therefore behind my arrest and today's examination, there stands a great organization. An organization which not only employs corrupt warders and fatuous supervisors and examining magistrates, of whom the best that can be said is that they are humble officials, but also supports a judiciary of the highest rank with its inevitable vast retinue of servants, secretaries, police officers and other assistants, perhaps even executioners—I don't shrink from the word. And the purpose of this great organization, gentlemen? To arrest innocent persons and start proceedings against them which are pointless and mostly, as in my case, inconclusive. When the whole organization is as pointless as this, how can gross corruption among the officials be avoided? That's impossible, not even the highest judge could manage that': Franz Kafka, *The Trial* (Penguin Books 1994) 36.
93. Criminal Assets Bureau Act 1996, s 10(7).
94. See John Meade, 'Organised Crime, Moral Panic and Law Reform: The Irish Adoption of Civil Forfeiture' (2000) 10(1) Irish Criminal Law Journal 11; Colin King, 'Hitting Back at Organised Crime: The Adoption of Civil Forfeiture in Ireland' in Colin King and Clive Walker (eds), *Dirty Assets: Emerging Issues in the Regulation of Criminal and Terrorist Assets* (Ashgate 2014).

95. See Tom Brady, 'CAB Uses New Powers to Target Lower-Ranking Gang Members' *Irish Independent* (Dublin, 17 September 2016).

96. Ruth Costigan and Philip Thomas, 'Anonymous Witnesses' (2000) 51(2) Northern Ireland Legal Quarterly 326, 335.

97. For consideration of the CAB, see Colin King, 'Follow The Money Trail: 'Civil' Forfeiture of 'Criminal' Assets in Ireland' in Petrus van Duyne and others (eds), *Human Dimensions in Organised Crime, Money Laundering, and Corruption* (Wolf Legal 2013).

98. *CAB v PS* [2009] 3 IR 9, 32.

99. See *Van Mechelen v Netherlands* [1998] 25 EHRR 647, para 61. But, see *Doorson v Netherlands* [1996] 22 EHRR 330, para 71.

100. John Peter Andersen, 'The Anonymity of Witnesses—A Danish Development' [1985] Criminal Law Review 363, 366. See also Stefano Maffei, *The European Right to Confrontation in Criminal Proceedings: Absent, Anonymous and Vulnerable Witnesses* (Europa Law Publishing 2006) 48.

101. Costigan and Thomas (n 96) 342.

102. *Van Mechelen v Netherlands* [1998] 25 EHRR 647, para 56. But see the dissenting opinion of Judge Van Dijk, which is receptive to anonymous testimony by State officials.

103. Steven Churches, 'Is There a Requirement for Fair Hearings in British and Australian Courts?' in Greg Martin, Rebecca Scott Bray, and Miiko Kumar (eds), *Secrecy, Law and Society* (Routledge 2015) 102.

104. There are many references to abuse of power in secret trials, most notably the Star Chamber, though there has also been criticism about 'myths' attached to that court. For further discussions, see, for example, Daniel Vande Zande, 'Coercive Power and the Demise of the Star Chamber' (2008) 50(3) American Journal of Legal History 326; Thomas Barnes, 'Star Chamber Mythology' (1961) 5(1) American Journal of Legal History 1.

105. Of course, each of these reasons can also be criticised. For an excellent discussion of such reasons see, for example, Judith Resnik, 'Due Process: A Public Dimension' (1987) 39 University of Florida Law Review 405; Antony Duff and others, *The Trial on Trial, vol.3: Towards a Normative Theory of the Criminal Trial* (OUP 2007); Claire Baylis, 'Justice Done and Justice Seen to Be Done—The Public Administration of Justice' (1991) 21(2) Victoria University of Wellington Law Review 177.

106. Duff and others (n 105) 260.

107. John Jackson, 'Justice, Security and the Right to a Fair Trial: Is the Use of Secret Evidence Ever Fair?' [2013] Public Law 720.

108. Miiko Kumar, 'Secret Witnesses, Secret Information and Secret Evidence: Australia's Response to Terrorism' (2011) 80(4) Mississippi Law Journal 1371.

109. David Ormerod, Andrew Choo and Rachel Easter, 'Coroners and Justice Act 2009: The "Witness Anonymity" and "Investigation Anonymity" Provisions' [2010] Criminal Law Review 368.
110. Kevin S Bankston, 'Only the DOJ Knows: The Secret Law of Electronic Surveillance' (2007) 41(4) University of San Francisco Law Review 589.
111. John Ip, 'The Rise and Spread of the Special Advocate' [2008] Public Law 717.
112. Gabrielle Appleby, 'Protecting Procedural Fairness and Criminal Intelligence: Is There a Balance to Be Struck?' in Greg Martin, Rebecca Scott Bray, and Miiko Kumar (eds), *Secrecy, Law and Society* (Routledge 2015) 94.
113. See Heffernan (n 51).
114. For further discussion, see Colin King, 'Using Civil Processes in Pursuit of Criminal Law Objectives: A Case Study of Non-Conviction Based Asset Forfeiture' (2012) 16(4) International Journal of Evidence and Proof 337, 358ff.
115. *Quicunque aliquid statuerit, parte inaudita altera, aequum licet statuerit, haud aequus fuerit*—where natural justice is violated, it is no justification that the decision is, in fact, correct. Cited in Christopher Forsyth, *Administrative Law* (11th edn, OUP 2014) 406. See also *Boswell's case* (1605) 6 Co Rep 48b.
116. Kennedy (n 7).
117. Criminal Assets Bureau, *Annual Report 2015* (2016) Chapter 8.
118. Van Harten (n 6) 16. See also David Cole, 'Enemy Aliens' (2002) 54(5) Stanford Law Review 953, 1002.

Colin King is Reader in Law at the University of Sussex and Co-Founder of the Crime Research Centre. He was an Academic Fellow at the Honourable Society of the Inner Temple from 2014–2017. In March 2016, Colin gave oral evidence at the Home Affairs Select Committee Inquiry into the Proceeds of Crime Act. Colin is co-editor of *Dirty Assets: Emerging Issues in the Regulation of Criminal and Terrorist Assets* (King and Walker, Ashgate, 2014). Also with Clive Walker, King led an Arts and Humanities Research Council (AHRC)-funded research network (2014–2016) entitled 'Dirty Assets: Experiences, Reflections, and Lessons Learnt from a Decade of Legislation on Criminal Money Laundering and Terrorism Financing'. In 2017, he was awarded a prestigious AHRC Leadership Fellowship to conduct empirical research on proceeds of crime legislation.

25

International Asset Recovery and the United Nations Convention Against Corruption

Dimitris Ziouvas

Introduction

According to the former Secretary-General of the United Nations, Kofi Annan:

> Corruption undermines democracy and the rule of law, leads to violations of human rights, distorts markets, erodes the quality of life and allows organized crime, terrorism and other threats to human security to flourish …The (United Nations) Convention (against Corruption) introduces a comprehensive set of standards, measures and rules that all countries can apply in order to strengthen their legal and regulatory regimes to fight corruption. … And it makes a major breakthrough by requiring Member States to return assets obtained through corruption to the country from which they were stolen. … These provisions—the first of their kind—introduce a new fundamental principle, as well as a framework for stronger cooperation between States to prevent and detect corruption and to return the proceeds.[1]

These words emphasize the importance of asset recovery for fighting the scourge of corruption and the pivotal role that the United Nations Convention against Corruption (UNCAC)[2] can play in fostering international cooperation in asset recovery. Corruption-related asset recovery is a prerequisite for

D. Ziouvas
Sussex Law School, School of Law, Politics and Sociology, University of Sussex, Brighton, UK

© The Author(s) 2018
C. King et al. (eds.), *The Palgrave Handbook of Criminal and Terrorism Financing Law*,
https://doi.org/10.1007/978-3-319-64498-1_25

global justice and the promotion of the international rule of law as backbones for sustainable development.

'Always follow the money' and make sure that 'crime doesn't pay' has been sound advice in anti-corruption law enforcement and policy makers' circles for decades. But the tracing, seizure, confiscation and return of corruption-related assets have faced many legal obstacles. These obstacles are particularly pronounced where corruption-related assets have been diverted from developing countries and laundered in foreign jurisdictions. Thus, procedural and evidentiary obstacles can be found in the anonymity of financial transactions, the lack of technical expertise and resources, the lack of harmonization of national criminal anti-corruption laws and of procedures for international cooperation, and the myriad of problems in criminal prosecution.[3]

The size of corruption-related wealth is hard to calculate. Estimating the amounts of corrupt assets that cross borders for money-laundering purposes relating to the proceeds of corruption is even harder.[4] The size of corruption must be clearly differentiated from the much higher and even more difficult to calculate economic cost of corruption. The European Commission estimates that corruption costs European Union member states around EUR 120 billion per year.[5] The United Nations Office on Drugs and Crime (UNODC) estimates that the total amount of criminal proceeds generated in 2009, including those derived from corruption but excluding those derived from tax crimes, may have been approximately US $2.1 trillion, or 3.6% of global GDP.[6] Out of this amount the money laundered was estimated to be close to US $1.6 trillion or 2.7% of global GDP in the same year. On the other hand, if only *transnational* crime-related proceeds were considered, the money-laundering estimates would be expected to fall to levels around 1% of GDP. The UNODC research report further concludes that the 'interception rate' for anti-money-laundering efforts at the global level remains low—much less than 1% (probably around 0.2%) of the proceeds of crime laundered. The yearly proceeds of corruption alone are conservatively estimated to be between US $20 billion and US $40 billion.[7]

The sheer size of the problem demonstrates the necessity for developing effective responses. The analysis that follows focuses on the UNCAC. The UNCAC was opened for signature on 9 December 2003 in Merida, Mexico, and entered into force on 14 December 2005. The current[8] 140 signatories and 181 States Parties make it the only truly global and legally binding anti-corruption instrument. The UNCAC addresses a wide range of preventive and deterrent provisions against corruption and sets out comprehensive provisions on asset recovery.

Asset recovery represents a relatively new field of international anti-corruption law and international cooperation. It serves mainly four essential purposes: it is a powerful deterrent measure, as it removes the profit incentive for people to engage in corrupt practices; it restores justice by taking away the profits from criminals; it plays an incapacitative role by depriving criminals and powerful criminal networks of their assets and instruments of misconduct; and it helps repair the damage done to victim countries and their populations.

For these reasons, Chapter V of the UNCAC establishes asset recovery as one of its 'fundamental principles' (Article 51 UNCAC). The respective provisions provide States Parties with a comprehensive set of tools to effectively prevent the transfer and laundering of the proceeds of corruption and a set of legal avenues for successful international cooperation in the tracing, seizing, confiscating and recovering of the proceeds of corruption.

This chapter briefly analyses the procedures and conditions for asset recovery set by the UNCAC. It is intended to serve as an introductory guide with regard to the various available legal tools for international cooperation in asset recovery. Before attempting a hermeneutical approach to the letter of the provisions of Chapter V of the UNCAC, the research explores, both from a criminological and a legal point of view, the systematic interconnection between the UNCAC provisions on the criminalization of corruption and other corruption-related offences on one side and the criminal and asset recovery provisions of the United Nations Convention against Transnational Organized Crime (UNTOC) on the other side. All respective provisions are systematically interpreted in combination with the UNCAC provisions on the prevention of money laundering as well as with the general provisions on international cooperation and mutual legal assistance.

Following the legal positivistic approach, the chapter then explores the sociolegal dynamics and, at the same time, the challenges for the UNCAC by addressing the problem of the unwillingness and/or inability of many victim states to recover stolen assets. The research goes on to identify some national (Switzerland and Canada) and regional (Arab Forum on Asset Recovery) best practices for overcoming these obstacles. Using the Ao case, a case where asset recovery efforts between Macao, Hong Kong and the United Kingdom came to a successful end, as an illustration for UNCAC's use as an autonomous legal basis for international cooperation in asset recovery, this chapter argues that UNCAC's full potential still remains to be discovered by recovering jurisdictions and practitioners.

The critical legal approach to the emerging issue of settlements in transnational grand corruption cases and their implications for corruption victims' rights, as well as an outlook on the future of international and domestic asset recovery practices with a view to determine whether the existing UNCAC framework is sufficient, or whether any other tools or amendments are necessary, round up the chapter.

Asset Recovery and the UNCAC in the Criminological and International Legal Context

UNCAC's Broad Scope of Application

Corruption crimes must be conceived and legally addressed in their broader criminal context in order to be fought effectively. The UNCAC, like all other international anti-corruption conventions,[9] understandably shies away from providing a general definition of corruption. However, Chapter III of the UNCAC on 'criminalization and law enforcement' lists specific offences as acts of corruption. Chapter III is the heart of the UNCAC. Not only does it ensure national suppression of corruption by creating a minimum anti-corruption criminal standard among States Parties, whose national laws diverge significantly, but it also enables both general and asset recovery-related international cooperation by ensuring satisfaction of the requirement of double criminality. UNCAC States Parties are obliged to criminalize bribery of national public officials,[10] bribery of foreign public officials and officials of public international organizations,[11] embezzlement, misappropriation or other diversion of property by a public official,[12] laundering of the proceeds of crime[13] and obstruction of justice,[14] while several other articles such as the ones on bribery and embezzlement of property in the private sector,[15] illicit enrichment,[16] abuse of functions,[17] trading in influence[18] and concealment[19] are non-mandatory provisions.

The broad spectrum of UNCAC's criminal provisions shows that corruption is much more than bribery. Actually, embezzled and misappropriated funds (Article 17) are unsurprisingly much higher sums than bribery-related assets. Looting the state proves to be much simpler, easier and also more profitable than just receiving bribes. Further, the UNCAC, by expanding the scope of application of the money-laundering offence of Article 23 'to the widest range of predicate offences'[20] including 'at a minimum a comprehensive range of criminal offences established in accordance' with the Convention, takes note of the symbiotic relationship between corruption and corruption-related money laundering.[21] By including predicate offences 'committed both within and *outside* the jurisdiction'[22] of the State Party criminalizing money laundering, the

UNCAC recognizes the transnational nature of both corruption and money laundering as predicate offences.

Applying the UNTOC to Grand Corruption

Grand corruption[23] cases are typically transnational and therefore multi-jurisdictional. Bribes for the award of public contracts or stolen public funds are usually paid into foreign bank accounts or used to acquire real estate or other assets abroad. The proceeds of corruption are usually laundered through a number of countries, both major financial (onshore) centres and offshore havens, to impede tracing and seizure. It comes therefore as no surprise that both 'corruption' and money laundering are included as core crimes[24] in the UNTOC.[25]

The UNTOC is the main international instrument in the fight against transnational organized crime.[26] Article 8 UNTOC obliges States Parties to criminalize (active and passive) bribery of national public officials.[27] Article 6 UNTOC requests the 'criminalization' of the laundering of proceeds of crime. The laundering of the proceeds of organized crime is useful to organized criminal groups because, on one hand, it disguises the illicit origins of their profits and, on the other hand, it makes the proceeds reusable for further investment in criminal activities. Corruption and money laundering support organized criminal groups (OCGs)[28] by enabling and facilitating their operations before commission of their crimes and by concealing their crimes after these have been committed. The profit-making and very diverse 'final' crimes of OCGs, which include trafficking in drugs, human beings, firearms or wildlife, offences against cultural heritage, fraud and other 'serious'[29] offences, could not be carried out without the organizational and entrepreneurial structures provided by the core crimes.

UNTOC becomes applicable only when the offences of bribery and money laundering are both 'transnational in nature and involve an organized criminal group'.[30] But most grand corruption and money-laundering cases will fulfil these criteria.

Practical Implications of Grand Corruption's Transnational Organized Nature

UNTOC's applicability on corruption and money-laundering cases is of significant importance for asset recovery. First, and from a procedural point of view, it allows for the application of UNTOC's quite extensive provisions on international cooperation for the purposes of seizure, confiscation and actual recovery of the proceeds of transnational organized corruption. Article 12 UNTOC ('Confiscation and Seizure') requests States Parties to adopt 'such measures as may be necessary to enable the identification, tracing, freezing or seizure' and the consequent confiscation of the proceeds of crimes derived from offences covered by the UNTOC. Article 13 UNTOC ('International Cooperation for purposes of Confiscation') requires that States Parties cooperate with each other 'to the greatest extent possible within their domestic legal system' to enable confiscation of the proceeds of crime. Article 14 UNTOC ('Disposal of confiscated proceeds of crime or property') regulates how confiscated assets shall be disposed of. Finally, Article 18 UNTOC ('Mutual Legal Assistance') contains extensive provisions on asset recovery-related tools of mutual legal assistance.

Secondly and from a substantive criminal law point of view, UNTOC's framework allows for the punishment of a group of criminals participating in transnational organized corruption and money laundering. The depiction of corruption crimes, including the laundering of the proceeds of corruption, as the purpose of the establishment and the continuing operations of such organized criminal groups (OCGs) helps to address the role of kleptocrats' associates and legal and financial service providers as criminal accomplices. In large-scale grand corruption cases, the focus of law enforcement should not be limited to convicting the offender, usually a senior government official, and recovering and repatriating the respective proceeds of corruption. Addressing the role of international business partners as well as banks and other gatekeepers is equally important. Asset recovery should not be used just as a tool for depriving the bribees of their profits but also for identifying and dismantling the global support system of corruption. Autonomous criminalization of the offence of participation in a transnational OCG aiming to commit corruption crimes can also lead to serious criminal procedural benefits, such as the very effective special investigative tools that can be utilized in cases of OCGs.[31]

Thirdly and from a criminological point of view, UNTOC's anti-corruption legal framework helps us to conceptualize bribery as an integral part of a much bigger criminal picture. Bribery does not occur as a stand-alone offence. It prepares the act of breach of duty or abuse of function by the bribee and often enables, as shown above, the commission of a series of further 'final' serious crimes by the briber or his accomplices. When these profit-motivated serious crimes are committed by an organized criminal group across national borders, corruption becomes much more than a crime against integrity: it is used to facilitate or conceal TOC and so becomes indirectly a threat for a myriad of legal interests and goods including the rule of law and public order.

The strong dependency of the application of UNCAC's asset recovery provisions on the very broad criminal provisions of the UNCAC and the UNTOC reveals the importance of national jurisdictions criminalizing all UNCAC and UNTOC offences and extending their legislative confiscation framework to all of these offences.

Despite the above theoretical and practical benefits for asset recovery of establishing a systematic interconnection between the UNCAC and the UNTOC, there are significant limitations to UNTOC's applicability in corruption-related asset recovery cases. Besides the vast difference in terms of content and in-depth analysis between the asset recovery provisions of the two international legal instruments,[32] as well as UNTOC's limited scope of application to corruption cases of transnational and organized nature, UNTOC has two further main weaknesses compared with the UNCAC. First, UNTOC's provisions allow compliance-averse States Parties an 'escape hatch'[33] by requesting them to take only measures that are 'appropriate', 'consistent' and 'permitted' within their domestic legal system. UNTOC's asset recovery provisions are non-mandatory, whereas the basic UNCAC provisions are legally binding. Secondly, UNTOC's enforceability is limited by the lack of an effective review mechanism.[34] By contrast, state compliance with the UNCAC is supported by an extensive set of tools and guidance for implementation provided by UNODC.[35]

The UNCAC as a Legal Basis for International Cooperation in Asset Recovery

International cooperation aims to ensure cooperation between prosecution and judicial authorities of different countries in various cross-border situations. The main instruments for international judicial cooperation are extradition (in criminal matters) and mutual legal assistance (MLA). The purpose of MLA is to facilitate gathering and exchanging of information and obtaining evidence in one ('requested') country in order to assist judicial proceedings in another ('requesting') country.

Domestic jurisdictions generally require one of the four legal bases to provide formal MLA in asset recovery cases: international conventions containing provisions on MLA in asset recovery, such as the UNCAC and the UNTOC; domestic legislation allowing for international cooperation in asset recovery; bilateral mutual legal assistance agreements; or a promise of reciprocity through diplomatic channels (known in some jurisdictions as letters rogatory).

International cooperation on the legal basis of the UNCAC can take two forms depending on the constitutional requirements of each State Party for the transposition of international law into domestic law.[36] In some jurisdictions the mere act of ratification of a self-executing international convention such as the UNCAC makes the convention provisions part of domestic law. In these jurisdictions, MLA in asset recovery may be granted directly based on the UNCAC provisions. In dualist countries, the provisions of international treaties must be transposed into domestic law by virtue of national legislation before they acquire legal force.

Outline of UNCAC, Chapter V

Chapter V (Articles 51–59) of the UNCAC codifies international asset recovery best practices. State Parties are obliged to take the necessary measures, including legislative and administrative measures, in accordance with the fundamental principles of their domestic law, to ensure compliance with the UNCAC.[37] The special provisions of Chapter V must be read in combination with a number of general provisions contained in Chapters II–IV of the UNCAC and referring directly or indirectly to asset recovery. Particularly relevant for asset recovery are: Article 14 on the prevention of money laundering; Article 31 on the establishment of a regime for domestic freezing and confiscation of the proceeds of corruption as a prerequisite for international cooperation and the return of assets; Article 39 on cooperation between national authorities and the private sector; Article 43 on international cooperation; and Article 46 on mutual legal assistance.[38]

Actual recovery of the corrupt assets by returning them to the victims of corruption[39] requires different phases of asset recovery. In general three different procedures can be used for asset recovery: criminal confiscation or forfeiture,[40] non-conviction-based confiscation or forfeiture[41] and civil proceedings.[42]

Prevention of Laundering the Assets

An effective anti-money-laundering environment is a prerequisite for asset recovery. Consequently, Article 52 UNCAC requires States Parties to take a series of measures in order to prevent the transfer of the proceeds of corruption crimes. Article 52 must be read in conjunction with Article 14 UNCAC on the prevention of money laundering. While the basic operational principles of an anti-money-laundering (AML) prevention system are foreseen in Article 14, Article 52 will, ideally, prevent the proceeds of corruption from leaving the State Party of origin or at least will alert the authorities of the relevant transactions. Even when the transfer cannot be prevented by the institutions of the State Party of origin, state compliance with the provisions of Article 52 will help the institutions of the receiving State Party either to refuse the property transfer or to report it. The main requirements introduced by Article 52 are discussed below.

Verification of Customer Identity

Verification of a customer's identity by financial institutions goes much further than a mere formal identification. AML 'know-your-customer/client' (KYC) rules, when applied in a strictly formal way, can be limited to obtaining a copy of a customer's identity card or company formation document.

'Verifying' customer's identity includes confirming the authenticity of the identity documents, obtaining certified (by a public notary or another financial institution) copies of the identification documents particularly in cases of non-face-to-face establishment of the client relationship, or in the case of legal entities obtaining an updated copy of the documents of incorporation from the public companies' registries, official bulletins or gazettes.

Identification of Beneficial Owners of High-Value Accounts

By requiring States Parties 'to take reasonable steps to determine the identity of the beneficial owners of funds deposited in highly valued accounts',[43] the UNCAC aims to impede the use of third persons holding the proceeds of crime on behalf of corrupt individuals.

Beneficial owners are *natural* persons who ultimately own or control a fund or an asset and/or natural persons on whose behalf a transaction is being conducted. The term also includes those natural persons who ultimately exercise *effective* control over a legal person or arrangement.[44] In cases of beneficial ownership the ultimate ownership/control is exercised through a chain of ownership or by means of control other than direct control. Establishing such a long chain of ownership/control can serve legitimate purposes of tax planning or be abused to provide anonymity to criminals and slow down law (asset recovery) enforcement procedures.

In complying with their Convention obligations States Parties may consider prohibiting financial institutions (mainly banks) from accepting as an asset holder a corporate vehicle or a legal entity, the identity of which cannot be established as a beneficial owner, or may oblige their home financial institutions to require that corporate clients lift their so-called corporate veil.

Determining what minimum amount makes an account qualify as a 'highly valued account' remains within the discretionary power of implementing States Parties. So does applying the requirement not only to bank accounts but also to other financial products. Special attention must be given to joint bank accounts, joint securities accounts, investment companies and other collective investments, as well as to assets held by 'offshore' companies having their registered seat in 'tax havens'.[45] In the case of offshore companies, States Parties must compel their financial institutions to require, in addition to a certified copy of the incorporation documents verifying their identity, a written declaration indicating the beneficial owner(s) of the assets concerned.

Enhanced Scrutiny over Accounts Held by Politically Exposed Persons (PEPs)

Article 52 of the UNCAC next requires States Parties to compel their financial institutions to conduct enhanced scrutiny of accounts maintained by so-called politically exposed persons (PEPs). PEPs are defined in Article 52(1) as 'individuals who are, or have been, entrusted with prominent public functions, as well as their family members and close associates'. Individuals exercising public functions include, for example, Heads of State or of government, senior politicians, senior government, judicial or military officials, senior executives of state-owned corporations and important party officials.[46] PEPs can be domestic, foreign PEPs or individuals working for an international organization. The precise definition of PEPs remains with the States Parties. While defining the spectrum of family members based on the degree of family, kin and marriage relationships can be clear and easy, the definition of 'close associates' is very difficult and poses many interpretative challenges. According to the FATF Recommendations the definition of PEPs shall not cover middle ranking or more junior individuals in the categories mentioned above.[47]

Record-Keeping

Article 52(3) requires that advisories issued in accordance with Article 52(2) (a) must specify a special record-keeping obligation for high-risk customers and PEPs going beyond the general duty in Article 14(1). The records must be 'adequate' and maintained over an 'appropriate' period of time, thus leaving to States Parties a lot of discretionary power in concretizing the respective obligations of financial institutions. In any case it is advisable that national regulators establish timescales for retention of records that go well beyond the statutes of limitations for corruption offences. Significantly prolonging the time limits of record-keeping obligations for PEPs is a further best practice.

Preventing the Establishment of, and Correspondent Relationship with, Shell Banks

One of the most used financial vehicles to hide assets in the international financial system is a so-called 'shell bank'. According to Article 52(4), shell banks are 'banks that have no physical presence (in the country where they are incorporated and licensed) and are not affiliated with a regulated financial group'. Maintaining an office run by a local agent or by low-level staff is not enough for establishing a physical presence in a jurisdiction. The physical presence of a financial institution is usually understood as the place where 'the mind and management' of the institution is. Shell banks have their management located in a foreign jurisdiction, so preventing the regulator at the jurisdiction of incorporation from exercising its supervision and control.

The second element of the definition of a shell bank is the lack of affiliation with a supervised financial services group. Due to the consolidated nature of banking supervision, such an affiliation would extend regulatory supervision to the shell bank. Because of this lack of supervision and the anonymity offered to their clients, shell banks are frequently used to channel proceeds of crime out of a jurisdiction and are a popular money-laundering tool in major corruption schemes.[48] Consequently, Article 52(4) requires States Parties to adopt measures to prevent the establishment of shell banks in their jurisdictions.

Funds rarely remain deposited in a shell bank for long. Shell bank accounts are usually a 'transit' destination for corrupt assets. For this reason, the UNCAC recommends that States Parties also prohibit their banks from establishing correspondent banking relationships with shell banks.[49] A correspondent bank is effectively acting as its respondent's agent, processing payments or other transactions for the respondent's customers. Foreign correspondent banking can be abused to circumvent strict supervision conditions for respondent financial institutions and to facilitate money laundering.

Financial Disclosure Systems for Public Officials

Following up on Article 8(5) UNCAC,[50] Article 52(5)–(6) recommends States Parties to establish financial disclosure systems for appropriate public officials, including information on ownership of foreign accounts.

Detecting and Freezing the Assets

When it has not been possible to prevent the laundering of corrupt assets, then rapidly identifying, locating and freezing the assets becomes the most important stage of asset recovery. The chances of successful detection are in most cases higher before MLA has been formally launched.[51] Article 56 UNCAC introduces the innovative and very useful concept of spontaneous sharing of information without prior request by the victim State Party. States Parties are encouraged to advise each other of information that could lead to investigations, judicial proceedings or requests for assistance to recover the proceeds of corruption.

Determining the Proceeds of Corruption

Determining what exactly constitutes 'proceeds' of corruption is the next step in asset recovery. Proceeds of crime are defined as 'any property derived from or obtained *directly or indirectly* through the commission of an offence'.[52] Direct proceeds would include funds paid for by a bribe or amounts stolen by an official from a national treasury or governmental programme. Indirect proceeds would include the appreciation in the value of the bribery payments or real estate or a stock portfolio purchased with the stolen treasury fund.

The following simple case scenario[53] shows how quantifying the direct and indirect proceeds of corruption works in practice. Mr. X is a corrupt official who accepted a cash bribe of US $100,000. A series of transactions subsequently took place to launder the funds: (1) Mr. X deposited the bribe into a bank account in his wife's name; (2) Mr. X caused his wife to transfer the money into the trust account of a lawyer in London, UK. This lawyer was already holding US $900,000 on behalf of Mr. X (the origins of which are unknown); (3) the lawyer purchased a property worth US $1 million in the name of an investment company controlled by Mr. X; and (4) three years later, Mr. X sells the property for US $2 million and has the proceeds returned to an account controlled by him in his home country. In this case the capital gain on the sale of the house (doubled in value) must be added to the amount *directly* derived from the bribe (US $100,000) to make up the *total proceeds of crime* in value of US $200,000.

Freezing the Assets of Corruption

Once the exact amount of the proceeds of corruption has been estimated, it is pivotal for the effectiveness of international asset recovery that the involved states cooperate in freezing or seizing the assets temporarily. Articles 54 and

55 follow up on the general provisions of Article 46[54] regarding MLA by specifying the asset recovery-related procedures.

Article 54(2) of the UNCAC requires States Parties to take all necessary provisional (or interim) measures to enable the eventual permanent confiscation of corrupt assets. For this States Parties are required to cooperate in the recognition and enforcement of foreign freezing orders and in the issuance of domestic freezing orders. The freezing order can be issued by a court or competent authority of the requesting State Party (a) where either provides a reasonable basis to believe that there are sufficient grounds for enforcing it and that the property will eventually be subject to a permanent order of confiscation, or (b) upon a request by the victim State Party on the same basis.[55]

Article 54(2)(c) recommends that States Parties take not only measures of seizure but also other provisional measures of asset recovery so that assets are preserved for eventual confiscation.

Confiscating the Assets

Seizure of the corrupt assets is to be followed by their permanent confiscation. Confiscation (also known as forfeiture) can take the form of criminal (conviction-based) confiscation, non-conviction-based/civil confiscation and administrative confiscation. Under domestic laws, confiscated assets are typically payable to the state, although they can also be used in some jurisdictions for restitution or compensation of victims.

Articles 31, 54 and 55 of the UNCAC are applicable in cases of criminal forfeiture. The required criminal liability for the underlying corruption offences is to be established by States Parties on the basis of the criminalization provisions of Chapter III of the UNCAC ('criminalization and law enforcement').

Article 54 aims at establishing procedures for States Parties to secure the confiscation of the proceeds of corruption originating from another State Party. The scope of international cooperation in confiscation is broadened significantly by including forms of property not only 'acquired through' but also 'involved in the commission' of a corruption offence.

The obligation of States Parties under Article 54(1)(a) to enforce an order of confiscation issued by a foreign court can be fulfilled, as is the case with seizure orders, by way of two procedures. The requested State Party may either recognize and enforce the foreign confiscation order or else initiate proceedings on behalf of the requesting State Party or issue a new domestic confiscation order in accordance with its own law. The latter option will in most cases prove very complicated, politically sensitive and less effective than the first, since it transfers criminal proceedings to a foreign jurisdiction: 'experience in this area clearly demonstrates that the direct enforcement approach is much less resource intensive, avoids duplication and is significantly more effective in affording the assistance sought on a timely basis'.[56] Nevertheless, sometimes the institution of new confiscation proceedings may be the only possible legal resolution, such as when the State Party requested to enforce a confiscation order against a legal person does not recognize the criminal liability of legal persons.

Article 54(1)(b) reflects the immense significance of prosecuting money laundering for effectively fighting predicate corruption offences. States Parties, to whose jurisdictions the corrupt proceeds have been exported, are required to legally enable the confiscation of the proceeds of foreign predicate offences through money-laundering-related proceedings.

Article 54(1)(c) complements the arrangements for criminal confiscation by recommending that States Parties put in place instruments for non-conviction-based confiscation. The implementation of this recommendation depends on the punitive or restorative character that each State Party assigns to the concept of confiscation. Non-conviction-based confiscation is the only way to recover assets when a criminal conviction cannot be obtained by reason of death, flight or absence.

Next, Article 54 enables the implementation of Article 55. Article 55(1) mandates States Parties to provide assistance 'to the greatest extent possible' within their domestic legal system, when they receive a request from another State Party having jurisdiction over a corruption crime for the confiscation of proceeds of crime situated in their territory. The formal details are set out under Article 55(3).

Returning the Assets

The provisions of Articles 54 and 55 regarding international cooperation in seizure and confiscation pave the way for Article 57 on the return and disposal of assets. There can be no effectiveness in prevention, no confidence in justice and the rule of law and no faith in the notion that corruption does not pay, unless the proceeds of corruption are taken away from criminals and returned to the rightful owners. For this reason, Article 57 lies at the heart of asset recovery. Article 57 of the UNCAC establishes some *mandatory* requirements and general rules upon which States Parties shall base their procedures for the return and disposal of confiscated assets, once the proceeds of corruption have been traced, frozen and confiscated.

States usually dispose of or return confiscated assets in two ways. The first is by 'sharing' confiscated assets with a foreign state that participated directly or indirectly in the investigation leading to confiscation. This will be in most cases the victim state, but it can also be any other state whose jurisdiction was affected directly or indirectly by the transborder transfer of the corruption-related assets. The state in whose territory the assets were confiscated will retain only that portion of confiscated assets to recoup the costs incurred in the confiscation procedure. Confiscated assets are 'shared' between states on the basis of respective ad hoc agreements. Another option is for states to 'remit' the confiscated assets to the victims of the criminal activity upon which confiscation was based (so-called 'underlying' criminal activity).

Returned assets fall within three main categories: First, there are embezzled or misappropriated (and later laundered) funds in accordance with the criminal provision of Article 17 ('Embezzlement, misappropriation or other diversion of property by a public official'). The bulk of the recovered assets recorded in the Asset Recovery Watch database[57] fall under this category. Secondly, there are other proceeds mainly resulting from foreign bribery (Article 16 on 'Bribery of foreign public officials and officials of public international organizations') and related cases. Asset Recovery Watch reports only a small number of foreign bribery cases. Lastly, there are other funds, such as voluntary reparation payments. Reparations are gratuitous or voluntary payments made by a wrongdoer to atone for harm caused. Such amounts are payable to the victims but could also be payable to a third party, such as a humanitarian organization. Minimal funds have been repaid so far for reparation on such a voluntary basis. One of the most notable cases is BAE Systems, in which the company agreed to make an ex gratia payment for the benefit of the people of Tanzania.[58]

For the first set of assets (embezzled or misappropriated funds), Article 57(3)(a) provides for the *mandatory* return of the confiscated property to the requesting State Party. The confiscated proceeds of embezzlement and the laundered embezzled assets must be returned to their rightful owner after reasonable confiscation expenses have been deducted.

In the case of all other corruption offences, Article 57(3)(b) requires that assets be returned if the requesting state establishes prior ownership or if the requested state recognizes damage to the requesting state.

In all other cases Article 57(3)(c) recommends that State Parties shall consider 'compensating the victims of the crime'. Compensation must be interpreted in its broadest sense to include all forms of 'restitution'. The principle of restitution requires that a person who has suffered loss as a result of wrongdoing against him/her must be restored as nearly as possible to their circumstance before the damage took place. Restitution can be either civil or criminal. In some jurisdictions, the court has the power to order the guilty party to pay restitution to the victim as part of a criminal conviction in an amount equal to the costs incurred by the victim as a result of the guilty party's actions. Compensation is a formal way of restitution, in that a court may issue a compensation order in a criminal case where a victim has been identified in the proceedings and has proved he or she suffered damage. The compensation order will often form part of the confiscation.

Article 57 is complemented by Article 53 on the direct recovery of dirty assets through civil proceedings. Prior ownership, damage recovery and compensation are different legal grounds for the victim State Party to claim in the civil courts of the State Party where the assets were located. Article 53 mandates States Parties to ensure in their jurisdictions that other States Parties have legal standing for claiming misappropriated assets by initiating civil actions and other direct means to recover illegally obtained and diverted assets. The UNCAC requires that victimized States Parties are granted appropriate legal standing in a civil action on property, as a party recovering damages caused by criminal offences, or as a third party claiming ownership rights in any civil or criminal confiscation procedures.

Articles 57(3)(c) and 53 must be read in conjunction with Article 35 ('Compensation for damage'), which requests States Parties 'to ensure that entities or persons who have suffered damage as a result of an act of corruption have the right to initiate legal proceedings against those responsible for that damage in order to obtain compensation'.

Asset Recovery in Cases of Inactive (Unwilling or Unable/Failed) Victim States

Chapter V contains innovative, and most importantly mandatory, provisions regarding the return and disposal of corruption-related assets, but nevertheless gives States Parties discretion to make their own arrangements between themselves on a case-by-case basis. Article 57 clearly envisages that victim states will want stolen assets returned or will be able to claim such recovery.[59] Yet in many international grand corruption cases the actual recovery of stolen assets fails because there is no real interest on the side of victim states to recover their assets. It often occurs that victim states do not even submit a request for asset recovery.[60]

The UNCAC itself does not oblige victim states to prosecute corruption domestically or to initiate international cooperation proceedings by requesting fellow States Parties to offer mutual legal assistance in the recovery of the proceeds of corruption. This could never be the declared aim of an international convention. Putting 'law in books' in 'action' is the sole responsibility of the national law enforcement agencies. UNCAC's purpose is to oblige States Parties to enact a minimum set of anti-corruption laws and to harmonize the national anti-corruption law *enactment* practices.

Barriers to Asset Recovery

The reasons why victim states remain inactive in recovering their stolen assets vary. When corruption becomes systemic and endemic, victim states often lack the political will to expose their corrupt political elite.[61] Most developing countries also lack the institutions and law enforcement mechanisms to *effectively* seek restitution by initially prosecuting corruption at home and then supporting their developed fellow UNCAC countries in substantiating claims of seizure and confiscation.[62]

In many cases victim countries are undergoing political transition or situations of war, or civil unrest, making interstate cooperation in complex asset recovery procedures impractical or impolitic. The cases of Arab countries like Libya, Egypt and Tunisia transitioning from their previous corrupt regimes[63] following the 'Arab Spring' (2011) demonstrate the major challenges for asset recovery in countries in transition. Despite the strong political impetus to repatriate stolen assets to the victim states, only minimal assets have been recovered so far.[64]

For successful international cooperation in asset recovery, two states must cooperate effectively. The 2015 UK asset recovery case of former Ukrainian natural resources minister (under former President Viktor Yanukovych), Mykola Zlovesky, highlighted a crucial flaw in countries' efforts to cooperate in asset recovery cases across borders: 'Even in the rare cases when the UK does freeze a foreign official's property, it is dependent for evidence from colleagues abroad who usually have fewer resources, less training and a decades-long tradition of institutionalized corruption'.[65] Despite the United Kingdom's commitment to confiscate misappropriated money belonging to Yanukovych's allies and return it to the people of Ukraine, Ukrainian prosecutors failed to support the United Kingdom's Serious Fraud Office (SFO) in its efforts to confiscate USD 23 million of Zlovesky's London-based assets by providing adequate evidence that the temporarily frozen money is related to a specific corruption crime.

Absent the victim state being willing or able to take effective asset recovery action, questions remain about the possibilities for the international community and the countries of location of the dirty assets to do justice and the role of civil society.

Best National, Regional and International Asset Recovery Practices

In cases of troubled or failed victim states asset recovery efforts remain a work in progress that requires a coordinated and comprehensive strategy involving governments, the private sector, civil society and the international community. The (usually developed) countries of location of the corruption-related assets should not wait for a request from the (usually developing) victim country before freezing assets located within their territories. Developed countries should adopt a proactive approach towards asset recovery for the best interest of the people of looted troubled countries and global justice.

There are some national laws which adhere to this best practice of unilateral asset recovery. The 2011 Swiss Restitution of Illicit Assets Act (RIAA)[66] (known as the 'Duvalier Law')[67] permits Switzerland to freeze and confiscate ill-gotten assets, when it believes that 'the country of origin is unable to satisfy the requirements of MLA proceedings owing to the total or substantial collapse, or the unavailability, of its national judicial system (failure of state structures)'.[68] The Swiss law allows the freezing of contentious assets for up to ten years before launching action to confiscate them in order to later return them. The Swiss example is followed by Canada's 2011 Freezing Assets of Corrupt Foreign Officials Act which targets assets of foreign politically exposed persons when in the foreign state 'there is internal turmoil, or an uncertain political situation' and the freezing of assets is 'in the interest of international relations'.[69]

A success story from the Arab region shows that strong regional commitment and continuing efforts for cooperation based on the rule of international law can bear fruits. In April 2013 US $28.8 million corruptly acquired by Tunisia's former President Ben Ali and held at a Canadian bank in Lebanon by Ben Ali's wife was handed over to Tunisia's President by the Attorney General of the State of Qatar and the United Nations Special Advocate for the Prevention of Corruption, Dr. Ali bin Fetais al-Marri.[70]

The recovery of stolen assets taking place within the Arab World is the result of much hard work done within the Arab Forum on Asset Recovery (AFAR). AFAR is an initiative in support of asset recovery efforts by Arab countries in transition.[71] It was established in 2012 and is supported by the G7, the Deauville Partnership with Arab Countries in Transition, as well as key global and regional financial centres. Since its first meeting in November 2012 in Doha, Qatar, AFAR has addressed the key needs of Arab states in recovering assets and has served as a forum for practical action and cooperation. Mobilizing both policy makers and practitioners, the Arab Forum has generated political momentum, raised awareness locally and internationally of effective measures for asset recovery, promoted domestic coordination and facilitated international cooperation in asset recovery cases.

Including Corruption's Victims in the 'Bargain'

Even in cases where victim states actively pursue recovery, and assets are successfully located, frozen and confiscated, a series of technical legal issues and competing states' claims complicate things and often result in leaving the true victims of corruption 'out of the bargain'.[72] Despite the imperative to repatriate stolen and corrupt assets to the countries of origin, problems have often arisen with the actual return of assets. But as it has been noted emphatically, 'in the end, the UNCAC is and must be about actual recoveries'.[73]

Defining 'Victims'

In this context one should first address the complex question of who is or should be considered a *victim* of corruption. In a particular foreign bribery case, whether harm was suffered, by whom, and where, may prove very difficult to identify and quantify. Things get even more complicated when dealing with various corruption-related offences. For these reasons, there is currently no commonly agreed upon legal definition of corruption victims at the global level. The UNCAC uses the term 'victim' when addressing participation as a civil party to a criminal action[74] and the conditions for qualifying for restitution,[75] but it intentionally avoids further definition of the term.

The concept of a *victim or affected country* is even more complicated and deserving of such a thorough debate, that would go well beyond the scope of this chapter. For the purposes of this study a victim or affected country is understood as any country that may claim harm as a result of transnational bribery, which includes in particular the countries whose officials were allegedly bribed. Countries whose facilities are used, whose nationals serve as intermediaries or whose markets are touched by transactions may also take the position that they are affected. At an individual level the victims of bribery shall be sought on the basis of the principal-agent theory[76] in the circle of the (public or private sector) principals of the corrupt agents/bribees and possibly be extended to competitors of the bribers and other third parties. The broad spectrum of corruption's victims at both a collective and an individual level clearly contradicts the myth that 'corruption is a victimless crime'.

Settlements in Foreign Corruption Cases

A study by the StAR Initiative on the implications of settlements in foreign bribery cases for asset recovery[77] and the respective database of foreign bribery cases,[78] which supplements and extends the study, show that of more than US $6.9 billion realized worldwide between 1999 and mid-2012[79] in monetary sanctions for settlements, only 3.3% (US $197 million) had been returned to states whose officials had been bribed and where corrupt transactions had taken place.[80]

Settlements can be defined for the purposes of this study broadly to include various procedures for concluding foreign bribery cases short of a full trial. These abbreviated and negotiated procedures, in which the two sides (prosecution and defendant) reach a mutually acceptable agreement, can take different forms from one legal system and jurisdiction to the other: guilty pleas, out-of-court restitution arrangements, civil settlements in the United Kingdom and deferred- and non-prosecution agreements in the United States.

From a domestic enforcement perspective, law enforcement and judicial authorities consider settlements an efficient and effective tool to handle complex cases of foreign bribery in a timely manner. The StAR study indicates that settlements are increasingly being used to resolve cases of foreign bribery and related offences. Most recovered through settlement assets relate to embezzled and misappropriated assets (under Article 17 of the UNCAC). The settling jurisdictions are mainly developed countries,[81] whereas the victim countries are mostly developing countries. The reported settlements have been concluded, for the most part, without the involvement or cooperation of the jurisdictions whose officials were allegedly bribed.

The StAR data reveals a huge gap between the amounts realized through settlements and other alternative mechanisms and those returned to the victim countries. Overall the victim jurisdictions were very infrequently and only occasionally informed, consulted or in any other way involved in the conclusion of settlements.[82] These findings demonstrate that the victims of transnational grand corruption, mainly developing countries, have so far been left out of the settlement 'bargains' made mainly by developed countries.

The UNCAC does not explicitly deal with settlements. However, Chapter V of the UNCAC establishes as a fundamental principle the recovery and return of assets to prior legitimate owners and those harmed.[83] Transparency is a further underlying principle of the UNCAC. The trends in the current settlement and asset recovery practices, as outlined above, contradict one of the main functions and purposes of asset recovery: repairing the damage done to the victims. Such practice is in clear contradiction with the basic principles and the true spirit of the UNCAC.

Correct implementation of the UNCAC by States Parties implies the need for greater transparency in settlements. The negotiation of settlements typically takes place between the authorities and alleged offenders, with little oversight by a judge and sometimes without any public hearing at the conclusion. Victims should be allowed access and participation and generally more involvement in the settlement process. There is also a need for more public information on settlements globally. Once an agreement has been reached, it should be made public. Most importantly States Parties must achieve higher rates of actual repatriation of corrupt assets, restitution and compensation of victims.

Last but not least, the needs of civil society must be considered when deciding upon the use of recovered assets. If civil society participation as a preventive measure provided by the UNCAC in Article 13 is to be taken seriously, a notable proportion of recovered assets should be invested in strengthening the capacities of civil society, anti-corruption education and youth empowerment. Youth anti-corruption education in integrity ethics must become one of the main recipients of recovered assets. In any case, the post-recovery use of assets by victim countries must guarantee transparency and accountability.[84]

UNCAC in Practice: The AO Man-Long Case

In 2008 Ao Man-Long, former Secretary of Transport and Public Works of the Macao Special Administrative Region (SAR) of China, was convicted of bribery and bribery-related offences involving approximately US $103 million. He was found guilty of receiving bribes from the Hong Kong real estate tycoon Joseph Lau for favouring Lau's company, Chinese Estates Holdings Ltd., in relation to the acquisition of land in Macao.

In order to launder the bribes, Ao had set up shell companies and a network of secret bank accounts in Hong Kong and the British Virgin Islands with the help of friends and family members. Thirty-nine bank accounts and a safe deposit box for cash were used to hide the corrupt assets at several banks in Hong Kong. Substantial funds were also sent from Hong Kong to the United Kingdom for the purchase of real estate.

Part of the corruption-related assets was recovered in Hong Kong on the basis of private civil action. Due to the absence of an MLA Treaty between Macao and Hong Kong, Macao had to file a civil suit in Hong Kong to recover Ao's illicit assets. Informal MLA channels were used in order for the Hong Kong Independent Commission against Corruption to trace the corrupt assets. Subsequently Hong Kong issued a confiscation order of approximately US $32 million.

The procedure followed for the recovery of the UK-based assets is an exemplary case of the successful implementation of the UNCAC as a basis for international cooperation. Both the MLA Treaty between Hong Kong and the United Kingdom and the UNCAC were used in parallel as independent legal bases for asset recovery. The UNCAC offences implicated were the ones established by Articles 16, 18, 19, 20 and 23. On the basis of the money-laundering offences committed in the United Kingdom, the requesting authorities could freeze the UK real estate asset. Eventually the property was sold under a court order. Under an agreement signed on 3 November 2015 between the government of Macao and the United Kingdom, the latter committed to return GBP £28,718,752.63 to the government of Macao.

Challenges and Outlook

The UNCAC is the most applicable multilateral treaty for international cooperation and MLA in the recovery of the proceeds of corruption. It obliges 181 States Parties to afford one another the widest measure of assistance in investigations, prosecutions and judicial proceedings concerning corruption matters. The UNCAC undoubtedly guides the design of the international asset recovery regime. Its asset recovery provisions present a well-established and supported, in terms of guidance for State Parties and practitioners, mechanism for international asset recovery.

However, the international framework can only be implemented and put to work through its implementation at the domestic level and through the action of national authorities. In this context, the coverage and convergence of national systems are critical in determining the effectiveness of UNCAC as a whole and its asset recovery provisions in particular. Part of the legal doctrine criticizes this dependency and the respective flexibility in UNCAC's provisions.[85] Yet, it must be acknowledged that in 2003, the UNCAC entered unknown territory with its detailed mandatory provisions on asset recovery and as a truly universal legal instrument it had to seek consensus and make compromises amid conflicting countries' interests.[86]

Unfortunately, many States Parties still do not comply fully with their direct (MLA-related) and indirect (criminalization-related) obligations under Chapter V of the UNCAC. Criminal law-related compliance suggests that national jurisdictions expand their anti-corruption and AML criminal provisions to the widest range of offences established both under the UNCAC and the UNTOC and ensure that the scope of their domestic legal framework for seizure and confiscation encompasses all offences under the international conventions.

With regard to MLA-related compliance, a few States Parties do not have a domestic MLA framework in place at all, while other states frequently fail to allow in their domestic MLA laws for all types of assistance (especially assistance in NCB and civil confiscation)[87] as set out in the UNCAC, provide for overly broad grounds for MLA refusal or apply overly stringent evidentiary requirements.[88] Even in jurisdictions where transposition of international self-executing provisions, such as many of the ones contained in Chapter V of the UNCAC, is not required, practitioners are often unfamiliar with the UNCAC provisions on asset recovery and rarely use them as an independent legal basis for cooperation.[89] The direct applicability of the UNCAC as an autonomous legal basis for transborder asset recovery is an invaluable tool, which is often overlooked in theory and practice.

Consequently, States Parties are encouraged to put in place legislation that provides for the widest possible range of asset recovery tools in accordance with the UNCAC. Particular attention should be given to mechanisms for non-conviction-based forfeiture and civil proceedings. In most jurisdictions these legal avenues require a much lower evidential threshold than criminal forfeiture, they are quicker and they don't have to meet the problematic pre-condition of dual criminality.

The challenges posed by money laundering and the flaws in effectiveness and efficiency of the global AML legal framework and regulatory policies should not discourage us from further strengthening international cooperation in asset recovery. Asset recovery theory and practice need to adopt the broadest possible approach and further explore and intensify synergies between the international laws against corruption, money laundering and transnational organized crime.

With regard to the repatriation of confiscated corrupt assets to the victim countries, this chapter argues that respect of victims´ rights for compensation should be the guiding principle in international asset recovery. The current practice contradicts this finding. Despite the good deal of progress made by countries to foster asset recovery, much more work needs to be done if the international community truly aspires to fulfil the promise of the UNCAC: global justice in line with victims' rights for restitution.

The fact that Chapter V of the UNCAC (together with Chapter II on 'Preventive Measures') is currently (2015–2019) undergoing review by the Implementation Review Group of the Conference of States Parties to the UNCAC presents an ideal opportunity to strengthen compliance at the national level by helping countries identify and address any implementation gaps and expand national and regional (e.g. Arab Forum on Asset Recovery) best practices in asset recovery. As experience and expertise will improve, more and more countries are expected to base their requests for international cooperation in asset recovery on the UNCAC. As the US Attorney General Eric Holder noted,

> it is only with a truly international and cooperative response that we will be able to achieve success in recovering the proceeds of corruption.[90]

Notes

1. United Nations Convention Against Corruption (adopted 31 October 2003, entered into force 14 December 2005) (UNCAC), Foreword iii–iv.
2. The text of the UNCAC is available at <http://www.unodc.org> accessed 10 April 2017.
3. For further discussion, see Kevin M Stephenson and others, *Barriers to Asset Recovery: An Analysis of the Key Barriers and Recommendations for Action* (World Bank 2011); Indira Carr and Robert Jago, 'Corruption, the United Nations Convention Against Corruption ('UNCAC') and Asset Recovery' in Colin King and Clive Walker (eds), *Dirty Assets: Emerging Issues in the Regulation of Criminal and Terrorist Assets* (Ashgate Publishing 2014).
4. For discussion of illicit financial flows from developing countries, see Dev Kar and Joseph Spanjers, *Illicit Financial Flows from Developing Countries: 2004–2013* (Global Financial Integrity 2015).
5. EU Anti-Corruption Report, 'Report from the Commission to Council and the European Parliament' COM (2014) 38 final, 3.
6. UNODC, *Estimating Illicit Financial Flows Resulting From Drug Trafficking and Other Transnational Organized Crimes* (UNODC 2011); For criticism of the UNODC report, see Chap. 15 (van Duyne, Harvey, and Gelemerova) in this collection.
7. UNODC and World Bank, *Stolen Asset Recovery (StAR) Initiative: Challenges, Opportunities, and Action Plan* (World Bank 2007) 1.
8. As of 10 April 2017.
9. For a brief overview of the anti-corruption Conventions, see Carr and Jago (n 3) 206–10, and for more detail, Marco Arnone and Leonardo Borlini, *Corruption: Economic Analysis and International Law* (Edward Elgar Publishing 2014) 219–270; Jan Wouters, Cedric Ryngaert, and Ann Sofie Cloots, 'The International Legal Framework Against Corruption: Achievements and Challenges' (2013) 14(1) Melbourne Journal of International Law 1.
10. UNCAC art 15.
11. UNCAC art 16.

12. UNCAC art 17.
13. UNCAC art 23.
14. UNCAC art 25.
15. UNCAC arts 21 and 22.
16. UNCAC art 20.
17. UNCAC art 19.
18. UNCAC art 18.
19. UNCAC art 24.
20. 'Predicate offence' means according to UNCAC art 2(h) any offence as a result of which proceeds have been generated that may become the subject of money laundering.
21. David Chaikin and Jason C Sharman, *Corruption and Money Laundering: A Symbiotic Relationship* (Palgrave Macmillan 2009), argue correctly that failure to properly understand the corruption-money laundering nexus undermines the success of policy measures to tackle them.
22. UNCAC art 23(2)(c).
23. *Grand* corruption as opposed to *petty* corruption is a non-legal term, which describes corruption occurring at the highest levels of (public or private) power and usually involving high sums of bribes or value of other undue advantages.
24. UNTOC itself proscribes four types of 'core' crimes: participation in an organised criminal group (Article 5), corruption (Article 6), money laundering (Article 8) and obstruction of justice (Article 23).
25. See United Nations Convention Against Transnational Organized Crime (UNTOC) (adopted on 15 November 2000, entered into force on 29 September 2003). The Convention has 147 signatories and 187 Parties as of 10 April 2017. For a comprehensive overview of the criminal provisions of the UNTOC, see Neil Boister, 'The UN Convention Against Transnational Organized Crime 2000' in Pierre Hauck and Sven Peterke (eds), *International Law and Transnational Organised Crime* (OUP 2016).
26. See generally Roger S Clark, 'The United Nations Convention against Transnational Organized Crime' (2004) 50(1) Wayne Law Review 161; David McClean, *Transnational Organized Crime: A Commentary on the UN Convention and its Protocols* (OUP 2007); Dimitri Vlassis, 'The United Nations Convention Against Transnational Organized Crime and its Protocols: A New Era in International Cooperation' in International Centre for Criminal Law Reform and Criminal Justice Policy (ed), *The Changing Face of International Criminal Law* (International Centre for Criminal Law Reform and Criminal Justice 2002).
27. Article 8 UNTOC corresponds to Article 15 UNCAC, although it has a much broader title: 'criminalization of corruption'. Criminalizing bribery of *foreign* public officials or other forms of corruption remains a non-binding recommendation towards UNTOC States Parties.
28. The definition of 'organized criminal group' is set out in UNTOC art 2(a).

29. As defined in UNTOC art 2(b).
30. See UNTOC art 3(1). For the criteria of 'transnationality', see UNTOC art 3(2).
31. See UNTOC art 19 ('Joint investigations') and art 20 ('Special investigative techniques').
32. UNTOC's provisions are generally phrased and very basic when compared with UNCAC's thorough and clearly outlined procedures for international cooperation in asset recovery, as outlined below.
33. See Philippa Webb, 'The United Nations Convention Against Corruption: Global Achievement or Missed Opportunity?' (2005) 8(1) Journal of International Economic Law 191, 204. UNTOC's lacking precision and consequently enforceability is also seen in the loose definitions of 'organised criminal group' and 'serious crime'. See Boister (n 25) 149.
34. The Conference of Parties to the UNTOC has no clear powers: reviews need only be made 'periodically', and there is no process for verifying country reports. See Webb (n 33).
35. See, UNODC, *Legislative Guide for the Implementation of the United Nations Convention Against Corruption* (2nd edn, United Nations 2012) <http://www.unodc.org/pdf/corruption/CoC_LegislativeGuide.pdf> accessed 10 April 2017; UNODC and United Nations Interregional Crime and Justice Research Institute (UNICRI), *Technical Guide to the United Nations Convention Against Corruption* (United Nations 2009) <http://www.unodc.org/documents/corruption/Technial_Guide_UNCAC.pdf> accessed 10 April 2017.
36. See Stephenson and others (n 3) 50.
37. UNCAC art 65(1).
38. Mutual legal assistance may be requested according to Article 46 for various purposes, including: '(j) Identifying, freezing and tracing proceeds of crime in accordance with the provisions of chapter V of this Convention; (k) The recovery of assets, in accordance with the provisions of chapter V of this Convention'.
39. UNCAC art 57.
40. UNCAC arts 31, 54, and 55 in conjunction with Chapter III on corruption crimes.
41. UNCAC art 54(1)(c).
42. UNCAC art 53.
43. UNCAC art 52(1).
44. See FATF, 'International Standards on Combating Money Laundering and the Financing of Terrorism and Proliferation—the FATF Recommendations' (2012, last updated 2016), 113 <http://www.fatf-gafi.org/media/fatf/documents/recommendations/pdfs/FATF_Recommendations.pdf> accessed 10 April 2017.
45. OECD, 'Global Forum on Transparency and Exchange of Information for Tax Purposes' <http://www.oecd.org/tax/transparency> accessed 10 April 2017, has identified a list of jurisdictions as 'tax havens'.

46. Public functions are exercised by 'public officials'. The latter are defined in UNCAC art 2(a).
47. FATF (n 44) 123.
48. See the Cayman Islands Guardian Bank and Trust case (Russo Cable case) in OECD, *Behind the Corporate Veil: Using Corporate Entities for Illicit Purposes* (OECD 2001), 93 <http://www.oecd.org/corporate/ca/43703185.pdf> accessed 10 April 2017.
49. For further discussion of correspondent banks, see Chapter 11 (Ramachandran, Collin, and Juden) and Chapter 12 (Levi) in this collection.
50. '… requiring public officials to make declarations to appropriate authorities regarding, inter alia, their outside activities, employment, investments, assets and substantial gifts or benefits from which a conflict of interest may result with respect to their functions as public officials': UNCAC art 8(5).
51. Stephenson and others, (n 3) 55, recommend that jurisdictions should introduce mechanisms that allow for prompt tracing and *temporary* freezing of assets before a formal MLA request is filed.
52. UNCAC art 2(e). The same definition is adopted in UNTOC art 2(e). For 'property', see UNCAC art 2(d). Converted or mixed property is dealt with by UNCAC art 31(4)–(6).
53. Adopted from the training Module of the World Bank, *Asset Recovery Process and Avenues for Recovering Assets* (complementing the *Asset Recovery Handbook: A Guide for Practitioners* (World Bank 2011)), 12 <http://pubdocs.worldbank.org/en/824561427730120107/AML-Module-5.pdf> accessed 10 April 2017.
54. According to UNCAC art 46(1), 'States Parties shall afford one another the widest measure of mutual legal assistance in investigations, prosecutions and judicial proceedings in relation to the offences covered by this Convention'.
55. UNCAC art 54(2)(a)–(b).
56. UNODC, *Legislative Guide* (n 35) 255.
57. StAR Asset Recovery Watch is a project of the Stolen Asset Recovery (StAR) Initiative of the UNODC and the World Bank. The database compiles, systematizes and publishes information about completed and active asset recovery efforts around the world. For more information, see their website <http://star.worldbank.org/corruption-cases/arwcases> accessed 10 April 2017.
58. See further Chapter 26 (Lord and Levi) in this collection.
59. Some see in this assumption a fundamental weakness of the UNCAC: Tim Daniel and James Maton, 'Is the UNCAC an Effective Deterrent to Grand Corruption?' in Jeremy Horder and Peter Alldridge (eds), *Modern Bribery Law: Comparative Perspectives* (CUP 2013) 322.
60. This was the case with the assets of Zaire's (now the Democratic Republic of the Congo) corrupt President Mobutu Sese Sisoko. See Daniel and Maton (n 59) 321; Konye Obaji Ori, 'Swiss Court Approves African Kleptocracy: Mobutu's Loot to Go to his Family' *Afrik News* (15 July 2009) <http://www.afrik-news.com/article15923.html> accessed 10 April 2017.

61. Stephenson and others (n 3) 24 define lacking political will to mean a lack of a comprehensive, sustained, and concerted policy or strategy to identify asset recovery as a priority and to ensure alignment of objectives, tools, and resources to this end.

62. Daniel and Maton (n 59) 316 name Indonesia and Kenya as states which request assistance abroad but fail to produce evidence of any will to prosecute at home and the Democratic Republic of the Congo (DRC), Haiti, Equatorial Guinea, Gabon and the Congo Republic (Congo Brazzaville) as victim states which fail to take any action whatsoever.

63. Muammar Gaddafi, Hosni Mubarak and Zine El-Abidine Ben Ali, respectively.

64. See *The Economist*, 'Making a Hash of Finding the Cash' *The Economist* (Cairo, 11 May 2013) <http://www.economist.com/news/international/21577368-why-have-arab-countries-recovered-so-little-money-thought-have-been-nabbed> accessed 12 May 2017.

65. Oliver Bullough, 'The Money Machine: How a High-Profile Corruption Investigation Fell Apart' *The Guardian* (London, 12 April 2017) <http://www.theguardian.com/world/2017/apr/12/the-money-machine-how-a-high-profile-corruption-investigation-fell-apart> accessed 12 May 2017.

66. See full text of the 'Federal Act on the Restitution of Assets illicitly obtained by Politically Exposed Persons' (RIAA) <http://www.admin.ch/opc/en/classified-compilation/20100418/201102010000/196.1.pdf> accessed 10 April 2017.

67. For a discussion of the case of former (1971–1986) Haitian dictator Jean-Claude 'Baby Doc' Duvalier, see Daniel and Maton (n 59) 320ff, and the StAR, 'Asset Recovery Watch Report' <http://star.worldbank.org/corruption-cases/node/18515> accessed 10 April 2017.

68. RIAA (n 66) art 2 (c). For a detailed analysis of the RIAA, see Frank Meyer, 'Restitution of Dirty Assets: A Swiss Template for the International Community' in Katalin Ligeti and Michele Simonato (eds), *Chasing Criminal Money: Challenges and Perspectives on Asset Recovery in the EU* (Hart Publishing 2017).

69. Article 4(2)(b)-(c). See full text <http://laws.justice.gc.ca/PDF/F-31.6.pdf> accessed 10 April 2017.

70. Jean-Pierre Brun and Richard Miron, 'Tunisia's-Cash-Back: The Start of More to Come?' *StAR Asset Recovery Blog* (12 April 2013) <https://star.worldbank.org/star/news/tunisia's-cash-back> accessed 10 April 2017; The Guardian, 'Tunisia Recovers $28m From Wife of Deposed President' *The Guardian* (London, 11 April 2013) <www.theguardian.com/world/2013/apr/11/tunisia-28m-wife-deposed-president> accessed 12 May 2017.

71. For more information about AFAR <https://star.worldbank.org/star/ArabForum/About> accessed 10 April 2017.

72. See Jacinta Anyango Oduor and others, *Left Out of the Bargain: Settlements in Foreign Bribery Cases and Implications for Asset Recovery* (World Bank 2014), 2 <http://star.worldbank.org/star/sites/star/files/9781464800863.pdf> accessed 10 April 2017.

73. Daniel Claman, 'The Promise and Limitations of Asset Recovery Under the UNCAC' in Mark Pieth (ed), *Recovering Stolen Assets* (Peter Lang 2008) 350.

74. Article 32 (Protection of witnesses, experts and victims) para 5 requires that States Parties 'enable the views and concerns of *victims* to be presented and considered at appropriate stages of criminal proceedings'.

75. Article 57(3)(c), as already discussed, asks States Parties to 'give priority consideration to returning confiscated property to the requesting State Party, returning such property to its prior legitimate owners or compensating the victims of the crime'.

76. For the principal-agent model as perceived by neo-institutional economics, see among others Niko Groenendijk, 'A Principal-Agent Model of Corruption' (1997) 27(3) Crime, Law and Social Change 207.

77. Oduor and others (n 72).

78. StAR Corruption Cases Search Center <http://star.worldbank.org/corruption-cases/assetrecovery> accessed 10 April 2017.

79. The database reports a further US $4 billion of monetary sanctions imposed between mid-2012 and mid-2016.

80. The concluded settlements in the corruption cases of Ferdinand Marcos in the Philippines, Sani Abacha in Nigeria and Muammar el-Qaddafi in Libya (ongoing) and the individuals and entities associated with them make up the biggest portion of the recovered amount.

81. The United States, Germany, the United Kingdom and Switzerland lead the list, with approximately two-thirds of the cases having been settled by the US Department of Justice (DOJ) and the US Securities and Exchange Commission (SEC).

82. Conference of the States Parties to the United Nations Convention against Corruption, Open-ended Intergovernmental Working Group on Asset Recovery, 10th Intersessional Meeting (Vienna, 25–26 August 2016), Note by the Secretariat on 'Settlements and other alternative mechanisms in transnational bribery cases and their implications for the recovery and return of stolen assets' CAC/COSP/WG.2/2016/2 (2016), 18.

83. Due consideration of victims' rights is not a novelty of the UNCAC. It is also manifested in UNTOC art 14(2).

84. The James Giffen—Mercator Corporation oil mining case (see the StAR Asset Recovery Watch report <http://star.worldbank.org/corruption-cases/node/18528> accessed 10 April 2017, and the subsequent establishment in Kazakhstan of the BOTA foundation for the repatriation of US $ 115 million following a MoU between the governments of the United States, Switzerland and Kazakhstan is a successful case of assets invested in affected local communities and overseen by the World Bank. See Aaron Bornstein, 'Key Lessons of the BOTA foundation' *The FCPA Blog* (5 April 2017) <www.fcpablog.com/blog/2017/4/5/aaron-bornstein-key-lessons-of-the-bota-foundation.html> accessed 10 April 2017.

85. Arnone and Borlini (n 9) 258 argue that 'the drafters of the UNCAC gave "too" high a priority to flexibility with the purpose of accommodating an agreement meeting the various contracting parties' positions'.

86. See Dimitri Vlassis, 'The United Nations Convention Against Corruption: A Way of Life' in Nikos Passas and Dimitri Vlassis (eds), *The United Nations Convention Against Corruption As a Way of Life: Selected Papers and Contributions from the International Conference on 'The United Nations Convention Against Corruption As a Way of Life' (Courmayeur, 15–17 December 2006)* (ISPAC—International Scientific and Professional Advisory Council of the United Nations Crime Prevention and Criminal Justice Programme 2007) 15, 32 <http://ispac.cnpds.org/publications-22-the-united-nations-convention-against-corruption-as-a-way-of-life-22.html> accessed 10 April 2017.

87. For the importance of domestic legislation permitting NCB confiscation, see Stephenson and others (n 3) 66. For a list of jurisdictions permitting NCB confiscation and relevant legislation, see Theodore Greenberg and others, '*Stolen Asset Recovery: A Good Practices Guide for NCB Asset Forfeiture*' (World Bank 2009).

88. Stephenson and others (n 3) 50.

89. Ibid. 50.

90. Speech at the Opening Plenary of the VI Ministerial Global Forum on Fighting Corruption and Safeguarding Integrity (Doha, 7 November 2009) <https://www.justice.gov/ag/speeches/2009/ag-speech-091107.html> accessed 10 April 2017.

Dimitris Ziouvas (LLB Athens, LLM Freiburg, Dr. iur. Cologne) is a Reader in Criminal Law and Compliance at Sussex Law School. In 2016 he was awarded the Sheikh Tamim bin Hamad Al Thani Anti-Corruption Excellence Award in support of the United Nations Office on Drugs and Crime for his research, social impact and work as President of the 'Eurasian Integrity Youth Academy'. Dimitris has served on the Advisory Board of the Greek Anti-Corruption Authority. He participates at the Conference of States Parties to the UNCAC and the UNCAC Intergovernmental Review Group on Asset Recovery. Dimitris, a certified fraud examiner, practises international financial criminal law as a compliance officer, an ombudsman and a lawyer admitted in Greece and Germany.

26

In Pursuit of the Proceeds of Transnational Corporate Bribery: The UK Experience to Date

Nicholas Lord and Michael Levi

Introduction

As we began writing this chapter on the proceeds of corporate bribery and their confiscation, recovery and disgorgement, the UK[1] Serious Fraud Office (SFO), the lead authority for the investigation and prosecution of corporate corruption, secured approval from Lord Justice Leveson for a third Deferred Prosecution Agreement (DPA) for a company implicated in the bribery of foreign public officials.[2] The company concerned is Rolls Royce PLC, the UK's leading manufacturing multinational corporation, and the DPA, announced in January 2017, involved 12 counts of conspiracy to corrupt, false accounting and failure to prevent bribery. The company, specifically its Civil Aerospace and Defence Aerospace businesses and its former Energy business, used a network of agents to bribe officials in at least seven different countries[3] to win lucrative contracts over a period spanning three decades.[4] Consequently, the company agreed to pay a financial settlement of £497.25m (plus £13m prosecution costs) to the SFO in addition to agreeing a number of terms such as cooperation in the prosecution of individuals.[5]

N. Lord
School of Law, University of Manchester, Manchester, UK

M. Levi
School of Social Sciences, Cardiff University, Cardiff, UK

C. King et al. (eds.), *The Palgrave Handbook of Criminal and Terrorism Financing Law*,
https://doi.org/10.1007/978-3-319-64498-1_26

Less than a year earlier, the SFO concluded its first successful prosecution of a corporation, Sweett Group PLC, for a failure to prevent an act of bribery intended to secure and retain a contract in the course of its business in the United Arab Emirates, contrary to section 7(1)(b) of the Bribery Act 2010.[6] The SFO investigation revealed that its subsidiary company, Cyril Sweett International Limited, made corrupt payments to Khaled Al Badie, the Vice Chairman of the Board and Chairman of the Real Estate and Investment Committee of Al Ain Ahlia Insurance Company (AAAI) to secure the award of a contract with AAAI for the building of the Rotana Hotel in Abu Dhabi. Sweett Group received a criminal fine of £1.4m in addition to a confiscation order of £851,000 and a requirement to cover prosecution costs of £95,000. These cases provide clear insight into the policy direction of the UK Government and the SFO in how it intends to respond to UK corporations implicated in transnational corporate bribery. As we can see, a central component of this policy is to disgorge, confiscate, recover or otherwise reappropriate the benefits of the corruption in addition to other financial penalties that can potentially be used for compensation, reparation or other financial needs.

In the UK Government's Anti-Corruption Plan 2014, the section concerned with tackling illicit financial flows linked to corruption was fronted with a quote from the then Home Secretary, Theresa May, stating that '[c]racking down on corruption, and working to recover stolen assets, is an issue which has increasingly gained international importance and is one we must continue to work hard on'.[7] When Mrs May made this statement, it appears she did not have in mind those proceeds of corrupt transactions instigated by otherwise respectable 'UK Plc' as part of their legitimate business operations, but instead those corrupt foreign officials and 'organised crime'-associated 'bad guys' who are laundering their corrupt funds through the UK's financial system and property market, or demanding payments from UK businesses in their own countries. While the section includes an overview of 'foreign bribery', there are no questions raised over how we might disincentivise the giving of bribes by confiscating the proceeds generated in these corrupt business transactions. This chapter focuses on this very issue, exploring how the proceeds of bribery generated for those corporations on the 'supply side' have been targeted and what more could be done.

We begin with a brief overview of how we define and conceptualise transnational corporate bribery and consider related legal developments at the domestic and international levels for the pursuit of the proceeds of corruption. Next, we analyse the finances of transnational corporate bribery, thinking about what needs to be financed for such bribery and of course the finances that are generated from such bribery. This is important for understanding the financial orders that are levied against corporations for these offences, and here we include an analysis of all cases of corporate bribery to have been sanctioned for substantive bribery offences in the UK since the emergence of corporate bribery as a criminal offence. We also consider the mechanisms that are utilised by corporate offenders to conceal the finances of their bribery. Additionally, we turn to the specific control mechanisms available for targeting the proceeds of corruption, including confiscation, civil recovery, disgorgement, compensation, reparation and restitution, criminal/civil fines and voluntary payments. We also consider where these monies actually go and for what purpose. Finally, we conclude with a discussion of key issues in dealing with the proceeds of corruption and consider likely future scenarios in this area.

What Is Transnational Corporate Bribery?

Transnational corporate bribery involves legitimate corporations and commercial enterprises that operate in licit transnational markets and use illicit (financial) transactions/exchanges to win or maintain business contracts in foreign jurisdictions.[8] This form of bribery involves the bribing of foreign (public) officials by corporations operating in international business and is organised across jurisdictional boundaries (e.g. via intermediaries or third parties; money laundering). For instance, in some cases, bribery will be used to win or maintain multi-million pound contracts for the corporation involved. Such illicit arrangements are often referred to as 'grand corruption' and can involve monetary or non-monetary inducements such as cash payments and kickbacks through contracts, or the provision of gifts, favours and services. The bribery may also occur on a smaller scale, often referred to as 'petty corruption', where we see small payments to facilitate and expedite necessary business procedures and operations, such as the timely crossing of borders. In the aggregate, these small bribes can be very substantial, particularly where payments are made systematically in the course of business over time. The UK criminalises such 'facilitation payments', but other jurisdictions, such as the US, have created legal exceptions in order not to 'unfairly' jeopardise the competitiveness of their international businesses.

In all cases of bribery, there is an inherent illicit transaction (a specific event) or relationship (an on-going state) between at least two willing or at least consenting active/passive actors that leads to an advantage in business for the corporation.[9] Those on the 'recipient side' gain varied benefits. The intention is to clandestinely ensure the commission or omission of certain acts that breach an individual's duties primarily for the benefit of the corporation though individual gain usually accompanies this either directly, as a 'cut', or indirectly, via promotion or job retention for those on the 'supply side'. There are few direct, identifiable victims although there are substantial political, social, economic and environmental harms.[10]

Since the late twentieth century, corporate bribery has emerged as a priority concern internationally for organisations such as the OECD, UN and EU as well as non-governmental anti-corruption organisations such as Transparency International and Global Witness, amongst others. Such organisations have over time sought to create and harmonise normative anti-bribery frameworks and international standards in order to facilitate credible domestic responses to bribery in international business.[11] This international dialogue, largely influenced by the USA,[12] led to the creation of the Organisation for Economic Co-operation and Development's (OECD) Convention on Combating Bribery of Foreign Public Officials in International Business Transactions 1997 (OECD Anti-Bribery Convention) and its associated programme of peer-review monitoring and expert evaluations coordinated by intergovernmental organisations[13] and the evaluative reports of (inter)national non-governmental organisations. Consequently, nation states are under pressure to respond to transnational corporate bribery.

The UK has signed and ratified the two main global anti-corruption conventions: the OECD Anti-Bribery Convention (signed December 1998 and ratified February 2002) and the UN Convention against Corruption 2004 (UNCAC) (signed December 2003 and ratified February 2006). Offences of bribery and corruption abroad were introduced via sections 108–110 of the Anti-Terrorism, Crime and Security Act 2001 which imported a foreign element to the ageing Prevention of Corruption Acts (1889–1916).[14] These amendments brought the UK's legal framework in line with international legal requirements. In the UK, the introduction of the Bribery Act 2010 consolidated and strengthened the previously fragmented framework and created the most wide-reaching anti-bribery legislation on the globe. This legislation created discrete offences of 'bribing another person' (offering, promising or giving a financial or other advantage), of 'being bribed' (requesting, agreeing to receive or accepting a financial or other advantage), and of 'bribing foreign public officials' in addition to making it a criminal offence for a commercial organisation to fail to prevent bribery within or by their organisation.[15] Our focus here is on the UK as a generator and venue for bribery. We focus primarily on the 'supply side' of bribery, that is, those UK corporations, or employees, subsidiaries and/or agents acting on behalf of these corporations, that give, offer or promise a bribe or inducement to a foreign public official usually to lead those officials to breach their duties. We assess the monies that are confiscated from these corporate actors.

Table 26.1 provides an overview of all cases of actual transnational corporate bribery to have been sanctioned in the UK since it became a criminal

Table 26.1 The finances of transnational corporate bribery

Sanctioned business (criminal and civil)— lead agency/year	Nature of case	Sanctioned offence	Business advantage obtained	Financial penalty
Balfour Beatty SFO—2008	Payment irregularities during execution of construction project in Egypt.	Inaccurate accounting records in breach of s.221 Companies Act 1985.	– No apparent financial benefit. – Alleged construction contract worth £100m.	Civil recovery of £2.25m plus unspecified prosecution costs.
Amec Plc SFO—2009	Receipt of irregular payments associated with a project in which AMEC is a shareholder.	Breach of duty to keep accounting records contrary to s.221 Companies Act 1985.	Approximately £5m received as a result of bribery and corruption elsewhere in a project in which AMEC is a shareholder.	Civil recovery of £4.9m plus costs.
Mabey and Johnson Ltd SFO—2009	Corruptive payments to influence decision-makers in public contracts in Jamaica and Ghana. (Also sanctioned for breaching UN sanctions in Iraq.)	Conspiracy to corrupt contrary to s.1 Criminal Law Act 1977 and s.1 Prevention of Corruption Act 1906.	Contracts worth £60m–£70m.	£6.6m in financial penalties including £1.5m criminal fine for corruption offences in Ghana/Jamaica plus £2m for Iraq. A Confiscation Order of £1.1m, compensation of £618,484 to UN Development Fund, reparations of £797,000 to Ghana/Jamaica and £350,000 prosecution costs.

(continued)

Table 26.1 (continued)

Sanctioned business (criminal and civil)—lead agency/year	Nature of case	Sanctioned offence	Business advantage obtained	Financial penalty
BAE Systems SFO—2010	Failure to keep adequate accounting records of corruptive commission payments relating to the sale of an air traffic control system to Tanzania.	Breach of duty to keep accounting records contrary to s.221 Companies Act 1985.	£28m in radar contracts with the Tanzanian military.	£500,000 criminal fine plus £225,000 prosecution costs. Plus ex gratia payment of £29.5m to Tanzanian Government.
Innospec SFO—2010	Corruptive payments to public officials of the Government of Indonesia to secure contracts for sale of tetraethyl lead.	Conspiracy to corrupt contrary to s.1 Criminal Law Act 1977 and s.1 Prevention of Corruption Act 1906.	Up to US$160m [£104.9m] in contracts and benefits.	$12.7m [£8.3m][a] incorporating confiscation order ($6.7m [£4.4m]) and civil recovery ($6m [£3.9m]) plus prosecution costs.
DePuy International Ltd (UK subsidiary of Johnson and Johnson in the USA who also faced bribery charges) SFO—2011	Corruptive payments to Greek medical professionals relating to the sale of orthopaedic products.	Not specified. No corporate criminal prosecution so to avoid 'double jeopardy', as company criminally sanctioned in the USA. Former Director John Dougall prosecuted for conspiracy to corrupt contrary to s.1 Criminal Law Act 1977 and s.1 Prevention of Corruption Act 1906.	Retention and enhancement of market position. Greek government paid approximately £33.5m to DePuy for products (£14.8 passed back to DePuy, £14.8m represents unlawfully obtained property).	Civil recovery of £4.8m plus unspecified prosecution costs (plus fines of US parent company Johnson and Johnson). Recovery limited by SFO in light of US fines.

(continued)

Table 26.1 (continued)

Sanctioned business (criminal and civil)—lead agency/year	Nature of case	Sanctioned offence	Business advantage obtained	Financial penalty
MW Kellogg Ltd SFO—2011	Used by US parent company to distance itself from a special purpose vehicle used to make corruptive payments to Nigeria.	No predicate offence. Civil recovery under Part 5 Proceeds of Crime Act 2002.	N/A	Civil recovery of £7m in recognition of sums that MW Kellogg was due to receive from criminal activities of third parties plus prosecution costs.
Macmillan Publishers Ltd SFO/OACU—2011	Corruptive payments to influence public tender processes in Rwanda, Uganda and Zambia for the supply of educational materials.	Not specified beyond general corruption offences.	Contracts to supply products (educational materials) valued at approximately £11.2m.	Civil recovery of £11.2m plus prosecution costs.
Oxford Publishing Ltd SFO—2012	Kenyan and Tanzanian subsidiaries of company offered and made payments, directly and through agents, intended to induce the recipients to award competitive tenders and/or publishing contracts for schoolbooks.	Not specified beyond general corruption offences. S.266 Proceeds of Crime Act used for civil recovery.	Unspecified but dividends and fees paid by subsidiaries to OPL, and therefore revenue created, from bribery and corruption.	Civil recovery of £1.9m plus prosecution costs.

(continued)

Table 26.1 (continued)

Sanctioned business (criminal and civil)—lead agency/year	Nature of case	Sanctioned offence	Business advantage obtained	Financial penalty
Smith and Ouzman Ltd. SFO—2014	Corruptive payments to influence the award of business contracts (related to security documents, e.g. ballot papers) to the company in Mauritania and Kenya.	Conspiracy to corrupt contrary to s.1 Criminal Law Act 1977 and s.1 Prevention of Corruption Act 1906.	Award of contracts of unspecified amount.	£2.2m (consisting of £1.3m criminal fine, £881,158 confiscation order and £25,000 in prosecution costs).
Standard Bank SFO—2015	Failure to prevent bribery by its sister company, Stanbic Bank Tanzania, to a local partner in Tanzania, Enterprise Growth Market Advisors (EGMA) to induce members of the Government of Tanzania.	Failure of a commercial organisation to prevent bribery contrary to Section 7 of the Bribery Act 2010.	Gained favour for a proposal for a US$600m [£398.8m] private placement to be carried out on behalf of the Government of Tanzania. The placement generated transaction fees of US$8.4m [£5.6m], shared by Stanbic Tanzania and Standard Bank.	Deferred Prosecution Agreement (DPA) with financial orders of US$25.2 m [£16.2m] including payment of compensation of US$6m [£4m][b] plus interest (US$1 m [£0.66m]), financial penalty of US$16.8 m [£11.2m], payment of costs of £330k and disgorgement of profit of US$8.4 m [£5.6m].

(continued)

Table 26.1 (continued)

Sanctioned business (criminal and civil)—lead agency/year	Nature of case	Sanctioned offence	Business advantage obtained	Financial penalty
Sweett Group SFO—2016	Failure to prevent bribery by its subsidiary company intended to secure and retain a contract with Al Ain Ahlia Insurance Company in the UAE.	Failure of a commercial organisation to prevent bribery contrary to Section 7(1)(b) of the Bribery Act 2010.	Not specified.	£1.4m criminal fine plus £851k in confiscation and £95k prosecution costs.
Anonymous SME SFO—2016	Company's employees and agents involved in the systematic offer and/or payment of bribes to secure contracts in foreign jurisdictions.	Conspiracy to corrupt, contrary to section 1 of the Criminal Law Act 1977, conspiracy to bribe, contrary to section 1 of the same Act and failure to prevent bribery, contrary to section 7 of the Bribery Act 2010.	The total gross profit from the implicated contracts amounted to £6,553,085.	DPA with financial orders of £6,553,085: comprised of a £6,201,085 disgorgement of gross profits and a £352,000 financial penalty. (The SFO agreed not to seek costs.)

(continued)

Table 26.1 (continued)

Sanctioned business (criminal and civil)—lead agency/year	Nature of case	Sanctioned offence	Business advantage obtained	Financial penalty
Rolls Royce PLC SFO—2017	12 counts of conspiracy to corrupt, false accounting and failure to prevent bribery. The company, and its associated persons, used a network of agents to bribe officials in at least seven different countries.	Six offences of conspiracy to corrupt, contrary to section 1 of the Criminal Law Act 1977; five offences of failure of a commercial organisation to prevent bribery, contrary to Section 7(1)(b) of the Bribery Act 2010; and one offence of false accounting contrary to s. 17(1)(a) of the Theft Act 1968.	Profit gained equated to £258,170,000.	DPA with disgorgement of profit of £258,170,000, a financial penalty of £239,082,645, and payment of costs of £13,000,000.

Sanctions have also been imposed on individuals engaging in foreign bribery, including Julian Messent (PWS International), Bruce Hall (Alba), Neils Jorgen Tobiasen (CBRN) and four employees from the Swift Group as well as those breaching UN Sanctions, for example, Mark Jessop (Bureau Ltd and Opthalmedex Ltd), amongst others, but the focus here is explicitly on *corporate* bribery. In addition, cases involving sanctions for having inadequate systems to prevent bribery (and thus where no bribery may have occurred) such as in the case of AON Ltd have also been excluded, although suspicious payments were recognised

[a] The SFO recorded the figures in US Dollars. These were converted using an exchange rate of US1$: £ 0.6555227689. This was the exchange rate on the day of the announcement = 18 March 2010

[b] The SFO recorded the figures in US Dollars. These were converted using an exchange rate of US1$: £ 0.6646439742. This was the exchange rate on the day of the announcement = 30 November 2015

offence in 2002. Despite being criminalised in 2002, the first case to be sanctioned in the UK was not until 2008 when Balfour Beatty received a civil recovery order of £2.25m for payment irregularities during the execution of a construction project in Egypt. Enforcement was not immediately forthcoming following criminalisation. This reflects practical issues, in that these cases are not immediately identifiable as bribery occurs, but often come to light much later. In addition, political will to support investigation and prosecution was lacking, and we saw this in the case of BAE Systems in 2006, when the then Prime Minister Tony Blair intervened with the investigation on security grounds in the context of counterterrorism (and perhaps to protect the UK's economic interests).[16] However, since 2008, cases have more regularly been investigated and sanctioned. As the table indicates, these cases relate to varied offences, such as inaccurate accounting, conspiracy to corrupt and failure to prevent bribery. The small number of cases means enforcement trends or patterns cannot be discerned, but cases have predominantly been dealt with through non-criminal sanctioning mechanisms, such as civil recovery. Since 2015 there has been a shift towards the use of DPAs, and it is expected this will continue to be the case.

The Proceeds of Transnational Corporate Bribery

There are different aspects of looking at the finances inherent in transnational corporate bribery.[17] We can consider the finances required *for* the illicit transaction. Here we might question what needs to be financed, how much finance is needed, and how the bribes can be generated and distributed by the business to its intended intermediaries and ultimate recipients in the public and/or private sectors. We can also consider the finances *from* the illicit transaction. Here we can investigate the different forms of proceeds that emerge, how offenders can and must conceal the derivation of funds from these crimes while also retaining control over them, and how they must overcome particular obstacles and problems posed by controls (such as anti-money laundering) in their own countries and/or overseas. In this chapter, we are primarily concerned with the latter questions, although understanding the former has implications also for the recovery, confiscation and disgorgement of the proceeds of corruption. For instance, how well concealed is the generation and diversion of internal corporate funds via variably complex means to fund the bribes and inducements (such as slush funds hidden within obscure accounts to make cash pay-offs, or the inclusion of 'kickback' schemes as part of contracts) directly impacts on how much law enforcement authorities know about the level of finances involved, particularly when those implicated do not cooperate.

Studies of money laundering and the proceeds of crime generally are concerned with the movement of illicit finance in illicit or 'grey' markets, but in the case of transnational corporate bribery, we see the concealment and movement of illicit finance in the context of legitimate markets undertaken by otherwise legitimate businesses.[18] Opportunities for bribery emerge within legitimate organisational settings and in the course of legitimate business practices, processes and procedures. Occupational actors may realise these opportunities and are able to conceal their behaviours within ready-made markets, structures and social networks. The dynamics of bribery under these conditions vary and create different requirements for concealing, converting and controlling the proceeds of bribery.

Those involved in corporate bribery must not always 'launder' the finances generated from the illicit transaction. In other words, they must not actively place, layer or integrate the proceeds into the established financial system as in the commonly understood notion of 'money laundering'. The finances generated are automatically returned as part of the transaction, such as through the awarding of a contract, and to external observers this appears otherwise legitimate as the underlying bribery is concealed. More challenging is for 'bribers' to ensure the funds transferred to third-party agents or recipients are actually used to ensure the advantage sought is provided. When the advantage sought is not given in return, the briber has little opportunity to retrieve the monies invested as the courts and authorities will not enforce an illicit contract. Thus, ensuring the bribery is well concealed and, retaining control over the finances involved is a primary issue for bribers.[19] Further research exploring the risks of being complained about by losing bidders for contracts, or the risks of the whistle being blown by internal employees or external auditors, in addition to the costs incurred in managing such risks, would further inform the dynamics of bribery.

Publically available data, such as those presented in Table 26.1, indicate that the finances required for bribery are substantial. Furthermore, it is likely that the gross profits generated out of the bribery are much greater than the bribes themselves, or at least equal to them. The valuation of such profits is not always straightforward. For instance, in the context of 'grand' bribery, it might be that we can assess the value of a particular contract gained, but determining the financial value of gaining access to a particular market for business is more difficult. Table 26.1 indicates that contracts worth up to £398m have been received as a result of bribery.

At the 'petty' level, assessing the financial value of gains also has obstacles. For instance, if we consider facilitation payments, we can see that the advantages gained are direct, such as swift border crossings or a speedy permit application response. In all cases there will be some form of financial advantage but what value do we place on these gains? Gross gains may also be reduced as in reality, the unexpected and inconsistent payment of facilitation payments may increase business operating costs although it is likely that corporations will seek to identify when such risks may arise. Nonetheless, in the aggregate, these 'bribes' can be costly but, in contrast to the financial gain at the high-end, they remain worthwhile 'expenses' as the value of contracts gained substantially outweighs that of facilitation payments.

Other tangible, but more indirect, advantages may include the creation of fees, dividends and revenues provided by subsidiaries that were directly involved in the bribery. Two cases are of note here: Amec and Oxford Publishing. These companies were not direct perpetrators yet their associations through ownership structures generated financial gain. Furthermore, in the case of Mabey and Johnson, the SFO was able to agree a repayment settlement of the benefits received via dividends for the shareholder that amounted to £131,201 under Part 5 of the Proceeds of Crime Act 2002: this demonstrated that even if unaware of the criminal behaviour, firms can be made subject to civil action.[20] Thus, there is scope to pursue ill-gotten gains that were indirectly obtained, even if those profiting were not directly involved in the alleged bribery.

Methods of concealment are shaped by how pervasive and organised the corporate bribery is. For instance, an offender's hierarchical position in the corporate structure is significant. Whether the bribery involves 'ordinary employees', 'middle-managers' and/or senior board-level employees and executives would shape the available opportunities for concealment practices and cooperation that would be required. For example, if illicit profits were directed via the use of corporate vehicles, then this would likely require senior collusion and notable organisational support/ignorance, and it can be expected that offenders' behaviours in such cases would require a certain level of pre-planning to ensure that profits and gains can be concealed. To conceal the profits, some form of collusion and/or cooperation with external actors such as accountants and lawyers may be required to facilitate these processes[21] though informational shielding and distortion may reduce the risks from them. In this sense, involved actors must place their trust in other people, whether family members or reliable contacts, or in an institution such as a bank, money service business or legal firm in order to circumvent likely scrutiny.[22] Trust is central across the process of the illicit transaction, as offenders may abuse the trust given to them by employers or shareholders (unless they are 'amoral' and have no conception of such abuses), but must also trust others themselves to ensure the bribery is sufficiently concealed and profits usefully diverted and controlled. Establishing trust based on personal relationships reduces the risks of disclosure in addition to ensuring reliable and expected performance when payment and quid pro quo are separated in time.[23] These concealment practices are important when considering the difficulties faced by the SFO in obtaining a full and clear understanding of the proceeds of the bribery for enforcement purposes. For this reason, the SFO has made cooperation a central requirement to the negotiation of any non-criminal sanction by a corporation, such as civil settlements or more likely now Deferred Prosecution Agreements (see below).

In order to conceal the monies obtained from corporations through bribery and make them usable within legitimate financial structures, those public officials at the demand-side of the transaction or relationship may utilise various mechanisms to assist in the movement of the monies. The Financial Action Task Force[24] created a 'typology' on laundering the proceeds of grand corruption and identified the following central mechanisms that can be used to facilitate this process: the use of (1) corporate vehicles and trusts, (2) gatekeepers (meaning facilitators and enablers), (3) domestic financial institutions, (4) offshore/foreign jurisdictions, (5) nominees and (6) cash. The concern in the report is with 'grand corruption', defined by Transparency International[25] as consisting of '[a]cts committed at a high level of government that distort policies or the central functioning of the state, enabling leaders to benefit at the expense of the public good', and politically exposed persons (PEPs). There are clear commonalities in the modus operandi of control and concealment by both briber and bribee. The SFO must seek to understand these practices but often cannot do so without corporate cooperation.

Reappropriating the Proceeds of Corporate Bribery: International and Domestic Law

The emergence at the international level of various legal frameworks for the enforcement of corporate bribery has created a context of legal convergence and harmonisation, though principles of enforcement do formally diverge at the level of nation states and national authorities.[26] For instance, Article 3 of the OECD Anti-Bribery Convention requires that legal persons, in this case corporations, involved in the bribery of foreign public officials shall be 'punishable by effective, proportionate and dissuasive criminal penalties' in all signatory countries. A debate could be had over how we conceptualise what is 'effective', 'proportionate' or 'dissuasive', whether underlying principles can or should converge given divergent contexts, and whether or not all three are even necessary—if a sanction is effective, is that not enough? In any case, incorporated within this framework is the use of financial penalties and sanctions as part of criminal justice responses (or 'non-criminal' justice in those jurisdictions such as Germany where corporations cannot be criminally liable) although in reality the UK authorities are able to use a wider array of non-criminal financial sanctions.[27] More specifically, Article 3 Paragraph 3 of the OECD Convention states that:

> Each Party shall take such measures as may be necessary to provide that the bribe and the proceeds of the bribery of a foreign public official, or property the value of which corresponds to that of such proceeds, are subject to seizure and confiscation or that monetary sanctions of comparable effect are applicable.

Similarly, the UN Convention Against Corruption incorporates several articles that provide for the recovery of assets and their return to prior legitimate owners and/or the compensation of victims.[28] Thus, there is an explicit focus on the confiscation and seizure of the monies involved in the bribery that is required across State Parties. There is currently uneven enforcement of these requirements. For instance, Transparency International's[29] most recent progress review of the OECD Convention indicates that only four jurisdictions—the USA, Germany, Switzerland and the UK—are actively enforcing the convention. That said, analysing the UK as an 'active enforcer'[30] does provide insight into the ways in which proceeds of corporate bribery can and are being recovered and confiscated.

Table 26.2 provides an overview of the legal mechanisms available for targeting the proceeds of bribery in addition to other allied financial penalties that have been used in cases of corporate bribery including data on the actual monies involved. The small number of cases does not permit anything more than descriptive analysis, but out of the 14 cases at the time of writing, civil recoveries have been the most used sanction, followed by confiscation orders and criminal fines. (See below for further analysis of the figures involved in these cases.)

In England and Wales, since 2008, the SFO has been able to draw on the Proceeds of Crime Act (POCA) 2002, Part 2 (Confiscation Orders) and Part 5 (Civil Recovery Orders) specifically. This legislation was originally intended primarily for confiscating and recovering the proceeds of organised crime activities, rather than of the criminal activities of otherwise legitimate business. Nonetheless, as stated on the SFO website,[31] the powers in POCA are now being used in order to:

Table 26.2 Financial penalties in cases of transnational corporate bribery

Type of financial sanction	Explanation	Total amounts (no. of times used out of/no. of cases to 2017)
Criminal fine	Financial penalties for violations of the criminal law reflecting seriousness of the offence.	£4.7m (4/14)
Confiscation order	Post-conviction sanction to obtain the benefit of the crimes.	£7.2m (4/14)
Civil recovery	Non-conviction-based mechanism for obtaining the benefit of the crimes.	£36m (7/14)
'Financial Penalty'	Broadly comparable to a fine that the court would have imposed following a guilty plea, not a criminal fine, and also considered as voluntary and therefore mitigating. (Compensation given priority over a financial penalty.)	£250.7m (3/14)
Disgorgement of profit	Non-conviction-based mechanisms used as part of DPAs to remove profits of bribery.	£270m (3/14)
Compensation order	Used as part of, but not confined to, DPAs to redistribute monies to victims, usually foreign governments.	£5.2m (2/14)
Victim reparation/ restitution	Form part of conviction-based financial penalties; likely to be part of DPAs.	£0.8m (1/14)
Prosecution costs	Used in both conviction- and non-conviction-based sanctions to cover prosecuting authorities' costs.	At least £13.71m (13/14)
Voluntary contribution	Financial payments where no conviction for substantive bribery offences but self-recognition of corporate fault.	£29.5m (1/14)

- Carry out confiscation investigations and seek confiscation orders against those convicted
- Obtain compensation orders for victims
- Enforce the confiscation orders obtained
- Seek civil recovery orders in the High Court in respect of property which represents the proceeds of criminal conduct, even if there is no criminal conviction

In brief, POCA creates provisions for the use of Confiscation Orders, Civil Recovery Orders, cash forfeiture and criminal taxation. In the case of transnational corporate bribery, the SFO has until now utilised both Confiscation Orders and Civil Recovery Orders (see Table 26.1) against corporations.

Confiscation Orders

A confiscation order is 'an order made against a convicted defendant ordering him to pay the amount of his benefit from crime'.[32] There are two key points here: first, confiscation requires conviction, but prosecutions and convictions of corporations involved in foreign bribery are rare due to varied obstacles, whether ideological (including political preferences to avoid harmful economic consequences) and normative (such as a preference to negotiate with offenders), practical (such as the associated costly and time-consuming processes) or pragmatic (such as obtaining sufficient evidence from less developed jurisdictions).[33] Second, in cases of corporate bribery, the benefits for the offenders are not solely equal to the profits made from the contracts gained but the value of the contracts themselves.

As Table 26.1 indicates, by September 2016, confiscation orders have been used against four corporations: Mabey and Johnson, Innospec, Smith and Ouzman and Sweett Group PLC. Table 26.2 indicates that a total of £7.2m has been confiscated from companies involved in bribery. A closer analysis of these cases indicates that £1.1m was confiscated from Mabey and Johnson, despite benefits in the form of contracts worth over £60m. That said, the bribery here related to three jurisdictions. A further £4.4m was confiscated from Innospec, despite the large estimated 'benefit' of £104.9m obtained through the bribery. This raises questions over whether the level of confiscation is adequate to reflect the illicit benefit received, but confiscations are shaped by the financial ability of companies, such as Innospec in this case, to pay the penalties without becoming insolvent. The level of the confiscation was further complicated due to a simultaneous plea agreement being made in the US with the Department of Justice (DoJ), the Securities and Exchange Commission (SEC) and the Office of Foreign Asset Control (OFAC). The financial penalties agreed with Innospec were determined through this process ahead of obtaining court approval in the UK. Consequently, Lord Justice Thomas approved the sentences despite considering the amounts to be 'wholly inadequate' to reflect the level of criminality in the case. This case became a key moment in ensuring that without the permission of the Courts, the SFO is not permitted to enter into such agreements with corporate offenders. In the Smith and Ouzman case there was a confiscation order of £881,158. This case was the first prosecution of a corporation for a substantive bribery offence. The benefit obtained from the bribery was unspecified in the publicly available documentation. In the case of Sweett Group PLC, a Confiscation Order of £851,000 was brought. It should be noted that this offence related to a 'failure to prevent bribery', rather than a substantive bribery conviction as in the case of Innospec.

Civil Recovery Orders

The SFO obtained civil recovery powers in April 2008 following provisions in the Serious Crime Act 2007 that merged the Assets Recovery Agency into the Serious Organised Crime Agency (SOCA, now the National Crime Agency (NCA)) and transferred its recovery powers to other agencies.[34] Foreign bribery is a criminal offence, but since the SFO increased its enforcement activity in 2008, civil solutions for these activities became a part of the 'default position' and this raised concerns about the use of civil responses for criminal behaviours.[35] This was particularly the case between 2008 and 2012 under the previous SFO Director, Richard Alderman, who recognised that criminal conviction was improbable and sometimes politically/economically undesirable. (This of course raises important questions over the extent to which enforcement considerations were shaped by factors other than criminal *justice*—domestic economic and political considerations are prohibited by the OECD Convention.) These civil solutions primarily took the form of civil recovery orders.

A civil recovery does not require conviction or for a criminal offence to be established and instead permits asset forfeiture (including money) in civil proceedings before the High Court of property obtained through unlawful conduct (e.g. often profits from contracts won but also revenue).[36] The proceedings are against the property itself (in rem) rather than against an individual (in personam). Finality can therefore be obtained without a costly criminal prosecution as the proceedings are a form of civil litigation where the civil standard of proof applies (i.e. the balance of probabilities). For corporations, the stigma is less and debarment is avoided. However, sufficient evidence is still required to demonstrate that the property was most likely the proceeds of unlawful conduct, even if no crime commission needs to be proven.

At the time of writing, 7 of the 14 concluded cases had been completed using civil recovery orders: Balfour Beatty, Amec Plc, Innospec Ltd, DePuy International Ltd, MW Kellogg Ltd, Macmillan Publishers Ltd and Oxford Publishing Ltd. As Table 26.2 indicates, a total of £36m has been recovered from corporations implicated in bribery cases. In October 2008 in the first case of this sort, Balfour Beatty was required to pay £2.25m as part of a Civil Recovery Order relating to payment irregularities during the execution of a construction project in Egypt,[37] and more recently Oxford Publishing Ltd paid a £1.9m civil recovery in relation to its Kenyan and Tanzanian subsidiaries offering and making payments, directly and through agents, intended to induce the recipients to award competitive tenders and/or publishing contracts for schoolbooks.[38] Interestingly, the underlying offences associated with these recoveries were not only related to corruption but also accounting irregularities or breaches under the Companies Act 1985 in addition to there being no predicate offence identified.

The use of civil recovery by the SFO was scrutinised when the current Director, David Green, took over in April 2012, given the narrative he pursued around criminal prosecution. However, Green acknowledged that civil recovery can play a part in appropriate cases and we quickly saw the conclusion of the Oxford Publishing case to reinforce this. However, the use of civil recovery has lacked transparency over the decision-making process to pursue the option, the informal and hidden negotiations involved, and, as orders were not disclosable prior to April 2012, in relation to subsequent case details that were not made public beyond a brief press release. For instance, one key recommendation from a HM Crown Prosecution Service Inspectorate review of the SFO in 2012 stated that 'The SFO needs to design and document a transparent process for deciding to pursue civil recovery, and negotiating/agreeing any consent order'.[39] A follow-up review in 2014 noted that the SFO had made substantial progress with this recommendation but that transparency and clarity remains a concern.[40]

Disgorgement of Profits as Part of Deferred Prosecution Agreements (DPAs)

In February 2014, the use of DPAs became available to the Director of the SFO following their legal establishment through the Crime and Courts Act 2013. The decision to introduce DPAs was based on their perceived 'success' in the USA where they are now widely used (following the 'disastrous' prosecution and initial conviction of Arthur Andersen) by the Department of Justice and by the Securities and Exchange Commission as an opportunity to restore equilibrium in the prosecution of corporations.[41] Concerns have been put forward that DPAs 'limit the punitive and deterrent value of the government's law enforcement efforts and extinguish the societal condemnation that should accompany criminal prosecution'.[42] Furthermore, Koehler argues that such 'alternative resolution vehicles' are not authorised by the Foreign Corrupt Practices Act (FCPA) 1977, nor by any other Congressional legislation, and that their use, while increasing the quantity of cases dealt with, have lowered the quality of FCPA enforcement.[43]

However, notable differences exist in the UK system such as the requirement of early judicial oversight and court approval in the UK.[44] Critique in the US has indicated abuses of prosecutorial discretion due to a lack of judicial oversight,[45] raising concerns that prosecutors' use of DPAs is inconsistent with the rule of law.[46] A core theory failure in the policy transfer to the UK was the failure to acknowledge that difficulties of corporate criminal liability—though mitigated somewhat because of the Bribery Act 2010—and the severity of sanctions in the USA generated a motivation to agree to a DPA that is largely lacking in the UK.

Following a consultation on DPAs in 2013, the UK Government responded by recognising 'the pernicious and damaging effect of corporate economic crime on our economy,' and referred to the "general recognition" that options for dealing with offending by commercial organisations are currently limited and the number of outcomes each year, through both criminal and civil proceedings, is "too low"'.[47] The outcome of this was the introduction of DPAs to the legal system.

A DPA is a discretionary tool that enables a formal, voluntary agreement between a prosecutor and a corporation to be reached whereby a criminal prosecution for alleged criminal conduct can be deferred in exchange for the fulfilment of certain 'terms'. Possible terms of a DPA include a financial penalty, compensation to victims, donations to charities/third parties, disgorgement of any profits made, implementation of a rigorous internal compliance/training programme, cooperation in any investigation, payment of reasonable costs to the prosecutor, prohibition from engaging in certain activities, financial reporting obligations, robust monitoring, cooperation with sector-wide investigations. The prosecutor would only need to have 'reasonable suspicion' that the corporation has committed an offence and there would only need to be 'reasonable grounds for believing' that with further investigation the evidence collected would establish a realistic prospect of conviction in accordance with the Full Code Test[48] (i. evidential stage, ii. public interest stage) in a reasonable amount of time—DPAs therefore permit a substantially lower burden of proof which circumvents many practical/pragmatic obstacles.

A criminal charge is initially made, but at the end of the deferment period, the charges will be dropped if the requirements of the DPA are met. Alternatively, if these requirements are not met, the prosecutors maintain the right to prosecute at this time. Any agreement reached between the prosecutor and the corporation is subject to court approval where it must be demonstrated at a preliminary and final hearing that the agreement is in the 'interests of justice' (and the public) and that the proposed terms are 'fair, reasonable and proportionate'. The Code indicates that the SFO expects a high level of cooperation, honesty and proactive engagement (i.e. a self-report[49]) from the corporation in order for a DPA to be suitable. There are several concerns over the use of DPAs in the UK system. For instance, in the USA, where DPAs have been deemed a 'success', the principle of vicarious liability applies—this means a corporation can be held criminally liable for the acts or omissions of its individual employees as the criminal intent, and the performance of the legally prohibited act are automatically attributed to the corporation.[50] There is a clear issue of policy transfer across jurisdictions here—decisive in the success and impact of such transfers are the cultural, sociopolitical and institutional contexts at the receiving end[51]—the absence of a credible threat of corporate prosecution in the UK undermines the tool. It might also be argued that DPAs reflect normative preferences for the principal role of corporate criminal enforcement to be about the structural reform of corrupt corporate cultures rather than indictment, prosecution and punishment.[52] DPAs may also hinder the development of case law and precedent which can establish the boundaries of permissible behaviour, creating regulatory uncertainties that can increase the costs to corporates investing abroad as they attempt to determine efficient and optimal legal frameworks.[53] For such reasons, 'there is increasing scrutiny of these agreements in the US and a larger debate about the appropriate use of such enforcement tools by regulators',[54] and this reflects prosecutors' willingness to compromise when corporations are 'too big to jail'.[55] Thus, the fledgling use of DPAs in the UK coincides with increased scrutiny and criticism in the USA.

At the time of writing, DPAs have been approved for three companies: Standard Bank, an Anonymous SME and Rolls Royce. A central part of all three DPAs was the disgorgement of profits made from the bribery. Essentially, disgorgement operates as a blend of confiscation order and a recovery order, as DPAs do not involve a conviction even though a criminal offence has been established (though there is no admission of guilt by the corporation at this stage, just an agreement to a 'statement of facts'). As Table 26.2 indicates, a total of £270m has been disgorged. In the context of huge guesstimates of the extent of transnational bribery, and despite the inflation of the figure through the record financial penalties in the case of Rolls Royce (see Table 26.1), this looks very modest indeed.

Victim Compensation

Compensation orders may be part of confiscation orders or a stand-alone mechanism and are likely to be a common condition in any DPA. In both cases, the corporate defendant is required to pay a specified amount for the victims of the criminality. Such orders ensure reparation and/or restitution for the victims of the bribery. The amount of compensation to be paid by the defendant is determined by the judge and depends on the value of any available realisable assets and on the amount of money obtained illegally from victims. Their use is governed by sections 130–133 Powers of Criminal Courts (Sentencing) Act 2000. Compensation requirements have been used in one case, the DPA with Standard Bank.[56] In this case, the SFO and Standard Bank agreed that Standard Bank would pay compensation to be held initially by the SFO for the benefit of the Government of the United Republic of Tanzania in the amount of £4.66m (including interest), and a failure to do so will constitute a breach of the DPA. Importantly, Standard Bank also agreed that no tax reduction would be sought in the UK or elsewhere in connection with the payment of compensation. Compensation was also ordered in the case of Mabey and Johnson, where £618,484 was paid to a UN Development Fund in addition to reparations of £797,000 to Ghana and Jamaica.

BAE Systems made a 'voluntary' payment of £29.5m to the Tanzanian Government as part of a 'plea-bargain'. Formally, the financial penalty was £500,000 for failure to keep adequate accounting records of corruptive commission payments relating to the sale of an air traffic control system to Tanzania. However, although BAE admitted only to relatively minor accounting offences and not bribery, the agreed ex gratia payment of £29.5m to Tanzania was formally voluntary. Furthermore, it was agreed that all SFO investigations into BAE would be terminated and that the SFO would not investigate or prosecute any member of BAE for any conduct (disclosed or not) preceding 5 February 2010. The sentencing judge, Mr. Justice Bean, expressed several concerns over the settlement that had been agreed with BAE.[57]

Destination of the Recovered Proceeds of Bribery

Except for victim compensation, monies obtained through confiscation, civil recovery and disgorgement are now passed directly to the Government's Consolidated Fund or to the Home Office for reinvestment in proceeds of crime work. However, while these monies do not stay with the SFO, they do receive funds back from the Treasury. For instance, the Government's Asset Recovery Incentivisation Scheme (ARIS) stipulates that enforcement authorities with involvement in the confiscation, forfeiture and recovery of proceeds and assets are permitted to obtain a share. Up to 2013–2014, the SFO, as both the investigating authority and prosecuting authority in corporate bribery cases, was able to obtain 37.5% of the recovered and confiscated funds (i.e. 18.75% each for investigation and prosecution). However, this income stream, due to it involving infrequent and highly unpredictable funds, proved difficult to manage for the SFO. Consequently, since April 2014, the SFO agreed with HM Treasury that all ARIS receipts would go to central funds and that they would receive a fixed sum in return to be added to the SFO's core funding. This additional funding amounts to the costs of running the Proceeds of Crime Division.[58]

Conclusion: Key Issues in Recovering the Proceeds of Corporate Bribery

This chapter has explored how the proceeds of bribery generated for those corporations on the 'supply side' have been targeted by the SFO. This has involved an overview of key mechanisms such as confiscation, civil recovery, disgorgement, compensation and reparation. International conventions require that signatories pursue the proceeds of corporate corruption, and the legal framework in England and Wales permits this. In absolute terms, the use of civil recovery has been the most used tool for targeting the proceeds of corporate bribery and has also produced the most monies. This reflects a vigorous period of enforcement by the SFO between 2008 and 2012, where the former Director, Richard Alderman, actively pursued non-criminal solutions to cases of corporate bribery. From here on, it is more likely that DPAs will become central to the enforcement response, with the proceeds of corruption likely to be targeted through disgorgement. It can also be expected that victim compensation, reparation and restitution will be foregrounded as campaign groups continue to reinforce the need to compensate victims and as those victimised countries become more aware of their 'victim status', right to restitution and/or ability to litigate. Thus, 'there is a clear balance to be struck between the desire to express society's ultimate disapproval of poor business practice while making DPAs a constructive outcome, both for affected corporates and the public at large'.[59]

It is of course important to deprive offenders of the fruits of crime, ideally in addition to criminal fines or other sanctions that reflect the seriousness and harm of corporate bribery. The monies recovered and confiscated have rarely equated to the value of the contracts gained from the bribery, although disgorgements have better reflected the profits made. For credible deterrence, and according to the legislative intent, the full value of the contracts should be 'recovered', but this may generate too much 'collateral damage' domestically for many British companies, which are at risk of insolvency if the amounts to be paid are too great. Those who argue for general deterrence might be content that it is precisely this that is needed to keep businesses on the path of righteousness and that without such damage, corporations have insufficient incentive to obey the law. However, this disregards the legal and other 'business conduct' costs associated with major investigations, self-reporting and so on. Furthermore, given the difficulties of criminal prosecution, small and medium enterprises remain more likely to be convicted and face not only confiscation but also the stigma attached to the 'criminal' label. Addressing this disproportionality between the response to SMEs and larger multinational companies poses difficulties for the SFO. The enforcement mechanisms outlined in the chapter, whether used on their own, or combined with each other, all have a role to play as determined by the specifics and contexts of each case. However, the arbitrary and inconsistent use of such mechanisms needs to be avoided, and a more coherent policy framework guiding their use would be beneficial for SFO. Whatever the future direction, the key is to ensure transparency in the discretion, (de)prioritisation and decision-making practices of the SFO and allied authorities to ensure appropriate public scrutiny of the enforcement response.

Notes

1. Jurisdictionally, this chapter covers only England, Wales, and Northern Ireland. Scotland, although covered by the UK-wide Bribery Act 2010, constitutes a separate legal system with enforcement undertaken by the Crown Office and Procurator Fiscal Service, Scotland's Prosecution Service.
2. The SFO's first DPA was given to Standard Bank in November 2015 <www.sfo.gov.uk/2015/11/30/sfo-agrees-first-uk-dpa-with-standard-bank/> accessed 5 December 2016.
3. Indonesia, Thailand, India, Russia, Nigeria, China and Malaysia.
4. For the SFO's press release on the Rolls Royce DPA, see <www.sfo.gov.uk/2017/01/17/sfo-completes-497-25m-deferred-prosecution-agreement-rolls-royce-plc/> accessed 13 March 2017.
5. Rolls Royce also reached agreements with the US Department of Justice and Brazil's Ministério Público Federal. These agreements result in the payment of approximately US$170m to the USA and $25m to Brazil.
6. See SFO, Press Release (19 February 2016) <www.sfo.gov.uk/2016/02/19/sweett-group-plc-sentenced-and-ordered-to-pay-2-3-million-after-bribery-act-conviction/> accessed 9 November 2016.
7. Home Secretary's Opening Speech, Ukraine Forum on Asset Recovery (April 2014) quoted in HM Government, *UK Anti-Corruption Plan* (Crown Copyright 2014) 41 <www.gov.uk/government/uploads/system/uploads/attachment_data/file/388894/UKantiCorruptionPlan.pdf> accessed 9 November 2016.

8. Nicholas Lord and Alan Doig, 'Transnational Corporate Bribery' in Gerben Bruinsma and David Weisburd (eds), *Encyclopedia of Criminology and Criminal Justice* (Springer 2014).

9. Nicholas Lord, *Regulating Corporate Bribery in International Business: Anti-corruption in the UK and Germany* (Routledge 2014).

10. Lord and Doig (n 8); Lord (n 9).

11. Nicholas Lord, 'Establishing Enforcement Legitimacy in the Pursuit of Rule-Breaking "Global Elites": The Case of Transnational Corporate Bribery' (2015) 20(3) Theoretical Criminology 376; Ian Clark, *International Legitimacy and World Society* (OUP 2007).

12. When the USA introduced the Foreign Corrupt Practices Act 1977, it was expected that other nation-states would follow suit. This did not immediately occur and so enforcement of the Act did not follow until the creation of the OECD Anti-Bribery Convention, which created international pressure for other countries to implement analogous legislation.

13. GRECO, *Evaluation Report on the United Kingdom on Incriminations* (ETS 173 and 191, GPC 2 2007); OECD, *Phase 3 Report on Implementing the OECD Anti-Bribery Convention in the United Kingdom* (OECD 2012).

14. These changes are fully explained in Clive Walker, *The Anti-Terrorism Legislation* (OUP 2002) para 6(10).

15. Bribery Act 2010, ss 1, 2, 6 and 7.

16. David Leigh and Rob Evans, 'How Blair Put Pressure on Goldsmith to end BAE Investigation' *The Guardian* (London, 21 December 2007) <www.the-guardian.com/world/2007/dec/21/bae.tonyblair> accessed 20 March 2017.

17. Nicholas Lord and Michael Levi, 'Organizing the Finances for and the Finances from Transnational Corporate Bribery' (2016) European Journal of Criminology (advance access).

18. Lord (n 9).

19. Michael Levi, 'Money for Crime and Money from Crime: Financing Crime and Laundering Crime Proceeds' (2015) 21(2) European Journal on Criminal Policy and Research 275, 284.

20. See SFO, Press Release, 'Shareholder Agrees Civil Recovery by SFO in Mabey & Johnson' <www.betterregulation.com/external/Civil%20Recovery%20of%20Dividends%20from%20Shareholders.pdf> accessed 5 December 2016.

21. For discussion of lawyers and money laundering, see Chap. 6 (Benson) in this collection.

22. Levi (n 19) 284.

23. Susan Rose-Ackerman, *Corruption and Government: Causes, Consequences and Reform* (CUP 1999) 98.

24. Financial Action Task Force, 'Laundering the Proceeds of Corruption' (2011) <www.fatf-gafi.org/media/fatf/documents/reports/Laundering%20the%20Proceeds%20of%20Corruption.pdf> accessed 20 March 2017.

25. Transparency International, 'The Anti-Corruption Plain Language Guide' (2009) 23 <www.transparency.org/whatwedo/publication/the_anti_corruption_plain_language_guide> accessed 5 December 2016.

26. Nicholas Lord, 'Responding to Transnational Corporate Bribery Using International Frameworks for Enforcement: Anti-bribery and Corruption in the UK and Germany' (2014) 14(1) Criminology and Criminal Justice 100.

27. Lord (n 9).

28. UN Convention Against Corruption (adopted on 31 October 2003, open for signature on 9 December 2003), Chapter V.

29. Transparency International, *Exporting Corruption—Progress Report 2015: Assessing Enforcement of the OECD Convention on Combatting Foreign Bribery* (2015) <www.transparency.org/exporting_corruption> accessed 20 March 2017.

30. Though the arbitrary formulation of these categorisations is problematic. See Lord (n 9); Nicholas Lord and Michael Levi, 'Determining the Adequate Enforcement of White-Collar and Corporate Crimes in Europe' in Judith van Erp, Wim Huisman, and Gudrun Vande Walle (eds), *The Routledge Handbook of White-Collar and Corporate Crime in Europe* (Routledge 2015).

31. See SFO, 'About Us' <www.sfo.gov.uk/about-us/> accessed 25 November 2016.

32. See CPS, 'Confiscation and Ancillary Orders pre-POCA: Proceeds of Crime Guidance' <www.cps.gov.uk/legal/a_to_c/confiscation_and_ancillary_orders/#whatis> accessed 9 November 2016. For discussion of the law governing confiscation orders, see Chap. 19 (Hopmeier and Mills) in this collection.

33. For analysis, see Lord (n 9); Lord (n 26).

34. For discussion of civil recovery powers, see Chap. 22 (Alldridge) in this collection.

35. Nicholas Lord, 'Transnational Corporate Bribery: Anti-Bribery and Corruption in the UK and Germany' (2013) 60(2) Crime, Law and Social Change 127; Lord (n 9).

36. Attorney General's Office, 'Guidance for Prosecutors and Investigators on Their Asset Recovery Powers Under Section 2A of the Proceeds of Crime Act 2002' (November 2012) <www.gov.uk/guidance/asset-recovery-powers-for-prosecutors-guidance-and-background-note-2009> accessed 9 November 2016.

37. David Leigh and Rob Evans, 'Balfour Beatty Agrees to Pay £2.25 m Over Allegations of Bribery in Egypt' *The Guardian* (London, 7 October 2008) <www.theguardian.com/business/2008/oct/07/balfourbeatty.egypt> accessed 20 March 2017.

38. See SFO, Press Release, 'Oxford Publishing Ltd to Pay Almost £1.9 Million as Settlement after Admitting Unlawful Conduct in its East African Operations' <www.sfo.gov.uk/2012/07/03/oxford-publishing-ltd-pay-almost-1-9-million-settlement-admitting-unlawful-conduct-east-african-operations/> accessed 25 November 2016.

39. HM Crown Prosecution Service Inspectorate, *Report to the Attorney General on the Inspection of the Serious Fraud Office* (2012) <www.justiceinspectorates. gov.uk/crown-prosecution-service/wp-content/uploads/sites/3/2014/04/ SFO_Nov12_rpt.pdf> accessed 2 December 2016.

40. HM Crown Prosecution Service Inspectorate, *Follow-up Inspection of the Serious Fraud Office* (2014) <www.justiceinspectorates.gov.uk/hmcpsi/wp-content/uploads/sites/3/2014/11/SFOFU_Nov14_rpt.pdf> accetessed 2 December 2016.

41. Robert J Ridge and Mackenzie A Baird, 'The Pendulum Swings Back: Revisiting Corporate Criminality and the Rise of Deferred Prosecution Agreements' (2008) 33(2) University of Dayton Law Review 187, 197; Peter Spivack and Sujit Raman, 'Regulating the "New Regulators": Current Trends in Deferred Prosecution Agreements' (2008) 45 American Criminal Law Review 159.

42. David M Uhlmann, 'Deferred Prosecution and Non-Prosecution Agreements and the Erosion of Corporate Criminal Liability' (2013) 72(4) Maryland Law Review 1295, 1302.

43. Mike Koehler, 'Measuring the Impact of Non-Prosecution and Deferred Prosecution Agreements on Foreign Corrupt Practices Act Enforcement' (2015) 49 University of California, Davis Law Review 497.

44. For discussion, see Michael Bisgrove and Mark Weekes, 'Deferred Prosecution Agreements: A Practical Consideration' [2014] Criminal Law Review 416.

45. Ridge and Baird (n 41) 203.

46. Jennifer Arlen, 'Prosecuting Beyond the Rule of Law: Corporate Mandates Imposed Through Deferred Prosecution Agreements' (2016) 8(1) Journal of Legal Analysis 191.

47. Monty Raphael, *Bribery: Law and Practice* (OUP 2016) 73.

48. For an explanation of the Full Code Test, see the Code for Crown Prosecutors <www.cps.gov.uk/publications/code_for_crown_prosecutors/codetest.html> accessed 2 December 2016.

49. While the first two DPAs with Standard Bank and the Anonymous SME involved 'self-reports', this was not the case with Rolls Royce as SFO became aware of the corruption via whistleblowers. This has led some to suggest the SFO had 'a failure of nerve': Corruption Watch, A Failure of Nerve—The SFO's Settlement with Rolls Royce <www.cw-uk.org/2017/01/19/a-failure-of-nerve-the-sfos-settlement-with-rolls-royce/> accessed 13 March 2017.

50. Ved P Nanda, 'Corporate Criminal Liability in the United States: Is a New Approach Warranted?' in Mark Pieth and Radha Ivory (eds), *Corporate Criminal Liability. Emergence, Convergence and Risk* (Springer 2011) 65.

51. Susanne Karstedt, 'Creating Institutions: Linking the "Local" and the "Global" in the Travel of Crime Policies' (2007) 8(2) Police Practice and Research 145.

52. Spivack and Raman (n 41) 161.

53. Allen R Brooks, 'A Corporate Catch-22: How Deferred and Non-Prosecution Agreements Impede the Full Development of the Foreign Corrupt Practices Act' (2010) 7 Journal of Law, Economics and Policy 137, 156.
54. Raphael (n 47) 166.
55. Brandon Garrett, *Too Big To Jail: How Prosecutors Compromise with Corporations* (Harvard University Press 2014).
56. See *SFO v Standard Bank* Case no U20150854 [39].
57. See *R v BAE Systems* Case no S2010565.
58. The ARIS agreement with the SFO is explained on the SFO's website <www.sfo.gov.uk/about-us/> accessed 2 December 2016.
59. Raphael (n 47) 169.

Nicholas Lord is a Senior Lecturer in the Centre for Criminology and Criminal Justice in the School of Law at the University of Manchester. Nicholas has research expertise in white-collar, financial and organised crimes and frauds. He is the President of the European Working Group on White-Collar and Organisational Crime hosted within the European Society of Criminology. His book *Regulating Corporate Bribery in International Business* (2014) was the winner of the British Society of Criminology Book Prize 2015. In 2014 he received the Young Career Award of the National White-Collar Crime Research Consortium hosted within the American Society of Criminology. He is currently undertaking funded research into domestic bribery, corporate vehicles and organised crime, food fraud and counterfeit alcohol.

Michael Levi has been a Professor of Criminology at Cardiff University since 1991. He has been conducting international research on the control of white-collar and organised crime, corruption and money laundering/financing of terrorism since 1972. He is an Associate Fellow of RUSI and a Senior Fellow at RAND Europe. He advises Europol on the Serious and Organised Crime Threat Assessment and on the internet-enabled Organised Crime Threat Assessment, and other public positions include membership of the European Commission's Group of Experts on Corruption. In 2013 he was given the Distinguished Scholar Award by the International Association for the Study of Organised Crime, and in 2014 he was awarded the Sellin-Glueck prize for international and comparative criminology by the American Society of Criminology.

27

In Search of Transnational Financial Intelligence: Questioning Cooperation Between Financial Intelligence Units

Anthony Amicelle and Killian Chaudieu

Introduction

Establishing an FIU [Financial intelligence unit] is an important step in combating financial crime. [...] In this connection, it is useful to note that one of the critical functions of an FIU is the exchange of information with other FIUs. In addition to the contribution the FIU can be expected to make in combating domestic crime, it will also be called upon to respond to requests for intelligence from other FIUs.[1]

The first national agencies, today referred to as financial intelligence units (FIUs), were created at the turn of the 1990s, starting with the Australian Transaction Reports and Analysis Centre in 1989 (operational in January 1990) and the Financial Crimes Enforcement Network (FinCen) in the USA in April 1990[2]—the same month that the Financial Action Task Force (FATF—established in 1989) issued its original 40 recommendations.[3] The number of FIUs has now climbed to more than 150, and the FATF recommendations are recognised as the global standard for dealing with money laundering and terrorist financing in 194 jurisdictions. One of the key recommendations (R. 29) states that 'countries should establish a financial

A. Amicelle
University of Montreal, International Centre for Comparative Criminology, Montreal, QC, Canada

K. Chaudieu
University of Lausanne, Lausanne, Switzerland

© The Author(s) 2018
C. King et al. (eds.), *The Palgrave Handbook of Criminal and Terrorism Financing Law*,
https://doi.org/10.1007/978-3-319-64498-1_27

intelligence unit (FIU) that serves as a national centre for the receipt and analysis of: (a) suspicious transaction reports; and (b) other information relevant to money laundering, associated predicate offences and terrorist financing, and for the dissemination of the results of that analysis'. FIUs are the critical agencies at the core of the finance-security assemblage[4] which deals with flows of illicit money, widely known as dirty money. 'In their simplest form, FIUs are agencies that receive reports of suspicious transactions from financial institutions and other persons and entities, analyse them, and disseminate the resulting intelligence to local law-enforcement agencies and foreign FIUs to combat money laundering [and terrorist financing]'.[5]

The overlap between national and international initiatives is worthy of note in the field of financial intelligence.[6] The development and evolution of national FIUs and international norms regarding 'dirty money' have been closely related for over 25 years. Both emerged in the early 1990s to track the money from drug trafficking and are now being promoted as a way to fight against all forms of illicit financial flows, from terrorist financing to tax evasion. Consequently, FIUs around the world have increased considerably not only in number but also in their sphere of action. They are seen as 'knowledge centres' or information hubs to provide actionable intelligence against crime and terrorism at large.[7]

Moreover, the original connection between FIUs and international activity took an operational turn as early as 1995 when a number of national agencies—then called 'financial disclosure units'—decided to create an informal forum and worldwide network to explore ways to cooperate: the Egmont Group. In a similar vein, information exchange between the FIUs has been a European objective since the second half of the 1990s, culminating in the Council decision of 17 October 2000 'concerning arrangements for cooperation between financial intelligence units of the member states in respect of exchanging information'.[8]

However, the historical and multifaceted internationalisation of FIUs should not be overemphasised. On the normative side, an FIU is not a 'one size fits all' organisation, either at the international level or within the European Union (EU).[9] On the operational side, transnational cooperation between FIUs is still regularly criticised as inadequate.[10] The chapter precisely aims at questioning FIU-to-FIU exchange of information that is presented as 'the cornerstone of the international efforts to counter money laundering/terrorist financing'.[11] How does the transnational sharing of financial intelligence operate in practice?

This chapter looks at the range of devices, channels of communication and related difficulties involved in developing cooperation between FIUs. It draws on document analysis (official reports and statistics from the Egmont Group, the EU, the FATF, and FIUs) and ten semi-structured interviews with officials from Europol and from four FIUs in late 2016 and early 2017: two FIUs from the EU

(France and UK), one non-EU FIU from a European country with a major financial centre (Switzerland), and one North American FIU (Canada).[12] Recent fieldwork in these four countries is also used to complement the analysis.[13]

The chapter has two main sections. The first section sheds light on the cooperation channels that the FIUs use and how they use them, at European and international level. The second section focuses on the main tensions and difficulties in transnational financial intelligence.

European and International Communication Channels

Given the growing internationalisation of financial flows, we really cannot manage with national financial intelligence alone. We have to be able to look for information abroad very quickly. The importance of cooperation has exploded compared to what was envisaged in the 1990s. (Interview FIU 1, 2016)

Transnational cooperation between national FIUs is promoted as a way to prevent the internationalisation of financial flows from being used to make it more difficult to discern criminal activity. In accordance with international standards and 'follow-the-money methods',[14] any FIU will follow the money to determine (1) the origin of financial flows, (2) their destination, (3) the economic reason for the transaction(s)/operation(s), and (4) the beneficial owner(s) of the assets. In this context, different types of situations encourage FIUs to cooperate with foreign counterparts.

First, the request for information from another FIU can be initiated by proactive analysis of suspicious transaction reports (STRs). In this case, one or several reports include an international element, such as cross-border transactions, bank customers of foreign nationality, or national citizens living or working in another country, that justifies the request. A request for international cooperation is sent when access to further information at the national level is deemed insufficient to determine whether the reported transactions are relevant for intelligence and/or judicial purposes. For example, a reporting entity justifies a disclosure to the FIU by arguing that it concerns a customer of foreign nationality who is party to legal proceedings in his country. The FIU analysts will first access national databases and, if they cannot verify the assertion of the reporting entity, then they will ask their foreign counterparts if they have any relevant information, using their right to request confirmation that they need to analyse STRs. If, in a similar case, FIU analysts can confirm through national databases or open source information that the flagged client is party to legal proceedings in a foreign country, they can decide to share information spontaneously with the foreign FIU:

> Here, we are not asking for anything. We tell them that we have received a suspicious transaction report in relation to a person who is currently party to legal proceedings in their country and we give them the information we have on the basis of the report. (Interview FIU 2, 2016)

As stated in the international principles for information exchange between FIUs, 'FIUs should exchange information freely, spontaneously and upon request, on the basis of reciprocity'.[15]

Second, FIUs can receive sensitive information or requests from their national law-enforcement partners that lead them to follow the money trail abroad through international cooperation. FIU officials can either be asked by their partners to make a request for information from another FIU or they can proactively seek information from foreign FIUs in order to be able to help their national partners. In the case of an explicit demand from a national partner, some law-enforcement officers see cooperation between FIUs as providing a faster channel for information exchange in a criminal matter than international legal assistance. They often use the FIU channel as a first step to determine if it is worth sending a request for international legal assistance in order to collect evidence. In proactive searches, before using information provided by a national partner to justify a request to foreign FIU(s), FIU officials must generally obtain the national partner's permission.

Third, the FIU channel can be used for 'diagonal cooperation':

> I think there is also another approach and we practice it a lot with close partners. This is diagonal cooperation. It is not necessarily from FIU to FIU only. I mean, if we know that the information we want is held by a specific law-enforcement agency, we can specify this to the foreign FIU, which is thus being used as a postal box. And the reverse is also true—the foreign law-enforcement agency will ask their FIU to ask us if we have information on X or Y. Diagonal cooperation is very frequent between us and them. We actually have relations with police forces and intelligence services in this country and they use our financial intelligence as long as there is a link with our country. (Interview FIU 3, 2016)

In this case, one of the FIUs acts as a facilitator since it mediates the cooperation between its national partners and a foreign FIU.

Regardless of the motive for requesting information, the FIUs use from one to three cooperation channels depending on geographic location, legal framework, and technical capacity, as described hereafter.

The Egmont Secure Web

In accordance with the FATF recommendations, FIUs are expected to apply for membership of the Egmont Group. The Group arose in 1995, when FIU representatives met at the Egmont Arenberg Palace in Brussels and decided to create a global forum. More than 20 years later, this 'informal network' is now largely formalised in the 'Head of financial intelligence units' (HoFIUs—the governing body of the Egmont Group), four working groups, the Egmont committee (the consultation and coordination mechanism for the HoFIUs and the working groups), and a secretariat established in 2007 in Toronto (Canada). The secretariat, committee, and working groups meet three times per year, including the Egmont annual plenary session. The governance and standards of the Egmont Group rely on a set of key documents such as the 'Egmont Charter', the 'Egmont Principles for information exchange', and 'Operational Guidance for FIU activities'. In general terms, the Egmont Group aims to improve both international cooperation in the fight against dirty money and national implementation of financial intelligence programs in the areas of information exchange, training, and the sharing of expertise. This includes the goal of 'fostering better and secure communication among FIUs through the application of technology, presently via the Egmont Secure Web (ESW)'.[16] In this regard, following James Sheptycki's interpretation, 'it might be accurate to characterise [the Egmont Group] as a prototype for a transnational superstructure for co-ordinating information exchange emanating from the surveillance of financial transactions records'.[17]

As members of the Egmont Group, 156 FIUs can make and respond to requests via the ESW, which is promoted as a secure and reliable FIU-to-FIU channel of communication. 'The ESW is an electronic communication system that allows encrypted sharing among members of emails and financial intelligence, as well as information of interest to members and to the functioning of the Egmont Group'.[18] The use of this channel is not limited to operational purposes. It 'permits members to communicate with one another via secure e-mail, requesting and sharing case information as well as posting and assessing information on typologies, analytical tools, and technological developments'.[19] One FIU may have several ESW email addresses, including one for operational purposes, one that allows the director to contact foreign FIU directors directly, and others to deal with international strategic and policy issues. The ESW is maintained technically by FinCen (the US FIU) on behalf of the Egmont Group.

Regarding operational communication, any FIU receiving a request for information is encouraged to respond as soon as possible—with or without bilateral memoranda of understanding—'consistent with the urgency of the request, or within a month if possible. Additional time is reasonable if there is a need to query external databases or third parties'.[20] Following the official Egmont query form, the FIU can indicate if the request for information is urgent. 'For me, there are two types of requests: in the case of urgent requests, we try to reply within a week. With normal requests, it can take a month' (Interview FIU 2, 2016). FIUs usually classify their requests from 'normal' to 'urgent' and even 'very urgent' in some cases, but the definition of urgency can be a matter of debate:

> When we are told that it is urgent, we tend to respond more quickly. Now the problem is that certain FIUs think that everything is urgent ... Therefore, it is useful to contact them to know if it is really urgent and we often nuance the degree of urgency when we talk to them. Nonetheless, we do try to process the urgencies first, the real ones. (Interview FIU 1, 2016)

Informally, phone calls often complement email messages to either specify the degree of urgency or give further contextual details if necessary to allow the request to proceed more quickly. According to certain FIU officials, the meaning and implication of the indication 'urgent' should be further specified to avoid everyone ticking the same box, which poses a challenge for the prioritisation of information sharing. In practice, however, the degree of responsiveness is not linked only to the degree of urgency of the incoming request but also to relations and experiences between two FIUs:

> We often receive demands with 40 or 50 names. We need to have an analyst working on them and this is a very difficult kind of request. Consequently, if we really want to reply, we categorise the request. Does it come from our top 5 partners, yes or no? If so, we will do it, notwithstanding the time and effort. If not, or if it comes from a partner who is very slow to respond to our own requests or who does not respond at all, its priority will be downgraded. We will reply in the end but we will probably limit ourselves to providing information about five to ten key people rather than the forty or fifty persons mentioned in the request. (Interview FIU 3, 2016)

There is also criticism of 'phishing expeditions'—sending the same request to 'everyone'. 'We still receive lots of requests that make no sense and there are also FIUs sending their requests to everyone everywhere and we struggle to find a link with us' (Interview FIU 1, 2016). The FIUs under examination criticise the use of phishing expeditions except in cases of 'maximum urgency', such as after a terrorist attack.

If there are manifest and recurrent problems with cooperation in relation to a particular FIU, the HoFIUs of the Egmont Group may eventually take countermeasures. 'When an FIU joins the Egmont Group, it is required to sign the Egmont Charter and commit to working according to its founding documents. However, countries that join Egmont are not part of any treaty or convention; therefore, no international sanctions or legal action can be taken against a non-complying country' although 'the Egmont Group has an internal Compliance Procedure that defines the actions to be taken against an FIU that does not comply with the Egmont Charter and Principles for Information Exchange document'.[21] The governing body of the Egmont Group (HoFIUs) has the power to suspend and/or expel non-compliant FIUs.[22] In July 2011, the HoFIUs accused the Swiss FIU of insufficient international cooperation and issued a warning of suspension.[23] As a result, Switzerland's anti-money laundering act was amended in 2012 to enable the exchange of financial information from FIU to FIU.[24] The legislative amendments came into force in 2013 and the warning of suspension was lifted the same year.[25]

Compliance does not mean that FIUs are systematically obliged to respond to a request, and their national legislation generally specifies an FIU's differential obligations to national and international partners. Usually, the FIU 'must' reply to the requests of national partners, while it 'should' respond to the international requests. National and supranational laws also mention exceptional situations in which the FIU may refuse to exchange information. For instance, the Swiss legislation underlines that 'a request for information from a foreign reporting office shall not be granted if: c. national interests or public security and order will be prejudiced'.[26] The fourth European Money Laundering Directive stipulates that 'an FIU may refuse to exchange information only in exceptional circumstances where the exchange could be contrary to fundamental principles of its national law'.[27] Exceptions vary slightly among countries in practice but can include refusal to exchange information about political opponents in 'non-democratic states', with the countries of origin of asylum seekers, about persons who can be jailed for a crime of opinion, or about individuals who are liable to be sentenced to death on the basis of the information provided. Interviewees all mentioned specific cases in which they had not replied based on those situations, although the reason for non-response was not always made explicit to the requesting agency. It is recognised that exceptions are legitimate, but there are also complaints that the 'political argument' is occasionally used to mask non-compliant activities that ultimately protect corrupt foreign politicians. In this regard, the fourth European Money Laundering Directive specifies that 'those exceptions shall be specified in a way which prevents misuse of, and undue limitations on, the free exchange of information for analytical purposes'.[28]

The exchange of information between FIUs is systematically associated with explicit determination of 'appropriate conditions of use'. The rules for information dissemination include three main options. First, the default option always indicates that the FIU cannot 'disclose the [received] information outside its agency without the prior written permission of the disclosing FIU.[29] Second, the disclosing FIU can authorise its FIU counterpart to disseminate the information outside its agency but for intelligence purposes only, for example informally, not for evidence purposes. Third, the FIU agrees that their counterpart can disseminate and use the information beyond informal intelligence, for instance as evidence.

FIU.NET

In October 2000, Council Decision 2000/642/JHA was adopted concerning arrangements for cooperation between FIUs of EU Member States with respect to exchanging information. While the arrangements already adopted by EU Member States in relation to the Egmont Group and the ESW were mentioned, the community legislation noted that 'it is necessary that close cooperation take place between the relevant authorities of the Member States involved in the fight against money laundering and that provision be made for direct communication between those authorities'.[30] This resulted in the FIU.NET initiative led by the Dutch Ministry of Security and the Dutch FIU, joined in 2002 by FIUs in France, Italy, Luxembourg, and the UK. FIU.NET was launched as a pilot programme in 2004 with the financial support of the European Commission and has been officially operational since 2007.[31] It is now accessible to the 28 Member States. FIU.NET is promoted as 'a decentralised and sophisticated computer network supporting the FIUs in the European Union in their fight against money laundering and the financing of terrorism'.[32] Since 2004, it has been governed mainly by a board of FIU partners with several meetings a year to set policy rules and establish priorities. Until the end of 2015, the budget of the FIU.NET depended on European Commission grants (95 per cent of its budget) and FIUs financial contribution. Since then, maintenance of the network has been integrated into Europol's budget.[33]

Although the ESW and FIU.NET are based on the same goal of information sharing between FIUs, there are a number of differences between them.

First, 156 FIUs around the world can use the Egmont secure web while the FIU.NET is restricted to EU member states only, with potential extension to other European countries such as Iceland and Norway in the near future.

Second, on the technological side, the sophistication of FIU.NET compared to the Egmont Secure Web is largely acknowledged within the EU and by

Egmont Group representatives, especially with regard to easier retrieval of data that can be directly integrated into FIUs databases.[34] 'The ESW is a technology of the twentieth century, a bit old and it would be helpful to change the current query form for something more dynamic or automated for data retrieval. The ways of sharing intelligence at the international level with Microsoft Word documents ... We are no longer convinced' (Interview FIU 3, 2016).

Third, the sophistication of FIU.NET compared to the Egmont Secure Web is also coupled with the possibility of multilateral exchanges. The Egmont Secure Web and FIU.NET both allow bilateral exchanges between FIUs but only FIU.NET really permits multilateral operational cooperation. It allows FIUs to exchange information bilaterally, multilaterally, or even 'in full' with all connected counterparts, from 'known/unknown requests' to 'case files'. If the response to an FIU's request regarding whether an individual or organisation is known or unknown is positive, it can move to what is called the case file approach, providing further details and justifications to obtain information from the other FIU(s). Taking a case-centric view, the FIU can then link different entities to its case file. The case file is like a box and inside the box the FIU can put information on a person, ID documents linked to a person, a company, or an account, and transactions linked to the account without needing to re-send the message via FIU.NET:

> You can share different elements in that case with different FIUs depending on relevance. For instance, you have a person in Italy who you are interested in because of a suspicious transaction report (STR) you have received. You send a known/unknown to, let's say, the UK, because you see that the transaction is going there. They [the UK FIU officials] reply that the person is known and you start building a case file and it becomes a joined case file, with user protocols that state precisely how it can be used. (Interview Europol, 2017)

In 2012, FIU.NET introduced 'Ma3tch technology' as an option to allow encrypted data exchange, and a Ma3tch-engaged pilot was launched in 2013. The 'a3' stands for autonomous, anonymous, and analysis. FIUs have a number of options available to them for using the Ma3tch process, including sending simple 'know/unknown' or 'hit/no hit' requests to one or several counterparts. To do this, the FIU translates the subject (usually individuals) under examination into an anonymised entity (such as a 'filter') and shares the result with one or several selected FIUs through FIU.NET to determine if there are any positive matches. Such requests work only for names and dates of birth according to the director of the Dutch FIU, who insists on the 'anonymous' and 'autonomous' dimension of the analysis through the Ma3tch process:

As a simplified example, an information resource contains: Philip Tattaglia (12/28/16), Luka Brasi (3/13/26), Johnny Fontane (10/7/27). The anonymization algorithm minimizes these 3 individual records into a single combined anonymous 4-character fuzzy logic data structure: 'tnUG'. This 4-character code captures the 'characteristics' of the combined original sensitive information, making it impossible to recover the individual records. The extreme data minimization enables (configurable) false positives (collisions) that enhance anonymity. In addition, the information owner controls which data are included in the filter, and if, when, and where filters are shared (multiple filters can be created for a single dataset, for example with lower accuracy for sensitive data). Other parties that receive the filter can use it to ma3tch local sensitive data against the anonymized data structure 'tnUG' without knowing the underlying data. ... Positive hits are optionally or automatically followed up for (anonymous) validation, compliance check, and/or a fully detailed 'need to know' information exchange.[35]

More generally, the underlying logic of the Ma3tch functionality encourages automated cross-matching practices between EU FIUs' filters. Personal data is normally shared only if there is a hit:

Some of the FIUs put their entire suspicious transactions reports' database into a match filter which batches the names and dates of birth and encrypts them. You share that filter with another FIU or with all of the FIUs and depending on what they put into their filters it will match and tell you if any of those names are known by another FIU. So it is effectively doing the 'known/unknown' but in mass. (Interview Europol, 2016)

The automated logic of cross-matching is thus available via FIU.NET but is far from being part of FIUs' daily routine. It depends on the creation and sharing of larger encrypted data-sets (filters) between FIUs. According to one supporter, 'automated cross matching means that I make available a data-set and FIU.NET tells me that persons 1, 2, and 3 are also targeted by an STR in the Czech Republic, for instance. This is central because I will make requests for information to places I would have never thought of' (Interview FIU 1, 2017). Other FIU officials remain reluctant about this possible evolution of the European computer network, in particular because they consider that the nature of the fairly new link between FIU.NET and Europol is not sufficiently clear. Issues concerning information security, confidence, and data processing are regularly expressed by some FIUs that fear more extensive police and judicial involvement in financial intelligence and FIU.NET in connection with Europol.

Matching subjects through FIU.NET is also performed with connected data sets other than FIU filters, starting with commercial databases. Europol currently provides open source tools such as World-Check, a data company that is now part of Thomson Reuters. As described by Marieke de Goede and Gavin Sullivan, this company

> ...collects, collates and sells listing information and due diligence compliance solutions to clients within (and beyond) the financial industries. Its main rationale is to compile into one master database the more than 400 sanctions lists, counterterrorism watch lists, regulatory and law enforcement lists in existence worldwide ... However, World-Check does not only compile pre-existing list entries. It also "value-adds" by adding their own nominations of heightened risk banking clients—including, for example, persons indicted for fraud or terrorism and persons otherwise publicly associated with, but not necessarily convicted of, such offenses. .... Protocols for database inclusion are recognised to be subjective and listing categories are flexible and overlapping.[36]

Subscriptions to World-Check can cost up to one million euros annually. For the FIU.NET, Europol officers put WorldCheck list entries into a filter accessible to FIUs. When an FIU creates a case file or a filter, the Europol filter is supposed to alert them if there is a match with sanctions lists, lists of politically exposed persons, and so on.

Finally, for the last few years, FIU.NET has also included a cross-border reporting function in connection with a pilot project with FIU Luxembourg under the pressure from other European FIUs. This project is associated with the ambiguous situation of several reporting entities registered and established in Luxembourg: PayPal, Amazon, and IPay. While these business companies operate commercially largely in other EU Member States, they do not have the same legal presence in those states as compared to Luxembourg, given that their registered offices in Europe are limited to this country. Consequently, they are legally obliged to send their STRs to the Luxembourg FIU, even if the transactions are related to other member states such as France and UK. The pilot project was launched to require FIU Luxembourg to share spontaneously 'all STRs filed by Amazon, Paypal and Ipay with other national FIUs via the FIU.NET Crossborder system. 90 percent of cross-border reports were transferred to another FIU within 24 hours and 99 percent within 3 days'.[37] Following this logic, the fourth EU Directive now mentions that when an EU FIU receives a report that concerns another member state, 'it shall promptly forward it to the FIU of that Member State'.[38]

Other Recognised Cooperation Channels

Certain FIUs also use other channels—secure emails or even fax messages—to exchange information with the minority of their counterparts that are neither members of the Egmont Group nor FIU.NET.

Information Sharing in Numbers

Chart 27.1 and Table 27.1 reveal that both UK and France's FIUs receive and send more inquiries than MROS (the Swiss FIU) and Fintrac (in Canada) even though the number of inquiries sent to MROS is high,

		2010	2011	2012	2013	2014	2015
Canada's Fintrac	Inquiries received	228	329	202	241	222	240
	Inquiries sent	46	74	105	116	140	147
France's Tracfin	Inquiries received	711	849	814	952	1 051	1 346
	Inquiries sent	1 147	1 485	1 891	1 950	1 569	2 195
Switzerland's MROS	Inquiries received	577	564	598	660	711	804
	Inquiries sent	157	159	205	426	545	579
United Kingdom's NCA	Inquiries received					1 482	1 566
	Inquiries sent					1 359	1 801

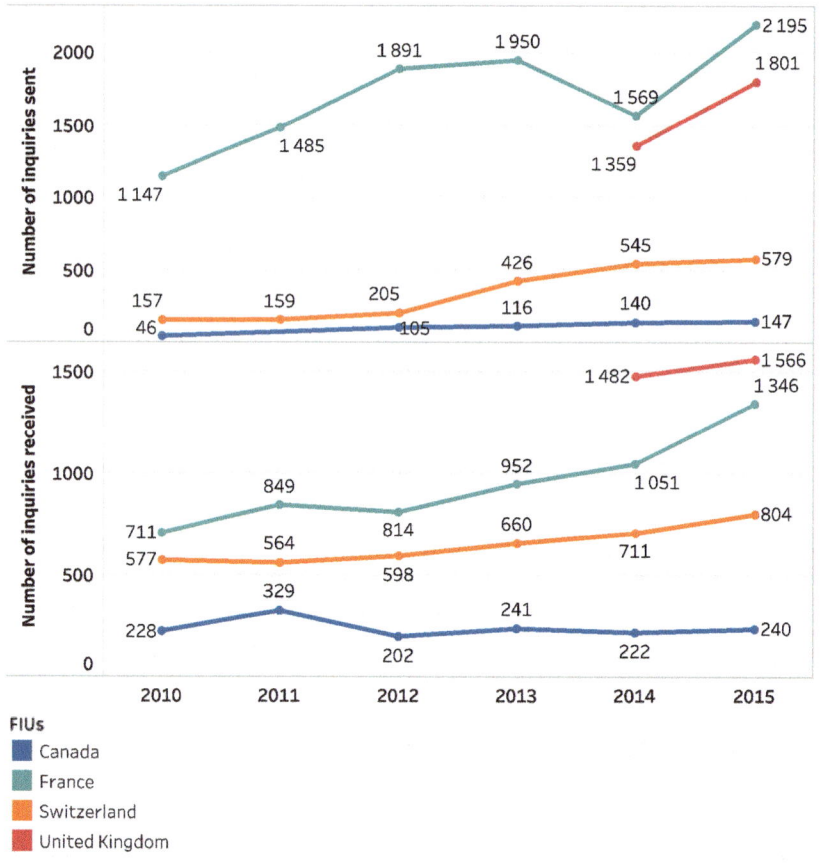

Chart 27.1 FIUs in Canada, France, Switzerland and the UK: Inquiries received/sent

Table 27.1 FIUs in Canada, France, Switzerland, and the UK: Inquiries received/sent

		2010	2011	2012	2013	2014	2015
Canada's Fintrac	Inquiries received	228	329	202	241	222	240
	Inquiries sent	46	74	105	116	140	147
France's Tracfin	Inquiries received	711	849	814	952	1051	1346
	Inquiries sent	1147	1485	1891	1950	1569	2195
Switzerland's MROS	Inquiries received	577	564	598	660	711	804
	Inquiries sent	157	159	205	426	545	579
United Kingdom's	Inquiries received					1482	1566
NCA	Inquiries sent					1359	1801

especially regarding the inquiries sent compared to the number of STRs received by the Swiss FIU annually (in 2015, 579 inquiries compared to 2367 STRs). The ratio can be largely explained by MROS's dependence on foreign information in relation to Switzerland's position as a major financial centre. The relatively low number of inquiries to Fintrac can be partly explained by the collection of tens of millions monetary threshold-based reports annually. The reporting of suspicious transactions is at the heart of financial intelligence, but some FIUs such as Fintrac also rely on other reporting obligations, based largely on monetary thresholds, including 'electronic funds transfer reports' for the transfer of $10,000 or more out of, or in to, Canada. In this context, Fintrac collected over 23 million financial transaction reports in 2015, including over 14 million 'electronic funds transfer reports', over 9 million 'large cash transaction reports', approximately 114,000 'suspicious transaction reports', and 172,000 'casino disbursement reports'.

Chart 27.2 and Table 27.2 reveal that the vast majority of inquiries received by Tracfin (France's FIU) are from European Partners (both EU and non-EU). Those from the EU are received largely via FIU.NET; around 60 per cent of all inquiries received by Tracfin come from EU member states. There is almost no overlap between this cooperation channel and ESW. In other words, these channels of cooperation are complementary/compatible.

Chart 27.3 and Table 27.3 reveal that, in contrast to Tracfin (France's FIU), the UK FIU seems to either receive and send a majority of extra-EU inquiries or face duplication and overlap between the FIU.NET and the ESW.

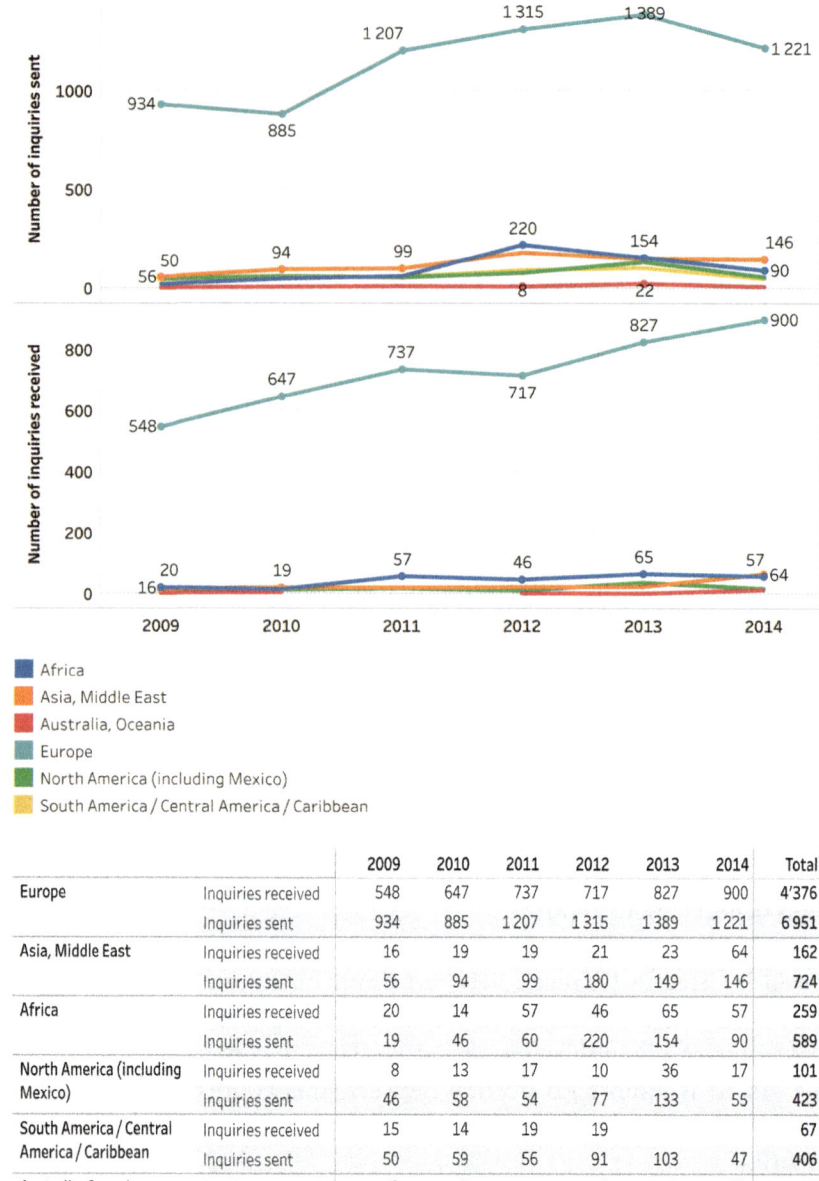

Chart 27.2   France's FIU: Information exchanged

		2009	2010	2011	2012	2013	2014	Total
Europe	Inquiries received	548	647	737	717	827	900	4'376
	Inquiries sent	934	885	1 207	1 315	1 389	1 221	6 951
Asia, Middle East	Inquiries received	16	19	19	21	23	64	162
	Inquiries sent	56	94	99	180	149	146	724
Africa	Inquiries received	20	14	57	46	65	57	259
	Inquiries sent	19	46	60	220	154	90	589
North America (including Mexico)	Inquiries received	8	13	17	10	36	17	101
	Inquiries sent	46	58	54	77	133	55	423
South America / Central America / Caribbean	Inquiries received	15	14	19	19			67
	Inquiries sent	50	59	56	91	103	47	406
Australia, Oceania	Inquiries received	2	4		1	1	13	21
	Inquiries sent	1	5	9	8	22	7	52

Table 27.2 France's FIU: Information exchanged

		2009	2010	2011	2012	2013	2014	Total
Europe	Inquiries received	548	647	737	717	827	900	4376
	Inquiries sent	934	885	1207	1315	1389	1221	6951
Asia, Middle East	Inquiries received	16	19	19	21	23	64	162
	Inquiries sent	56	94	99	180	149	146	724
Africa	Inquiries received	20	14	57	46	65	57	259
	Inquiries sent	19	46	60	220	154	90	589
North America (including Mexico)	Inquiries received	8	13	17	10	36	17	101
	Inquiries sent	46	58	54	77	133	55	423
South America/ Central America/ Caribbean	Inquiries received	15	14	19	19			67
	Inquiries sent	50	59	56	91	103	47	406
Australia, Oceania	Inquiries received	2	4		1	1	13	21
	Inquiries sent	1	5	9	8	22	7	52

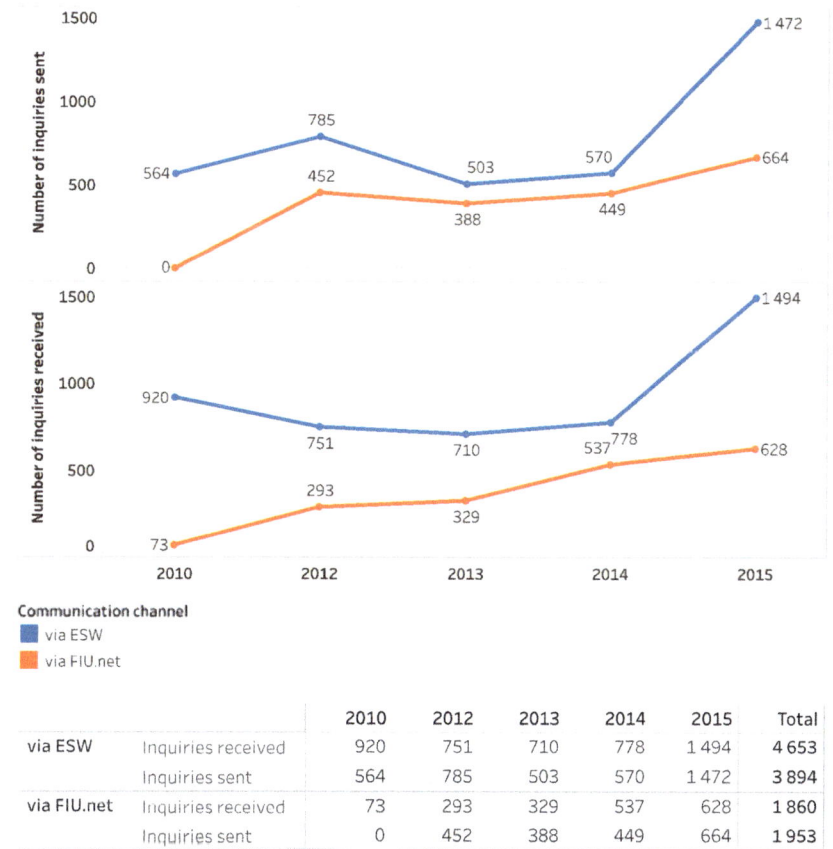

		2010	2012	2013	2014	2015	Total
via ESW	Inquiries received	920	751	710	778	1 494	4 653
	Inquiries sent	564	785	503	570	1 472	3 894
via FIU.net	Inquiries received	73	293	329	537	628	1 860
	Inquiries sent	0	452	388	449	664	1 953

Chart 27.3 UK FIU: Information exchanged

Table 27.3 UK FIU: Information exchanged

		2010	2012	2013	2014	2015	Total
Via ESW	Inquiries received	920	751	710	778	1494	4653
	Inquiries sent	564	785	503	570	1472	3894
Via FIU.net	Inquiries received	73	293	329	537	628	1860
	Inquiries sent	0	452	388	449	664	1953

Financial Intelligence Cooperation in Face of Tensions

> We try to organise ourselves to better understand how exchanges work with each FIU and to understand how another FIU is organised. Because when, after a request, we are told "I don't know!", we have to determine is there no information because the other FIU has looked for it and did not find anything, or because it did not look for it, or because it could not have looked for it, or because it looked for it but did not have the resources to really look for it? (Interview FIU 1, 2016)

Cooperation practices between FIUs regularly come under fire in relation to a series of difficulties. These difficulties are often associated to existing differences in the ways that FIUs operate. Nevertheless, the main differences are not where they might be expected to be. The International Monetary Fund's highly influential 2004 report—*Financial Intelligence Units: An Overview*—insisted on 'variations' between FIUs. According to the authors, the fundamental distinctions relate to the legal nature of FIUs, which fall into four models: (1) the administrative-type FIU; (2) the law-enforcement-type FIU; (3) the judicial or prosecutorial-type FIU; (4) the mixed or hybrid FIU.[39] These four models of FIUs are currently mentioned by the Egmont Group as follows:

> The Judicial Model is established within the judicial branch of government wherein "disclosures" of suspicious financial activity are received by the investigative agencies of a country from its financial sector such that the judiciary powers can be brought into play e.g. seizing funds, freezing accounts, conducting interrogations, detaining people, conducting searches, etc.

> The Law Enforcement Model implements anti-money laundering measures alongside already existing law enforcement systems, supporting the efforts of multiple law enforcement or judicial authorities with concurrent or sometimes competing jurisdictional authority to investigate money laundering.

> The Administrative Model is a centralized, independent, administrative authority, which receives and processes information from the financial sector and transmits disclosures to judicial or law enforcement authorities for prosecution. It functions as a "buffer" between the financial and the law enforcement communities.

The Hybrid Model serves as a disclosure intermediary and a link to both judicial and law enforcement authorities. It combines elements of at least two of the FIU models.[40]

The IMF classification has been largely used to shed light on key differences when assessing the comparative advantages and disadvantages between FIUs. For instance, it is regularly stressed that there is an information gap between law-enforcement and judicial FIUs on the one hand, and administrative and hybrid FIUs on the other. In the EU, for example, law-enforcement and judicial FIUs, on average, have better access to national police and judicial data.[41] However, the classic typology is not sufficient to identify the key operational differences between FIUs and it masks numerous critical elements that make a difference in practice, including those between FIUs that fall into the same model. It gives the mistaken impression that every question relates to status problems. On the contrary, being grouped into the same model—like Canada, France, and Switzerland, which are all in the administrative group—often means very little in practice with regard to the three core functions of FIUs (such as information collection; information analysis; information dissemination). The main issue is not a matter of status as defined by the IMF typology. There are major differences between FIUs in the same model while 'administrative FIUs', such as France's Tracfin, Canada's Fintrac, and Switzerland's MROS, sometimes have better access to police and intelligence databases than some law-enforcement FIUs.

Ultimately, tensions in transnational financial intelligence are due either to a lack of capacity to respond to a request, to the low level of spontaneous dissemination, or to 'abusive' restrictions on the use of information, three key issues which will now be examined.

On the Capacity to Respond to FIU Requests

First of all, a number of FIUs have been criticised for their inability to obtain information from 'reporting entities' (mainly financial institutions) following requests from foreign counterparts. Such criticisms can be broken down as follows: a general inability to request information from reporting entities, or a conditional (in)ability to obtain information from reporting entities. In relation to the former, some FIUs cannot request and obtain additional information from reporting entities, even after the submission of one or several related STRs. For example, the 2016 FATF evaluation of Canada notes that 'Fintrac may request the person or entity that filed an STR to correct or complete its report when there are quality issues such as errors or missing information, but not in other instances where this would be needed to perform its functions properly. According to the authorities, Canada's constitutional framework prohibits Fintrac from requesting additional information from reporting entities'.[42]

On the other hand, with the latter, other FIUs cannot request information from reporting entities on behalf of foreign FIUs without related suspicious transactions in their own database. In other words, a prior report on client or transaction 'X' from bank 'Y' in the database of FIU 'A' is a pre-condition for cooperation with FIU 'B' that requests information on client or transaction 'X' from bank 'Y'. FIU 'A' will not contact bank 'Y' for further details without such a prior report. The recent FATF evaluation of Switzerland notes that 'an important limitation in the effectiveness of international co-operation results from MROS not having the power, in the case of a foreign request, to request information from a financial intermediary unless the latter has previously submitted a suspicious transactions report or has a link with a STR received by MROS. This limitation, which was also raised by numerous delegations who shared their experience in co-operating with Switzerland, appears particularly important in the Swiss context'.[43] By contrast, there are also concerns that FIUs' request for information from reporting entities on behalf of a foreign counterpart may compromise the confidentiality of the foreign investigation. 'Information security is sometimes a cause for concern when our counterparts (foreign FIUs) need to contact a reporting entity to obtain information. They contact the reporting entity and say: 'we are looking for the bank accounts of Mr X'. And the banker or the accountant or the lawyer might contact Mr. X. From experience, there is no guarantee that this will not happen' (Interview FIU 3, 2016).

Secondly, FIUs may complain about an inability to get access to beneficial ownership information. The lack of information about beneficial ownership by legal persons and arrangements established in another country is widely recognised as a critical issue. In accordance with the international standards against money laundering and terrorist financing, the notion of 'beneficial owner refers to the natural person(s) who ultimately owns or controls a customer and/or the natural person on whose behalf a transaction is being conducted. It also includes those persons who exercise ultimate effective control over a legal person'.[44] In light of international financial operations, especially for tax-related requests, FIUs often depend on beneficial ownership information available in another country. Parties involved in targeted transactions often cannot be identified without access to accurate and reliable information because of the lack of transparency in legal arrangements:

> This is at the heart of the Panama Papers! What do I see as the core issue of the Panama Papers? Yes there are suspicious financial flows but the main issue is to show that shell companies are used to conceal these financial flows ... Because

the financial flows—we see them! We can see them! But we cannot see who is the benefical owner and what is the economic reason behind the legal arrangement. There are structures of opacity that do not permit us to know who the operator really is. (Interview FIU 1, 2016)[45]

Without access to information on beneficial owners and control of legal persons, it is not possible to match financial traces to an identity. The misuse of corporate entities for illicit activities was largely acknowledged before the Panama Papers,[46] and frequently recalled in the aftermath of the scandal, but the identification of beneficial owners through FIU-to-FIU cooperation is still a predominant concern among practitioners. Along these lines, law-enforcement agencies in Canada recently stated that 'they encounter difficulties in identifying beneficial owners of Canadian companies owned by entities established abroad, particularly in the Caribbean, Middle East, and Asia. [...] Also, in a number of cases that have been investigated and where Canadian companies were owned by foreign entities or foreign trusts, it was not possible for law enforcement agencies to identify the beneficial owners'.[47]

Thirdly, FIUs often complain about a lack of (access to) information databases. According to the FIUs examined, one of the main issues is related to the ability to get access to police databases in order to respond to foreign FIUs requests. The lack of access to such databases is presented as an 'international handicap'. However, the issue of direct or indirect access to national databases is not limited to police information, particularly for tax-related money laundering. In this regard, the FATF's mutual evaluation of Canada suggests that it should 'consider granting Fintrac access to information collected by the CRA [Canada Revenue Agency] for the purposes of its analysis of STRs'.[48] Current discussions in the EU are not restricted to access to existing national databases but also focus on the systematic creation of new databases, such as the central registers for all holders of bank accounts—registries that exist in some member states, including in France, which has FICOBA (*Fichier National des Comptes Bancaires et Assimilés*). Every bank account, savings account, and trading account opened in France is listed in FICOBA. The register contains information on the account's opening, modification, and closing. This includes: (1) the account owner's name, date and place of birth, and address (in the case of natural persons, the related code, names, legal form and address are registered); (2) the name and address of the financial institution holding the account; and (3) further details about the type and nature of the account as well as the account number. Financial institutions must provide and update this information, which is stored in the national register throughout the entire life cycle of an account and for ten years after the account is closed. In 2016, 80,000,000 individuals were registered in FICOBA, which processes 100 million account reports (opening, modification, closing) annually.[49] FICOBA is directly accessible to officials from financial administrations (tax administration, customs, Tracfin, and so on), the securities regulator, social security agencies, banks, judges, and criminal investigation officers, the '*huissiers de justice*', and notaries in charge of a succession. In relation to financial intelligence, the promoted added-value relies on the ability to determine if a person related to a STR has more than one account in more than one bank. FIUs without such central registers are criticised for 'insufficient capacity' to map the possible multiple accounts held by an individual in various financial institutions. In this respect, the fourth EU Directive mentions that 'in accordance with Union and national law, Member States could, for instance, consider putting in place systems of banking registries or electronic data retrieval systems which would provide FIUs with access to information on bank accounts without prejudice to judicial authorisation where applicable'.[50]

Fourthly, there are timeliness issues and lack of reciprocity. While responsiveness to FIU requests may vary from one country to another, it may also vary from one type of illicit flow to another:

> Of course there have been some improvements but the fact remains that there are problems with some countries, including the largest ones such as the US, if we do not talk about terrorism. Most of the time, the answer is limited to 'known/unknown'. (Interview FIU 4, 2017)

In the field of financial intelligence, as elsewhere, national prioritisation matters and the focus on counter-terrorism has not necessarily had a positive impact on the fight against financial crime in general. This question is at least a matter of debate.[51] For some, the primary focus on terrorism has created a new dynamic that provides a 'major leverage effect against financial crime as a whole' (Interview FIU 1, 2016). In this context, current national, European, and international action plans to strengthen the fight against terrorist financing should be highly beneficial for dealing with any kind of natural and legal persons linked to money that is 'dirty' because of either its origin or its use and destination, from terrorists to tax-related white-collar criminals. Others, however, question this idea of general progress:

> The question of terrorism is the number one priority and there are many things, many legal developments, that will allow us to share more information on this topic. But in terms of money laundering, it is… it has lost its cachet … When cooperating at the international level with financial intelligence units on tax evasion versus terrorism, we are not in the same galaxy here, it is completely different, even with the same close foreign partners. (Interview FIU 3, 2016)

Some are concerned that the effort to deal with terrorism is to focus on one tree and to ignore the wood. They argue that FIUs should not be used primarily as counter-terrorism tools at the expense of other missions. This debate questions the assertion that FIUs are now officially at the heart of a fight against all forms of illicit financial flows.

Moreover, response time is still a concern for all the FIUs we examined, which sometimes receive the requested information but several months too late to be relevant. Response time and number of responses from an FIU, however, deserve very careful assessment. An FIU may have good statistics on timing and number of exchanges but these results may include a wide range of quick responses such as, 'we are not in a position to reply'. It can also mask a lack of reciprocity that is a shared concern among FIUs:

> There is an issue of real importance in international cooperation: reciprocity. We have a problem in terms of reciprocity. Most of the time we do not succeed to obtain the same thing as what we provide. (Interview FIU 2, 2016).

On Spontaneous Dissemination and 'Abusive' Restrictions

> I have had some clashes with my analysts who used to tell me: 'Suspicious Transactions Reports—STRs not relevant, no link with our country' while for me it was critical to spontaneously send these STRs to foreign FIUs. (Interview FIU 4, 2017)

This quote illustrates current discussions regarding spontaneous dissemination. Spontaneous dissemination is encouraged in international standards but is far from being the norm in practice. While some FIU officials would like to see increased dissemination, others support an automatic information exchange every time an STR has an 'international' element. This support is especially explicit in the EU, where the internal market facilitates opening a bank account in a member state other than the country of residence.

Finally, the ways in which the exchanged information can be used can also be a matter of significant tension between the FIU making the request and the FIU receiving the request, in particular on tax issues:

> Actually, when we make a request for information to this European FIU on tax-related money laundering, there is no problem with getting the information, they are doing their job. They reply in a timely manner but … They always write at the end: 'You cannot use this information for tax purposes'. It is too bad because it is exactly for tax purposes that we made the request! How do you want to exchange information post–Panama Papers? All the difficulties involved in getting access to the information and then at the end you receive the information with this kind of restriction! (Interview FIU 1, 2016)

As already mentioned, international standards of information exchange require that any further use of information must be authorised by the FIU providing the information. The argument of abusive use of this basic principle, especially on tax-related issues, is debated on a daily basis in the field of financial intelligence, in the EU, and abroad.

Conclusion

'Money laundering is the process of making illegally gained proceeds ("dirty money") appear legal ("clean")'.[52] This clear and straightforward definition of money laundering is now available on the website of the US FIU but could have been written, published, and widely accepted in 1990. Meanwhile, the scope of the notion of 'dirty money' has been radically extended from the proceeds of drug trafficking to illicit flows of money in general, including, after years of explicit exclusion, tax evasion. The striking definitional malleability of 'dirty money' has largely transformed financial intelligence practices.

FIUs' powers have continued to increase significantly over the last 25 years and the tremendous development of financial intelligence capabilities has been justified largely in the name of counter-terrorism. While this prioritisation of terrorist financing is very often associated with an increased effort in the fight against illicit financial flows as a whole, there are much more mitigated results in practice with regard to 'mutual benefits'. More generally, while international norms and European legislation now officially cover all forms of illicit financial flows, the differential management of predicate offences still deserves further analysis.

Furthermore, as the meaning of 'dirty money' has changed since the early 1990s, what an FIU is and what it does has evolved over time but still varies from one country to another. In other words, the expression 'dirty money' now tends to be increasingly understood in the same way across countries, but this relative convergence is far from being the case for 'financial intelligence unit'. Given the many differences between national agencies and their impact on international cooperation, critical discussions of FIUs should go beyond a focus on the four traditional models (administrative, hybrid, judicial, law-enforcement). This classic distinction between FIUs remains important for identifying and understanding a number of national variations and international tensions, but these are certainly not the only issues at stake.

Notes

1. IMF, *Financial Intelligence Units: An Overview* (World Bank 2004) 5–6.
2. Liliya Gelemerova, 'On the Frontline Against Money-Laundering: The Regulatory Minefield' (2008) 52(1) Crime, Law and Social Change 33; Saskia Hufnagel, *AUSTRAC Report* (Unpublished Study on Demand 2011)
3. These recommendations have since been revised and updated—the most recent version being: FATF, *The FATF Recommendations* (FATF/OECD 2012, updated in October 2016).
4. For discussion of such assemblages in this collection, see Chap. 31 (de Goede).
5. IMF (n 1) 4.
6. Eric Helleiner, 'State Power and the Regulation of Illicit Activity in Global Finance' in Peter Andreas and Richard Friman (eds), *The Illicit Global Economy and State Power* (Rowman and Littlefield 1999); Michael Levi and Peter Reuter, 'Money Laundering' in Michael Tonry (ed), *Crime and Justice. A Review of Research* (Chicago University Press 2006); Gilles Favarel-Garrigues, Thierry Godefroy, and Pierre Lascoumes, *Les Sentinelles de l'Argent Sale: Les Banques Aux Prises Avec l'Antiblanchiment* (Édition La Découverte 2009); Jason C Sharman, *The Money Laundry. Regulating Criminal Finance in the Global Economy* (Cornell University Press 2011); William Gilmore, *Dirty Money—The Evolution of International Measures to Counter Money Laundering and the Financing of Terrorism* (4th edn, Council of Europe 2011).
7. Petrus C van Duyne, 'Money Laundering Policy. Fears and Facts' in Petrus C van Duyne, Klaus von Lampe, and James L Newell (eds), *Criminal Finances and Organising Crime in Europe* (Wolf Legal Publishers 2003); Ioana Deleanu, 'The Role of Information for Successful AML Policy' in Brigitte Unger and Daan van der Linde (eds), *Research Handbook on Money Laundering* (Edward Elgar Publishing 2013); Jef Huysmans, *Security Unbound. Enacting Democratic Limits* (Routledge 2014), Chapter 5.
8. Council Decision of 17 October 2000 concerning arrangements for cooperation between financial intelligence units of the Member States in respect of exchanging information [2000] OJ L271/4.
9. Jean-François Thony, 'Processing Financial Information in Money Laundering Matters: The Financial Intelligence Units' (1996) 4(3) European Journal of Crime, Criminal Law and Criminal Justice 257; Brigitte Unger and others, Project 'ECOLEF': The Economic and Legal Effectiveness of Anti-Money Laundering and Combating Terrorist Financing Policy (funded by the European Commission—DG Home Affairs JLS/2009/ISEC/AG/087) *Final Report* (2013) <www2.econ.uu.nl/users/unger/ecolef_files/Final%20ECOLEF%20report%20(digital%20version).pdf> accessed 4 May 2017.

10. Clifford Williams, 'Artificial Harmony: Why Cooperative Efforts to Create a Global Financial Intelligence Unit Have Faltered' (2014) 17(4) Journal of Money Laundering Control 428.

11. Egmont Group of Financial Intelligence Units, 'Annual Report 2015–2016' (2017) 14 <https://egmontgroup.org/index.php?q=filedepot_download/1660/45> accessed 29 May 2017.

12. For other academic comparative analysis but more in terms of evaluative and/or policy-oriented research, see Milind Sathye and Chris Patel, 'Developing Financial Intelligence: An Assessment of the FIUs in Australia and India' (2007) 10(4) Journal of Money Laundering Control 391; Musonda Simwayi and Muhammed Haseed, 'The Role of Financial Intelligence Units in Combating Money Laundering: A Comparative Analysis of Zambia, Zimbabwe and Malawi' (2011) 15(1) Journal of Money Laundering Control 112; Mohammad Al-Rashdan, 'An Analytical Study of the Financial Intelligence Units' Enforcement Mechanisms' (2012) 15(4) Journal of Money Laundering Control 483.

13. Anthony Amicelle, 'Towards a 'New' Political Anatomy of Financial Surveillance' (2011) 42(2) Security Dialogue 161; Anthony Amicelle and Gilles Favarel-Garrigues, 'Financial Surveillance: Who Cares?' (2012) 5(1) Journal of Cultural Economy 105; Anthony Amicelle, *The EU's Paradoxical Efforts at Tracking the Financing of Terrorism. From Criticism to Imitation of Dataveillance* (CEPS Liberty and Security Series 2013); Anthony Amicelle, 'Differential Management of Economic and Financial Illegalisms: Anti-Money Laundering and Tax Issues' (2014) 10 Penal Field 1; Anthony Amicelle, 'Management of Tax Transgressions in France: A Foucauldian Perspective' in Judith van Herp, Wim Huisman, and Gundrun Vande Walle (eds), *The Routledge Handbook of White-Collar and Corporate Crime in Europe* (Routledge 2015); Anthony Amicelle and Elida Jacobsen, 'The Cross-Colonization of Finance and Security through Lists: Banking Policing in the UK and India' (2016) 34(1) Environment and Planning D: Society and Space 89; Anthony Amicelle, 'Policing Through Misunderstanding: Insights From the Configuration of Financial Policing' (Forthcoming) Crime, Law and Social Change; Killian Chaudieu, Anthony Amicelle, and Quentin Rossy, 'Follow the (Dirty) Money in Switzerland: Remarks About Financial Policing' (Forthcoming) Penal Field.

14. Robin Thomas Naylor, 'Follow-the-Money Methods in Crime Control Policy' in Margaret Beare (ed) *Critical Reflections on Transnational Organized Crime, Money Laundering and Corruption* (University of Toronto Press 2003).

15. Egmont Group of FIUs, 'Principles for Information Exchange Between FIUs' (2013) 4 <www.ppatk.go.id/backend/assets/uploads/20160930143939.pdf> accessed 29 May 2017.

16. Egmont Group of FIUs, 'Benefits of Egmont Group Membership' <https://egmontgroup.org/en/content/membership> accessed 4 May 2017.

17. James Sheptycki, 'Policing the Virtual Launderette: Money Laundering and Global Governance' in James Sheptycki (ed), *Issues in Transnational Policing* (Routledge 2000) 153.
18. Egmont Group of FIUs, 'Charter' (2013) 8 <https://egmontgroup.org/en/filedepot_download/1658/36> accessed 29 May 2017.
19. FinCEN, 'The Egmont Group of Financial Intelligence Units' <www.fincen. gov/resources/international/egmont-group-financial-intelligence-units> accessed 4 May 2017.
20. Egmont Group of FIUs, 'Operational Guidance for FIU Activities and the Exchange of Information' (2013) 5 <https://egmontgroup.org/en/filedepot_download/1658/38> accessed 29 May 2017.
21. Egmont Group of FIUs, 'FAQ' (2017) <http://forum.techbizlines.com/view-topic.aspx?tno=31177> accessed 29 May 2017.
22. Egmont Group of FIUs (n 18).
23. Money Laundering Reporting Office Switzerland (MROS), 'Annual Report' (2012) <www.fedpol.admin.ch/dam/data/fedpol/kriminalitaet/geldwaescherei/jabe/jb-mros-2012-e.pdf> accessed 29 May 2017.
24. MROS, 'Annual Report' (2013) <www.fedpol.admin.ch/dam/data/fedpol/kriminalitaet/geldwaescherei/jabe/jb-mros-2013-e.pdf> accessed 29 May 2017.
25. MROS, 'Annual Report' (2014) <www.fedpol.admin.ch/dam/data/fedpol/kriminalitaet/geldwaescherei/jabe/jb-mros-2014-e.pdf> accessed 29 May 2017.
26. Federal Act on Combating Money Laundering and Terrorist Financing (October 1997-January 2016), art 31.
27. Directive (EU) 2015/849 of the European Parliament and of the Council of 20 May 2015 on the prevention of the use of the financial system for the purposes of money laundering or terrorist financing, amending Regulation (EU) No 648/2012 of the European Parliament and of the Council, and repealing Directive 2005/60/EC of the European Parliament and of the Council and Commission Directive 2006/70/EC (Text with EEA relevance) [2015] OJ L141/73, art 53(3).
28. Ibid.
29. Egmont Group of FIUs (n 20) 22.
30. Council Decision of 17 October 2000 concerning arrangements for cooperation between financial intelligence units of the Member States in respect of exchanging information [2000] OJ L271/4, para 6.
31. David Carlisle, *Making Information Flow. Instruments and Innovations for Enhancing Financial Intelligence* (RUSI 2016).
32. Europol, 'Financial Intelligence Units—FIU.NET' <www.europol.europa. eu/about-europol/financial-intelligence-units-fiu-net> accessed 4 May 2017.
33. Ibid.
34. European Commission, *25th Meeting of the EU FIUs Platform* (2015) 8; Interviews FIUs, 2016 2017.

35. Udo Kroon, 'Ma3tch: Privacy AND Knowledge. Dynamic Networked Collective Intelligence' Presentation at the IEEE International Conference on Big Data (Silicon Valley, 6–9 October 2013).

36. Marieke de Goede and Gavin Sullivan, 'The Politics of Security Lists' (2016) 34(1) Environment and Planning D—Society and Space 67.

37. European Commission, *26th Meeting of the EU FIUs Platform* (2015).

38. Directive 2015/849 (n 27) art 53(1).

39. IMF (n 1) 9–17. For an earlier but rather similar classification, see also Valsamis Mitsilegas, 'New Forms of Transnational Policing: The Emergence of Financial Intelligence Units in the European Union and the Challenges for Human Rights' (1999) 3(2) Journal of Money Laundering Control 147.

40. Egmont Group of FIUs, 'Financial Intelligence Units' <https://egmontgroup.org/en/content/financial-intelligence-units-fius> accessed 4 May 2017.

41. Unger and others (n 9).

42. Financial Action Task Force (FATF), *Mutual Evaluation Report of Canada* (FATF 2016) 184.

43. Financial Action Task Force (FATF), *Mutual Evaluation Report of Switzerland* (FATF 2016) 150.

44. FATF (n 3) 113.

45. The Panama Papers scandal dominated news headlines in more than 60 countries in April 2016. It refers to the leak of 11.5 million financial and legal records from one of the world's biggest offshore law firms, Mossack Fonseca—based in Panama. The German newspaper *Süddeutsche Zeitung* obtained and shared these leaked records with the International Consortium of Investigative Journalists (ICIJ) 'to expose the offshore holdings of world political leaders, links to global scandals, and details of the hidden financial dealings of fraudsters, drug traffickers, billionaires, celebrities, sports stars and more': ICIJ, *Panama Papers* <https://panamapapers.icij.org> accessed 22 May 2017.

46. Michele Riccardi and Ernesto U Savona, *The Identification of Beneficial Owners in the Fight Against Money Laundering* (Transcrime 2013).

47. FATF (n 42) 103.

48. Ibid. 36.

49. Commission Nationales de l'Informatique et des Libertés (CNIL), 'FICOBA: Fichier National des Comptes Bancaires et Assimilés' (2016) <www.cnil.fr/fr/ficoba-fichier-national-des-comptes-bancaires-et-assimiles> accessed 29 May 2017.

50. Directive 2015/849 (n 27) para 57.

51. Valsamis Mitsilegas, 'Countering the Chameleon Threat of Dirty Money: "Hard" and "Soft" Law in the Emergence of a Global Regime Against Money Laundering and Terrorist Finance' in Adam Edwards and Peter Gill (eds), *Transnational Organised Crime: Perspectives on Global Security* (Routledge 2003); Michael Levi, 'Combating the Financing of Terrorism: A History and Assessment of the Control of 'Threat Finance'' (2010) 50(4) The British Journal

of Criminology 650; Jayesh D'Souza, *Terrorist Financing, Money Laundering, and Tax Evasion: Examining the Performance of Financial Intelligence Units* (CRC Press 2011); Marieke de Goede, *Speculative Security. The Politics of Pursuing Terrorist Monies* (University of Minnesota Press 2012).

52. FinCEN, 'History of Anti-Money Laundering Laws' <www.fincen.gov/history-anti-money-laundering-laws> accessed 4 May 2017.

Anthony Amicelle is Assistant Professor in Criminology at the Université de Montréal. His research examines practices of policing, surveillance and intelligence at the interface of finance and security, especially with respect to counter-terrorism and anti-money laundering. His recent publications include (with Vanessa Iafolla) 'Suspicion-in-the-Making: Surveillance and Denunciation in Financial Policing (British Journal of Criminology, 2017); 'Policing through Misunderstanding: Insights from the Configuration of Financial Policing' (Crime, Law and Social Change, 2017); (with Elida Jacobsen) 'The Cross-Colonization of Finance and Security through Lists' (Society and Space, 2016).

Killian Chaudieu is a doctoral student in the School of criminal sciences at the University of Lausanne and in the Department of criminology at the Université de Montréal. Trained in forensics and criminology, his research is focused on a comparative analysis of financial intelligence apparatus in Canada and Switzerland.

28

Taxing Crime: A New Power to Control

Raymond Friel and Shane Kilcommins

Introduction

It is said that 'The power to tax involves the power to destroy.'[1] Accordingly, this chapter deals with the taxation of criminal activities. In addition to tracing the development of the relevant jurisprudence across a number of jurisdictions, it examines the increasing regulation, and thus control, of criminal activity through the tax authorities as distinct from the police. In that way it reflects a general trend towards the 'civil'ising—the flow of power from the criminal realm in to the less jurisprudentially constrained civil realm—of the criminal process. The traditional criminal process is now viewed as only one part of a wider spectrum of tools available to the state. These tools are geared towards controlling the criminal environment through regulation rather than correctional interventions.[2] This more regulatory approach embodies many actuarial tendencies: it perceives crime as a normal occurrence, where the wrongdoer needs to be 'managed' as a 'risk object' rather than normalised as a 'biographical' individual. The classic example of such regulation is the case of Al Capone, who was successfully prosecuted for tax offences rather than the criminal activities he directed.[3] In Ireland, a more modern counterpart can be found in the case of Thomas 'Slab' Murphy. Murphy was engaged in criminal activities used partly to fund terrorism across two or more jurisdictions:

R. Friel • S. Kilcommins
School of Law, University of Limerick, Limerick, Ireland

© The Author(s) 2018
C. King et al. (eds.), *The Palgrave Handbook of Criminal and Terrorism Financing Law*,
https://doi.org/10.1007/978-3-319-64498-1_28

677

If Capone was Chicago's gangster Mr Big then Murphy was Provisional republicans' Border godfather. Chieftain might be a more fitting description, because in many ways that is what he is, a leader who commanded loyalty and felt safest in his south Armagh tribe.[4]

His story provides a microcosm of the issues that this new power to control creates.

Though never convicted of terrorist activity, Murphy was allegedly an important figure in the South Armagh Brigade of the IRA in the 1970s and 1980s before being elected Chief of Staff of the IRA in 1997.[5] His farm straddles County Armagh and County Louth, the border between Northern Ireland and the Republic of Ireland. In December 2015, Murphy was found guilty on nine counts of tax evasion following a lengthy investigation by the Criminal Assets Bureau (CAB). In February 2016, he was jailed and sentenced to 18 months in prison.[6] What seems striking about this is that for all of the legal, extra-legal and military powers of the authorities in Northern Ireland, England and Wales, and the Republic of Ireland, it was civil and criminal tax provisions that were ultimately used to bring him to account.[7] In this chapter, we discuss the taxation of crime using Murphy's case as a vignette.

Conditions of Possibility

Though the instrument of tax has long been advocated as a powerful tool to be employed against criminal enterprises,[8] it is only in the last few decades that we see its increasing use.[9] Taxing the proceeds of crime is authorised in a number of jurisdictions including the US,[10] Australia,[11] Canada,[12] New Zealand,[13] the Republic of Ireland,[14] South Africa,[15] and England and Wales.[16] In *US v Sullivan*,[17] the justification for taxing criminal activity was expressed as follows: 'It does not satisfy one's sense of justice to tax persons in legitimate enterprises, and allow those who thrive by violation of the law to escape. It does not seem likely that the legislature intended to allow an individual to set up his own wrong in order to avoid taxation, and thereby increase the burdens on others lawfully employed.'

In the Republic of Ireland, although power to tax proceeds of crime already existed, it was only with the establishment of the CAB in 1996 that tax powers really came to the fore.[18] Indeed, and in something of a reversal of the established position of political imitation and policy transfer from other jurisdictions, it has been suggested that the 'structure and modus operandi of the Criminal Assets Bureau have been identified as models for other countries which are in the process of targeting the proceeds of crime'.[19] The CAB Act

1996 was introduced as part of a package of measures designed to tackle organised crime. While it is CAB's civil forfeiture powers[20] that garner most attention,[21] it is the tax powers of CAB that are, in practice, its most potent (and widely used) weapon.

Under section 5 of the CAB Act, CAB is required to ensure that the proceeds of criminal activity are subjected to tax. Significantly, it had previously been thought that profits derived from a criminal enterprise could not fall within the contemplation of income tax legislation.[22] It was only with the enactment of section 19 of the Finance Act 1983 that permission was given to the state to assess and collect tax on profits that arose from unlawful sources or activities. This proved difficult initially as the Revenue Commissioners were ill-equipped to deal with the challenge of hardened criminals. It was only with the increased protection provided by the CAB that the taxation instrument became fully effective.[23]

The Jurisprudence

For 'Slab' Murphy, the criminal justice system would intersect with tax law in ways which would prove immensely effective from the state's point of view. But the introduction of this novel approach could not have come without a significant evolutionary jurisprudence which would lead the way and provide the backdrop to a rapidly developing field of socio-legal theory.[24] Taxing the proceeds of crime brings into sharp focus certain legal, ethical and moral considerations. First, which criminal activities, if any, should be susceptible to tax? Second, even if the criminal activity is susceptible to tax, does that mean we *should* tax it? Third, how should such taxation deal with allowable expenses in the calculation of tax liability in these situations? And finally, to what extent, if any, would such taxation impact upon the behaviour of those engaged in criminal activity? These questions are not merely interlinked but part of an overall spectrum and this division, while useful in terms of exposition, may conceal the intellectual totality of the process. For example, a determination on the ethical issues involved in the first question might be different if the answer to the fourth question is that it would lead to a significant reduction in crime. We turn now to consider each of these four questions.

Which Criminal Activities Might Be Susceptible to Tax?

Tax is a state levy imposed on natural or legal persons for certain types of activities or events related to that natural or legal person. The most common form of tax today is income tax, which is generally considered to be the fairest form of tax because it is a percentage of the amount by which one's wealth has increased over a given period of time or on the happening of a certain event.[25] By contrast, property taxes are often perceived to be unfair because it is a 'state of affairs' tax not related to ability to pay. Income tax is a tax which shares in the taxpayers' benefit whereas property tax is a tax which imposes a cost on the taxpayer.

Generally, crime can be divided into two very broad categories: crimes against the person (murder, rape, assault, etc.) and property crimes (theft, deception, destruction, etc.).[26] Of course the commission of one type of crime may result in the contemporaneous commission of the other, for example, a mugging will constitute an offence against the person (or victim) as well as a crime against that person's property. In a way, crimes against the person have state costs imposed upon them, traditionally through custodial sentences but more recently in addition through monetary fines. In that way, the state already 'taxes' crimes against the person. In any event, these crimes are normally not susceptible to the normal taxation process because by definition there is no 'proceed' upon which to levy the tax.

Property crimes are entirely different. Property crimes can be divided into two categories. First there are non-consensual crimes of acquisition and second there are consensual criminal activities which generate an income. Mugging an individual on the street and stealing his or her wallet is an example of the former, whereas selling illicit narcotics to the same individual is an example of the latter. There are two fundamental differences between each of these activities: consent and utility. For the non-consensual crime of acquisition, it involves an unwanted asset transfer from the victim to the criminal. The transaction lacks true consent. Economically, it is a zero sum game: the criminal has gained, the victim has lost, and from a narrow viewpoint, society is unaffected. In these cases, alongside criminal prosecution, the appropriate remedy is seizure of the non-consensually acquired property and its return to the dispossessed victim. The subject matter of the crime is not a 'proceed'.[27] Even where the property has been sold, the property in essence can still be traced into the proceeds of the sale and those proceeds should be seized and returned to the victim. Where there has been a mingling of the proceeds of many such crimes, then the state may have no option but to seize these proceeds and retain them for the benefit of society at large. It could, for example, choose to funnel such proceeds into enhanced policing or victim compensation schemes. Most modern legislation that seeks to confiscate the proceeds of crime is reflective of this civil forfeiture approach.[28] The difficulty with this approach is twofold: first the illegality relates to the property and not the person and, second, because the action is for seizure of property, civil procedure and burdens of proof are being used as surrogates for establishing criminal liability. This is characteristic of taxing the proceeds of crime in general.

Consensual income generating criminal activities are reflective of normal economic activities. They are usually consent based and provide individual, although not necessarily social utility. This is so irrespective of whether the activity is unlawful. Selling alcohol to a minor is consensual and brings utility to both parties although society may want to prohibit such transactions as it looks beyond the individual utility to the greater good of society. Another way of looking at consensual income generating criminal activities as distinguished from non-consensual acquisition of property is through the prism of property rights. The latter bestows no beneficial interest in the criminal and requires confiscation and return of the property to its rightful owner whereas the former is beneficially owned by the criminal. There is no basis for confiscation, but it does potentially give rise to a tax assessment on the income, or increase in wealth generated by that activity. Every day of the week a large percentage of economic activity arises from illegal acts and it is this income which theoretically can, and usually is, the subject of taxation as if it were no different from any other legal activity.

Is Taxing the Proceeds of Crime Acceptable?

At a very fundamental level, taxing such activities bears all the hallmarks of living off immoral earnings, which in many jurisdictions is a crime in its own right. Even if it were not, there must be strong ethical objections to the state becoming an accessory after the fact to criminal activity. The better ethical approach would be to confiscate the proceeds of any activity which has resulted in a profit to the accused.[29] To do otherwise results in the state sharing in the proceeds of ill-gotten gains, using the apparatus of the state including the civil service and the judiciary to conspire to take a share of the profits from activities which it has determined are prohibited. Even in the absence of any ethical consideration, there is a tension between inconsistent state objectives with one agency seeking to curtail activity (by prohibiting an act) which another agency seeks to maximise a financial return from (by sharing in the spoils of that activity).

This conundrum was traditionally addressed by Irish courts in a very straightforward and robust fashion. In *Hayes v Duggan*,[30] the Irish Supreme Court explicitly rejected the taxation of criminal activities. The Court made two primary arguments in support of this proposition. First, it held that any tax process would create new criminal offences, such as accessories after the fact, from the filing of returns to the claiming of allowances, and these disclosures themselves would obligate the state agencies to pursue the relevant individuals through the criminal process. Second, the state could not be seen to be profiting from, or condoning, criminal activity.[31] This remained the position in Irish law despite its subsequent rejection by English courts[32] and remained in operation until specifically overturned by statutory provision in 1983.[33] Even then, the Supreme Court's approach found support from some legislators. As one member of the Dáil (Irish parliament) said: 'the very idea of putting such a provision in legislation seems to suggest an acceptance and blessing of such illegal activities'. An alternative approach of confiscation of all the proceeds of crime was suggested.[34] Nonetheless the legislation permitting the Revenue Commissioners to tax the proceeds of crime, albeit under the misleading return of 'miscellaneous income', was passed and is now settled law.[35] There remains, however, both an admirable clarity of reasoning and a purity of principle in the original Supreme Court's approach.[36]

However, the overwhelming international approach is very much in favour of the taxation of the proceeds of crime. In the US, the argument that filing a tax return on income earned from criminal activities would in itself constitute a crime came under consideration in the *US v Sullivan*.[37] That argument was stronger in the US due to the Fifth Amendment of the US Constitution which protects an individual against self-incrimination.

In *Sullivan*, the US Supreme Court rejected the argument that an individual was exempt from declaring income on a tax return merely on the basis that it would involve self-incrimination. The illegality of the source of the income did not relieve the taxpayer of the requirement to declare that income. The Fifth Amendment did, however, protect the taxpayer from being forced to disclose its criminal origin when filing the return. Curiously in *US v Garner*,[38] the Supreme Court decided that where the taxpayer voluntarily declared the illegal source of the income thereby incriminating oneself, the Fifth Amendment would not prevent the use of that information outside of the taxation process. This was on the basis that the tax return was a voluntary waiver of the taxpayer's rights under the Fifth Amendment.[39] Similar to the Irish provisions enacted in 1983, US tax returns relating to proceeds of crime are generally filed under 'miscellaneous income'. It is possible for the taxpayer to make a return expressly claiming benefit of the Fifth Amendment when declaring the source of their income, but this is unlikely.

In England, the courts rejected the Irish approach in *Mann v Nash*.[40] The King's Bench concentrated on the strict application of the taxing statutes using literal interpretation. The taxing legislation taxed all income arising from a trade and made no distinction on the nature of that trade or the source of the income in general. The ruling of the court dealt with the second issue raised in *Hayes*, namely that taxation of the proceeds of crime would involve the state condoning or becoming partners in the criminal activity. Rowlett J rejected the argument that the state would effectively be condoning or participating in criminal activities. As he put it, Inland Revenue was doing no more than dealing with an 'accomplished fact',[41] namely the income of the taxpayer arising from his/her trade or profession whether that trade or profession is legal or illegal.[42]

In fact, most English jurisprudence revolves around what constitutes a 'trade'. Under statute, the term 'trade' has a rather circular definition: 'a trade is … every trade, manufacture, adventure or concern in the nature of a trade'.[43] In *IRC v Aken* HM Revenue raised an assessment of tax on the income of a prostitute. The taxpayer argued that since her attempt to register a company whose business was that of prostitution was refused on the basis that it contravened public policy, HM Revenue could not tax an act that the state had declared was contrary to public policy. The court rejected this argument, stating that a trade was taxable under the tax statutes whether that trade was lawful or not.

Although English jurisprudence represents a general view now shared in many jurisdictions,[44] it appears somewhat strange that all the moral and ethical issues can be avoided through an almost blind application of the rules of statutory interpretation. The courts have long held that a contract for prostitution cannot be enforced by the courts because it offends public morality, but they are willing to facilitate the 'sharing' of these illicit proceeds by the state. Further, *Aken's* case involved prostitution, which of itself is not criminal. Would the same approach be taken if the income had arisen from the 'trade' of a hitman? Arguably in New Zealand, the answer is a clear 'yes', given as it has been said that taxation knows no morality: it is not a question of fairness or morality but of statutory application.[45]

There are two suggested reasons for taxing the proceeds of crime: control and equity.[46] By taxing criminal activities one can control the 'industry' as one would control a lawful enterprise. Increased taxation on criminal proceeds may deter or lower existing criminal activity and in that way should be seen as part of an integrated strategy including confiscation of criminal assets and money laundering crimes. This 'control' rationale (or deterrence) is not without its critics.[47] The primary criticism centres on the dominant role of taxation which is to raise revenue and not control behaviour. Blurring the distinction between the two is inappropriate. Taxes on cigarettes—aimed at reducing smoking—raise significant revenue creating an inherent conflict of interest for the state. On the other hand, the equity rationale is more straightforward.[48] All generated income should contribute to the state coffers regardless of the source of that income. To do otherwise would be to discriminate income from one source compared to another and, in the context of not taxing the proceeds of crime, that discrimination would reward illegal income over legal income.[49]

There are two additional arguments which support the view taken by US, UK and other countries with respect to the taxation of the proceeds of crime. First, as a matter of practical reality, the tax take of most jurisdictions includes a not insignificant amount derived from money laundering of income earned by criminal activity.[50] Most money laundering will attempt to legitimise the income by putting it through the tax system.[51] The use of high cash turnover businesses—such as casinos, laundromats and so on—involve creating fake sales upon which both sales and income tax is levied—is a staple of the money laundering process. There are few questions concerning the appropriateness of such taxation, even if the 'laundering' is suspected or known about. Cleaning the proceeds of that criminal activity may lead to further scrutiny by the security agencies, but the revenue authorities are only concerned that they secure at least the amount which the taxpayer is willing to declare. They are concerned about taxpayers not declaring income rather than over-declaring their income. If the state is willing to tax the proceeds of crime where the source of that income is knowingly fabricated, why should it not tax similar proceeds where the source is not specified or admits to illegal activity?

Second, the Organisation for Economic Co-operation and Development (OECD) and other international agencies now accept that income generated by illegal activity must be included in the national accounts as part of the national product of that country.[52] The argument is straightforward: this activity is an integral part of the economic statistics of the country. The OECD details the sorts of activities that should be included and they can be grouped as follows:

> Production of illegal goods such as drugs, pornography, counterfeit goods, IP violative goods etc.
>
> Illegal or immoral services, e.g. prostitution, claims to be a medical doctor etc., smuggling, fencing of stolen goods, bribery, hit man.

The cumulative effect of the US, UK and other comparative jurisprudence and statutory provisions, together with the OECD recommendations, establishes a key conclusion. The one common thread is that income generating crime is, and should be, reported and is subject to tax by the authorities. What remains to be answered is how this income is to be calculated for tax purposes: specifically what if any would be an allowable expense in a criminal activity?

Allowable Expenses for Criminal Activities

All tax codes provide for expenses which can be set against income. Expenses reduce income for the taxpayer and thus there is a clear and understandable difference between gross and net income. Exactly what expenses are allowed for tax purposes is however a matter of significant debate. Large parts of any tax code are in fact dedicated to defining such allowances in specific detail. However, the underlying assumption is that all expenses arise from the acquisition of a legal service or good albeit being used to conduct an illegal activity which is giving rise to the income being taxed. Legitimate expenses involved in the operation of an illegal income generating activity have to be regarded as an allowable expense.[53] Since, in general, tax codes make no distinction between legal and illegal income, any distinction as to the treatment of legally incurred expenses would run the risk of a rights-based analysis with the criminal justice sphere rather than a simplistic tax offence.[54] Thus rent, wages, insurance and other expenses can be set against gross income for tax purposes.[55] Curiously, so too can the legal costs in defending a criminal case arising from the activity concerned since it is an expense paid for the acquisition of a lawful service necessitated by the income generating activity.

The more interesting question is whether illegal expenses can be claimed against income: for example, can a bribe be claimed as an operating expense, or indeed ammunition for a weapon? The US tax code specifically deals with this.[56] Criminal expenses are non-deductible for the purposes of income tax under the public policy exception. At first glance, this may appear somewhat incongruous but in essence if the taxation of the proceeds of crime is treated identically to that of legal activity, then the treatment of expenses must also be identical and a criminal expense incurred in a legal income generating activity would also be disallowed. At a more abstract level, tax is simply a levy on declared income, regardless of the source of that income. Allowable expenses are choices made by the state as to what expenses, if any, can reduce the income liable to tax. It is therefore legitimate for the state to choose not to allow some expenses while allowing others. Choosing not to allow criminal expenses as a legitimate cost is a valid state choice in the same way as choosing not to allow depreciation of assets as a cost against income. It is essentially a matter of public policy.

The final issue is whether or not fines or penalties incurred in the criminal activity should be an allowable expense. There are two primary justifications why fines and penalties should not be allowed as deductions. First, as a matter of public policy similar to that outlined above. Second, the fines may be viewed as personal to the taxpayer and not part of the expenses of conducting the business. In *Tank Truck Rentals v Commissioners*,[57] the plaintiff sought to reverse the decision of the Internal Revenue Service (IRS - the US federal tax authority) not to allow deductions for the fines imposed on the plaintiff's drivers for operating their vehicles in excess of statutory weight limits. This decision itself represented a reversal by the IRS which until 1950 had allowed such deductions. The court found for the IRS, stating that it would not permit the frustration of expressly stated and sharply defined state policy by allowing such fines to be set against income for taxation purposes. However, it is important to note that the ruling did not preclude all fines and penalties from being allowable expenses, but only those which would frustrate a sharply defined state policy. The plaintiff in that case had argued that these fines were analogous to a tax on an overweight vehicle rather than a penalty but this was rejected by the court on the facts of the case. Thus, a fine which is not penal in nature may in fact be an allowable expense although the US tax code was subsequently altered to expressly prohibit deductions for fines or penalties regardless of whether they are penal or not.[58]

Does Taxation Policy Affect Criminal Behaviour?

There are many reasons why individuals commit criminal acts which are discussed in detail below. In this section, the analysis focuses primarily on an economic approach that motivates this behaviour. The issue is whether taxation impacts upon the decision to engage in criminal activities. The impact of taxation policy on criminal behaviour has not been satisfactorily addressed, although there is a body of law and economic theory which purports to do so.

Returning to our case study of 'Slab' Murphy in Ireland, from a behavioural point of view, this case raises a very simple question: why did Murphy seek to evade all tax liability since it was evasion combined with the subsequent admission that he in fact had an occupation that was to be his undoing? Murphy was under observation by the security services in any event, so simply declaring income from 'miscellaneous sources' would hardly have raised a flag with the authorities that was not already flying at full tilt.

One argument in terms of rational response is that the taxation of illegal activity may alter the risk position of the taxpayer. In other words, an individual is less likely to engage in the inherently risky business of criminality if the potential rewards are lessened by the imposition of a tax: I will not deal in contraband cigarettes if my projected income from this is not €100 gross but only €60 after tax. The rational taxpayer, even one engaged in criminal activity, alters their acceptance of risk based on potential return from that activity.

However, most of the law and economic analysis assumes that those involved in criminal activity are risk neutral.[59] Risk neutrality means that the individual does not alter their position based on the level of risk to the return. Risk neutrality is, however, based on two assumptions. First, criminals who engage in inherently risky activities are risk neutral because it is believed that they will engage in an activity regardless of the risk. This means that they are as likely to engage in lawful acts as unlawful acts despite the risk associated with the latter. Second, the criminal is motivated by the amount of potential income arising from either activity. In theory, therefore, taxing the proceeds of crime should reduce the incidence of crime as individuals switch into lawful activities for which post taxation income might be higher due to more allowable expenses. But the economic theory behind this is based on the underpinning assumptions holding true, a view that has been criticised. Most of the literature deals with the impact of *either* taxation or criminal sanctions on the individual's risk profile but not with the impact of both.[60] In any event, the analysis changes dramatically if risk neutrality is replaced with risk aversion.[61]

Moreover, the law and economic analysis overlooks two very important factors. First, taxpayers may actually increase their criminal activity simply to ensure that their illegal income level rises to compensate for income lost to taxation in the same way that an employee may work additional overtime to compensate for a raise in the tax rate. Second, that many criminals will culturally, or for practical reasons, not declare illegal income in any event. Presumably, Murphy was driven by the latter and not the former.

Given that Murphy did not declare his illegal income, the potential incidence of tax cannot have been a factor in determining the volume of illegal trade, which was clearly driven by personal needs and/or that of any organisation to which he might provide funding. What is more likely is that Murphy failed to declare his income either because he denied the validity of either state and/or was fearful that any such declaration would open him to prosecution as a potential admission of a criminal act or acts.

Catch 22: Taxing the Proceeds of Crime Imposes an Obligation to Disclose and Thereby Incriminates the Taxpayer

Taxing statutes generally puts the obligation on the taxpayer to declare his or her income to the authorities based on the premise that the authorities will accept the taxpayer's declaration subject to a potential audit of their validity. Audits may be targeted because the declaration is regarded as unsatisfactory, inconsistent, incomplete or lacking in credibility or, alternatively, simply on the basis of random control checks on a percentage of returns which both seeks to promote compliance and assess the rate of non-compliance across the population. A person who earns an income from illegal activity which is clearly the subject of a tax liability must therefore choose either to make a return, which will highlight to state authorities the illegal source of their income or fail to declare an income in violation of their civil obligation to so do. Neither choice works in the individual's favour. Declaring large amounts of illegal income as 'miscellaneous' opens the taxpayer to a targeted audit since the nature of the information supplied is normally incomplete or lacking in credibility as the taxpayer seeks to avoid self-incrimination.

The smart response is to 'launder' the money through a legitimate commercial activity or business. A charge to tax will arise in either event but if the illegal income can be hidden among legitimate business income then tax returns are unlikely to result in a targeted audit. The taxpayer is then only concerned with randomised audits, the risk of which is relatively low and where the initial investigation is somewhat superficial and can normally be relatively easily satisfied.

The more instinctive response, but by far the most dangerous, is not to declare any of the illegal income. It was this that caused the difficulty for Murphy. His refusal to make tax returns on the basis that he had no occupation was defeated by a public admission that he was a farmer. By definition, as a farmer he was obligated to make a return. His failure to do so allowed authorities to initiate a tax case against him.[62] The battle had moved from the criminal sphere to the civil process where the rules of the game had changed considerably in favour of the authorities.

The Offences Against the Person Act 1861 Way of Knowing

What is also striking about the Murphy vignette is the absence of any 'real crime' elements—what we refer to as an '*Offences against the Person Act 1861* way of knowing'. Such an approach focuses on traditional real crime and criminal law: homicides, violent assaults, sexual offences, the requirement of *mens rea* and *actus reus*, and general defences. It emphasises the significance of crimes against *persons*. This way of knowing, which is closely tied to a police-prosecutions-prisons mode of operation, is expressive in orientation. It can still be employed to describe many practices in the criminal process. It cannot however explain the emergence of more instrumental, regulatory strategies which can be used as alternatives to or in association with a more traditional real crime approach. Nor can it account for the employment of specialist agencies such as CAB or the Revenue Commissioners.[63] The provisions employed against Murphy should be seen as a new approach involving more 'networked governance' strategies that employ civil, administrative and regulatory mechanisms alongside expressive criminal law instruments.[64] This extended, somewhat fluid, institutional arrangement is very different from the traditional bifurcated representation of wrongs as either civil or criminal harms, with almost mutually exclusive formal processes for knowing and handling conflicts. For example, strict distinctions have traditionally been drawn between regulatory wrongdoing and ordinary crimes on the basis that the former are *mala prohibita* (prohibited wrongs) and the latter are *mala in se* (moral wrongs). The former, it was suggested, should be thought of in 'instrumental means-ends terms', as not embodying quasi-moral values such as 'justice, fairness, right, and wrong'.[65] They were to be viewed as 'quasi administrative matters' that did not attract 'significant moral opprobrium or stigmatise'.[66]

This conceptualisation remains in the ascendancy, as evident in many criminal law textbooks and syllabi.[67] Nevertheless, the employment of these new strategies suggests that it is time to abandon the traditional divisions which have so structured our thinking and teaching. Our conception of criminal law should be extended beyond a focus on a relatively narrow taxonomy of offences and contestable principles—such as subjective culpability—to incorporate regulatory criminal wrongdoing. Rather than being afforded exceptional or epiphenomenal status, its extensive use, infrastructural arrangements and modes of operation requires us to reconsider the purposes, principles and boundaries of criminal law, and how it fits with other parts of the institutional architecture.[68] Particular emphasis should be placed on the proliferation of hybrid enforcement mechanisms that can be employed by the agencies or, on occasion, by private parties. These mechanisms have all contributed to a more general 'blurring of legal forms',[69] conflating the functional distinctions that exist between criminal and civil law, and between regulatory wrongdoing and ordinary wrongdoing.

Moreover, and as noted, the techniques employed in Murphy are not exclusively *in personam* in orientation (though they can be targeted at individuals who are perceived as dangerous), as one would expect with conventional criminal law practices. Rather they also contain strong 'in rem' system management elements. This shift from 'personal references and towards system relations'[70] is an acknowledgment that the former approach to criminal law—as embodied in the Offences against the Persons Act 1861—cannot adequately contend with the harm which can be caused by 'systems risks', such as global finance, terrorism, organised crime, money laundering, food production, cyber-crime and environmental destruction.

'Civil'ising Crime

The Murphy vignette is also revealing in that it demonstrates that the employment of criminal law as the monopoly mechanism for dealing with deviant behaviour is beginning to fragment and blur. In particular, the diversification and diffusion of the State into the civil sphere as a means of crime control is becoming more visible. This move away from the traditional condemnatory 'prosecution-conviction-sentencing' approach to deviant behaviour may to some extent be seen (through a benevolent lens) as a willingness to move beyond the harsh consequences of criminalisation.[71] It seems more likely however that recent embrace of civil measures is more closely connected with the perceived ineffectiveness of the criminal law mechanism. The principled protections of the criminal process—premised on a criminal sanctioning model of justice—can more easily be circumvented by directing the flow of power into this parallel system of civil justice.[72]

Throughout the nineteenth century, subjects increasingly ceded 'their authorisations to use coercion to a legal authority that monopolises the means of legitimate coercion and if necessary employs these means on their behalf'.[73] In monopolising the investigative and prosecutorial functions in crime, the State obviously imbalanced the equilibrium in power relations. Though constituted as a rational being, the accused in such circumstances was now seen as vulnerable in that he or she was pitted against the unlimited resources of the State. In this context, it is not surprising that a whole corpus of exclusionary rules and fairness of procedure rights emerged to ensure that the accused was afforded the best possible defence against unfair prosecution and punishment. Since, and to paraphrase Stephen, the State was so much stronger than the individual citizen, and was capable of inflicting so very much more harm on the individual than the individual could inflict upon society, it could afford 'to be generous'.[74] The State could draw upon a centralised police force and a public prosecutor's office which would gather and present evidence in the public interest. As a consequence, in part, of this process of State monopolisation, a discourse and practice of liberal legalism emerged (emphasising the universality, liberty and sameness of the individual person) to rebalance power relations in the justice arena. For the accused, this meant that the justice network was restructured to incorporate a clearer and more substantive body of due process rights that would guarantee, as far as practicable, both substantive and procedural justice. The Leviathan criminal justice system, thus created, required an 'equality of arms' framework to ensure the proper regulation of power. Garland neatly encapsulated the 'social contract' framework which emerged in the nineteenth century when he suggested:

The offender is defined as a legal subject, a citizen inscribed with rights and duties, entitled to equal treatment before the law. The State which punishes does so by contractual right in accordance with the terms of a political agreement. Its power to punish has its source in the offender's action—it is the agreed consequences of a contractual breach. The State has here no intrinsic or superior right. It meets the citizen on terms of equality and must not encroach upon his or her rights, person or liberty except in circumstances which are rigorously and politically determined in advance—*nulla poena sine lege*. In this penal vision we meet the ideology of the minimal legal state, the liberal dream, guardian of the free market and the social contract.[75]

Taxing crime deviates from this equality of arms, due to process framework. It is premised on efficiency and as few restrictions as possible on fact finding. It seeks to ensure that process is not 'cluttered up with ceremonious rituals that do not advance the progress of a case', as is often the case with the criminal process which 'insists on the prevention and elimination of mistakes to the extent possible'.[76] This practice of pursuing the money trail through the civil jurisdiction of taxation relieves the State from the strictures of criminal due process requirements in relation to certain obligations (such as discovery) and rights (such as silence, the presumption of innocence and the giving of evidence at trial). In raising a tax assessment, authorities in various jurisdictions have developed considerable powers to require a taxpayer to furnish details of earnings and assets, to obtain orders freezing monies and assets, and to seek information from third parties and financial institutions. The taxpayer often has limited time within which to appeal the assessment. Moreover, before an appeal can take place, the taxpayer may have to pay an amount of tax not less than the amount which would be payable on foot of his/her own tax returns. Non-payment of this tax renders the assessment final and conclusive.[77] If anything, 'the procedural tax rules greatly favour the state: [a] tax assessment, once levied, is assumed to express the truth about a situation'.[78]

Though this phenomenon is rapidly occurring, our due process defences have remained static, firmly fastened to the place inhabited by criminal law. They remain enmeshed in the fixity of definition and are incapable of contending with the plasticity and fluidity of the flow of power into civil spaces.[79] Concerns about such powers to seize and tax are counterpoised by the simple legal appeal to the civil as opposed to criminal design of the provisions. This reasoning, which has judicial imprimatur, is, to some extent however, an exercise in obfuscation. As was noted in another context: 'merely redefine any measure which is claimed to be punishment as regulation and, magically, the Constitution no longer prohibits its imposition'.[80] It is difficult to dislodge the perception that such devices permit states to achieve late-modern criminal justice goals—public protection, targeting, non-inflammatory stigmatisation and threat neutralisation—in a more 'jurisprudentially unconstrained' civil setting.[81]

Such measures might best be described as falling under a schema of criminal administration, a cost-efficient form of legitimate coercion which jettisons the orthodox safeguards of criminal law (the requirements of criminal guilt, proof beyond reasonable doubt, obligations of discovery in criminal proceedings, proportionality to offence seriousness and the presumption of innocence), but which continues to embody criminal indicia including the moral opprobrium associated with the prohibited conduct and the capacity of the measures to stigmatise.[82]

Criminal Regulation

In addition to this flow of power in to the civil sphere, the techniques adopted above will often include reliance upon regulatory criminal law. This operates in opposition to the general trend of paradigmatic criminal law which permits general defences, demands both a conduct element and a fault element, and respects procedural standards such as a legal burden of proof beyond reasonable doubt. Pure doctrines of subjective culpability and the presumption of innocence are increasingly abandoned within this streamlined regulatory framework to make up for difficulties of proof in complex cases.[83] The increasingly instrumental nature of criminal legal regulation is evident, for example, in the introduction of 'reverse onus' provisions that require the accused to displace a presumption of guilt. The system of justice that applies in the regulatory realm is thus more exculpatory in orientation than its ordinary criminal counterpart. The attachment of subjective mental element to wrongdoing in conventional criminal law is also often severed in the regulatory criminal arena where more objective standards of culpability apply. Moreover, any defences that might exist in the regulatory area are more specialised than the general defences that apply in criminal law. Very wide powers of entry, inspection, examination, search, seizure and analysis are given to regulatory crime agencies including the power to demand the production of books, records, other documents, which may contain information relevant to liability.[84]

Provision is often also made for information sharing with other agencies and authorities. In some instances individuals are required to become 'information reporters'. Solicitors, for example, are required to report clients' suspicious transactions to agencies including the police and Revenue Commissioners. The financial services industry and professional service providers (including auditors, accountants, liquidators and tax advisers) must also do the same.[85] This is somewhat akin to a pre-modern system of law enforcement which was heavily reliant on a network of rewards, victims, thief-taking and accomplice-driven prosecutions. In an industrialised setting, this system of enforcement was increasingly viewed as a 'badly regulated system of power'.[86] The state, as will be discussed further below, increasingly in the course of the nineteenth century began to monopolise investigative and prosecutorial functions, and to enforce the law on behalf of the 'people'. As much as possible recourse would not be had to local networks; where these practices continued—for example, with informants—they were downplayed. The centralised state apparatus—as expressed through the police and public prosecutors—thus completely monopolised the crime conflict. These new circuits of information gathering throw up techniques and strategies—particularly the emphasis on legal compulsion[87]—beyond the traditional reach of the police and prosecution agencies. In addition to facilitating exchange of information and compelling certain parties to become information reporters,[88] the authorities are increasingly also seeking to protect and encourage witnesses to come forward and provide evidence.

As these regulatory criminal practices become more embedded, they are subjected to judicial scrutiny given their instrumental desire to maximise efficiency, enhance control and minimise risk. The flow of power into these civil and regulatory spheres is challenging for a due process system that emphasises the primacy of individual accused rights. When due process, regulatory values and outlooks meet, as they increasingly do, it makes for an interesting battleground, a site for struggle and competing claims about security, instrumental effectiveness, governance and principled protections. These tensions occur in relation to justiciability; legal privilege, definitions of crime; double jeopardy; privacy; the privilege against self-incrimination; the burden of proof; proportionality of punishment; and culpability requirements.

The meeting and mixing of these different approaches is often not captured in the orthodox account of criminal law, which, rooted in the 1861 Offences against the Person Act conception of wrongdoing, continues to perpetuate the myth of regulatory exceptionalism (usually in relation to strict liability offences only). It also continues to present criminal law through a 'police-prosecutions-prisons' lens, giving rise to the false assumption that the sanctioning and expressive function is the exclusive preserve of that discipline. In doing so, it maintains the myth that the traditional criminal law and criminal justice process is the exclusive conduit for the expression of collective outrage[89] against morally culpable conduct, as it alone embodies censuring and stigmatising elements. This hierarchical, narrow approach ignores the extent to which civil, regulatory and administrative mechanisms also employ sanctions[90] in addition to seeking to restore the *status quo ante*. It also does not capture the extent to which compliance strategies—facilitated by a wide range of strategies that favour the employment of negotiation, consultation, persuasion and settlement—often work in tandem with such sanctioning strategies. In our vignette above, the outcomes were that Murphy settled his civil tax liability, had a significant proportion of his assets confiscated though a civil process, and was subjected to a regulatory criminal infrastructure that resulted in his imprisonment. The nuances and circuits that run through this rhizomatic structure incorporate both compliance and sanctioning strategies, facilitating very different objectives such as the promotion of instrumental effectiveness and the expression of collective outrage. It is a fluid rather than binary arrangement which generates a range of possibilities for the relevant authorities.

Governance

The emergence of this governance structure is also significantly different from the unified monopolies of centralised control underpinning policing and prosecution in the modern State. Arguably these new techniques and strategies can be seen as part of a pattern of more, rather than less, governance, but taking 'decentred', 'at-a-distance' forms.[91] Throughout the nineteenth century, the State very gradually began to monopolise and separate the prosecutorial and policing functions, particularly for serious crimes. Previously strong stakeholder interests in the prosecution and investigation process, such as victims and the local community, were gradually colonised in the course of the nineteenth century by a hierarchical State apparatus which acted for, rather than with, the public.

Now, however, public prosecutors and public police are, to some extent, increasingly losing their monopoly role. The number of agencies that have entered the arena, colonising the power to investigate in specific areas and to prosecute summarily, has increased dramatically in recent years. This intrusion has occurred in areas such as revenue, but also competition, consumer affairs, environmental protection, health and safety, and corporate enforcement.[92] Significantly, these agencies have both investigative and prosecution functions, with each pursuing their own agendas, policies and practices. All of these agencies represent more governance by the State, rather than any 'hollowing out' of the State.

This enlargement in scope, however, is fragmented and heterogeneous in nature, occupying diverse sites and modes of operation. Governance therefore is no longer defined by centralising tendencies. Rather it is much more dispersed: 'it flows through a network of open circuits that are rhizomatic and not hierarchical'.[93] Information trails and information gateways cut across civil, administrative, criminal and regulatory domains of action, no longer limiting or fixing the reach and potential for effective intervention. In the same way that these new governance strategies seek to move beyond the limiting effects of over centralisation in policing and prosecution functions—and the fixity of traditional criminal law—they also cut across territorial boundaries. The phenomenon of organised crime now extends far beyond national territories. The Offences against the Person Act 1861 model of justice is ineffective in respect of such transnational developments, anchored as it is to sovereign and person referents. It is not surprising therefore that new strategies have emerged. These new practices are less concerned with the 'territorialization of national spaces'.[94] Increasingly a network of power is being developed that can reach beyond national state borders—the Murphy case, for example, involved multi-agency collaboration across three jurisdictions. The surveillance practices themselves can be molecular and subtle, because, as Rose points out, 'the securitisation of identity' is dispersed across everyday life[95]:

They overcome the barriers of space and time involved in physical surveillance; they are not labour intensive; they are of low visibility; they are of high durability; they are of high transferability across domains; they are largely involuntary or participated in as an uncalculated side effect of some other action.[96]

All of this involves a trend away from a hierarchical command and control apparatus of State policing and prosecution. It constitutes a new form of 'networked governance' involving the increasing 'regulation of civil society'.[97] The tax mechanism is a very good example of this more rhizomatic approach. It can cut across civil, criminal and regulatory domains. Because its focus, in large part, is on the *person's identity* rather than the *person simpliciter*, it can be employed as a high-transferability, low-visibility hybrid technology of governance. It stands in marked contrast to the traditional view that criminal law and prison isolates a small group who can be controlled, 'a delinquent milieu, closed in upon itself, but easily supervised'.[98] It is appropriate to view it as part of a new model of governance, involving a 'hybridisation of techniques' that involve 'a multiplication of possibilities and strategies deployed around different problematisations in different sites and with different objectives'.[99]

The Abiographical Wrongdoer

The Murphy vignette also, however, displays another important difference from traditional criminal law and correctionalist criminology outlooks. Provisions that seize or tax the proceeds of crime are not designed to re-orient human behaviour or to reintegrate those that are deviant. Their focus is more 'apersonal' in orientation (albeit with the sanctioning potential to stigmatise and exclude). They are tailored to sweep up the material proceeds of the crime rather than fit the broad range of individuated circumstances of wrongdoer. It is not expected that the range of techniques employed against Murphy will result in his 'normalisation'. They are not part of a 'perfectability of man' trajectory which wishes to know the 'field of reality' to which his offending belongs to, or seeks 'to assign the causal process that produced it', or which concerns itself with his 'future development'.[100] The civil tools employed against Murphy dismantled the enterprise by removing money, property, laundering units and equipment. This was further buttressed by a tax demand. The regulatory criminal tool resulted in an 18-month prison sentence, a relatively modest sentence perhaps, but one which still permitted the expressive, censuring qualities of the stratagem to be revealed.

Taxation practices in a criminal setting are largely agnostic to the wrongdoer's personality, environment, associations, family background, opportunities or to the State's complicity in his or her wrongdoing. Its practices replace the 'biographical criminal' with *homo economicus*, the rational choice individual who thinks in cost/benefit terms.[101] As Rose notes:

> In such a regime of control, we are not dealing with individuals but with dividuals: not with subjects with a unique personality that is the expression of some inner fixed quality, but with elements, capacities, and potentialities…In our societies of control, it is not a question of socialising and disciplining the subject *ab initio*…It is not a matter of apprehending and normalising the offender *ex post facto*. Conduct is continually monitored and reshaped by logics immanent within all networks of practice. Surveillance is 'designed in' to the flows of everyday existence.[102]

Taxing crime taps in to these networks by following the flow of money across time and space. What can be more routine or everyday than spending money? It is this personal and financial information which is the 'raw material of successful investigations'.[103]

Reliance on tax provisions regulates wrongdoing not by identifying pathological individuals but by altering the environments in which they operate.[104] This approach to wrongdoing manages disturbances according to risk principles. It employs discourses and technologies which focus on removing the 'possibilities of action' by the wrongdoer.[105] It is not (exclusively) 'carceral' and does not have the 'soul' of the individual as its *raison d'etre*. Nor does it seek to render the 'body' docile via an 'economy of suspended rights'.[106] Rather it attempts to permanently alter the social, financial and physical structures around the individual—the enterprise, its financial structures, its working capital and the proceeds arising therefrom. It is a more efficient and permanent form of power, one that can permeate illegal structures more easily than earlier methods of criminal investigation and intervention. It assumes that the transformative individual effects of criminal law are quite limited: 'changing people is difficult and expensive'.[107] It is in this sense an adaptive response,[108] a recognition that traditional crime enforcement agencies can no longer win the 'war on crime'. It accepts that crime is a normal social phenomenon,[109] something which is with us, and which needs to be managed as efficiently as possible. Moreover, by not seeking to change the individual, and by using civil and regulatory strategies, there is minimal potential for resistance.[110]

This 'retreat from the social' also bypasses professional social expertise. Taxing the proceeds of crime does not require the knowledge of social experts such as probation officers, psychiatrists, counsellors, psychologists, educationalists, correctionalist criminologists or social workers. It embraces instead new forms of expertise—accountants, auditors, tax consultants, lawyers, estate agents, data analysts, bankers and financial consultants. None of these forms of expertise are orientated to 'normalising' the wrongdoer. Instead knowledge of this kind is employed as part of 'the power to destroy' the criminogenic structures that exist around the wrongdoer.

Conclusion

The taxation of crime is part of an emerging actuarial approach to criminal wrongdoing, one which employs civil, administrative and regulatory mechanisms. Its appeal lies in its permanency and low-visibility efficiency. It forms part of a networked rather than hierarchical model of governance, one that is not limited by national boundaries. It adopts a fluid arrangement which ensures that it can penetrate most aspects of everyday life, making resistance very difficult. This is copper-fastened by the disequilibrium in power relations—the onus is very much on the subject of a tax audit to demonstrate compliance. Moreover, the taxation of crime is not designed to produce a 'socially engineered solution', to make the deviant better by correctionalist intervention and normalisation. Unlike modern criminal justice practices which focus on the 'soul' of the offender, taxation instruments attempt to permanently alter the criminogenic networks that exist around the individual, thereby neutralising the possibility of future bad choices. In this regard, it is pessimistic about the normalising potential of modern criminal justice practices. It is also pessimistic about the capacity of States to 'win the war' on crime. In taxing crime, there is an implicit acceptance that it will always occur. Sharing in the profits of such activities is simply a late-modern, pragmatic response to the reality of living in 'criminal enterprise' societies.

Notes

1. *McCulloch v Maryland* 17 US 316 (1819), 4 L Ed 579 [607] per Chief Justice Marshall.
2. See, generally, Performance and Innovation Unit, *Recovering the Proceeds of Crime* (Cabinet Office 2000).
3. *Capone v US* 56 F 2d 927 (1931), cert denied 286 US 553 (1932); *US v Capone* 93 F 2d 840 (7th Cir 1937), cert denied 303 US 651 (1938).
4. Gerry Moriarty, 'Thomas 'Slab' Murphy Jailed Over Tax Like Chicago Gangster' *Irish Times* (Dublin, 26 February 2016) <www.irishtimes.com/news/ireland/irish-news/thomas-slab-murphy-jailed-over-tax-like-chicago-gangster-1.2550298> accessed 17 February 2017.
5. Ed Moloney, *A Secret History of the IRA* (Penguin Books 2007) 160.
6. Murphy appealed his conviction, submitting 48 grounds of appeal. In January 2017, the Court of Appeal dismissed his appeal against conviction. See *DPP v Murphy* [2017] IECA 6.
7. However, the mode of trial was the Special Criminal Court, as approved by the Supreme Court in *Thomas Murphy v Ireland* [2014] IESC 19.
8. Robert Baker, 'Taxation: Potential Destroyer of Crime' (1951) 29(3) Chicago-Kent Law Review 197.
9. David Lusty, 'Taxing the Untouchables Who Profit from Organised Crime' (2003) 10(3) Journal of Financial Crime 209.
10. See, for example, *US v Sullivan* 274 US 259 (1927).
11. See, for example, *Magna Alloys and Research PTY Ltd v FCT* 49 FLR 183 (1980).
12. See, for example, *Minister of Finance (Canada) v Smith* [1927] AC 193.
13. See, for example, *Maney and Sons v CIR* [1967] NZLR 41.
14. See s 19 of the Finance Act 1983, as amended.
15. See, for example, *CIR v Delagoa Bay Cigarette Co.* (1918) TPD 391.
16. See, for example, *IRC v Aken* [1990] 1 WLR 1374.
17. *Sullivan* (n 10).
18. For consideration of the role of the CAB in taxation, see Liz Campbell, 'Taxing Illegal Assets: The Revenue Work of the Criminal Assets Bureau' (2006) 24(20) Irish Law Times 316.
19. Criminal Assets Bureau, *Annual Report* (Stationery Office 2000) 5.
20. Proceeds of Crime Acts 1996–2016.
21. See Liz Campbell, 'Theorising Asset Forfeiture in Ireland' (2007) 71(5) Journal of Criminal Law 441; Francis Cassidy, 'Targeting the Proceeds of

Crime: An Irish Perspective' in Theodore Greenberg and others (eds), *Stolen Asset Recovery: A Good Practice Guide for Non-Conviction Based Asset Forfeiture* (World Bank 2009); Colin King, 'Civil Forfeiture in Ireland—Two Decades of the Proceeds of Crime Act and the Criminal Assets Bureau' in Katalin Ligeti and Michele Simonato (eds), *Chasing Criminal Money in the EU* (Hart Publishing 2017).

22. *Hayes v Duggan* [1929] IR 406; *Collins v Mulvey* [1956] IR 223.
23. Cassidy (n 21) 159.
24. See Joe McGrath, *Corporate and White Collar Crime in Ireland* (Manchester University Press 2015); Shane Kilcommins and Ursula Kilkelly (eds), *Regulatory Crime in Ireland* (Londsdale Law Publishing 2010).
25. Adam Smith, *An Inquiry into the Nature and Causes of Wealth of Nations* (Encyclopaedia Britannica 1952).
26. For the purposes of this chapter, we are excluding crimes against the state which attack the interest of the state alone, such as treason. However, very many crimes against the state may also fall into either or both of the two categories of used in this analysis and there is no reason to treat this differently.
27. In *Southern v AB Ltd* [1933] 1 KB 713 [719] the proceeds of a burglary were not taxable as an income. In New Zealand, the proceeds of an embezzlement were held not to be taxable in *Grieve v CIR* (1984) 6 NZTC 61 and *A Taxpayer v CIR* (1997) 18 NZTC 13 [350] (CA). Statutory measures were introduced to over-rule these decisions and avoid a taxpayer avoiding tax by categorising their income as stolen.
28. See, generally, Nicholas Ryder, *Financial Crime in the 21st Century: Law and Policy* (Edward Elgar Publishing 2011).
29. This view is not universal, see Robin Thomas Naylor, 'Wash-Out: A Critique of Follow-the-Money Methods in Crime Control Policy' (1999) 32(1) Crime, Law and Social Change 1, although his primary argument appears based on efficacy rather than ethics.
30. *Hayes* (n 22) [417] per Kennedy; [420] per Fitzgibbon.
31. For a similar view, see the judgment of Judge Manton in the case of *Steinberg v US* 14 F 2d 564 (2nd Cir 1926). In an interesting side note, Judge Manton was later to be prosecuted for accepting bribes and in an ironic twist of fate, had to pay tax on those bribes!
32. *Mann v Nash* [1932] 1 KB 752.
33. Finance Act No 15 of 1983, s 19.
34. Dáil Debates, 11 May 1983, Vol 342, Col 1022 per Mr Ahern.
35. Taxes Consolidation Act 1997, s 58.
36. Indeed this approach was evident in an early Canadian case, *Smith v Minister for Finance* [1925] 2 Dom L Rep 1137 which rejected taxing the proceeds of crime.
37. *Sullivan* (n 10); note *CG v Appeal Commissioners* [2005] IR 472 where the Irish High Court held that the right against self-incrimination was not

infringed where there was an agreement that the disclosure would not lead to additional inquiries by the Criminal Assets Bureau.

38. *US v Garner* 424 US 648 (1976).
39. In Ireland, see In *Re Irish National Bank and the Companies Act 1990* [1999] 3 IR 145 where information obtained under a statutory provision is only admissible if it was voluntary.
40. *Mann* (n 32).
41. Ibid. [758].
42. Note also that even in jurisdictions which levy tax based on the source of the income, the definitions are generally so wide as to encompass illegal activity income, see Vern Krishna, *The Fundamentals of Canadian Income Tax* (6th edn, Carswell 2000) 152ff.
43. Income Tax Act (8 and 9 Geo c 40) s 237.
44. For example, in Canada, the decision in *Mann* has been cited with approval in *No 275 v Minister of National Revenue* 13 Tax ABC 279 and in Australia the Tax Office has ruled that receipts from a systematic activity … are income irrespective of whether the activities are legal or not: TR 93/25, 5.
45. Committee of Experts on Tax Compliance, *Tax Compliance, Report to the Treasurer and Minister of Revenue* (1998) Part IV: Operational Issues, Ch 16: Relationship with Taxpayers.
46. Michelle Gallant, 'Tax and Terrorism: A New Partnership?' (2007) 14(4) Journal of Financial Crime 453.
47. James Calder, 'Al Capone and the Internal Revenue Service: State Sanctioned Criminology of Organized Crime' (1992) 17(1) Crime, Law and Social Change 1.
48. See Smith (n 25) and one of his four canons of taxation: equity.
49. See generally, Ann Mumford and Peter Alldridge, 'Tax Evasion and the Proceeds of Crime' (2005) 25(3) Legal Studies 353.
50. Although figures are notoriously imprecise, in 1998 the IMF estimated that money laundering accounts for 2–5% of global GDP, or between $1 and $2 trillion per annum. See Price Waterhouse Cooper, 'Adjusting the Lens of Economic Crime: Preparation Brings Opportunity Back in to Focus' (PWC 2016) 41 <www.pwc.com/gx/en/economic-crime-survey/pdf/GlobalEconomicCrimeSurvey2016.pdf> accessed 16 December 2016. For criticism of such estimates, see Chap. 15 (Van Duyne, Harvey and Gelemerova) in this collection.
51. Less than 1% of laundered money is seized, see Price Waterhouse Cooper (n 50).
52. See OECD, *Measuring the Non-Observed Economy: A Handbook* (OECD 2002), Chapter 9 Illegal Production <www.oecd.org/std/na/NOE-Handbook-%20Chapter9.pdf> accessed 21 December 2016.
53. For example, the cost of a hotel room for a professional hitman, phone costs for a drug dealer or the purchase of tools used by a thief.

54. Michelle Gallant, 'Tax and the Proceeds of Crime: A New Approach to Tainted Finance?' (2013) 16(2) Journal of Money Laundering Control 119.

55. In the US case of *Commissioner v Tellier* 383 US 687 (1966), the US Supreme Court held that the tax acts were intended to tax net income and if the US wished to use the tax code to punish illegal activity then it would have to expressly pass legislation to that effect. Thus deductions are available for both legal and illegal activity.

56. 26 USC 162 (f).

57. *Tank Truck Rentals v Commissioners* 356 US 30 (1958).

58. 26 USC 162 (f); see also the New Zealand case of *Robinson v CIR* [1965] NZLR 246, where Tompkins held that fines and penalties are inflicted upon the individual as a personal deterrent and/or punishment. The emphasis is on the personal penal nature of the fine.

59. Ivan Png and Eric Zolt, 'Efficient Deterrence and the Tax Treatment of Monetary Sanctions' (1989) 9(2) International Review of Law and Economics 209.

60. See Joseph Stiglitz, 'The Effects of Income, Wealth and Capital Gains Taxation on Risk Taking' (1969) 83(2) Quarterly Journal of Economics 263, which does not deal with the impact of criminal sanctions on risk; and Gary Becker 'Crime and Punishment: An Economic Approach' (1968) 76(2) Journal of Political Economy 169, which does not deal with the impact of taxation on risk.

61. Avraham Tabbach, 'Criminal Behavior, Sanctions and Income Taxation: An Economic Analysis' (2002) John Olin Program in Law and Economics Working Paper No 169 <http://chicagounbound.uchicago.edu/cgi/viewcontent.cgi?article=1151&context=law_and_economics> accessed 17 February 2017.

62. In October 2005, Mr Murphy's solicitor made a statement to the effect that he had nothing to do with particular properties under investigation and that he was 'just a farmer'. Reports indicate that this statement allowed members of An Garda Síochána to react: 'F*** me, we've got him.' 'For years he's been refusing to put in tax returns, saying that he had no occupation. He has just admitted on national tv that he is a farmer. We now have enough evidence to open a tax-evasion case against him.' Moriarty (n 4).

63. John Braithwaite, 'What's Wrong with the Sociology of Punishment' (2003) 7(1) Theoretical Criminology 5.

64. The phenomena of more 'networked governance' is dealt with more fully in the 'governance' section of this chapter.

65. Nicola Lacey, 'Criminalisation as Regulation: The Role of the Criminal Law' in Colin Parker and others (eds), *Regulating Law* (Oxford University Press 2004) 145.

66. Finbarr McAuley and Paul McCutcheon, *Criminal Liability* (Round Hall 2000) 341.

67. James Chalmers and Fiona Leverick, 'Quantifying Criminalisation' in Robert Duff and others (eds), *Criminalisation: The Political Morality of Criminal Law* (Oxford University Press 2014).

68. Shane Kilcommins, Susan Leahy and Eimear Spain, 'The Absence of Regulatory Crime from the Criminal Law Curriculum' in Kris Gledhill and Ben Livings (eds), *The Teaching of Criminal Law* (Routledge 2016) 194–205.

69. Andrew Ashworth, 'Is the Criminal Law a Lost Cause?' (2000) 116(2) Law Quarterly Review 237.

70. Jurgen Habermas, *Between Facts and Norms* (6th edn, Polity Press 2008) 432–35.

71. Andrew Ashworth, 'The Criminal Justice Act 2003 Part 2: Criminal Justice Reform: Principles, Human Rights and Public Protection' [2004] Criminal Law Review 516.

72. Shane Kilcommins and Barry Vaughan, 'Reconfiguring State-Accused Relations in Ireland' (2006) XLI Irish Jurist 90.

73. Habermas (n 70) 12.

74. James Fitzjames Stephen, *A History of the Criminal Law of England* vol I (Routledge/Thoemmes Press 1883) 354.

75. David Garland, *Punishment and Welfare: A History of Penal Strategies* (Gower 1985) 18.

76. Herbert Packer, *The Limits of the Criminal Sanction* (Stanford University Press 1968) 159.

77. Lorna Gallagher, 'The Criminal Assets Bureau and Taxation—More Recent Developments' (2003) 16(4) Irish Tax Review 391; Simon Sweetman, 'Why Worry? Are We Overreacting to HMRC's New Powers? (2008) 162 Taxation 459; Peter Vaines, 'Where Will it End: Her Majesty's Revenue and Customs' Powers to Obtain Information' (2009) 163 Taxation 4; Allison Plager 'Not so Finely Tuned: Opinions on HMRC Powers Vary' (2016) 176 Taxation 13.

78. Gallant (n 54) 123.

79. Barry Vaughan and Shane Kilcommins, *Terrorism, Rights and the Rule of Law* (Willan 2008) 135; Manuel Castells, *The Power of Identity* (Blackwell 1997) 243–308.

80. *United States v Salerno* 481 US 739 (1987) [760] per Judge Brennan.

81. Lucia Zedner, 'Security for Whom? Reducing Risk by Eroding Rights?' British Criminology Conference Glasgow (5–7 July 2006); see also Anthony Kennedy, 'Justifying the Civil Recovery of Criminal Proceeds' (2005) 12(1) Journal of Financial Crime 8.

82. See Kilcommins and Vaughan (n 72).

83. Abraham Goldstein, 'White Collar Crime and Civil Sanctions' (1992) 101(8) Yale Law Journal 1895, 1899.

84. John Considine and Shane Kilcommins, 'The Importance of Safeguards on Revenue Powers: Another Perspective' (2006) 19(6) Irish Tax Review 49;

Gupta Ranjana, 'Inland's Revenue Powers of Search and Seizure and Taxpayers' Constitutional Rights' (2013) 15(1–2) Journal of Australian Taxation 133.

85. See, for example, Shelley Horan, *Corporate Crime* (Bloomsbury Professional 2011) 1529–40.
86. Michel Foucault, *Discipline and Punish: The Birth of the Prison* (2nd edn, Penguin 1991) 79.
87. John Lea, *Crime and Modernity* (Sage 2003) 168.
88. Anthony Kennedy, 'Winning the Information Wars' (2007) 14(4) Journal of Financial Crime 372.
89. Emile Durkheim, 'Two Laws of Penal Evolution' (1969) 38(1) University of Cincinnati Law Review 32.
90. Kenneth Mann, 'Punitive Civil Sanctions: The Middle Ground Between Criminal and Civil Law' (1992) 101(8) Yale Law Journal 1795; Robert Baldwin, 'The New Punitive Regulation' (2004) 67(3) Modern Law Review 351.
91. John Braithwaite, 'The New Regulatory State and the Transformation of Criminology' (2000) 40(2) British Journal of Criminology 222, 225.
92. See, for example, the Competition and Consumer Protection Commission in the Republic of Ireland, or the Competition and Markets Authority in England and Wales.
93. Nikolas Rose, *Powers of Freedom: Reframing Political Thought* (Cambridge University Press 2008) 234.
94. Ibid. 34.
95. Ibid. 241.
96. Nikolaos Rose, 'Government and Control' (2000) 40(2) British Journal of Criminology 321, 326.
97. Adam Crawford, 'Networked Governance and the Post Regulatory State?: Steering, Rowing and Anchoring the Provision of Policing and Security' (2006) 10(4) Theoretical Criminology 449.
98. Foucault (n 86) 281.
99. Rose (n 93) 240.
100. Foucault (n 86) 19.
101. Pat O'Malley 'Risk, Power and Crime Prevention' (1992) 21(3) Economy and Society 264.
102. Rose (n 93), 234.
103. Kennedy (n 88) 372.
104. Markus Dubber, 'Policing Possession: The War on Crime and the End of the Criminal Law' (2002) 91(3) Journal of Criminal Law and Criminology 150.
105. Barbara Hudson, *Justice in the Risk Society* (Sage 2003) 75; Barry Vaughan, 'Neo-liberalism, Crime and Punishment' in Deirdre Healy and others (eds), *The Irish Handbook of Criminology* (Routledge 2016) 486–99.
106. Foucault (n 86) 11.
107. Jonathan Simon, 'The Ideological Effects of Actuarial Practices' (1988) 22(4) Law and Society Review 771, 773.

108. David Garland, *The Culture of Control: Crime and Social Order in Contemporary Society* (Oxford University Press 2001) 113–31.
109. Malcolm Feeley and Jonathan Simon, 'Actuarial Justice: The Emerging New Criminal Law' in David Nelken (ed), *The Futures of Criminology* (Sage 1994) 173–201.
110. Rose (n 93) 236.

Raymond J. Friel is a graduate of UCC, the University of Exeter and was called to the Bar in 1986. He joined the School of Law at the University of Limerick in 1989. He has held visiting professorships at Boston College Law School, Western University Law School in Canada, the University of New Hampshire Law School and the University of Kansas Law School. His areas of specialisation are contract and commercial law, and he has authored leading treatises on contract, tax and business law. He has published extensively both nationally and internationally in prestigious law reviews, including the International and Comparative Law Quarterly. He is Director of the International Commercial and Economic Law Research Group at the University of Limerick.

Shane Kilcommins is a graduate of UL (BA in Law and European Studies, 1994), the University of Wales, Aberystwyth (PhD 1999) and UCC (MA in Teaching and Learning, 2007). He joined the Law School, University of Limerick, in 2014. He lectures in evidence law, criminal law, jurisprudence, penology and criminology. His areas of specialisation are penology, evidence law, criminal procedure and victimology.

29

The Disposal of Confiscated Assets in the EU Member States: What Works, What Does Not Work and What Is Promising

Introduction

An issue often overlooked in the discussion of confiscation proceedings is the disposal phase—that is, the phase in which a final confiscation order is enforced and confiscated assets are disposed of. There is a notable lack of knowledge about the disposal of confiscated assets and their reuse, despite the importance of the topic for the effectiveness of the overall confiscation system.

Theoretically, different forms of reuse are possible. These range from the traditional transfer of ill-gotten gains into the State coffers and its use as any other public money/resources, to more innovative forms of disposal such as the reuse of the assets for social purposes or for incentivisation schemes for law enforcement agencies.[1] Recently, some EU institutions have more closely scrutinised the issue by showing interest towards a peculiar form of disposal, which involves giving criminal proceeds back to the communities affected by (organised) crime and promoting their use in line with communal needs: social reuse.

This chapter advances the discussion of the disposal phase through the following questions:[2] how are confiscated assets disposed of across the EU Member States? In particular, what does not work (key obstacles) and what works (best practices)? Is social reuse a promising disposal option? The chapter is organised as follows: the current state of the art of asset disposal within the EU is first

B. Vettori
Faculty of Political and Social Sciences, Università Cattolica del Sacro Cuore, Milan, Italy

© The Author(s) 2018
C. King et al. (eds.), *The Palgrave Handbook of Criminal and Terrorism Financing Law*,
https://doi.org/10.1007/978-3-319-64498-1_29

reviewed. Disposal options in the Member States are then mapped, and the key problems and best practices are highlighted. Attention is then focused on those Member States that envisage social reuse, so as to present and compare existing legislation and practices. Some conclusions are then put forward to discuss if social reuse could be a promising option that other Member States might be interested to adopt.

The Current State of Asset Disposal in the EU

Existing Studies

With some exceptions, very few studies have addressed the issue of asset management and disposal. In 2006 the author of this chapter mapped legislation and practices in the then 15 Member States, focusing on the three key phases of confiscation proceedings, that is, the investigative, judicial and disposal phases.[3] That study identified the key problem of the long duration of the disposal phase, often as a result of the inadequate resources dedicated to it. While there are few problems when confiscation orders relate to money, problems arise with other types of assets, such as real or personal property. Often these assets are sold at public auctions where the prices tend to be low. A further issue here is that criminals may be able to buy the assets back. Another criticality is that the sale procedure can be overly complex and lengthy, especially when real property is to be disposed of. The study also highlighted practical difficulties with legislation on the use of confiscated assets for social purposes: such provisions 'are either rarely applied (Belgium and Luxembourg), or when they are applied, the procedure is excessively complex and time-consuming, and the assets are not always in the best condition when given to the recipients […]'.[4]

In 2009 a study commissioned by the European Commission reviewed investigative, judicial and disposal phases of criminal asset recovery in the EU and identified good practices and obstacles. That study concluded that 'management and disposal of assets generally suffers from a lack of capability and capacity especially in relation to: real estate; movable high value goods; vehicles of all kinds where depreciation and storage is an issue; and operating companies that are ongoing'.[5] Disposal issues were addressed in 2012 in another study—commissioned by the European Commission—whose aim was to suggest policy options for EU-level intervention. One proposed option refers to social reuse and states that 'to promote social reuse in other Member States, the EU could require Member States to establish mechanisms allowing confiscated assets, in appropriate cases, to be returned to deprived and victimised communities through social reuse schemes'.[6] Another 2012 study, carried out by the Basel Institute on Governance for the European Parliament, analysed in depth the legal framework on asset recovery, both at the EU level and at the level of six selected Member States (Bulgaria, Germany, Italy, France, Spain and the United Kingdom), with a view of assessing the feasibility of establishing EU regulations on the use of confiscated assets for social purposes. The study also analysed the advantages of social reuse; it concluded that 'there is a clear need for a coherent European approach'.[7]

EU Developments

Scant attention has been paid to the disposal phase not only by the research community but also by policy makers. Over the past five years, however, EU institutions have shown an increasing interest towards the reuse for social purposes of confiscated assets. First, Directive 2014/42/EU invites Member States to 'consider taking measures allowing confiscated property to be used for public interest or social purposes'.[8] The Directive also specifies that such measures may comprise earmarking property for law enforcement and crime prevention projects, as well as for other projects of public interest and social utility. In 2011 the European Parliament highlighted that

> the re-use of confiscated assets for social purposes fosters a positive attitude to strategies aimed at tackling organised crime, since confiscating an asset is no longer regarded solely as a means of depriving a criminal organisation of resources but is doubly constructive in that it both helps to prevent organised crime and has the effect of boosting economic and social development.[9]

That Resolution urged the Commission 'to accept and support the urgent need for European legislation on the reuse of crime proceeds for social purposes [...], so that the capital of criminal organisations or their associates can be reinjected into legal, clean, transparent and virtuous economic circuits'.[10]

In 2010 the Justice and Home Affairs Council stressed that attention should be focused on all phases of the confiscation procedure and recommended the adoption of measures aimed to ensure the preservation of assets during the confiscation process and their reuse.[11] Also in 2010 the Commission requested Member States to make by 2014:

> the necessary institutional arrangements, for example by creating asset management offices, to ensure that frozen assets do not lose their value before they are eventually confiscated.[12]

The same year the European Council called upon the Member States and the Commission 'to identify assets of criminals more effectively and seize them and, whenever possible, consider re-using them wherever they are found in the EU common space'.[13] In 2008 the Commission recognised that 'different practices exist in the Member States with regard to the destination of the assets confiscated and recovered'.[14] The document adds that 'it is desirable to promote practices which have proven to be effective at national level',[15] including some forms of institutional and social reuse expressly mentioned in the document, such as those existing in the United Kingdom and in Italy.

Disposal of Confiscated Assets in the EU: Mapping Legislation and Practices

This section presents the key findings from the mapping of existing legislation (including current institutional building arrangements) and practices on the disposal of confiscated assets in the EU Member States carried out in the RECAST project.[16] In doing so, this section also devotes attention to how seized assets are managed, because this may have a great impact on their subsequent disposal, once these assets are finally confiscated.

It is first important to provide some background information about confiscation systems in the EU. The vast majority of Member States only have criminal confiscation. Just in eight Member States is it possible to confiscate outside criminal proceedings as well. These are Bulgaria, Greece, Ireland, Italy, Romania, Slovakia, Slovenia and the United Kingdom. Furthermore, property-based confiscation seems to be the rule, although several countries favour value-based confiscation (Cyprus, Finland, Netherlands, United Kingdom and Sweden).

Legislation and Institutional Building Arrangements

What follows is a comparative overview of legislation and institutional building arrangements on asset disposal in the Member States.

First, provisions to promote effective management of seized assets have been introduced in most Member States: in all but four (namely Denmark, Lithuania, Luxembourg and Malta) there are legal provisions on the management of seized assets aimed at optimising their value and/or minimising their deterioration.

Second, sale is the main disposal option in practically all the Member States. That notwithstanding, most of them (about two-thirds) have introduced—almost never as first choice—different forms of reuse of the assets/proceeds, via their transfer to State/local institutions (institutional reuse, via incentivisation schemes) or to society/NGOs (social reuse). These reuse practices vary a lot in terms of beneficiaries, modalities and asset typologies involved. Institutional reuse seems to be more frequent than social reuse. Destruction is the third most commonly applied option, although only for certain items (e.g., drugs, excise products) or under certain conditions (assets are unusable or depreciated).

Third, the main social reuse experiences are in Belgium, France, Hungary, Italy, Luxembourg, Scotland and Spain. Social reuse differs in form across the EU, and this is analysed in depth below.

Fourth, in terms of institutional building arrangements, in all but three Member States there is not a specialised approach to the disposal of confiscated assets, that is, there is not a unique entity exclusively charged with the task. A confiscation order is executed as any other penalty, with the involvement of a variety of actors, which may comprise a key central authority charged with the collection of tax duties (e.g., the Patrimonial Services within the Federal Public Service of Finances in Belgium, the National Revenue Agency in Bulgaria, the National Agency for Fiscal Administration in Romania), the management of public property (Office of Government Representation in Property Affairs in Czech Republic) or the enforcement of criminal and administrative penalties (e.g., the Legal Register Centre in Finland, the Land Registration and Estates Department in Luxembourg, the Registry of the Courts of Criminal Judicature in Malta, the Public Prosecution Service in the Netherlands, the Enforcement Authority in Sweden). On the other hand, many Member States rely on more decentralised systems, where the tasks related to management and disposal are distributed among several institutions or managed on the local level by the court.

A trend towards specialisation is emergent, and so, in a minority of Member States, a dedicated agency has been established. The countries that have adopted this approach are France, Italy and Cyprus. In France, AGRASC (*Agence de gestion et de recouvrement des avoirs saisis et confisqués*) is a public administrative body under the Ministry of Justice and the Ministry of Budget, established in 2010.[17] AGRASC is vested with various tasks designed to improve seizure, management and confiscation; it also plays a key role in the disposal of confiscated assets, since it is tasked with the sale or destruction of all assets that the agency previously managed. In Italy, ANBSC (*Agenzia nazionale per l'amministrazione e la destinazione dei beni sequestrati e confiscati alla criminalità organizzata*) was established in 2010.[18] It is tasked, amongst others, with the management and disposal of assets confiscated from organised crime. In Cyprus, MOKAS is the Unit for Combating Money Laundering, operational since January 1997. It is an example of Asset Recovery Office (ARO) that has a unique overview, from investigation to disposal. Among other things, it is charged with the execution of confiscation orders.

Fifth, in most of the Member States legal provisions do not specify the timing of the disposal phase—notwithstanding the importance to dispose of assets within a reasonable time so as to reduce the risk of depreciation. The only exceptions are Greece (disposal must take place within 3 months from seizure), Hungary, Italy (maximum recommended duration of the disposal phase: 90 + 90 days), Lithuania (the bailiff has to transfer the assets to the competent Territorial State Tax Inspectorate within 10 business days from the date the judgment to confiscate has come into force), the Netherlands (execution should be completed in a timeframe equal to the statute of limitations for a given offence, plus one-third), Romania (the assignment should take place within 180 days from the disposal order) and the United Kingdom (via 'time to pay' limits).

Practices: What Does Not Work (Key Problems)

Looking at existing practices on asset disposal, a vast array of problems have been reported by Member States. First, regarding asset management, even in those countries where provisions to promote effective management of seized assets exist, problems arise in their implementation. For example, these regulations sometimes have a limited scope of application (Ireland) or are limited to certain asset typologies, as it happens in Belgium, where real estate is not covered by regulations and only movable seized assets can be sold. In some countries, administrators are excessively expensive (United Kingdom), so that often the costs of management receivers outweigh what is recovered. In addition, administrators are not always competent, as in Italy, and courts in different regions take different approaches (in regions such as Calabria, notwithstanding a legal framework encouraging active administration, a passive administration is promoted). Similarly, in Greece seized assets are just stored and not used at all. A recurrent problem is the poor conditions of seized assets: for example, in Estonia they are frequently unusable or damaged. Furthermore, asset registration systems are not always properly working, as in the Netherlands, where registration of seized assets is not always up to date or complete. Effective management might be hampered, as in Portugal, by a scant sensitivity towards the importance of the issue among prosecutors and judges, as well as by lack of sufficient means to properly take care of the assets or by the delay with which interim measures are adopted (Romania).

Second, the legal framework on asset disposal is often poor (Bulgaria, Denmark, Poland), unclear (Italy) or outdated (Luxembourg). For example, in Luxembourg legislation dates back to 1844, while in Italy legislation is not entirely clear about ANBSC competences. Third, in the few Member States with legal provisions specifying the timing of the disposal phase, problems still arise. For example, in Italy the recommended duration of the phase is 90 + 90 days. In practice, however, in more complex cases the disposal phase can last for five or ten years, if mortgages have to be sorted out.

Fourth, it is often the case that not enough property has been seized to cover the amount of the confiscation order. And when further assets are looked for, it might be hard to find them, especially if assets are located abroad (Belgium, Cyprus, United Kingdom, Netherlands, Spain). A fifth problem arises where confiscation orders are unclear, incomplete or provide no or insufficient or outdated information on the assets to be disposed of: this has been reported by Belgium, France and the Netherlands. For example, in France the final confiscation orders do not always include all the necessary information for disposal, and this creates problems for AGRASC when executing an order regarding cash and bank accounts. In Belgium key details on the assets are often missing (e.g., cars without information on their location, documents or keys). There have also been problems in relation to real estate: for example, there are occasions where the property cannot be immediately identified (e.g., a real estate asset is confiscated for the amount of €5000, and the Patrimonial Services will then have to find the assets or more details/information). The sixth problem arises as a result of depreciation or deterioration of the assets: this happens in many countries (e.g., Bulgaria, Greece, Hungary, Italy, Portugal, Romania). Depreciation and/or deterioration can also occur as a result of the excessive length of the court proceedings. A seventh problem relates to transcription issues (for real estate): this problem has been reported in Belgium and France. For example, the disposal of complex real estate in France requires AGRASC to bring together complete files (including extracts from the Land and Mortgage Registry) to transfer ownership, and this is sometimes problematic.

The eight problem stems from the lack of a dedicated centralised register on restraint measures. In Luxembourg this sometimes leads to assets remaining frozen even after the court has issued the final confiscation order, because the attachment of property is only indicated in the court records. Related to this, the ninth problem is that, more generally, there is a lack of data management systems and of statistics. A key topic is if, and how, information on the disposal of assets is gathered, and in particular the existence of data management systems. This issue is strictly connected to statistics, since it boosts the development of a statistical apparatus to monitor disposal and assess its effectiveness. In most countries, data collection regarding disposal is on paper. A few countries have developed a data management system. These include France (where a system was set up by the AGRASC in 2011), Ireland (where a system is held by the Criminal Assets Bureau), Italy (where a data management system has been developed by the ANBSC (REGIO) and by the Rome Tribunal), Romania (IMIS, for drug trafficking only), Slovenia and the United Kingdom (JARD, Joint Asset Recovery Database). Even though many Member States have some statistics regarding final confiscation orders, not much information is available on asset disposal.

A tenth problem arises from parallel, and often uncoordinated, proceedings on the assets due to third-party claims, such as bankruptcy or matrimonial proceedings: this happens in Hungary (where other enforcement procedures have priority over criminal confiscation), Belgium, Cyprus, Italy and the United Kingdom. For example, in Belgium, in many cases, the Patrimonial Services are confronted with occupants who were not officially informed about the criminal case and, when they are informed at the disposal phase, take legal action against the Patrimonial Services (e.g., the wife living in the family house confiscated from her husband or third parties neither involved nor invited in the criminal case). Problems also arise when real estate owned by companies is confiscated. In many cases, these companies go bankrupt and the Commercial Courts appoint a judicial external liquidator over their assets. These commercial proceedings take place without knowledge of the Criminal Court, and Commercial Courts are more ready to satisfy the claims of the creditors of the apparently innocent companies than the confiscation order.

Eleventh are communication problems related to timely and proper notifications to the relevant asset management office: these occur in Belgium, Bulgaria, Finland and Italy. For example, in Italy, first-degree confiscation orders are sometimes notified with (much) delay to the ANBSC. A twelfth problem stems from a lack of cooperation between the institutions involved: this is reported in Greece and Italy (where state administrations and local entities are not always cooperative with ANBSC), as well as Slovenia. Also in Italy, the existence of regional superstructures, which can be considered copycats of the ANBSC (e.g., ABECOL, *Agenzia regionale per i beni confiscati alle organizzazioni criminali nel Lazio*, in the Lazio Region), sets the ground for coordination problems and inefficiencies.

The thirteenth problem relates to real estate: many Member States report that there are plenty of cases where the confiscated real estate has mortgage liens or is subject to other executive procedures (Belgium, Bulgaria, Cyprus, Italy, Portugal, United Kingdom), also linked to third-party interests. The aggravating factor is when the value of the mortgage is higher than the real market value of the property. The contraction of the real estate market during the economic downturn that started in 2008 has made the sale of these properties difficult because there is a lack of buyers (Bulgaria, Greece) and because their sale bears more costs than the expected returns (Belgium, Bulgaria, Cyprus). The lack of an ad hoc sale procedure for public auctions of confiscated property has also been reported, since it creates 'grey zones' and legal gaps negatively affecting the outcome of these sales (Bulgaria). Similar problems arise with the following typologies of real estate: properties under instalment sale agreements (Portugal), property under joint ownership (Belgium, Bulgaria, Denmark, Italy, Portugal, Slovenia), confiscated pro-quota (e.g., a cellar used to produce drugs underneath a property that was not confiscated) (Belgium, Italy), unlawfully occupied property (Belgium, Italy) and property with unresolved issues with tenant owner's rights (Belgium, Sweden) or with permit/environmental problems (Belgium, Italy). For example, in Belgium many confiscated houses were built without a construction permit. This means that the house will have to be demolished, at the expense of the State. In Denmark you can buy a small house placed at a so-called allotment garden (the person owns the house and has the right to use the garden, through membership of the allotment garden): the house can be confiscated, but not the right to use the garden, so the sale of such a house can be difficult. In Hungary the major problem with real estate is the lack of any information about this type of property during the criminal procedure so that its existence remains hidden until the moment it must be disposed of. Certain types of immovable properties are also reported as more difficult to sell, such as high-value real estate (Portugal). The reputation of the previous owner is reported as another detrimental factor for potential buyers of real estate (and of movable assets as well) (Bulgaria, Denmark, France, Sweden). A specific problem reported by Portugal concerns the possibility that the private seller charged by the court with the sale deals with it in order to obtain a private profit; there are some pending proceedings, and the crime most commonly investigated is the appropriation by the private agent of the difference between the real offer that s/he got and the offer s/he referred to the judge.

Fourteenth are problems related to financial assets (e.g., shares, stocks and bonds) and companies: such assets can be difficult to evaluate and sell (Czech Republic). The shares of small family businesses rarely attract interest and, unless other family members decide to redeem them, are practically unsaleable (Denmark). Problems also arise in relation to concurring bankruptcy proceedings against confiscated companies (Cyprus, Italy). Industrial and agricultural properties are also problematic to be disposed of, since it is difficult to keep them operating and guarantee occupational levels (Spain).

Fifteenth are problems related to movable assets: the main critical factors are often related to rapid deterioration, considerable value depreciation and disproportionate storage costs, which are often exacerbated by the prolonged judicial trials (e.g., Estonia, Hungary, Portugal, Slovakia, Sweden). For example, in Slovakia the main problems are related to objects, equipment or vehicles that are very difficult to reuse due to their obsolescence or depreciation; sporadic difficulties are also caused by large volumes of movable property (e.g., thousands of cartons of cigarettes or thousands of bottles of alcohol) as involved subjects have limited financial and human resources to handle their disposal. Another source of difficulties is the requirement that criminal assets must be liquidated by authorised personnel. In Germany the most critical cases are those involving animals (exotic animals, fight dogs). In Hungary practical problems arise in the disposal of computer hardware due to quick depreciation. Machines and processing lines are also difficult to transfer, and their maintenance is troublesome. In Romania precious metals and stones are difficult to dispose of due to the complex handing over and disposal procedures: they have to undergo expert valuation, the pool of eligible buyers is limited and the number of individuals and legal entities authorised to trade such items is limited. In Slovenia the greatest difficulties are encountered with the sale of vehicles, mobile phones and other movable property. In Sweden food and other perishables that quickly devaluate cannot always be promptly sold, while alcohol and cigarettes fall under a complicated tax regulation regime. Other assets difficult to sell are those having a limited market, such as very technical machinery (France), as well as assets without any real value but which are expensive to destroy (used items) (Belgium). The issue with counterfeited goods is more complicated, as the infringement of intellectual property rights precludes their sale and makes it quite cumbersome to dispose of them in some other way than destruction (e.g., Hungary, where brands and logos on clothing have to be removed).

A sixteenth problem is the lack of resources devoted to the disposal of confiscated assets: in about one-third of the Member States there are no dedicated resources, or available resources are insufficient. The seventeenth, and final, problem is the lack of training: in most countries there is a lack of ad hoc training on disposal (also due to the fact that confiscated assets are treated as any other State property).

Practices: What Works (Best Practices)

The following best practices emerged from the analysis. First, it is a best practice to reduce management costs by using mechanisms similar to the so-called seizure without dispossession (France). AGRASC does not administer seized complex assets that require very high administration costs; since 2010, there is provision for seizure of property without dispossession which makes it possible to leave seized assets in the custody of the owner, who must bear maintenance costs.[19]

A second example of best practice is the use of databases supporting asset management, network building and disposal (Italy). The Tribunal of Rome has developed a dedicated database to map all seized assets; it was created in two months, at no cost.[20] That database includes detailed geo-localised information about the assets, including any critical issue (e.g., bankruptcy). It is accessible to registered users, including law enforcement agencies and other relevant entities (e.g., Libera, that supports allocation of the assets by identifying suitable users; ABI (*Associazione Bancaria Italiana*), the Italian banking association, to ensure that seized and confiscated companies can continue having access to credit; ANCI (*Associazione Nazionale Comuni Italiani*), which is the national association of Italian municipalities that are bodies heavily involved in asset disposal). It therefore builds a network of actors, promoting prompt management and disposal. Other tribunals are developing a similar system (e.g., Bari, Naples, Reggio Calabria, Trapani, Turin). This database also supports a best practice developed by the same Tribunal of Rome, that is, the provisional assignment of seized or provisionally confiscated assets for social reuse (that will be discussed later).

A third example of best practice is to assess the value of properties under mortgages before seizing them (Sweden): if the value of the real estate does not cover both the mortgage and the cost of the sale, no freezing measure is imposed.

Fourth, setting up dedicated and centralised institutional building arrangements (Italy, France and Cyprus) seems also to be a best practice: the existence of centralised and dedicated authorities—as long as they do not suffer from understaffing as some of the current central agencies do—can significantly boost asset disposal.

Fifth, it is a best practice to promote interagency cooperation (Sweden): the Swedish Justice Department issued an order for closer cooperation between the police, Economic Crimes Bureau and the Prosecution Service which resulted in the establishment of the National Function for Proceeds of Crime, intended to act as an advisor to the different authorities.

Sixth, it is a best practice to set up ad hoc offices to sell confiscated assets at auction (Belgium): this has made it possible to sell, practically speaking, any type of movable asset in a very short time (e.g., Finshop Brussels).[21]

Seventh, setting up an ad hoc office for the centralised management and sale of confiscated real estate (Belgium) seems to be a best practice too: after the final confiscation order, the Patrimonial Services take over the management of the confiscated real estate. A special central office, named FINDOMMO, has recently been created to ensure a more efficient management of all real estate, which is property of the Belgian State. This management concerns real estate destined to be sold within a short period of time. This office prepares property for sale, and when the property is ready (no further occupation, cleaned, new locks, etc.) FINDOMMO gives a sale order to the competent real estate committee, specialised in the sale of real estate.

Eighth, promoting protocols between relevant local stakeholders and/or associations to facilitate effective reuse of the assets (Italy) is another best practice: for example, on the occasion of a conference organised by Libera in Rome in October 2014, agreements with seized restaurants in the city centre were signed to offer participants meals at reduced prices.[22]

Ninth, it is a best practice to promote synergies among confiscated companies so as to maintain businesses in operation and avoid staff being made redundant (Italy): for example, in Rome, workers from a confiscated restaurant near the beach were hired in the winter in a confiscated restaurant in the city centre, which had a staff shortage, and vice versa.

The tenth best practice is to coordinate criminal and non-criminal proceedings involving third parties (United Kingdom): there are some local arrangements (not consistent yet) where matrimonial issues are held in the same court as asset disposal.

Focusing on Current Social Reuse Experiences in the EU

In addition to the traditional transfer of ill-gotten gains into the State budget, some Member States envisage a more innovative form of disposal that is attracting increasing attention at the EU level: the reuse of confiscated assets for social purposes. Its attractiveness is the visibility of confiscated assets among citizens. As noted above, the key social reuse experiences within the EU are in Belgium, France, Hungary, Italy, Luxembourg, Scotland and Spain. Before analysing them in detail, these experiences can be seen to fit one of the following two models: direct social reuse or indirect social reuse.

Direct reuse of confiscated assets for social purposes operates in Italy, Belgium (Flemish Region) and Hungary. With direct reuse, assets are reassigned for the public benefit through a change in their intended use (e.g., conversion of the house formerly belonging to a criminal boss into a playgroup).

Indirect social reuse is where the proceeds of crime (or from the sale of confiscated assets) are distributed via specialised funds that use them either (1) in crime prevention projects or (2) in incentivisation schemes for law enforcement agencies so that these entities may have a further incentive to keep on fighting crime—always, even if indirectly, in the interest of society. Under this mechanism, confiscated assets are not straightforwardly passed on to society, rather the proceeds from their sale are. In addition, the proceeds may not always be reused for the immediate, but rather the mediate (via incentivisation schemes) interest of society. This model is in place in France, Spain,[23] Luxembourg and Scotland.

We turn now to consider experiences of social reuse—direct and indirect—in different Member States.

Key Social Reuse Experiences in the EU

Belgium

In Belgium social reuse for real estate is envisaged in the Dutch/Flemish Region only. The 1997 Decree containing the Flemish Housing Code[24] provides for the right of the municipalities to temporarily manage unsuitable/uninhabitable or abandoned property from its negligent owners, on the condition that the property will be restored/renovated and used for social housing for a certain period of time. The owner keeps his rights over the property, but the municipality acquires the right to temporarily manage the buildings for nine years or longer, depending on if more time is needed to regain investments made to improve the real estate and to rent them to needy people. The idea to apply this regime to confiscated real estate came about after the Federal Public Service of Finance had confiscated some derelict properties with illegal occupants and did not know how to handle them. Social management appeared as a win-win option: on the one side, it provides the local authorities with a chance to invest in these properties, to regain the investment via the rents and to improve the housing problem; on the other side, the federal government benefits from preventing further deterioration of the estate and from regaining it in the end, renovated and free of illegal occupants, and not bearing any management cost.

A decision by the Municipal Council starts proceedings for social management. The municipality hires the repairmen and undertakes renovation works, and the property is then rented in accordance with social housing rates. The municipality itself does not deal with the renting of the properties—instead, the properties are transferred for management to a provider of social housing (such as social housing companies, the Flemish Housing Fund for Large Families, social housing ('tenants') associations, social rental agencies and public centres for social welfare). Although the Decree specifically lists these eligible providers, it does not provide for a selection procedure.

France

The Interministerial Mission in the Fight Against Drugs and Drug Addiction (*Mission interministérielle de lutte contre la drogue et la toxicomanie*, MILDT) was established in 1982. Its mandate is the organisation and coordination of national activities regarding the fight against drugs and drug addiction (particularly in three key areas: monitoring, research and prevention of drug use; treatment and reintegration of drug users; training for those involved in the fight against drugs). The MILDT manages the fund—so-called *Fonds de concours*—established in 1995 to collect the proceeds of confiscated assets in connection with drug trafficking.[25]

The procedure is as follows: a final confiscation order—including a specific statement that certain movable or immovable assets confiscated in relation to drug crimes are to be forwarded to the MILDT—is issued. AGRASC manages the auction sale of the assets and the proceeds are transferred from the AGRASC bank account to the MILDT one. MILDT waits until the end of each year for the presentation of the '*Fonds de concours*' annual budget. At the same time, the several public institutions involved in the redistribution of the proceeds submit their projects. Proceeds are distributed as follows: (60%) Ministry of Internal Affairs; (20%) Ministry of Justice; (10%) Ministry of Economic Affairs and Finances; and (10%) MILDT. These proceeds are distributed by MILDT among several entities (i.e., Ministry of Social Affairs, Ministry of Health, Ministry of Agriculture, Ministry of Education, etc.), according to their needs and to the projects submitted. MILDT has the exclusive power to select the projects that should be financed with the *Fonds de concours*. While the quotas assigned to other ministries can be regarded as an incentivisation scheme, and are largely used to buy equipment to fight drug trafficking, the 10% MILDT quota is directly used for social purposes. Most of it is addressed to the Ministry of Social Affairs and the Ministry of Health for promoting social and medical campaigns against drug abuse, as well as other forms of addiction. The Ministry of Superior Education and Research or the Ministry of National Education usually uses these proceeds for prevention campaigns in universities and schools, and the Ministry of Agriculture uses them for prevention strategies at the workplace.

Hungary

Since 2000 confiscated goods may be offered for charitable purposes.[26] The procedure for offering these goods for charitable purposes is referred to as 'use in public interest'. It applies to personal assets only and cannot cover either vehicles or real estate. Goods suitable for social reuse must fulfil one of the following purposes: nutrition, clothing, sleeping gear and fixtures, grooming/hygiene, cleaning, washing, education and culture. In addition, assets meeting one of these purposes can be socially reused: provisional housing, house maintenance, home equipment, household appliances and tools, kitchen equipment and utensils, communications equipment, toys and leisure sport.[27] In practice, 98% of all goods offered for charitable purposes are counterfeited commodities (e.g., clothing, shoes or toys). End users must be individuals in need (not public institutions or private organisations). The law also defines the timeframe of the procedure (about two months).

The Charity Council is responsible for initiating and coordinating these proceedings. The procedure starts either with a final confiscation order issued within criminal proceedings or with a confiscation decision for infringement by the National Tax and Customs Administration within tax and excise proceedings. The goods are transferred to the management offices of the territorially competent courts to take custody over them; these offices assess if social reuse is possible; if so, they inform and offer them to the Charity Council. The members of the Charity Council review the offers on a monthly basis and decide whether to accept them against certain criteria, such as if the goods can fulfil any actual needs, as well as feasibility and cost-effectiveness. The members of the Charity Council are well-experienced charity organisations with proven logistic capabilities and a wide network of local offices that collect requests for donations, so at any given time they have good knowledge of local needs. Once the Charity Council accepts an offer, a charity organisation is assigned to take care of distribution to end users.

As the vast majority of goods offered for social reuse are counterfeited commodities (clothing, shoes, etc.), distribution cannot be initiated before the brand owner consents to the procedure. Should the brand owner not consent, the Charity Council could initiate judicial proceedings before the competent court.

Italy

In Italy, since 1996, it is possible to socially reuse assets confiscated from mafia in civil/preventative proceedings and in certain criminal proceedings instituted under article 12-sexies of Law 356/1992.[28] The key institution involved in the decision-making process is ANBSC, which intervenes after the first-degree confiscation order to deal with asset management and disposal. A notification is made to ANBSC by the court of the final confiscation order. The decision related to their social reuse must be adopted by its Executive Committee within 90 days from notification of the order (or within 180 in more complex cases).

Assets suitable for social reuse are immovable assets, movable assets (also registered ones) and companies. To delve further into detail regarding immovable assets, within six months from the adoption of the final confiscation order lists of real estate available for social reuse are published by ANBSC on its website, so as to make potential beneficiaries aware and to enable them to put forward applications. Real estate may be:

- used by the State for justice/public-order purposes or to respond to other governmental or public needs related to the institutional activities carried out by state entities, fiscal entities, universities or cultural institutions;
- used for economic purposes by ANBSC, with the approval of the Minister of the Interior;
- transferred for institutional purposes or social reuse to local entities (the municipality where they are located or, alternatively, to the related province/region). The local entities must keep and regularly update a list of the assets transferred to them, which shall be made public. They can directly manage the asset or assign it for free to social communities/associations (e.g., youth centres, charities or therapeutic communities and rehabilitation centres), based on an agreement detailing duration, modalities of reuse and related monitoring procedures, renewal modalities, and so on. Assets that are not allocated may be used by local authorities for profit-making aims and the income must be reused for social purposes. If within one year the local body has failed to assign the asset, the agency shall revoke the transfer and appoint a commissioner with substitutive powers.

Regarding social reuse of companies, these can be rented by ANBSC to worker cooperatives (for free); alternatively, they can be rented to public or private enterprises (upon payment of a rental fee), sold or liquidated. Movable assets (also registered ones) can be used by ANBSC in institutional activities or can be assigned to other State bodies, local entities or charities.

Assets are assigned by the ANSBC to local entities (and by local entities to social communities/associations) based on their needs and on the projects of reuse they submit. Even if the assignment decision is largely discretionary, equality of treatment must be assured.

Luxembourg

Since 1992, the so-called *Fonds de lutte contre le trafic de stupéfiants* (Fund to fight against drug trafficking) has aimed to foster the development, coordination and implementation of instruments to fight drug trafficking, drug addiction and all their direct and indirect effects.[29] The Fund is made up of all real and personal property, divided and undivided, confiscated under section 8.2 of the Act of 19 February 1973 on the sale of medicinal substances and the fight against drug abuse, as well as under art. 5, par. 4, of the 1988 United Nations Convention against Illicit Traffic in Narcotic Drugs and Psychotropic Substances. Following the enactment of new legislation in 2010,[30] the Fund now also gathers the proceeds from other crimes, such as money laundering and other serious crimes, and has been renamed *Fonds de lutte contre certaines formes de criminalité* (Fund to fight against certain forms of criminality).

The Fund is therefore the government institution that receives confiscated proceeds from drug trafficking and money laundering and supports programmes in fighting 'certain forms of criminality'. Its beneficiaries include international organisations, national institutions and NGOs. Since being set up in 1993, the Fund has funded projects worth over €36 million.[31] In 2014, its beneficiaries included, for example: (1) UNODC (for projects in Africa and Asia); (2) the national public sector, that is, the police and justice areas, with projects that supported the public prosecutor offices and the Police Grand-Ducale (with training and new equipment to fight drug trafficking), and the health and youth sectors, with, for example, a project with the Health Ministry to build a drug treatment centre and to run a prevention project within schools; (3) the finance sector, with a training project on money laundering and (4) NGOs and other organisations, such as Caritas, with a project for the treatment and rehabilitation of drug addicts in Bangladesh, and the Pompidou Group (Council of Europe), with a project for drug prevention and treatment in the prisons in Moldavia, Ukraine, Romania and the Balkans.[32] The Fund constantly monitors the financed projects and eventually stops them.

Scotland

In Scotland, recovered criminal assets are invested in the 'CashBack for Communities' programme. This programme is a Scottish Government initiative that takes the ill-gotten gains of crime, recovered through the Proceeds of Crime Act (POCA) 2002, and invests them into community programmes, facilities and activities largely, but not exclusively, for young people at risk of turning to crime and anti-social behaviour as a way of life. Since its launch in 2007, the vast majority of POCA receipts have been allocated by the Government to this programme (some funding has been provided to Police Scotland and to the Crown Office for the specific purpose of maximising POCA receipts), subject to a cap of recoveries up to £30m in any one year. Over £74 million recovered from proceeds of crime has been so far invested in sporting, cultural, educational and mentoring activities for young people and their communities. The programme is intended to be (1) positive (healthy, fun, active, engaging), (2) open to all (accessible, well advertised, free of charge, of interest to all irrespective of age, gender, ethnicity, etc.), (3) developmental (aims at changing behaviours and attitudes and at developing skills) and (4) sustainable.

The procedure is as follows: a confiscation order is placed on an individual or a company by the Scottish Courts Service (SCS). Monetary payments of orders are made to the SCS, which then transfers monies to the Scottish Government. The Scottish Government utilises the money to fund partner organisations and associations to deliver programmes of activities or to construct community sports facilities over three-year programme blocks. Payments to partner organisations are made by grants. Applicants for CashBack for Communities funding range from large national associations and organisations to small individual third-sector organisations. All funding applications must deliver activity that aligns with the aims of the programme. Also, they are subject to standard financial and organisational due diligence checking and monitoring. CashBack for Communities can provide additional discretionary funding to build delivery capacity, if reasonably necessary, within partner organisations.

The current list of successful project partners for the CashBack for Communities programme through to the end of 2016/2017 are Scottish Football Association, Scottish Rugby Union, Scottish Sports Futures, Basketball Scotland, Princes Trust Scotland, Creative Scotland, Youth Scotland, Youth Link Scotland, Glasgow Clyde College, Sportscotland, Street Soccer Scotland, Action for Children, Celtic Foundation and Ocean Youth Trust.

All individual CashBack projects and the overall programme are subject to evaluation for the impact and diverse range of outcomes that are being delivered. Evaluation reports of individual initiatives are on the CashBack website.[33] An independent external evaluation of the programme was published in June 2014,[34] which demonstrates how CashBack is changing individual young people's lives for the better and that significant impact is being made on participation, diversion and progression pathways and engagement outcomes for young people and communities across Scotland. Also, the programme is well advertised and its activities attract comprehensive regional press coverage across Scotland.

Spain

The disposal of proceeds from drug trafficking is regulated by Law 17 of 29 May 2003.[35] This statute has established a Fund financed out of the assets confiscated in drug trafficking and related offences. This Fund is used (1) to finance programmes for drug addiction prevention, assistance to drug addicts and their rehabilitation; (2) to promote and improve measures to prevent, investigate, prosecute and repress drug-related crimes; and (3) to promote international cooperation on such matters. That said, any asset typology confiscated in relation to the above crimes can be disposed of socially: movable and immovable assets as well as companies. The Fund's beneficiaries are law enforcement agencies charged with counter-narcotics activities; NGOs and non-profits working in the substance abuse field; regional and local governments and authorities; Government Delegation for the National Plan on Drugs (*Delegación del Gobierno para el Plan Nacional sobre Drogas*, DGPNSD); and international organisations and institutions.

The DGPNSD—which is a body under the Ministry of Health, Social Services and Equality—is in charge of this social reuse mechanism. When the final confiscation order is adopted, notification is made to DGPNSD, together with a list of the assets. The key entity tasked, within DGPNSD, with the management of the Fund is the *Mesa de Coordinación de Adjudicaciones* (Coordinating Bureau for Allocation). Its tasks include the identification of the assets to be allocated to the Fund and the adoption of decisions regarding their destination to beneficiaries.[36] Unless the assets have to be abandoned (due to deterioration or high management costs), or are definitively assigned to the law enforcement agencies authorised by the court to temporarily use them for pending legal proceedings, two key options are foreseen for their social reuse: (1) sale, with the profits from the sale flowing to the Fund (indirect social reuse) or (2) assignment for free to potential beneficiaries (direct social reuse), upon their request. In practice, most assets are sold rather than directly assigned.

In the period 1996–2014, apart from money (about €230 million), the Fund gathered 31,945 assets, as follows:[37] 46% of these assets were vehicles, 2% was real estate, 8% were boats, 6% was jewellery and 38% objects (i.e., assets not falling under any of the above categories, such as hardware, appliances, clothing, audio-visual equipment, phones, furniture). In the same period (1996–2014), 26,394 assets have been disposed of, as follows: 53% have been abandoned, 7% have been finally awarded to law enforcement agencies (mostly vehicles), 16% have been sold and 8% have been assigned for free.

Comparing Social Reuse Experiences in the EU

The above-mentioned social reuse experiences vary significantly in terms of beneficiaries, modalities and asset typologies involved. First, beneficiaries include international organisations and institutions (Luxembourg, Spain), national institutions (France, Italy, Luxembourg, Spain), local entities (Belgium, Italy, Spain) and charities, civil society organisations, associations and cooperatives (Belgium, Italy, Hungary, Luxembourg, Spain, Scotland). Second, the allocation of assets under the direct reuse model (Italy, Belgium, Hungary) is decided by the competent authority upon formal request/expression of needs by eligible beneficiaries. Third, with the allocation of proceeds under the indirect reuse model (Luxembourg, France, Spain and Scotland), some Member States (e.g., France) do not envisage any competitive procedure, since the redistribution of the revenues is ultimately prescribed by law. In contrast, others (e.g., Luxembourg, Scotland and Spain) give more discretionary powers to the bodies managing the funds, and the repartition involves a competitive procedure.

Fourth, there are different typologies of confiscated assets suitable for social reuse. In some countries social reuse is used for movable assets only (e.g., Hungary), while in others it applies also to companies, lands and real estate (e.g., Italy, Spain). Fifth, in some countries social reuse is possible only in relation to the proceeds from certain offences (typically drug trafficking, such as Spain and France), while others (e.g., Luxembourg, Italy) envisage it in relation to all (serious) crimes. And, finally, it is important to note distinctions between national and local scope for application: social reuse typically applies to the entire territory, with the exception of Belgium where it is envisaged in the Dutch/Flemish Region only.

Social Reuse Practices: What Does Not Work (Key Problems)

Looking at existing practices, a series of problems have been reported, which can be grouped as follows: (1) problems related to the legal framework; (2) asset-related problems; (3) problems related to implementing institutions and procedures; (4) beneficiary-related problems and (5) problems in terms of public information and policy evaluation.

First, we consider problems related to the legal framework. Some Member States experience a lack of interest in assets available for social reuse by potential beneficiaries: in Belgium most of the social housing providers are not interested in the social management scheme, as it only allows for temporary management and sub-renting. In Italy some articles of the Anti-mafia Code discourage potential beneficiaries from applying for the assets (e.g., art. 46, which—should the assets be given back to their owner—requires beneficiaries to pay back a sum of money equivalent to their value). In addition, there are legal limitations in terms of potential beneficiaries: in Hungary the law allows only for individuals to be recipients of the social reuse regime, thus reducing the eligible target groups (e.g., schools or hospitals cannot benefit from it).

Second, there are asset-related problems. This can include issues of third-party claims in relation to properties under joint ownership and other asset-related obstacles. To provide an example, in 2011, Antwerp, Belgium, took a property under the social management scheme and discovered that a share of it was forfeited by the Federal Public Service of Finance. One of the landlords claimed that he was still in possession of his share, which resulted in legal disputes between him and the Federal Public Service of Finance and an appeal against the social management procedure. So too have difficulties arisen in Italy, where assets may be either of too little value, in bad condition, subject to third-party claims (including mortgages, which occur in nearly 50% of immovable assets) or to parallel proceedings; also, there are assets confiscated pro-quota, as well as obstacles due to technical and logistical features of the assets (e.g., difficult access to an estate, unsafe buildings).

Still, with asset-related problems, some Member States have experienced problems related to the sale of certain assets, feeding the indirect social reuse system. In France AGRASC is in charge of the sale of the assets confiscated in drug-related cases, whose proceeds flow to the fund managed by MILDT. While movable assets are sold quickly, the sale of immovables is more difficult. In one case, the convicted owner, in reaction to the confiscation, vandalised his property. So too are there limitations, in daily practice, to the typologies of assets suitable for social reuse. In Hungary the typologies of confiscated goods suitable for social reuse are defined by law and also include goods with auxiliary scopes of use (e.g., provisional housing, house maintenance, home equipment, household appliances and tools). In practice, the offerings to the Charity Council mainly include clothing and shoes, since the other suitable goods are usually of higher value and public sale is preferred.

Third, we consider problems related to implementing institutions and procedures. This includes shortage of human resources. For example, Italy and France—where ANBSC and AGRASC were established as centralised bodies dealing with asset utilisation—report that currently the agencies are suffering from understaffing, which is also due to difficulties in finding competent experts. Hungary also reports a shortage of human resources due to budgetary constraints. In addition, there can be uncertainties at the court level on how to ascribe crime proceeds to dedicated funds. For many years the French fund managed by MILDT was not able to gather all the money, because the fund was almost unknown to practitioners. The situation has improved since 2008.[37] Relatedly, there might be issues of limited practical application: in Belgium the procedure has not been widely applied so far. It is however expected that the social management procedures regarding forfeited properties will run more smoothly compared to the ones against private owners, since the Federal Public Service of Finance is a public institution (there should be fewer obstructions against the procedures).

There can also be problems where procedures are overly complex, costly and not always transparent: in Italy procedures are excessively complex and do sometimes lack transparency; also, a wider direct involvement of associations in the assignment of assets, without the filter of the local authorities, would be advisable. Related to this are problems associated with the lengthy duration of the social reuse procedure: in Hungary a clear timetable is set. However, in practice, this timetable is respected only when dealing with original products (2% of all cases), while with counterfeited goods (the remaining 98%) it is hard to keep these deadlines, and the duration varies depending on the response of the brand owner, the capacity of the contracted de-branding company and the amount of the goods. Sometimes brand owners often do not respond within the prescribed deadline because they are informed by the authorities with delay about the current status of the assets. So too can there be problems with the lengthy duration of confiscation proceedings and negative impact on social reuse: in Hungary judicial proceedings on average take three years, some others up to six years: as a result, some 20% of seized goods are not suitable for social reuse purposes due to deteriorated quality, and this precludes reuse of food, as well. A final point to mention in relation to problems related to institutions and procedures concerns intellectual property rights issues and related costs: in Hungary the removal of brands is expensive and in many cases unfeasible. Most of the brand owners refuse to cooperate or do not respond within the deadline. This also narrows down the range of goods that can be utilised.

Fourth, there can be beneficiary-related problems: such as a lack of economic and technical capacity on the side of beneficiaries; in Italy beneficiaries are commonly local authorities that seldom have enough economic resources for their management. Also, most of them lack any dedicated office for managing confiscated assets. As a consequence of this, in many cases local authorities submit reuse projects that are impracticable or not feasible.

Fifth, and finally, it is important to consider problems in terms of public information and policy evaluation. Often notable is a lack of any systematic publicity about the social reuse scheme: for example, in Hungary, even if some statistics are produced, there is no systematic mechanism in place to inform the general public. There is also poor quality of information regarding assets available for social reuse: in Italy, notwithstanding legal provisions, most local entities do not publish the list of assets they have been assigned. And, there is a lack of any systematic policy evaluation of the outcomes of the social management regime: apart from some evaluation of the direct results of the individual social reuse projects—via some monitoring/reporting activities (Hungary, Italy, Luxembourg)—the overall outputs and outcomes of the social reuse scheme are not systematically assessed. In some instances, this can be due to limited experience and recent implementation (Belgium). In most cases, just some statistics are produced (e.g., Spain). In France a purely formal financial, *ex post*, check over the use of the proceeds is performed.

Now that we have outlined some of the key problems in how social reuse operates, we turn to consider some examples of best practice.

Social Reuse Practices: What Works (Best Practices)

Looking at existing best practices, these can be grouped as follows: (1) preventing assets' deterioration; (2) empowering beneficiaries and institutions; (3) preventing criminals from buying the assets back and (4) public information and policy evaluation. We discuss each in turn.

The first one to consider is best practices preventing assets' deterioration. This includes provisionally assigning seized assets to prevent deterioration and to promptly respond to social needs. In Italy the Rome Tribunal provisionally assigns to social reuse seized/provisionally confiscated assets, based on a temporary loan for use agreement. This practice has been developed on the basis of regulations making it possible to assign seized movable assets (e.g., cars) to the police and other public bodies. The Rome Tribunal extended this practice beyond moveable goods to also include real estate. This is in order to immediately use the assets that will eventually be given back (not vandalised or depreciated, etc.) to the defendant at the end of the proceeding.

The second area of best practice relates to empowering beneficiaries and institutions. This can include enhancing beneficiaries' capability to implement social reuse projects: in Scotland, through the CashBack for Communities programme, individual partner organisations are provided with assistance on project accountability, output outcomes monitoring and reporting, evaluation and capacity to deliver. This is outsourced to an external Delivery Partner that puts arrangements in place to support project partners to provide the core functions (e.g., management, finance, administration, communications and evaluation) necessary to implement the programme. Empowerment can also take the form of setting up a mechanism linking institutions and acknowledged charity organisations. For example, the strong point of the Hungarian system is the link, via the Charity Council, between government and acknowledged charity organisations. This affirms the credibility of the model and ensures cooperation from local partners (which provide for better assessment of needs and more effective distribution of the goods) and brand owners (that are increasingly consenting to the distribution of counterfeited goods carrying their trademarks without their prior removal). Empowerment can also include the provision of external funding to support social reuse: in Hungary charity organisations must bear all costs related to the utilisation of the goods. However, the Ministry of Human Resources provides financial support through grants amounting to one-third of all costs. The other two-thirds are covered through the organisations' own resources, fundraising, volunteer work, grants or in-kind contributions from local government.

The third area of best practice relates to the importance of preventing criminals from buying the assets back. One way of doing this is by providing for disposal monitoring: in Italy art. 48 par. 15 of the Anti-mafia Code envisages that when—based on reports by citizens or information held at *Prefetture* (prefecture)—it emerges that confiscated assets have been reacquired by the criminal, then the act that assigned the assets is revoked. An interesting revocation case happened in the Municipality of Formia where the former mayor, upon having received a confiscated estate, falsely declared the indigent status of the mobster's wife, allowing her to continue living there. In relation to confiscated companies, another method of preventing criminals from reacquiring a company is by identifying a strict list of prerequisites that applicants must meet: in Spain, in the so-called Pazo Baión case,[38] a confiscation order was pronounced in 2006 and included the palace and other buildings and a couple of companies producing wine. To avoid the former owners buying the property back, the Award Board set strict requirements for companies interested to submit a bid, such as: at least four years in vineyard activities; an average annual turnover not lower than €5 million; agreement to respect all workers' rights; to continue the vineyard activities for at least 15 years; to employ over a 15-year period workers who suffered drug addiction; and to devolve at least 5% of the profits for the first 15 years to programmes oriented to drug addictions. One Galician company presented the best offer and the whole property was sold for €15 million in July 2008. Since then the company has met all of the obligations.

Fourth, and finally, it is important to consider best practices in terms of public information and policy evaluation. This can include setting up mechanisms for the evaluation of the social reuse scheme: in Scotland all individual

CashBack projects, and the overall programme, are subject to self- and independent evaluation for the impact and diverse range of outcomes that are being delivered. All evaluation reports are available online.

Conclusion: Is Social Reuse a Promising Disposal Option?

It is clear that social reuse is not immune to the plethora of practical obstacles that affect more traditional disposal options. Still, it seems that it can bring about a significant added value, not least by the visibility of confiscated assets among citizens and by its strong social impact. Social reuse operates differently from traditional forms of reuse—whereby assets are used for public purposes (since they become part of the State budget) but, since they are mixed up with other public resources, citizens cannot see that they are derived from confiscated assets. Social reuse makes this link explicit: what stems from crime is openly given back to society and is used in accordance with community needs. By doing so, it can be seen not only as a social rebalance mechanism (what was previously illicit becomes a benefit to the community) but also as a tool to tangibly spread the message 'crime does not pay'. Citizens who are well aware of this message and who can concretely see how the administration of justice can respond to the needs of their communities will tend to value legality over illegality; be more likely to trust the State; and tend to report suspicious activities/behaviours and to raise law-abiding kids; in short, social reuse will be an effective barrier to crime. For all these reasons, social reuse can be seen as a worthy means of utilising assets at the disposal phase, one that that may incentivise local communities to take a stance against (organised) crime, thus activating a 'social fight' against it. Social reuse can therefore be regarded as a promising disposal option.

In order to fully assess, however, how promising this disposal option is, it should also be understood how willing other Member States are to incorporate it into their national legislation. To assess the feasibility of the adoption of social reuse by other countries, taking into consideration the overall benefits it could bring about as well as the potential obstacles, a data collection protocol was administered to 12 of the 20 countries not having at all, or not having, as the Member States analysed in depth in this chapter, a well-developed social reuse system in place.[39]

The potential benefits that social reuse can bring about include meeting certain social needs, especially via direct social reuse; making explicit the willingness of the State to combat crime; greater awareness of asset seizure/confiscation; a more effective communication about confiscation to the wider public;

making more visible to the public the activity of law enforcement agencies; and a better reuse of certain assets, that would otherwise not be used/be damaged if not reused, such as perishable goods and cars.[40] These benefits were widely recognised by respondents. At the same time, they expressed concerns about how to guarantee fairness in the selection process, that is, in giving preference to one cause/beneficiary over another. Another significant issue that was raised relates to the overall economic efficiency of such systems, which seems to be impaired by the bad conditions of confiscated assets in most countries, with the consequence that extra money from the state budget might be needed to restore them. Costs might exceed benefits, in economic terms, in the end. Of course, this shall be weighed against overall benefits of social reuse, including the cultural message that it spreads and the contribution that it could give, in the long run, to the fight against crime. Needless to say, these intangible benefits can hardly be measured, but should nonetheless be taken into account.

The social reuse model that seems to best fit the needs of other countries is, according to all but one respondent, the indirect reuse model, since it overcomes some key problems associated with the direct reuse of the assets: not all assets are in good conditions and/or can be directly reused (e.g., Rolex watch); overall, the reuse of the proceeds is regarded as simpler, it better satisfies diverse and general needs of citizens or institutions and can be more easily incorporated in value-based confiscation systems.

It is now up to the Member States and EU institutions to decide if and how to keep on discussing the issue and to eventually turn it from a promising option to a real-world one, taking into account the lessons learnt from current experiences. Focusing on the role of the EU, European regulations could encourage a diffusion of social reuse across the EU and help resolve some of the above issues by promoting social reuse systems that are both effective and fair, with transparent procedures for assigning the assets and for monitoring them after assignment, for making all information publicly available, and with procedural safeguards for everyone involved. This might ultimately contribute to finally put a (so far) very much neglected actor, that is the citizen, at the heart of confiscation policies in the EU.

Notes

1. Under these schemes—that aim at incentivising asset recovery and enabling the involved agencies to recoup some of the costs incurred in confiscation proceedings—the entities that contributed to seizure and confiscation get back a percentage of confiscated assets. See, for example, the Asset Recovery Incentivisation Scheme (ARIS) in England and Wales.

2. This chapter presents the results of the EU-funded project 'RECAST—*REuse of Confiscated Assets for Social purposes: Towards common EU standards*'. The project was awarded to the University of Palermo—Department of European Studies and International Integration by the European Commission, DG HOME under the 2010 ISEC Programme. It was carried out in the period November 2011–November 2014 in cooperation with the Center for the Study of Democracy and the FLARE Network and with the support of Agenzia nazionale per l'amministrazione e la destinazione dei beni sequestrati e confiscati alla criminalità organizzata and the United Nations Interregional Crime and Justice Research Institute. The results of this study were presented at the conference 'Successes and Failures of Proceeds of Crime Approaches' at the University of Manchester (Manchester, 3 October 2014).
3. Barbara Vettori, *Tough on Criminal Wealth. Exploring the Practice of Proceeds from Crime Confiscation in the EU* (Springer 2006).
4. Ibid., 115–16.
5. Matrix Insight Ltd, *Assessing the Effectiveness of EU Member States' Practices in the Identification, Tracing, Freezing and Confiscation of Criminal Assets—Final Report* (2009), 84.
6. Rand Europe, *Study for an Impact Assessment on a Proposal for a New Legal Framework on the Confiscation and Recovery of Criminal Assets—Technical Report* (2012), 74.
7. European Parliament, Directorate General For Internal Policies, Policy Department C: Citizens' Rights and Constitutional Affairs, Civil Liberties, Justice and Home Affairs, *The Need for New EU Legislation Allowing the Assets Confiscated from Criminal Organisations to be Used for Civil Society and in Particular for Social Purposes* (2012), 54 <www.europarl.europa.eu/RegData/etudes/note/join/2012/462437/IPOL-LIBE_NT(2012)462437_EN.pdf> accessed 4 April 2017.
8. Directive 2014/42/EU of the European Parliament and of the Council of 3 April 2014 on the freezing and confiscation of instrumentalities and proceeds of crime in the European Union [2014] OJ L127/39, 43.
9. European Parliament, Resolution of 25 October 2011 on organised crime in the European Union (2010/2309(INI)) [2013] OJ C131E/08, 71.
10. Ibid., 73.
11. Justice and Home Affairs Council, Conclusions on Confiscation and Asset Recovery [2010] 7769/3/10 REV 3.
12. Communication from the Commission to the European Parliament and the Council of 22 November 2010—The EU Internal Security Strategy in Action: Five Steps Towards a More Secure Europe [2010] COM(2010) 673 final, 6.
13. The Stockholm Programme—An Open and Secure Europe Serving and Protecting Citizens [2010] OJ C115, 23.
14. EU Commission, Communication from the Commission to the European Parliament and the Council of 20 November 2008—Proceeds of organised crime: ensuring that 'crime does not pay' [2008] COM(2008) 766 final, 9.

15. Ibid.
16. The main tool used to gather relevant information was a questionnaire jointly developed by the University of Palermo and by the Centre for the Study of Democracy and administered to one (or more) national expert in each Member State. All Member States, excluding Latvia, replied.
17. See Law 768 (9 July 2010).
18. See Law Decree 4 (4 February 2010).
19. See Code of Criminal Procedure, art 706.158.
20. Two officers from the Guardia di Finanza developed it; Aste Giudiziarie, a company, did the software for free, since they get profits from the sale of the assets on auction (mainly cars).
21. For more information, see <www.finshop.belgium.be> accessed 26 October 2016.
22. For more details, see <www.libera.it/flex/cm/pages/ServeBLOB.php/L/IT/IDPagina/10512> accessed 26 October 2016.
23. The Spanish model envisages both direct and indirect social reuse. In practice, the second option is predominantly used, and for this reason Spain is herein classified in the related category.
24. See Décret contenant le Code flamand du Logement (15 July 1997), art 90.
25. See Decree 322 (17 March 1995).
26. See Act XIII (2000) and Government Decree 65 (2000).
27. See Act XIII (n 26), art 2.
28. This was originally envisaged by Law 109 (1996). Relevant regulations are now in Legislative Decree 159 (2011) (Anti-mafia Code) and subsequent amendments.
29. See Law of 17 March 1992, art 5.
30. See Law of 27 October 2010, art 5.
31. Grand Duche de Luxembourg, Fonds de lutte contre certaines formes de criminalité, *Rapport d'Activité 2014* (2015), 2 <www.mf.public.lu/publications/FdL_contre_trafic_stupefiants/fdl_rapport_2014.pdf> accessed 4 April 2017.
32. Ibid., 5–11.
33. See <www.cashbackforcommunities.org/impact> accessed 26 October 2016.
34. ODS Consulting, *National Evaluation of the CashBack for Communities Programme (April 2012–March 2014), Final Report* (2014) <www.gov.scot/Resource/0045/00452165.pdf> accessed 4 April 2017.
35. This statute further develops rules originally contained in Law 36 (1995) (the so-called *Ley del Fondo*).
36. For more information <www.pnsd.msssi.gob.es/delegacionGobiernoPNSD/organigrama/funciones/coordinacion.htm> accessed 21 March 2017.
37. The statistics herein presented are taken from Delegación del Gobierno para el Plan Nacional sobre Drogas, *Informe Sobre la Actividad del Fondo Procedente de los Bienes Decomisados por Tráfico Ilícito de Drogas y Otros Delitos Relacionados Durante el Año 2014* (2015) <www.pnsd.msssi.gob.es/delegacionGobiernoPNSD/

fondoBienesDecom isados/InformesFondo/pdf/Memoria__FONDO2014. pdf> accessed 21 March 2017.

38. In order to overcome this problem, for example, a dispatch was circulated on 4 August 2008 asking the courts to establish an annual list of goods confiscated in cases of narcotics and to verify that payments to the Fund of competition were made well. This initiative contributed to an increase in the Fund of more than 400% compared to the previous year.

39. For more information on this case, see Elisa Lois, 'El Pazo del Narco Se Convierte en Hotel de Lujo' *El País* (Madrid, 2 January 2011) <http://elpais. com/diario/2011/01/02/domingo/1293943956_850215.html> accessed 4 April 2017; Ignacio Calle, 'Los Millones de los 'Narcos' Se Pudren en un Almacén' *El Mundo* (Madrid, 27 September 2014) <www.elmundo.es/grafico/espana/2014/09/27/542433a5ca4741d9278b4585.html> accessed 4 April 2017.

40. The countries were Austria, Bulgaria, Cyprus, Estonia, Finland, Ireland, Latvia, Lithuania, the Netherlands, Poland, Portugal and Sweden.

41. This was also noted by the Belgian respondent when commenting on the Flemish social reuse experience. In his opinion, social reuse is an option preferable to sale for real estate in unattractive areas: in Belgium, many of the confiscated properties are located in 'problematic' and therefore unattractive areas. Hence, sale to the general public proves difficult and often results in property going back in the hands of organised crime. In this regard, social management seems to be an alternative that prevents confiscated properties from going back to organised crime via sale and that, at the same time, still provides value for money. It also seems to be an option preferable to sale for low-value real estate: in Belgium, much of the confiscated real estate has a very low value, because of its poor conditions. Handing them over to the local authorities, the Patrimonial Services can reduce the operational costs for their management and get back the real estate renovated and with higher value at the end of the procedure. At the same time, municipalities can address the needs for more affordable housing.

Barbara Vettori is Assistant Professor of Criminology at the Faculty of Political and Social Sciences, Università Cattolica del Sacro Cuore, Milan, and a member of the Department of Sociology of the same university. Her main research interests are organised and economic crime and the evaluation of related counter policies, in particular proceeds from crime confiscation. Since 2007 she has been a member of the Informal Expert Group on Confiscation and Assets Recovery of the European Commission, DG Home Affairs and, since 2013, of the ARO Platform Subgroup on Asset Management established by the same DG. She has also been a member of the ARO Platform Subgroup on the Reuse of Confiscated Assets of the European Commission, as well as an international expert for the OSCE on confiscation.

Printed by Printforce, the Netherlands